PATRICK WHITE

by the same author

BARWICK
THE IVANOV TRAIL

PATRICK WHITE

A Life

DAVID MARR

ALFRED A. KNOPF   NEW YORK   1992

To my father, Ewan

THIS IS A BORZOI BOOK
PUBLISHED BY ALFRED A. KNOPF, INC.

Copyright © 1991 by David Marr

Originally published in Great Britain by
Jonathan Cape, London, in 1991

Library of Congress Cataloging-in-Publication Data
Marr, David.
Patrick White : a life / David Marr. — 1st American ed.
p.   cm.
Includes bibliographical references and index.
ISBN 0-394-57435-4
1. White, Patrick, 1912–   —Biography.   2. Novelists,
Australian—20th century—Biography.   I. Title.
PR9619.3.W5Z76   1991
823—dc20
[B]   91-57913
CIP

Manufactured in the United States of America

First American Edition

I am the stranger of all time . . .
                              Patrick White

Contents

PART FOUR *The Pavement and the Crowd*

Picture sections follow pages 216 and 376. Family tree is on page 5, map of the Upper Hunter on page 17 and map of Castle Hill on page 263.

PART ONE

Out and Back

P. 'Where are you from?'
E. 'From here.'

The Twyborn Affair

ONE

Ruth

THE BRIDE WAS a plain woman in a big hat. She stood at the altar of St Philip's, Church Hill in Sydney a few days before Easter 1910 dressed for a voyage that would carry her across the world to Europe. She was thirty-two and this was a late and magnificent match for a woman on the threshold of spinsterhood. Great prospects lay before her, yet as Ruth swore to take her husband 'for better for worse, for richer for poorer' the crease of her mouth across that Withycombe jaw gave her the look of a woman who was faintly aggrieved. She carried that look for life.

Autumn, according to the calendar of Sydney society, always arrives in time for the Easter races. The salty, tropical winds that smother the city after Christmas are supposed to give way to crisp and brilliant weather for the Carnival and the Royal Easter Show. This old rule took no account of those abstruse calculations that decide when Easter falls, and 1910 was a year when the bush came to town for its holidays while the city still sweltered in damp summer heat. But they danced on Bellevue Hill, shopped at Horderns, and made their annual rounds of shirtmakers, tailors and milliners. Mothers rescued children from boarding schools for a few days while husbands and fathers retreated in heavy tweed to the Members Bar at the Show.

'The Easter call of the horse is being answered by thousands of humans,' reported the *Bulletin* that year. 'Sydney – that section which takes paying guests and lets apartments – is wishing it were elastic. The money it has to turn away makes it cry. Most of the Pure Wools are in town already and the racehorse owner is large in the vestibule of his hotel.'[1] Easter, when this crowd of graziers and horse breeders assembled every year in Sydney, was a practical time for bush families to marry. The small congregation at the ceremony on Church Hill was drawn from all over New South Wales, but most of the couple's relatives and friends were in town from the Hunter Valley and the cool Highlands south of the city.

The man at Ruth Withycombe's side topped the *Bulletin*'s list of 'Pure Wools'. Victor Martindale White was known by everyone as Dick. He stood half a head shorter than his bride and looked about him with the milky-blue eyes of the Whites. He was a cheerful little figure, chubby, vague and ten years older than Ruth, whom he vowed in his nasal, high-pitched voice 'to love and to cherish' until death. By the standards of families not known for impulsive or passionate marriages, this was a romantic match. Bride and groom were second cousins, yet between them were many differences. As Mrs Victor White, Ruth would lead a life she had so far observed only from its edge. To the rich existence that lay before her she would bring ambition, energy, imagination and a trace of Withycombe wariness. Above all, Ruth was determined never to be bored.

After a brief celebration the Victor Whites took a train to Adelaide, where they boarded the *Otranto* and sailed to the Middle East. Their honeymoon took them up the Nile, through the Aegean and across Europe, where they skied in the Swiss Alps, punted on the Thames, watched the shooting at Bisley and went to the races everywhere. Horses were the focus of Dick's life but he showed his wife other surprising, half-stifled enthusiasms: he loved the fjords and took her north to explore them. Ruth bought furniture, took Dick to the theatre, which was her passion, and augmented the collection of hats that became Mrs Victor White's trademark in society.

London was their base. In a Knightsbridge flat overlooking Hyde Park, their son was born at 11am on 28 May 1912. The baby had his mother's grey-green eyes. He was circumcised and Ruth was prescribed a nauseating diet of raw beef and celery sandwiches to bring on her milk. Her breasts would not fill as the child sucked 'first at one unresponsive teat then the other'.[2]

In Patrick White's world there are no accidents of birth. We are what we are born to be, free only to shape the lives fate has given us. What we inherit can never entirely be denied. Escape is impossible. In middle age he once remarked expansively, 'I feel more and more, as far as creative writing is concerned, everything important happens to one before one is born.'[3] He believed in blood and ancestors. He was delighted by the legend that a Withycombe was fool to Edward II.

By the time of Ruth's birth the Withycombes had been farmers for as long as anyone could remember. Withycombes are tall, hot-tempered, lithe, possessive and bronchial. Paradoxes define them: they are independent but love routine, gossips who are deaf to gossip, sceptics with a vivid streak of religious enthusiasm.

WHITES AND WITHYCOMBES

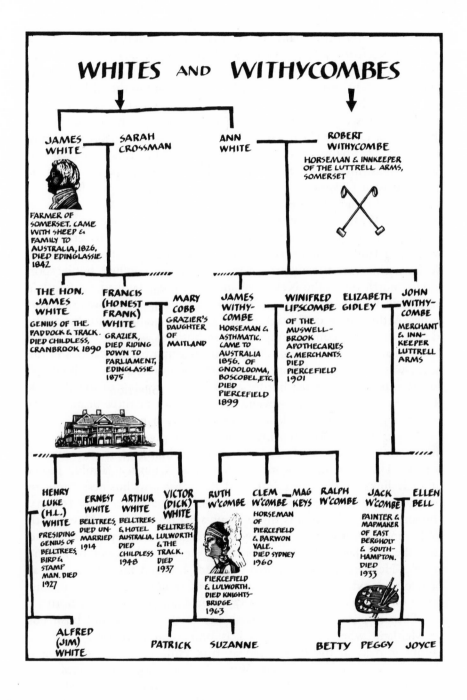

JAMES WHITE — **SARAH CROSSMAN**

FARMER OF SOMERSET. CAME WITH SHEEP & FAMILY TO AUSTRALIA, 1826. DIED EDINGLASSIE 1842

ANN WHITE — **ROBERT WITHYCOMBE**

HORSEMAN & INNKEEPER OF THE LUTTRELL ARMS, SOMERSET

THE HON. JAMES WHITE

GENIUS OF THE PADDOCK & TRACK. DIED CHILDLESS, CRANBROOK 1890

FRANCIS (HONEST FRANK) WHITE — **MARY COBB**

GRAZIER, DIED RIDING DOWN TO PARLIAMENT, EDINGLASSIE 1875

GRAZIER'S DAUGHTER OF MAITLAND

JAMES WITHYCOMBE

HORSEMAN & ASTHMATIC. CAME TO AUSTRALIA 1856. OF GNOOLOOMA, BOSCOBEL, ETC. DIED PIERCEFIELD 1899

WINIFRED LIPSCOMBE — **ELIZABETH GIDLEY** — **JOHN WITHYCOMBE**

OF THE MUSWELL-BROOK APOTHECARIES & MERCHANTS. DIED PIERCEFIELD 1901

MERCHANT & INN-KEEPER LUTTRELL ARMS

HENRY LUKE (H.L.) WHITE

PRESIDING GENIUS OF BELLTREES. BIRD & STAMP MAN. DIED 1927

ERNEST WHITE

BELLTREES. DIED UN-MARRIED 1914

ARTHUR WHITE

BELLTREES & HOTEL AUSTRALIA. DIED CHILDLESS 1948

VICTOR (DICK) WHITE

BELLTREES, LULWORTH & THE TRACK. DIED 1937

RUTH W'COMBE

PIERCEFIELD & LULWORTH. DIED KNIGHTS-BRIDGE 1963

CLEM W'COMBE — **MAG KEYS**

HORSEMAN OF PIERCEFIELD & BARWON VALE. DIED SYDNEY 1960

RALPH W'COMBE

JACK W'COMBE — **ELLEN BELL**

PAINTER & MAPMAKER OF EAST BERGHOLT & SOUTH-HAMPTON. DIED 1933

ALFRED (JIM) WHITE

PATRICK   **SUZANNE**

BETTY   PEGGY   JOYCE

The family came to Australia from Somerset, where there is a village called Withycombe in the hills looking out over the Bristol Channel. Withycombe families were scattered along the coast for a dozen miles from Watchet to Porlock, the village from which a man on business rode to interrupt Coleridge in an opium haze at Ash Farm. Dunster was the centre of the family's operations. In the early years of last century they owned small farms around the town, a general store, butchery, brewery and mill. Robert Withycombe ran the pub under the walls of Dunster Castle, franked the local mail and supplied staging horses. In 1827 he married Ann White and twenty years later their son James, an asthmatic, left for New South Wales to escape the damp air of the Bristol Channel and the epidemics of tuberculosis which were sweeping through the West Country in the 1850s.[4]

James Withycombe never settled anywhere for long in his new country, but moved from station to station, managing properties and trading in land. He may have worked for a time for his cousins the Whites, who were already prospering in the Hunter Valley, but he soon moved north on to the New England tablelands. He had his family's great skill with horses and was extraordinarily strong: it was said that James Withycombe could tighten the girth of a saddle with his teeth. He had the Withycombe temper, and in business was reckoned 'rather unreasonable in his demands'.[5] He dealt in a number of stations in the north-west of the state before taking up Gnoolooma, a run of about 200 square miles north of the border on the upper reaches of the Barwon River. At the age of thirty-seven, after only two or three years in that remote expanse of Queensland, he came south to marry.

His bride was Winifred Lipscomb the daughter of an apothecary, druggist, bookseller and seed merchant at Maitland in the Hunter Valley. The Lipscombs were another West Country family, proud of their links to the great Pitt, and the Lipscomb business came to be one of the most prosperous in the town, 'having a large country connection, which extends throughout a great portion of New South Wales and Queensland'.[6] Winifred Lipscomb was thirty and it is said that she and James Withycombe made an imposing and handsome couple. Her temper was reputed to match his, and they would 'fly at people with whips'.[7] A year after their marriage they lost a son, but while on holiday in England in 1877 their daughter Ruth was born.

They returned not to the harsh life of the Queensland bush but to Maitland where a son Clem was born, and then for a time the family moved to the homestead at Box Hill behind Sydney where they had a second son Ralph. When Withycombe sold Gnoolooma he bought land on the Hunter River near Denman. Piercefield cost £15,000 and was heavily mortgaged for the next thirty years. Most of its 6,500 acres covered hilly cattle country, but there were some hundreds of acres of rich flats along the river. It might have been expected that Withycombe would now settle at Piercefield, but instead he took his family down to the Highlands south of Sydney. Perhaps his health compelled this move, for the cool air of the Highlands was thought to work wonders for asthmatics. The Withycombes settled at Sutton Forest in an elegant rather stiff house called Boscobel with a garden and a few acres for horses and cows.

Sutton Forest is pale, washed-out country where khaki paddocks fade in winter to 'pale watered silk'.[8] Snow falls on the bleakest days of August and fires burn most of the year. This was the nearest thing to England in New South Wales and the gentry of Sutton Forest pursued a fantasy of English life. Dressed in tweed, they planted damp English gardens, read London magazines, and hired Irish servants. Half a dozen big houses sheltered behind windbreaks of black pines,

> which poured into the rooms the remnants of a dark green light, and sometimes in winter white splinters, and always a stirring and murmuring and brooding and vague discontent.[9]

Ruth Withycombe was ten when she arrived in this odd corner of Australia, a hill station that bred the ease, envy and snobbery of hill station life. Near Boscobel was Hillview, where the governors of New South Wales came every summer to avoid the muggy New Years of Sydney. Propinquity to Hillview was worth £40 an acre, according to the *Illustrated Sydney News*, for in the absence of thundering waterfalls and great ravines Sutton Forest offered visitors 'an enjoyable climate, pretty surroundings, a peep at the outside of the beautiful houses owned by the country gentry, and, if it conduces to your pleasure, an occasional glimpse at the representative of Her Gracious Majesty'.[10]

Two Sutton Forest families have an important place in this book. Across a shallow valley from Boscobel stood Mount Valdemar where Etienne de Mestre had come to live after losing his fortune. He had enjoyed an immense success on the track and his all-black silks were a famous sight on Australian race courses. Down on the coast in the 1870s he had bred or trained five winners of the Melbourne Cup, but he had paid too much for horses, bet too much on losers, and threw money into huge and unprofitable Queensland stations. To try to avoid ruin, he placed 'the biggest single bet ever written in Australia to that date'. The first leg of the double came in. The second failed.[11] He was sold up to pay his creditors and, with the proceeds of a benefit race meeting, moved up to the Highlands renting various houses until he reached Mount Valdemar. His young wife ran the place as a guest house. The boys did the milking, the girls scrubbed floors. The youngest son, sheltered from drudgery by his adoring mother, was Le Roi Leveson de Mestre, who grew up to be the painter Roy de Maistre.

At Browley, an old house of pink brick, lived the Morrice family. Mrs Morrice was a stringent and forbidding German who had nine children and wrote serials for the Sydney papers. A portrait of her survives as old Mrs Goodman in *The Aunt's Story* and the house became Meroë, an honest Australian country house 'flat as a biscuit' which stood on a rise looking out over the tussocks,

> grey in winter, in summer yellow, that the black snakes threaded, twining and slippery, and the little unreliable creek, whose brown water became in summer white mud.[12]

One of the Morrice daughters married a de Mestre. Another was Gertrude, very beautiful, rather dour and a couple of years older than Ruth. The two women became great friends. Gertrude Morrice, in later life a formidable spinster, was a witness at Ruth's wedding, and godmother to her son.

Ruth was plucked from the faded society of Sutton Forest by her father's decision to take the family back to the Hunter Valley. Why he did this is unclear. James Withycombe was fifty-eight and spent the last years of his life suffering terribly from asthma at Piercefield. On a windy rise he built a bungalow and planted a garden of olives and feather-green pepper trees. From the veranda the Withycombes looked down on their more opulent neighbours, for the house commanded a great sweep of river flats that merged, many miles upstream, into the grey hills behind Muswellbrook. Thunderstorms roll across this landscape, and it is said that James Withycombe built the chimneys of Piercefield out of bricks from a demolished church in the belief that blessed bricks would never be struck by lightning. They were, however, as the first storm passed over Piercefield after the family arrived some time in 1894.[13]

A polo field stood on the boundary between the Withycombes' land and Edinglassie, which was the headquarters of the Whites in the Hunter Valley. Withycombe borrowed from his cousins to set up a butter factory in a disused flour mill on the outskirts of Muswellbrook. The Millgrove Butter Factory and Cool Store was soon 'a flourishing industry'.[14] But after only five years back in the Hunter, his heart weakened by asthma, James Withycombe died at the age of sixty-three mourned by the *Maitland Daily Mercury* as 'one of the leading and most highly respected residents of the district . . . a high-minded gentleman, with a genial disposition . . . respected and honoured by all who were brought into contact or had dealings with him. He was an enterprising settler with progressive instincts, and his demise will be generally regretted throughout the district.'[15]

The writer of Withycombe's obituary was under an obligation to be generous, for the Lipscombs now controlled the *Mercury*. Withycombe was 'enterprising' and 'progressive' but not rich. He died heavily mortgaged after a lifetime in which great fortunes had been made around him. No flags flew at half-mast in Muswellbrook to give an official stamp to the 'general feeling of sadness' which was said to have swept the town on receipt of the news of his death. Under his will, two Whites became trustees of Piercefield and the butter factory until the younger boy came of age. Clem ran Piercefield and Ralph became the butter maker. All of them were rather hard up for the mortgages ate nearly £700 a year. Their mother, after only two years of widowhood, died and a couple of Lipscomb maiden aunts, Grace and her anti-Papist sister Lucy, arrived to help with the household.

Withycombe blood, London birth and a Sutton Forest upbringing determined Ruth to live a more exciting life than Piercefield offered. She was twenty-four when her mother died and for the next eight years lived in a household of orphans and spinsters. She made her own clothes and helped Grace about the house. She was not fond of Lucy. On frosty mornings Ruth washed the separator and complained, as Mrs Hunter was to complain in the hard years before her marriage, 'How blunt, red, hideous, fingers can become!'[16] Ruth loved the theatre, was musical – she crossed her hands most elegantly at the piano – and kept in touch with the family in Somerset. At Piercefield she grew into a gay and determined woman. Clem's sardonic joke was that she spent those years walking down the road to Edinglassie 'hoping to catch a White'.[17]

Ralph, who grew quickly stout and coached local footballers, exits from this story in 1906. He had to an exaggerated degree the temper of the Withycombes and it was said that he threw himself on the floor in seizures of rage. This was too much for his siblings and aunts. He left Piercefield and the butter factory for Sydney, and later lived in the south of the state on properties covered, according to his nephew, in Mexican thistle.[18] Thereafter Ralph had virtually no contact with his immediate family. These sudden and lasting estrangements are part of a family pattern, for the Withycombes brood over differences, sometimes for years, until a petty incident becomes the catalyst for a breach. More Withycombes had reached Australia by this time and a cousin Robert was never spoken to again after his brief stay at Piercefield. He complained the sheets were damp and went out to sleep on a haystack. Later he invented a useful rubber toothbrush with revolving discs that massaged the gums as it scoured the teeth. Withycombes displayed a talent for dentistry for a couple of generations, but for a time Robert made his living travelling around the shearing

sheds selling patent medicines. He appeared in *The Tree of Man* as a
stranger with a long nose selling Bibles and bottles labelled,

Thompson's Genuine
Magnetical Water
Guaranteed Killer of Most Pains
Safe but Sure
(No Humbug)[19]

Horses mattered most of all to the Withycombes, and their great
skill was horsemanship. They bred horses, raced, hunted and played
polo in Somerset and Australia. Clem, who had grown into a tall young
man with a hawk nose and the manners of a Hunter River gentleman,
was a superb polo player and it was the boast of the district that
'Clem Withycombe never misses'.[20] On the Muswellbrook team
Clem captained there were always a couple of the local Whites. The
Withycombes and Whites were relatives, neighbours and financially
entangled, but polo was the strongest link between the families and
their common ground was the polo field.

In June 1909 Clem Withycombe took his team up the valley to play
Scone, and it seems Ruth went with him to the game. It was showery
and cold, and for a time they feared the ground would be too slippery
to play, but the wind turned to the west and conditions were judged
tip-top for a game of 'magnificent recklessness' which ended in a rare
defeat for Muswellbrook.[21] A month later Clem was back to referee a
match in the presence of a large gathering of spectators. Dick White
and his brother Ernest, who had come in from their property Belltrees
to watch the June game, were here again in July and went on to the
'social function' in Scone that night. Ruth and Dick met at that polo
ball on 15 July 1909.[22]

A fortnight later Dick went down to the Muswellbrook club's
dance. No match was held in the town that day, and for a White to
make such a journey only for a party suggests a strong compulsion.
The School of Arts was artistically arranged for the occasion with
palms, flags and drapery. 'The gathering was a brilliant one, the music
superb, and the dance generally being one of the brightest of the
season, was much enjoyed by all who participated in it. The supper
room was exquisitely planned, the tables being covered with a pro-
fusion of delicacies of various kinds, arranged amidst a lovely assort-
ment of choice flowers in a manner that reflected the greatest credit
upon the ladies who supervised and directed the work.'[23] Dick
countered a month later with a party at Scone. He and his brother
Ernest were the hosts, and the local hall had seen nothing to rival the
event. The arrangements were perfect, 'the popular hosts, who are

nothing if not thorough, sparing neither trouble nor expense to have them so'. A Sydney florist installed 4,000 paper roses and daffodils. 'Dancing was kept up until the approach of daylight.'[24] Some time in the weeks that followed, Ruth and Dick announced their engagement.

'We are all pleased about it,' Dick's brother Henry wrote, 'and think they are well-suited if they agree to give and take a little.'[25] Henry White (known by his dry initials H.L.) was a shrewd man, but he underestimated the care Ruth would take to make her husband happy and the pleasure it gave Dick to let Ruth take the helm. They were to become devoted to one another, a perfect couple: Dick and Bird. Most of the difficulties that might have caused trouble in the years ahead were avoided by Dick leaving all the decisions to Ruth. He was happy to do as he was told.

In London it was Ruth who chose the curious name Patrick for their son: Patrick Victor Martindale White. Victor and Martindale made sense for they were Dick's Christian names, but in Australia at this time Patricks were Irish servants, Labor politicians and Catholic priests. The name was not yet fashionable in France and survived in England only among the children of the royal family as a dynastic claim to Ireland. None of this explains Ruth's choice and no one now knows what she had in mind when she made this gesture. Certainly it set her son apart from the White boys christened by family tradition James and Edward and Francis. It was bound to cause some confusion and in later years White was sometimes put with Yeats, Shaw and O'Neill on the list of Irish writers who had won the Nobel Prize, but this Patrick had not a drop of Irish blood. He maintained he loathed his own name. A passionate namer – of dogs, houses, books, people – he felt he could have done much better than Ruth given the chance. Yet in the end this name came to fit him all the better for being both distinguished and incongruous. Meanwhile, for his first twenty years, he was known even to Ruth and Dick as Paddy.

He was a child of the Empire, born in London to Australian parents who took pains to see that his upbringing confirmed the puzzling circumstances of his birth. 'It is not that I am not Australian,' he remarked. 'I am an anachronism, something left over from that period when people were no longer English and not yet indigenous.'[26] At whichever end of the Empire he lived, he always knew there was another home for him on the other side of the world. It angered him to be mistaken for English, yet it mattered a great deal to him that he was born in London, and he believed the first months of his life spent in the flat overlooking Hyde Park left their traces. 'It was in a formative period.'[27] He was to live in London and came to love it with the exasperation of a native, returning when he could for as long as he travelled. Yet London was denied him. Australia, he remarked bitterly late in his life, 'is in my blood – my fate – which is why I have to put up with the hateful place, when at heart I am a Londoner'.[28]

As a man he came to put his faith in many small superstitions, in saints and lucky charms, omens and coincidences. That he was born a Gemini meant a great deal to him, for the sign of the twins seemed an emblem of his own divided and often contradictory nature, not one man but a kaleidoscope of characters trapped in a body both blessed and cursed, proud and wracked by doubt, rich and mean, artist and housekeeper, a restless European rooted in the Australian soil, a Withycombe and White, man and woman. His trust in astrology was sustained in later years as he came across men and women who shared his stars and his divided nature. Three Geminis he felt in tune with from the moment of discovery were Pushkin, Henry Lawson and Marilyn Monroe.

In the London summer of 1912 there were no omens to indicate the life the boy might lead. Indeed, the fate of Ruth's cousin Jack pointed the other way. Jack Withycombe was the only artist among Whites or Withycombes, a minor Impressionist, etcher and map maker. For some years he had been living a kind of Augustus John idyll in East Anglia, his wife entertaining duchesses and their three little girls getting about barefoot. 'The Withycombes were the intellectual, or to be more precise the "avant garde", family of the neighbourhood,' recalled the illustrator Edward Ardizzone, who played with the Withycombe girls in East Bergholt in those years. 'Withycombe was a painter and a good one, whose work never had the recognition it deserved. His wife was clever and charming. Both were Fabian socialists, great lovers of the countryside and believers in the virtue of the simple life.' At the Withycombes' farmhouse, there was a sense of freedom and excitement unknown in the houses of their more conventional neighbours. 'We rarely left the Withycombes without some new idea for our childish minds to feed on.'[29] Withycombe had sold his silver, sold everything to keep going, but about the time Ruth and Dick were preparing to return to Australia, Withycombe was forced to pack up his paints and go out to Malaya to become a surveyor in the tin mines. But later Jack and his wife Ellen and their daughters Betty, Joyce and Peggy came to take a central role in this story as Patrick White's other, English, family.

The boy was four months old when Ruth and Dick embarked on the *Otranto* for the voyage to Sydney. They had engaged a nanny for the child, 'a white, hour-glass figure divided by a buckram belt' who once worked in German princely houses.[30] Whatever qualities this cool and sentimental woman brought to the care of little Paddy, she knew protocol and the art of walking backwards through doors. The *Otranto* reached Sydney on 7 November 1912. Dick's brother H.L., who had not come down to Sydney for the wedding, now cut short a Scone Shire Council meeting to be on the wharf to welcome them back. It was an important event, for Ruth and Dick were bringing home an heir.

Dick made a couple of trips alone to the Hunter that summer while his family remained behind in Sydney. After Christmas they went down to the Southern Highlands to escape the heat. According to family legend their hotel was engulfed by a fire from which the boy was saved by Nanny Galloway. To this brush with death at about the age of nine months White liked to attribute his persistent apprehension of danger, his native resilience and pessimism, 'Perhaps my being the greatest pessimist on earth'.[31]

In May Dick brought them up to Belltrees. The train reached Scone very early in the morning. H.L.'s car was waiting. The road skirted the lucerne flats of Segenhoe and swung into the narrow valley through which Voss would lead his party towards 'the ultimate stronghold of beauty'.[32] The Daimler splashed across a couple of shallow crossings and rattled across the wooden bridge into Gundy past a pub and a few cottages and St Matthew's weatherboard church, for which the Whites always hoped to find horse-riding, English clergymen. By Gundy they were already in White country.

For six more miles the road climbed gently until it reached the lip of a great valley, a broken triangle of river flats and gentle hills that fold back beneath the scarp of the Mount Royal Range. The prospect is magnificent. This is fat, rich land, olive and brown under a blue sky. Over the valley stands the black, comfortable bulk of Mount Woolooma. The Hunter flows out of sight along the foot of the mountain, its bed marked by a line of she-oaks and willows. Below them lay the long wool shed like a tin cathedral straddling a small hill. Somewhere near the river behind a screen of European trees was the new homestead, still hidden from sight as the Daimler changed into first and started down the side of the valley, sending out a spray of dirt and stones.

The road forked when it reached the river and the car turned along the bank past scattered cottages, the school, a tiny post office, the village hall and church, a blacksmith's shop, stables and greenhouse, along the high fence of H.L.'s paddock of kangaroos and wallabies, and into a garden of lawns and flower beds cut in crescents and triangles and lozenges, to pull up at a house the size of a town hall with walls of red brick and forbidding tiers of wood and iron verandas.

TWO

The Happy Valley

THE STORY OF the Whites in Australia is the history of a fortune, a river of money that flowed through New South Wales from Belltrees and Edinglassie, Martindale, Havilah and Saumarez, Baroona Station, Narran Lake, Timor, Ellerston and Waverley, Bando, Segenhoe, Merton and Dalswinton.

> exotic names . . . that have eaten into the gnarled and aboriginal landscape and become part of it . . . [1]

On the edge of the desert or in the swamps of the Northern Territory families could boast holdings as big, say, as Belgium. That was poor country. The Whites had hundreds of thousands of acres of the best land in Australia: in the Hunter Valley, across the Liverpool plains and up through New England. When Dick was a young boy Whites boasted they could ride from Edinglassie on the Hunter to the Queensland border and sleep on their own land every night. Dick was the grandson of the first White to reach Australia, and nephew of the man who had made his family's fortune.

The Whites were Somerset farmers like their cousins, but they arrived thirty crucial years before the Withycombes. The Whites' business was sheep. Once Europe settled down after the Napoleonic Wars, cheap Prussian wool reappeared on the English market and the wool industry in England began to slide towards ruin. In 1826 James White sold his farm at Crowcombe and left for New South Wales with a wife, a flock of sheep and about £500. He arrived just as the great wool boom was about to begin. Like the best of the Corsican's generals, the Whites had luck.

He worked briefly as a flockmaster for the Australian Agricultural Company on its million acres at Port Stephens until the shady James Bowman, surgeon-general of the colony, recruited him to manage his

sheep at Ravensworth in the Hunter Valley. Settlement came late to
the valley, for a convict prison barred the mouth of the river for many
years. When the convicts were shipped north, settlers hacked through
the cedar forests and set about clearing the Kamilaroi people from the
alley. Some of the bloodiest engagements took place at Ravensworth
in the months before James White arrived in 1829. The Aborigines
fled west and up on to the Liverpool plains where they were massacred
later that summer. They had bequeathed to the settlers pouring
into the empty valley a landscape perfectly suited to sheep. The
Aborigines had fired the land for centuries to hunt kangaroos on
new grass, and stretches of the Hunter Valley were so lightly
timbered that settlers drove their flocks into country as open and
rich as an English park.

With Bowman's help White was granted 1,280 acres at Gundy
and given convict servants to work the land, but this small grant was
not the source of the wealth he acquired in these years. White stayed
at Ravensworth where it seems he was working as Bowman's partner
through the mad boom of the late 1830s. At the height of the boom
Bowman was dismissed from his post in Sydney and came to live
on Ravensworth for the first time. White moved his seven children,
2,000 sheep and 300 cattle to Edinglassie, a property of 35,000 acres
that ran north to the Hunter near Muswellbrook. The government
assigned him convicts to work the place. They were fed and clothed
but paid no wages. 'Edinglassie took its place in the van of the young
industry, and boasted one of the leading flocks . . . Mr James White
proved himself an able sheep-breeder and station manager. He did
remarkably well with his flocks, securing additional holdings as his
position improved.'[2] But White then died at the age of forty-one just
as the boom began to break, leaving a widow, nine children and stock
worth £15,000.[3] It seemed his family would be wrecked.

'Bankruptcy was almost universal.'[4] The boom had been fed
by an 'excess of English capital, the ridiculous accommodation
of the banks, the speculative mania, the boundless extravagance
of all classes.'[5] The old seigneurs of New South Wales, including
the Bowmans, were ruined and their flocks sold for tallow. 'The
boiling vats were soon bubbling merrily round the chief towns. A
ring of tallow houses tainted the breeze in all directions.'[6]

James's widow Sarah saved the family from this general disaster and
proved herself 'a most capable manager in the interests of her sons'.[7] The
oldest of these, another James, was only fourteen at his father's death but
he was taken from school to learn the business. He had a genius for sheep
and land. With the help of his young brothers this second James worked
his way out of the depression 'through unwearied industry and intelligence, devoted year after year to the improvement of stock and of land'.[8]

Wealth was measured in livestock rather than acres until the graziers engineered constitutional changes to give themselves better title to their land. In 1848, when James White was only twenty, he had leased Belltrees from the orator, ex-democrat and gun-runner William Charles Wentworth. When the land laws changed soon after, White was able to snap up the freehold title to the family's single richest holding. Here the Whites' luck was crucial: suddenly the state was for sale and they were there at the right time, in the best country, with a lot of cash and a shrewd eye for land. James White was not a pioneer who drove mobs into the unmapped bush, nor did he amass land through political intrigue as the Macarthurs and their colleagues had done in the early days of the colony. He bought his empire as big estates came on to the market through the 1850s and 1860s.

Belltrees stood next to the family's original grant at Gundy and spread north, following the rivers back into the foothills of the Mount Royal Range until Belltrees took in all the best land on the upper reaches of the Hunter River and its tributaries, the Isis and Page. The range at the head of the valley was thick with cedar, and in those forests the young Ludwig Leichhardt had joined a party of woodcutters in 1842 to collect flowers and butterflies and try to learn bush skills. Like Voss, the fiction that grew from this life, the young Prussian was a model of incompetence. He lost himself, his horse, his pencil and most of his specimens in the forest. But, somehow, Leichhardt survived the odds he stacked against himself and convinced his backers to let him lead an expedition into the interior of the country.

For forty years James White dominated his family. Though he married he had no children, and his holdings were managed by his brothers, who were known to one another, like kings of the bush, by Christian name and territory: Frank of Edinglassie, George of Belltrees, Frederick of Booloominbah, Henry Charles of Havilah and Edward of Martindale. On their acres the Whites pursued tenacious, hard-working lives relieved by polo and marriage. They were loyal, temperate, unsociable, rather mean, conservative and cool-blooded. If they suffered any spiritual hunger, it was satisfied by the Church of England. They were not readers. 'Whites are only interested in what they are interested in.'9 The stud book was the only volume they took willingly from their shelves. The family was soon large – a cousinage that stretched across New South Wales – but White caution and loyalty kept the fortune turning back on itself. Acres were not left to women. Whites did not borrow except from one another and lent on sound security. They survived droughts, rode booms and prospered in busts. They did not – at least in the early generations – dissipate their fortunes by marriage into the English gentry. They kept no contact with the

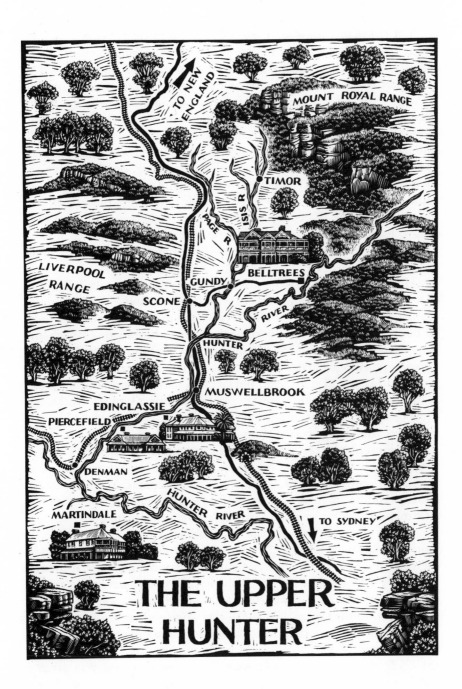

THE UPPER
HUNTER

Whites of Somerset out of fear, it was said, of poor relations. They considered themselves Australian.

But the man who made their fortune was the least typical member of his tribe. James entered the New South Wales Parliament while he was still in his thirties, retired from day-to-day work on the land to travel abroad and poured both cash and energy into his ambition to dominate the Australian track. South of Sydney he built his racing headquarters, a 'fairy castle' called Kirkham in which Miss Hare might have recognised the outlines of Xanadu perched above Sarsaparilla.[10] No one had carried on the racing business in Australia with such success. 'You have only to read the long roll of names in order to have the glories of the blue and white banner of Kirkham brought vividly to mind. Chester, Martini Henry, Nordenfeldt, Trident, Ensign, Dreadnought, Palmyra, Segenhoe, Iolanthe . . . Abercorn, Volley, Victor Hugo, Rudolph, Singapore and Democrat . . . During James White's career there were no stars of heaven which approached him in magnitude.'[11]

His architect at Kirkham was a difficult American called Horbury Hunt. The Whites were his first and best patrons and Hunt's buildings are the family's other legacy to civilisation in a new land. For them he built the brick pile Booloominbah at Armidale, made Havilah and Edinglassie into country houses, and turned Cranbrook on Bellevue Hill into an opulent city mansion for James White's retirement. The Whites would rather spend money on horses than themselves, and the stables Hunt built for the family are among the architect's finest works. He drew up the great shearing shed that straddles the hill behind the house at Belltrees. Along the Hunter Hunt designed Anglican churches to which Whites subscribed large sums. Here they commemorated themselves in English stained glass. 'Feed my Sheep,' commands a White window in St Alban's, Muswellbrook. 'I am the good shepherd,' says a bearded Christ standing in an orange grove in the east window of St James's, Belltrees. 'The good shepherd giveth his life for his sheep.'

The Whites' empire needed dry roads and high bridges, orderly workmen, local hospitals and an anti-Catholic clergy untainted by radical ideas. So they sat on shire councils and synods and the magistrates' bench. By the 1870s their grip on the upper Hunter was such that one of Sir Henry Parkes's supporters complained it was no use putting respectable candidates against the White family, 'hence for some time we have had men opposed to them who were without private or political character and each defeat of such opponents by the White family has made the latter more dominant than ever'.[12] James was given a seat in the Legislative Council, and his brother 'Honest Frank' White of Edinglassie stood for a seat in the lower house at elections hurriedly called in 1874.

Frank assured the men of the Upper Hunter that he put himself forward reluctantly because 'no candidate has offered himself who I believe
entertains political opinions in accord with those of the majority of the
electors of this important constituency'.[13] He appealed to the free
selectors, tradesmen, storekeepers, working men and mechanics of the
constituency,

VOTE

for

FRANCIS WHITE!

AN ACTIVE INTEREST

in your

LOCAL AFFAIRS

who

Has always contributed,
both by his Intelligence
and his Purse (and in a
princely manner), to
promote those Local
Institutions which have a
tendency to elevate you in
the social scale.[14]

A few days before Christmas the candidates gathered on
hustings outside the Scone courthouse to address the men of the town. A
hot westerly wind blew over the valley. The heat and clouds of dust made
outdoor work that day excessively uncomfortable. In the view of the
Mercury reporter, the heat sapped the energy of the crowd and
'shortened the speeches to a slight extent'. Frank White faced an uproar as
he came forward on the platform. He was a big man of forty-four with a broad
forehead and a beard like matted tobacco. He assured the crowd of his
diffidence, high patriotism and determination to tell only the truth.
'The truth has carried me through all sorts of difficulties. It has
changed opponents into supporters.'

A voice called, 'Many a poor man you put on his legs after
shooting his horse.'

'I can answer that,' said the candidate when the laughter and noise
had died away. 'Many a poor man I have helped upon his legs. I see
before me men, selectors on my runs . . .'

'Dummies!'

'I appeal to them whether I am not speaking the truth . . .'

'Who are they? Let us hear now?'

'I come forward wishing to assist in making laws for the benefit
of the electors, of myself, and of the whole country. I have no other
object.'

He battled on against the heckling. 'You might try to howl me down, but you had better trust a man who has enough, and whom you know to be honest, rather than a man who wants to grab all he can get. You have never known me to break my word.'

He pledged himself in favour of the erection of public schools in the bush at the entire cost of the public revenue but he opposed universal free education; he was not disposed to legislate for the eight-hour day because he thought labour should regulate its own market; he would legislate for the repression of Scotch thistle and seek to prevent destruction of grass by sparks from railway engines.[15]

Frank White's success in the ballot rested heavily on the votes of the men employed by his family. At Belltrees he had seventy-seven votes to his opponents' four. He took his seat in the New Year as an independent supporter of the New South Wales government. If the eulogies about to be delivered can be believed, here was a most promising young legislator: a thorough gentleman of sterling integrity, eminently useful, of good abilities, education and social position. Yet Frank White did not plunge into the affairs of Parliament. He rarely attended a division. He never uttered. Then in autumn, as he was riding down from Saumarez to Edinglassie, he contracted a fever which at first was attributed to overwork, but rapidly assumed the character of typhus. He died on 4 May 1875.

Frank White's funeral was one of the largest ever seen in Muswellbrook and he was buried with the highest honour a country town can bestow: all stores and hotels shut their doors. 'Business in the town was entirely suspended.'[16] As his body was brought in from Edinglassie, the cortège was joined by vehicles, horsemen and citizens on foot. After a service at St Alban's, he was buried in the family vault and honoured in newspaper prose up and down the valley. In Sydney Sir Henry Parkes took the unprecedented step of opposing the motion that the House adjourn as a mark of respect. He lost. Parliament rose for a day.

Dick was seven when his father died. His mother Mary Cobb raised him as her spoilt youngest son, the favourite of her seven children. The Cobbs of Maitland were graziers and Cobb daughters had married into the Whites along familiar lines: White brothers found sisters of good stock and married them all. Mary was a tiny woman with a little humpback. Nothing was *said* about the hump or the scandal of her brother caught servicing young men in a lavatory in a country town. The certain genetic contribution of the family to this story is the milky-blue stare they gave to all the generation of Whites since then and, through them, to a more scattered and elusive family of Patrick White's imagination. Alfreda Courtney had such eyes of 'mineral blue'; the mother of the Browns of Sarsaparilla prised open her children's secrets with her 'ice-blue ancestral stare'; and the German explorer Voss saw the dead heart of Australia through the 'peculiarly pale blue' eyes the Cobb sisters bequeathed the Whites.[17]

Dick was sent away to school in Parramatta. The King's School was an institution for sons of the bush and there were many Whites there when Dick arrived. King's was not anxious to open wide horizons or kindle ambition, for the boys had acres to go home to. They were drilled, instead, with enough learning to emerge numerate, literate and well-mannered. Discipline was random and harsh. Older boys enjoyed the privilege of beating younger boys. Dick was a slight boy and his ordeal at King's left him determined never to put a child of his own through the same mill. He turned out to be a sprinter, and at seventeen won a set of silver salt cellars and the title of All Schools Champion of Sydney. He was champion once again the following year, his last at King's, and took home to Edinglassie an oak writing set mounted in silver with cut-glass ink stands.[18] His trophy saw little use: desk work rather defeated Dick, and for the rest of his life he found letter writing an awkward business. He read only stud books, detective novels and the *Sydney Morning Herald*.

Soon after his return to Edinglassie – and some time before the Withycombes moved into their house on Piercefield – Dick left to join three of his brothers up the river at Belltrees. Originally, the Edinglassie Whites moved there only for the shearing, sending furniture and servants ahead to open up the simple homestead. But while Dick was still at school, the sons of Honest Frank began to sort out among themselves their share of White possessions while remaining accountable still to old James living in sumptuous retirement at Cranbrook. The four youngest sons – Henry or H.L., Arthur, Ernest and Victor – took Belltrees.

Dick's role in the rise of 'the finest estate in the settled districts of the colony' is rather vague.[19] In accounts of those early years, Dick's name is not bracketed with hard work. He was a bit of a dandy, a daredevil, at times a buffoon. The brothers called him the playboy of the team. Scraps of stories survive: how Dick put an unbroken mare into harness and smashed a buckboard to pieces in front of the house, and how he took the men down to the river to eat watermelons. His brothers disapproved of such familiar behaviour and they wore him down. Dick became their amiable, shy companion, a sweet man and quite without side. He was a hay-fever sufferer and spoke with a high nasal drawl. After a while his sprinter's body thickened, but he kept a boy's face and those astonishing blue eyes.

Horses were his passion. Just before old James died at Cranbrook, he gave the four brothers twenty blood mares. From that time Dick put much of his energy into the track and polo ground. The core of the Scone polo team in those years were the Belltrees brothers Dick, Arthur and Ernest White and it is said they were Banjo Paterson's model for the Geebung Polo Club, the 'irregular and rash' team who met the Cuff and Collar men from the city in a game so ferocious it ended with all players dead and a spectator's leg broken 'just from merely looking on'.

And on misty moonlit evenings, while the dingoes howl around,
You can see their shadows flitting down that phantom polo ground;
You can hear the loud collisions as the flying players meet,
And the rattle of the mallets, and the rush of ponies' feet,
Till the terrified spectator rides like blazes to the pub –
He's been haunted by the spectres of the Geebung Polo Club.[20]

Dick, Arthur and Ernest lived in the shadow of their brother H.L., a small, reclusive and forthright man, with a strong and original intelligence. He ran Belltrees on a feudal scale and in his hands it grew to 140,000 acres. For the 250 people on the place he built a school, post office, hall, store and church. The village celebrated Empire Day with bonfires, fielded a cricket team and sent detachments off to war. 'Who made the world?' asked a clergyman visiting the Belltrees public school. 'Please sir,' answered a boy, 'Mr H.L. White.'[21] H.L. was their boss, the local magistrate and President of the shire. His taste for dispute was sometimes extreme: when a tutor absconded to a softer post down south, he instructed his solicitor to see the man 'heavily fined or imprisoned' and was baffled to be told this was impossible.[22]

His temperament was scientific. He became a famous ornithologist. He stocked the river with fish, supplied the Sydney zoo with animals, and kept a menagerie in his garden. He bred new strains of wheat and grew flowers. His chrysanthemums were never beaten at the Horticultural Society in Sydney, but 'Like Alexander I had no more fields to conquer so gave the hobby up.'[23] Belltrees subscribed to the *Emu*, the *Captain*, *Wide World*, *Royal*, *Strand*, *London*, *Pearsons*, *Ladies Field*, *Sporting and Dramatic*, the *Sketch* and *Scientific American*.[24]

He dealt with the world by correspondence and for nearly forty years kept a station diary. His letters to his family and politicians, providores, agents, bankers, lawyers, newspapers, bishops, scientists and bird collectors filled over fifty volumes in his library. His prose is cool and unremarkable except when recording droughts and rain. Then he broke into a kind of poetry: 'Everything is wet at last, all water holes full, all creeks and gullies running.'[25]

Belltrees had no heir when the new century began. Dick was unmarried. Ernest had a taste for Muswellbrook seamstresses and was the despair of local matchmakers. He was an asthmatic, the most handsome of the four and the only one of the brothers to match the hard work H.L. put into the place. Arthur had married sweet, dim Milly Ebsworth of Bronte House in Sydney. They built a bungalow a little way from the homestead and called it Kioto to celebrate their passion for Japan. Twin boys were stillborn. Arthur and Milly had no more children. They travelled, and spent much of their time away from Belltrees at the races and watching cricket.

H.L. married Maude Ebsworth. The Ebsworths supplied wives to the Whites as the Cobbs had in their parents' generation. Maude was a big woman with sad eyes. Small children loved her, but living at close quarters with her bustling husband had thwarted her. Their first two children were daughters and then, in 1901 when Maude was nearly forty, she had a son. He was named after his uncle Alfred Ebsworth, shot leading a contingent of Belltrees' stockmen in the Boer War. The boy was known as Alf.

To celebrate the birth, H.L. ordered a new homestead. Horbury Hunt was dead, so he turned to a firm of architects in Maitland. 'The whole brick building must be made to look well,' H.L. ordered. 'Nothing of the barn appearance about it.'[26] Bricks were baked on Belltrees; the slate came from Wales; a foundry in Maitland supplied iron for the verandas. The house H.L. built from 1907 to 1908 was old-fashioned even for its day, but Belltrees became one of the most famous country houses in Australia, a confident pile of red brick encased in iron and lattice. Light filtered into the gloomier rooms through art-nouveau windows of rambling flowers. Even on days of blazing summer sun, the hall that runs a hundred feet from front door to kitchens lay in a cream and silver twilight. An opulent staircase with cedar columns, screens, urns and balconies, built like the companionway of an ocean liner, leads up to an acre or two of bedrooms. To fill the place new furniture was ordered from Beard Watsons store in Sydney, shipped up to Morpeth on the river and then hauled overland to Belltrees on five wool wagons. The Whites moved across the garden from the old homestead to the new in October 1908.

H.L. now had the space to display his collections of birds' eggs and skins, stamps and old Australian books. The collections dominated life in the new house.[27] He employed the corpulent ornithologist Sidney Jackson as his curator and collector for twenty years and sent him on expeditions to obscure corners of Australia searching for eggs and skins. H.L.'s nephew was to invent a great explorer, but H.L. employed one. Jackson's trophies were catalogued and stored in cabinets in the billiard room. H.L. judged his guests by their response to his collections. Sir Walter Davidson, the governor of New South Wales, lasted three hours with the eggs and stamps and was rated 'very easy'.[28] To bishops, governors and Japanese princes who wanted to pass through Belltrees, H.L.

was a reluctant host. He preferred his guests to speak English and be in and out of the place in daylight. Only the family was welcome to stay. He never entertained on any scale. For the two decades he lived in the new house, there is no record of a party or ball. The hall runner frayed only as far as his office door.

Dick was restless. In 1907 he turned forty and spoke of getting out of the partnership from which he was drawing huge dividends. Only horses and racing seemed to engage his interests. Early in 1908 he set out for Japan with Arthur, Milly and H.L.'s daughter Dorothy on a world tour that kept them all away from Belltrees for over a year. He returned in March 1909. H.L. noted in the station diary that Dick arrived home looking pale and thin.[29]

That winter Dick met Ruth. His family seemed happy at the prospect of his marriage, though aware that a financial gulf lay between them and their Withycombe cousins. By H.L.'s demanding standards, the late James Withycombe's wandering life was a failure. Whites were settlers but Withycombes were nomads: 'the stayer', said H.L. of men and horses, 'is what pays best'.[30] Piercefield was not a rich estate, and there were mortgages. H.L. was in a position to gauge Ruth Withycombe's financial position very accurately, for he had been both guardian and trustee for her younger brother Ralph.

Ruth was always suspicious of the Whites' attitude to her, ready from the start to see slights and hostility. She did not come to the altar a pauper. Shortly after she met Dick, the Withycombes decided to sell their property and the local press announced 'the celebrated Piercefield Estate' would be auctioned in September 1909.[31] The sale was miscalculated. Too proud, perhaps, to see Piercefield become a map of little dairy farms, the siblings offered the place in a few large parcels. 'One required to have a substantial banking account to purchase any of the lots,' explained the *Muswellbrook Chronicle*. There were few bids at the auction, but the land was eventually sold, the mortgages discharged, the butter business wound up, a loan repaid to the Edinglassie Whites, and the Millgrove factory leased as a rabbit-freezing works. Clem Withycombe bought land out on the Barwon near Walgett. So sick of cows was he by this time that he never allowed one on Barwon Vale, and he remained so loyal to horses that he never owned a car or tractor. He married Mag Keys, whose family lived over the Hunter from Piercefield, and for some years still came down from Walgett by train to captain the Muswellbrook polo team.

H.L. came to have an amused affection for his sister-in-law, but it was not reciprocated. Withycombe pride was uncomfortable in the face of White money. The whole capital Ruth brought to her marriage was about the same as Dick's income from Belltrees in 1910. The last season had been wonderful: 124,000 sheep were shorn and 2,000 bales of wool went under the hammer. The *Scone Advocate* noted that this was 'a record day's offering for one station for Australia – if not the world'.[32]

H.L. had sent congratulations to London on the birth of Ruth and Dick's son. Misfortune and the mathematics of White family loyalty, made Paddy heir to half Belltrees. Maude could have no more children, for her kidneys failed after Alf's birth. She was an invalid living in half-darkened rooms at the homestead and she spent most of the summer at Terrigal House, the family's place on the coast. Her daughters would have no share in the family acres. At Kioto Arthur and Milly were childless and Milly was past having children. Ernest was unmarried. He and Arthur would plough their shares of Belltrees back into the partnership when the time came. Paddy and Alf stood to inherit it all – yet Ruth could not bear the thought of living in the valley.

The Daimler carrying 'VMW, wife, child (Pat) and nurse' arrived on a dull cold morning in May 1913. The family had gathered for the event, and with them was Jackson, sorting eggs after the great hardships of an expedition to the uninhabited southern coast of Western Australia.[33] There were no celebrations. Later in the week the Edinglassie Whites – James of Edinglassie had married the third Ebsworth sister Emmeline – came up to inspect the baby but returned home the same day. Uneventful days passed.

Ruth was bored by the society of Belltrees. Of all the Whites she liked Ernest best: he was dashing, he had given her a diamond and sapphire brooch when Paddy was born. She thought Milly a joke and pitied Maude for being overborne by H.L. The wives lived in the shadow of their men, and the high points of their existence were afternoon teas with one another. If Ruth lived at Belltrees she would have to accept H.L's authority and Ebsworth company. Something of Ruth's response to this was echoed by Elizabeth Hunter at Kudjeri and reappeared in Alfreda Courtney's rejection in the early days of her marriage of the prospect of living in the country, 'I mean, I couldn't endure the idleness, when there is so much in life to tackle.'[34]

Dick felt life in Sydney would quite suit him, though he might never have had the courage to suggest such an arrangement to his brothers if Ruth had not made up her mind. In Sydney he could be close to his racehorses at Barden's stables, make himself useful to H.L. in town and come up to Belltrees every few weeks when he was wanted. The brothers were only anxious he did not break entirely with the partnership, for that would mean finding the cash to buy him out.

After a fortnight it began to rain. 'Rained without ceasing from 6 pm yesterday to 5 pm today 420 points falling,' H.L. wrote in his diary. 'This is the heaviest fall since 1899 . . . water all over the place.' At nine that night the river was at its highest – a new record – roads were cut, telephone lines carried away and the river downstream washed out the railway line to Sydney. But for a packhorse bringing in the mail, Belltrees was cut off for three days. Jackson rearranged eggs. H.L. worked on his stamps. He wrote, 'All hands repairing flood damage and clearing debris from horse yards; cutting the drift wood into engine fuel. Great damage reported to fence crossings all over the place.' Two Russians battled through the waters to sell H.L. some skins. 'I bought a "Russian Pony" coat for Maude for £50. Still repairing flood damage.'

After three weeks at Belltrees, and the rivers having fallen, 'V M White, wife, child and nurse left per car to catch the 11 am train to Sydney.'[35]

THREE

The Bunya Bunya Tree

THEY LIVED FOR a time in two flats on Phillip Street and the baby was left in his nanny's cool hands. He was a puking child and Galloway cleaned up the mess. She wheeled his pram through the Botanic Gardens where other nurses and their children played by the water, and at night she carried the baby, clean and spruce, into Ruth and Dick's apartment. He was dimly aware of being taken from a dull brown daytime world into the pink glow of his parents' sitting room. One day on the balcony while he was having his toenails cut, a maid called Alice showed him a double-yolker in a bowl. The egg in the bowl was his first clear memory.

The balcony at Cromer seemed so high to the child. Cabs clopped along the street far below. He could see the bald patch on the German who lived in a flat in the basement. The wind that blew from the gardens was warm but when it snuck from behind the building it was cold and he was brought inside to play. The maids let him ride on their backs as they scrubbed the floors. One gave him a wand, a magic wand though it was only a broken beach spade wrapped in silver paper. He danced with the wand. He remembered being on the Harbour with his father, and later finding himself in the garden at Belltrees where there were little umbrellas over the flowers. An old man, one of his uncle's workmen, played with him in the sun.

> The whole of the visit . . . was more dream than real life, though Father took it so seriously. Somehow the light and colour were more important than what you were doing: that was the real importance of the dream–visit.[1]

He was two and a half on this second visit to Belltrees. Often that year the boy had been left with Galloway in the Sydney flat while Ruth and Dick went up and down to the Hunter Valley, for Dick's brother Ernest had died suddenly in January and the Whites were coping with a disaster that had far-reaching effects on their lives.

Ernest died a true White. At first he thought the pain in his stomach came from drinking iced water in the heat. Soon he suspected appendicitis but went on working for another day just to make sure. He collapsed. A local doctor advised an immediate operation in Scone, but the brothers summoned a special train instead to take him down to the most distinguished surgeon in Sydney. Dick sat with his brother on the journey south. At some point on the way the appendix burst and Ernest died a couple of days later in Sydney.

Flags flew at half-mast on the Moorefield track. H.L. wrote in his diary: 'Cool morning, hot muggy day, showers in the afternoon. Left home at 5 am . . . in the Hudson car . . . and went on to Edinglassie. Attended poor Ernest's funeral and returned home by 1 pm bringing VMW with me. AGW returned to Sydney. I had hired the motor lorry and McGruder's car to take as many men from here as cared to attend the funeral: about 20 went from here. No work done of course today. Sold 50 cows in Sydney @ £7.10.3 market firmer.'[2]

Dick was given the job of culling Ernest's papers. 'I have not questioned Dick upon the subject,' H.L. wrote to Arthur, who was in mourning at the Coogee Hotel, 'but I understand that very little of a strictly private nature was found.'[3] While H.L. took Maude for a hot, unsatisfactory month in Tasmania, Ruth and Dick were left in charge at Belltrees. The outcome was regrettable. Ruth had a passion for furniture. In her later, grander existence she liked to hint that Queen Mary shared her tastes and would remark, pointing to the green porcelain artichokes on her fireplace, 'The only other pair are owned by the Queen.' Surviving among the wagon-loads of Beard Watsons furniture at Belltrees were good old pieces from the original homestead. Dick, as one of the partners, owned a share of the furniture: it had been a quarter but was now a third. In the weeks after Ernest's death Ruth picked some of the best pieces to take down to Sydney. Her culling of the furniture became a complaint that survived generations to drive a wedge between the Victor Whites and Belltrees. Forty years on Alfred White was still saying, 'She got off with the best of it.'[4]

Belltrees was now more than H.L. could manage. Dick was in Sydney, and Arthur spent more time chasing the Australian cricket team to London than working in the paddocks. Even before Ernest died H.L. had complained to one of his ornithologist friends that he was tired of the worry of management. 'The trouble is that it is too big.'[5] He was also troubled by the fear that the Labor Party, which was in power for the first time in New South Wales and the Commonwealth, might start cutting up the big estates. So H.L. persuaded his brothers in the aftermath of Ernest's death to sell large chunks of Belltrees. One block of 35,000 acres was sold within a few months, and they sold about 10,000 acres a year for the next four years, cutting Belltrees down to a huge 64,000 acres. Dick was left freer and richer.

In May 1915 Ruth had a daughter and life changed at Cromer. She gave her exuberant baby, born with her husband's blazing blue eyes, the name Suzanne. It was another of her innovations. 'I am pretty certain . . . my mother is responsible for all those "Soooes" who have littered Australia ever since.'[6] She found the name, it seems, in the hit musical *The Girl in the Taxi*,

> Suzanne, Suzanne,
> We love you to a man,
> We yearn for you,
> We burn for you,
> Our sweet Suzanne.[7]

Paddy was now three, irritable and sickly. The appearance of a sister threw him into a jealous rage which was compounded by the departure of Nanny Galloway and the appearance of Lizzie Clark, a tiny, no-nonsense woman not quite five feet tall, with sharp eyes and a tough Scots accent. For all her swank, Nanny Galloway was a soft touch: she fed all the animals on the nursery fireplace before making Paddy eat his brains: 'The camel! You missed out the camel on the other side.' Lizzie refused, so the boy stamped her tube of toothpaste flat, squirting paste everywhere. It was an act of revenge little Rhoda Courtney was to take when Hurtle Duffield appeared in her nursery. As Lizzie closed her eyes to say grace, Paddy (and Rhoda) silently unscrewed the cap from the hot dish: 'When they looked up there was a map in water spread across the tablecloth.'[8] Lizzie was fiery, loyal, tricky, shy and dour. She could deal it out. With sharp reprimands and wet kisses she won the little boy's heart, though she always found him a difficult kid to manage. The boy directed all 'the genuine love' in him to Lizzie and even as a child it worried him that he loved her too much and his real mother not enough.[9] Love would not obey the rules.

The Clarks were golfing Scots from the sands of Carnoustie on the Firth of Tay. Lizzie's brother was the pro and her father the caddy master at Royal Sydney, the course on the sand flats between Rose Bay and Bondi where the best families played golf. Lizzie had gone into service with the Campbells then the McDonalds before coming to the Whites where she stayed for the rest of her working days. The Clarks were loyal to the Empire. Lizzie's brothers volunteered to fight in France and Paddy remembered them coming one day to Cromer to say goodbye. Robert the youngest went off to fight lying about his age like Oliver Halliday and Hurtle Duffield. He was only sixteen but, 'Nobody would have known. He was big.'[10]

The day Germany declared war on Russia, H.L. had written in his diary, 'A bad lookout generally.' But Belltrees prospered through tough seasons and despite the difficulty of finding stockmen. In this H.L. made matters worse by hiring a recruiting officer to scour the district for men to send to the Western Front. H.L. despatched these men from Scone with a gold watch and a life insurance policy. Belltrees itself sent men and horses, even an aeroplane. Maude organised the women on the place into teams knitting socks for the Red Cross; Ruth sent gifts to the Belltrees sports day in aid of Belgium; and the brothers put a good deal of the capital realised after Ernest's death into War Loans. Dick invested £30,000, but he baulked when H.L. suggested a second plane in 1917. H.L. answered his objections: 'By the end of May we shall have about £50,000 to our credit, some £20,000 of which will probably be required for the payment of taxes etc.; from the balance I think we might very well afford to give another £3,700. If we were able to do anything in the actual fighting line, I'd not press the point, but as we can assist only with donations I think it is up to us to give all we can possibly spare.'[11]

War was a strange business for the young boy. 'German neighbours were pelted with rotten vegetables and fruit. Dachshunds were stoned.'[12] Lizzie took the boy on long walks to Darling Point to spit on the gates of the castle built by the beer baron Resch. One of her brothers was gassed. Young Robert was killed. One afternoon at Cromer, the child found Lizzie 'a heap of crumpled white on the bed'. He saw anguish for the first time in his life and crept away from the sight of this immense, puzzling grief.[13]

Lulworth was a big, ramshackle house at the back of Kings Cross looking across Rushcutters Bay. The Victor Whites paid £6,000 for the place in 1916 and engaged the architect Howard Joseland to carry out repairs. Joseland's work was fashionable but solid: he had made his name adapting the English businessman's mansion to the climate of Sydney's North Shore. He shaved the iron off the verandas and put a pediment over the front door, but Lulworth resisted his attempt to turn it into a smart city mansion. It remained comfortable and rather incongruous, like a homestead perched oddly at the back of the Cross. Instead of paddocks, the house looked across the bay and the park to the spire of St Mark's on Darling Point. Joseland neglected the hidden shortcomings of Lulworth, for the walls stood on rock without foundations or damp courses. The rooms were always damp and mould grew in corners. The Whites moved into the new house in the spring of 1916.

A few palms stood in front of the veranda, and a lawn of spiky buffalo grass ran to the lip of a little cliff. Down a flight of stone steps – 'the moss so thick in places his feet felt they were trampling flesh' – was a wild garden which became the boy's private territory and, in turn, the secret garden of Hurtle Duffield. An old wooden summer house decayed in a tangle of hydrangeas and guavas and custard apples. The air had a thrilling smell 'of crushed insects, or sickly fruit' and the sunlight lay in patches on the damp earth. It was always damp down there, a little world of rotting leaves and slime.[14] Through the undergrowth the boy stalked cats stalking lizards and, hidden in the summer house, said prayers to the god of the great bunya bunya.

The fleshy, spiked bunya bunya pine stood at the elbow of the gravel drive. One day the tiresome Mr Voss stood beside that tree to interrupt the Bonners on their way to a picnic. The fallen spikes, lying neglected on the gravel, caught Harry Courtney's eye as he drove Hurtle Duffield to the door. Aunt Theo, who came out with the most surprising remarks, liked to joke that she had left her breath under the bunya bunya. The tree was Paddy White's protector. If the larrikins of Darlinghurst were shouting at him through the privet hedge, all he had to do was run to the bunya bunya and he was safe. He wondered if paradise was somewhere in its branches, a thought that crossed the mind of the poet Le Mesurier as Voss's party passed Aborigines heading out of the desert for the soft country where they could pick the bunya nuts. The boy wondered did God live up there? Did he tear His pants climbing to the sky?[15]

One day watching a wild cat eat a lizard on the path, the boy found himself fighting for breath. The blood drained from his face and he was left grey, coughing, weak and frightened. From birth he had been wheezy but in the first summer at Lulworth his condition revealed itself as asthma. This awful discovery he later assigned to Eddie Twyborn whose childhood, like Paddy White's, was suddenly menaced.

> The future threatens very early. The growing threat which I'll always associate with unruly masses of purple lantana, and cats lying on hot asphalt as they died from eating too many lizards . . . Or was that a parent's diagnosis?
> MOTHER: Don't look, darling. Patches is sick from eating lizards. They somehow poison cats. We'll take her to the vet and he'll make her better.

But the cats never returned, and the wheezing boy was grief-stricken at their deaths.[16]

It was terrible for Ruth to find she had an asthmatic child. The

Withycombes' weak lungs had brought them out to Australia, and asthma killed her father at Piercefield. The Whites were asthmatic too: Ernest had been a sufferer and Dick had hay fever. She feared the worst for them all. Dick was vague, benevolent and helpless in the face of his son's condition. Ruth, on the other hand, fussy and germ conscious, set about fighting for the child's survival.

There was no mystery then about what happens in an attack: the lower airways to the lungs, the bronchi, close and fill with mucus, cutting the passage of air in and out of the lungs. The victim is left suffocating when the attack is severe. But at that time very little was known about what *triggered* attacks. Some said it was nerves and that asthma was to be mastered by exerting the will. Others blamed the air: Sydney was said to be a bad city for chests, but out in the country doctors recommended bracing sea air for sufferers. That allergies might be a cause was barely suspected then, and it was forty-five years before it became clear that damp and mould triggered this asthmatic's attacks. Water seeped over the cliff behind Lulworth into beds of lilies and camellias, into deep buffalo lawns and up into the walls of the house. Shoes left in cupboards grew a bloom of mould.

Ruth burnt belladonna leaves in a bowl in the boy's bedroom when he was wheezing, and the sweet smoke gave him relief but left him queasy and exhausted. Later he had asthma cigarettes to smoke which made him feel sick all the time. In severe attacks a doctor appeared at Lulworth to pump adrenaline into his arm. The drug immediately relaxed the bronchi and restored normal breathing. Sometimes the child was given a little morphine to calm his terror. His earliest memory of treatment was Wilfred Fairfax, a physician from a distinguished Sydney family, giving him a sticky white solution of ephedrine sulphate to drink. It was like semen, the boy later reflected, and was supposed to get the adrenaline to the lungs without breaking down in the stomach. It did little good. Whenever the boy was hit by a severe attack the doctor returned to Lulworth with a fat hypodermic of adrenaline.

The boy lived with the fear of asthma. No one could protect him or explain this curse away. He was always pale. From the age of five he had hints that he might not last, though he did not fear death: 'All that I saw, all that was happening around me, was far too vivid for me to believe in the event which carried off old people and pets.'[17] He grew languid and stubborn and angry – the asthmatic's anger with himself and his treacherous body and the uncomprehending, hostile world of the well.

Ruth was torn by two impulses: one was to smother her boy, the other to make him tough it out. She swaddled him in singlets and made him sleep on a hard, hair mattress. The boy clung to her and fended her off. Asthmatic children have a certain power over their parents. Asthma can be wielded as a weapon, often as not in self-defence. Paddy began to tangle with his mother. A contest of wills developed in which they exercised a shared Withycombe temper. As a last resort he retreated inside himself, beyond her reach. She was a difficult mother. He was a difficult and unusual child – but as Stevie Smith once remarked: 'The moral seems to be if you want to remain an individual you must arrange to have an invalidish childhood.'[18]

Paddy did not mix easily with other children. He played with them but made no friends. The swarm of his Lipscomb cousins frightened him, though he loved the pony and cow they had in their Darling Point garden. He was a private and solitary child, uneasy when he was away from Lulworth and the private kingdom among the guavas and *Monstera deliciosa*. He was always pessimistic, preparing himself for the worst: 'I had a mental list of things I would throw out of the window and in what order if fire broke out.'[19]

His sister Sue was still too young to play. His companion at Lulworth was Solomon Rakooka, the black watchman. He was an islander and drunk, a figure from 'Miss Root's' childhood at Piercefield. Sol was always around, 'in the Douanier Rousseau garden of my child-hood. We planted a mango stone together. We watered it. We dug it up every other day to see whether it had germinated. It had. What happened to our mango I can't remember. It probably died of too much loving care from our black and white alliance.'[20] In his dirty room at the back of the house, near the rubbish bins where lantana hung over the damp cliff and stank of tom cat, Sol kept a box of souvenirs from his years at sea: shells, a rubber tobacco pouch with a twist top and, the best thing of all, a knife that smelt of clean, oiled metal. Ray Parker held that knife, 'and supposed with cold fasci-nation what would happen if he closed his hand, just that bit closer, and closed. His skin was pricking.' And Hurtle Duffield felt the power a few trinkets, a signet ring and a lump of coral, had to conjure lives from other worlds.[21]

Near the summer house one evening the boy came across a woman tearing at the guelder roses. She was part-tramp, part-witch and drunk. In terror he called his mother, and Miss Root called Sol. 'Now Sol and the Mad Woman were wrestling and spinning in the dusk, she hissing, Sol shouting through his ragged moustache and brown stumps of teeth. Then the Mad Woman's skirt fell off. I did not see what happened after that. I ran away. I ran upstairs. I lay on my bed. The glass above the dressing-table showed me palpitating in green waves. My heart was beating, a wooden, irregular time.'[22]

At the age of five the little boy began at Sandtoft, a kindergarten in Woollahra. Sol came every afternoon to bring him home, 'my small white hand in his large black spongy one as he helped me aboard the tram'.[23] No one else had a black attendant. Sol bought him sweets. That was their forbidden secret, for Ruth was a figure fanatic – one had, she said, to choose between face and figure, and she had opted for figure – and brought her children up without sweets and to look on potatoes as a mortal sin. One afternoon she appeared at Sandtoft in Sol's place and Paddy demanded sweets. She refused. He spat in her face in Ocean Street and back at Lulworth she beat him with the handle of her riding crop.

Mrs Victor White was one of Sydney's antique collectors. In the hall at Lulworth stood a buhl table where the boy hid to smoke Dick's cigars. Off to the right was her small 'French' sitting room of gilt and tapestry, and through the doors straight ahead was a long, elegant room she called her salon, the maids called 'the salong', and the boy remembered as 'the desert of their mahogany drawing room'.[24] Copies of *Tatler* and the *Sketch* lay about. On the walls were landscapes of good grazing country. Ruth admired the rural vitality of Hilda Rix Nicholas's paintings, and somewhere in the house there hung a portrait of herself by Agnes Goodsir, a graduate of the Bendigo School of Mines and resident of Paris who returned to Australia from time to time to paint women like Mrs Victor White. The painting has disappeared, but in the memory of those who saw it in those years, the buhl rather crowded Ruth off the canvas.

French doors opened from the salon on to the veranda. The Harbour lay ahead, through the trunks of the palms with the bunya bunya on the right. One end of the veranda was open, but the other, behind which lay the dining room, was screened with lattice and fly wire. The dining room was dark and cool. The table was set with the Georgian family silver Ruth and her fellow collector Mrs Eadie Twyborn 'lovingly acquired at auction'.[25] The Whites' china, stored in tall cupboards in the pantry, was white with a broad green rim and a big gold W in the centre of each plate.

At the far end of the house, in what seemed from the garden to be a separate cottage, was Dick's study, sometimes called the smoking room. Photographs of racehorses and fat rams in lucerne hung on the walls. His magnificent desk was bare: 'All was disposed for study in this room except its owner . . .'[26] Dick retreated here in the mornings to read the *Sydney Morning Herald* or doze after lunch in his leather armchair.

The kitchens, on the far side of the green baize door that 'sighed like a human being', were run by Ruth's major-domo who had a cook and two parlour-maids working under her. Lulworth did not follow the protestant standards set at Belltrees for Ruth had her own prejudices. She would not have Australian servants in the house but would have

Catholics. The boy was Master Paddy to the Irish girls, and in the kitchens he could depend on their simple care and the wonderful smell of soap and beeswax, rising bread and starched aprons. He discovered those plain objects – bowls, a table, a wooden chair – that came to have an extraordinary power to console him in later life. 'This table is love,' said the landlord, spreading his hands on the table-top, 'if you can get to know it.'[27]

Australian was not the boy's first language. He learnt a little from delivery men at the back door and larrikins who pestered him through the hedge, but in the kitchens he heard more Cockney and Irish brogue: 'Nora Barnacle could have been one of the stream of Irish maids that flowed through our house.' On the other side of the baize door he spoke Ruth's proper English and she nagged her son to keep his accent and his grammar pure. Like Waldo Brown he was forbidden to use 'sloppy Australian vocabulary'.[28]

At the top of the stairs – the terrible basalt stairs which Voss's party descended in Laura Trevelyan's fever, the hooves of their horses striking sparks from outcrops of jagged rock[29] – were the children's bedrooms where Ruth came to hear her 'baa-lambs' say their prayers. They prayed to 'Gentle Jesus, meek and mild' and asked Him to bless 'Mummy and Daddy and Nursie' and each other. Paddy prayed for Sue, and Sue for Paddy. Ruth sat on their beds and told them stories which seemed to glow with the light of early morning. 'At Piercefield,' she began, 'when I was a girl . . .'

Ruth and Dick's bedroom and dressing rooms were at the far end of the hall. Sometimes the boy was allowed to watch his mother working at the high altar of her dressing table. He was dazzled by the scene: the little bottles rattling on the table, the stench of crimping irons and the powdery smell of dresses waiting in the open cupboard as Ruth curled and pouted in the mirror. She was shedding bulky Edwardian flesh, but it was said of Ruth that her mouth was now set for ever at twenty past seven. Maids pulled furs from bags, blew powder into long kid gloves and hovered over the jewels: diamonds, sapphires and Ruth's favourite rope of pearls. With every hair in place, she took a fur, kissed her son, checked her mouth in the mirror and went down to the waiting car.[30]

The war put a premium on the organising energy of women like Mrs Victor White. She made her mark in Sydney raising money for wartime charities, working with two women who became close friends. Ethel Kelly and Margaret Gordon had both come to Australia as actresses and each made a splendid match while on tour. Margaret Gordon was a Welsh singer who married a Sydney barrister. Ethel Kelly was a Broadway starlet who had a huge success in Australia

playing Cio-Cio San in Belasco's *Madame Butterfly* in 1903 before
marrying T.H. (Bertie) Kelly, the son of an industrial tycoon. Both
women had had to leave the theatre but the war allowed them to
return. While their neighbours were sewing pyjamas for the Light
Horse, Ethel Kelly and Margaret Gordon gave charity galas in aid
of the Red Cross, the Comforts Fund, the Belgian Fund and Jacks
Day.

Ruth moved in their wake, her young son bobbing behind. He
thought Ethel Kelly was wonderful and Ethel admired Ruth: 'How
vivid the women of the White family have been in social country
life, and how like meteors they have shot across the pages of social
Sydney. At any town and country matrons' ball that includes Mrs
Victor White's name you will find a perfect organisation, a scheme of
decoration original and charming, for she is a past-mistress of the art
of entertaining.'[31]

Kelly's finest effort in the war was an Elizabethan water pageant.
One cool spring evening, a steam ferry carried Elizabeth and her
court across the Harbour. A flute band played on deck where Ethel
as Elizabeth stood in a pool of electric light in rose silk and a red wig
with 'a Medici collar of silver tissue, a lace ruff, and ropes of pearls'.
All 'gloriously arrayed' around her was a party of Tudor courtiers.[32]
'A poignant touch was given to the festivity when in mid-harbour
the procession paused while an outward-bound troopship tramped
past, and across the water came the coo-ees of a company of our
boys going light-heartedly forth to fight for their country.'[33] Ethel's
party disembarked before a large crowd waiting in the grandstand of
the Clifton Garden baths. She knighted Bertie, who was dressed as
Drake, and Neptune's daughters in skirts of seaweed swam about in
the black water. 'A procession, consisting of over 100 persons in rich
and historically correct costume, preceded by Yeomen of the Guard
in vivid scarlet tunics bearing the banner of England, paced between
a double row of white pillars tied with red and blue streamers . . . to
the pavilion, where a galliard was danced by 22 ladies and knights to
the strains of 12 flutes, led by Mr Arloni, after which the younger set
fox-trotted and one-stepped.'[34]

Ruth's taste in clothes, jewels, theatre, music and travel were all
changed by Ethel Kelly – up to a point. Ruth was, in her bones, a
conventional woman and loved Ethel for being what she could not be
herself. The Kellys' house, Glenyarrah, on a headland in Double Bay
was the Gothic setting in which Ethel pursued her vivid existence. She
had a real talent for making people enjoy themselves. On their way
through Sydney the great and the promising called at Glenyarrah. Melba
was a dear friend. Bertie Kelly had had a few lessons from Joachim after
Oxford and played the fiddle in his own quartet. There was a story,

perhaps a malicious invention, that a famous pianist engaged to play with the quartet left in disgust. This became an embarrassing episode in the life of Elizabeth Hunter's friends the Radfords,

> They engaged Moiskovsky? the Russian pianist – to play sonatas with Sidney – but Moisenstein got up and walked out. Stuck to the cheque, and Sidney and Gladys were too ashamed to ask for it back.[35]

Mrs Kelly's favourite charity was the Italian Red Cross, for which she staged *tableaux vivants* of Sydney women 'suggesting the frescoes and pictures of the old Italian masters'. Ethel knew where to find, in Edgecliff or Vaucluse, just the right face. So high were her standards that she would even go to the North Shore for the woman she needed to bring a Gainsborough or a Claude to life. The results were said to be astonishingly accurate. Ethel herself appeared over the years as a painted Jezebel, Lady Nelson, Lady Macbeth and once, most memorably for Ruth's son, as Madame de Pompadour. The sight of Ethel Kelly striding along George Street to the Artists Ball rigged out as the Primrose Pompadour made an indelible mark on the boy.[36]

Ruth came that night as Rubens' second wife. She had none of Helena Fourment's elfin beauty but her breasts in the low-cut dress were fleshy in the Rubens manner. On her head she had something like a Light Horse hat, turned up at one side and stuck with feathers and pearls. The great sensation of the ball was the decor of bushland with cardboard Aborigines. 'It was the Abo's night,' reported the *Daily Guardian*. 'He was everywhere. He, and the Teddy bear, and the laughing jackass, and the kangaroo and the birds of the bush. Whatever the Artists Ball was not, it was Australian. And that makes up for a whole lot.'[37]

At the age of six, Ruth took her boy to watch Mrs Kelly as Portia in a charity matinée of *The Merchant of Venice*. Ethel noted in her memoirs that Bertie slaved over early manuscripts to achieve the 'most beautiful effects of plucked lute accompaniments, that gave rich value to my spoken words in the casket scene, and lent romance to the last act serenade'.[38] As she took her curtain call, Paddy White, holding a bunch of red roses provided by the committee, rushed down the aisle and threw them at her feet.

Ruth had taken him to the theatre from an early age, beginning with pantomimes and musicals at the Grand Opera House and Her Majesty's. 'We were always going, and I cannot be grateful enough for that. It filled some of the gap in what was by normal standards my solitary childhood and youth.'[39] He was almost sick with excitement every time they set out. The stage was magic, terror, delight, the same world of illusion glimpsed in Sol's box of treasures and Sunday scenes at St James's with music and marching and fainting women, and the thrilling horror of the Mad Woman in the garden. One day the woman was caught stealing from the garbage bins behind the kitchen, and in the aftermath of such excitement the boy's visit to the theatre that night was disappointing. The audience ate chocolates and cried over a waif on stage. The scene at the bins was better than this, when 'the stinking fish skeletons and heads she was sorting and wrapping in greasy paper had undergone some magic change'. Later he recognised this as 'the illusion referred to as art'.[40]

He danced for Ruth's friends. They looked alarmed but settled back to watch him prance about bashing saucepan lids together. The child was a terrible show-off. The performances became more sophisticated. He collected an audience in the salon, wound up the gramophone and disappeared through the curtains into the hall, where he climbed on to an upturned waste-paper bin and struck a pose. The curtains opened at his signal, the needle hit the record, and he climbed down to dance to 'The Dutch Kiddies' Two Step' or John McCormick in 'I'll Sing thee Songs of Araby'. These performances went on long enough for *Chu Chin Chow* to contribute something to his efforts. He saw the show when he was nearly ten. Oscar Asche himself was in the cast, and a very old actress called Maggie Moore who was said to be a heart throb of Dick's, and Louise Pounds, who Paddy learnt had nursed him when he was a baby in the flat in London.[41]

Ruth took him to the theatre, but Lizzie taught the boy to read. 'She infected me about the age of five: "The fat cat sat on the mat . . ." and all that. I never looked back. I was soon in a fever, while not understanding half of what I read, but reading and reading.' The miseries of *Dot and the Kangaroo* gave him morbid pleasure; *The Secret Garden* was entrancing; then he fell in love with 'the lithe and muscular form of Deerfoot, my infallible Red Indian hero'.[42] The little boy dreamed of a tame red Indian with feathers who would play with him in the jungle at Lulworth. He read whatever lay about the house with the help of a dictionary to find his way. 'I might not have understood what country people were exploding about if I hadn't consulted the dictionary. My own explosive vocabulary was born in my early childhood – by life out of the dictionary.'[43]

'Dear Father Xmas,' he wrote when he was six. 'Will yoy please bring me a pistol, a mouth organ, a violin, a butterfly net, Robinson Cruso, History of Australia, a little mouse what runs across the room. I hope you do not think I am too greedy but I want the things badly. your loving Paddy.'[44]

The boy's favourite book was *The Swiss Family Robinson*: 'Everything happened so easily on that island without tears.' He was more than absorbed, he found the book stayed alive in him even after it was finished and back on the shelf. Why? What was it about these books he came to cherish? 'One seems to pass over and go on living in them for ever after. I think possibly it is because they give one glimpses of a heartbreaking perfection one will never achieve, whether it is the rather comic, homespun achievements of the Swiss Family, the perfect refuge of *The Secret Garden*, the interiors and scenes of family life in Tolstoy.'[45]

Once Paddy was reading, Ruth engaged Madame Marie-Thérèse Henri to teach him French. Madame Henri turned up at Lulworth with picture books. 'Qu'est-ce que c'est que ça?' she asked the restless child as she pointed to trees, cats, dogs and castles. They battled over pictures of the châteaux of the Loire. The boy's vocabulary was strong on towers and moats. He did not find these lessons easy, and his fits of dumbness exasperated Ruth. She once burst out: 'I'd rather be a German prisoner of war than a child's governess.'

Ruth wanted the best for her children. With the White fortune behind them, what life would not be open to them on the wider stage of the Empire? Dick saw his son as an heir to Belltrees, but Ruth never imagined he would grow up only to crutch sheep. She badly wanted a genius. Her son had to aim in all things above Australian standards. Paddy must be a better boy, a perfect boy, drilled in the knife and fork, toothbrush and hairbrush. He must shake hands, look people in the eye, greet them by name, stand up straight and tell the truth. The sick boy must be well, and the glum child happy. Paddy must love his mother more. But love was a knotty problem.

He loved Lizzie, and she treated Paddy and Sue as her own. The smell of her clean cheeks – like the cheeks of Stavroula who suckled Angelos Vatatzes in Smyrna – was what you knew 'as earthly evidence of sanctity'. She taught the boy right and wrong in the light of her plain Presbyterian upbringing. Sin did not count: what mattered were the *failings* little boys must try to overcome. She was not to be crossed. She expected truthfulness at all times, and the child absorbed the idea that he had a right – indeed an obligation – to speak his mind. People must be faced with the truth. 'If I was shy and withdrawn, it was only till provoked. Then I could answer back.' She was not a forgiving woman. That people should get what they deserve was one of Lizzie's axioms, though she tempered this with pity for those less fortunate than themselves. For her the purpose of life was fulfilment not enjoyment. She kept a sharp eye for signs of pride. Paddy was forbidden to 'blow his own trumpet'. How comfortable it might have been, he later reflected, if he had had an Irish Catholic nurse instead.[46]

He was a proud boy. Ruth used just to laugh at the conceited things he said, like the time he came home from Sandtoft and announced he had the best voice in the school. How do you know? 'Because I've

listened to my voice, and listened to their voices, and I know which I
like best.' Vanity was deeply rooted in him.[47] Ruth was a proud woman
and Lizzie had her own pride, not least in serving the Victor Whites. She
passed to the boy something of the Presbyterian quandary about pride:
the obligation is to fight, to keep it in check, not to conquer. There is
such a thing as false humility, and proper pride.

The day the war ended, Paddy stood with Sue and their parents in
a cheering crowd watching soldiers march down George Street past
the Post Office. The sound of bands came and went with the soldiers.
Everyone was happy. This moment of high celebration was spoiled
when someone blew a paper whistle in Ruth's face. She recoiled. Germs!
Fifty years later the reveller was identified as simple Arthur Brown,

> Who blew out his blower with the pink feather on the end . . . In
> particular, he enjoyed the retreat of the sterner noses. Always when
> his blower had recoiled, again, there was someone to kiss him on
> his large face, slobbery with the joy of fulfilment, of recognition.
> Everybody was being and doing.[48]

The war was over, but Ruth's efforts reached their climax with
the Peace Ball of 1919 postponed because of the Spanish flu and the
dilatory negotiations at Versailles. Germany had still not signed the
treaty in August but Sydney couldn't wait. Ruth rallied the women to
put together an extravagant scheme of decoration for the Town Hall.
It was a task her son later assigned to Alfreda (Birdie) Courtney, who
shadowed in so many particulars Ruth's early career.[49]

Sunflowers sprang from the pillars; garlands of anemones ran
round the hall turning dark alcoves into bowers of blossom; baskets
of hollyhocks and poppies hung from the galleries. It was all paper
and the *Bulletin* observed it must have taken 'all the crinkled paper in
the land'. The band was put in a grove of real orange trees and played
a little jazz to mark the new age. Ruth wore a brown toilette relieved
with gold embroidery. The only jarring note was caused by the pencils on the dance programmes, each stamped 'Made in Austria'. Sixty
débutantes, forced to cool their heels through the war, were presented
to the Governor-General in one batch. 'It was the ceremonial and official
announcement that the days of our mourning were over, and that we
may once more be sanely gay.'[50]

The role of Mrs Victor White came to fit Ruth like a glove, but it
remained a performance and there was always something a little forced
about it. She provoked people to wonder what the *trouble* was. Perhaps
a difficult son? That her boy was sickly and hard to handle was widely
known, and stories of his truculent, precocious behaviour circulated in

Sydney while he was still a little boy. But Ruth encouraged her little performer. A dreary husband? No. Dick was just the man she wanted and they were what they seemed in these years, a happy couple: Dicky and Bird. Could it be – and here voices were lowered – because her mother's family was in trade? Ruth went at her new life with such determination she seemed to be climbing from somewhere far less secure than her Withycombe and Lipscomb past.

Ruth's problem was simple. She was a woman of drive, ideas, taste, courage of a kind and eccentric generosity. For all these remarkable qualities she lacked intuition. Ruth was very funny, especially about the foibles and vulgarity of those beyond her circle; her acid descriptions were remembered and quoted for years; but she never really understood people, and had little grasp of why they were as they were or, perhaps more to the point, why they were not as she was. What she could not grasp she mocked. Without an easy understanding of people she was uncertain how to win their trust, so she set out instead to dominate. Ruth grew into one of those generous but overbearing women who can hardly help enslaving people. She gathered a coterie of stylish young men to keep her amused and one or two poor relations as attendants.

The rhythm of life at Lulworth was set by Dick's obligations to Belltrees. The partners had bought 12,000 acres on the coast side of the Mount Royal Range as a protection against drought. This holding, Terreel, was Dick's responsibility. From Belltrees cattle were sent a hundred miles over the Barrington Tops to the grass on the coast, a journey that took eight to ten days through rough country. Dick met the mobs as they came in over the range and looked over the fattened cattle as they were taken out to market. The drover who spent his life taking cattle back and forth across the mountains was called Clay. The manager of Terreel was a drunk. Dick never took his son there. Terreel was an unknown, man's place from which he returned to Sydney smelling of work and horses. The little boy was roused by Dick's leggings in the hall: they seemed the most exciting thing about his father.[51]

Dick was at his brother's polite disposal. 'I wish . . .' H.L. would write and Dick would honour the wish: to see the clip auctioned and wire the results to Belltrees, to buy a gun for a hunter, to inspect Lincoln rams at Wagga and grass at Wodonga, to buy a bull at the right price, to show samples of Belltrees wool to 'some of your friends', to send him fruit from Santamaria's 'all on the unripe side', to interview butchers, bookkeepers and clerks for Belltrees – 'Don't want a R.C.' – and when H.L. came to town they ate together at the Australia Hotel, 'which after all is the best place in the Commonwealth'.[52] At first he consulted Dick with formal care about partnership business: do you agree to this dividend? should we sell this paddock? Later the tone changed. Dick was informed of the decisions made by his brothers, and reproached for taking initiatives at Terreel.

The end of the war saw difficult times: the flu, the worst drought in twenty years and the worst strikes. H.L. helped break the strikes by sending fifty Belltrees men and horses to assist the New South Wales mounted police. Dick and Arthur scabbed in Sydney: one of the brothers worked on the wharves, the other drove a horse lorry. But against the drought, the family could do nothing but wait and pray for rain. Dick's boy wrote, 'Dear Fairies, would you give me a book I don't mind what kind it is can I have it on my birthday it is on the 28th of May. I hope you will have a nice danse to night I expect you have tea on the toad stools at night. Do you live in the flowers. Could you please make it rain in the country soon it is very dry up there the sheep and cattle are dieing. And would you make the influenza better I wish you would with love from Paddy.'[53]

A touching affection grew up between the child and H.L., who frankly admired brains: Paddy had them but Alf did not. H.L.'s son was a great fast bowler – it was said he might have played for Victoria while he was still a boy at Geelong Grammar – but only scraped through school and was now having trouble finding a place at Cambridge. In many ways Alf was a disappointment, and when he lost interest in his father's collections, H.L. gave them away. The birds went to the National Museum of Victoria, and the stamps to the Mitchell Library in Sydney. H.L. refused, characteristically, to attend the ceremonies that marked the handing over of these gifts, but his nephew Paddy was taken to the Mitchell to see the big cabinets of stamps in their new positions in the reading room. 'I got out of hand, as I usually did, and ran clattering over the polished floor, till the Librarian – her name was Miss Flower, I seem to remember – came up and said, "SSSSSh! All the poor people are reading." She seemed to imply they were in some way sick. I looked round and couldn't see any signs of sickness in the readers. It rather puzzled me, but she didn't give me time to work it out or ask questions. She led me up to an enormous, yellow-brown globe, and set it spinning to attract my attention. I found it momentarily of far more interest than any sheets of black old stamps or sick readers.'[54]

H.L. tried to interest him in stamps. 'I have a small nephew (Master P. White, Lulworth, Roslyn Gardens, Darlinghurst) who has taken to collecting postage stamps, and I wish to help him,' he told his dealer. 'Please send him *on my a/c* £1 worth of stamps; a set of unused of some particular country preferred: something that will increase in value. I persuaded the boy's mother to do business with you in future, instead of with your friend near The Australia: she knows nothing whatever of stamps but is very keen for her son's sake.' Paddy sent his uncle a 'very nicely written letter' of thanks for the gift and H.L. promised more stamps 'when it rains'.[55]

The boy's enthusiasm failed, but it brought him close to the man from whom it seems he inherited, amongst other qualities, prodigious diligence and faith in words. Uncle Arthur was a blur. Frank of Saumarez, still wearing a great beard, rarely appeared from Armidale. James of Edinglassie was never seen, for he was pursuing an obscure feud with Ruth, which began when she received him at the Phillip Street flat in a short-sleeved frock. His maiden aunts Grace and Lucy Lipscomb appeared at Lulworth from time to time. The boy's hero was Clem, with a face the colour of brick and a nose like an eagle.

H.L. began to call for lunch at Lulworth on Sundays and take the family afterwards to visit the stables where he and Dick kept their horses in training. This became the Sunday ritual at Lulworth: St James (with ladies fainting), lunch (perhaps a little dance) and then the drive to Randwick where Paddy watched

> the lads in their singlets, swinging buckets of shining water, and the older men, bandy-legged, and the glistening, muscular, trembling horses.[56]

H.L. courted Ruth. She loved food and had good cooks. H.L. sent her pigeons, black duck and kangaroo tails from Belltrees. 'I have tried hard but unsuccessfully so far to get a hare for Ruth,' he told Dick. 'Can never put one up when carrying a gun.' When he succeeded he heard with alarm that she was leaving the hares hanging in the garage at Lulworth until the flesh was so rotten it could be spooned out.[57] He never won Ruth over but was undeterred. He commended her when her photograph appeared on the social page of the *Bulletin*; when he sent his brother a large photograph of sheep in lucerne for the 'smoking room' at Lulworth, he asked wryly, 'Did Ruth approve of it as a work of art?'[58]

The usual custom of their class was to find somewhere to escape the worst months of Sydney's summer. Their boy's asthma made this imperative for the Whites. Arrankamp was a guest house not far from Sutton Forest run by a fierce Miss Brennan with an army of maids to occupy the children while their parents motored around the Highlands. On their stays at Arrankamp, Ruth took the boy over to the Morrices' old, honest house staring 'surprised out of the landscape'.[59] His godmother Gertrude baked little cornflour cakes on these visits, and there was a kangaroo dog called Jack. Paddy met their friend Mr

Bagot who was old and had a big white beard and looked like God. One summer Dick was struggling to find a name for his new racehorse by Seremond out of Microbe. Paddy said, 'Vaccine'. Dick never had a finer horse, and the name his son chose was famous on the Australian track.

In mid-December 1919, as Sydney sweltered in a heatwave, the Whites and their friends the Gordons took a steamer to Tasmania to stay at Browns River near Hobart. It was an idyllic summer, the last of the boy's early childhood, and he remembered Tasmania as 'a kind of paradise lost' which he might someday regain.[60] Apart from the hotel and a few wooden houses there was nothing at Browns River but a beach and a jetty and fields of raspberry canes where Ruth sent him early in the morning to bring back punnets of fruit.[61] Paddy and Sue buried oyster shells on the beach, jagged edges up in the sand, to watch the guests stumbling over them in bare feet.

Lizzie was left in charge when the Whites and Gordons motored off round the island and she walked the children up to Mr Adams' shot tower on the hill and round to the next bay to see the blowhole after a storm. She had a taste for the macabre. Stuffed heads of dogs hung in the Old Curiosity Shop like hunting trophies. These were the dogs which mauled convicts at Port Arthur, and the little boy was so thrilled and terrified by the sight of them that he had nightmares.

The voyage home was terrible. He broke into a case of apricots and ate so many he was ill as the ship ploughed through rough seas in Bass Strait.[62] Back at Lulworth, after unpacking the starfish and anemones he left to rot on his windowsill, he dragged out the big dictionary downstairs to check a word overheard when he was hiding in the raspberry canes at Browns River. Margaret Gordon was saying, 'I can't believe he's one of theirs. He's like a changeling.' He did not know the word, but he caught the tone and was shocked. The dictionary proved him right. It was awful to think he was mixed up for someone else's boy and not Ruth's and Dick's at all. The idea was horrible at first, but it came to promise escape.

FOUR

The Best Years

ELABORATE PREPARATIONS were made for Paddy's education. Cranbrook came on to the market during the war, and Mr Victor White was a member of the syndicate that outbid the Papal Legate to buy the house and its acres of garden for a new Anglican boys' school.

After old James White died at Cranbrook in 1890, his widow married a young man and disappeared to Scotland with the pictures and plate. She was killed in Roxburghshire the following year when her gig overturned on a mountain road. The Whites muttered darkly of murder, and their version of the scandal passed down through the family until it appeared in *A Fringe of Leaves*. Garnet Roxburgh, driving the rich widow he married in Van Diemen's Land, 'overturned the gig. Her neck was broke!'[1] At the turn of the century Cranbrook became the official residence of the governors of New South Wales until the wartime Labor government, in a Bolshevik gesture, turfed out the Viceroy and put the house on the market.

Dick joined the syndicate to save his son from the King's School. Cranbrook, the new and distinguished school that opened late in the war, had as a founding purpose the need to keep Patrick White from the hell of the graziers' school in Parramatta. On the opening day there were several Whites among Cranbrook's sixty-four pupils, and Mr Victor White – 'a generous benefactor' – sat on the council. The school became one of Ruth's charities and the *Bulletin* later reported the art and antique fair organised by 'Mrs Victor White, one of the Hunter River clan' to raise money for the school. 'Every pawn shop-keeper and antique dealer in and around Sydney has made the energetic lady's acquaintance in the last few weeks,' wrote the paper. Stalls were set up along the drive. 'Dancing girls and crystal-gazers and a magic carpet will fleece the sheep and the lamb as closely as a champion shearer.'[2] The fair was ruined by a hailstorm.

Paddy White arrived at Cranbrook a few weeks after his return from Tasmania in early 1920. He was seven and a half, a pale child with bright eyes, pointed ears and long skinny arms. His asthma had grown worse and there were whole days he spent wheezing and gasping for breath. He was resilient, polite, pessimistic and curious. Even then people were provoked to ask what on earth would *happen* to this little boy.

While he wrestled with algebra at Cranbrook, he was introduced to Shakespeare in the Morrices' flat on Darling Point, where old Mrs Morrice received him sitting on the edge of a sofa, always in black, with rows of tiny jet buttons down her arms. She was the first person to fire the boy's literary imagination. As they talked about *Hamlet* he felt he was being treated as an equal. He did not understand all the words, 'but would pick out the stories, the bloodier the better'. Anyone could understand people killing one another. 'It's in the papers every day.' The boy loved the battles, the blood and thunder of the plays, and shared young Rodney Halliday's dreams of the Egyptian queens who 'put a pearl into a cup of vinegar and rank it right off'. Early in the mornings before breakfast, hiding from Lizzie under the sheet, he worked his way through the plays. The word EXEUNT was magic.[3]

The Morrices were important in his life even apart from the raw material they gave him for his work. Old Mrs Morrice's husband had died in 1918 and she came down to Sydney with her books and a little furniture, her miniatures and the withered apple that was found in her son's pocket after he was killed at Gallipoli. She set up in a flat in Tredegar House on Darling Point with Minna and Gertrude, her two unmarried daughters. Minna was cheerful and outgoing. Gertrude, Ruth's old friend and the boy's godmother, was more beautiful, more intellectual and aloof. The women lived on their investments, shopped at David Jones, smoked, read and looked after their mother. This was a women's household: the Morrice boys never stayed at Tredegar House on their visits to Sydney. No man had been good enough for her daughters – or none had the acres to match her snobbery – so now Gertrude and Minna waited on her. They came 'when the voice called'.[4] She was a tiny monster with frizzy hair, a tough nose and small, fine, dark, riveting eyes. They were eyes at once laughing and demanding, and her mouth had a way of being about to smile or bite without warning.

She had grown up in an atmosphere of high literary seriousness into which she initiated the boy. She was German, though she had lived as a child in Sutton Forest before being taken to Europe to study music in Heidelberg and Geneva, where she became 'a good singer and pianiste'. One uncle in Dresden was a great friend of the translator of Shakespeare, Wolf Graf von Baudissin, and wrote many dull novels under the pseudonym Waldmüller. Another uncle was the poet Julius Duboc, who escaped Germany in the aftermath of the 1848 revolutions and put his Romantic sensibility to the test in Australia. Duboc was ruined on Kangaroo Hills near Armidale, a heartbreaking slab of land owned for a time by James Withycombe, and he came to hate Australia where even the blue skies seemed 'celestial lavishness bestowed upon a withered dying corpse'. He returned to Germany to become an earnest philosopher of Life without God.[5]

Walter Morrice married her at the British Embassy in Bern and brought her back to Browley on the edge of Sutton Forest, where she had nine children and wrote serials like *The Wilfulness of Winnie* for Sydney and country newspapers. Her writing was sharp, witty, rather cold and sentimental. A collection of her bush poetry, *The River and Other Verses*, was published the year Ruth's boy was born.[6] When the war broke out and Germans were interned a few miles from Browley in the jail at Berrima, she burnt all her German books except one kid-bound volume of Duboc's poetry, *Fruh- und Abendroth*.[7]

German was the first language of the Morrice children, and they spoke English always with a faint, attractive burr. The girls, though Protestants, were educated by the nuns at Moss Vale in a school established by the de Lauret sisters, daughters of a former member of Charles X's Garde du Corps who had settled to the south of Sutton Forest at Goulburn.[8] These Dominican nuns, extraordinary women in the Anglo-Saxon world of rural New South Wales, educated two important figures in Patrick White's life: his godmother Gertrude and Roy de Maistre. Through them White was in touch with a demanding European tradition in which art was taken very seriously.

Gertrude Morrice took up the education of the boy begun by her mother, unobtrusively opening windows in his 'often desperate' mind. Gertrude was in her forties. She left to her sister Minna the role of aunt to their tribe of nephews and nieces. It was Minna who took the children to pantomimes and the zoo. Paddy was drawn to Gertrude, who lived most of the time out of sight in her room, preferring her own company, thinking a lot and saying little. 'She took her godmotherhood seriously, though I don't think she had a religious faith. She introduced me, book by book, at birthdays and Christmas, to Aldous Huxley and D.H. Lawrence, starting me off on whatever intellectual life I have had.'[9] Her hair was bobbed, she wore rather shapeless dresses and smoked cigarettes held in a pair of tongs. When she travelled – even before old Mrs Morrice died at last – she took cargo boats, an eccentric preference in the age of passenger liners. They took her to places she would otherwise never see. She spent a difficult year in England minding a family of de Mestre nephews. 'I regret to say that we made her life an absolute hell,' Richard de Mestre recalled. 'The three of us fought the whole time, so much so that she almost had a nervous break-down when our parents returned. She must have been a really tough old bird to have hung on . . . Incidentally, Auntie G. bore us no ill will and always came up with birthday and Christmas presents and I especially remember a 20-foot stock whip which she had made as a special order for me and which unfortunately I later lost in a poker game to an American when I was working in the oil world in Burma in 1938.'[10]

The track to the Morrices' flat lay across Rushcutters Bay Park and Paddy came to know every inch of it: the stone wall curving round the harbour, the big Moreton Bays and the rancid figs that lay like a carpet beneath them ready to stick to your shoes, the field where the circus set up its tent, and the seats where strangers sat waiting, perhaps to abduct little boys. He was warned against strangers. Ruth and Lizzie considered the park safe in the mornings, but he was not allowed to cross it alone at any other time. By the sea wall in Rushcutters Bay Park at night was the exact spot where Hurtle Duffield met his whore Nance Lightfoot. Parks and park benches were potent images, full of fears and possibilities. Even more frightening was the boxing stadium over the road: 'Little boys were always being nabbed there. I used to walk back home from Cranbrook with a fat, red-faced Ryrie boy and we used to skim the pavements outside the Stadium. I spent a lot of time as a kid running away from things, running away from Larries.'[11]

He began to learn the map of Sydney, and the 'brown summer heat and the cracks in the Sydney asphalt became part of me, to last for ever'.[12] He was too young to manage the tram into town alone, so he explored the city with his mother, who seemed to know every second face in Pitt Street. Sydney had an odd shape for Ruth: she was reluctant to go over the Bridge. The North Shore was rather against her principles. Darling Point and its hinterland Woollahra, Point Piper and Bellevue Hill, were Ruth's territory.

Dick was keen to go places. He took his son on the ferry down the Harbour to Manly, and to the little boy these voyages seemed like journeys to the other side of the world. Father and son stood together on the outside deck as the ferry rolled across the Heads in rough weather. Paddy was never seasick. The trip to Manly became linked in his imagination with confession, shared understanding, points in life when decisions are reached.[13] At Manly the Norfolk pines sighed in the salt wind and strange faces thronged the esplanade. One summer they all came over to the Pacific Hotel for a few days. Paddy ran wild along the beach. Dick was sick from sunburn and sat eating big ice creams with his son and daughter. Ruth suspected Manly was rather common: servants swam and made love on the sand under cover of darkness, and simple country folk like Stan and Amy Parker came here for holidays.[14]

The boy was allowed gradually to explore on his own and his solitary wanderings, 'mooning, dreaming' through Sydney, staring at faces encountered in the street, 'observing, always observing', were a lonely, happy part of his childhood. Much of Sydney was an Irish town, which he only discovered in the pages of Richard Ellmann's biography of Joyce, where the atmosphere of Dublin at the turn of the century 'recalled Sydney during my childhood years later. The men in the street looked and sounded the same.'[15] He came to know Darlinghurst and the Cross best, the scruffy territory that lay behind his house like a ratty fox on Lulworth's respectable shoulders.

Madame Henri's flat where he now took his French lessons lay along Woolcott Street where the prostitutes lazed in doorways after their night's work. The sight of these tarts at rest was mysterious and thrilling, and if he stood staring at them long enough they shouted obscenities at him across the street. On Saturday afternoons he slipped out the back and cut through the Cross to the pictures, petrified of being stopped on the way by the larrikins who hung about waiting to taunt little boys. Ruth thought the pictures common but no harm, and seemed unaware of the tarts and larries, the hazards of the Cross. To the boy this territory was his tribal land, filled with associations of the spirit: 'I seemed to spend more of my early life trudging these streets on errands of one kind or another. So that in a sense I, too, am part of the neighbourhood – spiritually part of it.'[16]

Mumps broke out at Lulworth in 1921 and Paddy was bundled off to his cousins the Wynnes in the Blue Mountains to escape the infection. They were obliged to leave Mount Wilson soon afterwards on a motoring tour of the Riverina and the boy was left in the care of their manservant and cook.

These weeks at Wynstay were wonderful. Matt and Flo Davies were 'black English rather than sunny Australian' and they cut through the politeness and rectitude that cocooned the boy at Lulworth. At home he was Master Paddy. On the mountain there was none of that. In the kitchen at Wynstay he felt in contact with real life, 'as opposed to the counterfeit offered children by most grown-ups of our class.

Every moment in their company was vital: the jokes, the laughter, the anecdotes, the smell of Matt's little black pipe, the scent of Flo's scrupulously laundered aprons and dresses.'[17]

In their book life was grim and hilarious. Matt was a Yorkshireman, once a footman and later Owen Wynne's batman in France. Wynne offered him a place in Australia after the war if he brought a cook with him. Matt married Flo, a maid from Blenheim Palace, and they came out to live the rest of their lives on Mount Wilson, always full of stories of the high life they knew: 'how Lord Louis went out leaving the front door ajar and a candelabrum burning on the doorstep'.[18]

If Ruth's altar was the dressing table, the Davies' was the kitchen bench. The smell of ironing, bread, bees' wax, soap and starch intoxicated the boy. Whatever love he was offered as a child, he found the love of devoted servants the easiest to accept. From Lizzie Clark and in the kitchens of Lulworth and Wynstay he absorbed the conviction that service is love, the truest form of love, and the more menial and selfless the service the greater that love. He put out of his mind the complicated consideration of money, that whatever sincere affection grew up between servants and masters they were paid to love him and paid to serve.

The boy had never known the unconditional affection of grandparents; and the fondness of his White uncles, aunts and cousins for this odd little boy came filtered through Ruth's suspicions. Dick's love was a benign mystery to him, and he was becoming fearful of his mother's love and fighting in a moody and stubborn way to keep her at a distance. But all this time, through his early childhood from the time he was three until he was thirteen, the boy was attended by saints. Their love, their service, fell short only in this respect: they could not save him from his asthma. In those attacks he was entirely alone.

Tattered copies of the *News of the World* lay about the kitchen at Wynstay, arriving months late from London bringing the truth about Life. Paddy pored over the paper:

Brief but Ardent
Ill-fated Courtship of Milliner & Engineer

The Midnight Lover
Chapel Luminary in Divorce Court
Bible Reading & Kisses for Another Man's Wife

Fickle Chauffeur

Holiday Camp Scandal
Boys' Instructor Committed on Grave Charges

Quaint Love Token
Lover Jilted after Beautifying Girl with False Teeth

Cupid in Caravan
Wealthy Furrier's Wife & Entertainer
Four Divorce Cases Follow Concert Party Trip

The Wynnes returned from the Riverina to find the boy's head in this trash. Mariamne Wynne, anxious to improve his nine-year-old mind, gave him a volume of the *Myths of Ancient Greece* to read, 'substituting the gods' adulteries, feuds, and murders for those of the wider-ranging British social system'.[19]

He was well on Mount Wilson, but when he returned to Sydney in June he had an attack of asthma so severe that Ruth and Dick were convinced he must be kept in the mountains as much as possible. When a cottage with seven acres of garden came up for sale on the mountain later in the year, Ruth bought it for £2,000. It was called Beowang after the native tree ferns that grow on Mount Wilson. But Ruth, who hated that 'dreary' Australian name, modestly rechristened the place Withycombe. The Whites moved in that Christmas.

On Mount Wilson the boy found the paradise of his childhood and youth. Most of his holidays from this time were spent at Withycombe. 'The first day was always particularly wonderful, and one clung on to it as long as one could.' He came to know it all, 'not only the elms and maples but the sassafras, blackwood and scrub.'[20] It seemed the most wonderful place on earth.

At 3,000 feet, the air is clear with a tang of eucalyptus. 'A real miracle worker', wrote an English traveller when the area was first being opened up. 'We have one of the finest opportunities ever given to a country for attracting wealthy sufferers.'[21] Wild bush surrounds the mountain on all sides. Down in the gullies are creeks and waterfalls of icy, fine spray falling into black pools. Parrots and lyre-birds live in the dark bush and at times lyre-birds built nests in the wilder gardens above. The top of the mountain is an English world: eight gardens of rhododendrons, wistaria, azaleas and elms growing in deep chocolate-red soil. In spring daffodils flower along the drives and in autumn the trees turn colours never seen in the steamy air of Sydney. Among the gardens stands the peculiar fibro church of St George, with a squat tower and barely any windows. A paddock of graves and tall beowangs lies to one side of the church and the gravestones bear evidence of long, easy lives. Servants are buried next to their masters.

The League of Friendship had a page in the Sydney *Sunday Times* where 'President' gave small prizes and perfunctory encouragement to the literary efforts of 'Tickletoe', 'Australian Lassie', 'Brunhilde', 'Circe', 'Shellpink', 'Red Admiral', and so on. 'Red Admiral' was Paddy White aged nine of Sydney. The Red Admiral was his favourite butterfly, and this was his debut with the League,

> I shall tell you about Mount Wilson. One gets off the train at Bell. Bell is the proud possessor of four houses. From Bell there is a long uninteresting drive, till one comes to a place in the road called the Zig Zag. On either side of the road after the Zig Zag are thick trees and vines. Then there is another stretch of uninteresting road and then a beautiful avenue of elms. Our house is nearby the first you come to. It has lovely oaks, elms, pines and cypresses. There is also an orchard. My cousins live up the road a little way. They have a beautiful old garden. There is a mile and a quarter of stone wall around it. My cousin's grandfather built a turkish bath, and had a little black boy stoking it all day.

'President' replied: 'Dear Red Admiral, – What a sport the grandfather must have been.' This was the first piece by Patrick White to be published. 'President' rated his effort well below essays on floods and fires and 'Velta's' description of a nasty accident on the Terrigal bus. Paddy White, unlike the boy with warts in *Three Uneasy Pieces*, won no prizes with his essay yet it was a flag Ruth waved above her little genius: published and not yet ten.[22]

Red Admiral had more to say the following spring,

> This time I am going to tell you about a moonlight picnic at Mount Wilson. We started off at about 7 o'clock and walked for about a mile till we reached the picnicking spot. A fire was built and we cooked chops and sausages over the blaze. The waterfall nearby looked like silver in the moonlight, while the tree ferns made weird noises as they swayed to and fro in the breeze. The hanging vines glistened with the spray showered upon them from the waterfall, and the grass rustled as if a snake army was creeping along in its depths. We did not return from this beautiful picnic till quite late, and then I was very sorry to go.[23]

Withycombe was a rather shabby cottage until Ruth got to work. It was built of weatherboard but covered in pressed tin to imitate stone and stucco. Behind the big wide veranda were a sitting room and two rows of bedrooms, each side of a courtyard which some earlier owner roofed to make a billiard room. Ruth had a fumed-oak cover built for the table, and the billiard room became their dining room. She furnished the house simply but beautifully; this was a holiday house, somewhere to relax from the elegance of Lulworth. Fires in big stone fireplaces were their only heating in winter and on the cold summer nights of Mount Wilson. Out the back was a long kitchen with a huge iron stove and windows that looked north over the bush to the broken horizon. Ruth installed a generator in a shed which was once the local post office, and it puttered away at night to give them electric light. Her diesel could be heard across the mountain.

She set out passionately to make a perfect English garden which Sydney's fug denied her at Lulworth. Cedars and holm oaks already grew at Withycombe and stands of old beowang ferns were rooted out of the paddock to make way for a new plantation of European trees. Ruth laid out hedges of cypress and laurel around the cottage and planted roses in a sunken bed edged with strawberries. Paths and dry-stone walls appeared at her command though she bossed the gardener to the point where he smashed the flagstones in exasperation. There was a practical side to Ruth and her new herbaceous border, the plants tagged with elegant lead labels, was designed to provide cut flowers for Lulworth.

The sight of a woman walking along such a border, her hem trailing through the flowers, stuck in the boy's mind. From when? Probably even before Withycombe, when hems were longer. Madame Vatatzes and Joany Golson 'sauntered down the silver borders' at the pink cottage at Hyères, 'their skirts drawing a perfume from them'. Hem-dragging, it seems, happens at moments of unrequited affection. Mrs Standish confronted her son on such a path,

> Sometimes I think you're a bad-tempered little boy, said Mother. Sometimes I think you don't love me any more.
>   She pulled the head off a dead flower. Her dress spread out round her, copper-coloured, as she stooped, it caught on the spikes of winter flowers, it shook and caught the beads of dew. She was so beautiful that he would have liked to touch her. But he did not know what to do, or say. He stood kicking at the frosted ground.[24]

Suzanne was seven when they came to Mount Wilson. Though they bickered and fought like most small children do, the two of them grew close on their mountain holidays. Yet they were so different: she was easy, cheerful and a bit gullible, a fat little tomboy, a White to Paddy's Withycombe. The boy was cautious and mean. Lizzie observed that when Sue's money box was full she bought something, while Paddy lined his full boxes up along his chest of drawers. When he was exiled from Mount Wilson a few years later, the boy wrote some heartfelt, awkward verse about 'darling Susan' playing in the

creeks on the mountain, and a long 'Reminiscence' about a time
when

> life was but a game from morn till night,
> When Sue and I disputed for some toy
> And nurse was forced to come and stop the fight.
> Our morning walks come back so vividly
> When I refused to act constrainedly,
>
> But must rush ahead and, falling, skin
> My knees, or Sue must bark her sturdy shin;
> And there were picnics near the waterfall
> Where tadpoles swam about in pebbled pools,
> Just meant for every childish hand to maul
> And gaily cram in jars, where, as a rule,
> They only live to die in muddy dregs.
> The picnic done, we ran on hastening legs
>
> Down to the saw-mill in the sassafras.
> How loved we then to watch the steely mass
> Of that giant moon, eating the fallen logs
> With gaping teeth, while sawdust fell in showers,
> Comingling with the oily stench of cogs
> And toiling wheels, the scent of forest flowers
> Floating upon the limpid summer air
>
> . . . we ranged the garden o'er
> And caught the frisking fireflies, if perchance
> Unwary they became; but when we saw
> Nurse sweeping down to pack us off to bed –
> No hour from out of twenty four so dread –
>
> We climbed up high into a sycamore,
> With not a thought for all the clothes we tore,
> And there sat cowering close against the stars
> With bated breath . . . [25]

Mount Wilson had rustic simplicity and a rigid social structure.
At the top were half a dozen families: the Whites and the Wynnes,
the Marcus Clarks who had a big store in town, the lawyers Stephen,
who were cousins of the Stephens of Bloomsbury, the Manns who
had hotels in Sydney, and the Valders, who ran Nooroo next door to
Withycombe as a farm and orchard. Young Mrs Valder had Morrice
connections. These few households were organised into a village by

Mariamne Wynne. Her relentless energy was sometimes resented, but she gave everyone something to do. There were dinner parties, tennis parties, bridge, dances – often in fancy dress – and a sports day to mark the New Year. At fetes and flower shows all classes mixed, and the mountain kids joined the big families for picnics and expeditions through the bush. Ruth was never keen to picnic for she was reluctant to eat sitting on a log.

The Wynnes were building a new Wynstay, something big and English in stone to replace the old wooden house. They had made their money importing cement to Australia, and Owen Wynne's grandfather had directed him to learn a trade before he could inherit his fortune. Now he was putting his training as a cabinet maker to use making furniture for the new house from mountain timbers. Paddy saw him ankle deep in shavings, 'this picture of an English officer and gentleman: clipped moustache, ruddy complexion, hair crinkly as an Airedale's coat' and this became an image in the boy's mind of profound satisfaction: 'the sweet smell of blond timber suggested all safety and virtue'.[26]

He liked steady Owen Wynne, but was dazzled by his wife Mariamne and her don't-give-a-damn upper-class haughtiness. This rich and independent spirit, who had driven ambulances in France during the First World War, now found herself marooned on an Australian mountain. Paddy remembered first seeing her – it was at lunch at Lulworth – wearing a cloche of monkey fur. The look and manner of Mariamne Wynne belonged, in time, to the dowdier Marcia Lushington of Bogong, first seen eating alone in the dining room of the Australia,

> Her dress proclaimed her a rich dowdy, or fashionable slattern. If the monkey fur straggling down from a Venetian tricorne gave her head the look of a hanging basket in a fernery, the suit she wore was buttoned and belted in a loosely regimental style, an effect contradicted in turn by several ropes of pearls which she slung about while studying the menu.

That was Mariamne Wynne, a great snob, a woman of the world who could impersonate the great actresses the boy read about in English papers. She helped him make a toy theatre with actors and dancers cut out of English magazines. 'Lopokova was one of my stars.'[27]

Two tribes of servants worked on the mountain. The English servants lived quite isolated lives in the big houses, but the Australians were part of the landscape. The Kirks knew the place better than anyone for they had brought early settlers to the mountain and stayed on to work while others played: 'We were the ones who made Mount Wilson tick.' Sid Kirk ran the sawmill. He showed the Whites' boy where lyre-birds danced in the scrub and taught him to track wombats. He took him exploring the gullies and hunting zircons in the creek, and told fantastic stories about the mountain and the war and the past. 'He taught me to unravel bush silence.'[28]

Tom Kirk, later a champion axeman, was a boy of seven when the Whites arrived on the mountain. He worked in the garden at Withycombe: 'Paddy was nervy. He always had asthma, a nervy kind of asthma. Little things set him off, like people not walking fast enough or walking too fast. Once he shouted at me, "You're only working class." Then Sue got stuck into him for that. A lot of the time you couldn't get him out of the house. He was never a robust boy. The asthma had him.

'Sue was the opposite. She was bubbling with fun. She was like her father, always fat and laughing. She was just about the nicest person I ever met. When we were children we decided we'd get married when we grew up. One day Ruth heard me calling her Sue and Ruth said, "You will call my daughter Miss Suzanne." You don't forget things like that. Ruth was the queen of snobs. She was the sort of woman who enjoyed insulting you, enjoyed getting you going. An unpleasant woman. She would only employ English servants. Australians weren't good enough. She didn't like them and she said so. She laid down the law about everything that was going, especially gardening. Fred Swainson the gardener would keep on saying "Yes ma'am" as she blew the tripes out of him.

'You wouldn't know she was mother of those children – Lizzie treated them like her own – Ruth patted them on the head like they were pet dogs. They never expected anything from her. You'd think they were strangers. You could see the antagonism between Paddy and her, but you didn't see them fighting. He must have felt like putting in the boot, but he didn't.

'Horses was all Dick could talk about. He always had a smile on his face. Dick was a water diviner. He cut a green stick and wandered round the paddocks. He got his men to dig a well on the side of a gully. A most unpromising place. He said they'd find water at 60 feet and they struck it at 59. He sounded Australian, not like her. There was no class distinction with him. One of my jobs was to ride Sue's pony to keep it quiet when they were away. Dick saw me one day and said, "You shouldn't be riding that pony without a saddle." I thought I was being reprimanded, but the next time Dick was up he brought a saddle with an English pigskin seat. It was one of the most beautiful things I ever owned.'[29]

Twice Paddy made the journey out to Clem Withycombe's place at Walgett. Once he travelled with Ruth but the second time alone.

She gave the guard endless instructions as she put him on the train at Central. Next morning his ancient great-aunts Grace and Lucy Lipscomb were waiting at Maitland to take care of him for the day. They lived in a brown weatherboard cottage with a pepper tree in its yard. A steam tram ran to East Maitland where they visited the Withy-combe rector of St Paul's. His aunts put him back on the train that night for the second leg of the journey. Above the window of the sleeper, 'The slimy water went slip slop inside the big, railways' water-bottle.'[30] At Narrabri in the morning he climbed down in starlight, bought himself breakfast in the Railway Refreshment Room and waited for the little motor train, the rattler, to take him west to Walgett.

He reached the end of the line in the afternoon and Clem was there in a sulky. 'Would you like to take the reins, old man?' his uncle asked. It was a moment of triumph for the boy. The road took them past the Aboriginals' shanties clustered on the outskirts of town. 'There's nothing you can do for these people,' his uncle said. Because he was fond of his uncle, he dismissed the blacks from his mind.[31]

The house on Barwon Vale stood by a lagoon in flat country about a mile from the river. It was a spartan set up, except for his Aunt Mag's pretty little parlour, where she read novels in the afternoon. They had no children. The boy listened to his uncle's endless country stories of marriages and divorce; he rode the great Vaccine which was having a spell out at Walgett; and he had his come-uppance from the Withycombes' cook to whom he had boasted childishly that he liked drinking vinegar. Perhaps he had Cleopatra in mind and Shakespeare saying she downed a glass of vinegar and pearls. The cook poured Paddy a tot and he drank it, his eyes smarting with tears and his stomach shrivelling. Of this (self-inflicted) humiliation he later wrote, 'I was sure I was going to die – but recovered, as from all the cups of vinegar I have been forced to drink in later life.'[32]

The Victor Whites had now to find somewhere out of Sydney's unhealthy climate to send their son to school, and chose Tudor House. This was the first of the lung schools on the Southern High-lands, advertising discreetly for Anglican boys with weak chests. They never mentioned asthma in their prospectuses – let alone TB – but the clue to the business was the offhand mention of altitude. 'The school site is an ideal one,' said Tudor House. 'It is 2208 feet above sea-level. The climate is unsurpassed. The School buildings are surrounded by 150 acres of beautifully undulating country.'[33] Summers were hot and short up there and the winters cold. Misty rain drifted up from the coast, and when the wind turned to the west in winter, it cut like a knife and brought light snow. This was held to be a tonic climate, invigorating, just the thing to put the glow of health in a young boy's cheeks.

The school had taken over another of Horbury Hunt's country houses. It sat on a ridge looking across paddocks of 'yellow grass, under the skeleton trees', towards the stump of Mount Ashby, which had once run with fire, 'its black cone streaming'.[34] Sutton Forest was only a few miles away, the other side of Moss Vale. Ruth knew this country well.

No school in Australia was like Tudor House. The boys were rich, the bias was privileged but it was not a fake-English prep school: the temper was Australian. The place was a shambles. Not much had been done to the old house for twenty years, still lit by gas and with water pumped by steam engine from the dam.[35] The school farm supplied a glut of apples, potatoes and milk to the kitchens. They were short of staff: maids came and went. Pupils were just as hard to come by, and by this time only thirty boys slept in dormitories that once took fifty. The headmaster, Thomas Skuse, had one assistant teacher and Miss Babbington, who looked after the 'bubs' like Paddy White, who arrived in early 1922.

He was terrified. On the first night he thought of selling his pencils and making a break for the railway station at Moss Vale, but he survived and found he liked the place. Homesickness died away, but he missed Saturday afternoons at the Kings Cross pictures and wrote some 'serials' of his own which were passed round the class in half a dozen handwritten magazines. In his first months at the school he wrote a bloody, swashbuckling play called 'The Mexican Bandits'. 'There was a good girl and a bad girl . . . The good one was called Ida Rowe and everyone started shooting everyone else in a court scene.' Hardly anyone was left alive by the time the curtain fell.[36]

Skuse was about to come a cropper. He was a big, red-faced old man, a great sight in cricket flannels, who had a habit of calling little boys to his room late at night. One remembered being woken and brought down to Skuse still too sleepy to know what was being tried. 'Someone before me had proved unsatisfactory. I, too, proved unsatisfactory.'[37] The new boy had a single encounter with Skuse which he remembered with gratitude. Paddy had been called to Skuse's study to be punished and arrived quite terrified, but Skuse put down the cane and embraced him, much as Alf Dubbo was to be embraced by the Rev. Timothy Calderon,

> At this point an alarming, but not altogether unexpected incident, the boy realised, began to occur. Mr Calderon fumbled at Alf's head, then pressed it against his stomach. They were standing in awkward conjunction in the semi-darkness and familiar smells. Although at first doubtful how he ought to behave, Alf decided to submit to the pressure. He could feel buttons and a watch-chain eating ravenously

into his cheek, and then, deep down in the rector's stomach, he heard a rather pitiful rumble. The sound that uncoiled itself was both apologetic and old. The boy visualised an old, soft, white worm slowly raising its head, swaying, and lolling, before falling back.

In this inconclusive embrace with Skuse sex was a matter of punishment forgiven and the boy 'dissolved in a mingling of gratitude and anti-climax'.[38]

The previous summer, walking home to Lulworth from the Rushcutters Bay baths with Dick, the boy had had his first erection. 'While looking down I suggested to my father that something unusual was happening. He became prim and embarrassed, shifted his wet bathers from one shoulder to the other, and told me to step out. At the same time there was the passing glimmer of a smile.'[39] The same day, by strange chance, he met Banjo Paterson. The great Australian poet had married one of the Whites' cousins and was visiting Lulworth. Dick brought him down into the wild garden to meet his son. A red-letter day: his first poet – even if Paterson had a face like a shrivelled lemon – and his first erection. The boy discovered masturbation in his bath, bewitched and troubled by the tiny spurt of white in the water: 'shamefully realised, deliciously seeping, orgasm'.[40]

Skuse disappeared in May – Tudor House announced tersely, 'Mr Skuse has decided to go to England' – and the headmaster of Suva Grammar, who was married to a delicate wife, grasped the chance of getting to a school 'which enjoys a perfect climate'.[41] Arthur Mann had served in the Balloon Corps on the Western Front, was pink-cheeked, clean-shaven, an Oxford graduate and very English. His arrival marked another of Tudor House's fresh starts. Hot water was piped to the bathrooms and a women's committee supervised disinfecting, repainting and refurbishment. After a couple of painful years Mann was also to 'go to England', but his failure was an influence of a different kind on Paddy. 'He would now be called a nut case,' one of the boys recalled. 'He dived into problems with blather and puff and came up with answers that were completely off the beam. He was ignored. He was never at grips with the practical running of the school. Indeed the possibility of him running a school satisfactorily was nil.'[42]

The boys ran wild. Within the easy routine of Tudor House Paddy White was free for the first time in his life. Mann had some control over the boys for only about half the day. They woke to a bell at 6.45, dressed and cleaned their shoes on the brick veranda. The older boys, in a democratic gesture, made their own beds before the whole school trooped in to a breakfast of porridge, salmon and rice, or scrambled eggs. Prayers were held in the old ballroom before lessons began. Blackett Smith's cockatoo, in a cage outside the window, learned to squawk, 'for ever and ever, amen'. They learned hardly anything from Pendlebury's *New School Arithmetic*, Palgrave's *Golden Treasury*, and Mann's extraordinary French classes. Paddy White was the brightest boy in the school, his French was the best, but he hooted along with the others as Mann tried with little mirrors to teach them to shape their mouths around French vowels. Lessons were over by early afternoon and the boys were free.

Clutching a handful of fruit and biscuits – each boy had his own square tin of Arnott's Monte Carlo, Iced Vo Vo, or Zu Zu Mixed locked in the store – they took their ponies and bicycles and roamed over the country. There were a few rules they were expected to obey: not to head towards Moss Vale, not to break into people's gardens, and not to use bows and arrows in the pitched battles they fought in the bush. Boomerangs were allowed. Bird nesting was the great craze of Tudor House. The boys worked in pairs,

> How Clem shone, blowing a maggie's egg for Harold on a clear morning of spring, ankle-deep in dead grass, against the huge stringy bark. Held to his more-than-friend's lips the speckled eggshell increased in transparency, and reddish, palpitating light.

Those rare, red-speckled eggs were innocent treasures, precious gifts, something 'round and whole and desirable and good'. Stan Parker's boy and Theodora Goodman also came to know the language of maggies' eggs.[43]

Paddy was no shot but he liked holding a smooth, clean, oily rifle and the *smell* of shooting, 'its serious pungency'. The paddocks round the school were full of rabbits which the boys shot and hunted with ferrets, the little predators 'turning and rattling' in their boxes until the moment of their release into the netted warrens.[44] They fried the carcasses over fires in bush cubby houses, and an old man appeared every few weeks to buy the skins. It was good pocket money. Below the house, through the improvised golf course, ran a muddy creek where the boys caught leeches. 'It was simple,' recalled one of the hunters. 'You put in your leg, leeches grabbed it and you pulled them off.' Sixty years on he remembers the sight of 'a fair Paddy White dangling very, very white legs into the creek'.[45]

The boy grew in this exhilarating freedom, 'Dashing about on ponies and screwing in the long grass'.[46] From his time in this oasis of sensuality, grass and sex were forever coupled in his imagination. 'Sex was the theme developed in the dormitories, in the tunnels of drought-stricken laurels, and the long grass hedged by hawthorn. Often barely explicit, like a crush on the music mistress as she smelled a bunch of violets or guided one's hands at the piano, or spasms of admiration for a sportsmaster's hairy, muscular arms, there were also brutal, boyish orgasms. I imagined I was in love. I suffered my first agonies of sexual jealousy.'[47] There were few facts of life of which he was not aware by the time he was twelve. 'I was always watching dogs and bitches, bulls and cows, even men and women in the long grass, and had had sexual experience myself by then.'[48]

He was curious, a stickybeak, drawn to the unexplained, the moments when adults fall silent. Tudor House had a second clientèle, those who arrived at the school because of 'family pressures', and the boy saw what lay behind that label: divorce, death, adultery. He was precociously confident of his knowledge of the world and felt this set him apart. When Dorothy the maid collapsed in the dining room he explained to his companions that she was pregnant. Falling maids – like Pearl Brawne, who fell at Meröe, and Rose Portion collapsing at the Bonners on Potts Point – were a hazard of life in the Whites' circle.[49] The boys laughed when Dorothy disappeared and Paddy laughed with them, but he remembered the maids stepping over the body and smashed plates and custard slops to get on with their work.

He read whatever he could lay his hands on, and found some very odd books tucked away in the school library, 'strange jewels in Ethel M. Dell and Maurice Hewlett's *The Forest Lovers*'. He was forbidden to read *Wuthering Heights* but he found a copy and got through it, though without great enjoyment. Ruth was startled to find him at Lulworth one day with *Lady Windermere's Fan*, but he found it very dull too. By the time he was twelve he had finished Galsworthy's *The Man of Property* and surprised his puzzled parents by discussing the charms of Irene Forsyte with Mrs Charles Ebsworth at lunch.[50]

Sometime in his second year at the school he wrote a play called 'Love's Awakening': 'There were only three people in it. A man and a woman decided they were going to have a divorce, and he goes out to buy the divorce and that's the end of Act One. Act Two, he has supper with the other woman and decides he's not going to have a divorce after all because he doesn't care for the other woman and he goes back in Act Three – and Love Awakens.'[51]

Every Monday an elderly Anglican clergyman came in a buggy to teach Scripture, and every month the boys, dressed in boaters and grey suits, walked or rode over the paddocks, dodging the magpies in spring, to hear him preach in the narrow, dusty Christ Church, Bong Bong. Nailed above the altar was a tin banner, loose at one end, announcing in patent-medicine script that GOD IS LOVE. God was the light blue of that banner.[52] When Theodora Goodman sat in such a church with the girls of Spofforth's Academy she washed her hands in the purple light of St George slaying the dragon, but the boys of Tudor House shuffled and scratched under windows of lilies, iris and roses.[53] Bong Bong's idea of heaven was an English garden. The service was reduced to Church of England essentials. No ritual or mystery interrupted the old man's amble through psalms and hymns to a sermon in which the children, the Governor – when in residence at Hillview – and citizens were urged to repent and be reborn in Christ's love. A last hymn released them into the outside world, where

> the trees smelt of sleep, and smoke, and crushed ants and the thin grey, distilled smell that is the smell of trees that have stood a long time in the sun.[54]

Parents taking their children out for the day collected them from the churchyard. The George Whites of Mittabah came occasionally for Paddy. George was Dick's first cousin and lived in the Highlands not far away at the end of a drive of black pines in a vast house overlooking wild country. The boy hated Mittabah. He was always overwhelmed by big families and here were thirteen cousins – including a Faith and a Hope, but no Charity – who shared one lavatory and were made to do chores. This seemed strange to the boy, for the only work he had ever done was collecting snails and calliopsis heads from the garden at Lulworth for a shilling a hundred. The children lived in awe of their father who, it was said, once despatched two of them to keep flies off a bull and forgot all about them out in the paddock. They were too frightened to move, and stayed with the bull most of the night.

Ivy White lay on a sofa as her children stoked the fire. Paddy found her particularly terrifying. She made him learn a Collect by heart every Sunday and recite it as she lay there. 'O God, forasmuch as without thee we are not able to please thee . . . mercifully grant . . . cast thy bright beam of light . . . keep us, we beseech thee . . . Stir up . . . pour thy grace . . . mercifully accept our prayer . . . through Jesus Christ our Lord. Amen.' The boy thought she was a monster. Her maiden name was Voss, and he kept the name in mind, waiting for thirty years to revenge himself on this 'Brunhilde who had left the Ring and joined the Salvation Army, taking with her, however, plenty of Wagnerian sex and hysterics – that was Ivy'.[55]

Tudor House was looking its best for the athletic sports meeting on 15 December 1923. Out on the field the Moss Vale Progress Band played selections from light opera, flags flew, the gardener had marked the field with white-washed tracks and the boys were wearing colours like young jockeys. Paddy White had chosen dark green. His friend Martin major was in cerise. With a twenty-yard start, Paddy came third in the under twelves' 220 yards. Over tea he was awarded the English prize and shared the trophies for general knowledge and religious instruction, justifying his uncle H.L.'s opinion that he was 'the brainy member of the younger generation'.[56]

When new buildings were opened at Tudor House early in the year and portraits of early headmasters unveiled – there was no oil of Skuse – Mann called for a 'spell of quiet work' to show what could be done 'in the new conditions'. He promised to discuss any remaining problems on sports day in December. That time had arrived, but Mann extricated himself from his difficulties by declaring the day too hot and the company too distinguished to linger over 'a formal report of the school's present position'. He thanked Mr Victor White for making Tudor House 'absolutely safe with regard to water supply', for Dick had divined a well in one of the paddocks when the school ran out of water in winter. The headmaster unveiled the War Memorial Sundial with a last few words about progress through wholehearted loyalty.[57]

Mann was trading on a diminishing stock of optimism. Parents might not know that his French classes were in chaos or that their children were running wild in the bush, but there had been public setbacks. Fifty parents had come on a sultry evening in October, with a storm approaching over the Highlands, to hear a concert on the radio Mann had bought for the school, a four-valve machine with knobs, coils and a great horn perched on top. The night was a fiasco. A reporter from the local paper wrote: 'Nothing recognisable as speech or music was reproduced through the loud speaker, though long distance morse messages were identified as coming respectively from Sydney, Melbourne and even from Funabashi in Japan.'[58]

Ruth's faith in Mann was unshaken. The Whites were not among those Australian families who sent their sons to school abroad, but Mann was now urging Ruth and Dick to send their boy away, and Ruth was impressed. Education was a matter that called into play the complex loyalties of Australians within the Empire. Ruth and Dick were, by instinct, pro-British but Dick was also an Australian chauvinist. This was not a contradiction: the two loyalties lay side by side. The Whites never forgot that Australia made them. This new land had earned their loyalty. H.L. White bluntly asserted, 'I look on myself as pure Australian on both sides.'[59]

Ruth loved England. On her dressing table was a box which held the glove she wore the night her hand was kissed by the Prince of Wales in Sydney. Her son kept a scrapbook of the doings of English royalty and during the Prince's tour was happy to wear 'a little pin with three ostrich feathers and the motto *Ich Dien*'.[60] In Ruth's eyes the Victor Whites counted for something anywhere in the Empire, and it was time to assert their place in English society. An English education for her brilliant son would be his – and her – foothold. Appropriate friends would be made.

The boy was brought up by parents who, in their hearts, wanted to be somewhere else: Dick in the bush and Ruth in England. Home was never indisputably *here*, for there was always somewhere else where life might be better or might be happier. His childhood was marked by a pattern of small exiles: from Belltrees, then from Lulworth, which was now only the scene of 'brief, violently asthmatic sojourns' on trips between the high air of Moss Vale and Mount Wilson.[61] Now he was faced with the prospect of the greatest exile of his life. He was exhilarated and terrified. He had been born in England: Matt and Flo and the *News of the World* all came from England; it was the world of his mother's imagination; it meant royalty and theatre; history happened in England. He could never be bored there.

Once they were back at Lulworth after the sports meeting, Dick sent off a form applying for his son to enter Cheltenham College in eighteen months' time. Cheltenham seemed the right place: it was a spa town near Bath and the climate was supposed to be good for weak chests. Their friend the barrister Beau Burdekin of Burdekin House in Macquarie Street went to Cheltenham College, on to Oxford and then rowed at the Stockholm Olympics. His was a model Anglo-Australian career.

Having cast this die, Dick took the family up to Withycombe for Christmas. The boy spent a lonely time that summer. If other children tried to swim in his pool in the river or share his bark hut he warded them off violently. He wandered alone into Happy Valley, a deep, cold valley on the far side of the mountain. On Christmas Day, locked in combat with his mother, he refused to go to church. Ruth and Dick were disgusted by the behaviour of their 'infernal child'.[62]

Scarlet fever broke out at Tudor House in the first term of 1924. Mann directed that all the rubbish round the school should be gathered into a bonfire and on April Fool's Day Miss Babbington lit the blaze. 'An effigy symbolical of the scarlatina germ was hoisted to the top of the bonfire and consumed to ashes,' Mann reported in the *Tudorian*. 'After that, however, the two last cases occurred.'[63]

Paddy and his friend Martin escaped the infection and entertained the sick, who were having a long and tedious convalescence. Mann wrote: 'Many forms of amusement were tried during the wet weather period of quarantine, and all card games were completely exhausted. Suggestions as to Postman's Knock were turned down, much to the disappointment of W[hit]e and M[arti]n. An impromptu concert was tried one night, and proved a "howling" success . . . Charades filled in one afternoon. Two parties, starring Martin ma. and White, went to a great amount of trouble in acting and make-up for their words.'[64]

The *Tudorian* had been revived by Mann, partly it seems as propaganda for his modern approach but also out of pride and affection for the boys he was teaching. That year the *Tudorian* published P.V.M.W.'s 'The Tramp',

> Up and down the highroads,
> In and out the by-roads,
> Slowly trudging on forever:
> His dreary journey never ending.
> His boots are worn and thick with dust:
> But onward, ever onward, go he must.
> His pipe between his lips so dry,
> He flicks aside a truant fly.
> Loth to work for his own living,
> He lives on those who are kind and giving.[65]

The sentiments are authentically White and priggish. Tramps would crop up again. The Tudor House tramp only wanders about smoking and taking advantage of people's kindness. Later tramps would prophesy, threaten, steal, trail a kind of broken-down glamour in their wake or demonstrate what matters, *in extremis*, in human life. These few lines are not extraordinary – though 'truant fly' is good – but not quite random either.

Dick took his son back to Belltrees that winter for the first time in ten years. The brothers had sold another great chunk of land below the Mount Royal range, not because the partnership was pressed for money but out of H.L.'s morbid fear of Labor governments. The fire-eating Jack Lang had taken over the New South Wales Labor Party and H.L. thought their money was safer in Commonwealth Bonds than paddocks. With the sale of the Ellerston block, Belltrees was reduced to a substantial rump of 30,000 acres.[66]

The boy was not free to roam the house, for H.L.'s library and the sitting room were both out of bounds and children never ate in the dining room at Belltrees. It was a dark house, for his Aunt Maude, like all Ebsworth women, disliked the light and windows were painted with cream paint to keep out the sun. There was no electric light and no radio. Every morning the boy was taken upstairs to his aunt, who lay dressed in white, rather gaunt, a martyr to her kidneys. Most of her life was spent on a glassed-in corner of the veranda. In the afternoons she was driven round the valley in a Supersix Speedster with her initials on the door. From time to time she invited the nurses from Scone Hospital to come out and pick flowers for their patients in the Belltrees' gardens. The Edinglassie women drove over to see Dick and his son. In the party was Dick's niece Ruth – known as Edinglassie Ruth – who was jolly, moon-faced and forty-one. She never married, lived very simply in a cottage on the grounds of Muswellbrook Hospital and gave most of her fortune away over the years. She was another of the kind, sexless, intelligent spinsters in the boy's life.

On the last morning at Belltrees, before the Nash arrived to take them to Scone, Paddy went upstairs to his Aunt Maude's suite to say goodbye. From her bed she presented him with a little pocket money to take back to school. That was the last time he saw her. He sent a dutiful letter of thanks which H.L. thought 'remarkably well written and expressed'.[67]

He was bored at school, in limbo waiting to leave. For a few weeks in early 1925, P.V.M. White was *dux* of the school and was given what the records call 'special instruction', for the exams he had to face once he reached England. He read, he clipped coupons from comic books and sent away for courses in shorthand and hypnotism. For a couple of terms he learnt the piano until the chilblains were too much for him. He joined the scouts, learnt to tie knots and got a badge for cooking porridge. When he was not allowed to go over to Adelaide for a jamboree he had a furious row with his mother. One day the big oak tree was split by lightning, and the boy was thrown unhurt to the ground. Later it seemed an omen: he was spared. 'If yer luck holds,' said the swaggie, 'nothin's ever gunner keep you down.'[68]

Madame Melba came up the drive one morning in a sulky. She was a dumpy woman in a brown dress and diamonds. 'Hands up everyone born in Australia,' she said to the boys assembled in the old ballroom. 'Where were you born?' she asked the pale boy in the front row. London, he explained. 'Not a bad place either,' said the old diva and gave the boys a half-holiday.[69]

Tudor House was in free fall. The time came that year for Mann to decide 'to go to England'[70] and the school faced yet another fresh start. Dick gave £1,000. A committee of local women carried out a survey of the housekeeping arrangements and the servants' quarters were sprayed with formalin. What became of Mann is not known though the boys spoke darkly of embezzlement and suicide. He disappeared having taken a crucial part in Paddy White's life: he gave the boy years of wild freedom he would recall with pleasure all his life, and then helped condemn him to England.

Lizzie was staying behind to marry Sid Kirk of the sawmilling family. Dick had given them a cottage on the mountain. The boy faced a difficult breach from Lizzie. Though they had been together only in the holidays for the last three years, he loved her and was adored in return. She seemed to be his 'real' mother.[71] But their separation would not end the unacknowledged tug-o'-war between Lizzie and Ruth over the boy. The claims of his two mothers were never resolved in his mind. Ruth wished him success, excitement and all the pleasure his fortune might bring him. He longed for Ruth's world, but there was also Lizzie's Scots' voice in his head, reminding him that pride has its pitfalls, that simplicity is the fundamental virtue, that pleasure must be earned. In Lizzie's Presbyterian world, the price of all that Ruth wished for the boy was a measure of punishment, pain and suffering.

Between them, the two women had managed to make Paddy feel children were beasts at heart. 'I have always believed there is more of a devil than an angel in the average child,' he later wrote. 'Perhaps I am judging them from knowing about myself.'[72] Among the many rules he came to lay down for the rearing of children – many and detailed rules for a man who had none of his own – were these: that children must be allowed to be bad, but that the good must then be dragged out of them. White believed it was wishful to think children were innately good. He complained about parents who treat their children as geniuses, and railed against mothers who thought they had an artist in their ranks.

Dick wrote the cheques but contributed little to the boy's moral education. If it seemed at any point that a three-way battle might develop over the boy, Paddy sided with the women against his father's sweetness, warmth and indolence. Dick was 'one of the Furlows of this world' and like Stan Furlow in *Happy Valley* he would sometimes look up from his paper and tell the women to leave the child alone.[73]

Lulworth was let weeks before the Victor Whites sailed so they made their farewells from an apartment in Park Lane Mansions. The day they embarked on the *Ormuz*, Paddy was particularly pale-green and asthmatic. That he was now a bit fat – 'going Sue's way' – made him an even more woebegone sight. 'I feel so sorry for those people,' he heard one of the passengers remark. 'That boy's going to die soon.'[74] The ship cleared the Heads on 23 April 1925. Behind him lay his childhood and the vivid world he knew through childhood's eyes. The boat was carrying him into an exile from which he would seek to return all his life. But there is no voyage home, except in memory and imagination.

FIVE

Exile

Vocab

driver	assistant house master
house filth	food
Lewisite	Southwood boy
new bug	new boy
pots	inter-house sports
satis	academic work report
shack	private study
sweatroom	general house study
toshroom	bathroom

They disembarked in confusion. Dick lost one of the trunks and the children took fright at the sight of the English. They swore an oath that night 'never to be Poms'. Ruth had chosen the Knightsbridge Hotel, for Paddy's birthday had fallen as the boat reached the end of the six-week voyage and their hotel was over the road from Wellington Court where he had been born thirteen years before. The morning after their arrival in London the Whites persuaded the caretaker to let them into the flat and they walked through the empty, elegant rooms. The view across Hyde Park in summer was one of the boy's first sights of England.

Dick disappeared to Scotland to buy an Aberdeen Angus bull for Belltrees[1] and the boy was sent to a tutor down at Portishead near Bristol to cram for the schools' Common Entrance exam which he sat, and passed, in June. With that hurdle cleared, the reunited family set out in a large car to spend the rest of summer touring England and Scotland.

They descended on Somerset. There were no Whites to visit because the Whites had allowed their connections with home to lapse, but the Victor Whites motored in state through the Quantock Hills and the towns along the Bristol Channel visiting Withycombes. Annie and Alice Lutley of Watchet were a pair of Victorian spinsters, wrinkled like pugs, who spoke in chorus. The two As spent all their ingenuity on small savings. Since the war they had been collecting dead matches to use as kindling. Ruth gave these cousins of theirs a pair of magnificent new rhododendrons, though the As had neither the soil nor space in their tiny garden. Ruth's generosity was blind. Duty visits killed Somerset for the boy: 'any response by my blood was firmly suppressed because of those Dunster-Watchet cousins'.[2]

After a few perfectly happy days on the Welsh coast they drove into Glasgow. Their car knocked an old woman down as they came through the slums and a mob poured into the street. The Whites sat tight and their chauffeur got out to deal with the situation. Paddy was terrified: this was a scene from the French Revolution. They drove on. The trip was not a great success for the boy. Travel for Ruth and Dick meant simple but expensive pleasures: entertaining friends, eating in good restaurants and days spent at the races. Ruth was also determined to introduce her children to the monuments of great art. They hushed their voices in cathedrals, and trudged solemnly through galleries. But buildings did not move the boy, and paintings bored him after a while. He never enjoyed long car journeys after this first summer in Britain. Most of the time he spent quarrelling with his sister.

They reached Cheltenham in September, and as the car drove up to the school Ruth declared it the proudest day of her life. But her son came to look on this occasion as a moment of fundamental betrayal. 'I lost confidence in my mother and . . . I never forgave.'[3] After presenting the matron with a certificate stating that P.V.M. White had not been exposed to infection during the summer, Ruth and Dick left him at Southwood House. He was not Paddy now, but White. In his baggage was a typewriter.[4]

Cheltenham had been a fashionable spa since the daughters of George III came to take its waters for their constipation. In the late eighteenth century a town of 'melancholy elegance' grew up around the springs at the foot of the Cotswold Hills, and in Queen Victoria's time Cheltenham became a favourite residence of retired officials whose health had been ruined in the colonial service.[5] When White arrived in the 1920s invalids were still pulled about the streets in wicker bathchairs built like rickshaws, bands played in the Montpellier gardens, and common folk were kept from the Promenade. Beside elaborate pump rooms, Cheltenham had theatres, a race track that came alive once a year and a handful of schools.

Cheltenham College, standing like a toy Gothic monastery on the edge of the town, was neither old nor very distinguished. This was not Eton or Marlborough, but a school set squarely in the second rank. Cheltenham fed half its young men into the British army, and for ninety years it had aimed to turn out good chaps who believed in honesty and fair play, 'the sort of qualities that typified the Indian Civil Service'.[6] Old Cheltonian dinners were held all over the Empire: in Shanghai, Cairo, Singapore and in the year of White's arrival at the school a particularly 'good show' was held in Simla.

Cheltenham had one odd connection with Australia. The poet Adam Lindsay Gordon was among its first pupils. His father taught Hindustani at the college in the 1840s, and the young Gordon spent most of his brief time at Cheltenham hunting. He was remembered as The Naughty Boy and The Awful Example of all that We were to Avoid.[7]

Southwood House was a Regency villa in a handsome street half a mile from the college. Here White lived in the care of the housemaster Arthur Bishop, a tall man with a long, sleepy face and eyebrows that met like a roof over his hooded eyes. Bishop was dangerous, unknowable and in the grip of a malign obsession to stamp out filth in Southwood. The fate of each boy at Cheltenham depended, more than anything, on the state of his house and since the scandal of 1924 life at Southwood had been wretched. 'Everything appeared to be going well,' records the prefects' log for that year, 'when it was discovered that immorality and indecency had been going on almost continuously . . . the result was that three fellows were expelled, one left and one was asked to leave at the end of the term.'[8] In White's first term the rumours were that half the house had been expelled, and that one of the victims had ended up in the chorus of *No, No Nanette*.

All friendships were now suspect. Bishop burst through doors expecting, and failing, to find boys *in flagrante*. He seemed to assume that every child was a liar, an idler, a potential drunkard, a bugger and a thief. His beatings were cruel even by the standards of English public schools. The verdict of a retired Major-General who suffered under him as a boy was that Bishop was 'an absolute sadist'. Lewisites wondered if the housemaster won his medals in the war for flogging German prisoners. They believed he came to the toshroom each night to check the pattern of welts on their backsides. To thwart their housemaster they turned to face him under the showers.

Southwood reeked of sex, fear and self-disgust. In a sense Bishop's campaign worked: he made sure that White had a bleak and fearful adolescence. The sensuality which had had free rein in the boy was now thwarted, and he was cut off from the physical affection that might have comforted him in England as it had at Tudor House. The long grass of Moss Vale gave way to bare rows of desks in the Southwood sweatroom. As a new bug he had no privacy, only a locker and desk. He withdrew behind a mask of remote detachment. Though he did not appear to be suffering acutely, he exuded no happiness. He was a pale, heavy boy who brushed his hair down flat behind fleshy ears, and spoke with a chesty wheeze. He was unobtrusive, had few friends and no enemies.

Once or twice early on he made his mark on the football field with a burst of energy, 'emerging with hair dishevelled and togs all muddied from the maelstrom of a scrum – struggling, with a frenzied vigour, courageous, tenacious, as he made ground for the House side in one of those highly competitive inter-House matches that brought out the unexpected in us. It was PVMW's zeal and great determination that surprised me. He was not, as far as I remember, interested in the world of sport – but at that moment he won great praise as he let himself go.'[9]

Ruth and her children might pass for English in Australia. But in England her son was Australian and sounded so to sharp ears at Cheltenham where family, money, county, regiment and accent mattered. The boy believed he was ridiculed for his accent, though Southwood at this time had boys from Chile, Armenia and India as well as Australia, and contemporaries do not recall Australians being the butt of such mockery. 'Never in all the years I was at Coll – we had one or two Australians – did I ever hear anyone being ragged or teased because they were Australian. The chaps who were given a bad time were the Jews.'[10] (Until the early 1920s Cheltenham had a house exclusively for Jews.) Whether or not this self-conscious boy was being ridiculed, he came to believe he was singled out, and grew afraid to open his mouth for fear of giving himself away. Cheltenham made him wary.

What set White apart in the eyes of the other boys were asthma, pale skin – he seemed extraordinarily pale for an Australian – and money. 'We all accepted that Paddy was one of the rich boys. I'm not suggesting there were any paupers at this time, but at the beginning of every term you went to your driver and banked the pocket money you had been given by your parents. If I or my companions might bank one or two or three pounds, Paddy would always be banking five or ten. He always had much more than anyone else.'[11]

Southwood was a long walk from the College, and Lewisites spent much of their day going up and back to the school. After house filth – a breakfast of an egg or a scrap of bacon, bread and margarine with jam – the sixty boys processed through the streets of Cheltenham walking in twos and threes. In winter they wore mortar boards and in summer boaters. Prefects on bicycles worked as outriders to keep stragglers in check, and Bishop rode beside the line on a machine built for his enormous frame. He was nearly seven feet tall. The procession ended at the chapel, an imposing piece of Victorian gothic. Prayers came first and lessons followed. Late in the morning a man sold penny buns from a tray in the yard that ran through the classroom block. When the temperature fell near to freezing, the boys were sent on a compulsory run before going back to the unheated classrooms.

Lewisites returned to Southwood for a lunch of meat and pudding. Most afternoons were spent at drill or sport. Both were compulsory. If snow and frost made the ground unplayable, the boys were sent for long runs over Leckhampton. White fought to keep up with the leaders. The day ended at Southwood with a light meal that left everyone hungry. Bishop fed them out of his own pocket and he was not generous, but they had hampers of their own food and could buy supplies from the tuckshop. Jam was rationed to two pounds a week per boy.

Upstairs in their shacks, the prefects' gramophones ground away at 'Frankie and Johnnie', 'Heavenly Father send thy Blessing', 'Drifting and Dreaming'. Downstairs forty junior boys did their homework in the sweatroom. White seemed to shudder trying to shut out the noise and unrest around him.[12] They were supervised by their house driver Clement Priestley, a mixture of clown and scholar, an enthusiastic sportsman known as the Jaw because of his bull chin. This strange but likeable man took some of the sting out of being in Bishop's house. Later he became *the* teacher of White's schooldays.

On Monday nights once a fortnight every boy had to show Bishop his satis, and a sense of dread hung over Southwood from early morning. In other houses little attention was paid to this ritual, but Bishop made each boy account for himself. If his work was satisfactory, Bishop dismissed him. He never praised. If it was unsatisfactory a beating followed automatically: six strokes of the cane, and a seventh if you straightened up too soon. He began with a thin cane to sting and changed to a thick one to rub it in. One night he smashed a light globe as he swung, and the boy had to sweep it up before the beating continued. White was rarely caned but confessed he didn't mind too much when it happened.[13]

One of his friends at Southwood, Ragnar Christophersen, later carried out an informal investigation into the fate of those Lewisites who passed through Bishop's hands. It revealed Southwood had 'more officers cashiered from the army, people who ended up on the wrong side of the law, solicitors who had embezzled money, and one chap who ended up in Salisbury lunatic asylum – than all the other houses at Cheltenham, and all ascribed to the rather sinister influence of our housemaster'.[14]

The Victor Whites had settled down for a prolonged stay at the Langham Hotel in Regent Street. Ruth and Dick were solid but unobtrusive figures in the Anglo-Australian community where businessmen, minor

royalty, the widows of former governors and other English with connections in Australia, mixed with Australians whose children, fortune
or family gave them a place, if only temporarily, in London society. In
December 1925 Dick attended the funeral of Queen Alexandra in the
Abbey. Ruth was presented at Court, a mature débutante of forty-eight
with a pair of solid ankles and a dress of 'deep biscuit lace over pink, train
of deeper shade of biscuit velvet, embroidered diamanté, diamonds and
pearls'.[15]

Christmas left these Australians at a loose end in London. Invitations dried up as the English retreated to their families in the country,
so the visitors had taken to gathering over Christmas and New Year
in Swiss hotels or on the Riviera. Ethel Kelly preferred Switzerland
when she came over every year to visit her sons. Ruth was always
predisposed to follow Ethel's lead and had an obscure prejudice that
le Midi was unsuitable for children. So Ruth and Dick collected their
children – Suzanne and her pet rabbit were boarding at a school on the
outskirts of London – and took the train to Pontresina near St Moritz
for a fortnight. The boy did a little clumsy skiing but his asthma often
kept him indoors and he loitered about the hotel keeping an eye on the
guests and staff, building fantasies from the scraps of talk overheard in
the corridors.

In spring the children were collected for a trip to Paris through
the Low Countries. At The Hague they had an excellent meal and saw
Juliana come out of the palace. Suzanne said, 'Oh, Mummy, is that a
princess?'[16] At the Belgian border Dick was appalled to be made to pay
duty on the wreath they were taking to the grave of Lizzie's brother
Robert. In Paris they visited Agnes Goodsir: a real artist's studio! And
Ruth took the family to the Théatre Sarah-Bernhardt to see Yvonne
Printemps as the boy Mozart. That was a potent memory. He never
forgot the sight of 'Mozart's blue eyelids and the smell of that red-plush
theatre'.[17]

Cheltenham had proved a disappointment to Ruth in only one
respect: the climate was terrible for her son's asthma. All year the
town was damp. Cold fogs banked up against the Cotswold Hills in
winter, and cleared to leave the town in a bowl of frost.

> Winters cracked with grey ice. The damp, feverishly green summers
> wormed their way into my lungs, then left them with the elasticity
> of perished rubber.[18]

The boy was not pampered, but wheezed his way through football
matches and long runs over the hills. He was often ill but welcomed
the privacy this won him. 'At fourteen I was seduced by James Elroy
Flecker's Hassan, and by sixteen had read most of the novels of Thomas

Hardy in a school sickroom. At that age what a luxury illness was!'[19] He tried and hated Dickens.

White was writing all the time. At about his fourteenth birthday he wrote a fragment of a novel he called 'The Maelstrom'. 'It was about a femme fatale.' That summer on the Sussex coast where the Whites had taken a house he wrote a melodrama in blank verse. 'The Bird of Prey' involved another femme fatale and a Florentine tyrant with a cellar full of lovers kept in chains. Sir Topaze 'in the course of many monologues' disembowelled his victims and flung their entrails to the winds.[20]

Turret House at Felpham was once the 'marine cottage' of the poet Hayley. It stood in a walled garden and from the turret the children could look out to sea and over the South Downs. William Blake had known the house, for Hayley was his patron and gave him a cottage by the beach in which he wrote the epic *Milton*. The Whites had taken the place not for its literary associations but the country air of Felpham and the resort of Bognor nearby. Paddy had a narrow room overlooking the vegetable garden. The room soon stank of burning asthma papers.

All summer Turret House was full of visitors and the boy concocted plays for an audience of 'amused, though proud parents, and their suffering friends' who gathered in the drawing room. Sue was his star, for he imagined his sister one day growing up to be a great actress. He would write the roles that made her famous. While Ruth, Dick and their Australian friends disappeared on motor tours, the children were left to play together. One of these was Pauline McDonald: 'Ruth was the most forbidding woman. We were rather frightened of her. Victor was a trick. Paddy was no fun. I never saw him play a game. We *tried* but he wouldn't play. There was no affection in him so you never got through. He never talked about what he was thinking or doing or planning, not to me and not to Sue.'[21] With mute distress the boy examined himself in the drawing room's great gilded mirror. 'I fluctuated in the watery glass; according to the light I retreated into the depths of the aquarium, or trembled in the foreground like a thread of pale-green samphire. Those who thought they knew me were ignorant of the creature I scarcely knew myself.'

He knew at least he was homosexual. He had no doubt: 'I never went through the agonies of choosing between this or that sexual way of life. I was chosen.'[22] He responded to this discovery with fear and self-disgust. There was little danger of being caught in the act at Southwood for sex was impossible in the crazy atmosphere of the house. But he feared the discovery of what he *was* and withdrew to an inner shell. The boy spoke to no one of this. He hated his appearance: he was plain and vain, and wished he were as 'handsome and strong, ordinary' as those boys he despised and envied. He was always scornful of obviously beautiful men and suspected the obviously beautiful in anything. When he was a child, asthma had brought out this jealousy and self-loathing and his sense of powerlessness in the face of a hostile world. Now this jumble of painful feelings was intensified as he came to grips with homosexuality. Once again he felt afflicted, set apart. But he accepted the verdict of fate: 'I settled into the situation.'[23] Though his fear could be overcome in time, a strong vein of self-loathing marked him for life.

Miserable and proud, the boy looked about for evidence that the human race was no better than himself. So he reached a bleak but reassuring view that people in the ordinary run of things are as shoddy, greedy, jealous, stubborn and contemptible as he, in despair, thought himself to be.[24] We are betrayers by nature; we disappoint high hopes; the healthy tear the sick apart; only those who suffer can understand what life is about. Illumination comes with pain, and the afflicted find truth through suffering. Behind this train of thought lay a great deal of self-pity, but it directed his compassion – as a boy and man – on to those he saw as fellow victims of fate. Permanent exceptions to the misanthropy that settled on him in his years at Cheltenham were loving servants and those strangers and sufferers whom he later called 'the burnt ones'.

The boy's sense of powerlessness, of being both alone and misunderstood, drove him to find a voice which would tell this hostile world the truth of what it was and, perhaps, bring it to order. Within the shell where he hid his feelings, the boy's innate sensuality continued to grow and be frustrated. How could he find release? So fearful of physical contact, so unsure of his own worth, he grew to doubt that any profound comfort could be given by one human being to another. Once he put out of his mind the hope of physical camaraderie – even rough-and-tumble friendship had been difficult for the boy – then what lay before him were a number of essentially lonely paths: reading, scribbling, dreams, the fantasy of living other people's lives, the theatre, an intense and sensual bond with landscape. Here he found ways of escaping the body that so distressed him.

Beyond repugnance and pain was the matter of working out what it meant to be homosexual. At the heart of his understanding of himself was the sense that there was woman in this man. This is not the common understanding of all homosexuals, but White grew to accept and take pride in this 'feminine sensibility' which he sensed the boys 'despised because they mistrusted'. He came to attribute much of his insight as a writer to the understanding his male-and-female nature conferred on him.[25] The dark side of this was the suspicion that he cut an incongruous figure, one out of kilter with itself and out of place in the world. Within him was a jumble of fragments shifting like glass in a kaleidoscope. At times he wondered who, if anyone, he really was. Yet he presented to the world one 'convincingly male' figure.[26] Would not anyone who came to know him well discover incongruity here amounting almost to deceit? How could he avoid feeling as he did, so often out of place, a foreigner anywhere, a stranger at heart?

As he stared into the great mirror at Felpham, resenting the face he saw in the flawed glass, the repercussions of his sexuality had only begun to work themselves out in him. Hair was beginning to sprout in unsatisfactory patches on his face, his voice had broken, but he was still a boy. He only knew that he barely knew himself.

After a bad term of slush and ice, White was rescued by his parents once again and taken off to Switzerland where Ethel Kelly had gathered a number of Sydney friends at the Palace Hotel in Villars-sur-Bex above Montreux. The party included the Whites, the McDonalds, the Gordons, and all their children.

The Australians reassured themselves that the Palace was not one of those smart Swiss hotels, just a comfortable pub up to its ears in snow. Yet life at the Palace called for many changes of costume: for the funicular and the slopes, for curling on the frozen tennis courts (the only time in their lives these women handled a broom) for *le Thé*, *le Thé dansant* and dinner,

> The general rout is trickling slithering pouring in. Slim young women in frothing georgette, squeaking taffeta, ice-blue green rose, all the colours of the crevasse . . . [27]

Between the *truite au bleu* and the profiteroles the band played and the little gilt tables emptied as guests streamed towards the dance floor. The Palace employed an ex-Air Force officer, down on his luck, to teach the Black Bottom. An Englishman of more mysterious origins appeared at Christmas to direct the guests' revue. The boy watched Margaret Gordon, now grown rather plain and deaf, take out her old box of make-up and transform herself into something like the stage beauty she once was for the New Year's Eve fancy dress ball. This was magic. Ethel Kelly drifted through the hotel, taking sleighs in the afternoons to dash about, bells jingling, wrapped in furs. Her thickening, raucous figure became, after sixty years' imagining, the Contessa del Castelmarino, alias Gladys (Baby) Horsfall of Gundy, New South Wales, having 'mad fun' on the verge of a scandalous switch to Catholicism.[28]

The ashen, unobtrusive boy wandered the corridors peeping through half-opened doors, hanging about as the musicians practised in the morning sunlight,

> In the ballroom at any time of day a musician can be heard
> trying out an instrument, plunk of guitar, metal idly brushed
> against a skitter of drums . . . [29]

Pauline McDonald, her hair glued down in Josephine Baker spit
curls, pursued a thirteen-year-old's desperate crush on the Spanish
guitar player. Her brother claimed her blood was 'mud' but she was
determined.[30] On behalf of a boy with a crush on Ethel's daughter
Beatrice, Paddy wrote love poems and put them in the shoes outside
her door. The stickybeak of the Palace Hotel had to leave to his
imagination the unravelling of these sub-plots, for he was often too ill
to leave his bed. He lay under his eiderdown, bored, masturbating,
listening to the steam radiators gurgle and crack,

> Beyond the window, the landscape, analogous to the hotel itself,
> the sumptuous, snowy mountains, the evergreens decorously lad-
> en with snow. None of this landscape ever quite escaped from the
> influence of the radiators. It suffocated, gently, slowly, luxuriously.
> You found yourself enjoying it, in spite of better judgment.[31]

Dick was restless. He had been away from his horses for nearly
two years and there were responsibilities to attend to at home. It was
time for Sue to settle down in an Australian school. H.L. had kept
in contact, reporting news from Belltrees, congratulating him on the
glowing reports of Paddy's success – 'From all accounts the boy has
plenty of brains'[32] – but the partnership had struck a rough patch. Dick's
income from Belltrees had been roughly £15,000 a year since the war,
but after a couple of years of drought it dipped to £6,000 in 1926 with
the prospect of less in the year ahead. From this point in the middle of
the 1920s, there is an indefinable sense in which the Victor Whites
never thought themselves quite as rich as they had been.

They planned to leave Switzerland for Naples, where they would
catch the *Otranto* for the voyage home. On the railway platform at
Villars they said goodbye to their son. It was a stiff farewell, a moment
of failed intimacy on all sides. As Paddy and his father plodded up
the platform in felt boots, breath streaming from their mouths, Dick
tried, rather late in the day, to explain something of the facts of life
to his fourteen-year-old son. He managed a few clumsy words about
lavatory seats and was silent. They were both relieved. The boy kept
his affection in check. 'Only the light was nagging at me, the sounds of
a train preparing to burrow through a Swiss landscape towards bleached
grass, eroded creeks, and the wounding blows from butcherbirds' beaks.
The wounds I suffered on the snowbound platform were of a duller kind
which promised suppuration. I was determined to keep my grief within

the bounds of that manliness I was being taught to respect, when I would have liked to tear off the rabbitskin glove he was wearing and hold the sunburnt hand to my cheek. I did nothing. I didn't cry. I only throbbed as a windowful of faces slid away through the Swiss dark.'[33]

Australian friends returned him to Cheltenham where, more than ever now, he felt he was doing time for some unnamed crime, serving a life sentence at the College. His work deteriorated. He slipped to twentieth place in a class of twenty-three. 'There was something slightly bleak about Paddy's attitude to life,' recalled Christophersen. 'He was never boisterous, he never exuded any particular mirth or happiness. He seemed to give the impression of a slightly mordant cynicism, tinged if you like with a certain amount of resignation.'[34]

The boy had not been abandoned entirely. A Withycombe great-aunt in Cheltenham had him to lunch on occasional Sundays. Her face was wrinkled and she drank too much sherry, encouraged by a maid who looked like a figure from the foot of the guillotine. This great-aunt Annie had the only photograph he ever saw of his mother as a young girl, and a fan tipped with flamingo feathers, a souvenir he put into the hands of Miss Hare of Xanadu.[35]

Ruth had arranged a number of holiday billets. There was a family of Christians near Reading whom he disliked very much. 'I used to bicycle over to Reading and go to the pictures as an escape: that was where I first saw Garbo in a film called *The Temptress*, Rudolph Valentino, Pola Negri and all the others of that period. Apart from the films the only thing I remember about Reading was its ugliness.'[36] There was Mrs Courtney Mitchell, who bred Airedales in asthmatic marsh country near Portsmouth. Her champion bitch was called Girlie, a name the boy saved for later use. Mrs Courtney Mitchell wrote to Ruth, 'Patrick made me desperate because he didn't seem interested in anything.' She was wrong. He liked expeditions to the theatre at Southsea and the naval officers he met when they toured the yards.

At Winchester was Helen Waddell, a prim widow who spent her life reading and embroidering. She was not the writer Helen Waddell, but a Havilah White whose name was famous among gardeners for the orange rose bred by her late husband. As a girl she was sent from Mudgee to finishing school in France, where she discovered First Empire furniture and a passion for French literature which she passed on to the boy who now turned up at Winchester on his holidays. *Decline and Fall* was her bedside book, and the Empress Theodora of Byzantium one of her strange enthusiasms. 'Poor dear Theodora,' she would whisper to the boy, 'just a prostitute.' A tiny woman, she lived in a spartan house with flint walls. Her housekeeper had a mania for dusting and the boy never had asthma in those absolutely clean

rooms. He and his Havilah cousin got on extremely well. She widened
his horizons, but was severe. She recognised 'the curse of self-pity'
in the boy and took him very sternly to task for this failure. 'I was
hurt at the time.'[37]

The Chapmans were the worst. On the boat to England Ruth
and Dick had come across one of this cricketing family returning
home after a tour of Australia with the English team. Their shipboard
friendship had flourished in England, so much so that the Chapmans
agreed to look after the Victor Whites' child in the holidays. 'I hardly
know which is worse – term-time or the Hols,' the boy complained to
Reginald Hailing, who ran Darter's Bookshop in Cheltenham. White
had an account and hung about the shop, a 'booky' boy who talked of
hating games and being often 'fed-up' with life. 'I reminded him that
holidays made a change. "I don't know," he added. "You see the
Chapmans have only one topic – cricket, and you can't eat without
it." '[38]

Ronald Waterall had ears like propeller blades and flaming red hair
which he doused with Yardley's lavender water. Hearty Lewisites
found him 'a really frightful wet' and disapproved of the change that
overcame young White when a friendship began between them. On his
first day at Southwood, White had been cheered by the sight of
Waterall dancing down the stairs singing,

> California here I come,
> Right back where I started from.

He was a couple of years older, so when their intimacy began it
came up against one of the taboos of Bishop's Southwood. Somehow it
was tolerated, despite disapproval. 'White was rather a quiet, retiring
individual until he developed a close friendship with one Ronnie Waterall
– a flamboyant character, completely obsessed with the stage and all that
went with it. Together, they would give practical demonstrations of
chorus girls' high kicks, with appropriate noises. We none of us thought
the friendship was good for Paddy.'[39] It lasted for over sixty years.

Both boys were stage-struck and wrote away for actresses'
photographs and autographs. This was a Southwood craze – even the
prefects hung photographs of these Edwardian beauties in their
shacks – but White and Waterall went about it with theatrical stealth.
They used assumed names and gave Darter's address as their mail
drop. White was potty about Dorothy Dickson and wrote her a long
ode. It was one of the earliest poems he wrote at Southwood. She
never replied.[40] The two boys spent hours concocting shows:
mapping out skits, designing the sets, casting great actresses. In
the sweatroom, White spoke as if he knew Beatrice Lillie, Hermione

Baddeley, Cicely Courtneidge and Jack Hulbert, the stars of these paper revues.[41]

The happiest times he spent in these years were with Ronald Waterall seeing shows in London. At the end of the Christmas holidays, the boys would gather in the sweatroom and ask each other how many shows they had seen. ' "Well, I went to five." "Oh, gosh, I went to six." We asked Paddy once and I remember he had been to thirty, which meant he must have been to the theatre or cinema on some days at least twice.'[42]

That Christmas, the first the boy had ever spent apart from his parents, he sent Ruth 'A Rustic Eclogue' in twelve verses, 'Dedicated to Mummy'. The boy had been studying Virgil that term. A troupe of antique figures wanders through a landscape of woods and mossy banks, thistles, cobwebs and mountain tarns, where sleepy cows chew the cud and spotted pigs twitch their tails. The poem ends on a note of wistful self-pity,

> So fade imaginings and visions flimsy.
> They come, delight and go,
> But a vain caprice, a poor mind's whimsy,
> A passing puppet-show.[43]

The poems he sent home to Ruth over the next few years were the work of a sad, very clever and rather affected child. There are a few sharp images: a saw like the moon, a lake of green cheese, winter trees standing in the mist like 'forgotten spinsters in a boarding house'. Acute homesickness appears to have been his spur, and perhaps he intended the poems to be read at Lulworth as a reproach. In 1928 he wrote his 'Reminiscence' about summers on Mount Wilson,

> I think it must have happened in a dream,
> So far removed, so distant does it seem,
> A dream which somehow buried in my heart
> At times creeps forth to soothe my troubled soul
> And all its buried fragrancy impart,
> The fragrance of fresh lilac in a bowl . . . [44]

He had a brief bout of religious passion after his Confirmation by the Bishop of Gloucester. For a couple of weeks he expected miracles, but then the enthusiasm died. He was a resilient boy. Despite the oppressive atmosphere at Southwood, he did not develop that sense of sin that frequently sends homosexual boys into tortured bouts of religiosity. The ground had not been prepared. Ruth was too proud, St James's, King Street where the Victor Whites worshipped was too

polite, and Lizzie Clark too Presbyterian to drum sin and hellfire into
him. A sense of secular failing, of flaws and shortcomings, preyed on
the boy but he was not moved by visions of Heaven and Hell. The
faith Cheltenham gave him was not in God but in the awfulness of
human beings.

All his life White spoke of his parents abandoning him at Cheltenham,
but after only eighteen months they reappeared in England and took
their son on a summer tour of the fjords and Baltic capitals. It was a
difficult reunion. One day before they set out from London he refused
to go to the cricket with Dick. White remembered as one of the worst
moments of his childhood Ruth's reproaches in a taxi in Oxford Street:
'I never thought I'd have a freak for a son!' It made him determined to
go on being just that.[45]

The *Otranto* sailed from Hull on 11 August 1928 carrying only
first-class passengers. Two hours out, in calm weather and clear light,
the ship collided with a Japanese freighter. The second sitting was at
dinner and fled to the deck across broken crockery as the ship heeled
over. There was confusion, panic in some quarters, until the *Otranto*
righted itself. That night the ship limped back to port and next morning the Whites joined the special train for London. *The Times* noted:
'The chief difficulty of many of the passengers is that they had closed
up their houses for the period of the tour and had sent their servants
away.'[46] After a few days back at the Langham, the Whites set off to
cover much the same ground by train. As they crossed the Channel,
their son lay in his bunk expecting the worst, waiting for the crash,
planning his escape.

White was sixteen, guilty and silent. The boy knew he was disappointing his parents' hopes, trudging along at the bottom of his class.
He only showed competence in English – not flair, just competence.
He was not one of the bright hopes of the college. He played football
in the House Thirds. Clean knees were punishable after a match.
Christophersen recalled: 'Some boys, and I know Paddy was one of
them, made quite sure they were not caught out in this way. Prior to
playing the game you would kneel down in the mud ostensibly to tie
up a shoelace, but to make quite sure their knees were muddy. Convicts learn certain tricks in prison and schoolboys learn certain tricks at
public school.' Ahead of White lay the prospect of even duller times,
for Waterall had left for Freiburg in Breisgau to study German.

From Copenhagen they crossed to Malmö. The lakes of Sweden
seemed dreamlike to the boy and in Stockholm he explored the quays
and the new Town Hall. He drank his first glass of red wine.[47] The
most thrilling part of the journey was the train over the mountains from
Christiania to Bergen: they climbed from summer into the glaciers,

through a snow storm and down to summer again on the far side. It was one of the great travel experiences of his life.[48]

White found his parents so 'deadly boring' he felt near suicide. 'I remember my mother used to burst into tears and say: "But you never say anything to us!" '[49] At last they had the conversation their son had been avoiding all summer. Paddy announced he wanted to leave school as soon as possible and become an actor. His parents were astonished. Ruth, with her mind on her own audience in Sydney, burst into tears and asked, 'What will I tell them?' The three reached a compromise: the boy could leave school early at the end of the following year without taking his final exams, but he would then come home to see if he was 'fitted' for life on the land. Final decisions would be post-poned until they could be made in the light of his experience back in Australia.

The idea of becoming an actor died with its expression. Perhaps it was no more than an early signal to his parents that he meant to make a life of his own. He knew he was too stiff, too self-conscious to go on the stage, though for the rest of his life he wondered if it might have been possible but for the deadening effect of Cheltenham on him. The boy still dreamed of being in theatre – but writing rather than acting. In Darter's one afternoon a group of friends were dis-cussing their future professions: the army, accountancy, law. White did not join in until towards the end, and quietly said, 'I'm going to be a writer.'[50] Some time that year the same subject cropped up with Robert Tod, who said he was going to university. 'You'll do well,' White said. 'You've got ambition, go, energy. I don't have energy, I don't have enthusiasm for things.'[51]

Once Ruth and Dick returned to Australia, the boy's work improved dramatically. Suddenly he was close to the top of his class. The prospect of early release from school and Waterall's absence in Berlin spurred him along. (Bishop forbade any contact between the two boys after some scandalous remarks in one of Waterall's letters got about the House.) But the fundamental improvement in the boy's mood coincided with the discovery of his cousins, the Jack Withycombes. They met in late 1928 when Helen Waddell took him to tea at their flat overlooking the County Cricket Ground in Southampton.

For them all this was an important meeting. The boy found in the Withycombes the sort of family he dreamed of having: 'They all painted and carved and wrote and did something, which was wonderful after coming out of the sheep world.'[52] Jack and Ellen Withycombe found a surrogate son to add to their family of daughters. The three girls became the boy's sisters, goads, confidantes and adversaries. At first Paddy was afraid they only accepted this mute 'schoolboy cousin from

Australia' as an afternoon's duty, but they clicked almost at once.[53] He upset Ruth by writing home soon afterwards: 'At last I know someone I can talk to – not like your friends.'

Jack and Ellen Withycombe had gone out to Malaya to repair their fortunes after his years painting in East Anglia. The war brought them home. Captain Jack Withycombe taught map-reading in Southampton to young officers on their way to France. Few returned. He stayed on after the war as a civilian at the Ordnance Survey to redraw the maps of Britain. His particular interest was the reform of lettering and he enjoyed a small public triumph in 1926 after the publication of the Ordnance's map of Roman Britain, which the *Daily Mail* declared 'one of the most wonderful maps ever produced'.[54]

Paddy felt at home with this silent, precise man though they did not have much to say to one another, 'we were in some ways too alike'.[55] Ellen, however, became one of the great loves of the boy's life. She was vivacious, original and rather a snob. Marriage had raised her in the world for she was the daughter of a bootmaker, Liberal and amateur musician in Herefordshire. As a free-thinking, literary young woman she taught in a village school before marrying a polo-playing Withycombe who surprised his family – they were the same Withycombes who ran the Luttrell Arms in Dunster – by deciding to be a painter. Jack and Ellen set up in Constable country, the *avant-garde* Withycombes of East Bergholt with three little daughters, Betty, Peggy and Joyce.

Ellen wished she were slim, tall and aristocratic, recalled Peggy. 'In fact she was fat, short and an intellectual. What she was, was much better than what she aimed to be. She wrote indifferent poetry in the Alice Meynell genre with a dash of Dowson and a great love and admiration for both Brownings.'[56] She wanted and tried to love her children, but was devoted to her husband. When they went out to Malaya – at about the time their cousin was born in London – she left her children behind in the care of a couple who ran a country school. From an early age the three girls had had to look out for themselves. They were bred to be independent, self-sufficient and game. The war reunited the family.

When Paddy White met her for the first time, Ellen Withycombe was 'expansive, slovenly if the truth is to be told, her hair always coming down, her seams bursting. At the same time she had her aesthetic principles, whether getting a room into shape for an arriving guest, in the books she read, in her approach to life. Never in the money, she had an instinctive taste which can conjure beauty out of the junk shop into the cottage. The meals she served were in the same tradition of conjuring and rightness.' Ellen Withycombe, in many disguises, became a figure in his work.[57]

The Withycombes' three daughters were already out in the world. Joyce, a painter who had trained at the Slade, was the youngest and wittiest. Peggy was away in South Africa setting up a department of sculpture in the art school at Cape Town. At twenty-three she was the 'most spectacular' of them, an accomplished sculptor with a tough and curious mind. Some months passed before the boy met her and twenty years before he came to know her well. Betty had the most immediate impact. She was the eldest of the Withycombe sisters, a dark and rather severe woman of twenty-six who had been to Lady Margaret Hall and was about to return to Oxford to work at the Clarendon Press. She seemed a 'tremendous bluestocking' to the boy who became her protégé, almost her possession.[58] Other women had introduced him to books, but Betty Withycombe was the first after Ruth to encourage him to write.

He was working on a novel at Cheltenham, but when they met he put it aside to concentrate on poetry. Betty was a poet: 'I followed the leader.'[59] At first he would show her nothing he wrote; instead they talked. 'None of the Whites or Withycombes he had known were educated people in the full sense,' she recalled. 'To say they didn't read was an understatement. We talked endlessly about books and music and pictures.' She did not need to get him going. 'The bug for writing was absolutely within himself.'

Betty Withycombe found him already set in his mould. 'Patrick always looked older than he was, not like a schoolboy at all. His hair was plastered down and cut short back and sides. He was not attractive and not happy. He didn't like himself very much, and had times of loathing himself. His mouth was always set very hard. He had a strain of stubbornness in him. Helen sent him over one day for a picnic on the Downs – we were going on to see Paul Robeson in *Showboat* – with his own sandwiches in a nasty tin sandwich box. He wouldn't join us or share our food but sat wrestling with the tin box. Once he made up his mind on something you couldn't persuade him to do anything else.' He had begun to show her some of his verse. 'Even at this age he could not take criticism of any kind.'[60]

He told her: 'Sydney and my mother gave me asthma.' He wrote every week to Lizzie. 'He loved and was grateful to her. She was his mother.' He confessed that he always wanted to be a Withycombe, though to Betty's eyes he did not quite look the part. He was stiff, not lithe like Withycombes, and she thought his jaw Australian.[61]

When Peggy arrived from South Africa, she thought this new cousin disturbed and depressed, 'He hung back and watched with very sharp eyes and if you met his eyes the expression didn't change.'[62] But the three sisters accepted him despite and perhaps to some extent because of his gawky unhappiness. Intelligent and open as they were, the three were no help to the boy about sex. He was too reserved to talk, and sensed a hostility to homosexuality. There was still no one to whom he could turn. Even with Waterall he found it impossible to admit his own feelings, and it was nearly ten years before they spoke of it together.

The poems he sent home to his mother kept their desperate edge. There was a lot of death, winter, bones, dust and tombs. The notion of hiding recurs in 'Requiem',

> I built me a garden small
>   Wherein to hide myself,
> And round it built a hedge so tall
>   That only birds could spy me.[63]

and 'The Birds',

> I am a stranger;
> I must veil myself;
> I must hide me.[64]

Privacy was one of the privileges of his last year at school. He had his own shack, which was heaven after the rough and tumble of the sweatroom. He sat in a fug of burning asthma papers listening to 'Chanson Hindoue' and 'The Blue Danube' on his gramophone. He was able to write in peace – two-fingered, for he never mastered touch typing – and to read more or less without being disturbed. He believed he was learning very little, except from his own private reading.[65] One of the favourite novels of his life, *Gentlemen Prefer Blondes*, was published at this time, and he knew *The Constant Nymph* practically off by heart. 'It was considered immoral. I remember the form master delivering a lecture on how such a story was ethically wrong because it showed the schoolgirl-mistress in a sympathetic light and made the injured wife out to be slightly ridiculous. I think nobody but myself had read the book, which made me feel very daring and unorthodox.'[66]

That year he discovered Chekhov, Ibsen and Strindberg. Bishop burst into his shack one day to find him indulging this 'morbid kink' and promised to stamp it out. He only stamped it deeper in. Chekhov's three sisters haunted White's adolescence 'to such an extent they became an actual part of it'. Years later he made the sweeping claim that Chekhov and Ibsen, 'discovered at the right age, prepare one as nothing else for life and the arts'.[67]

To his Cheltenham contemporaries White seemed to lead a terribly highbrow existence. 'We all knew pretty soon that Paddy had an account at Darter's bookshop, and he spent an enormous amount of his spare time there ordering books of various kinds, and notepaper and gramophone records. He was only happy in his shack – playing records and reading poetry – or shopping for books and records.'[68]

He spent the summer of 1929 in Dieppe with Waterall at the pension Les Aubépines, where the Le Grand family taught French to foreigners. They learnt little, for in the way of these places the students all spoke English. There were two schoolboys, a party of four very beautiful Swedish girls and an army officer with a chest like a 'burst hair mattress'. Lessons were conducted by Grandmère Vincent propped up in bed under a crucifix and sprig of yew. 'Grandmère's stomach rumbling with tilleul as she recited the lines of Le Lac in appropriately respectful tones.'[69]

They loitered in cafés smoking Gauloises and drinking Pernod. On the pebble beach, his skin streaked with tanning dye, White struggled with Madame Bovary but his French was not up to the task. It was both stimulating and frustrating to sense there were treasures behind the bars of the language, but he could not yet reach them. They took the Swedish girls to the opera at the casino for night after night of Massenet. He noticed Thaïs hid the hair in her armpits behind flesh-coloured rubber pads held in place with elastic straps. He wondered: is this a Roman Catholic habit? In the church of St Jacques he watched 'aged Popery' at work as a chambermaid went to confession,

> her worsted stockings
> Protrude from the confessional,
> As she pours out her petty sins
> Into the bosom
> Of our forgiving Church
> And the pocket of our blue-shaven priest[70]

Waterall left Dieppe early, not for Spain where he had expected to spend a year learning Spanish, but for London, where his stepfather had found him a job with British American Tobacco. Now alone in Dieppe, White concentrated his attentions on one of the Swedish girls. He fell for her. 'We embraced in doorways and on the sea-wall. I bought her a necklace of pink beads and a pink silk scarf. She must have found me amateurish, heavygoing.'[71] This crush left him jealous and wounded. For a while they exchanged letters but had no further contact. In his mind Dieppe became somewhere lovers put themselves to the test. Mrs Standish and Willy, then her daughter and the self-absorbed Maynard, cross the Channel to this 'damp French watering place' where a few days' fumbling led all parties to much the same conclusion: that husbands, lovers, slip away. Dieppe is a scene of quiet but fundamental failure.[72]

One term remained. He was now a prefect in the House, continued to run in the athletic team and play Rugby: 'Does his fair share of tackling and is generally well-up on the ball. Occasionally he has an off-day.'[73] P.V.M. White won the French Prize for Holiday Work with an essay on *Le Bourgeois Gentilhomme* and came equal top in French. Clement Priestley was now his English teacher. Most of the boys dismissed the Jaw as a clown and a queer, but with this teacher White felt he was at last learning. 'It may have been the man, or I may have been ready.' They studied Hardy's *The Dynasts*, Shaw's *St Joan*, Tennyson, *Richard II* and *Macbeth*. Priestley had his pupils write short stories for which he gave them the last lines. Two of White's efforts earned the accolade of a place in the headmaster's 'scrapbook'. In one a couple making love in a boat drift past a statue of Venus which suddenly falls into the lake and disappears. In the second a mad Messiah rushes through the East End of London in a great fire. It was not the Fire of London, but a fire to come. 'That happened in the war, and of course I wrote it.'[74]

The figure of the mad prophet appeared in the most memorable of the poems which survive from his school years. In 'Orchard Row', at the age of seventeen, he deals with images that fascinated him all his life,

> Squalor,
> All is squalor,
> Everywhere the stench of cabbages
> And overflowing garbage tins.
> Women,
> Blowsy and be-shawled,
> Sweat and swear in the tenements . . .
>
> The mother
> Is peeling potatoes
> By a lead sink. The room is hot,
> Hot as the very bowels of a ship.
> Potatoes
> And children
> Have killed the mother.

This is hell for the fastidious, but a fascinating hell; and down among the tramps and whores are those who claim (might they be right?) to be prophets,

> the mad Messiah
> The man with the wild eyes and flowing beard,

Cries out.
The children scatter.
'I am the Resurrection and the Life'[75]

The boy put Cheltenham behind him without a regret in mid-December after a Speech Day address by Lord Liverpool praising the trout fishing of New Zealand. At Cheltenham station White bought a packet of cigarettes and smoked all the way to London. When the jinxed *Otranto* left for Sydney in early January, the young man was nominally in the care of an amiable purser, who left him to muck about on his own for the voyage. He drank and slept,

> It was his habit to walk the deck before its holy-stoning, while the last wet kisses and the smell of sperm were evaporating. For miles he tramped, up and down and round the corner. He would have liked to think it was exorcism, whereas it was repetition.[76]

Making the voyage home was Dorothea Mackellar, poetess of the sunburnt country, the land of sweeping plains which White's homesick imagination, in the sleet and frigidity of Southwood, had turned into a paradise. He pictured himself returning to the freedom and sensuality of childhood, to the bush smelling of sun and smoke, and riding 'bareback through girth-high tussock, stripping leeches from my body after a swim in a muddy creek, my solitary mooning through a forest of dripping sassafras towards the sound of the waterfall'.[77] The young man was led up to meet the poetess. 'She was drifting about in veils, pissed.'[78]

SIX

The World of Sheep

Ruth and Dick were waiting on the wharf when the tugs nudged the *Otranto* into Melbourne. The reunited family took the train to Sydney, and their day together on the way north, travelling across the sun-stricken country, was 'fairly happy in a guarded way'.[1] Back in Australia he found he was Paddy again. They reached Lulworth late that night where his room was much as he had left it nearly five years before. Nothing had been disturbed, neither books nor trophies,

> nor the nightmares and unrealisable romances with which the narrow bed was still alive. He prodded it, and felt the same hair mattress on which he had done youthful penance.[2]

Lulworth seemed rather grand and he 'crept about' for a few days as he got used to the place again.[3] Theirs was the last of the big houses to survive in that part of town, hemmed in but intact. The Cross had changed: tall flats were going up around them and the hospital next door had built a wing against the fence, but the bunya bunya still stood above the wild garden, and from the upstairs veranda the Whites could look across to Darling Point as they always had, and see the little boats moored in Rushcutters Bay that 'jumped and fretted and pulled at their moorings to be away'.[4]

At the age of fifty-three Ruth had allowed a certain majesty to settle on her shoulders. Yet her face was the incongruous face of a woman who found life a hard slog. There was about her a sense of storms brewing, like a tropical mountain even on a clear day. Antagonism flickered between mother and son. Ruth had such plans for her boy. Those clever poems he sent home from Cheltenham she had printed and bound with a silk cord like a dance programme, with the title *Thirteen Poems* stamped on its cover. In the text she had left unchanged the boy's dedications, 'To Mummy' and 'To Mrs

Mrs Victor White with the author's compliments'. *Thirteen Poems* was for family consumption in the city and bush; the Whites were puzzled.[5]

Suzanne was fat and happy. Life at boarding school in the Highlands near Tudor House suited her down to the ground. She was a great sport. Brother and sister had not much in common and there were still spats and moody passages between them, but they found they laughed at the same things. That was their bond. He still imagined Suzanne White performing the great roles he would one day write. At Frensham, meanwhile, she was a memorable Bottom and a fair left-hand fast bowler.

The young man was defeated by his father without a struggle. Dick was sixty-two, tubby, sweet and indolent. He wore dark glasses now because they were supposed to protect him from hay fever. 'He exasperated me so much that I could scarcely stay in the same room with him, and the irritation was made worse by my having to admit the goodness and kindness behind the mediocrity. The trouble is I can never forgive mediocrity in anyone. I'd almost rather have a positive, flashy badness.'[6] Somewhere in his genial nature Dick had found a vein of sarcasm to explore. He could be tart with Ruth. It puzzled and offended their son to hear these quarrels and then see his parents a few hours later walking together in the garden as though nothing had happened. They played bridge together, he very badly. Over the cards Dick murmured, 'Yes dear . . . as you say dear.' He was happy enough, but Ruth was now such an imperious figure that she was known in Sydney as 'the White man's burden'.

Dick had little to do but read the *Sydney Morning Herald* exhaustively, keep an eye on his shares and check that his trainer was looking after his horses. The Sunday ritual at Lulworth was unchanged: church – now St John's in Darlinghurst – lunch with a few friends, and a trip to the stables to inspect the horses. The trainer Harry England, who got about the stables in a slightly yellow starched collar held together with a brass stud, had known Paddy since he was a small child. Now he found him 'the real gentleman', a remark that cut the young man with his authentic English accent to the quick.[7]

Ruth was uncompromising about what *had* to be done now that her son was home. He had to see the faith healer she'd found in George Street, a chiropodist with a shop near the cathedral. Paddy went twice for a laying on of hands. After the first visit to Ruth's miracle worker his wheezing disappeared immediately, but it returned. He came back to the shop once more, and again the wheezing went, but more slowly. He did not return a third time. The chiropodist was the first of a long line of quacks who promised miracle cures with coloured lights, grapefruit juice, comfrey, deep ray, acupuncture and prunes soaked in warm water. 'Quacks always did me good.'[8]

Ruth was determined to place her son in the Younger Set without delay. Society in Sydney was divided sharply between the married and unmarried. The Younger Set was a shameless marriage market, and photographs of girls from the country appeared in newspapers with pithy captions setting out name and property. Directories were available listing the acres that lay behind each of these women. Eligible men were sorted into ranks: at the top were the English aides–de–camp at Government House. The press scrutinised them ruthlessly: were they connected with royalty or only aristocracy, were they sporting or theatrical, did they have 'go'? In the next rank were men with acres or city men who gave good parties and perhaps owned a plane. The bachelors were frankly assessed by the press: 'Otway Falkiner, jun., dark, with gorgeous teeth and splendid physique is yet to be acquired by some lucky spinster, and Geoffrey Moss, a young bachelor of the Jewish community, has a merry smile and a very delightful station home . . . Mrs Harry Osborne's Denis is tall, was educated at Harrow, and a member of one of London's crack regiments, and manages four stations, Gordon Munro and John Spencer, too, are other country possibilities that must not be forgotten.'[9]

Paddy White had arrived home at the frantic end of the summer season, and Ruth threw him into the whirl. In his first fortnight the young man went to dances nearly every night. Hostesses forced him on to the dance floor cooing, like Frank Parrott's mother, 'You're wasting the music.'[10] He was looking for love, but aimlessly, too shy and cocooned to search for what he needed. For a young homosexual these parties were pointless. After nights at the Golf Club or the Lapstone Hotel he came home to be interrogated by Ruth.

'Tell me,' his mother asked, offering her face, 'there must be someone.'

'Someone? Who?'

'Why,' she laughed, 'you silly old boy! Some charming girl . . .'

On leaving the room he mopped his forehead with a handkerchief.

His mother had to wet her lips. And to return on frequent occasions to the inquisitions . . .

'Surely,' she said, 'I cannot believe there isn't some lovely girl. Otherwise it just isn't natural.'

She watched his mouth as it tried out shapes.

'There is no one,' he said.

And stuck to it.[11]

He hated Ruth for this, too harassed by her questioning to see her as 'more than a predator descending again and again to tear out an essential part of me'.[12] After a fortnight he dug in his heels and refused to go to any more dances.

Ruth still gardened furiously on Mount Wilson, though Dick had grown bored with the place. Lizzie was known on the mountain as Mrs Sid, a tiny woman, 'so Scottish it was ludicrous'.[13] The local children had their hair cut on the veranda of her cottage, for Sid Kirk was the only man on the mountain who could cut hair. Lizzie never appeared, never invited anyone in for a cup of tea. Occasionally she was seen walking briskly along one of the mountain roads in a coat, skirt and hat. She said 'Och, really?' to the children who spoke to her, and walked on. A child had been still-born; her children were Paddy and Sue.

After years of feeling Australian in England, the young man now felt a foreigner at home. He found himself unable to re-enter the child's Australia which had stayed so vividly in his mind in England that it became a permanent part of his imagination. Old Tudor House friends seemed daunted by his 'English' inhibitions. Fear and a strong dash of self-loathing aggravated his sense of suffering – as the Princess de Lascabanes later suffered on her homecoming – from 'the disease of foreignness'. He was at first alarmed and then permanently unhappy to find himself 'a stranger in my own country, even in my own family . . . However kind, generous, affectionate my family were on taking me back, they still did not understand the peculiar youth who had developed out of their difficult child.'[14]

He had his cousins. A cousinage of Whites stretched across New South Wales – the family tree was not long but wide, a document unrolled on billiard tables – and the young man spent much of his time in their company. They were easy dancing partners in that first difficult fortnight of parties; they played tennis together, not very well, but Paddy cut an elegant figure on the court in his Cheltenham blazer. He seemed to them a bit English but not remarkably so. His accent was exactly what was expected of him after those years away. There was no hint of his sexuality in his manner. Ruth was handing out copies of *Thirteen Poems*, so they knew he was writing, but they thought this would disappear once he settled down as a jackeroo. The most English thing about their cousin was the bulldog he bought and called Soames, and Paddy's peculiar way of dropping in at pubs for a sherry when he took them walking with the animal.

Dick warned, 'It won't be all violets.'[15] His son accepted that he must now go out into the bush to work for a couple of years, for he was still heir to a great chunk of the Upper Hunter. Dick had decided not to send him there for the time being, for Belltrees had everything, was too soft and his son would be treated by the men as one of the family. There was also the difficulty that H.L.'s son Alf, the other heir, was already in possession.

H.L. had died while White was at Cheltenham. By the time the young man arrived home, Alf had married Judy Coombe and they had a young son, Michael. Alf was now twenty-five, a stubborn, impetuous, quick-tempered man, father of a young family. The old arrangements that guaranteed Dick an income from the place, rankled with Alf. To meet death duties, he had sold his father's great library of Australian books, one of the finest in the country, and filled some of the gaps with volumes on the American West. He was a great fan of the Wild West. As the Depression slashed the profits from Belltrees, the young man found himself doing all the work while his uncles Dick and Arthur took two-thirds of the proceeds.

Alf did not mind paying Arthur and Milly, who lived with eccentric economy in a suite at the Australia Hotel. Arthur's meanness was a legend in the city: how he always took the tram, and cut a few sand-wiches for the cricket because the cost of a sandwich in the Members' stand was an outrage. Money to Arthur was as good as money in the bank for one day it would all come back to Belltrees. But the money that went to Lulworth was being spent! Alf stayed at Lulworth at this time and Paddy found him attractive 'throwing his body about', but Alf resented the Lulworth connection and complained later to his son Michael about the money ' "to pay Victor off" because that went on for years, and I think he just thought Ruth was spending it at the other end'.[16]

Dick arranged that his son would go south to jackeroo at Bolaro, a station owned by his friend Steenie Osborne, a genial man so fat that the steering column of his Cadillac was hinged to let him into the driver's seat. At Bolaro the young man would work on equal terms with Osborne's men and be paid nothing. He was doing this 'for love and experience'.[17] The Osbornes' place lay on the edge of the Snowy Mountains. In the early days, this landscape so reminded homesick Scots of the Highlands that families turned their backs on better land to sink their fortunes here. This noble, difficult country had rivers for trout fishermen, open grass for sheep, and bare hills for those who dreamed of home. Presbyterian fortunes were lost up here to drought and snow, wild dogs and hawks, but the Osbornes had prospered on their 18,000 acres along the Murrumbidgee.

The railway ended at Cooma, a town of brown granite pubs, sheltering in a hollow of hills. The road to Bolaro ran through rough country, with paddocks of boulders and ring-barked trees cleared out of the bush. But almost without warning the country changed, and the road reached the edge of a great, soft valley. Nothing stirred in this panorama of gold, rust and khaki except mobs of grey sheep and the shadows of high clouds drifting across the grass. There was hardly a tree in the whole valley, which gave the scene a childlike clarity but carried an ominous warning that winters here would be cold. Only a few crumpled hills lay between Bolaro and the Snowy Mountains to the south and west. The road ran down to the river in a few lazy swoops,

> a string of sheds, together with a huddle of cottages, their paintwork faded to a pale ochre, showed up amongst the white tussock on a river bank . . . Soon there was a bridge of loosely bolted planks buckling beneath the leaping car. Never had river waters looked glassier, more detached in their activity . . . above them in the middle distance a long low homestead, its windows dark and unrevealing behind a low-slung veranda, beneath a fairly low-pitched, red-painted roof, in corrugated iron. The homestead had a somewhat prim air, that of a retiring spinster of no pretensions beyond her breeding.[18]

The car did not make for the homestead, but drew up outside one of the two cottages in the woolshed paddock where the jackeroos lived. Paddy White (and his bulldog Soames) were given a room in the shabbier hut with the new men. He had a stretcher with army blankets, a deal table, a chest of drawers, an enamel candlestick, a frayed mat on the dusty boards and a mirror.

Outside the window the river ran in a jagged, silver S through the tussock grass. Wild hawthorns pressed against the weatherboard. Kitchen slops flowed into the yard and lay there in a rank pool. Out the back the lavatory leant sideways over a pit. Along a low rise that sheltered the cottages and the homestead was a double row of black pines which stirred, even on a still day, with a sad roar like the sound of an express in the far distance.

White was not among savages. For some time Steenie Osborne had been recruiting jackeroos from English public schools. This was the Bolaro Scheme, a mission on behalf of Australia: Osborne's argument was that Kenya should not attract all the best young men. He sent his manager, Colonel Charles Jones, over to England recruiting. Jones wore breeches, leggings, collar and tie even in the bush, and answered only when addressed as 'Colonel'. His recruits paid their own fares, brought out their dogs and horses, worked for the first year for nothing and were later paid a pound a week all found. White joined two young Englishmen at Bolaro: the randy, energetic Norris King and the sombre Arthur Ambrose. White bought a fine pony from one of the stockmen. She was dun with a light mane and he called her Spi after the French revue artiste Andrée Spinelli.

The jackeroos assembled early each morning to take their orders from the overseer George Irving. The sun was barely up and there was a smell of frost in the air even in late summer. Dogs whined and snapped. A few stockmen, one a half-wit with a cleft palate, waited to go out with the jackeroos. Their overseer was a dreary man made miserable by the departure of his wife and child.

'The winters were what the wife couldn't stand. She walked out on me – I'd better tell you before others do. It was the cold. Well, good luck to 'er! She was never much use to a man.'

His predicament became part of the history of Don Prowse, Eddie Twyborn's overseer at Bogong.[19]

The jackeroos were taught nothing, but picked up what skills they needed from the stockmen: how to dig out rabbits, strain a fence, work the Fordson tractor and harvest the oats. Flocks of white cockatoos flew, screeching and yabbering, out of a clear sky to tear down the stooks as soon as they were stacked. The young men worked mostly with sheep, those helpless, canny, obstinate, pathetic animals. Bolaro carried 11,000 Romney Marsh which had to be mustered, drenched, dipped, crutched, tailed, marked and dagged, 'snipping at the dags of shit, laying bare the urine-sodden wrinkles with their spoil of seething maggots, round a sheep's arse'.[20] The worst work was clearing briars. White tramped behind the tractor, slinging a cable round clumps of the obdurate plants. The Fordson heaved, and the team moved on. The job was never ending, tedious and backbreaking.

He returned exhausted each night to eat a joint of mutton cooked by Sally Venables, the motherly hag assigned to the young jackeroos. Venables had a husband somewhere and children all over the High Country. She loved a funeral, laid out the dead and signed her name with a cross. When she spoke,

she revealed two brown upper fangs with nothing but her tongue to fill the gap. She was dressed all in black, whether from grief or for practical reasons it was not possible to tell. She simpered a lot and hugged a bobbled crochet shawl round narrow shoulders. In the lower regions what had once been a laundered apron had failed to protect her practical black from a storm of flour.

He wrote her letters for her. She took him under her wing. Her food was terrible, mostly shoulders of mutton and mashed swede. There was always cake. 'I'd have cooked a pudding,' she used to say, 'but am fucked for fat.'[21]

He worked, ate and slept. His back ached and his hands were

raw. But he grew stronger and began to feel he was finding himself in the work. He let the sun soak into his back. His face and arms tanned deeply, and the asthma, nagging him since he arrived in Sydney, now left him alone. Like Eddie Twyborn, he was

> coming to terms with his body. He had begun to live in accordance with appearances. His hands no longer broke out in blisters; his arms, if not muscular, were at least lithe and sinewy. Sometimes on a calm day, by snatches of winter sunlight . . . he might take off his shirt, and the men would watch, not respectfully, but without showing too much disapproval. [22]

He began to read by lamplight. 'Gingerbread' Irving called the books that came up from Dymock's and Angus & Robertson's lending libraries by the box. The final volume of Henry Handel Richardson's *Fortunes of Richard Mahoney* was just out and Colonel Jones urged White to read the trilogy. It was the first great Australian novel the young man had read. He found it wonderful.

The jackeroos drove into the Bridge Club in Cooma to dance to the gramophone on Saturday evenings. White did not join in this simple social life. King and Ambrose found him friendly enough but recognised he preferred his own company. They called him Paddy. From time to time White was invited over to the homestead. He put on a jacket and sat with Leura Osborne, 'a charmer'[23] with a pack of fox terriers which scuffled and fought, clawing kapok from silk cushions. The Osbornes were not often at Bolaro, though Steenie, pear-shaped on his horse, appeared occasionally in the paddocks, stopping to talk to White as he worked. The men accepted this affectionate relationship between White and the boss as a matter of caste, in its way inevitable. Much of the time there was no one for the boy to talk to. Stockmen seemed to keep stale phrases handy for company, something familiar to have around like a horse and a dog. At first these men seemed to have the look of mystics or philosophers, but after a while White decided their far stare came from years spent scanning the horizon for sheep. [24]

Rather than return to Sydney for Easter, White took Spi over the mountains riding alone for a fortnight on a journey on which he 'lost and found' himself. Along the track he slept in pubs or cottages where travellers were taken in at night, and the walls were pasted with cartoons and corset advertisements. He was a good rider and he was happy. When Eddie Twyborn rode alone through these mountains,

> he could not remember ever having felt happier. At the same time he wondered whether he could really exist without the sources of unhappiness. [25]

From the ghost town of Kiandra, where a few people hung on in cottages bleached by snow and wind, he rode to Yarrangobilly. The resort was deserted for winter was coming. He slept in the Government Rest House, explored the caves and rode on towards Talbingo and down through apple country to Batlow and Tumbarumba – names he loved – to reach the Murray at Jingellic. From there he looped back along the river to a point where a track climbed the mountain wall to Kiandra. A hermit gave him directions. He rode all day without finding the track, reaching the top as night fell. He had no clue where he was. He had nothing to eat, and there was no feed for Spi. Like the Man who was Given his Dinner in *The Aunt's Story*, he wandered for hours, then sat 'under the shelter of a big dead tree, listening to the dingoes howl, waiting for the ghost. Cripes it was cold up there . . .'[26] At dawn he turned back down the mountain and found the hermit climbing, by chance, to Kiandra for supplies. So the two came back together. He was a civilised man and spoke well. He told White he had lived alone at the mouth of a steep gully lower down the mountains for years. They found the spot, only a few yards from the track, where White had spent the night and they rode together into Kiandra as the first snow of winter began to fall. White reached Bolaro next day, and Sally Venables rushed out to warn him that his worried mother had been ringing all round the mountains to find him. Ruth had kept the wires hot but missed him everywhere.

The beauty of the High Country came as a revelation in that fortnight alone in the bush. What had seemed hostile when he first worked in the paddocks now appeared austere and uncompromising. He longed, somehow, to become part of the country, to consummate this unexpected love which grew

> in spite of a sadistic wind, the sour grass, deformed trees, rocks crouching like great animals petrified by time. A black wagtail swivelling on a grey-green fence-post might have been confusing an intruder had he not been directing one who knew the password. The red road winding through the lucerne flat into the scurfy interior seemed to originate in memory, along with the wood-carving, boy-scout knots, and plasticine castle. For all the contingent's knowledgeable remarks on wool, scours, fluke and bluestone as they mounted the contours of Bald Hill, the scene's subtler depths were reserved for the outcast-initiate.[27]

He was seized by the need to find words to match the landscape. As the other jackeroos fished along the river in the evenings or shot quail in the tussock, he sat locked in his room with a stack of cheap

stationery and a kerosene lamp sweating over a novel. Sometimes he
wrote all night.[28] Landscape was not the only spur. He had no friends,
no theatre, no city in which to lose himself, no sex and no prospect of
sex. Exile and boredom were gnawing at him. His mother was out of
the way. In his imagination figures formed and took on a life of their
own, a life White was himself denied. Seeking an explanation for this
many years later, he admitted the importance of boredom in the process:
'All my life I have been rather *bored*, and I suppose in desperation I have
inclined to weave these fantasies in which I become more "involved".
Ignoble, *au fond*, but there have been a few results.'[29]

He called the book 'The Immigrants' and the plot posed a question much on White's mind: how could people stand this life? Some
immigrants arrive in the Monaro and have a tough time; one stays
because he finds something here in the land. There is a romance but
it falls through and the romantic woman goes away.[30]

Winter at Bolaro was bitter. On still days, even days that began
with a hard frost, the men might be working in shirtsleeves by noon.
But most of the winter the wind blew rain, sleet and snow down from
the mountains. The cold is not the deep, dry cold of Europe and North
America, but penetrating and damp. Men and animals backed into the
wind, their heads down, feet numb, blank with cold. With the cleft-
palated stockman for company, White brought a mob of sheep fifty
miles from Lanyon near Canberra, camping the night by the river at
Tharwa, and on next day through Naas to Bolaro. It amazed him that
'anyone should have had the idea of sending a half-wit and a boy of 18
on a journey through such country'.[31]

One of his jobs was to take the horses to be shod in Adaminaby,
a little town that had not much reason to survive now that gold had
given out at Kiandra and copper at Kyloe. By 1930 Adaminaby was
a spot on the map where the roads to Cooma, Jindabyne and Kiandra
met. If it was known to anyone outside the Monaro it was only as one
of the few towns in Australia where snow lay in the streets in winter.
Cold made it a curiosity. The main road, like a spine, climbed up the
hill, joined at sharp angles by a few bones of streets. As he rode through
the town White imagined padded cells in the cottages for the 'mads' who
walked the streets. He saw only meanness and illiteracy in the leftover
Irish and Germans who lived there. The jumble of cottages offended
his sense of order, as they did in the town he built on his memories
of Adaminaby,

> we are not particularly impressed by any beauty of design. Because
> somebody once built a house, I think it was probably old Quong,
> and someone else came along and built another, some little way
> off, just far enough to show there was no love lost in the act.

And it went on like that, just building here and there without co-operation. There never was co-operation in Happy Valley, not even in the matter of living, or you might even say less in the matter of living. In Happy Valley the people existed in spite of each other.[32]

Among the drab Europeans of Adaminaby were the exotic Yens, who became the Quongs of Happy Valley. Old Yen came down from the goldfields, and the family had set about making money without fuss. Bolaro got its supplies from Yen's general store and butchery. The Yens had the picture show higher up the street, as well as a garage run by wild Frank Yen, the disreputable member of the family, who had a way with women and lost the mail contract when he was caught one night in Cooma, drunk but purposeful, pissing through the keyhole of a shop.

White incorporated gossip and impressions of Adaminaby into the manuscript of 'The Immigrants', which he had finished by the time spring arrived at Bolaro,

> days of brilliant, slashing light alternating with a return to leaden rain squalls; the nights still crackled as he stood shivering, pissing from the veranda's edge on to frosted grass.[33]

He left Bolaro some time before Christmas. The verdict of the jackeroos on Paddy White was this: a loner who worked well enough, but he never looked as though he was going on the land. It wasn't unusual to see such city boys out in the bush in those days: jackerooing was a man's finishing school in Australia. The jackeroos had no idea he was writing. Sally Venables wept the day he left. In his luggage he had 'The Immigrants' and the beginnings of a second novel called 'Sullen Moon'.

The view from Lulworth was that Australian writers were teachers and public servants who scribbled at night. They were not in the Whites' class and Paddy neither made nor sought contact with them. 'They just did not belong to our world.' He did see the popular writer Hector Macquarie. 'He had just driven across somewhere in a Baby Austin – they were then a novelty – and was being lionised by the best people. I can remember him at a ball at the Golf Club sitting at the feet of Nesta Griffith – "the Embalmed Debutante", who writes books about the Stately Homes of N.S.W. I don't think she ever succeeded in coaxing him higher than her feet.'[34]

Ruth was curious about new books written by Australians though the notion of there being an 'Australian literature' was then considered odd and pretentious. Henry Lawson was dead, and it was over forty years before Patrick White read his stories. An English education left him untouched by, almost ignorant of, the writing which made up the Australian tradition: pastoral, realistic, democratic, with at its heart the figure of the battler. D.H. Lawrence had come and gone in 1922 while Paddy was still a boy at Cranbrook. When he read *Kangaroo* he found the slabs of politics dreadful, but he thought Lawrence's descriptions of the wild coast and the bush around Sydney were wonderful. Lawrence made little impression on local writers and none on Sydney society: it was as if he were never there.

Paddy owed to his mother the few discoveries he made in Sydney at this time. She had Katherine Mansfield's stories on the shelves at Lulworth. He became a passionate admirer of them, especially of 'At the Bay', and his enthusiasm was heightened by Mansfield's links with Lawrence. Ruth gave him a new novel by two women who wrote as 'M. Barnard Eldershaw'. The book was published just before his return to Australia, but a polite controversy about the accuracy of *A House is Built* continued in the newspapers. The novel became an important source for White when he became interested in the early history of Sydney, but it was twenty-five years before White met one of its authors, Marjorie Barnard.

He commissioned a bookplate from Adrian Feint: a naked lady, running past a dilapidated temple with a satyr hard on her heels. This image, however inappropriate it seemed, was supposed to represent man's striving after civilisation – the lady – and his failure to attain it – the broken temple. White always admired Feint's composition, but later came to think the plate was 'too exquisite by half' and scraped it out of his books.[35]

The satyr in pursuit was a better badge for the men who really set the tone of literary Sydney. About the time White arrived back in Sydney the police raided a bookshop in Martin Place and seized *All Quiet on the Western Front*, postcards of statues of naked women, birth control pamphlets by Marie Stopes, *The Decameron* and the complete works of Aristotle. Though they conceded the cards of Canova's 'Three Graces' were not objectionable, the police pressed the claim that the rest of their haul would have a tendency to deprave and corrupt Sydney's citizens, a danger mitigated only in the case of *The Decameron* because it was an expensive hardback out of the reach of the working classes.[36]

The talkies had reached Sydney but theatre was not quite dead. All the London successes came to town: *The Desert Song*, *Showboat*, *Rio Rita*, *Journey's End*. White had seen most of them before he left England, but while he was in Sydney he saw his first *Seagull* at Carrie Tennant's Community Playhouse and *Desire Under the Elms* at the Playbox. One of his aunt Mag Withycombe's poor relations danced in the chorus of musical revues, and talking to her for a few hours over coffee in Castlereagh Street made him feel as if he were in contact again with the wider world. 'She told me all about her life in the chorus, kicking up her legs, and I thought, how exciting, here I am talking to someone who's *really* been in the theatre.'[37]

Whatever relief theatre offered from the world of sheep was brief at best. He was caught, irresolute and uncomfortable, in the circle of his parents' friends. They were barristers, stockbrokers, a few graziers, store-owners: business, the law and the land.[38] They met at the races, ate at the Golf Club, played bridge and sat on the margin of the dances held to mark each stage their children took into the world: leaving school, turning twenty-one, engagement, marriage.

The Charles Ebsworths were important in this circle. Because Dick's brothers had married the three Ebsworth sisters of Bronte House, Chas and Fran Ebsworth counted as family at Lulworth. (According to an old joke Ruth only landed Dick because there were no more Ebsworths.) Chas was the Whites' family solicitor and like his shadow Arnold Wyburd – solicitor to the Hunters of Kudjeri – he was sinewy, handsome, upright to an almost ludicrous degree, a bit slow but devoted and understanding.[39] Ruth and Dick were grateful to him. His wife Fran was the sympathetic woman with whom the twelve-year-old Paddy debated the virtues of Irene of the Forsyte Saga. The Ebsworth daughters, who used to play at Lulworth when they were all children, came to have a role in the lives of Laura Trevelyan and Belle Bonner.

Ruth was shy of the social peaks. In principle she loved the vice-regal pomp of Government House, the gothic folly in the Botanic Gardens, but was nervous of it in fact. A new Governor had arrived from England, but the Victor Whites were not part of the Government House set under Sir Philip Game, a young English Air Force officer with a head like a fleshed skull.

In the Whites' crowd the men spoke of 'sheep, weather, racehorses and the Australian Moloch sport'.[40] The women drifted through music, books and theatre. Margaret Gordon's latest interest was Little Theatre. As Lady Gordon – for her husband was knighted when he retired from the divorce court – she was more than ever a force on charity committees, with Ruth as her lieutenant. Ruth was also a devoted supporter of the Australian Broadcasting Commission's new symphony orchestra.

The press kept track of the Whites, but it was a measure of their standing – right at the top, old money – that they were not reported slavishly in the papers. Ruth was known for food and the flowers she brought down from her Mount Wilson house to be arranged by city florists for parties at Lulworth. Frankly, the gossip columnists thought Lulworth was a bit slow, though Ruth was good for a paragraph every few months in *Truth*: 'Have you seen Mrs Victor White complete with monocle? She manages it in the real Chamberlain manner – screws it in with a deft twist, and just WINKS it out.'[41]

Ruth's position in Sydney allowed her some eccentricities. At that time she was one of the few hostesses to receive Charles Lloyd Jones and his new wife Hannah, married after a sensational Reno divorce. Their match, according to the conventional verdict of Sydney society, was no better than bigamy. Lloyd Jones was at heart a painter but he made a great success of the store he owned, David Jones. Hannah had once worked behind the counter. Patrick had a lifelong affection for the store, a landmark in his private geography of Sydney. David Jones' stood for comfort and vanity with a hint of social peril, for the girls on the bag counter were predators. They married young men of good family, and caught dotty old ladies like Alex Gray innocently shoplifting.[42]

Into the barely ruffled pool of Sydney society stepped Ethel Kelly, plump and eager after living for years in Florence. 'She looks like a Neapolitan fishwife,' reported Ruth on returning from the wharf, adding in a whisper to her son, 'and she's become a Catholic.'[43] Ethel's passion for fresh experience had led her to a late conversion. Sydney took it on the chin. Bertie Kelly left the tower at the Golf Club and, reunited with his wife, began to build an Italian villa on Darling Point. The town was delighted to see her back in action, pretentious as ever. *Tableaux vivants* reappeared, and the best families turned out for Ethel's eighteenth-century musicales dressed as figures from Watteau, Tiepolo and Boucher. The press reported their costumes with scientific precision and White loved the way the rhetoric of costume skewered these plain people, dolled up in Pompadour silks, blue moiré, taffeta and lace.

His letters to Waterall were full of funny, cruel vignettes.[44] Like Ruth, he gave no quarter. Mother and son would always share a laugh if someone grabbed the wrong knife and fork, but even as a bright and curious little boy, born with the intuition his mother lacked, Paddy realised her cut-and-dried rules of life were out of kilter with the world. As he grew up he had been faced with the choice all homosexuals must make between sticking to the rules – perhaps for a lifetime – or making sense of life by following the irrational, often painful truths revealed within themselves. Curiosity, scepticism and doubt are second nature to those who choose the second path.

What mattered to him were the more difficult truths found in the gap between what humans pretend to be and what they are. Find what we are hiding – especially from ourselves – and that is our character. The more hidden and defended our faults, the more they define us when brought into the light. White was reading his own predicament in the faces around him, but it left him nevertheless with the bleak conviction that character is largely a calculus of faults, deceit and pretence.

Mother and son were at odds over people. Any difference between them quickly became a point of friction, for it was almost as if the son's survival depended on him defending his truth against hers, either by fighting as the hunchback Rhoda Courtney fought her own mother 'with words and moods'[45] or by setting out on paper his contradictory version of the world. Setting his mother right was one of the spurs to White's writing, but to be a really effective, lasting stimulus he had to convince himself that Ruth misunderstood almost everything.

Both his parents seemed to be surviving in a daydream of self-deception. For instance Ruth's young men: she had collected around her a group of amusing men with gentle manners and good accents. She was at her best with them:

> As they hung about her in an esoteric group, and she fed them with their own wit, the young men would threaten to break at the hips. The old thing. They simply adored her.[46]

She spoke of them as her protégés, but to her son's gimlet eyes they were Ruth's 'crypto-queers'. They were elegant, if not aggressively successful architects and solicitors in Sydney. Some were to marry, some shrivelled up, some died of booze, a few escaped to Europe. They lived in terrified abstinence or extreme discretion.

Ruth's young men did not make her son feel at home in Sydney. Uncomfortable as he was at Lulworth, he sought no world of his own. Inactivity and frustration led him to despair. He hung about, shy and bored. He went to no more dances: 'However depressing the dance that you don't go to, the music in the street, and the sound of the people coming home, it is never so depressing as the one you let yourself be persuaded into.'[47] He was nearly nineteen. Standing under the showers at the Golf Club's annex at the beach, he watched with longing the men washing off Bondi sand. Loneliness filled him with frustration and self-disgust, not only from thwarted lust but at his own shyness that prevented him finding satisfaction.

Homosexual Sydney was a busy but invisible city. Initiates knew its customs and geography, but White was so cocooned that it was never apparent to him that Rushcutters Bay Park, where he took Soames every day for a walk, was one of the city's homosexual beats. Even that graziers' stronghold, the Australia hotel, was a place homosexuals traditionally met. Discretion was essential at the Long Bar. Sober clothes and a 'masculine' manner were all that outsiders observed but here at the Australia, on Friday nights at Madame Pura's Latin Café in the Royal Arcade, at Christ Church, St Laurence and the

Hot Sea Baths at Coogee were doors that opened on to a private city. Finding the door was everything.[48] Despite his loneliness and frustration, the young man failed to discover a way into that other Sydney. He was too shy, too fearful.

At Narrabri, after a breakfast of eggs and tea, White climbed on to the rattler for Walgett. The heat was fierce. All day the little train crossed a plain of black and gold: black soil, miles of summer grass drying to tinder, and a few trees like tin silhouettes on the horizon. Thunderstorms appeared over the rim in the afternoon, the clouds piling in tiers like the circle and gods of an immense theatre. Lightning flickered but made no sound. The hot air, full of fine dust, took on a sheen of gold as the sun began to drop.

At Eurie Eurie siding, a few miles short of Walgett, the rattler broke down. The passengers waited to be fetched. After a time White climbed into an old tank to find water. A steam engine appeared a few hours later to drag the rattler to the end of the line. Clem Withycombe was waiting with a couple of fine horses in the shafts of his wagonette. Uncle and nephew greeted each other with the stiff warmth they managed at such moments. The hero of the boy's childhood was still a man of great panache. The Whites admired him as a battler. It had been decided that Paddy would spend some time jackerooing for Clem at Barwon Vale. He was family, but out at Walgett there was none of the luxury that counted against a stint at Belltrees. Paddy was a little wary for he remembered his uncle's foul temper.

Barwon Vale was an hour's ride down the river from Walgett. At a plain iron gate they turned up the track that ran for a couple of miles through coolabahs to the Withycombes' wooden house by the waterhole. Scattered under the trees beyond were stables, a few workmen's huts and a shearing shed. The eccentricities of life on Barwon Vale, familiar to White from his childhood, were a source of entertainment and confusion to the district for twenty-five years. When neighbours with their broad verandas and tennis courts reproved Clem Withycombe for living in this cottage, he replied, 'You can't shear a house.' Mag never unpacked her wedding presents. Crated china marked the hope that some day they would have something better. They never did.

Barwon Vale was all horse. The stables were grander than the house, and Clem had built himself training tracks and a polo field. There was no car, truck or tractor on the place. Clem drove to town with a team of horses worth a thousand guineas each at a time when a new Buick cost £500. With this passion for horses came a contempt for cows. At Piercefield he had had enough of cows to last him a lifetime. They milked goats at Barwon Vale, and Mag Withycombe's narrow garden was double-fenced to keep them from the scrubby bushes that edged the house.

The district had to concede that apart from the house everything was well done at Barwon Vale. Nothing was curtailed, even in hard times. The Withycombes were judged rather grand: Clem 'always the Hunter River gentleman' and Mag rather distant. She had no children, and took little part in the tennis and dinner parties that made up the narrow social life of the district. Because she wore jodhpurs and rode astride she was criticised for letting standards slip. The Withycombes were ferocious snobs in their own way but deaf to this kind of prudery. They lived as they wished. In autumn and spring they 'jumped the rattler' for the Sydney races, and spent a week or so in summer, as they always had, at the Coogee Bay Hotel.

White shared a small room with the young overseer Frank Loder. Their beds were out on the veranda. Loder was twenty-four, ginger-haired and very strong. He came from what was called a 'good family', which meant he had an education but no money. Loder was willing. He did most of the work on Barwon Vale and lived with the Withycombes. In the age of the wireless, his cruel stammer earned him the nickname Static.

White was put to work with sheep again: castrating, dagging, dipping, mustering. The station diary records: 'Loder and White went through McKenzie's sheep for flies . . . the Boss and White burning track in Bore Pdk . . . Loder and White sorted all the "dead" wood in the shed and cleaning . . . White took mail down, and put Mr Cohen's mares and foals out of Little River Pdk into Big River Pdk.'[49] Around Walgett there is a folk memory that before riding off to work in the morning Paddy White used to put a book in his saddle-bag with his cold mutton chops. (An extreme version of the same story has it that he packed the book *instead* of the chops.) But he was treated as one of the men: 'He had to hit the collar the same as everyone else.' Withycombe was seen one day berating his nephew for mustering a paddock short. Steaming with rage, he sent White back for the missing sheep.[50] These attacks of foul temper, appearing out of the clear sky, passed entirely, leaving only the spectators shaken. White remembered one occasion when he failed to steady a nervous horse being examined by his uncle, a renowned amateur vet. 'Our relationship was temporarily destroyed when the man I admired became almost jellified with rage.'[51]

Barwon Vale's 18,000 (mortgaged) acres were desert in a poor year and survived a good summer only with artesian water flowing across the paddocks in 'drains' filled with emerald reeds. One boundary of the property followed the river. The Barwon curls its way through great stands of gums, their roots unravelling down the banks like old knitting. No underbrush clutters the simple lines of trees and grass and water with a great plain stretching beyond. Flocks of brilliant birds darted across patches of sun. Nowhere on Barwon Vale was more than a few feet above the level of the banks. In summer the temperature climbed above the century week after week, and as the mercury passed 110 degrees fahrenheit Withycombe would remark, 'It's getting to be a nasty day.' Work never stopped for the heat. Sunsets were slow and gaudy. Violent little storms moved across the land, tearing at trees and dumping patches of rain.

The landscape answered White's needs. He found it more passive than the Monaro, but more sensual. 'Perhaps because a rare commodity, water played a leading part in my developing sexuality. I was always throwing off my clothes to bathe, either at the artesian bore during a pause from mustering, the water ejaculating warm and sulphurous out of the earth, or in the river flowing between the trunks of great flesh-coloured gums, to a screeching, flick-knife commentary of yellow-crested cockatoos.'[52]

Once that year his uncle took him into Queensland. Withycombe was one of those men who don't drive a car but have a genius for organising lifts. Clem persuaded a stock agent to take them out to the opal mines at Lightning Ridge and then north over the border to a property called Brenda. It was the furthest Patrick White penetrated the Australian desert, except in his imagination. At Brenda black servants padded about in bare feet. He woke at dawn to see a wonderful sky and a garden full of birds. 'It was thrilling.'[53]

At Barwon Vale he lived simply and by strict routine. At precisely the same time each night everyone sat down to a quick meal of mutton and potatoes. Once there was a dish of stewed nettles during a dearth of vegetables.[54] Clem was a figure fanatic like his sister and held 'soup days' every now and again to keep his weight down. On these days he bolted from the table after a few minutes, unable to bear the sight of people eating. Meals at Barwon Vale took only fifteen minutes anyway.

Mag Withycombe read in her little parlour with an art nouveau fireplace at the front of the house. Loder mooned about for a while, then slept. Withycombe stood at the telephone in the narrow wooden hall, shouting down the party line. He was a great gossip, an Almanac de Gotha of the bush. 'He could go through people by the mile.'[55] To his stories he brought a punter's memory for bloodlines and the rough insights of a bush vet: beasts and men were all one in Withycombe's yarns. He would say, 'We had a horse like her.' He embroidered, but no one expected him to stick to the bare truth.

His nephew worked at the big table to finish 'Sullen Moon'. The plot was rudimentary: 'There were two sisters and a man, and the moon played a big part.' In the new novel the sky took something of the role played by the Monaro landscape in 'The Immigrants'. He felt he was 'beginning to get somewhere'[56] with 'Sullen Moon' even though he knew, like the jackeroo at Mumbelong, that he was not yet ready.

Out in the kitchen Col Forster was writing at something. There were pages of it amongst the grey-brown potato peelings. The lamp chimney had turned black.

'What are you writing?' Hurtle asked.

There was a breathing silence, while the insects batted round the glass chimney of the lamp, and Col held his hand to protect the paper.

Then he answered: 'Is it any business of yours?'

Hardly fair, when you only wanted to know.

Then Col thought better. He had a broad face, and spongy gentle fingers. 'I'm writing a book. A novel,' he said. 'The trouble is, I haven't yet experienced enough.'

'Can't you simply write it out of your head?'

'It wouldn't be real.'

It was difficult to see the point, only that the jackeroo was troubled.[57]

White poured his longing and frustration into 'Sullen Moon'. 'I wrote it off.'[58] In that airless house there was a strong sense of sex. Through wooden walls he heard the jangling of his aunt's and uncle's iron bed. His own lay close to Frank Loder's. As the months went by, this hard, young man began to enthral him: his chest had whorls of red bristle, and there were soft strands of red hair on his wrists. 'He was the first of the reds.'[59] The boy found the sight of wrists extraordinarily sensual, and red hair on wrists gave him a sharp thrill – and a pang of disgust – all his life. From the memory of this silent passion for Frank Loder grew all the red seducers of White's imagination, men like Frank Parrott who jackerooed on the Barwon, and the salesman who seduced Amy Parker, and Don Prowse the overseer at Bogong who raped the jackeroo.[60]

Nothing much happened at Barwon Vale. Beside the house lay the lagoon where the men who worked for the Withycombes swam on hot evenings. One night White found an old pair of high heels in the bathroom and tottered down to the water. The men 'turned the shoes into a ribald joke, acceptable because it was something we could share. We continued joking, to hold more serious thoughts at bay, while we plunged, turning on our backs after surfacing, spouting water, exposing our sex, lolling or erect, diving again to swim beneath the archways made by open legs, ribs and flanks slithering against other forms in the fishy school, as a flamingo moon rose above the ashen crowns of surrounding trees.'[61]

The Ridleys' Allawa was six miles from Barwon Vale, and that winter Paddy and the young overseer often rode over together, rackets strapped to their saddles, Soames puffing along in the wake of the horses, to play tennis with the Ridley girls. Clem was devoted to the old man, a cocky-farmer and battler, who had a bullock team and carted Barwon Vale's wool to the railway. In the district it was said that Ridley was once a circus acrobat. White took a fierce dislike to Mrs Ridley, 'a shrew and a machine, and the kind of woman I hate'. Her greatest fault, perhaps, was the determined way she was moving her family up the ladder. White liked people to stay where they were. For ever. Out of his undying dislike for this woman grew one of the great figures of his imagination, Girlie Pogson. 'There was a social barrier (invisible though accepted) between the cocky-bullocky and my uncle and aunt, although my aunt was also friendly with his wife and the two girls. It was something that always existed in those days between the cockies and the graziers . . . the wife was very hard headed, a shrewd bookkeeper, thin and wiry, with the tight perm that I always see Girlie Pogson as having – a hangover from the shingle days. The two girls were quite attractive giggly things in their late teens when I was in mine. They lived for the picnic races and the ball, were always whipping up sponges for tennis parties, and listening in to other people's conversations on the party line to see who was becoming engaged to whom. As I saw it later, *I* was supposed to become engaged to one of them.'[62]

After a day on the court the two young men had supper before riding home. White asked them all one night to sit round in the dark, their fingers resting on a little table, which they tried to raise with the power of thought. He told the Ridley girls how much he admired German women. They set out for Barwon Vale very late after one of these tennis days, and got home to find Withycombe 'raging on the veranda, afraid that I might be getting tied up to a cocky-farmer's daughter'. Uncle and nephew, for totally different reasons, were at one.[63]

Walgett was not much of a town, a grid of weatherboard houses on stumps, a court house and seven or eight pubs built by the river. Walgett was white. Aborigines of many tribes lived at the mission and in humpies along the river bed, but they were not allowed into town, unless they were going on an errand. The rule was: straight in and straight out with no loitering. Blacks were not allowed to drink, though not much notice was paid to the colour of a man's hand in the trapdoor at the back of the Royal, and whites took bottles of wine down to the camp to trade for ten shillings or a root. In his months at Walgett, White did not meet an Aborigine; they were everywhere but did not cross his path. Clem, alone of his neighbours, didn't take a black boy on the back of his sulky to open gates.

Light rain turned the fine black soil of the plain as slippery as grease, and a heavy shower made quagmires of the roads. Social life along the river was precarious. Rain wrecked weddings. At the sight of a bank of cloud, a line of Buicks and Fords headed for the gate, for otherwise the guests might be trapped for days. The Withycombes couldn't get far with a buggy, but they could always get through. In the winter of 1931 it rained heavily in the west and the Barwon overflowed its banks. 'White took ewes back to Bore Pdk from in Shed Pdk owing to flood water, and carting manure away from woolshed,' recorded the station diary in July. 'Loder and White went to see if any of the ewes and lambs had got bogged crossing the swamp in Slushhole . . . White brought up sheep from T.S.R. to polo ground.' Collecting the mail was one of his regular duties, and when the river rose he swam his horse across the flood-waters to the mail-box. He enjoyed the feat, and Frank Parrott was to boast to Fanny and Theodora Goodman how he swam his horse across the Barwon.[64]

Clem Withycombe remarked to one of his neighbours not long after White arrived: 'I don't know what's wrong with that boy. He's not interested in the place.'[65] His nephew was not shirking, the work was being done, but he was not keen. They were puzzled to see Paddy come in exhausted after a day in the paddocks and use his last energy to write all night at the table. Over those months at Barwon Vale, Withycombe realised his nephew was not cut out for the land. He convinced Ruth and Dick of this difficult fact sometime in the winter of 1931, a few weeks before the young man left to return to Sydney.

Dick was waiting at Scone when his son's train arrived from Walgett at midnight. Rather than drive out to Belltrees at that hour they took a room at the Royal. The publican was angry at being woken, but stifled his annoyance when he saw Whites on his doorstep. Father and son shared a big iron bed.

> 'I was so excited I lay awake all night listening to the noises in the pub yard. The moonlight, I remember, was as white as milk. It was hot. I pushed the bedspread off. It lay on the floor against the moonlight.'[66]

This night remained in his memory as an image of inexpressible intimacy. Eddie Twyborn shared that bed with his father the judge on circuit in Bathurst, and the son 'would not have regretted drowning in love' for the father. Mrs Elizabeth Hunter, on her way out to Kudjeri – to nurse the dying husband who, at long last, she realises she loves – spends this sleepless night alone at the Imperial Hotel, Gogong. Lying between rough sheets, she listens to the pub stirring,

A cock, a dog, and the moon were the major characters it seemed.
Till a cockatoo, evidently left uncovered, united its screeches with
the crowing and barking. A man was cursing as he first muffled,
then silenced, the cockatoo. Slippers slopped across the yard. There
was the sound of somebody making water against stone.[67]

Alf arrived early to bring them out to Belltrees. To Paddy it seemed
he had always made this journey along the river cliffs to Gundy in early
dazzling light, 'staring at the streaming golden paddocks on which the
sun was rising'.[68] They came not to the homestead but the cottage
Kioto, where Alf and his family lived. The homestead had been empty
since Maude's death a few years before but it was kept like a maharaja's
guest house, perfectly maintained for visiting polo parties. Paddy and
Dick stayed for a couple of days at Kioto with Alf 'bullshitting about'.[69]

When Patrick White explained his estrangement from the valley in
later life he would say the Belltrees Whites could not bear him
being a writer. This barely mattered. The nub of it was the mutual
dislike of two heirs: the martinet grazier and the failed jackeroo. Paddy
found his cousin bombastic and disagreeable, and his hostility was
amply returned. When Alf later learned his cousin was homosexual,
his enmity was cast in iron. Out in the bush they said Alf White was
'one hundred percent man'.[70]

The Whites, in turn, were to accuse Patrick of not loving the land.
They did not mean the landscape but the life they led on their acres:
working as labourers and living as grandees; spending their days in the
paddock and saleyard, and their nights talking sheep and politics and
polo and weather. Because the Whites read so little, few grasped how
deeply engaged he remained in his imagination with their lives and the
corner of Australia he always felt was his. And if the Whites sorted
him among the no-hopers for not sticking to the land, this, obscurely,
drove him on.

Ruth now had the upper hand in the matter of her son's career. She
wanted him to be a writer – she had always wanted him to write – but
he had also to have a career. She used to say when he was a child, 'He'll
probably go into the church,' for she had found him carrying round a
battered prayerbook in his pocket. That was long forgotten. She had
sketched a life for him at one stage as a doctor who wrote, and was
quite reconciled to the idea of him being a Hunter River grazier who
wrote. But after Barwon Vale Ruth's mind turned to the possibility of
her son becoming a diplomat and writer.[71]

Her enthusiasm for diplomacy was untouched by considerations
which might have daunted a less determined woman. Australia had
almost no diplomatic service, for Britain handled that sort of thing on

Australia's behalf; and her son had demonstrated as clearly as he could that he had no taste for society. Yet he did not tackle his mother at this point, for her plans offered him a way of escape from Australia. As Ruth saw it, the first qualification for this diplomatic life was a Cambridge degree.

This presented two immediate difficulties: cash and qualifications. Dick had been able to draw only £3,000 from Belltrees in 1931 and faced the prospect of drawing nothing in 1932. Capital was not a problem: Lulworth, Withycombe and Belltrees were all unmortgaged and the Victor Whites' investments were blue chip. But they were a little strapped for cash. As Ruth put it, 'The only people paying me dividends these days are the crematorium.'

She had made a few bad investments for she had a weakness for schemes promoted by men with good accents who were down on their luck. Major Poody Myles, once of the Indian army, persuaded her to speculate in the South Seas. She lost all she invested. The Major's wife had a pigeon's blood ruby which passed, in time, to Mrs Flack, Boo Hollingrake, Alfreda Hunter and the rubber-lipped General Sokolnikov. Rubies set in gold cufflinks inspired the Bonners' confidence in the bogus Dr Kilwinning, and Amy Parker's seducer Leo wore 'a very small ruby star' when he appeared at the farm selling lingerie and fancy buttons. That stone first appeared on the finger of Cissie Belper, and the Belpers were Paddy's revenge on his mother's behalf: Joe Belper, a bank manager and 'Captain Cook of platitude', lost all Alys Browne's money in the Salvage Bay Pearl Fisheries. So she was trapped, almost penniless, in Happy Valley. The ruby is always a warning.

The income crisis made no difference to the scale on which the Victor Whites lived. Dick still had his horses, a trainer and the astonishingly handsome chauffeur Brown; Ruth had her major-domo Mabel, a cook, maids and gardeners in Sydney and on Mount Wilson. But it did mean their son would have to wait until he could get away, and could not expect to live on the scale Alf had enjoyed in Cambridge a decade earlier, when H.L. gave his son a ducal allowance of £300 a quarter. Ruth and Dick rather hoped Paddy would win a scholarship.

Because the boy had left Cheltenham without matriculating, he would now have to take the university entrance exam. Ruth paid a tutor on the staff of Sydney University ten shillings a week to give her son a tutorial along Oxbridge lines. Fred Wood was a modern historian, a calm young man, polite, reasonable yet stringent. For about eight months from September 1931 he set White an essay each week – reviewing, perhaps, a new book of history – which they would then spend a few hours discussing.

'The curriculum called for him to grind through the ordinary drill of English and European history. He accepted this as a duty, but not with any personal enthusiasm.' Wood found no sign of real distinction or originality in his work, but compared with the young men he had been teaching at Oxford, White's thinking 'was fresh, quite active, not just a recipient of fact. Lively is too strong a word, but he came from a family circle where people spoke up and exchanged ideas and experiences. He had ideas of his own.'[72]

White made the common mistake of pouring his creative energy into the essays he wrote for Wood. 'I thought I'd put a bit of *something* into them. So boring otherwise.'[73] Wood was committed to clear and direct historical writing, in a style that was 'economical, not ornate or involved in words'. White recalls him tearing those essays to shreds. Wood was sure he pointed out lapses of taste but, precise as his recall was of this time, he had no memory of criticising White's writing harshly. Yet White awarded Wood the important symbolic role of being the first of all the academics who were 'very shocked by my style'.[74]

White liked his tutor. At first their sessions were held after dinner at Lulworth. Young men were offered beer rather than wine by Dick, and Wood found the atmosphere over dinner was easy, very natural and warm. Later there were lessons at Wood's mother's place on the North Shore, 'where there was a well-scrubbed, virtuous young wife, rather in the blonde, German, plaited style. The mother's house I remember quite vividly. It was full of brown furniture of no particular period, and standing in the midst of some gum trees. The air was very clear and breathable after that of Sydney. In one of the first novels I wrote, I used several of the Woods.'[75]

This was 'Finding Heaven', and he never confessed its existence to his tutor. He began the new novel at Barwon Vale after finishing 'Sullen Moon'; its theme was 'city life at the time of the Depression' and it involved 'a girl from the mountains and a flash man from the city'.[76] He worked on the book up at Withycombe, where he spent a lot of time on his own, wandering about the mountain, a standoffish figure in grey flannels with the slobbering Soames trailing behind him. The dog terrified small children by nuzzling their bare legs. Soames attacked Ruth's goat, which survived and was sent out of harm's way to keep down the Valders' blackberries.

Life on his own was primitive at Withycombe. He fed twigs into a roaring chip heater for his bath. The kitchen was too huge for him to crank into action, so his meals were brought over by the caretaker's wife. She was a bad cook. One night he buried a burnt curry in the garden rather than face her in the morning. Mount Wilson still seemed the most beautiful place in Australia, but the landscape no longer opened to him as it had in childhood. 'The sassafras I considered mine seemed to reject my intrusions; I was surrounded by a quizzical silence, watched by invisible birds.'[77]

He and Wood had some final tutorials in the mountains – interrupting Wood's honeymoon – before he took the exam down in Sydney. White passed but without winning a scholarship. Half-heartedly, he suggested to Ruth he might as well go to Sydney University now that he was here, but she insisted on Cambridge and he was relieved. He had, in retrospect, quite enjoyed his punishing stints in the bush which yielded three novels, but he had to run away. Isolation and the expectation of future loneliness were too much to face. 'It did not seem possible during those years that there could be anyone else who might share my own peculiar tastes.' Sex drove him away. 'There was nothing in Australia and no prospect of it.'[78]

He came to two resolutions. One was trivial. He would be called Patrick: 'I refused to go through life known as Paddy White, because it just wasn't me!'[79] The second resolution could not be put into effect immediately, and it was far from clear how it ever would be, but he knew he had to make a break from the White world and make a life of his own. Ruth had done that for herself when she brought Dick down from Belltrees to Sydney, and something like the same instinct propelled her son to the decision he now reached: he was determined not to be bored.

Soames was an ugly problem at the end. He found the goat tethered in the blackberries and tore the animal to pieces. The goat was shot. The neighbours wanted the bulldog off the mountain. They feared for the children. Here was a crisis to test Ruth White's mettle. Wasn't Soames a perfect mascot for the navy? She knew an admiral. She rang. It was arranged. The dog disappeared to Garden Island, and her son took the *Niagara* to Vancouver on the first leg of the voyage to England. He was rather frightened of what lay ahead, but expected never to return.

SEVEN

King's Men

White stood in the rain on Shanklin Pier as the audience of *My First Affair* wandered off into the dark. Soon he was alone by the stage door waiting for Ronald Waterall, whose name appeared well down the cast list that night as Ronald Waters. When British American Tobacco had tried to order the young man out to Java earlier in the year, he left tobacco for the West End. White admired him bucking his family's plans and setting out with a new name on this life of his own, but he wondered if Ronald had the talent. The show was pathetic. *My First Affair* had washed up on the Isle of Wight after a summer tour of seaside towns where the cast had had to go out selling tickets door to door. White greeted his friend with amused gloom and told him flatly, 'You shouldn't go on the stage.'[1] That night he stayed with the cast in a theatrical boarding house on the island, and was haunted by the sight of the leading lady coming down to breakfast next morning still in greasepaint, very red in the corners of her eyes.

It was wonderful to be away from Australia. His spirits had begun to revive once the ship left behind the Pacific islands, those 'gritty little lumps with the heads of tousled palms set in a leaden sea'.[2] He crossed Canada by train, spending a night somewhere in a neat little weatherboard town of such pristine simplicity he felt he might live there for ever. All his life he was tempted by these glimpses of paradise in Canada, New Mexico, Scotland, Tasmania or the Aegean. But he always kept moving. After a dull voyage through the Great Lakes, White caught the *Empress of Australia* in Quebec for his first Atlantic crossing. He was in London in September and on Waters's advice took a room in Ebury Street.

White was absorbed, once again, into Jack and Ellen Withycombe's family. Their headquarters was now an eighteenth-century country house outside Southampton. At West End the daughters pursued their difficult relationships with men, principles, art and one another:

'I vaguely floated in and out the oval drawing-room, sometimes providing a catalyst of sorts without my knowing. The drawing-room at West End was slightly reminiscent of the Long Room in Hayley's house at Felpham . . . but West End was never parent-ridden, nor did it have any of the frowsty Victorian accretions, the suffocating constriction of that other house, rented only for a season. In Ellen's house the stage was perfectly set. We made our exits to the garden between long curtains in amethyst velvet hanging from a gilded cornice.'[3] Jack Withycombe, always equable, was engaged on the great labour of his life: the fifth edition of the one-inch map of Britain. He had been ill, but appeared to be on the mend. Peggy was setting up a department of sculpture in the Bournemouth Municipal School of Art and was about to disappear to Majorca for a year. Betty, who had corresponded intensely with her cousin in Australia, was at Oxford University Press. White showed her one of the jackeroo novels, in which she found 'some quite good writing'.[4]

White wanted to find a publisher, and for help he turned to Joyce, the third of the three sisters, for she was to marry the writer and pacifist Richard Ward, whose first novel *The Compelled Hero* was then enjoying a success. More to the point, Ward read manuscripts for the literary agent David Higham. After returning from the Isle of Wight, White spent an uncomfortable weekend at Ward's cottage in Norfolk, and Ward agreed to send the jackeroo novels to Higham. They were later returned 'with a wry smile. He thought the works not worth sending to a publisher.' The weekend was not quite wasted: it introduced White to Norfolk on which he drew decades later when he wanted a landscape to match the sense of sexual threat he had felt in those days. And from Ward's landlady he took the name Kitty Goose for the first of the characters he built on the life of Ellen Withycombe.[5]

He signed the book at King's on 6 October 1932. The signature he had for life was already fully formed that day. At the last minute he had decided to abandon history in favour of modern languages. White always claimed that after Wood's tutorials at Lulworth he was unable to face 'another History essay and condemnation of my fanciful style'.[6] But he never lost his interest in history, researched keenly, and was determined that historical details in his work were always correct. This sudden decision to switch to modern languages dovetailed with his mother's diplomatic ambitions: diplomats needed French and German. Most of the important decisions he took at Cambridge for the next three years fitted Ruth's ambitions, which he left unchallenged until his last months at the university. He had been learning French since he was a child but had studied German for only four terms at Cheltenham. He was unfazed by the challenge he now set himself, for after those years in Australia he wanted to throw himself into hard, academic work.

Few students lived in at King's in their first year and White had rooms some distance from the college in a house run by a Mrs Cissy Mole, a good woman who tolerated the stench of burning asthma papers and dosed him with onion gruel when he had flu. White was always hungry. At twenty he was older than the men in his year and looked older still, for his face had aged when he lost his Cheltenham flab in Australia. Waters said: 'He was always old.'[7] He smoked and grew a moustache. His accent was unaffected by Cambridge. Asthma and Cheltenham had given him the rather toneless, foghorn voice that stayed with him for life. He bought two turtle-neck jumpers and wore the black day after day. To wear the red took more courage than he had, so he gave it to Betty Withycombe.

The term was short and all the lecturers dreary, except a Frenchman who renewed White's enthusiasm for the nineteenth-century French novel. That passion was with him then for life. White attended all lectures at first, dutifully taking notes that were 'a kind of automatic writing, but something to hold between you and doubt'.[8] He found the ritual of presenting an essay each week to his tutors as distressing in Cambridge as it had been in Sydney. For German tutorials he walked over to Emmanuel College where Henry Garland was encouraging. Donald Beves, his amiable and lazy French tutor at King's, was kind and did what he could to keep this touchy student calm.

Beves was, of all the famous monsters at King's in the 1930s, the only one White came to know well. When he first presented himself in Beves's rooms, he found a fat man in his late thirties who collected eighteenth-century glass. Beves was the rich son of a Brighton timber merchant, and he owed his position at King's to the murder of his predecessor by a crazed undergraduate. Beves was not a distinguished academic – indeed, a very languid teacher of French – but he was the best actor at Cambridge since the First World War.[9] He cultivated favoured undergraduates, but White was never picked to attend Beves's convivial dinners.

White did not enjoy his first term. He was trying to find his feet, dogged by loneliness and frustration. He took long walks in the afternoons through the flat country round Cambridge, a monotonous landscape to those

> who are deaf to the variations on it. A grey country . . . of many, many greys: boots clattering through grey streets; the mirror-grey of winter fens; naked elms tossing rooks into a mackerel sky.

Besides offering solace for his misery, this country proved surprisingly good for his lungs, 'perhaps too bracing for asthma to stand up to it'.

In such spare hours in these early months at Cambridge he probably wrote the play *Bread and Butter Women*, but it was some years before it saw the light of day.[10]

At Christmas he took a brief holiday on the Scilly Isles and wrote poetry. These islands off the coast of Cornwall are wild and almost sub-tropical in summer but battered in winter by cold Atlantic rollers. 'I stayed in a deserted hotel and the family that owned it took me into their lives. They had wonderful plain food.' He found himself

> happy here, happier than
> I thought was possible this side of Heaven . . .
>
> Now at last have I known beside the sea
> That bitterness can die, and joy instead
> Mount in the soft-spun bubbles of the spray.[11]

In the verse written in those few days on the Scillies, he confessed to hate, spite, bitterness and a gnawing sense of futility. He was grappling with the pessimistic conviction that homosexuality doomed him to a lonely life, for White was in love, but unable to declare himself.

He had, in his first term, drifted into the company of three young men. One was beautiful. R (as he has asked to be called) had come to King's to be an Anglican priest but was on the verge of abandoning his vocation and his faith. He was nineteen, slight and fair. In these lines written on the Scillies, White was reflecting on his unhappy and silent infatuation with this young man. For fear of provoking R's contempt, White flinched from declaring his feelings. The loss of friendship would be too much to bear,

> To know that day had been where night
> Unending drives her blinded share
> Into the furrows of my plight.
> Far better, then, to dull the light,
> And bear the pricking of the thorn.[12]

The best White expected for himself was a mix of joy and pain, loneliness relieved by undeclared affection. He resolved to survive by damping down his feelings.

He did not deny his homosexuality to himself. White knew what he was, knew that would not change and did not wish to be other than he was. It was a tentative mark of faith in himself, when he wrote on Christmas Day,

> The air, the earth, and the sea,
> Make mock of futile things like me.
> Yet surely there must reason be
> Even in futility . . .
> Crumbs related to the crust;
> Life to death; iron to rust.
> As naught can alter, then I must
> Be *Me*, until I change to dust.[13]

White was writing under the spell of A.E. Housman, trying to achieve something of the old man's clipped, lyrical style. He dreamed of meeting Housman and had wandered past the high iron fence of the poet's house in Cambridge, hoping he would show himself one day and invite this undergraduate in. He never did. White and R went together to the Senate House to hear Housman's famous public confession that beer and illness produced his finest verse. He told a surprised Cambridge audience that poetry's source is not the mind but the pit of the stomach, which he fed over lunch with a pint of beer ('beer is a sedative to the brain') and then went walking for two or three hours in the country thinking of nothing in particular until lines of verse, sometimes whole stanzas flowed into his mind. 'I have seldom written poetry unless I was rather out of health, and the experience, though pleasurable, was generally agitating and exhausting.'[14] Alcohol, fevers and long walks all became part of White's writing life, but Housman confirmed a more fundamental understanding in the young man: that writing is not willed, but boils up from within. Lines are given. For all the hard work that must be done to knock work into shape, essentially the writer is an inspired messenger.

Housman had another important lesson for White: the need for absolute discretion. The homosexual impulse of Housman's poetry was hidden in its resonant vagueness. The fears that stayed Housman's hand when he was writing *The Shropshire Lad* made it essential for White to cover his own tracks, for he was once again sending his verse – the laments and love poems of a young homosexual – home to his admiring mother Ruth.

Back at King's in the New Year of 1933 and in R's company once again, White was gripped by the conflict of pain and joy in the presence of the man to whom he could not declare his love. He wrote,

> Lovely, lovely you may be
> In your youth and clarity . . .
> Ah, but where's the charity
> In marble or in bronze?

> The fields reach vainly for the sky,
> To press their stubble on her cheek,
> And I as vainly, week by week,
> Pray that the rising day may seek
> The mirror of my eye.[15]

White said nothing and wrote verse, but R's faith was crumbling. In London, in the spring vacation, it collapsed when this 'untravelled provincial youth' visiting a school friend at University College tasted, for the first time, the pleasures of Soho restaurants, met fashionable Anglo-Catholic priests, and sat in the stalls at Colonel de Basil's Ballet Russe de Monte Carlo. But, recalled R, 'what is more to the point of this quite irrelevant story is that Waldo seduced me'.[16] R returned to Cambridge determined to experience all this new world had to offer. For the moment that meant sex.

One night in early summer, after the gates were locked, White and R were wandering through King's when they came across a couple of young women from the town. The four went to R's room for an awkward session of embraces, and then the two men helped them climb out over the wall. R remarked that this encounter had meant nothing to him. The ice cracked. White showed R his poem 'Lovely, Lovely You May Be'. Their affair began. After the frustrating, often desperate years at Cheltenham and in Australia, White at the age of twenty-one made 'human contact' at last.

> The sun smote my face with the sword of its glory
> And there was joyful pain in the wound,
> For I was no longer alone.[17]

But after only a few weeks he left to spend the summer in Germany to immerse himself in the language in preparation for the first oral exam he faced in the autumn. Mariamne Wynne of Mount Wilson had a brother in the Foreign Office who gave White access to the list of German families approved for coaching young British diplomats. White chose a family in Heidelberg and arrived in that ancient academic city in the first weeks after Hitler came to power.

The only Germany White ever knew was Nazi. They were burning books in Heidelberg, and one afternoon in a beer garden he drunkenly mocked a group of louts singing 'Horst Wessel'. White was rescued from a beating by a kind German who explained that this was only an Englishman who didn't understand. And he did not: the Reichstag had burnt, the Communist Party was disenfranchised, every institution in the country was being purged, but White barely noticed. He wrote

some poems about melancholy, frustration and the desolation of his
heart.[18]

Heidelberg was not a success for too much English was spoken
among the students. So White consulted the Foreign Office lists again
and passed over Eisenach, the birthplace of Bach, in favour of Hanover,
where the burgers claimed to speak the purest German. He used a pin to
pick the Oertel family from the list and arrived at their apartment on
the Holzgraben in August 1933. The Oertels were new to the business
of looking after students and this slim young man with *Märchenaugen*,
fairytale eyes, was only the second to live in their apartment. They found
him 'very introverted, from time to time almost sad, very humble but
also sometimes he loved a hearty laugh'.[19]

White found Rudi Oertel serious and good, an engineer who in
these hard years was supporting a large family. His wife was virtuous
and their boy was ugly but promising. The child was reaching that age
when he must join the Hitler Youth. Also living in the apartment were
Frau Oertel's three siblings: Walter and Wolfgang Lange and their sister
Lotte, who had a taste for make-up and *schnapps*, which did not fit in
with the new image of the scrubbed and dutiful *Bund Deutscher Mädchen*.
In the midst of this sprawling family White was once again a welcome
changeling. He loved Lotte's laughter, the clatter of cherry-wood chairs,
the deep feather beds, velvet upholstery, dark parquet and Frau Oertel's
Kartoffelpuffer and *Wurst*. The harmony of the apartment was ruffled
only by the visits of Herr Oertel's brother, who had been a prisoner
of war, and now

> liked to use the word *Volk*. It bristled from his small, intense
> mouth like the greyish stubble from his shaven head. He moved
> in a perpetual cloud of exasperation, at everything or nothing.[20]

White spent hours writing in his room, but what he wrote remained
a mystery to the Oertels for years until he gave them his book of poetry.
His bedroom looked into the Kleine Pfahlstrasse, where a few Jewish
families lived in a house known to the locals as the *Judenburg*. White
was only vaguely aware that Jews were having a tough time in the new
Germany. The sitting room of the apartment opened on to a balcony
over the Holtzgraben, where General Hindenburg had lived before
becoming President of Germany. A block away was the Eilenride,
and in this forest of oak and deer White took long solitary walks and
exercised horses lent to him by the bachelor army officer who lived in
the flat below the Oertels. This eccentric floated celluloid ducks in his
bath and had a habit of rebuffing callers by denying point blank that he
was there. As Oberstleutnant Stauffer in *Riders in the Chariot*, wearing
an apron trimmed with lace, he slammed the door of his flat on the

Jew Himmelfarb while remarking calmly, 'The *Herr Oberst* is not at home.'[21]

White felt himself taking root in Hanover, which became in time the Heimat of both Himmelfarb and the explorer Voss, and the town where Elyot Standish came to polish his Cambridge German.

> There was a balance and proportion in the blue and golden renascence town that went well with his frame of mind. He walked firmly down the streets. He was very receptive. He wanted to absorb, there was no chimney, no façade too distant to possess, to assimilate. He stood at the street corners and smelt with pleasure a gust of baking bread, or heard the dray rattle over cobblestones. All this had come to his senses for the first time.[22]

On the other side of the city, through the dark medieval streets at the old town's centre and past the Biedermeier mansions was the great alley of limes that lead to the baroque gardens of the kings who ruled Hanover and England until the accession of Victoria split the two kingdoms in 1837. For an Australian boy this almost English city was a potent, half-familiar mystery. He spent his weeks exploring the town and moving 'drunkenly' through the country that lay beyond: a landscape of forests and neat fields with Saxon farmhouses built of brick and black timber. Back on the Holzgraben, cosseted by Frau Oertel, he wrote secret verse about

> sadness that turns
> Its knickering knife
> In the heart of me

and struggled with the 'comic, hedgehog words constantly colliding' of the German language.[23] At the end of the summer he returned to Cambridge to take – and fail – his exam.

Fascist Germany made too little impact on White for him to be aware of the effects it was having back in Cambridge that autumn. The university was swept by a wave of political excitement as the repercussions of Hitler's rule became clear to more astute undergraduates. Donald Beves was accused, after his death, of recruiting Kim Philby, Guy Burgess and Donald Maclean to work for Russia. For this slander no evidence has ever been produced. All that 'security sources' argued when forced to explain themselves was that Beves's hospitality and idiosyncrasies made him 'admirably placed' to help the three men 'in disguising their treachery and planning their future careers'.[24] Beves's dinners were held against him.

White almost fitted the pattern of those young men: he was

rich, homosexual and was supposed to become a diplomat. But he was also politically illiterate, an Australian, and out of touch with those Cambridge circles in which this intellectual elite moved. All the time he was at Cambridge he was unaware of the Apostles, that secret society that nurtured the traitors. He once met Anthony Blunt at a dinner where the wine was good and the conversation was about painting. 'I kept quiet.' White spent the early 1930s almost untouched by European politics, unworried by Fascism, hardly aware of the fate of the Jews. Later he made amends.

On his return from Germany White was given a room in King's. Though the college is one of the most admired sights in Europe, and the great chapel perhaps the masterpiece of English Gothic, the great mass of King's is an ordinary Victorian pile in the back corner of which, above a narrow lane that ran down to the river, White was allocated a 'dark and rather nasty' room in the autumn of 1933. White spent only one term here in the Drain waiting to move into rooms with R in the New Year.

Alone at the end of the winter term White returned to Cornwall on a pilgrimage to the cliffs of Zennor where D.H. Lawrence in the summer of 1916 had set up a little literary community in a couple of stone cottages at Higher Tregerthen. The communards were Lawrence and Middleton Murry, who took long walks together in the mist discussing the Male principle, Frieda Weekley mourning for her children, and Katherine Mansfield. Lawrence was writing *Women in Love* at Higher Tregerthen, and the brilliant spirit Gudrun was his portrait of Katherine Mansfield in those months. Her portrait of him, in the letters and journals White so admired when they were published in 1927 and 1928, was a good deal less flattering. 'He's quite "lost". He has become very fond of sewing, especially hemming, and of making little copies of pictures. When he is doing these things he is quiet and kind, but once you start talking I cannot describe the frenzy that comes over him. He simply *raves*, roars, beats the table, abuses everybody . . . It is impossible to be anything to him but a kind of playful acquaintance.'[25]

The pilgrim was snowed in at the Tinners Arms in Zennor for a week and spent 'a rather miserable time with nothing more entertaining than Grillparzer to read while the innkeeper and his wife threw dishes at each other'. In Zennor White wrote remarkably gloomy verse about bitter tears and barren gorse. Once the snow cleared he made for Polperro by bus and found rooms in an empty hotel in the village. The food was good. With the hotel as his base, he took buses round that part of Cornwall, travelling with a stray dog that attached itself to him along the way. The dog's death under the wheels of a car inspired the overwrought 'Lines Written after an Encounter with

Death in a Country Lane'. One afternoon in Fowey, as he waited for a bus back to Polperro, he wrote thirty vivid lines about a ploughman working in a field by the sea,

> I saw a ploughman against the sky,
> The wind of the sea in his horses' manes,
> And the share it was shod with gold;
> Down to the sea, on the curve of the hill,
> A foam of gulls in the furrow . . . [26]

After returning to Cambridge for the new term, White typed a sheaf of poems and sent them to the *London Mercury*. Two were accepted by the magazine's eccentric editor Jack Squire who had spent the years since the war searching for writing that was, 'traditional yet experimental, personal yet sane'. The acceptance of his poems was a considerable honour for White, even though the magazine was rather a shambles by this time, and Squire was surviving on 'whisky and nothing but whisky for breakfast'. Squire's list of contributors had dwindled with the circulation, but they included three of the writers White most admired: Lawrence, Mansfield and George Moore. 'The Ploughman' and 'Meeting Again' appeared in June 1934, and the first was later selected for *The Best Poems of 1935*, an annual collection of verse from both sides of the Atlantic published by Jonathan Cape, where White found himself in the company of Robert Frost, Siegfried Sassoon, Edwin Muir and Roy Campbell. The appearance of the poems marked Patrick White's professional début, but they brought him no celebrity in Cambridge. 'I kept very quiet about them.'[27] Even R was unaware of the achievement.

The two men moved into a set of rooms on the first floor of Gibbs' Palladian masterpiece which stands at right angles to the college chapel. They had a sitting room looking into the quadrangle, and two bedrooms from which they could see over acres of lawn to the river and the Backs. White declared it was important to live up to the magnificence of the setting. They washed down the filthy panelled walls. White produced Persian rugs, a wing chair to stand by the fire, a Sheraton table for the long wall and a flamboyant old sofa, the kind of sofa on which, the two young men agreed, Madame Récamier might have reclined. Over the table, White hung a misty Chinese scroll. The typescript of one of the jackeroo novels lay on the window seat nearest the door. R never opened it.

They lived quietly. 'We were self-contained, perhaps too self-contained. Patrick was not outgoing. He did not find it easy to make contacts with people. He was recessive, dour. Shy is not the right word. It does not convey either his strength or the depth of feeling behind that austere frontage.' R admired both the refusal to mask this awkwardness with false *bonhomie*, and White's contempt for the idea of hobnobbing with the great of King's for the sake of it. Maynard Keynes was bursar; George (Dadie) Rylands was a tutor; E.M. Forster visited but was not yet living at King's. One afternoon the two invited Beves to tea and made elaborate preparations – brioche, Gentleman's Relish and a supply of Turkish cigarettes – but Beves did not appear.

After morning lectures they had a simple lunch every day of bread and cheese. One did not work in the afternoons. The hearties rowed and played Rugby. White was at pains to take no part in this, though some of the hearties fascinated him and were friends. Such men would have been impressed to know the hardships this pale aesthete had recently endured in Australia, yet White had drawn a curtain over his jackerooing past. He said nothing about it. Even R knew hardly anything of those years. Modesty was part of this but White, in fastidious recoil, was also disowning his past.

Every fine afternoon the two young men walked six or seven miles across the fields and returned to tea. In the hours before dinner, tutors had to be faced and essays presented. Dinner in hall was compulsory on five or six nights a week, but they ate cheaply in the town when they could, buying fish and chips wrapped in old pages of the *News of the World*. They drank at 'the Leo'. At the Cosmopolitan they saw all the French and German films as they arrived in England: everything of Jean Renoir, René Clair and Von Sternberg. Never forgotten was Marlene Dietrich in *The Blue Angel*, nor the silent horrors of *The Cabinet of Dr Caligari*. Each week in the repertory season they went to the Festival Theatre, and to concerts somewhere in the town. Cambridge had a passion for Handel, and White saw Beves dancing all but naked in a performance of *Jephtha*.

An exotic parade passed below their windows. King's men strolled through the court at strange hours in fancy dress; an heir to the Cunard line went about the quadrangle in lipstick and furs. White and R remained spectators of this extraordinary existence, for the aesthetes of King's were terrifying snobs, nocturnal creatures who played at night and slept all day in rooms draped with strange fabrics. 'The rooms were under-lit,' R recalled. 'It was very exciting and bohemian in those days to have underlit rooms.' Richard Gorer ran Salome, a drama and ballet society which went broke on lilies and magazines printed on silver paper. White recalled an undergraduate retreating, shattered, from a Salome party after asking Gorer if he knew Stravinsky's *Firebird*. Gorer replied, 'I know Stravinsky.'[28]

White showed no disappointment at not being absorbed into this world, yet he felt an undertow of regret that his early intellectual hopes were not being fulfilled at Cambridge. Lectures were tedious and he abandoned them; his tutors took no more than a routine interest in his work; he failed to find any intellectual or aesthetic mentors at the university. 'It must have been a sad and bitter disappointment,' R reflected. 'It would have been miserable and frustrating for him to have felt in *any* circumstances, that the high expectations of life in Cambridge, and not least of the finding of kindred spirits, were unfulfilled.'[29]

White's Cambridge world was defined by R's friends: a Yorkshire miner's son with a scholarship and a strong North Country accent, and a self-possessed young man studying science as a path to the Anglican priesthood. They made a nondescript band. Also scattered through the university were R's friends from his old school, and he took White to their parties. 'They involved lots of drinking, stripping and dancing, and climbing out of windows on ropes and into windows on ropes.' The two young men had a friend at Corpus Christi who owned a good gramophone, and they sat in his room listening to music and drinking until well past the hour when colleges locked their gates. So after hearing their favourite records over again – Mozart's piano concerto number 27, or *Bolero*, or one of the late Beethoven quartets – they drunkenly lowered one another into the street on knotted sheets.

Was it last night or tonight I tore off my clothes smelling of armpit and Ravel and was let down into the street by a rope?[30]

White introduced R to the three Withycombe sisters. Betty was dimly aware that R was his lover. She found him 'very pretty with good manners, a public school type, slightly insipid'.[31] R was impressed by the Withycombes but dumbfounded to meet Ronald Waters, who came up to Cambridge by bus every Sunday in February and March 1934 during his London run in O'Casey's *Within the Gates*. 'I could not imagine what my dour friend saw in this twittery, shallow, chattering creature.'

R had little money. On expeditions to London White met their expenses. Once he took his lover to dinner in Bayswater. 'Dinner was served by footmen. It was very grand. We were going on to the Ballet Russe at Covent Garden. In those days it was unthinkable to sit in a box at Covent Garden except in a white tie. But I had not brought my tails down to London. In support Patrick wore an ordinary suit as well. He was very interested in and conscious of dress, but he didn't need to be perfectly dressed to be comfortable. He had no fetish about correct dress. As we walked into Covent Garden together I whispered, "Now the ordeal begins." Patrick was very cross at me carrying on in this self-conscious way. As we sat in the box, there in the stalls were all the famous figures from King's: Rylands, Keynes, Lydia Lopokova, Forster.'

The poetry White wrote in these months records exalted happiness, but yet the lines are troubled: fear is felt for two, pain is burnt deep into the soul, when alone he feels himself doubly poor. He was jealous. When a friend of R's came to stay one night in Gibbs, White retreated to his bedroom, and as he sat listening to their voices in the other room

> brush together in their flight
> Out of the darkness

he wrote self-pityingly of

> The pain of day's long lingering,
> Still must I wait, and wonder why
> I sit forgot in Time.[32]

It became clear to both of them that their affair was based on a false premise. R was not homosexual. He was excited and flattered by White's love, and after adolescent years spent rather shackled in preparation for life in the Anglican priesthood, he had thrown himself into this adventure with enthusiasm. But R was aware that his response, however vigorous, fell short of White's desire. The physical side of love, he realised, was secondary for White. 'And for it not to have been enveloped into a warmth of tenderness and strong affection (though I certainly had affection) may have been repugnant.'[33] This first adult sexual relationship was evidence of what White took to be a truth: that human beings can never fully understand or find complete satisfaction with one another. Life with R was not the source of this fundamental notion, but shaped it at a crucial time. Their alliance seemed so nearly right but was, in reality, misconceived.

Again White said nothing, but wrote verse. In the course of 1934 the poems move from sheer exultation, through hints of doubt, to fears suppressed and then acknowledged, and reach the edge of disenchantment. When he read them, R judged the self-pity to be authentic.

> From trees are blown
> The fancies that were born of Spring;
> And in this panting solitude I stand,
> Untouched by momentary grief or joy,
> And wait the plunging of the sword,
> And wonder why I am.[34]

Cambridge gave White no gloss and offered no foothold in

literary England, but it taught him to read. When he abandoned lectures – 'a course in desiccation' – he dropped out into the library. Garland and Beves gave him 'a nudge' and he worked his way through those French and German texts he was supposed to read, and beyond them found the books he needed. 'It was a great eye opener.' He read in English, French and German, and felt he was at last making up 'for time lost, intellectually'.[35]

He pressed copies of *Howards End* and *Orlando* on R, but his urgent advice to R was to read Joyce, Lawrence and Proust. He could not then admit that the Albertine passages in *A la recherche* 'always bored me in my youth'. He broke into Heine because the German was easy. Later he came to the playwright Büchner, the poets Mörike, Hölderlin and Stefan George and to Thomas Mann. He also pressed translations of Mann on R. White shared a taste for Theodor Fontane's *Effi Briest*, a 'touching though slightly insipid story' with Reha Himmelfarb, wife of Himmelfarb who held the chair of English at the University of Holunderthal. But White came to hate two of the pillars of German literature: Kleist and especially Goethe, whom he came to think an appalling human being and a 'manufactory of German platitudes'.[36]

He read more widely in French than German and most admired the novels of Flaubert and Stendhal. He rediscovered *Madame Bovary*, which he had first struggled with on the pebbles at Dieppe, and found *L'Education Sentimentale* 'which has never been as popular because it's so very bitter and satirical', the wonderful *La Chartreuse de Parme* 'one of my six great novels', and *Le Rouge et Le Noir*. Alain-Fournier's fantasy of adolescence *Le Grand Meaulnes* was another favourite. White was then, but only briefly, a fan of Gide.[37]

To polish his French, White stayed for some weeks at Compiègne north of Paris in the home of an elderly Baronne, a relic of the Mexican Empire of Maximilian. The Baronne's father had been Chancellor to Maximilian's household, and her mother a lady-in-waiting to the Empress Charlotte, and the house was filled with mementoes of doomed Empire. Eton boys were the backbone of the Baronne's business. She doted on 'mes Eton boys', who repaid her by escaping to Paris to hang about the Folies Bergères and bring back erotic dolls made of rubber to frighten the servants. Compiègne was dreadful country for asthma and the Baronne's cook Mathilde tried the ancient remedy of cupping on the young man. To her disappointment, White did not purple as her husband did when she applied the hot cups to his chest. White was lonely in Compiègne but, wandering about, he came to know the place well. He watched the Rothschilds in eighteenth-century dress riding after stags in the forest. In the town he found one person to show him kindness: the cast-off wife of a Greek millionaire, who lived in a flat piled with oriental rugs. Madame Xenophon lived *under* the rugs in winter. He remembered her name and this habit nearly fifty years later when he was 'editing' the *Memoirs of Many in One* of Alex Xenophon Demirjian Gray. Despite his stint in the forests of Compiègne, White continued to speak French with a distinct English accent.

By the end of this second year at Cambridge, he knew he did not have a scholar's mind. His academic performance was solid, and his German tutor Henry Garland encouraged him to believe he might have taken a very good degree if he had begun studying German earlier, but he was not going to be one of the bright minds in modern languages. This discovery hurt him at first, and he was nagged by a sense of intellectual inadequacy until he came to see that he had another kind of intelligence, a 'magpie mind' that found ideas as he needed them and seized any image that caught his eye. Systems were never very attractive to him. Over the years he picked up bits of Freud, bits of Spengler, bits of the Bible, but was never a disciple and was always sceptical of those who had a scheme that gave all the answers.

When Betty Withycombe came up to Cambridge for weekends, the two cousins talked 'at enormous length, about books and plays and travel and a good deal of gossip about people – all that seemed to interest him. It did use to bother me that Patrick seemed to take no interest in his studies though he did not neglect them . . . he was not passionately interested in accurate information though he was much addicted to every sort of gossip about people – that I suppose is the difference between the scholar and the novelist.'[38]

The exams that year were a disaster for R, for his life with White had been all-absorbing. The college authorities decided to make him work by sending him out into digs, but R appealed to Beves who knew the situation. As a compromise, the two young men were moved to separate rooms close to one another in an undistinguished building by the river. Their friendship was seemingly unchanged. The affair continued; always, at White's insistence, in the dark.

Mrs Victor White was at work in Sydney promoting her son's poetry. She and Dick were the principal backers of P.R. (Inky) Stephensen, an abrasive charmer and chaotic businessman who was setting up a new publishing house to promote Australian literature. Stephensen had raised high hopes and moderate capital for his pioneering venture. The Whites put in £100 at first, and Ruth helped recruit backers and staff. Then as P.R. Stephensen & Company headed for the rocks in July 1934 the Whites threw in another £200. By the end they contributed nearly half his capital.

A few days after the Whites' second injection of cash, Stephensen accepted a printer's quote for *The Ploughman*, a book of poems by Patrick White, and urged the printers to have proofs ready by the following week. 'You will proceed with printing as soon as possible after we return the marked proofs,' Stephensen wrote, 'as we should like the job treated urgently.'[39] Ruth and Inky Stephensen were both taking care to behave as if this were not vanity publishing. Stephensen was the editor of the book. But Ruth paid, and it proved expensive in the end.

White also sent the publisher the manuscript of 'Finding Heaven' and Stephensen suggested general revision. 'I have not looked at it for some time,' White replied, 'and so could not say definitely whether I think it possible to revise the book. Perhaps you could give me some idea of what you consider its greatest weaknesses. But I am really uncertain whether I could bring myself to revise it after all this time. I wrote it in a frame of mind with which I cannot altogether sympathise today.'[40] Nothing more was heard of 'Finding Heaven' being published.

It was October before proofs of *The Ploughman* reached England. The original idea had been to combine in a single volume some of the old *Thirteen Poems* with the new work from Cambridge, but when White saw the proofs he decided to drop the surviving Cheltenham poems and substitute five fresh poems written on the literary pilgrimage he had made in the summer holidays to Thomas Hardy country.

Alone or with Betty Withycombe he returned to Wessex several times over the next few years, walking from village to village, staying the night in bed and breakfasts, exploring the territory of *Tess of the d'Urbervilles* and *Jude the Obscure*. He often suggested to Betty Withycombe that she should also spend some time on the Continent as he did, but England suited her and there was the matter of money: Patrick's allowance was bigger than her wage. At Corfe Castle on two of these Wessex expeditions he had terrible attacks of asthma, some of the worst of his life, and retreated to his cousin Helen Waddell's flint-walled, exquisitely clean house at Winchester. 'By this time a machine had been invented, a kind of pump driven by a motor that pumped a fine mist of drugs into the lungs. I hired one from the chemist in Winchester. They superseded disgusting asthma cigarettes and burning asthma papers.'[41]

Out on the Wiltshire Downs he was struck by doubts of an oddly revealing kind. Lizzie Clark had taught him as a child not to blow his own trumpet, but that did not mean White was indifferent to the possibility of fame. South of Chittern is a mark on the Downs known as Oram's Grave. White reflected that nothing was known of the man but his fame would last as long as the magic of his name, by which time

> my bones will be but the bones of the field,
> Even as Oram's bones, and my name
> A chilly whisper, a little sigh.[42]

White returned Stephensen's proofs to Sydney promptly, indicating the order he wanted the poems to appear. He asked Stephensen, 'would it be possible to place a few copies somewhere in London after publication? I might be able to get a sale for these. And a few cards for circulation might be a help.' But Stephensen was in deep trouble by this time. His cash was running out. After publishing over a dozen elegant titles, Stephensen was only surviving by refusing to pay his printers' bills. *The Ploughman* was not his first priority for he was desperately trying to produce Xavier Herbert's *Capricornia*. He knew this would establish him if only he could get it out, for this was the 'Great Australian Novel for which the world is waiting'.[43] Summonses began to roll in a little before Christmas. Stephensen tried without success to reconstruct the company. This time the Whites did not contribute. In February 1935 P.R. Stephensen & Company went into liquidation. Ruth and Dick lost £300.

Within a month Ruth had *The Ploughman* published by the Beacon Press, an imprint used by Boylan & Company, printers of Cunningham Street, to turn out volumes of Japanese woodcuts, verse and *belles lettres*. Only 300 numbered copies of *The Ploughman* were printed. The volume, 'Dedicated to My Mother', was handsome: a buff binding, creamy thick paper and twenty-three wood engravings by L. Roy Davies, who had made his name in Sydney with studies of swaggies and bush sheds. Men and women hold hands in sunlit gardens, an Australian ploughman pauses on the Cornish coast, a white swan in some confusion flies over 'A Gull Blown Inland by the Storm' and the gull decorates the swan's 'O Cold, Cold Rain'. Read together, the poems seem obsessed with rain, damp, snow, grey skies, loneliness, pain, disappointment. The awkward enthusiasms of the Cheltenham verse had been ironed out. The poet was cleverer, more careful, less brilliant.

When *The Ploughman* appeared in February 1935 at five shillings a copy, it made little impression in Australia and left no mark elsewhere. Ruth distributed copies to the family. Few sold. The *Bulletin* thought these 'chips and shavings of poesy' would be more vigorous and picturesque if the author had written in the manner of Byron and Longfellow. The characteristically Australian advice that writers should write like somebody else pursued White for half his life. Ruth's and Dick's paper the *Sydney Morning Herald* acknowledged 'dignity and a quiet music' amongst the juvenilia.[44] Good will was evident.

Stephensen had not deserted the Whites and wrote to Lulworth in early March asking to borrow the block of the frontispiece to use with a big review of the poems planned for his new literary magazine to be launched 'soon'. Ruth was 'only too pleased'.[45] Stephensen's creditors had him under siege and the *Literary Times* folded before it hit the streets. But in May his partner brought out a magazine called the *Opinion*, and it led with a long review of *The Ploughman* under the headline: PATRICK WHITE. BRILLIANT YOUNG AUSTRALIAN PRODUCES FIRST VOLUME OF POEMS. The writer was overcome with admiration: 'Patrick White, who is of the younger generation of Australians, now publishes in an excellently produced volume, a first book of poems, all of which are written and dated in Europe. Mr White is at present a student of Cambridge University, preparatory to his intended entry into the Diplomatic Corps.

'The poems suggest a sensitiveness, an appreciation of beauty, reminiscent of the late Rupert Brooke, and throughout many is a strange sadness, a weariness, which evidently reflects the atmosphere of so many of our youthful literati, who are hopeless of affecting the much needed change in modern life, from futility to happiness.' He concluded with the confident prediction that we can 'expect further and greater literary achievements from this brilliant young Australian'.[46] The *Opinion* never appeared again.

Sydney had another opportunity in these weeks to judge Patrick White, for Ruth had persuaded Bryants' Playhouse to open its 1935 season with her son's play, *Bread and Butter Women*. She would foot all the bills. Bryants' Playhouse had been going for three years. It was a finishing school for shy young women, and a club where young lawyers and architects could wait for work in the Depression. For a few radio actors it offered serious professional training. Beryl Bryant's forte was the voice. The film director Charles Chauvel sent his actors to Bryants' to purge them of their English accents.

Beryl Bryant, commanding but disorganised, dark and impetuous, had retired from the silent screen when she married Albert (Tweed) Mayor of Vanity Hosiery, makers of the first fully fashioned seamless silk stockings in Australia. Then the Mayors were ruined in the Depression. Tweed was crushed by the catastrophe; Beryl taught elocution in private schools; when she set up the theatre, she brought her father George out of retirement. He had been one of the leading stage villains of his day. Now he played ancients and elder statesmen as required. Ruth was touched by their plight. The Mayors lived on the box office and Beryl's lessons. Actors took nothing. Royalties were 'by arrangement'. Mrs Victor White installed herself as treasurer and publicity secretary of Bryants'. She manned the tiny box office in her silver fox and pearls; decreed that *everything* was possible on stage with hessian; and fed publicity to the social pages of Sydney newspapers. When the Mayors' furniture was about to be seized Ruth gave them £100 and, later, some of those inappropriate and splendid gifts for which she was known: a gold and amethyst pencil, a greenstone tiki, an antique chair.

Their theatre was in a basement under St Peter's church hall in Darlinghurst, entered through an iron gate in St Peter's Lane. The walls were white-washed and the curtain was raw burlap decorated

with abstract patches of red wool. The steeply banked tiers of old
school seats held only eighty-two customers. The hall upstairs was an
outpost of Ruth's charity in the Depression. There she held meetings
of her Fuchsia Club once a month, inviting the poor of Woolloomooloo
to come up the road for cake, tea and light entertainment. The club had
some vague political purpose on the conservative side. Ruth recruited
her poor relations to hand around the cake.

As *The Ploughman* was coming off the press Ruth was already
cranking up publicity for *Bread and Butter Women*. The *Sun* noted
that Bryants' would re-open in the New Year with a play by a young
undergraduate Patrick White. 'It deals with the life of a family in which
the men are artistic and idle, and the women are the breadwinners.
Suzanne White, sister of the author, will play a part.' Suzanne was cast
as May the maid. The action takes place over a couple of days in the
English house of a Mr and Mrs Winwood. Present are the Winwoods,
their pompous, poetic and feather-brained stepson Timothy, a poor
artist Andrew Smith, and the women who provide the 'bludging males
with their bread and butter'. In the end, the fortunes of the Winwood
family are rescued by marriage.[47]

The play was received with great enthusiasm on the opening
night, 23 January 1935, by an audience stacked with Ruth's friends and
relatives. Frank Crago the director was an unemployed architect and heir
to a flour-milling fortune. He usually designed the Bryants' sets, and this
was his début as a director. Most of the cast were amateurs, except for
Harry Harper, who played the poet and went on to a career in radio as
an actor and producer. The Sydney critics, after making allowances for
Ruth's cheer squad and the 'obvious immaturities' of the text, found a
great deal to praise.[48]

The *Sydney Mail* forecast a bright future for the young playwright:
'The comedy proved to be very well written, the author exhibiting a
mordant and lively humour which should carry him far upon the road
to dramatic recognition. Mr White is at present in England, so that
he was unable to be present at the undeniable success accompanying
the presentation of what I understand is his first play. If he can write
others as good as *Bread and Butter Women*, which is not only well
constructed but novel in theme and effective in situation, he should –
if merit counts at all – soon obtain recognition in England.' *Bread and
Butter Women* played every Wednesday night for seven weeks and Mrs
Victor White, noted *Smith's Weekly*, 'was as proud of it as if it had been
one of Galsworthy's best'.[49]

Ruth stood alone centre-stage for these minor triumphs in Sydney
in early 1935. Dick had been ill and was recuperating in the Lister
Private Hospital. The Victor Whites were due to leave Sydney shortly
to be present at Patrick's graduation in June, but now it was decided

that Suzanne would go ahead and they would follow when they could. Chaperoning a young Sydney woman across the world was not an easy business. Luckily one of Suzanne's friends, Sue Stogdale, was about to leave on the *Otranto*. Suzanne pulled out of *Bread and Butter Women* and sailed in February. She was 'simply thrilled to be going' reported *Smith's Weekly*. 'Her brother is at Cambridge and has promised to show both lasses the sights, unless he is too busy writing plays.' In London Suzanne would spend most of her time at the theatre, said *Smith's*, 'as she is mad on acting and hardly has a thought for anything else. It will be amusing to see which particular actress she will copy as regards appearance, and it will have to be a plump one, as Susie is no fairy.'[50]

At nineteen, Suzanne was a big girl full of breezy energy. She had that prized quality 'go', and faced the world with candid good humour. Friends said of her, 'She's a real White.' This observation was even truer in the last year, for after a car accident she developed asthma. Her convalescence was charted in the society columns of Sydney papers, as were her stage appearances and travel plans. She had done little to justify her brother's hopes for her stage career. He still dreamt of Sue dazzling audiences in the roles he would write for her but, though she adored the theatre, she loved cricket and the races more. About the best the critics said of her performance in *Bread and Butter Women* was 'Suzanne White made something of a maid's part.'[51]

On board the *Otranto*, the two Sues played deck quoits with the Prime Minister and Cabinet, travelling over for the King's Jubilee. At Cairo the girls rode camels. From Naples they motored with the Stogdales through Italy and France in an open car. Each morning the chauffeur Pasquale bought *vins de pays* for a picnic lunch, and afternoons were spent battling sleep, with Mrs Stogdale shouting at the girls, 'Wake up. I didn't bring you all this way to snooze.' The party reached London in April and the girls went up to Cambridge, where Sue Stogdale found her friend's brother odd, reclusive and far too anti-Australian for someone whose money came from the bush. He took them to the chapel and the Backs and they had tea in his cold room by the river. They did not meet R, nor did he know of their coming.

These were White's last months in Cambridge, and the final scenes of what he looked back to as his 'late-teenage *Sturm und Drang*'.[52] He realised that one way or another, being an artist was all he had ever wanted to be.[53] Now he wished to live in London and be a writer. After drifting for years in the wake of his mother's ambition, he had now to make his own course clear. Ruth was a woman of powerful will with a way of binding people to her, but her son was too like her to be happy with this. That he had to free himself as far as possible from this woman to whom he was closely bound – he had written to her every week at Cambridge – was the native instinct that saved him as a man and artist.

Cutting free from Ruth took stubborn courage. It was one of the great internal dramas of his life, and one he explored again and again in his writing. Most of his heroes are escapees, men and women who turn their backs on the lives laid down for them to follow their own paths towards fulfilment. Breaches are painful but a necessary part of this. Nor do artists break free once and for all: breaking free is what artists must do again and again, despite the pain, despite the cost, always breaking free and moving to fresh ground.

Ruth was keen to see her son succeed as a writer, had paid for the publication of two books of verse and the presentation of his first play but still, at this time, she was telling the Sydney press that Patrick White was to become a diplomat. Diplomacy, it seems, would be the frame in which he pursued his civilised talents. For all her energy, Ruth was not one who believed in diving in at the deep end. She lacked her son's social courage. Dick still hoped, in some muddled way, that his boy would come back to Australia and take an interest in the Whites' corner of the world up in the Hunter Valley. It was very painful for them all.

White drew strength from a new enthusiasm: the work of the Irishman George Moore. No book influenced White over the next two decades as much as Moore's double-decker novel *Evelyn Innes* and *Sister Teresa*, the story of a woman who turns her back on her family and conventional morality to become a diva and then, at the height of her fame, retires to end her days in humble service as a nun. The demands of art are absolute in her life. She is independent, passionate, talented and self-possessed. Success is earned painfully through the suffering she inflicts on herself, her family, lovers and those intimates she sheds along the way. After a hundred pages of inner struggle (we are now in volume two) she enters a convent on the edge of Wimbledon Common. In retreat from the world she does not forsake her art – performances of Gounod's 'Ave Maria' save the house from ruin after the nuns plunge on Australian mining shares – but devotes her life to destroying the 'terrible sensual beast within her'.[54]

The quest of Evelyn Innes, diva and nun, echoed and supplied some of the big themes in White's life as an artist. She sets a pattern for White's explorers, spinsters, dames, Jews, painters, Aborigines, farmers, washerwomen and tramps who shake off their past to pursue a calling and reach, in the end, some vision of the holiness, the wonder of life. Evelyn Innes's conflict between the stage and the convent echoed the old strain between Ruth's dedication to the world and Lizzie Clark's idea of service, between luxury and simplicity, the life of things and the life of the spirit. Innes suffers also from a resigned distaste for sex, and finds sex without faithfulness repugnant. She sleeps in a bare cell and scrubs the convent's floors. Through domestic mortification and the torments of chastity she finds holiness, the highest art and the knowledge that 'the sacrament is an eternal act in nature'.[55]

Moore's unfashionable style also made a potent impression on the young man, one that Betty Withycombe deeply regretted. Moore's prose is polished to a high sheen, wistful and prone to lyric outbursts. Moore had a taste for lengthy inner turmoil, and his heroine made no move in her career without pages of highly polished, racked introspection.

Moore had broken free from a landowning, racehorse-breeding family to become a writer and his parents had given him a handsome allowance to do so. Patrick White hoped for the same. Mustering all his courage, he wrote to Ruth and Dick in Sydney telling them his plans. He did not want to come home; he did not want to take up any profession; he wanted to stay in London and write. 'It was not a particularly brave act: I think I believed they wouldn't abandon the son who was letting them down.'[56] In case it came to the worst, he made a couple of trips to London to try to find a job. Theatre companies didn't want him; Bumpus Bookshop was not impressed. So his father was crucial to his plan to be a London writer, but for the moment Dick was still too ill to travel.

White took his exams in May and the results were respectable: second class honours, first division. Ruth begged him to stay up at Cambridge long enough to squire Suzanne to May Week balls, but White refused. They were not for him. He wanted to leave as quickly as possible. He packed his furniture and books, and gave R the Chinese scroll that once hung in their sitting room in Gibbs. On perhaps the very last night of term, they went to the rooms of an unconventional hearty who had a large collection of classical records. R recalled: 'On this evening he put his gramophone on, and almost at once Patrick started dancing. It quickly became rather wild, and I found this almost flamboyant expression of himself a strange revelation of a Patrick I had hardly known. The other man and I sat at the side of the room, at first amused, but then, as the dancing became more extravagant, rather embarrassed. When the music stopped – though there must have been several records played – there was silence. And this silence continued as Patrick and I walked down to our rooms by the river – the whole length of the college – and when we got there we parted, and went to our separate bedrooms. Looking back, am I inventing a false retrospective interpretation of this episode, in thinking that Patrick's wild dance was celebrating a release not merely from the narrow confines of the academic world in general and of King's in particular, but also from the affection and the bonds which had circumscribed so much of his life during those three years?'[57]

The Victor Whites left Sydney in style. Before embarking on the *Nieuw Zeeland* they held a cocktail party at the Golf Club attended by the senior judiciary, thousands of acres, the principal Sydney fortunes and several hundred friends. It was reported by the *Sydney Morning Herald* that Mrs Victor White 'received her guests wearing a frock of black delustred satin, with pearl ornaments, and a small black hat. The lounge of the club-house, and the drawing room were attractive with masses of autumn-toned flowers.'[58] They arrived in London in July.

Mother and son were soon locked in a brawl. The cause seemed trivial. Ruth held a dinner party at the Mayfair Hotel to thank the Stogdales for looking after Suzanne. She insisted that her son wear a dinner jacket. He refused. But in the end, recalled the other Sue, White came to dinner at the Mayfair in very bad grace, 'and in the much-despised dinner jacket. I think it was one up to his mother. It was a painful evening with Ruth telling him to get up and dance.'[59]

White had already dashed off a play as an argument for staying in London and showed the typescript to his parents. Ruth supported her son's decision to stay behind and write, but Dick found it hard. 'Poor Dick, who had never read a book unless a studbook, or one of the thrillers Ruth brought him from the library, to fall asleep over in his leather armchair after dinner, didn't know what it was all about.' He was vaguely impressed to be able to hold the play in his hand, the pages punched and bound neatly with a ribbon. But his son had written under the pseudonym Peter Withycombe, for the young man had concluded the Whites were barbarians and decided to abandon the 'pitiful name' of Patrick White. Dick accepted his son's plans reluctantly, but underwrote them by offering him a splendid allowance of £400 a year. He placed only one condition on this, that if his son must be a writer 'it had to be under the name White'.[60]

Patrick had effectively sabotaged Ruth's plans to launch his sister in English society. First there was the business of the May Balls, but then he persuaded Sue not to be presented at court with Sue Stogdale. Ruth had set her heart on seeing Suzanne in feathers and train at Buckingham Palace in June. So to mollify his mother, White agreed to take his sister on a trip through central Europe. They left for Hanover in midsummer. The Oertels' apartment on the Holzgraben had become another home for White over the past couple of years. He was there in the summer of 1934, and was back in the spring of 1935 on a trip that took him to Berlin at the time of Goering's wedding. 'I watched from the street this vast couple in a limousine lined with roses. Hitler arrived in another car. Everyone was going mad.' As a small gesture of defiance, White was carrying a parcel which he rather hoped might be mistaken for a bomb. It was an orchid specimen vase in a box. 'People looked at me, but no one opened it.'[61]

The time for such jokes had passed. When he arrived with Suzanne in the summer of 1935 he sensed the Oertels were pulling in their horns, and that his presence in Hanover made them a little nervous. Suzanne was keen on paint. She taught Lotte Lange the latest techniques of make-up. 'We laughed our heads off drinking schnapps on the safe balcony above the Holzgraben in Hanover, and Lotte overpainted her lips in defiance of the tin sabre.' The Oertels were prospering in the new Germany and had bought themselves a car which they first named Patrick, 'to honour our friend Patrick White'. But then they rechristened the car *Weltenbummler*, world-wanderer, 'for the poor Patrick would perhaps break down one day thinking that so many people are always riding on his back'.[62]

The two Whites went on to Munich, which was rather terrible 'with her makeup and Nazidom gathering force' and then to Vienna for *Heurigen*. Deciding it was too hot for Budapest, they struck north to Prague, where a peasant festival jammed the streets. The city was crowded and sinister. 'Everyone suspected everyone else. No English was spoken and my German didn't go down too well.' They took the train to Dresden. That exquisite city was a revelation, 'a dream landscape like a Dutch landscape, but less tangible. You couldn't explain it. It was like walking through a dream.' They saw *Die Walküre* at the great opera house, but more than the music, White loved the sausages and salad at interval and the sight of Brünnhilde riding round the stage on a real white horse. Theodora Goodman was to follow them to Dresden in the last days of peace, troubled by the sight of the great soprano singing up 'her soul for love into a wooden cup'.[63]

The family was together for the last time. Ruth rather pined for a white Christmas, but Dick was not well enough to face a European winter. Above all, he was keen to get back to see his great racehorse High running in Sydney. In the autumn of 1935 Ruth and Dick took Suzanne back to Australia leaving Patrick to start afresh in a city he found absolutely marvellous, somewhere 'you could burrow in and just lead your own life'.[64]

PART TWO

Letters of Introduction

'He was a human being, and
human beings aren't allowed
to choose what they shall
love: woman, man, cat – or
God.'

The Vivisector

EIGHT

The Mouse and Roy

EBURY STREET RUNS along the hem of Belgravia, from Chelsea down by the river, through shabby Pimlico, across a quarter that might pretend to be Belgravia itself and into the vortex that surrounds Victoria Station.[1] Ronald Waters introduced White to the street, for whenever the actor had work in London he lived here in a boarding house run by Inez Imhof. This became White's London headquarters from the time of his return to England in 1932. It turned out that his entire London existence was lived at Imhof's or within a few blocks of her establishment at 68 Ebury Street.

A room and breakfast cost about thirty shillings a week. Supper was extra, and the food was wonderful for Imhof ran the house in partnership with her brother Mario Maranta, a pastry cook and chocolate maker with a shop in Shaftesbury Avenue. They were Swiss-Italian. White discovered that Inez Imhof 'was one of the artists of domesticity . . . her basement kitchen was a warm womb in times of need, smelling of fresh laundry and the promise of delicious meals'. Below White's room lived 'a rackety creature' called Lady Mary Montagu, daughter of the Duke of Manchester. 'The whole family very unstable. They have always been my yardstick for titles where I have to use them in a novel.'[2] Domestic order was always a spur to White's writing, and within weeks of arriving back at the Imhof house in 1935 he finished the play that convinced Ruth and Dick to allow him to stay in London.

Ebury Street's plain brick houses were mostly turned over to flats and rooms, boarding houses and little hotels. This was not a celebrated address, but somewhere convenient and quite respectable, within walking distance of those more distinguished streets where its population of writers, actors, harlots, painters, aristocrats, antique dealers and refugees would rather live. To be on Ebury Street too long was a sign that one's life was coming to a halt. Noël Coward had abandoned 111 for Belgravia. Victoria Sackville-West and her husband

Harold Nicolson put 184 into the hands of V.S.-W.'s eccentric mother Lady Sackville and went to garden in Kent. Lady Sackville stayed on at 184 – once Mozart's house – with her staff and a pet blackbird. The journalist Godfrey Winn remained at 115. At the river end of Ebury Street, in a small flat, Oswald Mosley kept a curtained double bed for his seductions, and collapsed there in a fever after forming the British Union of Fascists. George Moore, recently deceased, lived at 121 with a Manet, two Monets and a housekeeper. Here he wrote *Conversations in Ebury Street*, a volume of pretentious essays which White admired. The young man was now thrilled to be living in Moore's literary shadow.

Once he had his allowance from Dick, White moved over the road from the Imhof house to a small flat on the top floor of 91. He had a couple of roughly partitioned rooms, a kitchen in a cupboard and a bathroom down a flight of stairs. He engaged a woman to look after him, arranged the antiques from Gibbs and had the phone installed: SLOane 3732. R came for one night, but the affair was over. 'He had decided he *wasn't*.' The two men never met again.[3]

This quarter of London with its 'obdurate maroon and brown' streets was to become a familiar landscape in White's writing. Somewhere in Pimlico in a vast, damp crumbling house, Mrs Lusty held a ham funeral for her husband. At 89 Ebury Street, on a block that might be mistaken for Belgravia, the painter William Standish and his wife Catherine bought a house at what was 'still a respectable and at the same time not too stuffy address, and close to Chelsea for Willy'. Their son Elyot Standish, who shared so many of White's experiences at Cambridge, in Germany and in London, pursued his barren life as a literary biographer at this address. Beyond the far end of Ebury Street, around the corner from the river in an imaginary Beckwith Street, the former jackeroo Mrs Eadith Trist established the magnificent brothel that served a better class of Englishman in war and peace.[4]

From 91, White ventured into London. Once more he was the new boy. He cut a quiet, formal and rather furtive figure, with his mouth set hard. 'You wouldn't have noticed him,' said Betty Withycombe. His sharp eyes watched from a pale, averted face. His skin was extraordinarily pale and his soft hair was brushed neatly back over the tips of long, flat ears. The uniform he wore was still sports coat, grey trousers and black turtle-neck jumper. Now he shaved his moustache and bought himself a pork-pie hat. London's climate was kind to his lungs, except down by the river in Chelsea which became, of course, a favourite quarter. He always carried an asthma contraption in his pocket. Waters called him 'the mouse'. He seemed morose, but full of hidden, wonderful humour. 'He didn't talk much until he got to know you – then he laid down the law.'[5]

At the Witts, a simple café in the West End, White sat with Waters and his friends, young actors and actresses who were poor but usually in work. In this bright company White felt tongue-tied and awkward. They performed their lives with all the confidence White could not find in his own as he muddled along, prey to shifting dreams. He wished he were an actor; he envied painters; at times only musicians seemed to have the integrity he craved. Stiff as he was, he even dreamt of himself as a great dancer. Of them all at the Witts, White suspected he was 'the only one who would never enter into life or art. I grew ashamed, but I don't think anyone else was aware.' Waters recalled him sitting there 'at the edge of the group wanting to be part of it'.[6] In time he was. He became their confidant, the one with whom they rehearsed their stories of love, jealousy, money, ambition, broken hearts and abortions. This was matter from the real world and White absorbed it, passive but alert.

At best, White's life was quietly outrageous. 'I was too frightened I suppose to be flamboyantly outrageous.' He had a brief affair with an old friend from Tudor House who turned up in London. They were never lovers as boys on the Southern Highlands but now they spent some hectic days together in Cornwall. When he disappeared White was once more alone and left to defend his loneliness. There seemed 'nothing else to do about it. You have to make the best of it, pretend that this is what you would choose.'[7]

Yet he wanted above all to find a companion, to be one of a couple. His failure to find that man over the next few years made White think there was something wrong with himself. He saw he was 'intense, possessive and jealous' and blamed his unhappy loneliness on his homosexual temperament, forced 'to surround itself with secrecy'. Pessimism made him resilient.[8] Soon after he came down to London, Joyce Withycombe's husband Richard Ward was charged with soliciting young men in a Hampshire village and sent to prison. The Withycombes were distraught. Joyce stood by him, and though Ward emerged well from the ordeal, the scandal cast a shadow of fear over White's life.

He made a timid attempt to work in the theatre. W. H. Auden's play *The Dog Beneath the Skin* was to be produced in London by Rupert Doone at the Westminster Theatre in early 1936. He met Doone through Peggy Withycombe, who had married Tom Garland, a handsome Rugby-playing doctor of radical left views who was with Auden at Gresham's School. The poet remained close to Garland, grateful for being rescued from the misery he suffered in his early days at Gresham's. In Auden's essay 'Honour' Tom Garland is the prefect portrayed affectionately as Wreath, and in the poet's *Last Will and Testament* Auden remembers both Garlands, wishing the sculptor Peggy,

someone real in every feature,
To Tom, her husband, someone to help . . . [9]

The Garlands, Auden, the shaven-headed Doone and Robert Medley
– a friend of Peggy's from the Slade – often ate at the Café de Flamme
in Euston Road. White offered Doone help with *Dog Beneath the Skin*.
'Nothing came of it. He wanted somebody who could "do things with
his hands" and I had to confess I was completely useless in that respect.'[10]
He shook Auden's hand at some point in these years, but never took up
the opportunity offered by the Garlands' friendship to come to know
the poet well. It seemed to Peggy that her cousin might be jealous of
the fame that settled so quickly and so effortlessly on Auden's shoulders.

White divided his days between writing in the morning and the
theatre at night. 'I used to wake up in the morning in a flat in London
and without getting out of bed, write till lunchtime, with no thought
for anything but what I was writing.'[11] He was writing into a vacuum.
Nobody wanted his plays, but with the stubborn determination of the
Whites, the family imperative of sticking at it, he continued to write.
One of these early London efforts was 'a bleak play about a spinster'.
Another was called, 'Into Egypt': 'It was about a whore trying to find
something else. She drowns herself in a temple.'[12]

There had been an upheaval in the Withycombe family: Jack had
died suddenly and Ellen had left West End to live with her daughter
Betty in Oxford. Before setting out on his last trip to Germany in the
summer of 1936, White spent the day in Oxford with Betty, punting on
the Isis. He found the town rather squalid after Cambridge – 'all those
bicycles and cheap furniture shops' – and a few hours in Oxford left him
feeling asthmatic. Back in London he wrote to Betty: 'This morning I
went straight to Cook's to make inquiries about the air service. But as
the fare is ten guineas to Berlin, I have decided to go by train after all.
It is difficult to give you anything definite in the nature of an address.'[13]

He was in Hanover at some point and it was, perhaps, on this last
visit that one of the Oertel uncles took him to his first brothel. 'There
are two types of women,' the uncle advised. 'Apples and pears. Never
go for the pears.' They sat about in the bawdy house and got drunk.
The young man was fascinated by the make-up on the tarts.[14]

As he made his way along the Baltic coast, White was still able
to pretend nothing much was afoot in this landscape of sand, pines
and sea. He was not travelling in the present Germany but in his
own 'romantic reconstruction of the past', moving through scenery
without politics. 'Even as fantasy it was not without its sinister side.'
In Königsberg a troupe of jeering, cropheaded boys pursued him along
the quay. Stettin was grim. But in Swinemunde, a Baltic resort for
the *hoch bourgeois*, White joined the fun, jumping on an Agfa ball and

having his photograph taken in the shallows. 'At night you marched round the bandstand where a tenor from Berlin sang the prize song from *Die Meistersinger*.'[15] Hints were made by the wife of an Essen arms manufacturer that her daughter Annie and a dowry might be available.

He made a literary detour to Rügen to see the schloss of the Gräfin von Arnim, formerly Mary Beauchamp of Sydney. The Gräfin was a cousin of Katherine Mansfield, and the author of two books he admired: *Elizabeth and her German Garden* and *The Caravaners* which he thought was one of the funniest novels he had read. From exquisite Lübeck he crossed into Denmark, travelling to Copenhagen, where he had an introduction to the family of the Court Chancellor and his three daughters, and then on as far as the tip of Jutland to watch Kattegat meet Skagerrak.

Back from Denmark that summer he smuggled a copy of *Ulysses*. He was already a fan of James Joyce's writing, though not the man, whom he always thought repulsive. Now, fourteen years after its publication, he read the Irishman's great work. Here was prose like music – making more sound than sense at times – and a dazzling technique that took him inside the vivid, wandering minds of these Dublin figures. He had to admit to himself that much of *Ulysses* bored him, but when it worked he was swept away. James Joyce became for him 'practically God'.[16]

Ulysses and Roy de Maistre entered his life in the same weeks. White met the painter, whose studio was at 104 Ebury Street, before leaving for Germany. De Maistre had given him those distinguished introductions in Copenhagen. Some time that summer, before or after his romantic tramp round the Baltic, White fell in love.

De Maistre was forty-two, tiny, tubby, balding and diabetic, but he became what White most needed at this time, 'an intellectual and aesthetic mentor'. His tastes and prejudices soon permeated the young man's mind, for which he remained loyal and grateful to him all his life. 'I always feel it was he who taught me to write, although he himself found it the greatest effort to put pen to paper.'[17] Another of the West End plays by Patrick White was doing the rounds of managements and nobody wanted it. White was prepared to go on down this dead end until Roy de Maistre convinced him it was the wrong way.

That they had not come across one another until now was a result of strange mischances. The painter had grown up in Sutton Forest, where his family rented a big place called Mount Valdemar across the paddocks from the Withycombes' Boscobel. A brother and sister de Mestre married a sister and brother of Gertrude Morrice. When Paddy White was a schoolboy at Tudor House, Roi de Mestre was riding about the Highlands on a red horse, his easel and paints strapped to the

saddle. They did not come across one another then, and by the time
White returned home from Cheltenham, the painter had made his final
break with Australia, a country he loathed as an outpost of the second
rate: second-rate painters and second-rate critics. Like White, he vowed
as he left that he would not return. He honoured the vow.

His life was a work of art, a skilful confabulation, yet the facts were
more interesting than his own inventions. The family was originally
French. The boy's grandfather had come to Sydney from China as a
tea merchant and, at the time of the Napoleonic Wars, faked British
nationality to avoid the inconvenience of being an enemy alien in
a British colony. From the acorn of that lie grew a bizarre family
tree. Prosper de Mestre shed his Catholicism, made a fortune and
was almost wiped out in the great crash of 1842, which the Whites
weathered successfully on the Hunter.

The next generation of de Mestres were great names on the
Australian track. The painter's father owned or trained the early
winners of the Melbourne Cup. He lost a second fortune and retreated
to the Highlands where he was reduced to running guest houses around
Sutton Forest. The painter later presented this as an elegant childhood
spent in vice-regal company. A sense of greatness, if only lost greatness, was at the core of the family's sense of itself.

Roy was the ninth child of the family, protected from the drudgery
of the guest houses by an adoring mother. He was always delicate,
remembered as 'a prissy little boy who wore a bow tie even when
playing as a child. He was obviously not the sort of boy his "manly"
horse-training, farmer brothers thought he should be. His family tells
stories of his sitting in church sketching the clothes of the vice-regal
party . . . and then coming home and making clothes from the sketches
to dress his dolls; and stories of his wheeling his pram of dolls through
the paddocks accompanied by his younger sister who was shooting
rabbits with an air gun.'[18]

The same French nuns who taught literature to Gertrude Morrice
gave Roy lessons in art and music. The painter was a second path by
which the influence of those severe and accomplished women reached
Patrick White. In Sydney, Roy took Dattilo Rubbo's classes at the Royal
Art Society of New South Wales, where the other students were so
impressed by the young man's hauteur and fastidious dress that they
called him 'the Duke'. He was dirt poor but they had the impression
he lived on a private income.

The war made him a Modern. All his life Roy was to lie that he had
been invalided out of the army with tuberculosis, but his medical records
rule out TB and put his exit down to 'general weakness and debility'.
Behind this euphemism lay something both Roy and the army wished to
hide. Perhaps he suffered a breakdown. His discharge papers say he was

not insane, but after leaving the army he spent a good deal of time with Dr Charles Moffitt, formerly of Sydney's Callan Park Asylum. Moffitt put the painter to work decorating wards for shell-shock victims in Red Cross Nerve Hospitals. So desperate were doctors to find some treatment for this intractable condition, that 'psychological investigation by psycho-analysis, hypnotism, etc, relaxation, re-education, reassurance, suggestion, persuasion, electricity, massage' were being tried in half a dozen Sydney nerve hospitals.[19] Colour was thought to soothe the men. Working from a scheme suggested in the *Lancet*, de Mestre painted a ward at the Russell Lea Nerve Hospital sky blue and primrose with a dark green floor. The patients reported sleeping peacefully.

De Mestre discovered in this a passion for the 'science' of colour. Composers, quacks and artists had for decades been seeking links between health and colour, the spirit world and colour, music and colour. None of this was new, but de Mestre and Adrien Verbrugghen, a colleague from the Sydney Conservatorium, worked out a mechanical scheme for 'translating' melodies into colour. They laid the seven colours of the rainbow against the notes of the scale. Yellow was C, and they called the scale of C major 'yellow major'. Higher octaves were brighter colours, and the lower were darker; colour chords were produced by direct translation from the keyboard. De Mestre gave his paintings titles like 'The Boat Sheds in Violet Red Key'. When the Mittabah Whites, the Dangars and Lloyd-Jones gave the Red Cross an old flower farm near Sutton Forest, de Mestre was able to apply his theories on a large scale, painting the shell-shock wards in colour-music keys 'which enabled patients to receive the full benefits of colour treatment without the retinal exhaustion produced by prolonged exposure to single colours'.[20]

He then took an important step: stimulated by the success of a joint exhibition of music-colour works with Roland Wakelin and by the mild applause of the critics – which he afterwards represented as abuse – he began to paint in whorls of pure colour. The first of these entirely abstract paintings, 'Rhythmic Composition in Yellow Green Minor', was, the critic Daniel Thomas claims, 'astonishing anywhere in the world at that time'. The press wrote, with admiration, 'In Sydney there is a young artist who can stand before any of his pictures and whistle it, or play its theme on a piano.'[21]

A decade of muddle followed. De Mestre spent part of that time in France, where this son and brother of New South Wales horse trainers discovered a 'preordained harmony between himself and his surroundings'. This was not a judgment shared by White: 'Roy was one of the least French people I have ever known. He was always darting across to France and had some French friends he was very fond of, but he was not French by any means.'[22] He never mastered the language. Despite everything he remained stubbornly, if oddly, Australian.

Back in Sydney the painter found a few patrons of modern art and survived as a teacher and interior decorator. Grace Bros sold his patented De Mestre Colour Harmonising Disc 'to facilitate the work of artists, designers or decorators who are concerned with schemes of colour'.[23] It was very popular. He had a room in Burdekin House in Macquarie Street, got by on nothing, wore a few beautiful clothes, played tennis at Government House and lived a life of extreme sexual discretion.

His farewell to Australia was the exhibition at Burdekin House, the fine mansion in Macquarie Street which was about to be demolished to make way for a fake gothic Presbyterian church. Downstairs de Mestre arranged antiques lent by Sydney collectors – Ruth was not among them – and upstairs he set aside rooms to be decorated in the Modern manner. His was the most uncompromisingly Modern: apricot walls, a 'skyscraper' bookcase, bare boards and a sharply patterned rug. The arbiter of Sydney taste, *The Home*, was enthusiastic: 'The hundreds of visitors to Burdekin House have only too eagerly asked the question, "Where are the modern rooms?" With a cry of relief they have almost leapt up the stairs.'[24]

Once he was in Europe he invented a name, a distinguished childhood and that youthful bout of TB. De Mestre became de Maistre: by changing 'e' to 'ai' he claimed a link with the family of Joseph de Maistre, the philosopher Balzac called an 'eagle among thinkers'. But the de Mestres and de Maistres came from opposite ends of France. Ignorant of – or perhaps undeterred by – this the painter explained thereafter that 'de Mestre is the *old* French form and it seemed an anachronism for a modern painter to appear to favour Medievalism when all the rest of my relations in France used the Modern Spelling.' He also awarded himself the philosopher's Christian name Joseph. Later he became convinced of royal blood. His friend, the critic John Rothenstein – to whom he never mentioned the family's bankruptcies and guest houses – admired the finished effect: 'aristocratic though he is, he is also a self-made man. His establishment in Europe is the consequence of acts of faith and will.'[25]

Though so much about him was fake, de Maistre had a knack of making young and talented men take themselves seriously. When he found Francis Bacon, this wild Irish boy was working as an interior decorator and furniture designer. In de Maistre's company he became a painter. They shared an old garage in West Queensberry Mews, polished the floors and hung the windows with white rubber sheeting. Bacon showed his first paintings here in a joint exhibition with de Maistre, but it was Bacon's steel and glass furniture that won the attention of the art press. At the Mayor Gallery in Cork Street they exhibited together again a couple of years later, but Bacon faded for a time as de Maistre was taken up by one of the gallery's proprietors, Douglas Cooper. This rich and bitchy offspring of an Australian family poured his share of the profits from Cooper's Sheep Dip into collecting Cubist works 'with the reverence and scholarship hitherto reserved for the old masters'. He was a difficult man to take, very flamboyant and self-important, but for many years he was a great friend of de Maistre and later of White: 'He has a good mind, great wit, and is loyal once he takes to you.'[26]

De Maistre found himself again, if only briefly, an *avant-garde* success at the Mayor, though the gallery sold none of his austere, fragmented paintings drenched in pure colour. In 1933 Herbert Read gave de Maistre a place in his magisterial survey *Art Now*. Read became his friend and, in time, an important contact for Patrick White in literary London. De Maistre had a talent for important friendships. His circle included poets and critics, musicians, politicians and royalty. In country houses he was thought 'great fun, and like Creevey, was always a *most* welcome guest'.[27] He never travelled without letters of introduction.

The contradictions in de Maistre's nature at the time he and White became lovers were deep but clear: he was a snob and an artist of integrity, a Modern who affected Edwardian manners, a homosexual of extreme discretion, and a melancholy man of great charm. He was poor but his friends were loyal. To survive in Ebury Street he painted portraits and flowers, and inspired a kind of maternal doting in women who 'would try to outdo one another with the most delicious jar from Fortnum's'.[28] He dressed with exquisite care, less like a painter than a bank manager of another age, and worked in a tailored smock.

Their affair was brief. 'He himself was trying to recover from something unhappy, but said that in any case an intimate relationship of ours wouldn't have worked because he was twenty years older. It wouldn't have worked either. We were both too irritable and unyielding.' The difference in their ages was not itself a barrier: Roy was the first of three lovers roughly twice his age who played important roles in his life. White liked older men and enjoyed their company, 'not because I thought they were wiser in the conventional sense, but because they held a sort of secret knowledge of the details of living that was very important to me'. From this brief affair with de Maistre, they emerged as friends, mentor and pupil, father and son. Looking back, White wondered if it had not been an attempt to consummate his stifled love for a father 'with one who was everything Dick was not'.[29]

De Maistre patiently drew out the young man's ideas and persuaded him they were worth expressing. It was an article of de Maistre's faith that serious artists were Modern. 'He persuaded me to walk in the present instead of lying curled and stationary in that over-upholstered cocoon the past, refuge of so many Australians then and now.' Serious artists must also absorb themselves in high art. One day a woman visiting the Ebury Street studio asked de Maistre to play the Schumann piano concerto on his gramophone. He did, and White went away 'seduced by the whole occasion. On another occasion when we were alone I asked him to play it again, and he turned on me and said: "Nonsense! You must only listen to the greatest!" And I suppose ever since I have resented having to listen to the easily seductive.'[30]

De Maistre's paintings were the great lesson for the young man. They were abstract, fractured and difficult, but de Maistre's aim was not to paint patterns on canvas but to show the real world in a fresh light. In France he learnt to admire the French for finding 'the Good, the Beautiful and the True' in the intimate and simple subjects of their everyday life. He believed that behind such simplicity might be found the unseen eternal. De Maistre encouraged White to set out on the same search, and mimic in prose the procedure White later called 'the fragmentation by which I convey reality'.[31] However complex the surface of de Maistre's paintings and White's prose, behind them lay the same quest for freshness, simplicity and truth.

'I began to write from the inside out when Roy de Maistre introduced me to abstract painting. Before that I had only approached writing as an exercise in naturalism. Anything else was poetry . . . Then came the terrors of abstract painting. As far as I was concerned, it was like jumping into space, and finding nothing there at first (the same thing when one first plunges into Zen.) Then gradually one saw that it was possible to weave about freely on different levels at one and the same time.'[32] He dug out 'The Immigrants', which he had finished by lamplight six years before in the cottage at Bolaro. He recognised here a more honest 'lumbering after truth' than in all his plays written since he came down to London.[33] He began to rework the Monaro novel under the title *Happy Valley*.

To turn away, now, from his London existence and begin to draw on that hidden Australian life, took considerable courage. He had hardly mentioned these years to his Cambridge and London intimates, but if he was going to be an artist they had to be faced. The writing was harsh, for White was returning to his jackerooing years not out of affection but need. And the book was all the harsher for him having absorbed de Maistre's great fear of sentimentality. White was afraid to relax in case he turned out a novelette, and that anxiety haunted him nearly all his life.

He had no writers to turn to for advice on technique. He learnt by reading. 'I don't think I ever asked anyone anything of that kind (anyway I didn't know any other writers) I simply read and blundered on with my own writing.' He had read Hemingway, but was finding the American unsympathetic and it irked him later to see Hemingway cited as a formative influence. Their prose had a common mother in Gertrude Stein. 'When I was beginning to write novels of any possibility I was very much under the influence of Gertrude. So I suppose she helped form me too!' Lawrence was important, but Joyce was his God and *Ulysses* his Bible. As he wrote *Happy Valley* he was 'drunk with the techniques of writing . . . and had gone up that cul de sac the stream of consciousness'.[34]

To drift with the thoughts of his characters, and switch at will from the mind of one to another, appealed particularly to White, for it meshed with the workings of his peculiar creative imagination. He *acted* all his characters at the typewriter, and in the theatre of his imagination he played everyone. To try to write a novel through the eyes of a single character seemed thoroughly boring. 'I can only endure the isolation and monotony of writing fiction by losing myself in a number of characters. I suppose this would not work if the writer's own character is not sufficiently fragmented.'[35]

White wrote under the influence of two other Modern enthusiasms. The first was Spengler, who 'gave me the gooseflesh in my youth',[36] and the pessimistic German's view that Western civilisation was in its death throes stuck with White for life. One of the fundamental assumptions in White's work is that all we value – society, relationships, even fortunes – is sliding into decay. The familiar situation of most of his novels is the lone figure seeking fulfilment in a world drifting towards ugliness and violence, loneliness and poverty. Ruth had in her own way prepared the ground for the gloomy German by drumming into her boy the proposition that fortunes last only three generations. Dick's was the third.

Though carried away by Spengler, White remained sceptical of Freud. He accepted much that psychoanalysis had to teach but never allowed himself to be analysed. In Freudian jargon, he was a heavily defended personality. Psychoanalysis, he later remarked, 'is a dark cave into which I'd never venture for fear of leaving something important behind'. The loss he feared was some part of his creative self.[37]

Freud did convince him that an imperious mother and diffident father were central to him being homosexual. Ruth was somehow to blame for his unhappiness as she was also, at some deep level, for his asthma. The discovery of Freud fed the antipathy between the boy and his mother. But he could not be a disciple. His dreams did not fit Freud's pattern. Dreams were important all his life. He dreamed vividly nearly every night and remembered his dreams. They fed his work. The casts of his books moved and spoke as he slept. He dreamed through the problems of his writing. But Freud's explanation of dreams seemed to White too much about sex, too systematic. White suspected all systems.

As he worked on *Happy Valley*, he had terrible bouts of asthma and began to cough blood. It was thought he had TB. This was now to be a recurring nightmare, and at its first appearance in the London winter of 1936 to 1937 it provoked a family panic. Ruth directed him to see one of his Lipscomb cousins who was a doctor in London, and Lipscomb sent him on to a Pimlico TB clinic. Wandering about the streets on these visits White noticed an elderly drunk he dubbed the Twitching Colonel and imagined a life for him: going to pieces in India, shipped back to Britain where he sinks through the suburbs – Maida Vale, Bayswater to Pimlico – boozing and dreaming about India, until he perishes in a fire,

> as climbing rope the window opens, I am climbing rope or smoke and the flame smiles with the warmth of smiles that welcome, no longer the half-guessed significance of smiles, of wave, of rope, of the brown eye of jewelled elephants, as slipping effortless and without elegy the world dissolves.[38]

'The Twitching Colonel' was accepted by the *London Mercury* and appeared in April 1937. This short story was White's first appearance in print since coming down to London. Squire would never have accepted such a piece, but the old editor had been sacked, and the magazine was now open to such mannered Modern prose under its new editor Rolfe Scott-James. 'The Twitching Colonel' was not much in itself – 'I was trying painfully to knock together a technique'[39] – but it marked the distance White had come since the *London Mercury* published his *Ploughman* poems three years before.

The valley of White's novel extends from Moorang to Kambala, that is, on official maps, from Cooma to the old gold-mining camp of Kiandra in the mountains. The town of Happy Valley stands midway between these two bleak poles, where Adaminaby stood when White was jackerooing in the Monaro. The sun sometimes shone over Adaminaby, but the weather is always foul in Happy Valley. White painted a yellow landscape: grass, dogs, faces, the autumn sun, posters curling on a paling fence, the moon, even bed sheets are yellow. Winter mud, nettles in the gutters, and the music teacher's passion for mauve would yield, according to the De Mestre Colour Harmonising Disc, the key of G Minor.

Out on Glen Marsh, the biggest property in the district, White installed Mr and Mrs Stan Furlow. They are the first of all the versions of Ruth and Dick he would write over the next fifty years. These figures became more complex and more appalling in time, but the Furlows of Glen Marsh have the clarity of a naïve painting. Stan Furlow's mind is 'only a mutual understanding between a number of almost dormant instincts', asleep much of the day under the *Sydney Morning Herald*, troubled only by passing flies.[40] His wife, who squabbles with her difficult daughter and dotes on a fox terrier so constipated it can hardly walk, is a thrusting figure who looks to Government House as the natural arena of her social ambition. Across Mrs Furlow's bosom hang the first of the strings and ropes and chokers of pearls worn by White's women. They are their badges of rank:

> When she swept into a room in an excessive number of pearls everyone said MY DEAR, which, if overheard, Mrs Furlow always interpreted to her own advantage. This because she held an innate belief in her own importance as a public figure. She liked to pick up the *Herald* and read a description of her dress. She had also a private passion for the Prince of Wales.[41]

There was more to Ruth than this, and White would grudgingly admit it. 'Some people see a lot of my mother in Mrs Furlow. I suppose she has some of those qualities, but also a great many remarkable ones that you don't find in Mrs F. She's positive and adds something by her life, which I could never feel my father did. (I suppose this all boils down to the same old boring complex!)'[42]

Escape is the common dream of everyone in Happy Valley except the Furlows and the Quongs. They know what they are doing there, for between them they own the place. The Quongs are taken raw from the Yens who ran most of the businesses in town when White was a jackeroo. Walter Quong is the notorious Frank Yen who pissed in the keyholes of Cooma. Arthur Quong kept a racehorse in a shed at the back of the shop as Arthur Yen had in Adaminaby, and both men shared the same white-rimmed eyes. Ethel Quong, like Minnie Yen, was a domestic at Government House before she made an unlikely and unhappy marriage. But White invented for her a child, Margaret, conceived out of wedlock. Margaret Quong is not a Yen, but an exotic version of Paddy White, a lonely, thoughtful and silent child with big eyes.

Here at the beginning of his career, White wrote his best plot. Plots interested him less over the years. 'My downfall is that I become interested in characters and want to explore each one of them too thoroughly.' But the plot of *Happy Valley* is packed: Dr Rodney Halliday is married without passion to a good, drab wife. He lives one of the lives Ruth sketched out for her son as a country doctor with (abandoned) ambitions to be a writer. White acknowledged, 'Rodney Halliday *has* quite a lot of the author in him – character not background; for I had what you might call an upholstered childhood.' Halliday falls in love with Alys Browne, an artistic spinster who teaches piano in a cottage on the edge of town. Browne is thin, plain, overwrought and lonely. She dreams of leaving for California but puts off her dreams day by day until she is ruined by Belper the bank manager. Alys is the first of White's spinsters, and another fragment of White himself. Her loneliness 'was very close to my own unfortunate experience'.[43] She and Halliday have music in common. Both fail the de Maistre test: they are fond of Schumann.

Two adulteries are afoot in the valley: the doctor with the music teacher, and Clem Hagan the Lawrentian overseer on Glen Marsh – he has the sure mark of sexual potency: red hair on the backs of his hands – with the sluttish wife of the schoolteacher Ernest Moriarty. The teacher was White's first asthmatic, his chest 'a ravine of pain, the breath rare and hot that struggled up, he could not get up far enough, he could not drag a weight'.[44] The reek of burning asthma papers hangs over *Happy Valley*, but Moriarty has the strength to strangle his wife and tear out her tongue in jealous rage. He wanders down the road and dies of heart failure, and his body is lying there as Halliday and Alys try to make their escape. The murder 'brings him back to his senses'.[45] Halliday turns back, recalled by duty and pity for his own wife's fate, though he knows the price of his decision will be emotional impotence.

One couple holds and a second forms. Hagan has been seen slipping from the Moriartys' house that night, but the Furlows' daughter saves him by swearing falsely that he was in her bed when the woman was murdered. The scandal rocks the Furlows, but Stan adores his daughter and buys her and Hagan a place up at Scone. So Sidney Furlow finds a way of breaking free from her family to live her own life. They will marry though Sidney already despises the man she has trapped. Ahead of them lies something like the appalling but enduring union of the Macrorys of Kudjeri.[46] Each will suffer, but not alone. White was always on the side of couples. Anything is better than loneliness.

> This is the part of man, to withstand through his relationships the ebb and flow of the seasons, the sullen hostility of rock, the anaesthesia of snow, all those passions that sweep down through negligence or design to consume and desolate . . . immune from all but the ultimate destruction of the inessential outer shell.[47]

He chose the name *Happy Valley* because it had a universal and desolate ring. White settlers in Kenya were drinking themselves to death in one Happy Valley, and on the edge of Sydney the unemployed had set up a shanty camp in another. The name was everywhere. Lunatic asylums, race tracks and dust bowls all over the English-speaking world were Happy Valleys. A property out beyond Bolaro had the name, but the Happy Valley Patrick White knew best was the deep, silent gully behind Mount Wilson. It was not the place but the name that mattered, for its sense of universal suffering, lost hopes and defeat. The book reads like a horror story. It is all recoil. The people of Happy Valley are trapped by poverty, habit, duty, timidity, and – the better ones – by pity. The author is the only one to make good his escape.

Roy disapproved of the theatre, but three or four nights a week White slipped away to the West End, usually with Ronald unless Waters dropped him in favour of an actress. 'You'd be dropped flat.'[48]

White loved actresses. He became a connoisseur of their offstage performances: he loved their shifting moods, their self-absorption, their passions. He envied them for all the vivid qualities 'the mouse' could never match. Yet they shared something important: as they acted their unlived lives on stage, White was realising his other fragmented lives on the page. Working alone at his desk, the actor manqué envied them the lights, the greasepaint and applause.

These women gave him intimate friendship without any sexual confusion. He valued this all his life. Through the Arts Theatre Club White met Ambrosine Phillpotts, the actress of his Ebury Street years. She was a niece of the playwright, daughter of an admiral and a stylish young comedienne. Phillpotts was original: on stage one bitter night, she tried to keep warm by placing a hot potato between her breasts. On a trip that had an epic flavour for White she brought him down from Hull where she was working for the local repertory theatre in an ancient car she could barely drive, their only luggage in the back was an alarm clock and a bunch of bananas.

He kept the theatricals away from de Maistre. But keeping friends apart was something they taught each other. Roy was dictatorial and finicky. He never introduced the young man to his grand English friends like Samuel Courtauld, who had put together one of the greatest collections of post-Impressionist paintings, 'loved and admired' de Maistre and bought a number of his works.[49] De Maistre painted Courtauld's abrupt daughter Sydney and her husband the Under-Secretary of State Rab Butler. The painter persuaded the couple to buy some of Francis Bacon's furniture. But White's path never crossed the Butlers'. De Maistre allowed him to meet Bacon, Henry Moore, Graham Sutherland and Douglas Cooper, 'who would start off genial and generous, then turn against those he had taken up'. The young man did not dare exchange a word with Moore and Sutherland, 'and would have avoided Bacon too, had he not been a friend rather than a guest at parties'.[50]

His own friends he kept in three watertight compartments: de

Maistre's studio crowd, theatricals and Withycombes. Though each knew of the existence of the other groups, separation was rigid. Waters 'didn't know de Maistre or that side of Patrick'. Betty Withycombe met de Maistre only once, 'and Patrick would have liked me not to'. She put this down to a chameleon quality in him. 'Patrick *feels* different with one person rather than another. His persona changes. I remember the bell rang one night when I was in his flat in Ebury Street. He went down and was away for ages. When he returned he said, "That was Ron Waters en passant." But he wouldn't bring him up.' She was astonished.[51]

White saw this in darker colours: he felt he had to keep the Withycombes away from his homosexual friends. 'Betty was always very anti-Roy, partly on artistic grounds but mainly because I loved him and she had a low tolerance for that. All the Withycombes did.' Even with them he remained very reticent, and all his life thought it strange that people would want to talk about their confusions. 'All my youth I was confused, but I never went telling people, because I didn't think anyone else could do anything about it: it was something I had to muddle along with.'[52] His reticence and the habit of keeping his friends apart left him a lonely figure. There was no Patrick White crowd. His few close friends were distanced from one another, oases separated by bare ground.

Late that winter Ambrosine Phillpotts finished her stint at Hull and joined White and Waters in Cannes, staying for a fortnight in March or early April 1937 in a cheap hotel in a back street behind the Carlton. 'We had no money,' Waters recalled. 'But to be in Cannes with an actress! It was very grand.'[53] They went gambling. Phillpotts had borrowed extravagant dresses from the Hull wardrobe, but their big entrance to the casino was reduced to fiasco when White stood on her train and tore it off.

White had put aside the manuscript of *Happy Valley* for a few weeks and written two theatre pieces. *Peter Plover's Party* was a monologue for a chatterbox in the manner of Ronald Waters: 'It was rather as I behaved at parties if I was nervous, throwing my arms about and talking non-stop.'[54] The mannerisms of Peter Plover were Waters's, but the target was their very camp neighbour in Ebury Street, the journalist Godfrey Winn,

Noppy, what *have* you got on your head? Don't tell me fish-net is really coming in? . . . Oh, well, I adore corks . . . And your work? Writing many beautiful things? You're looking so prolific. I mean . . . I read your last. It was such fun. Though personally, I don't think the woman would have eaten the potato. She would have kept it as a souvenir. Just a psychological point. And of course, your style's becoming a joy. So delightfully *raw*. One must come down to essentials, mustn't one? One must BE . . . Just look at that old trout Sir Humphrey telling poor Bernard about somebody else's gold standard . . . I *must* go. Much as I'd like to stay for ever with all you exciting people . . . Beryl, dear, marvellous! You must come to mine next week . . . Why here comes La Perle de la Couronne! Oh, no it's not. It's Godfrey Winn . . . Hullo, Godfrey. I certainly must fly . . . (*He exits.*)[55]

Waters had returned from the south of France to play Sir Benjamin Backbite in *The New School for Scandal*, an updated version of Sheridan's text. After five years in the theatre, Waters was always in work, but he hoped with this production to make his big break. The imposing Ellen Pollock was to play Lady Sneerwell. Perhaps it was the thought of this production that sparked White to write a one-act play called *School for Friends* which he sent home to Sydney to be entered anonymously in the annual Bryants' one-act play competition. All that's known of the second of White's plays to be performed was that it involved 'three bitching females'. After two performances at Bryants' in April 1937 – the author was identified as 'P.W.' – the play was selected for the final round of the competition in May. However, *School for Friends* ended unplaced by the judges behind Betty Adamson's *Call it a Date* and Lionel Shave's *That's Murder*. There were two more performances in June under White's name and then the play disappeared.[56]

'Cleverly written but ineffectively climaxed,' was all a critic ever said of the play. The gossip columns were kinder: 'Mrs Victor White is very proud of her son Paddy whose play *School for Friends* was recently produced at Bryants' Playhouse,' noted the Sydney *Daily Telegraph*. 'And very good it was too. A comedy in one act all built on the modern trend of thought. Paddy, who has made London his home for some years, finds things so very interesting on the other side that the family goes from here to visit him periodically, as "the Mountain will not come to Mohamet".'[57]

But no more. Dick had set about selling his share of Belltrees finally, convinced his son would have no place there. He 'retired' from the partnership on 30 June 1936 after nearly fifty years, selling his one-third share for £78,000. This caused considerable pain at Belltrees, as it was necessary to take a small mortgage of £25,000 to meet Dick's price. Whites did not mortgage. Between Belltrees and the Victor Whites it was another potent cause of bitterness.

As Dick was disentangling himself from the partnership at the age of sixty-eight, he was struck by the curse of the Whites. The hay fever he had all his life turned to severe asthma. Ruth took her husband north to take the waters in the bore baths at Moree but this brought no relief. She wrote to her son that it was terrible to hear the panting that echoed through Lulworth at night as Dick struggled to find breath. Despite her chipper interview with the *Daily Telegraph*, there was no prospect of Dick travelling to Europe. He was now an invalid.

NINE

Spanish Eyes

As it was then the fashion for writers to go abroad to finish their novels, White cast about for somewhere to spend summer polishing the final draft of *Happy Valley*. Roy de Maistre suggested St Jean-de-Luz in the Basque country near Biarritz.

The port of St Jean was part of de Maistre's France. He had taken a party of students from Paris down to St Jean on his first trip to France in 1924, and *Boat Harbour St Jean-de-Luz* was the painting he gave the Society of Artists in Australia to fulfil the terms of his travelling scholarship. Roy liked to boast in an exaggerated way that the painting provoked 'many protests from outraged citizens'.[1] Now he slipped over to St Jean from time to time to stay with rather grand English friends. The port had become a holiday resort for the English, an innocent version of Biarritz, somewhere to eat Basque food, gamble and play golf. When White fell in with de Maistre's suggestion, the painter was able to send the young man across with letters of introduction.

A mole across the bay takes the brunt of the Atlantic surf and shelters the mouth of the little river that runs between the boat harbour and the sea. The light is salty and pale, the air blustery. On the spit between the harbour and the beach stands a jumble of pale houses and gravel squares shaded in summer by dense plane trees. This is the old town where Louis XIV waited to meet the Infanta Maria Theresa, who was brought across the border from Spain for their marriage in the church of St Jean Baptiste. Roy slept one night in Louis's bed and sent a card to Sutton Forest to let his family know.[2] At the back of the harbour is Ciboure, once a separate village but now part of the town. Ciboure has one imperishable claim to fame: Ravel was born here in a house on the waterfront.

When White arrived in August 1937 the Spanish Civil War was a year old. The frontier lay only half an hour to the south, and the railway junction at Hendaye on the edge of St Jean was a principal point of supply to the Republican forces. St Jean was the Red Cross headquarters and it was from here that ships ran the Fascist blockade of Spain's northern coast. Bilbao, the nearest major Spanish city, had fallen to Franco's forces in June 1937. Early in the fighting the diplomatic corps had retreated from Madrid to St Jean, leaving only junior officers behind in the Spanish capital. The war proved a great boost to the local society of St Jean. The United States Ambassador set up his headquarters on the golf course.

On de Maistre's recommendation White took a room at the Jacquets' Hostellerie de Ciboure, a *relais gastronomique* with a few rooms upstairs for guests. To a shabby version of this little hotel White would one day send the spinster Theodora Goodman. The Hôtel du Midi had little of the Hostellerie's style, but it is recognisably the same small pub at the back of the boat harbour,

> a tight fit, between a garage and a confiserie. The Hôtel du Midi wore vines and a frill or two of iron. There were the blinds that furled and unfurled still, and the blind that evidently had stuck. Smells came in at the door, petrol and oil, fish, sea and the white, negative smell of dust.

In the hall stood sombre furniture, and from the salon which opened to the right came the sound of a clock, 'prim and slow'. A stair wound out of sight to upper floors where corridors led off at odd angles. The geography was complex, and the size of the little hotel difficult to grasp. Beside the Hostellerie was a walled garden where guests sat after lunch drinking coffee at iron tables or pacing the gravel paths to settle their digestions. Flowers – 'beaucoup de fleurs' – grew under the stubby palms and in the shade of the Jacquets' bay trees. But the *jardin exotique* of the Hôtel du Midi, where Theodora Goodman experienced in her disintegrating mind all the 'European cross-currents of the Thirties', was filled only with gravel, iron and cacti.[3]

White had found another domestic Eden in which to write. The Jacquets' nieces recalled Madame Jacquet was a most refined *cordon bleu* and her husband had a fine nose for wine. 'They had their own brand of hospitality, which was particularly warm and personal; and they knew how to treat their customers well, so that they always became friends afterwards.'[4] The food was Basque and French. In the 1930s the Hostellerie's dining room was patronised by painters, ambassadors, gourmands and the English community of St Jean. The Jacquets kept only a few rooms upstairs for guests. White was given a room on the first floor. As a gesture of thanks to the Jacquets he gave young Rodney Halliday's governess in *Happy Valley* their name.[5]

He spent that summer writing, eating, travelling through the

Basque country, watching bullfights in Bayonne, shopping for antiques and making love. One of de Maistre's letters of introduction was to Basil Leng, an Englishman with a farmhouse at Putchuteguia in the hills outside St Jean. White was at lunch there on 12 August and met a Spaniard, José Mamblas, who mentioned that night in his diary 'a Mr White, a young English writer who is correcting proofs in a quiet spot in Ciboure'.[6] In the next few days Mamblas became the lover of this 'big young man scarcely twenty-six years old, very tall, with a severe face whose expression was rigid to the point of being harsh, and with extremely penetrating eyes'.[7] Mamblas soon corrected his mistake about White's nationality and detected the 'colonial' pungency of Walt Whitman in the young man's poetry. Two stiff, Audenesque love poems reached the Spaniard a fortnight after they met.

> Those who have discarded truth for the lie of living
> who smile at the poor chipped torso in the attic ruin,
> and patronise argument at 2 a.m.,
> shudder still at its glance, the mirror-face,
> probing beyond the flesh to a hardened core,
> because they are afraid of the articulate
> mouth that condemns and offers judgment,
> because they no longer respect the simplicity of things,
> that the hand renders by touch, the beautiful
> lingering line that encircles peace.
> Love alone will accept the immaculate
> questioning of truth, will not reject
> the embrace without shame of the almost-forgotten,
> will lie in the nakedness of trust without
> regret for the moment of breath on breath.
> This I salute, the interpreter of truth,
> and one who has touched my body with his hands.[8]

They spent a month together and had a last lunch at the Hostellerie on 13 September before White returned to London. Mamblas wrote in his diary, 'This young man is intelligent, learned, with a head full of ideas which he explains very clearly and with elegance; but he is too sentimental, to the point where his super-acute sensitivity worries me. Could it be that Australians are like this? He comes from Australia. As he says, "a country of frustrations". Patrick is a young man who has to be treated with finesse because his nature always drives him to great heights or extremes. Today, when I said goodbye to him, I realised all this and the depths I have stirred in his affectionate nature without having understood or wished it.' A fortnight later he followed White to London.

Mamblas was a Francoist, an aristocrat and a Jew. His parents, friends of the King and Queen of Spain, had sent him to school in England, and he returned home to be a chamberlain to Alfonso XIII before pursuing a career in the diplomatic service. José Ruiz de Arana y Bauer, Viscount Mamblas, spent the 1920s in London, where he was remembered as a small man with perfect manners and exquisite clothes who gave beautiful dinners and was devoted to the Ballet Russe. He had a passion for aristocratic French novelists and was one of the circle of Princesse Edmond de Polignac. When he met the young Patrick White, he was forty-four and living in exile in France with his parents the Duke and Duchess of Baena.

'I found myself in the *pays Basque* in 1937, a man much battered about by the terrible events affecting both my country and my person. I was in Biarritz, in a state of acute anxiety, but also on active service, trying as hard as I could to save some, comfort others, and especially and above all to serve my country: Spain.'[9] He had left the diplomatic service and was biding his time, making occasional forays into Fascist Spain, waiting for the triumph of Franco.

Mamblas undermined the vague political loyalties of the lover he found in St Jean. White understood, by now, what was happening in Germany and had resolved, despite his affection for the Oertels, not to travel there again. London theatre had given him a kind of political education: he was impressed by the plays of Auden and Isherwood, particularly *The Ascent of F6* which had opened earlier that year in London.[10] But now White found himself with a lover who followed Franco and 'the ranklings of guilt perhaps intensified my sexual passion'.[11]

Mamblas recorded with romantic pride the inroads he made into the 'sentimental' politics of this 'young liberal Australian on the Left . . . On my side, I held no prejudices about him, having myself received a British education, and being very familiar with the reactions that the struggle in Spain produced in northern, protestant and democratic countries . . . the question of being Fascist or anti-Fascist, Catholic or protestant and still less Jewish, has never existed between us . . . We were both profoundly humanist beings, sharing broad perspectives about happiness and the decency that life required of us.

'Day by day, in the mind of my young Australian friend, the tempest raging so close by completely changed its meaning. It didn't take long for Patrick White to take into consideration in the conflict the virility of a strong race unmarked by degeneration, the unbridled reactions of individualists, sometimes accompanied by a punitive instinct that went as far as being ferocious in its punishment, backed up by an uncompromising idealism; and with it all, a natural, human generosity without any corresponding sense of calculation, often bordering on irresponsibility.

He especially and profoundly admired the spirit of independence which is innate in the Spanish. For the Patrick White I knew was an absolute independent. Everything he would do, write or say, would be based on his attitude of personal and human independence. "These are people who live and die with courage – independently – and are therefore real human beings." That's how Patrick White judged the Spanish then.'[12]

In London Mamblas introduced his young lover to homosexual high society and over the next year White was to sleep with some of these men. They were all much older than himself. Malcolm Bullock had married the Earl of Derby's daughter who died in a hunting accident and left him to pursue an undistinguished parliamentary career and a passion for theatre, feline gossip and the company of young men. Bullock lived in a vast house in Lowndes Square, where White ate opulent dinners à deux while the Russian Empire chairs cut into his kidneys.[13] Bullock was the model for Gerald Blenkinsop in *The Living and the Dead*: a splendid man

> even before the hairbrush, the final stroke of brilliantine. His face, smooth, pale, turned to eye if possible its own profile, had the formalism of a nineteenth-century silhouette. Emphatically nineteenth century, said his friends. Which was as it ought to be. The implication aesthetic of course, unless it was remembered, and most had forgotten, that Gerald's grandfather made bricks. Married to the daughter of a peer, Gerald had liquidated Blenkinsop's Bricks.[14]

Mamblas recorded those London weeks in his diary. 1 October: 'After leaving the Queen of Spain's flat in Porchester Terrace I had lunch with Patrick White in his Ebury Street studio. He gave me a delicious meal cooked by himself: this contrast between the palace and "la bohème" is the most precious thing in the world.' 11 October: 'I went and fetched Patrick and together we went to Gregorio Prieto's studio where we met Nadal – we spent a long time there, the three Spaniards and the Australian boy looking at Prieto's drawings . . . Patrick and I came back late halting for a meal in Sloane Square. We spoke late that night. You can talk to Patrick! He has a broad literary knowledge; he has ideas and good taste. A day like today, dedicated to talented and original young people, is something that comforts me.' 15 October: 'I had dinner with Patrick at the Café Royal and then we went to the Old Vic to see a production of Shakespeare's *Measure for Measure*. Very well played. Coming back along Waterloo Bridge and the gloomy district on the other side of the river, Patrick and I were astonished by that sordid part of London which a river keeps apart from the other bank, well-lit, rich, elegant; this appeared to Patrick and myself as something like a challenge.' 17 October: 'I left Victoria Station early with Patrick, going to Mayfield where we are going to spend the day with George Plank . . . So we took, Patrick and I, one of these small old English trains into Sussex . . . It was a day of complete rest, walking across peaceful, wavy, water-coloured country. Patrick, George, Alice and I didn't stop talking about books, artists, and that picturesque old friend who was called Lady Sackville.'[15]

Plank was the only man of real interest White met at this time. He was a graphic artist from Pennsylvania who had arrived in England with a considerable reputation won by his covers for *Vogue* magazine. Plank was one of the great passions of Lady Sackville, who commissioned Lutyens to build a perfect cottage for him at Five Ashes in Sussex. This was Marvells, a cottage of 'unexpected toy grandeur'.[16] Plank lived here in somewhat contrived simplicity at the beck and call of his patroness until her death in 1936. He told extraordinary stories about this wayward, dazzling woman. She used to call him in the middle of the night to come down to her cliff house at Brighton, where she would rummage through the garbage bins looking for scraps of fillet to prove the maids were cheating her. Lady Sackville contributed this incident and something of her elderly glamour to the portrait of Elizabeth Hunter in *The Eye of the Storm*.[17]

Mamblas returned to France a few days after their Sussex idyll. 22 October: 'I found shelter at last at Patrick White's; he gave me a meal. I could finally rest by the fire-side in his bachelor's establishment in Ebury Street and there, in slippers (my shoes are very wet) I was able to speak about Gertrude Stein, Picasso, Cambridge . . . I remember Patrick's words tonight: "You don't let the grass grow under your feet, do you?" I think he is right.' When White said goodbye to Mamblas next day at Victoria Station, he gave his lover a copy of *The Autobiography of Alice B. Toklas* to read on the return journey to Paris. 'For the only time in my life,' White later reflected, 'I felt like a mistress.'[18]

It seemed in those weeks that White's career in the theatre was at last getting somewhere. About the time of his return from St Jean-de-Luz, two of his skits including *Peter Plover's Party* were performed by Edward Cooper in the Arts Theatre Club revue *Copyright Reserved*. 'He beautifully satirises all the blither and blah of the district where Chelsea marches with Mayfair,' reported the *Sketch*. 'This is a real gem, and I hope it will be permitted to shine in some revue with a chance of a larger and more public life.'[19] Ronald Waters also performed *Party* about this time at a charity gala in a London hotel at which he appeared with Ellen Pollock.

White had been asked by Margaret Rutherford, an Ebury Street neighbour, to write some dialogue for the revue *It's in the Bag* which was

already in rehearsal at the Savile. Rutherford as Miss Penelope Prothero
weaved her way around a series of revue skits; she spun a lasso; there
was a murder; she was carried about screaming in a strait-jacket; later
she accepted a proposal of marriage.[20] White experienced for the first
time in those weeks the intoxicating dreariness of rehearsals: rats in the
stalls, the producer's mistress struggling endlessly with her one line,
the cast sitting about with colds. 'Dreariness, dreariness.' He watched
Rutherford performing the inexplicable, unconscious 'conjuring tricks'
of a genius. 'I can remember Margaret Rutherford changing shape in
the wings at the Savile during a rehearsal for that peculiar revue, when
she told me to go away and that she was so frightened: it was almost
as though I'd caught her naked or having a shit.'[21]

It's in the Bag had a try-out season at the Palace in Manchester,
but it is not clear how much of White's work survived when it opened
there with an 'International Cast of 60' on 12 October 1937. White had
no credit on the programme, but Waters believes some Patrick White
lines were still there, including the part of the stage manager written
especially for him. White did not go up for the opening. The *Manchester
Guardian* next day recommended further cuts: 'if it were not for the
ever-amusing Miss Margaret Rutherford one would feel those scenes
could be cut altogether'.[22] And they were before the show opened in
London at the Savoy. Rutherford and Waters were dropped from the
cast. The experience, recalled White, was 'trying for poor Margaret'.[23]

White tried to put the new access he enjoyed to London society to
the purpose of finding a publisher for *Happy Valley*. Since his return
from St Jean with the finished manuscript – dedicated to Roy de Maistre
– the book had been turned down by most of the big publishing houses
in London. White had found an agent, John Green at Curtis Brown,
but he had been unenthusiastic from the start, 'more insulting about
that book – before it was published – than anyone has ever been
about any of my work. After telling me the book could easily be cut
by half, that it was quite lacking in tension, humour, and practically
any literary justification or merit, he picked on the race week ball and
said: that should have been a high spot, but it means nothing. I could
write a chapter on that apart, but I'll leave him with the prize remark
he once aimed at me: People are writing in short sentences now.'[24]

After a lunch at the Reform Club, Dennis Cohen asked to see
the manuscript but the Cresset Press then turned it down. The great
John Macmurray – 'like D.H. Lawrence but very grey and calm'[25] –
assured him over lunch that Geoffrey Faber himself would read *Happy
Valley* which White considered a 'very satisfactory' arrangement.[26] But
Faber & Faber also turned it down. He wrote to Mamblas that he felt
he was going about the business of becoming a Literary Success all the
wrong way: 'In the first place, I don't take nearly enough people out

to lunch. That seems essential, and the more expensive the lunch the
more satisfactory the results.'[27] Good wine was rare. Good food was,
as Mamblas had warned him, too quickly whisked from English tables.
He encountered a race of middle-aged men who gave the impression of
'drifting from lunch to tea party – it always staggers me a bit, how they
manage to stay the course, and with such very little real ballast'.[28]

He took Spanish lessons and was able to read a little Spanish.
White's letters to Biarritz expressed sympathy for Franco's progress
in Spain, concern for his lover's stomach and 'a lot of pleasure' in the
possibility that Mamblas might become an official Fascist representative
in London. He sent sharp sketches of figures encountered on expeditions
into society: 'But you must forgive me, my dear, one of my greatest
faults is the tendency to caricature.' He met Sybil Thorndike and Lewis
Casson for the first time: 'I have never met an actress who acted so hard
off the stage, and yet with it all, a lot of sincerity – that was what I
could not understand – the queer mixture of sincerity and technique.
The conversation was mostly political. They are very ardently Left.
Sybil works herself into a frenzy which one suspects may develop into
an epileptic fit. She sits on the edge of her chair, trying to bring out
words which refuse to come, and clutching at the air as a substitute.
The uncomfortable part was that I found myself also straining to sit
on the edge of my chair and could almost feel my face growing into
the shape of hers. Lewis Casson sat there like a block of granite against
which, occasionally, she cannoned, to quiver off again. By the end of
the evening I was in a state of complete awe and exhaustion.'[29]

On 1 December, in the midst of this amusing and unproductive
round, White had a telegram from his mother to say that Dick
had died at Lulworth. Asthma had weakened his heart. He was
seventy. The news left White in turmoil. 'Even though he has had
a lot of illness lately one was not quite prepared for it. And since
that I have been trying to re-adjust myself to this new situation
and am feeling very tired and restless. I find I have the greatest
difficulty in making myself sit down in one place for more than
half-an-hour on end, which is an unusual state of affairs for me. I
think it would be much easier if I could feel what I ought to, and
what other people are expecting me to feel . . . now more than ever I
realise what little connection there always was between my father and
me.'[30]

Obituaries in the Sydney papers celebrated Dick's horses rather
than his life. Victor Martindale White of Belltrees and Lulworth,
was remembered for Vaccine, Charge, Golden Slipper, Early Bird,
The Brush, Spreadeagle and High, 'credited with having won more
races at Randwick than any other horse at present in training'.[31] After
a funeral service at St John's Darlinghurst, Dick was cremated in the

Spanish gardens of the Northern Suburbs Crematorium, then and now the point of last departure for the better families of Sydney.

Dick's will set generous bounds on his son's life for the next twenty-five years. Patrick White never had to undertake the literary chores that dominate the lives of most writers. He never reviewed a book and wrote no more than two or three pieces of journalism in his entire career. Nearly twenty years passed before a novel brought him any substantial income, yet he was free all that time to pursue his own style, sustained by dividends not the public. 'How disgusting all this money for writing sounds!' he said many years later. 'I have never written with that in view.'[32] Yet he was not rich as his parents had been. The great flood of White money that flowed through New South Wales reached him at the end of 1937 as a modest but sustaining stream.

Dick's estate was valued for probate at a shade less than £300,000. His son received £10,000 and the rest – apart from a few small bequests to Lizzie Clark, Charles Ebsworth and the trainer Harry England – was left for Ruth to enjoy for life unless she remarried. Only at her death would Patrick and Suzanne come into their inheritance.[33] Dick had also put money into a family company in order to avoid death duties. White enjoyed some income from this but, again, had no access to capital until his mother died. She was nearly sixty at Dick's death. White feared Ruth would now summon him to Australia. 'I do feel that to leave this side of the world just as I am getting my toe inside the door, would be to throw up all the progress made in the last two years.'[34]

Dick had died as his son was on the brink of his first public success. Herbert Farjeon, critic and producer of chic revue, had seen *Peter Plover's Party* at the Arts Theatre Club, and bought it for a West End show opening in early 1938. White sent Waters up to audition at Farjeon's house in Hampstead. Farjeon 'fell about all over the parquet laughing' and hired Waters for the cast, but when *Nine Sharp* opened at the Little Theatre in late January 1938 the Australian actor Cyril Ritchard played Peter Plover.[35]

'It was one of the most exciting evenings I have spent,' White reported to Mamblas. 'A couple of nights before I had been to the dress rehearsal at which most things that could go wrong, did. My sketch was done so shockingly that I almost sank under the seat with shame and the thought of having to face it with an audience was almost too much. I spent a miserable couple of days, not helped at all by my developing a violent cold. On the night I arrived at the theatre with my nose hanging on by a couple of shreds of red flesh and feeling as if I had dressed for a wake. But the moment I entered the theatre I knew this was going to be an evening, and it was – everything went with a swing – it is the most elegant revue I have seen, and I am sure it will be the talk of the town.'[36]

The show was an immense success and ran for a year, making Cyril Ritchard's reputation, and establishing Hermione Baddeley as 'queen of revue on the London stage'. White knew that to have one sketch in *Nine Sharp* did not mean he had arrived, but he was 'a little further on the way'.[37]

In Australia Ruth cranked the publicity mills for the last time on her son's behalf and under the weight of her persuasion the press got the impression that Patrick White had a big hand in the show's success. The fashionable magazine *Home* carried a studio portrait of the young man, his chin resting on his knuckles and his hair polished. He was credited with composing 'many of the sketches for the successful London revue'.[38] The *Sydney Morning Herald* reported that his success had 'elated the members of Bryants' Playhouse for it was in that snug little crypt in Darlinghurst that Mr White's first play *Bread and Butter Women* was first produced by Miss Beryl Bryant, and gave such promise of better things to follow'.[39] This was Ruth's last service for her son's career in Australia.

She was now free to leave for Britain. But for Dick's racehorses and his obstinate, gentle attachment to his native country, Ruth might have transplanted the family to London years before. Now she quickly set about preparations for departure. She sold Lulworth cheaply to the hospital next door on condition that it become a maternity wing. She gave Withycombe to the Church of England for ten shillings to be a mountain holiday house for poor clergymen. Patrick was furious: it was the one place in Australia he dreamed of returning to one day. By some foul up, the house was put in the name of the Archbishop of Sydney, Howard Mowll, who treated Withycombe – and later sold it – as his own. Ruth bought a cottage for her gardener near Rushcutters Bay Park on condition that he look after her terriers Binky and Barry until their deaths.

Foreign travel was just the thing Sue White needed, remarked one of the Sydney gossip columns. 'Though she has everything in her favour, she always gives the impression that she is content to sit back and play second fiddle to her brilliant mother. Mrs W. is, of course, the perfect example of the soignée matron, and no matter the occasion is never to be seen with so much as a hair out of place.'[40] With Suzanne, and the faithful major-domo Mabel in tow, Ruth left for Europe.

Roy de Maistre's patrons Sydney and Rab Butler had bought him the lease of a building round the corner from his little place in Ebury Street. At 13 Eccleston Street de Maistre set up a studio at the back of the ground floor in a long room which had once been a restaurant.

Here the painter achieved a kind of threadbare opulence with a few chairs and tables, old porcelain, signed vice-regal photographs, and his unsold paintings stacked around the walls. He was earning only a little income with flower paintings and portraits.

He offered White the two top floors of the building as a flat. 'I shudder in the middle of the night when I think of the money I shall have to spend,' White told Mamblas. 'But *tant pis*, it is going to look nice even if it takes me into the bankruptcy court.'[41] After battling tradesmen for a few weeks, White moved into Eccleston Street in early February 1938. The flat was still unfinished. On the first floor was his dining room, with a little kitchen and bathroom tucked into the back. Up a tight stair were two attic rooms: at the back a bedroom and at the front a studio, 'which I shall use as my work room and informal sitting room'.[42] Here he installed a brown-pink carpet, yellow curtains and a little coal-burning stove. The narrow bookshelves were filled with chaste lines of Gallimard editions and there was a chrome trumpet for a light. He had no radio. A journalist who saw the finished 'bachelor flat' reported that as a lover of music Mr White 'is not of the type that submits to forcible feeding by the BBC'.[43]

He shed his antiques. Betty Withycombe was given his French bed. The furniture for Eccleston Street was to be up to the minute. 'All this modern stuff one sees in the shops is so frightfully expensive,' he complained to Mamblas. 'But I think I may be solving that problem by having it designed by a painter I know called Francis Bacon, and made up bit by bit as my pocket allows in some workshop.'[44] Bacon designed him a magnificent desk with wide, shallow drawers and a red linoleum top. The Butlers had grown rather grand for modern furniture – Rab was about to be made Under-Secretary of State for Foreign Affairs – and White bought from them a glass and steel dining table and set of stools all designed by Bacon. In the course of setting up the flat at 13 Eccleston Street, White and Bacon became friends. He had 'a beautiful pansy-shaped face and rather too much lipstick. He lived in a house at the Chelsea end of Ebury Street, not far from the Mozart house, with an old Nanny who used to shoplift when they were hard up.' He was painting false teeth obsessively, but destroying almost every canvas. 'I can remember him going into a trance over lines scribbled on a hoarding – he was overcome with admiration for the perfection of these random arabesques.'[45]

On the walls White hung only the most severe works by de Maistre, the core of what became a large collection of his paintings. Over the dining-room fireplace hung 'On the Deck' painted from a newspaper photograph of Mrs Wallis Simpson and her lover cruising the Mediterranean. The odd passion of de Maistre and Bacon for newspaper photographs was one that White came to share. Each collected them; the painters took them as starting points for abstract exercises; the writer invented lives for these figures exposed so incongruously to public scrutiny.[46]

From the Imhof-Maranta house White recruited Hilda Richardson to look after him. Once more he was in the care of a devoted servant, though he enjoyed pottering about the flat and cooking little lunches for himself. 'There always seems to be plenty of domestic detail to attend to, or else I go out and look round the shops without finding what I am looking for. I suppose really I have the soul of a Hausfrau.'[47]

Thirteen Eccleston Street became another of the landscapes of White's imagination. At the front was an antique shop run by a crazed and boring White Russian who was once an admiral in the Czarist navy. He was now, unknown to himself, waiting for his greatest engagement, as General Sokolnikov in the *jardin exotique* of the Hôtel du Midi.[48] Below White on the first floor lived two Austrian refugees who made lampshades. Something of this situation emerged in *The Living and the Dead* where Mrs Standish's elegant but old-fashioned quarters were a floor above the milliner Mme Adorée, 'sleek and raucous with a goitre' in whose workshop of young women Willy Standish committed the final indiscretions of his married life.[49] The Austrians were Jewish, and White was irritated by their wheedling manner. The horror of the pogroms in Europe had not yet shaken his complacency. 'We still flickered with irritation meeting refugees on the landing; our buried anti-semitism flared over some drama of the dust-bins.'[50]

Once he was settled at 13 Eccleston Street he began work on a new book. 'Nightside' was a short 'novel of layers'. The central figure was a dancer from the Sydney Harbour suburb of Mosman. She was Lily in Australia, and Lys in Paris, where she was murdered by a perverse German. 'Nightside' was set mainly in France and all in the present day.[51] Lily/Lys was White himself in the guise of a dancer. On the stage of his red-topped desk Patrick White could play at being a dancer, psychopath, painter, servant, nun, explorer, grazier, whore and *soignée* woman of society. His characters took possession of him. 'I have not much say in the matter,' he told Mamblas, 'but get down and do the work.'[52]

By early March he was able to report, 'It is shaping nicely, and at the moment I am back at St Jean-de-Luz, drawing not on my own experience there, though I am trying to suggest some of the atmosphere. You will be able to give me some help with one point. In which month did they burn Irun? *Do please remember to tell me this when you write.* Because I don't want to make too many chronological mistakes.'[53]

Eccleston Street saw White's dandy phase. He ordered stiff writing paper, Jermyn Street shirts, fine suits and a cloak which he wore to the theatre with a gardenia pinned to his collar. To miss an opening night was death. He saw an immense amount of theatre in these years and remembered every detail of the performances. He was in some demand. The producer of a radio revue requested material, but White put him off to get on with 'Nightside'. 'People who took no notice before are beginning to consider me, a state of affairs which makes me see how difficult it would be to recognise genuine friendship if one achieved success.'[54] But neither his new connections in society, the modest fame brought by *Nine Sharp*, nor all his lobbying had found a publisher for *Happy Valley*. The book had been rejected by eight London firms.[55] But once he was settled in Eccleston Street, and with the help of a Hunter Valley connection, he finally found a publisher.

He had written a poem after dreaming one night that he was sitting in the hall of a house eating peaches. Aware that there was an angry mob outside, frightened by faces peering through the fanlight, the dreamer and a shadowy companion crept upstairs to hide in an attic. But death had already entered the house,

> At night I walk through the passages and expect to
> encounter death,
> A sudden cold clapping of the hand to mouth, taken not
> altogether by surprise,
> because I am still afraid to admit that this is not what
> I know:
> the way his body clattered on the market stones, the
> bowels hot,
> and that particular stink of blood from bones that were
> once a hand.[56]

The dream remained so vividly in his mind that he wrote it out in a single draft when he woke. He called the poem 'The House Behind the Barricades' and sent it off to Geoffrey Grigson's *New Verse*. Grigson's magazine was the most important outlet for poetry in England, though it never sold more than a thousand copies an issue. It was modern, tart, fresh, combative. Auden published in *New Verse*; so did MacNeice, Cecil Day Lewis, Edwin Muir, Dylan Thomas, Stephen Spender, Pound and, of course, Grigson himself. When 'The House Behind the Barricades' was accepted, White sent Grigson the manuscript of *Happy Valley*.

Grigson was, in a sense, family. His first cousin Robert had gone out to Australia and set up a practice in Muswellbrook, where he married Dick White's only sister Mary. They had a nephew called Patrick which greatly angered Ruth. The Robert Grigsons retired to Sydney and in Patrick White's childhood they were a grim presence in a flat at The Albany in Macquarie Street. Aunt Mary Grigson – she was Patrick White's only real aunt – was a frail asthmatic who fed her nephew forbidden sweets. The Grigsons seemed to do nothing but play patience. Both died when the boy was about ten. Geoffrey Grigson was fascinated by family matters of this kind and knew of the Hunter Valley connection to this unknown writer. Whether it clouded his judgment in the selection of 'The House Behind the Barricades' can never now be known, but the poem was only a forerunner to the novel.

At this time Grigson was earning a little money as a reader for the publishers George G. Harrap & Co Ltd, which pursued a humdrum trade in textbooks and light fiction. Grigson was trying to convert the Harraps to the idea of publishing some 'good books which would bring lustre to the firm'.[57] When he read *Happy Valley* he persuaded this most unlikely publisher to accept the novel. It was to appear in their '8/6 Fiction Series' early the following year, 1939.

White's interest in the Spanish Civil War was personal and perverse: for the sake of his affair he wanted it over. 'I fear *we* only begin where you are leaving off.' He urged Mamblas to take care of himself on his sorties into Spain. In the winter of 1937–8 Mamblas was plunging into the war every few weeks then returning to the calm of Biarritz. White did protest mildly over the bombing of Spanish cities. 'It ain't amusing,' Mamblas conceded. 'But on the other hand you know (because I have mentioned it to you) how intense life has become at the present moment for us all . . . everything is fundamental, pregnant with consequences for the future.' Franco's push into Catalonia drew a sharper protest from White. 'I must say the bombardment of Barcelona was a horrible business, Pepe. I can't see that any end can justify such a means. For the first time in the whole war I think I have been really conscious of what it signifies – I suppose really the events of the last few weeks have brought us much closer to it – one sees what may be in store for all of us.'[58] That week Hitler had marched into Austria.

White barely grasped the politics of Fascism and blamed the Civil War on the vileness of the human race. 'I have no head for international, or indeed any variety of politics,' he remarked lamely to Mamblas. 'One is either born with it or one isn't.' He simply wished the fighting to end, and sided against the Left. His support for Chamberlain's side of politics was instinctive, though he had little admiration for the figure cut by the Prime Minister. After sitting near him one night at a concert White reflected that Chamberlain seemed a 'dreary looking old nonconformist parrot'.[59]

The House of Commons lay only a few minutes' walk from Eccleston Street, and White was in the crowd that stood in Parliament Square the day Sir Anthony Eden resigned over Chamberlain's policy of appeasing Mussolini in Africa. 'There were as many people outside the House as for a royal wedding, or perhaps one should say a royal funeral,' he reported to Biarritz, observing that Eden had lost his nerve. A week later crowds marched down Regent Street shouting 'Chamberlain Must Go', but White thought the demonstration 'just an excuse for spending the evening en masse'. He worked his way to the front of the great anti-Fascist rally in Trafalgar Square organised by the publisher Victor Gollancz 'and his satellites'. Twenty yards from the plinth White could catch only about one word in twenty, 'so that of all those hundreds of people standing there no more than 5% can have caught anything intelligible. All the same the passive enjoyment of the crowd was immense and no doubt it went home feeling that it had taken part in something momentous.'[60]

White's response was not shared by his English family. Joyce Withycombe and her husband Richard Ward were pacifists and pillars of the Peace Pledge Union. Peggy was a Marxist and her husband Tom Garland had joined the Communist Party in 1937. They sheltered Communist refugees from Germany in their house in Hampstead. Auden remained their friend, and it was to Tom Garland that he turned for a supply of morphia and a warm coat before going off to Spain.[61] Garland was then the medical officer at the Carrera cigarette factory in Mornington Crescent. On one occasion he took White on his rounds, and the young man caught sight of real poverty for the first time in his life, in an 'earthly hell in the rotten tenements where most of his patients no more than existed in small overcrowded rooms smelling of poverty, sickness, and sewage'. He was not converted. 'I was too well entrenched behind my own egotism and my father's allowance to embrace Communism in any guise.'[62]

Betty, the third of the Withycombe sisters, had responded to the rise of Fascism by joining the Labour Party in Oxford. Deeply troubled by the course of events on the continent, she began to question her atheist certainties. White was to go up to Oxford to see her a day or so after the Gollancz rally, and admitted to Mamblas that he was not altogether looking forward to the visit, 'For I feel that I shall have a week-end of my cousin Betty in one of her Brontë-esque moods. Not that I am not very fond of her. But she is inclined to take up that "myself-at-war-with-the-universe" attitude and to think that no one else can ever be afflicted in the same way. In the long run it is very trying.'[63] The following year she was to be baptised and confirmed. She took this sudden plunge into faith without warning her family, and when she told White she had become a Christian he was taken aback and made no reply.

A few weeks after the bombing of Barcelona he returned to Leng's house outside St Jean-de-Luz and saw Mamblas for the first time in five months. 'I found him', Mamblas noted in his diary, 'with that "sooty" look that all those who come direct from London have, and find themselves all of a sudden in a bright and sunny atmosphere! the appearance of having popped out of a chimney.' To White's distress, he realized the Spaniard considered their affair finished. Mamblas wanted only friendship. 'There must have been someone else.'[64] White paid a last sentimental visit to Biarritz and as he approached Mamblas' hotel he saw the diplomat walk out on to a balcony, catch sight of him and dart behind the shutters. White was stung by this gesture of rejection.

Mamblas left for another of his expeditions into Spain which was now effectively in Franco's hands. White left the coast to pay a brief visit to the Haute Savoie for he had the idea of writing a novel about Roy's supposed ancestors Xavier and Joseph de Maistre. He put up at Chambéry, got soaked to the skin on Lamartine's 'lac' and had a thoroughly miserable time. He discovered, however, a good local wine. Nothing came of the de Maistre project.[65]

He returned to Eccleston Street: to his new novel, to scripts commissioned and rejected by the revue star Beatrice Lillie, and to write *Return to Abyssinia*, which was White's only play to reach the London stage.[66] He began work on this '*éducation sentimentale*' as he came to his political senses in the aftermath of his affair with Mamblas. In the summer of 1938 White began drifting back to the 'right' side. Mamblas appears in the play as a refugee Spanish marquis, the lover of an aged French actress Beauval in St Jean-de-Luz at the time of the Spanish Civil War.[67] When the actor-manager John Wyse read White's script he found it had 'great charm, was very flippant, a pastiche, well constructed, all about nothing at all.' He wanted to mount a West End production, but first he had to find an actress of a certain age and presence to play Beauval. White had modelled her on the ancient French comedienne Cécile Sorel, who had recently abandoned the Comédie-Française for a triumphant late career in music hall. Wyse needed someone who could snatch up a candlestick 'for no particular reason' and recite slabs of Racine.[68]

All that survives of *Return to Abyssinia* is a synopsis of the plot. 'The story concerns Mr Morland, a gentle Englishman living in the South of France, with a young and ingenuous daughter. Lucy Morland is a pretty thing, and possesses all the enthusiasms and ideals of youth. She cannot understand her father's complete indifference to the nearby rumblings of the Spanish Civil War, in which she is, in the purely passive sense, a strong pro-Government partisan. She is apt, occasionally, in a nice daughterly way, to reprove her father for his regrettable indifference, but these little scenes sound the only discordant note in the peaceful Morland household until two visitors arrive.

'Beauval, a beautiful actress from the Comédie Française, has a motor accident below the Morlands' terrace, and is brought limping into the villa. Mr Morland, all chivalry, invites her to stay until she recovers; she stays quite a while. Then Manuel arrives, a pro-Franco Spanish aristocrat of doubtful means and reputation. Manuel contrives, with remarkable ease, to make Lucy forget her political convictions, and it is left to the experienced and understanding Beauval to prevent a young heart breaking.'[69]

The title was taken from the last words of Samuel Johnson's *Rasselas*. White had only recently read Johnson's moral fable about the prince of Abyssinia who escapes the 'happy valley' of his birth to explore the known world. He ploughed through the prose rather grimly but seized on Johnson's native and sceptical conclusion with enthusiasm. The prince, having discussed with philosophers and rulers all known ways of life and systems of belief, concludes that none suits him so well as those he was born to, and he resolves 'to return to Abyssinia'.[70]

The affair with Mamblas, his toying with the Fascist cause and the discovery of *Rasselas*, crystallised one of Patrick White's key beliefs. 'What a pity that is such a boring book,' he remarked twenty-five years later to Geoffrey Dutton. 'Otherwise the truth of it strikes me over and over again as I come and go.'[71] In 1938 he read *Rasselas* as a fable about belief not geography: not that he had to head home, but that he must be what he was, not toy with enthusiasms that were foreign to himself. This was the theme of *Return to Abyssinia*.

In the summer of Munich White drew back from the sympathies Mamblas had encouraged, but he did not go on to join his cousins in the anti-Fascist cause. He kept his faith in appeasement and hoped to the very end that peace was possible. He was, in this, a true member of his generation.

He was beginning to tire of London. Ruth and his sister arrived from New York and he spent most of August in their company. The White world was closing in on him. The two women sat for Roy. Sue bored him, but Ruth drew a sharp response. He painted her as if lit by footlights, and her pink, waxy skin has the sheen of stage paint. This might be the face of a great actress, perhaps one of those imperious Sydney women who had retired from the stage to make a rich marriage. Under a hat like a tropical flower, she glances from the canvas with a look of acid regret. At her throat is a tangle of *vieux rose* silk and, on the lobe of each ear, a diamond. Ruth was pleased.[72]

Dinners and brief encounters with high society homosexuals were beginning to pall on White. There was something hardly alive about these occasions: wonderful food, a Poussin on the wall, footmen, cigar smoke and 'the tangle of remarks that strayed without point or purpose, except when camouflaged with claret'.[73] Roy stuck to his strange rules about who could and could not be introduced to the writer in the attic. White was searching for a man, someone to make sense of his life if only by saving him from his own loneliness. His parents' long and uneventful marriage had often seemed ridiculous but now he suspected something like that was what he wanted for himself. He wasn't going to find it in Belgravia.

At weekends he escaped to Ronald Waters' cottage near Maidenhead. That was a prosperous summer for Waters, who was still playing in *Nine Sharp*. He had a little car and rented the 'marmalade cottage' at Maidenhead from Mrs Keiller of the jam. Up the lane lived Beatrice Lillie and, though she turned down White's revue scripts, the two became friends. With great discretion, White began an affair with Lillie's pianist, the gentle American bald-headed Sam Walsh, who became the saxophonist Wally Collins, an unlikely lover for the aged Mrs Standish in *The Living and the Dead*.

> Wally Collins was at home in crowds, the slick and gaudy places where you lived high, round about Leicester Square and Piccadilly, the Metropole at Brighton, Broadway and 52nd, or Atlantic City. He got around. Because Wally Collins was a rootless one, an amoeba in the big green pool. His grips were only half unpacked, the ties hanging out, and a crumpled shirt or two, the photo of a girl emerging from a cloud of tulle . . . it was all natural and above-board, like waking with a mouth that felt like sawdust, like taking a swig from the bottle of gin. The racket was O.K. while it lasted, the drink, and the saxophone, and the faces of girls, tongued and moistened by the neon signs.[74]

Sam Walsh sparked White's curiosity about America, so alive, so raucous and uninhibited compared with the pale life he was tiring of in London. When Mamblas reappeared in October they lunched together and spent an afternoon trailing through the antique shops along the King's Road. They shared a sense of the emptiness of London society. Mamblas recalled with approval White's refusal to go along with the 'calculating happiness' which the diplomat thought was the way of life of the English Establishment.[75]

'He often joined me over a meal in my London clubs: the Travellers', St James and the Garrick Club. During these little sessions of British gastronomy, he would remark as much as I would the reserved air of the head waiter, clearly a little offended by a strong Australian accent a bit like London cockney. All these little things made him a bit confrontational, and he didn't try to conceal a certain contempt with regard to the social structure which was snobbish and therefore stupid.'[76] One night the two men strolled away from another dinner at Malcolm Bullock's in Lowndes Square. A yellow fog hung over the streets. Both had found the occasion tedious:

> England is very puzzling to me, the Spaniard said. I go into the houses of the rich . . . I eat their food, I speak their language. It is like an unpleasant dream. The dream language, hinting at things. Sometimes I think, not hinting. It is an elaborate charade that meant something once, a long time ago. When the figures, the gestures were related to enthusiasms.

This was the speech Elyot Standish heard from the Spanish attaché after a dinner at the Blenkinsops'. The attaché offered Standish, as he offered White in much the same terms, 'the choice of the two ways, of the living and the dead'.[77]

Nine Sharp closed in January 1939 and a week later *Happy Valley* was published in a plain blue jacket with white lettering. The author was kept extremely busy preparing for the event. The publishers gave him 450 postcards to stamp, address and send out as circulars. 'My publicity man wanted me to receive twenty-five picked journalists the day before the book appeared, but I drew the line at that.'[78] Geoffrey Grigson had circulated proof copies of the book to writers and critics, and advertisements for *Happy Valley* carried praise from Graham Greene, Elizabeth Bowen and Herbert Read. 'Life itself, grim and realistic,' wrote Read. 'But raised to the tragic heights by a style of unusual beauty and by the knowledge that nobility lies the other side of suffering.'

These endorsements compelled the critics' attention, and the reviews that began to appear in the first week of February treated *Happy Valley*'s appearance as an event. It was Book of the Day, Book of the Week and one or two critics predicted Book of the Year for 1939. The general verdict was that *Happy Valley* was the most interesting first novel for a while and Patrick White was greeted as a new talent who had, in the words of Pamela Hansford Johnson, 'sprung into literature Minerva-wise, fully armed'.[79]

This praise came with one general reservation: there were too many obscure and mannered passages, too much Lawrence and Joyce in White's style. R read these remarks and remembered, ruefully, White's advice to him to read 'Lawrence and Joyce, Lawrence and Joyce'.[80] V. S. Pritchett's response to *Happy Valley* summed up the critical verdict: 'The people are commonplace enough, but one sees into their odd minds and longings, one tastes their food, smells their domesticity, is thrust into the intimacy of their love affairs and into their ephemeral life-camp upon this ancient and hostile country. Their talk especially is good. If Mr White is sometimes obscure, jumpy and allusive, hates too much and has not yet got *Ulysses* out of his system, these mannerisms are the surplus of a biting, adroit and sensual talent.'[81]

The first printing of 2,000 copies sold out in February and Harrap gave the next printing what White called a '*War and Peace* build-up' with quotes on the dust jacket from Greene, Bowen, Stephen Spender, Read and Pritchett.[82]

Happy Valley had 'a fair sale' in Australia, where booksellers had taken five hundred copies.[83] The women of Sydney society bought the novel to see what 'Ruthy's boy' was up to, and *Happy Valley* confirmed all they thought of him: very difficult. The Whites in their houses on the Hunter read a few pages and gave up. Most never tried his books again and never saw the debt Patrick owed his family and their acres in his work.

The Australian critics were under no obligation to like *Happy Valley*. Most did not. They chided White for having a distasteful style and condemned his book for being unfair to Australian country towns. On behalf of the people of the Monaro, an angry Australian wrote to *John O'London's Weekly* to correct Richard Church's glowing review: 'I know the village where the story is supposed to happen and I can assure Mr Church that the people there live very busy lives and are not of the type that Mr White writes about. Far too many English critics seem to have the idea that bush people are preoccupied with sex and with drinking and are generally a thoroughly depraved lot. Bushwacker Bill is apt to be coarse and inclined to drink too much, but he lives a very active life, puts up with a lot of hardship, and is usually a very fine sort.'[84]

Patrick White was dogged all his career by the demand that he put aside his private vision and write optimistically about decent Australians. The *Adelaide Mail* said of *Happy Valley*, 'Surely a little hope, a little looking towards the future, might be advisable.' Australia shared the notion that literature was meant to aid, not sap, the will and enthusiasm for building a new nation. Even after Fascism and Communism had discredited this civic notion in Europe, it survived at the other end of the world, shared by the Right and Left. Only the jargon differed: the Right called him gloomy and affected while for decades the Left charged him with lacking 'consciousness of the militant optimism characteristic of Australians . . . his fundamental delusion about the inherent evil of humanity cuts him off from the hearts of the people'.[85]

No British critic cared a fig for this, nor for the Australian critics' assumption that they knew the shape, the style, the cast and mood of the Great Australian Novel which had yet to be written. *Happy Valley* was not It. 'A pervading sense of the futility of life is all very well. That is a matter strictly between the writer and his conscience, and not the critic's affair,' conceded the Melbourne *Herald*. 'But the great Australian novel, in its final and ultimate justification, must . . . stand on higher ground.'[86]

A myth sprang up over the years that Australian critics were unanimously hostile to Patrick White's early novels. Even in some of the papers there were lone critics enthusiastic about *Happy Valley*, and one or two literary magazines, puny though they were, registered the appearance of a new and promising talent. Frank Wilmot, writing as 'Furnley Maurice' in *Bohemia*, parodied White's style wickedly to praise his novel,

> Troubled minds of characters splash about the streets. Few streets in Happy Valley. Real vivid streets, real, moving characters. Profound earnestness. If Mr. Patrick White looked into your mind and published what you thought of parts of his book he would have to prosecute himself for libel. Attraction and repulsion means movement anyhow. If he found what you thought of the book's good qualities he'd think you were shook on his sister.[87]

In Paris, where she had gone to supervise Suzanne's French lessons in preparation for their new European existence, Ruth subscribed to a clippings service and pasted into her scrapbook reviews of *Happy Valley* as they arrived from Britain, Australia, Canada, Egypt, Palestine and New Zealand. In Ireland *Happy Valley* was banned by the Office of Censorship for being 'in its general tendency' indecent. In Stockholm *Bonniers Litterära Magasin* included Patrick White in its survey of new writing from the West by Steinbeck, Faulkner, Eliot, Auden, Isherwood, and so on. White was praised for a first novel in which 'all life moves laboriously, as though in a heavy sleep'.[88] The critic Artur Lundkvist then forgot Patrick White for twenty-three years.

'I can feel doors begin to open,' White wrote to Mamblas. 'People who used to cut me in the street now stop and speak. I think, if anything, I have come out of it slightly more contemptuous of my fellow beings than I was before! When I think of all the times I have waited, offering no less than I have to offer now, having rude things said by publishers who now try to blame someone in their firm for turning my book down, all this depending on a handful of reviewers – well, it does leave a bitter taste in one's mouth.'[89]

He granted one interview to the Australian journalist Guy Innes, who found at Eccleston Street 'the kind of flat you would have yourself if you were a bachelor and were let alone to enjoy it. There is evidence of the operations of a conscientious and tidy housemaid, but she is not allowed to disturb anything that matters; and Mr White himself has an orderly mind (for a novelist) which must rob housekeeping of half its evil by removing all its ill-timed interferences. Beyond this, the influence of a woman's hand is not particularly notice-able.'

'Are you fully satisfied with *Happy Valley*?' Innes asked.

'No, not altogether. I have great difficulty connecting it with myself. It just happened. I do not think that you can regard these things as stepping-stones. You do your work, and it does something for you; but in itself it is quite distinct and apart.'

'Do you want to go back?' the old journalist asked. White protested that he had only just arrived. What might Patrick White achieve, Innes wrote, 'if he returned to Australia, and was stimulated by the flood of local colour . . . This consummation, however, is unlikely, for this author exemplifies Australia's tendency to export its talent, and once that talent departs, it seldom returns.' Innes's remarks lodged somewhere deep in him.

'Nightside' was finished, he told Innes, 'a novel within a novel the scene of which was laid in France and Germany'. He spoke of publishing a book about Stendhal; perhaps in fifteen years' time. But the next novel would deal with London of the present day.[90]

'Nightside' was never shown to a publisher. Ronald Waters read it and hated it. Betty Withycombe found it 'beastly . . . all about a psychopath. It was a horrid book, nasty.'[91] White decided, under her influence, to put the book aside. Of the four unpublished and now destroyed novels White wrote as a young man, 'Nightside' is the only one he occasionally, late in his life, regretted. Its abandonment left him impatient with the constraints of life in London, for he believed his friends' disapproval of 'Nightside' sprang in part from the book's association with his homosexual life.[92]

He decided to sublet the flat, go over to New York and find a publisher for *Happy Valley*, then travel around for a few months before settling down somewhere in the States to start the book about London. Sam Walsh would be at home in Maine in August, and they could spend some time together before White returned to London for rehearsals of *Return to Abyssinia*, which John Wyse planned to open in the West End in autumn 1939.

'Patrick White, whose name is on everybody's tongue, has gone to Paris to wish his mother, Mrs Victor White, and sister Susan farewell before he sets out for U.S.A. at the end of the month,' reported a Sydney paper in March 1939. 'With publishers pounding at him for another book and a feeling that first he must at least regain the tempo of life which suits him, he is going to get right off the beaten track in

U.S.A. He will go all over the States in a bus. You well know the kind. They were made famous by Clark Gable and Claudette Colbert in *It Happened One Night*.'[93]

TEN

Crossings

HE ARRIVED IN New York in April 1939 with a couple of copies of *Happy Valley* in his bag and a smart new studio photograph for the American dust jacket. He imagined a publisher would take the book 'five minutes after I landed'[1] and to achieve this he planned to assault Manhattan from two fronts: through the New York branch of his agents Curtis Brown, and through letters of introduction he collected before leaving London. White had adopted Roy de Maistre's habit of never travelling without them.

John Macmurray had urged White to see Auden in New York – Auden and Benjamin Britten had arrived in America a few weeks earlier – but he decided against: 'I don't know why a jug and basin should remind me of Auden, but they do . . . I admire some of his work very much. Some of it not so much. And I have always disliked him, from what I have seen of him, as a public figure. He seems to me to *try too hard*, which only accentuates that moon-calf look he has. But no doubt this is all stupid and unjust prejudice.'[2]

Publishers did not snap up the novel and after a few weeks White thought of retreating to London. In that mood he sent a card to the Austrian lampshade-makers at 13 Eccleston Street, who replied with encouragement and reproach through his servant Hilda Richardson: 'They say you must not go so quick give it a little more time and you must be more boisterous in America as you are on the shy side and you are so nice.'[3]

With nothing decided about *Happy Valley*, White set out to cross America, not by bus as the Sydney press reported but by train. 'I got to know it the railroad way.' He kept a journal of the trip, a record of impressions and judgments, which he hoped one day 'might be worked up into something'. He headed south to Charleston then down to New Orleans and on across Texas to the promised land of California. 'I remember the patient negro car attendants, conversations into the night with naive middle-aged, middle-class citizens . . . humility . . . in the soft voices, soft palms of the pullman-car attendants.'[4]

Los Angeles struck him as one of the 'three arseholes of the world' and he never after wavered from that verdict, but San Francisco became one of his favourite small cities: fascinating, beautiful and peaceful. He met a writer called John Holstius and liked the sound of his name, which he remembered later when he was writing *The Aunt's Story*. From San Francisco he went out to the redwood forests and found Yosemite National Park 'horrifyingly touristy . . . You were taken round and shown bears. Hostesses put you at tables with other people and expected you to be matey with them. After dark there was a firefall and then you went to your cabins. All night people tried to break in on the offchance.' The turning door knob on the locked door became a small motif of nightmares avoided. Alex Gray on her theatrical tour of outback Australia lay in an Ochtermochty pub watching the knob turn, and Eddie Twyborn on ship returning to Australia lay on his bunk while

> All night, it seemed, giggles and explosions, a traffic of clumsy, spongy feet filled the corridor. At intervals a handle was rattled, at others almost wrenched off.[5]

On his way back east, White left the train at Santa Fe to make a pilgrimage into the Sangre de Cristo mountains where Lawrence had tried to establish another literary utopia, this time in a climate kinder to TB. He arrived by bus in Taos at dawn.

> The town was pink, mostly, of baked mud, an earth pink. A bronze cock on a wall shook his feathers into shape . . . there was a guest house farther up that was fine, with individual cabins, where people went, and artists . . . and there was a canyon, and an Indian pueblo, and an Indian that was petrified from falling down a cliff and lying upside down in the right kind of water for many years.[6]

White took a room on the plaza. When it was discovered he was a writer, someone sent for Brett. The eccentric English painter Dorothy Brett and Lawrence's widow Frieda divided between them the task of keeping watch over Lawrence's ashes and fame. Brett arrived like a pear in a sombrero, holding in front of her a little box covered in turquoise and Mexican silver. The box was wired to her ear. Brett was deaf, rather dirty, a timid painter and as devoted to D. H. Lawrence in death as she had been in life. She took White to meet Frieda at Lawrence's cabin above Taos.

The road climbed above an immense and simple prospect cut across by the canyon of the Rio Grande. The air was pure, 'the emptiness of this landscape was a fullness, of pink earth, and chalk-blue for sky. And the rim of the world was white. It burned.'[7] The track reached a forest of stunted conifers with an undercover of dead grass, twigs and needles. As they climbed higher the trees grew taller. Animals moved in the undergrowth. They reached Lawrence's house set behind a wire fence and surrounded by barking dogs, and White found not the log cabin he expected but a cottage from the German mountains. Frieda gave him the key to Lawrence's shrine. She was a second swift surprise, not at all the turgid earth mother he imagined he would find guarding the shrine but a witty and amusing woman. He took the zigzag stone path that climbed up to the chapel with a phoenix perched on its gable. The pilgrim entered and paid his respects to Lawrence's ashes, mixed, to secure them against thieves, in a ton of concrete.

Brett's log cabin was five minutes down the trail Lorenzo had ridden every day to fetch letters and milk. She had had huge windows put in each wall of a plain log cabin and added an 'upper-storey studio built almost entirely of glass. The Tower Beyond Tragedy she called it.'[8] White made it into the Lantern House, the deserted cabin where Theodora Goodman found her reassuring ghost companion Holstius,

> a thin house, with elongated windows, like a lantern. The lower part was black slabs of logs with paler clay or adobe slapped into the interstices, but higher up the house became frailer frame, with the elongated windows . . . that had the blank look of deserted houses.[9]

White felt he could spend the rest of his life quite happily in that clean, dry mountain air living 'above the disintegrating world' in one of these plain cabins. He spent a memorable day with a family of farmers in

> a house that had been built purposely for living, the clutter of sheds, hutches, corral, cans, hessian tatters, and broken toys that such houses accumulate.

The hospitality of the Jacksons was simple. There was a son Zac, a dark, serene child with whom the visitor felt a brief, intuitive alliance. In time, White turned the Jacksons into the Johnsons, into whose lives the spinster Theodora Goodman wanders before climbing higher up the mountain to the Lantern House.[10]

White's companion in Taos was Walter Willard (Spud) Johnson, a wiry man of forty-five, cool and waspish, with a face that reminded White of an early Picasso.[11] Johnson had brought a little magazine called the *Laughing Horse* east from Berkeley fifteen years before and become an identity in the town, a friend of the painters and writers who arrived in Taos in the wake of the Lawrences. He published a little hand-set local newspaper called the *Horsefly*, wrote poetry and lived by literary odd jobs. Mabel Dodge Luhan, monster and patroness of New Mexican arts who married one of the Indians from the pueblo, employed Spud Johnson to type her manuscripts. In one of the last issues of the *Laughing Horse*, which appeared the summer before White was in Taos, Johnson published an old sketch by D. H. Lawrence set in the pretentious chaos of Mabel Dodge Luhan's kitchen. The cast of 'Altitude' includes Spud, Mabel and various house guests. The curtain rises on a woman chanting a loud 'Om'.

MARY. This country is waiting. It lies spell-bound, waiting. The great South-West, America of America. It is waiting . . . what for? What for?
(*Enter Spud, taking in the situation at a glance.*)
SPUD. Hello! Hasn't the cook come?
MARY. Good morning! No sign of her as yet . . . Isn't morning wonderful, here at this altitude, in the great South-West? Does it kindle no heroic response in you, young Intellectual?

Johnson makes the coffee while the women yabber on about the perfect rhythm of the American earth and the life pulse of the Indian. Mabel pauses to send Johnson out to get the poppies before the sun spoils them.

IDA. Spud's queer this morning.
CLARENCE. Spud always seems queer, to *me*.
MABEL. Spud *is* queer. – I wonder what it is; whether we can't fix it.
MRS SPRAGUE. He has such a swell disposition. I wonder what it can be?
CLARENCE. I don't know. Of course it mayn't *mean* anything, but I heard his door banging *all* night last night . . . (*etc*)[12]

White and Spud Johnson became lovers, but despite this turn of events White left Taos in late June after three exhilarating weeks. As usual in his life the schedule triumphed over happy accidents: *Happy Valley* had still to be dealt with in New York and he wanted to be well underway on the new book before Sam Walsh arrived in Maine. Time was running out. Waiting for the train in Santa Fe he watched the population 'trailing up the streets in a tipsy Corpus Christi procession' and then left for Chicago. The train seemed full of Elks from Oklahoma who yawned and passed remarks about Mr Roosevelt, the rainfall and Japan. The Kansas plains seemed to go on for ever.

> All through the middle of America there was a trumpeting of corn. Its full, yellow, tremendous notes pressed close to the swelling sky. There were whole acres of time in which the yellow corn blared as if for a judgment . . . [13]

'It is difficult', he wrote to Johnson on the train, 'not to be crude in words and say all the things I would like to say – to you and about you – but I think you have felt them as much as I have – so there is no need. The last few days have meant a great deal to me. I didn't realise how much till going away. *We've got to see each other some more* – I hope some day. I'm sure we shall. Because I know I don't discover such a perfect complement at the end of the earth for nothing, just to throw it away again. I hope you are going to feel the same. If you don't, you can blame the plains of Kansas . . .

'My pyjamas did arrive back from the laundry in the end, but almost unrecognisable. Like a piece of brown paper more than anything else, and cobbled up the back into the bargain. We had a last minute row over the telephone after which the laundry consented to pay 2 dollars 50.'[14]

He stopped at Kansas City, and again in Chicago, where he saw the slaughteryards and was sickened by the smell of blood: 'I went there because it *is* Chicago and I felt I ought to do it.' Arriving back in New York he found rejection slips from Harcourt Brace, and Farrar and Rinehart, 'with letters complimentary about the substance, but timid when it comes to publication'. After throwing himself into a round of Fourth of July parties, he collapsed in his room at the Hotel Sutton on East 56th Street, 'a cheap hotel, the sort of place where you went for a divorce, a screw and that sort of thing. And it was near Sutton Place, very up-market.'[15]

A letter arrived from Johnson when he was at a low ebb, and White, who had been nervous of the declaration he made the week before, wrote back: 'I did think perhaps after writing to you that I had said too much, about something you hadn't felt in the way I had, and that you might be surprised, or bored, or irritated. I find it's a rare enough experience for two people genuinely to react to each other. Then your letter came and I was glad I had my train-impulse! It put me right back into our meetings at Taos, which I think can speak for themselves.'[16]

His agent having had no luck with *Happy Valley*, White deployed the letters of introduction he brought across the Atlantic. One produced an invitation from Mrs Sage Holter to a weekend party at Mount Kisco, where she promised to pull two publishers out of her hat. White was sceptical of these conjuring tricks, but the woman seemed determined. He found a rich house, servants and swimming pools. 'On the Saturday night we went to a dance, which I hated, at another large white house, owned by one of the publishers. And of course I didn't have one word with the publisher. Finally, I got into a corner with a bottle of champagne and watched and listened to the gaggle of Long Island geese till I almost fell asleep. The next day there was another large party, a luncheon, at the house of the second publisher, with whom I had possibly seven words.'[17]

George Plank had given him a letter to Jean Starr Untermeyer, poetess, who hailed from Zanesville, Ohio, but now lived in New York, married, divorced, remarried and again divorced from the anthologist Louis Untermeyer. Ben Huebsch, a partner in the Viking Press and publisher to the American *avant-garde*, had issued her first book of poetry *Growing Pains* in 1918. She now said to White, 'Show me your book and if I like it I'll give it to Huebsch.' It had not occurred to White to aspire to the Viking Press which was then considered 'practically the best publisher in New York'.[18] He gave Starr Untermeyer a copy of the novel and she did as she had promised.

In the second week of July White left New York to find a quiet hotel on Cape Cod to start work on the new novel. The fate of *Happy Valley* was still undecided when he set out for Boston, where he took a literary bus tour to Lexington, Concord and the houses of Longfellow, Emerson and Louisa May Alcott. Boston was tediously English. 'I don't know why the Bostonians should be less attractive than other Americans,' he remarked to Johnson. 'Low-Church views perhaps. These are always inclined to breed physical ugliness.' Curiosity took him to the original Church of Christ Scientist, 'an excrescence in Bostonian romanesque, with St Peter's, Rome, growing miraculously out of one side. The interior smells predominantly of floor polish. Everything *very* clean. All the walls covered with texts from Mary Baker Eddy. I was shown round by two jaunty, uneasy women, whom I found increasingly sinister, like the whole atmosphere in fact.'[19]

He settled down in the quiet of Sandwich, a weatherboard village on the edge of the dunes and salt marshes of the Cape. Some corners of the Daniel Webster Inn survived from the 1690s; Webster himself and Thoreau were once guests; in the 1930s it was a plain summer hotel for the prosperous vacationer. Al and Molly Govoni offered good food, clean rooms and a Wurlitzer Multi-Selector in the bar where taciturn natives sat around playing cribbage. White had a large room with 'rather ramshackle, ugly, but personal furniture, and a closet with a jug and basin inside'.[20] As soon as he unpacked he began to write.

'It all suddenly came pouring out – a novel that has been fermenting for the last three years. So now I am going through all the misery and elation attached to the business . . . I realise now that one should never publish a novel until everything that has to be written is well out of the system. I am now as nervous as a cat about every word. So that I feel the result will be dead and self-conscious.'[21]

He began with huge ambitions. The chief character of the book was London itself and White imagined he was embarking on something to match the scale of Joyce's portrait of Dublin in *Ulysses*. The trouble was that White was more than ever out of love with London since finding himself in America. Here, especially in the West, he felt continually alive, 'and for the first time I felt I was communicating continuously with other people.' To imagine himself living in damp England again after experiencing the colour and energy of America, 'would be like living with one's senses damped down to half their capacity.'[22]

At the core of the book is the Standish family of Ebury Street. The story of Katherine Standish, née Kitty Goose, has many parallels with Ellen Withycombe's life, though White was not conscious of drawing on them as he wrote. Katherine Standish grows into a dowdy, energetic woman, intellectually alive while bursting at the seams. She was one of the few things about the book White eventually thought 'not badly done'.[23]

Her son Elyot, the literary biographer, drifts through the elegant world which Pepe Mamblas had taken White into after St Jean-de-Luz. Mamblas has a walk-on part in the novel as the unnamed Spanish attaché, and the title White chose was an echo of his lover's complaints one night about the charade of London society as they left one of Malcolm Bullock's opulent dinners at Lowndes Square. 'I am thinking of calling the novel *The Living and the Dead*,' White wrote to Mamblas. 'I'm more and more conscious . . . of people being divided into two categories – the people who are aware, and the people who are – well, just dead. That's something the political labellers will never take into account.'[24] The title is also a tribute to Joyce: White was always struck by last words and these are the last of Joyce's *Dubliners*,

he heard the snow falling faintly through the universe and faintly falling, like the descent of their last end, upon all the living and the dead.

White knew he was writing a big book, and as the weeks on the Cape went by he worried that its shape was getting out of control. 'I am working in fits and starts at what promises to be a *very* long novel. I keep discovering a fresh layer and that leads to something else, with the probable result that nobody will ever find the thread. But on the whole, I am enjoying the process. And I also find I have become more tolerant. Perhaps *America* has done that!'25

White wrote every morning in bed, which was 'very delightful, with the trees just outside the window. There is nothing like that particular kind of *golden* light that comes through lindens.' In the afternoons after his work was done, he would lie 'naked on the sand, in a line of dunes that remind me of the North coast of Norfolk. Or explore the lanes, which are full of blueberries and wood ticks and surprisingly green beetles.' After a time he felt he was no longer a tourist in this sedate village. Old ladies did not pause in their rocking chairs as he walked by. Sandwich was unconcerned with the outside world. White offered Molly Govoni his copy of the *New York Times* one morning, but she declined. 'No thank you, I don't know any people in New York.'26

His letters of introduction extended to one or two families on the Cape. 'I fell into a sophisticated party here in Sandwich, which was something of a surprise – background music, supper on the terrace, diplomats, Clifton Webb, and my hostess in a white satin dress waving a white ostrich feather fan. A hostess at a party should always carry an ostrich feather fan, I think. It provides just the right touch of light insincerity.

'The only other outstanding event of my week was a midnight swim in one of the many Cape lakes. A strange effect. One walked over white sand, through black pines, into the water, which ended in a white mist. Something of a Corot effect. But the scene was prevented from becoming too insubstantial by my companions – the carpenter, the policeman, the sanitary engineer, and the bartender from the inn. It was almost like playing all the scenes from *A Midsummer Night's Dream* at once. Afterwards everyone stood about on the sand, drinking neat whisky.'27

The bar of the Daniel Webster Inn was the marshalling point for the volunteer fire brigade. In the heat of mid-August, White went with them to a forest fire burning twelve miles out of Sandwich. 'Hanging on to the back of a big, clanging Ford fire engine as it goes fifty along a country road is quite a sensation. And then five exhausting hours at the fire, crawling through smoking undergrowth with a hose. I have just had a hot bath and a large meal, and am feeling aggressively healthy and extrovert – but ready enough to return tomorrow to my sedentary existence.'28

He travelled all over the Cape, along the sandy roads that wind through dunes and marshes towards villages marked by the spires of weatherboard St Martins-in-the-Fields. On Nantucket, 'lodged in the period of mahogany and bibles', he found beautiful houses with solid white porticoes, 'the best bits of domestic architecture I have seen in this country outside Charleston – but more solid and bourgeois than the South Carolina version. And the family names that you read on the door plates are in keeping with the houses – the Starbucks and Coffins that recur all through the town, and again in the whaling museum which has a lot of poetry in it.'[29]

Sandwich was celebrating its tercentenary that summer with fire-works, Puritans marching down the street, clambakes ('there is surely nothing more disgusting, more reminiscent of a bad drain than a baked clam') and a Grand Ball featuring a floor show from New York.[30] 'To-day it has rained, to make the place greyer than it would be ordinarily after the music. It is the sort of evening when the only thing to do is to shut oneself in with somebody one loves very much, and ignore it. But what am I to do in the circumstances?'[31]

White's letters were cautious at first, and in the early days on the Cape he asked Johnson to write to General Delivery, Sandwich, Mass. 'I think that would be safer than this address.'[32] But under the pressure of Johnson's declarations, he thawed. 'My dear Spud, I love you and I love you more tonight than I ever have, and I hope it goes on like that, getting more and more.'[33] A fortnight later he wrote, 'Whenever I have been in love before, it has always seemed so one-sided, even when I have known that a certain amount was being returned. I had begun to believe that it was inevitable for two people to speak in two different languages. And both of those pretty limited. Why are people so afraid of *saying things*? I suppose it's due principally to their unwillingness to commit themselves definitely – because it might suggest permanency. Then this happens, and it feels as if everything is happening for the first time. That is why *I* am so happy, my dear. Incidentally, people have also been telling me that I look well.'[34] Despite the great distance between them, White discovered, as Laura Trevelyan found when writing to Voss in the hinterland of Australia, that the man he loved was, in a sense, present: 'the last couple of weeks, even on the days when there haven't been letters, you have been extraordinarily close. I could almost put out a hand.'[35]

Though White regretted by this time leaving Taos so quickly, he did not rush back. A more fundamental purpose was forming in him: that he would return to live in America. 'There is still so much that we're going to be able to do together in the future. Frankly you're the only person I ever thought I might live with successfully. We might try – and I'd like to – if you're willing, to wait a little and take the risk. But I've got to get back to London in the fall, as I think my play is going to be done, and then I have to do something about my apartment, which I have on my hands till February. Is all this too rushed?

'If all goes well I could get out to Taos by March. It depends a little on my mother's plans. She will be going out to Australia about March or April, and I don't want her to feel I am washing my hands of her by rushing off before she leaves. But I want to be with you Spud. I've never been so certain of anything in my life.'[36]

This was August 1939 and all White's plans depended on peace. *The Living and the Dead* was conceived on a scale that presupposed years of quiet work, and *Return to Abyssinia* was to open in London in late autumn. The producer John Wyse had been over to Paris that summer to persuade the great actress Françoise Rosay to make her London debut playing the part of Beauval. White's agent reported in early August that Rosay liked the play and was rereading it before deciding whether to take the part. White wrote to Johnson, 'I might feel elated if I hadn't already had some experience of actresses' minds.'[37] There was a berth booked on a boat leaving New York on 20 September, which would land White in England in time for the start of rehearsals.

All that late summer in America White held firmly to the hope that war was impossible. No one would be mad enough, he felt, to start a war now. Even as the *New York Times* reported the Poles' determination to defend Danzig and the corridor, White wrote to Johnson, 'There's still some little nucleus of peace that's got to be made to spread.' His decent hopes grew stronger as August went by, but in a moment of pessimism White suggested a plan to Johnson: 'If I'm all wrong, and I have to go back suddenly, I shall have to see you, Spud, for a couple of days. If it happened, could you meet me at, say, Albuquerque? I could get there in a day by air, and it would be worth it if all this is going to happen.'[38]

August was nearly over when White heard that Sam Walsh was waiting in Maine. He made formal farewells, found space in his luggage for a fisherman's present of sea clams and scallop shells, and left Sandwich for Bridgton-on-the-Lakes. In this brief reprise of his affair with Walsh, swimming in the lakes and watching summer stock theatre, White's hopes rose once more. Hitler had signed the non-aggression pact with Stalin and made formal demands for Polish territory, but on 29 August White read in the *New York Times* that Britain was trying to force Poland to negotiate. He wrote to Taos, 'I have an idea there is not going to be a war. We have been waiting too long, and everyone is ready, and now I think there will be a more rational solution after a lot more talk. But I wanted to see you again, anyhow, before going back. A war was to have been only something of an excuse. So now – I hope – I shall be coming excuseless.'[39]

He wired Johnson to meet him at Albuquerque airport at 8.15am that Sunday. Johnson made several drafts of his reply. He rejected 'Yes

yes yes yes yes yes yes yes yes yes, Spud', and 'Of course certainly absolutely yes with Daimler and liveried chauffeur', also 'Yes, unless I fall down an elevator shaft or get run over by a subway.' He sent: 'Try to stop me.'[40]

But that Friday morning came the news that Germany had invaded Poland. White was still in Maine and spent part of the day watching *The Wizard of Oz* and reflecting on the fate of his literary hopes now 'carried away by the flood of history'. That Sunday morning he flew west, and his plane touched down in Albuquerque a couple of hours after Britain and France declared war. The two men had two days together in Albuquerque, then Johnson drove back to Taos and White caught the plane to New York. 'I'm so glad we did it,' he wrote. 'I don't mind now how soon I sail for England and whatever I shall have to do there.'[41]

The next few days in New York were all turmoil. He was restless and unable to settle down to anything. Cunard had cancelled all bookings and could not tell him when he might sail. Then Ruth cabled to say Suzanne had married. White was very upset at the news. He had met her husband Geoffrey Peck and could 'never find half a dozen words to say'. This was not the kind of match he had in mind for his sister. Peck was English but a New South Wales Osborne on his mother's side, and worked at the BBC broadcasting cricket and football matches. White wrote in a rage to Spud Johnson, 'This is another grudge I have against this damn war. I can see how this probably came about in a fit of heroics – the send-them-to-the-front-happy attitude which women always are inclined to adopt on the outbreak of war. But that is that and I can't alter it.'[42]

Men were no different. Waiting for a boat, killing time eating and drinking with friends, White met Joe Rankin from Georgia. Rankin was a handsome man of his own age, with ante-bellum manners and a Manhattan medical practice treating men with venereal disease. At their meeting White found all the certainties of the last summer overturned. He fell in love and once again thought he had found 'the other half of the permanent relationship' he was searching for.[43] But in letters to Taos White said nothing of this defection to Joe.

On 15 September he heard suddenly there was a berth for him on a ship leaving New York next day. He sent his American journal to Taos for safe keeping, and embarked on the *Vandyck*, which sailed to Halifax and sat in the harbour for five days waiting for a convoy. The passengers were allowed ashore only the night before the convoy sailed. White spent the evening 'in a kind of genteel brothel – very chastely, nevertheless – talking to a madam in flowered chiffon with a bust reaching to her knees. Her name was Margery and her conversation stuck to the oh-my-yes-dear technique. Finally I left, after she had suggested for the third time that she should send out for a girl, and was almost on the verge of offering herself.'[44]

As the *Vandyck* crossed the Atlantic, he worked at *The Living and the Dead*. At night he got drunk, 'walking the darkened decks in an Atlantic gale not worrying about a thing'. He felt happily cut off from the world. What lay ahead was a mystery in which only one or two trivial points were clear: fresh taxes on booze, and income tax at 7/6d in the pound. 'I shall be left with a pittance. Who cares?'[45]

London was so calm after the clamour of New York that White wondered if the war wasn't going to end soon 'if it hasn't even ended already'. Winter was early. On nights of moonlight and frost he wandered about the blacked-out streets and squares. It was extraordinarily beautiful. By day the city was empty and formal. 'I have been for a long, autumnal Sunday walk this afternoon round the Park and Kensington Gardens – a very subdued landscape in blacks and browns and dead greens, with a mist over the ponds, and clouds of noisy gulls, and one rather floppy balloon hauled down out of the sky for a fresh consignment of gas. The balloons are really a great addition to London. They add a nice formal detail to the sky, and in the early morning or at sunset are particularly beautiful. I believe children are referring to them as Heavenly Cows.' The worst of the war in these months for White was the sense of wasted time. 'There is so much I want to do.'[46]

He volunteered as a switchboard operator with the fire brigade but there were no bombs. Nothing happened. He was bored, felt useless and left. Civil Defence turned him down. Twenty-seven-year-olds would not be called up for a year; as a severe asthmatic it was unlikely that he would be taken even then; but as a Belltrees White he was able to call on the help of the Agent-General for New South Wales. This man knew the British Censor personally, but nothing came of White's attempt to find work in the Censor's office.[47] He was left alone to write. The Eccleston Street flat was still let, but he moved in downstairs where the Viennese ladies once made lampshades. He never re-occupied the elaborately decorated rooms above.

The first casualty of White's war was *Return to Abyssinia*. Françoise Rosay was no longer available, for 'all the French actors have been commandeered by their government for some kind of national entertainment scheme'. To Mamblas he confided, 'I shall never get over the disappointment of this.' The *Sydney Morning Herald* reported White's difficulties under the headline BAD TIME FOR PLAYWRIGHTS: 'In the meantime, the author is working on another book which has London as its setting this time, and doesn't mention Australia or Australians.'[48]

He was ill. That winter was particularly wet and cold, a time of insinuating bitterness. In a blizzard the pipes at 13 Eccleston Street froze. He wrote to Johnson, 'Why we go on living in this primitive, unprepared way, I don't know.' He had trench mouth and then a vicious bout of flu. The misery of those months worked its way into his prose. He confessed he had begun to dislike it. 'The book is going on for ever. Sometimes I like it, but more often I hate it. There are so many limits to what I can do. What I suggest is so much paler than what I see, that sometimes I feel there is nothing left but to give up altogether.'[49]

Instead, he decided to pare the book down so it might be finished before he became involved in the fighting. He lopped two years from the task. The scale would have been larger, the characters explored more deeply. 'It should have been the Novel of London, but haste made it only a sketch.'[50] Time was not all he lacked: there was also the problem of candour. In writing *The Living and the Dead* White was involved in two issues he found very difficult to speak about with any clarity: his shifting loyalties during the Spanish Civil War and homosexuality.

Elyot Standish, the dry and indecisive literary biographer, is a fragment of the London Patrick White: educated at Cambridge, living in Ebury Street on an allowance of £400 a year, finding no sustained passion, seeing out the decade against the offstage noise from Spain. Standish is also homosexual. But this is always muffled in the writing. One day Standish senses the truth when he meets his sister's lover, a carpenter called Joe Barnett. This decent and beautiful man is the only hero of *The Living and the Dead*,

> It was funny, it was satisfying. Like arriving from abroad after a long time. Everything was all right then, you felt, looking at Joe Barnett, you approved the short, cropped hair and, rising from the shirt, the solid tower of an uncovered neck. There was no hurry. Soon you would begin to say the many things that waited. But you liked to enjoy the waiting, to taste a presence.

Elyot is finally unconvinced by any of his women. Not by argument, but by a passive process of elimination, he grasps at last that he must expose himself to profound emotional risks in order to escape the fate of being one of the living dead of London. Into his orderly, sophisticated, intellectual life he must allow 'the drunken disorderly passions of existence'. Though he *knows* this by the end of the book, there is no more than a bare possibility that he might now go on to start living.[51] Had White been able to state Standish's predicament bluntly, the end of *The Living and the Dead* might have been the opening pages of a more profound novel.

As he worked he was brushing up his German, 'in case there is some chance of me using it in a job'. He read Stefan Zweig's latest novel, and realised with regret how much German life and culture still meant to him. He poured his thwarted affection for Germany into a portrait of the Oertels of Hanover who became the Fiesels of Aachen in *The Living and the Dead*. White took the name Fiesel from Frau Oertel's old governess, but he took only the name. His Frau Fiesel was, like Frau Oertel, so kind that Elyot felt 'on the verge of trespassing' in her apartment. For the purposes of the novel Frau Fiesel is widowed and given a sinister brother who shares the Germanic bitterness White found in Frau Oertel's brother-in-law. That character in the novel is given Herr Oertel's name Rudi and the profession of engineer, but nothing else of the *ernst*, good man White knew in Hanover. Frau Fiesel has a daughter Hildegard, a *Bunddeutscher Mädchen* with

> pale eyes, the colour of mackerel freshly caught . . . the golden, shining face of the young German girls. She had the sleek, shining hair . . . She was very firm, a golden brown.[52]

Into the confrontation of Elyot and Hildegard, White put something of his own tussle with the Swedish girls at Dieppe.

The landscape of London eluded him. The country of Happy Valley had emerged clear and whole in his writing, but London was as foggy on the page as it was that winter in life. The book did catch some sense of a city waiting as London was during the phoney war, 'You could feel the waiting. For a cataclysm perhaps.' And its dull colours in White's prose were influenced by his passion for Sickert. 'He did a lot of sordid paintings of Kentish Town, whores, murdered whores on beds, Dieppe – one of my places – and personages in the theatre down to the young Peggy Ashcroft. He did a wonderful painting called "Ennui" – a woman with her back turned away and a man with a beer and cigar. It got the feeling of London on a Sunday. He was a very important influence in my London life.'[53] For all this, London does not emerge in *The Living and the Dead* as a vital presence. Something was missing.

Theatres had reopened after the first panic, 'into a wilderness of farce and nude revue'. He was robbed of his own first night, but still attended others. After one he found himself at Lady Oxford's. She turned out to be much less of a dragon than he expected, 'in fact, a nice, rather pathetic, rather dotty old lady, who seized my hand when I left and insisted on escorting me down the steps into Bedford Square in case I slipped on the ice. At supper I sat between her son, Anthony Asquith, who directed *Pygmalion*, and *French Without Tears* – from the play by Terence Rattigan who was the other side of me. Asquith is charming. Altogether quite a gay evening, and unlike wartime.'[54]

He was 'refurbishing' revue sketches unsuccessfully that winter, and offered a lyric to Bea Lillie which she turned down. But Hermione Gingold accepted an old lyric for her new revue *Swinging the Gate*, which was to open in spring. 'La Grande Amoureuse' was written in St Jean-de-Luz in 1938.[55] It is the confession of an old tart whose

> life has been rather gaseuse
> I've tasted the waters of so many spas
> I've been patted by princes, tortured by shahs
> My diamonds are only outdone by my scars
> Quel-le vie!
> You'll agree . . .

The old tart has recorded in her album the vices of each lover, his income and shoe size:

> He had a mole . . . I can't say where!
> He made restoratives for hair,
> Page eleven . . . he was heaven!
> Hermann whipped me black and blue,
> Such a demon lover!

> George gave roses. Serge a diamond ring.
> Alphonse – he was a jeweller – said it was no such
>   thing.
> Pedro – Pedro was puritanical.
> And Bebe – well, he turned out to be botanical.
> Each had his charm, and yet it might be said
> Their common theme was just . . . 'And so to bed.'[56]

De Maistre began to paint White's portrait not long after he arrived back from America. 'I'm afraid I'm a very bad sitter,' he reported to Taos. 'I find I can't *relax* when it comes to the point.' He sat every afternoon for a week in a grey double-breasted suit, an ox-blood tie, a handkerchief stuffed in the breast pocket and the fingers of his right hand resting on the silver tip of a cane. The mouth is prim. His face stares into the light, but his body seems to flinch from scrutiny. De Maistre has given him the eyes of someone biting back emotion, like a schoolboy afraid he's about to weep. It is the wooden face of a sensitive and private man. At first White judged the painting a great success achieved despite the difficulties of having him as its subject. 'It reminds me a bit of one of the looser Goyas in a more contemporary idiom.' But later he turned against the portrait and swore he had always hated it.[57]

Spud Johnson sent over a tin of chilli powder for Christmas and it sparked vivid memories of their nights in Taos. When the collector Douglas Cooper called at Eccleston Street after returning from New Mexico, White wrote to Johnson, 'it all came back to me in a glare of pink earth and blue mountains in spite of the fog outside. It is odd in London at this time of year to remember the smell and feel and even the look of heat.' Ruth came to Eccleston Street for lunch on Christmas Day with Suzanne and her new husband Geoffrey Peck. 'We are having a goose, as I refuse to live on bits of dry wood done up in different ways for weeks after, which is the inevitable evil attending on a turkey. And I also refuse to eat plum pudding. We have finally decided on a chocolate mousse, and a lobster soup I learnt in New Orleans to start off with. All this shows we are not yet in a state of starvation.'[58]

Gentle, wry Ben Huebsch accepted *Happy Valley* for Viking and White heard the news in the first weeks of 1940. The book would appear in New York in June. White wanted to be there on publication day. There was also a chance he could do something with *Return to Abyssinia* in New York, and above all he was anxious to return to his lover, for his feelings for Joe Rankin were 'building up'[59] in the months he struggled with *The Living and the Dead* in London. Johnson was still unaware of White's defection, but sensed something was amiss, for all the intimacy had disappeared from White's letters.

As Australians, White and his mother were still free to travel. Ruth joined the droves making for safety on the other side of the world, and her son applied for a permit to cross the Atlantic. 'Personally I can't see the difference between sitting on my behind here or in New York till I am called up at the end of the year.'[60] He was back in New York on 27 March for a tempestuous reunion with Rankin.

White could no longer delay explaining matters to Spud Johnson. A few days after settling into Rankin's apartment at 48 East 53rd Street, he wrote to Taos: 'This is a letter that I hate, and have put off writing, Spud. Now there seems nothing to do but go at it baldly in the way of explanation – which should have come earlier anyhow. You've noticed a change in me, and there *has* been a change. I haven't explained before because I was waiting to see if time would do something to either of us, and it hasn't worked that way.' He told him, briefly, about Rankin; who he was and how they had met. 'Is this too unpleasant a letter? I hope not. Because I *am still* very fond of you and I hate hurting you. I know I am to blame for this. But there it is – I suppose I'm made that way.'[61]

White's elegant and reflective letters continued intermittently through the war. Johnson showed remarkable forbearance and White wrote, early on, thanking him, for he was grateful to be able to keep in contact with a man for whom he continued to feel affection and respect. Their correspondence mattered to White: 'There are so few people on which one can work off abstractions, that one has to take the rare opportunity.'[62]

The prospect of meeting Huebsch for the first time rattled him. As a pioneer of the *avant-garde* in America, the old man had published the early novels of White's heroes Joyce and Lawrence. The previous year Huebsch and T. S. Eliot had jointly published *Finnegans Wake*. Huebsch was the son of a German rabbi, studied music and was at one time music critic for a New York paper. He was also apprenticed to an uncle who was a printer and later set up his own firm which, by degrees, became a publishing house. Its trademark was a seven-branched candlestick. Huebsch had absorbed the radical and civil libertarian traditions of the printing trade and for a few years put out an independent radical weekly. When other American publishers were too timid to publish Joyce's work, Huebsch took it on. He introduced new German writers to America – he spoke German fluently – and championed local writers like Sherwood Anderson and Upton Sinclair. He merged his firm with the new Viking Press in 1925. Harold Guinzberg of Viking Press was the business genius, Huebsch did the 'literary crystal-gazing'.[63]

White found, rather to his surprise, a simple man who was softly spoken, direct, intelligent but worldly. 'One of a breed of noble Jews.' Mr Huebsch, as White called him for the next twenty years, was the rock on which Patrick White's career was built. 'He took me seriously,' White recalled after his death. 'He saw something in my book and then began a relationship which lasted until he left us. Ben stuck to me through the unacceptable years. He became as much a part of my writing as those other necessaries, paper and ink. It was so important in my uncertain youth, to say nothing of my vacillating middle-age, I realise now, to feel that here was one of the certainties.'[64]

Huebsch left White free to express himself in his own style, though the publisher would haggle at times over his grammar. Huebsch was not deterred by length. The manuscripts of authors like White were not to be cut. He put no pressure on authors to be commercial, and was happy for the Viking Press to carry unprofitable writers in whom he had faith. Huebsch's interest in literature was – though he hated the word – idealistic. Though he took pains to win good reviews for White's work, he was phlegmatic about the bad. 'Ben Huebsch used to say: reviews don't matter; in the long run a book will reach the people for whom it's intended.'[65]

Working on *The Living and the Dead* in Joe Rankin's tiny apartment, White thought himself 'more or less an adopted American', though he had his doubts about New York. 'It strikes me as being lacking in a dimension, and the people are without roots. But it has a queer, irritating fascination about it. I repeatedly get the kind of sick feeling in my stomach I used to have as a child going to the theatre in a taxi. That's what I feel is wrong with New York. One's reactions are feverish and intestinal.'[66]

Rankin and his friends urged him to stay in the United States. Why go back, they asked. What use would an asthmatic be at the Front? 'The War stays perpetually at the back of my mind and just manages to spoil every bit of happiness I am enjoying at the moment. Even so that is considerable, and I wouldn't miss any of it, though it is, as I say, just spoiled. When I shall be called up, I don't know. Or what my attitude will be when I am. I'm inclined in the evening to decide that nothing is going to be allowed to spoil my own personal life, and in the morning I read the news and have a fresh fit of wretched patriotics. It is all very difficult.'[67]

He had brought from London the second draft of *The Living and the Dead* – finished on 15 February – and in New York he was typing the third and final draft. The novel, the flat and the affair were by turns exhilarating and stifling. He became jealous of Rankin's patients and suspicious of his affected Southern charm. At night White roamed the bars, at times alone, quarrelsome and drinking heavily. 'Sometimes my companions would have to kick me in the ribs to persuade me to get up out of an Eastside gutter.'[68] He went up to Harlem to watch the 'orgiastic dancers' at the Savoy Ballroom. Men danced on their chests. The bands of Chick Webb, Count Basie and Nat Pierce were electrifying:

here was nothing like the deep bass notes of the sax, or the higher, climbing, shining ones for burning up the guts. This nightly burning of the guts was the *raison d'être* of Wally Collins, a brief, orgasmic almost death under the glare of chromium, more important this than sex, though appreciated too, the pursuit of skin through lingerie. But nightly the bowels rose in the sad surge of saxophones, the skin eroded by a white light, the mouth grown round and moist on a persistent note. He could feel his whole body shaped by a chord in music. His whole body writhed to burst its casing of black tailor's cloth. It drained the sockets of his eyes. By 2 a.m. these were bone dry.[69]

The first reviews of the Viking edition of *Happy Valley* appeared the week France fell. 'It is a great pity', he told Huebsch, 'that the book should appear at just this moment.'[70] But he could not have hoped for a better reception. The critics liked the book and predicted the brightest future for Patrick White. They praised the strength of his characters and the beauty of his prose. His style, which had been greeted with scepticism in London and hostility in Australia, was very much to taste in America. The *New York Times* added, 'Stream-of-consciousness is only one of the weapons with which he attacks the citadel of personality. Much of the story is told in straight narrative that is both simple and effective.'[71]

The fall of France and then Dunkirk intensified the guilt he felt at being safe on Manhattan. Ruth was writing from Australia about the ambiguous position he was in as a Britisher in America. From Huebsch he felt wordless pressure to return to England and face his responsibilities. He put his quandary to Betty Withycombe: what could he do in England? His asthma probably left him unfit for service, and he did not see the point of sitting about with the fire brigade, once again bored and useless. Withycombe's advice was crucial. He was free to remain in America if he wished, she said, but must not fudge the question of *why* he was doing so. The key was his own motive for staying, not whether he would be useful in the war. He replied that her advice made more sense than any he had received.[72]

The war of *The Living and the Dead* is the Spanish Civil War, but in tracing the shifts that determine why the carpenter Joe Barnett goes to Spain to fight for the Republic, White was drafting an unheroic formula for his own resolve. As Barnett and Eden Standish walk one day along the Medway they stumble on the corpse of a dog, its guts hanging out on the ground. Barnett reflects on the ordinariness of death. It is expected. 'Man was born to this, no other dignity.'[73] He resolves to go. On the afternoon of his departure he explains to Elyot Standish:

> There was a time, said Joe, when I could read the papers and keep things in their place. That's where they belonged, in the papers. It was other people's business. It was foreign names. Then it got to being part of yourself . . .[74]

White was unhappy with the novel. It seemed to him 'the drabbest, dreariest thing ever written', though here and there it held his interest and he hoped readers would find it better than 'I, as its author, am ready to believe'.[75] He dedicated the book,

TO

JOE RANKIN

FOR HIS

SELFLESSNESS

AND

PATIENCE

and delivered the finished typescript to his agent in late June. Huebsch accepted the book. Another copy of the typescript went to Harrap in London. Harrap rejected it. So a pattern was set for the next fifteen years: immediate acceptance of White's work in New York and a struggle to find a publisher in London.

White felt 'immense if also fearful relief' once he decided to return to Europe. Huebsch approved as silently as he had early reproved and the two men drew closer. The prospect of departure fanned White's affair with Rankin into a last blaze. Their parting was painful. He wrote to say farewell to Johnson: 'My plans are no more definite than to go to London and offer to do something. Then when it is over I shall come back here and probably take out my papers. Anyway, I know from my last six months in England that I can't breathe in Europe any more.'[76]

ELEVEN

Love and War

WHITE STOOD HALF-naked for an hour and a half in a Wembley drill hall while a military board tried to make up its mind about his chest. A plump old doctor took off his glasses and asked quietly, 'You don't really want to get into it, do you?' White said he did.[1] He was to return for their verdict some time before Christmas.

London was hardly touched by the war. This was the golden summer of Mrs Trist's triumph when the former jackeroo reached 'the apogee of her career or fate' in a brothel by the Thames. The bombing had not yet begun. By night the city was a whore's paradise and by day the planes overhead seemed only to be writing vapour trails on blue summer skies.

> Figures strolled in the parks in their shirtsleeves, lolled in deck chairs at lunchtime, offering their cheeks to an indulgent sun . . . One could accept the smell of khaki and sweaty socks mingling with the stench of duck droppings and urinals when so many healthy lads from the Dominions had arrived to defend all that is most worthy of defending. In the circumstances, it was easy to accept adultery, perhaps even sodomy – more difficult their dreadful accents.[2]

White found a bed-sitter in Ebury Street next door to the Imhof Maranta house and slipped back into the disconnected worlds of his London: actors and actresses, high society homosexuals, the Withycombes and Roy's studio crowd. *The Living and the Dead* had been turned down by Harrap, Faber and Chatto; now his agent was trying Jonathan Cape. He worked at his American journal, but suspected it was 'too trite and too personal' to be published. If the journal found a publisher it would be dedicated to Spud Johnson, for playing 'an important – but not embarrassing – part in it'.[3]

At de Maistre's suggestion, White spent the next few months

working for the Red Cross while he tried to find a place in Air Force Intelligence. 'But this takes time, much time,' he wrote to Huebsch. 'I think even longer than it does to place a novel by Patrick White.' The Red Cross put him to work at St James's Palace in the Postal Message Scheme, which gave members of families separated by war a way of keeping in contact. White came across interesting and often tragic stories, 'letters asking us to trace families and lovers, and often letters which the senders hope will go direct, with very intimate messages, and sometimes even pressed flowers'. But he could send only formal cables through Geneva, 'and all the flowers and *chauds baisers* are wasted on our office files'.[4] For one purpose or another he was to spend much of the next few years eavesdropping in the service of the Allies. White fought a novelist's war.

Any hope of seeing *Return to Abyssinia* in the West End had been abandoned. On the evening of 7 September 1940, one of the most memorable nights of his life, White dined with the play's would-be producer John Wyse at the Café Royal in Regent Street. They did not know each other well. As they ate, the first bombs began to fall on London and the two men emerged to find the city alight. The scent of Wyse's cigar 'mingled with a stench of burning. The eastern sky was ablaze, fire engines clanging. It was not yet dark. The west was a cold ice-green as opposed to the Wagnerian glow eastwards, the play of light paradoxical as our world was turned upside down.'[5] They could not find a taxi, so the two men set off together towards Ebury Street, hunching their shoulders against the metal rain pattering on the pavements.

The raid grew worse. As they reached the corner of Ebury and Eccleston Streets at about 11pm, a bomb screamed towards them and they fell into a heap on the footpath with a couple of soldiers coming from the opposite direction. One of the soldiers offered his helmet to shelter these two fops. The bomb hit Victoria Station, but even a couple of blocks away the impact was terrific. 'There we lay with shrapnel spattering round us and the building rocking against our ribs.' In such a 'perverse sunset' Edith Trist perished as she crossed London to join her mother in a Piccadilly hotel, and Himmelfarb walked through this fire storm falling on his city of Holunderthal:

> Then wheels were arriving. Of ambulance? Or fire-engine? The Jew walked on, by supernatural contrivance. For now the wheels were grazing the black shell of the town. The horses were neighing and screaming, as they dared the acid of the green sky. The horses extended their webbing necks, and their nostrils glinted brass in the fiery light. While the amazed Jew walked unharmed beneath the chariot wheels.[6]

White and Wyse were unhurt. The producer was making for his mother's place in Battersea, but White suggested he shelter with him in Ebury Street until the raid finished. They reached the room. Wyse asked White what they should do. He had never seen White so carefree. Bombs were still falling. White suggested they get under the bed. 'He went to a chest of drawers and took out a pair of white silk pyjamas. I said that I had never met anyone who had such beautiful pyjamas, and he said, "These are for you". We got under the bed like two white rabbits. At an affectionate moment, Patrick said he had to get his asthma thing. He crawled out from under the bed, then there was the worst bang of the lot. He came back with his machine. It was very pleasant.'[7]

The raids continued every night after that. The worst were those in the early morning when the sirens sounded at 3am and White woke wondering if this was his last moment, 'or shall I find myself in the next half hour walking away from a pile of rubble in my dressing gown with a cardboard box full of salvaged belongings'.[8] In the early days of the Blitz he went to the crowded cellars when the sirens sounded, but he was too restless to stay underground. After a month of raids, he wrote to Johnson, 'I have been out most nights, as the alternative seemed to be extinction by staying in, and the deserted streets have been very beautiful, in a white moonlight and yellow flashing of guns.'[9]

At some point in those apocalyptic weeks, sitting in his room swigging Calvados as the bombs fell, White read the journal of Edward John Eyre, a young man who walked across Australia along the cliffs and dunes of the Great Australian Bight. Eyre was a name known from childhood, one of those explorers who left a dotted line across the map of the continent. Familiar as the story of Eyre was to White, he was now 'electrified' as he read his journal. Eyre was a romantic who never lost sight of the beauty of a landscape so terrible it seemed set on destroying him. The journal gave White an itch to see Australia again and the vague ambition to write a novel about an explorer. The Blitz, Eyre's journey and his own approaching part in the war made White wonder about the nature of heroism.[10]

'The last two or three days I've been forced to believe we are at war,' he wrote to Naomi Burton, his agent in New York. 'Four air raids a day make our average. But even so there is something ludicrous about death even when it's right on top of you or perhaps more so the closer it comes. I'm inclined to believe that heroism is probably also a myth and that the ones who go out and face death are as indifferent to it as the civilians who continue to work with the planes overhead, or at most, sit under the stairs with a cup of tea.'[11]

London lost the last of its inhibitions, for every night might see the end of the world. On any dark street there was a chance 'something lively may come round the corner or out of the skies at you at any moment'. Life was dangerous and encounters easy for White in the West End, on Ebury Street, and in the vortex of Victoria Station. 'I learned a lot about the whore's mentality, and the variations on her one client, in fact the whole tragi-comedy of sex.'[12]

He had a long letter from Joe Rankin in November, then never heard from his Southern lover again. He kept writing for a while before realising it was over. White was wounded by this defection, particularly hurt that Rankin gave no reason for his silence. White kept writing to Spud. He was only writing letters now. Huebsch asked for an introduction to the Viking edition of *The Living and the Dead* but White found it impossible. 'If you were here, you would understand how difficult it is to make the brain function creatively.'[13] Jonathan Cape had rejected *The Living and the Dead*, and Curtis Brown was trying Heinemann.

The Air Force called him to an interview in November and after a session 'guaranteed to scare the daylights out of the brashest aspirant',[14] he was told to buy himself a uniform and report for duty as a pilot officer in the Administrative and Special Duties Branch (Intelligence) of the RAF Volunteer Reserve. The uniform embarrassed him. He hated saluting. In the hope of 'some sun and peaceful nights'[15] he asked to be posted to the Middle East, but found himself instead in the underground ops room of Bentley Priory, compiling reports on the bombing of Britain. The job called for more concentration than anything he had ever done in his life. With his eyes falling out, he sat from 8.30pm to 8.30am watching the ops table, and at the end of each duty he wrote a report and answered calls from all over the British Isles. He had to work out the rules as he went along, terrified of the repercussions of the simplest error. The worst fear during his month inside the war machine was that Churchill might ring. He never did.

'When I come off duty I am not good for much more than a hot bath and bed,' he wrote to Spud Johnson after a fortnight at the Priory. He had that day been told to expect to leave for the Middle East before the end of the month. White made a couple of guesses about his destination but these were censored from the letter. 'Personally I seem to get a great deal more out of small things – like seeing my friends, chance encounters, a few minutes in which to do nothing, even bacon rations. And above all I have come to the conclusion that there is no material tie worth hanging on to, that nothing matters, nothing is harmful or annihilating, except something that touches what I think one has to call one's personal integrity.'[16]

The railway that runs from Khartoum to the Red Sea crosses the

river Gash at the town of Kassala, where a few mud huts and the
railway yards stand under the Gebel Kassala, a black rock rising out
of the plain. The Italians had occupied Kassala for six months before
being pushed back over the Eritrean border in January, when the town
then became the base of the No. 1 Squadron of the South African Air
Force. The squadron's job was to give air cover for the Allied drive
through Eritrea to the Red Sea while Haile Selassie with 3,000 mules
and 15,000 camels re-entered his kingdom. Patrick White arrived by
Wellesley from Khartoum on 1 March 1941 to take up duty as squadron
intelligence officer.

The journey from London had taken him over two months. His
boat zigzagged down the Atlantic from Greenland to the Azores, finally
dropping the men at Takoradi on the Gold Coast, where they waited
for a fortnight for aircraft. 'Every evening at sunset we went down to
bathe in a grey, languid sea, in company with the resident whites and
their guarded or overtly hungry female attachments, before the nightly
gin session.'[17] He read *The Possessed* as he flew over Allied Africa in an
old bomber. From the Sudan he was posted briefly to Cairo and then
brought back to Khartoum, where he spent February 1941 directing
interception of Italian cargo planes flying into Eritrea. Off duty, he
tried without success to learn Arabic.

When he joined the 'Billy Boys' at Kassala, he was the third White
in the squadron. They called him Bruin White, because of the colour
of his hair, to distinguish him from White White and Black White.
The history of the squadron records that Bruin White did 'fine work'
and was very popular. In the company of the South Africans, his
habitual shyness turned into confidence. 'I was soon enjoying hearty
extrovert, totally unreal relationships with several of the pilots. It
is always agreeable to discover one is liked by unlikely people. I was
touched by their trust. They told me in detail about their wives,
children, sexual exploits. From being a diffident young misfit chained
to a demanding telephone and an even more demanding, petulant
monkey nobody else wanted, I was changed by circumstance into
a hen fluffing out wings to accommodate a half-fledged, frequently
troubled brood.'[18]

The airmen lived in the old district commissioner's house set
in a garden behind a high wall. A shepherd grazed a flock of sheep
and goats among the trees. One morning at dawn, as the sun rose
behind the Gebel, White watched as a lamb was born and the mother
casually resumed cropping on the grey grass. The pilots drew water
from a well in the garden in the depths of which lived a huge barbel
that ate kitchen scraps. In the evenings, the men lounged in the
mosquito-proof eyrie the Italians had built on the roof when the
house was briefly occupied by an enemy general; or they wandered

into town to drink at the rival Greek cafés, the Acropolis and High Life.[19]

On the Gebel Kassala grew a single tree which was said to confer immortality on anyone who could pluck a leaf from its scraggy branches. White never made the climb, for the Gebel was another of the peaks he gazed at but never conquered. Early on there was Mount Ashby seen from the veranda of Tudor House, later the Eagle Nest in Taos, the White mountains in Maine, and the volcano on Aiyina. It was in Maine he first noticed how he *made* places like this wherever he went: 'I want to go, but we don't seem to make the move.'[20]

He fought the Eritrean campaign on the telephone, relaying orders from RAF operational headquarters inside Eritrea to the dozen fighter pilots of the squadron. After the sorties he collected optimistic accounts of destruction and sent these back to headquarters. The RAF and South Africans had destroyed all the Italian airfields in Eritrea, and the No. 1 Squadron faced no opposition in the air as they escorted bombers over the mountains to strafe the road that ran down to Massawa on the Red Sea. In the middle of March the Allies began the battle of Keren, an extremely ferocious attack over heavily defended mountains, and the No. 1 Squadron returned to the Massawa road, slaughtering the Italians trying to make their way down to the coast.

White had his head shaved in preparation for the heat and dust storms of the Sudanese summer, but the next day came orders posting the squadron to Alexandria. The Italians were beaten in Eritrea and the South Africans were needed to help defend the Delta. White followed the planes down by rail. Somewhere between Khartoum and Alexandria, in a railway junction where the train had stopped at night, he lost the squadron monkey. After a hectic chase among the carriages, he stood sweating and wheezing in the moonlight. 'It was one of those moments when you are encouraged to feel you have escaped from what is ordained . . . Detached from my past, real life, and with no clue to the future, I was temporarily a free being.'[21]

In Melbourne the members of the Australian Literature Society stood for a few minutes' 'respectful silence' to mark the death of Banjo Paterson. Then the 1941 annual general meeting in a room on Collins Street was called to order. The society had pledged in 1900 to engage in the systematic study of Australian literature but by now its flag flew much of the time at half mast. The bush poets to whom the society was devoted were dying out and the members feared 'infection from the prevalent degeneration into the abnormal as exemplified by the school fathered by D. H. Lawrence'. In their lifetimes these men and women still hoped to see the arrival of 'The Great Singer' in Australia. That was their faith.[22]

Meanwhile the society awarded each year the Colonel Crouch Gold Medal for fiction. The novels of Martin Boyd, Henry Handel Richardson, Eleanor Dark and Xavier Herbert had won the honour. When the members of the society resumed their seats on 17 February 1941 the principal item on the agenda was the award of the Gold Medal to Patrick White for *Happy Valley*.

The prevailing taste of the society made White an unlikely winner; the rules disqualified him because he lived abroad; and the award of the medal – containing gold to the value of £5 – contravened wartime regulations. But the society was guided to the choice of White and *Happy Valley* by three judges whose taste was ahead of the rank and file. Percival Serle was compiling the first *Australian Dictionary of Biography*; Arthur Phillips was a critic, teacher and literary patriot who later defined Australia's 'cultural cringe'; and Frank Wilmot was the poet 'Furnley Maurice' who had published that enthusiastic review of White's novel in *Bohemia* eighteen months before: 'It's funny. Painstakingly vulgar too. The new humour. Stirring the mental stew with a deft and deliberate cynicism and an emblazoned ladle. Why not? you say. Yes. Well, why not?'[23]

The society had no idea where to send the medal and over the next six months meetings heard progress reports on the search for Patrick White. Finally he was located in the Middle East and the Perpetual Trustee took possession of the prize on his behalf.

As Australia honoured White's first novel, his second appeared in New York. Viking had paid *The Living and the Dead* the high compliment of a jacket by the illustrator McKnight Kauffer which suggested, rather oddly, that this was a novel about the war. Once again New York critics credited Patrick White with passion, honesty, sharp eyes, originality, precision and 'bedrock strength'. There were those who dissented from the general verdict, and even those critics who praised the book highly had reservations. But the prevailing mood was, as Jane Spence Southern wrote in the *New York Times*, that the difficulties were 'only a milestone on the road to greater things'.[24]

A fortnight before these reviews appeared in New York, Heinemann turned the novel down in London. Anticipating this, White had arranged for Herbert Read to see the typescript once Heinemann was finished with it. Read was a friend of Roy de Maistre, an enormously influential critic and an editorial director of George Routledge & Sons. He read and accepted *The Living and the Dead* in a few days.

Routledge was another odd perch for Patrick White, for Routledge's fiction list was never large. The strength of the firm lay in the fields of psychology and social studies. But Read's enthusiasm in this case was decisive and the book was published very quickly. Routledge was able to set from the New York edition as Viking had not Americanised White's spelling, and *The Living and the Dead* appeared in London in July. The edition was small: only 1,428 copies to supply the British and overseas markets. It 'sold right out' within a year, and plans for a second printing were cancelled only because of wartime paper shortages. White's total royalty earnings on the Routledge edition were £55 11s 2d.[25]

London was lukewarm. Notices were brief and critics respectful, but they found the book 'somehow dowdy, a little belated'. In the second year of the war the static introspection of *The Living and the Dead* seemed a luxury of peace. Standing apart from the critical ruck was the poet Edwin Muir, and his review in the *Listener* became one of Patrick White's cherished possessions. 'Mr White has a passionate spirit of exploration . . . He examines, or rather enters into, the world of experience, ordinary and extraordinary, with an insistence which itself is a gift; for the essential mark of the writer who illuminates life for us is that he does not stop where other writers stop, content to reach an approximate stage, but pursues his search for meaning . . . the close investigation of thought and feeling is never pursued for its own sake; in all the parts there is a sense of the whole. For this combination of qualities Mr White required an exceptionally flexible style. It has some displeasing idiosyncrasies; it is sometimes restless; but at its best it has the closeness and the imaginative venturousness of poetry, and sometimes an astonishing flow of invention. Compared with what he does in this book with the raw material of experience, most novels seem to do nothing at all.'[26]

The Living and the Dead was barely noticed in Australia. Fewer than 350 copies made the wartime journey from London.[27] Only the poet Douglas Stewart in the *Bulletin* tried to come to grips with it. Stewart, who had recently taken over the magazine's influential 'Red Page', found the novel frozen and obscure. In his generally damning review Stewart posed a question which was already in White's mind: 'Would the color and vigor of the Australian scene forcibly projecting itself into his work, bring light and warmth and strength?'[28]

Not till a year after its New York publication did a copy of *The Living and the Dead* reach White in the desert. He was delighted with the job Viking had done: 'binding, type and jacket all very good. I enjoy looking into it sometimes, for it is all so old now that it begins to be new.'[29]

At Amiriya, a waste of rock and sand on the desert road outside Alexandria, White and his pilots had little to do. Only half the squadron was at Amiriya, replacing pilots sent north to defend Greece. With Egypt stripped of men for this adventure, Rommel easily reconquered the North African coast. Greece fell and the Allied survivors limped back to Alexandria. White's pilots were then reunited with the rest of

the squadron at Sidi Haneish, fifty miles from the Libyan border. Their
task was to give air cover to the ships carrying supplies from Alexandria
to besieged Tobruk.

White's existence was monotonous but tense. He worked twenty-
four hours on and twenty-four off, once again chained to the telephone.
At the other end of the line were the pilots waiting in the officers' mess
to scramble when he warned that enemy aircraft were approaching.
He cranked the air-raid siren. When the squadron returned to base he
compiled a report of enemy ground and air forces then rang this through
to Air Headquarters. The squadron was now suffering casualties, and
White believed he could detect 'a certain fated look' in the eyes of those
about to die.[30]

> FLO. I didn't tell you, Eureka . . .
> EUREKA. You didn't need to tell me, I knew.
> FLO. Did someone else?
> EUREKA. Nobody. Denzil was marked – he had it in his eyes.[31]

Life was informal, dress was slack. He slept on a stretcher in a
bell tent with two other men and stored his clothes in an old petrol
box. He was smoking a pipe heavily. He shaved every other day. 'I am
flybitten, flea-ridden, sweating and stinking – washing my own socks
in an inch of muddy water. I doubt if I shall ever sink much lower
than this.' In fact, he took some pride in being able to do without.
'My consolation is that for ever after I shall be able to cope with a
lack of material things.' The officers' mess was a big tent with a hessian
floor, trestle tables and more abandoned petrol boxes to store crockery,
booze and the bottles of sauce that made their food palatable. The pilots
played rummy, drank, wrote letters and read. They read anything they
could lay their hands on: old newspapers, Army 'rags', the Bible, the
Everyman classics. Sandstorms were the worst hazard at Sidi Haneish,
and when the *khamseen* blew the war stopped. Flying was impossible;
sand invaded everything, sifting into food, into the folds of clothes,
between the pages of books. White wrote, 'Gregariousness is getting
me down. I want a room to myself and all day to think my thoughts
. . . It's a long time since I even spoke my own tongue.'[32]

Sidi Haneish lay in sand dunes by the sea. This was the true desert
which he had hankered after romantically for years, and despite war and
dust storms the scene was idyllic. It was spring and the days were warm
and dry. At Sidi Haneish he began to think of home. 'I was obsessed
by memories of the Australian landscape. The landscape became for
me the Land, images around which my own patriotism formed more
positively: frosty mornings in the Monaro, with sulphur-crested cockatoos toppling the stooked oats; floodwaters of the Barwon and Namoi

through which I swam my horse to fetch the mail; the pepper trees and cracked asphalt of steamy Sydney streets.' Swept with this unexpected nostalgia, he felt an impulse to return to the scenes of his childhood, 'the purest well from which the creative artist draws'. He wrote home, 'I am thinking of coming out after the war – first to the States, then to Australia. I *have* to go to Central Australia, for some reason. Europe, I don't think I could live in any more. It will have to be the States or Australia.'[33]

The South Africans sent one of their own men, Nick Nicholas, to replace White at Sidi Haneish and the two became friends in the brief time they had together. The young South African wrote in his diary: 'He is an R.A.F. pilot-officer attached to the Squadron, about 29, fair, comes from Australia, but the sole defect in his accent is his asthma. That and a natural caution gives a slow decision to his voice. His eyes laugh frequently, but the most his body can produce is a chesty chuckle. He is an author, if a poem and two published books make a man an author: the second, just-published, is *The Living and the Dead*, and very well reviewed in the *New York Times*.'[34]

A party was held in the mess to celebrate White's birthday and his departure from Sidi Haneish. The night was such a success that it is recorded in the history of the No. 1 Squadron SAF, and Nicholas gave a full account in his diary. 'Most people had a great deal to drink.' Bruin White appointed himself 'servile barman' and saw to that. A professional accordion player was brought over from a nearby ack-ack camp and the singing went on late into the night:

> We called on the major to sing us a song,
> We called on the major to sing us a song,
> So sing you bastard sing,
> Or show your fucking ring.

Down by the sea, ack-ack shells burst and searchlights sprayed the sky. Wildly drunk, White and another officer set out to drive the accordion player home. They were soon lost in the desert, ran out of petrol and wandered back over the dunes at dawn. A few days later White left for a British squadron at Idku on the bay of Abu Qir near Alexandria. 'I found the South Africans more stimulating than anyone else I have met in the Service,' White wrote. 'They have a very strong sense of nationality and great enthusiasm. Returning to the English was like taking up a position behind a locked door.'[35]

Cosmopolitan Alexandria would soon be as dead as Troy, celebrated in Greek verse and English novels, yet this city was never so like itself as in its last, wartime years. There was no rationing, no restraint, no martial law in Alexandria. Egypt was not at war but hosting the Allies' campaign. Farouk was King. The presence of Rommel's armies out on the Libyan border in the summer of 1941 did not touch Alexandria's complacency. The city still thrived on fabulous extremes of wealth and need. Poverty was Egyptian; wealth was Greek, Jewish, Syrian, French and British. This was the great market of the Middle East, selling whores for masters and whores for servants, coffee, cotton, dates, cocaine, boots filched from the Allied armies, carrots fresh from the Delta and oranges piled on the gutters in golden pyramids.

White had come to Alexandria with a letter of introduction to one of the great Jewish families of the city. The Menasce were Sephardim who made a fortune in the cotton trade and were awarded a Hungarian title at the turn of the century for handling the Egyptian investments of the Habsburg family. Alexandria had a Rue de Menasce, the family Banque de Menasce, a palace of that name, and an eye hospital given by the family to the city. George de Menasce collected yellow diamonds and Persian daggers and gave stiff musical parties where the drink was vile and the food very good. His cousin the baron Charles lived in a large apartment in the *quartier grec*. Here White found shelter whenever he came to Alexandria on leave. They were lovers.

'For the most part, while I was his guest, each of us went his own way. He was seldom at home. I felt oppressed in his silent, shuttered flat amongst the Gobelins, chinoiseries, and *fin de siècle* bibelots as ugly as they were valuable. The best part was turning on the bathroom taps and watching the water gush out in a cloud of steam . . . There were also the receptions in one of the minor salons of the flat.'[36]

Charles was bald and simpering, an exquisitely dressed little man with cold black eyes. He had a passion for eating duck, and White imagined his little body full of cold duck as, in time, were the bodies of General Sokolnikov and the cook's friend at Durilgai, 'and when they cut him open — would you believe it? — it was duck. He was stuffed full.'[37] Menasce showed unusual generosity towards White, and the airman roused the jealousy of his host's sycophantic friends. Menasce graded these friends with calculated finesse. Alexandrians of his circle rang every month or so to ask if Charles was 'in' and they were invited for tea or drinks — but never a meal. Second-class members of this coterie were served local Bolonaki whisky in the *salon japonais*. The first class had Scotch in the *petit salon*. In July 1941, a few weeks after White left the South Africans, Menasce arranged an afternoon tea. 'I've got an Australian officer and I'm asking a few friends,' he told Manoly Lascaris on the telephone. Lascaris accepted his invitation.

'A Greek, is he?' White asked.

'Yes,' Menasce sighed, 'a Greek from here.'[38]

A dozen men were drinking tea and eating sweet cakes. Lascaris found this crowd rather effeminate and stood back in the doorway of a balcony covered with vines and flowers. When White entered in his blue Air Force uniform 'the queens cooed', but Lascaris saw from White's eyes that he liked none of them. The party was successful enough for Menasce to send everyone on for drinks in the *petit salon*. Again Lascaris hung back, pausing to look at the portrait of a cardinal that hung in the corridor. As he stared at the old priest, White came behind him, put his arms around his chest and embraced him.

The alliance that began that afternoon in the Menasce apartment continued to the end of White's life. The Australian airman and this 'small Greek of immense moral strength'[39] were born within weeks of one another at the opposite ends of Europe; an Australian in London and a Greek in Cairo. They were both twenty-nine, yet Lascaris always seemed the younger of the two: more relaxed, more generous and amused. From his Greek father and American mother he had a most beautiful voice with a deliberate, musical, hesitating cadence. What provoked black pessimism in White caused Lascaris no more than amused despair; his calm matched White's temper; he softened his lover's outbursts of rage against the world with his Levantine acceptance that things had always been so; and the human race which White met with such suspicion, kindled sympathy and wry forbearance in Lascaris. White wrote, 'He is my sweet reason.'[40] In July 1941 they were both looking for permanence and found it together amongst the hideous bric-à-brac of Menasce's Alexandria.

White gave Lascaris a copy of *Happy Valley* and Lascaris thought he had found another D. H. Lawrence. The English speakers of Alexandria were devoted to D. H. Lawrence at this time, and Lascaris showed the book to his friend the novelist Robert Liddell who was lecturing at the Egyptian University. Liddell's verdict was this: Patrick White was a 'terribly good writer' but Lascaris might end up strangled like Mrs Moriarty. Lascaris decided to take that chance: 'This may be the end of me, but it has to be.'[41]

The two men found themselves a flat in the Rue Safîa Zaghloul, a street of shops that runs a crooked course from the corniche, past Cavafy's Billiard Palace, across the Rue Fouad – the old Rue Rosette – and up the hill to the railway station. The flat was on that last hill. Behind them lay the slums of Kom el Dik. Down a side street on a little square was Pastroudis, the wonderful Greek restaurant, and a few minutes' walk along the Rue Fouad was the Alexandria Water Company, the Moya, where Lascaris was working while he waited to be taken into the Royal Greek Army. For the next six years as the war drove them back and forth across the Levant, they kept the flat on Safîa Zaghloul as their base. They had two large rooms and a veranda with a marble floor that led by a few steps to a small garden. It was a mess when they took the lease, but a Smyrna Jew over the road put in cupboards and bookshelves, a French upholsterer made curtains and a peacock-blue cover for their bed, and an Egyptian further up the street painted the rooms which, for a time, looked smart before the paint began to peel.

Through Manoly Lascaris, White entered a world that seemed waiting to receive him. He found his imagination fired by the Greeks and stories of the Byzantine past, a history both splendid and miserable, of marble veined with blood, all so at odds with the Anglo-Saxon existence of Whites and Withycombes. Greece helped White shed the imaginative constraints of his own background, and his life with Manoly Lascaris, who had this history in his bones, enriched and freed him.

The Lascaris family had lost almost everything in the twentieth century except an antique name, imperial snobbery, Athenian connections and the adaptive strength that allowed them to survive centuries of wandering. Their story linked two Greek misfortunes that came to haunt White: the loss of Byzantium and the Catastrophe of Smyrna. There was much exotic, bloody detail to master. 'As for Greek family history,' complained Eudoxia Vatatzes in *The Twyborn Affair*, 'outsiders cannot hope to penetrate what they are expected to accept.'[42]

When Byzantium was dismembered by the Fourth Crusade, Theodore Lascaris and his successors became emperors in exile in Nicaea. By the end of the reign of the great John III, Duke Vatatzes, the family held vast territories including most of the old empire up to the edges of the city of Constantinople. But when the empire passed to the boy John IV Lascaris Vatatzes, the throne was usurped by his general, Michael Paleologus, who led the Nicaean forces on the reconquest of Constantinople where the Paleologi reigned for two hundred years until the city was overthrown by the Turks. The Lascaris family survived out of reach of the Paleologi through marriage into the ruling houses of Hungary and Savoy. Over the next centuries they appeared in France, Sicily and Egypt, where Napoleon encouraged the Chevalier Théodore Lascaris to fan a Coptic insurrection on his behalf. It failed.

Except by blood and name, the grandfather of Manoly Lascaris was hardly Greek. He was born in Paris and studied law at the University of Paris before going out to Smyrna to practise in the commercial courts of the city. Under Turkish rule the courts conducted their affairs in French. Lascaris prospered in Smyrna and rented the Athenogenes house on the Rue Franque, then married the only Athenogenes daughter. Marriage Hellenised him. He learnt Greek and converted to the Orthodox faith. The house came to him as part of a large dowry, for the Athenogenes family owned great estates in Anatolia. He began to live opulently, fathered eight children, and died in the aftermath of an appendectomy performed without anaesthetic in the kitchen at the Rue Franque.

The oldest son fell in with one of the sons of Albert de Dion at university in Aix-en-Provence and they went out together to New York to promote the family car. George Lascaris came to visit his elder brother in America and met a Roman Catholic New Englander, Florence Mayhew, whom he married and took back to Smyrna. The Mayhews were farmers and among their cousins were the protestant Coolidges, farmers and storekeepers of Vermont. The young bride bore the Oriental despotism of her mother-in-law on the Rue Franque for a few years, then insisted on a move to Cairo. Her fourth child, Emanuel (Manoly) George, was born in Cairo in August 1912. Two more followed.

During the First World War, the Lascaris marriage fell apart, but it was impossible for Florence to escape. Her husband was in cotton, and they lived on some scale with a house in the Cairo suburbs and a flat on Solimon Pasha in the city where they changed for evening parties. Here Florence had her babies, for the German hospital was nearby. The children spoke Greek to their father, English to their mother and English in the presence of both. To the governess they spoke French. The older girls were sent to a French boarding school and fell into the habit of speaking French to one another. An Austrian nanny looked after the babies.

Once the war was over, Florence left for New York. Her husband followed, but never rejoined his wife.

First mother went away. Then it was our father, twitching from under our feet the rugs, which formed, he said, a valuable collection. We were alone for a little then. Not really alone, of course, for there was Fräulein Hoffmann, and Mademoiselle Leblanc, and Kyria Smaragda our housekeeper, and Eurydice the cook, and the two maids from Lesbos. The house was full of the whispering of women, and all of us felt melancholy.[43]

Manoly was six. He was sent to his aunt the Marchesa Anastasia Giustiniani in Alexandria, but was brought home when two Lascaris aunts appeared from Smyrna to rescue the children. Both were spinsters. Elly Lascaris took charge. She decreed that only Greek would be spoken in the house; that in order to keep the respect of the servants the children had to be dressed and down to breakfast at 7am every day of the year. Only the *nouveaux riches* rose late and drifted about undressed. 'She was strong, a great disciplinarian, very religious, terribly scholarly. When she helped me with my ancient Greek homework she never used a dictionary. She read Goethe every day as a discipline.'[44] Her sister Despo

affected delicate health, read the poetry of Tagore, ate raw carrots, and
was a prey to migraine. Every year she took the waters in Europe,
whence she returned with trunks of new clothes.

They were now living in the family's summer house in Alexandria
in the bare suburb of Ramleh where Bedouin still tethered camels and
pitched their tents. There was also a Lascaris beach house nearby in the
sandhills behind Stanley Bay, and the Austrian nanny marched the children every morning to the beach calling 'Ein! Zwei!' to keep them in step.

> The garden was never so cool and damp as when they brought
> us back from the beach. The gate creaked, as the governesses let
> us in through the sand-coloured wall, into the dark-green thicket
> of leaves . . . I believe we were at our happiest in the evenings of
> those days. Though somebody might open a door, threatening to
> dash the light from the candles on our aunt's piano, the flames soon
> recovered their shape. Silences were silenter. In those days, it was
> not uncommon to hear the sound of a camel, treading past, through
> the dust. There was the smell of camel on the evening air.[45]

After four years in Alexandria, the aunts decided to take the children
home to Smyrna, where the Athenogenes' house on the Rue Franque
stood empty. Despo went ahead to install bathrooms and electric light.
This was 1922. The Great Powers had allowed the Greeks to occupy
the city after the war, and the Greek army had driven the Turks back
into the hinterland. But in the late summer of 1922 Kemal launched a
counter-attack. Despo went to the front to distribute comforts to the
troops and was injured when she was thrown from her horse. The
Greeks withdrew into Smyrna.

As the Turks entered the city, the great harbour was full of Allied
warships waiting to evacuate the foreign communities. There were no
ships for the Greeks. Massacres began in the Armenian quarter. The
Metropolitan of Smyrna was hacked to pieces by the mob, and a
legend grew up that he was crucified on the doors of his own cathedral.
Fire spread through the wooden city and a quarter of a million people
crowded the waterfront, the Prokymaia, to escape the blaze. Only a
handful of Greeks reached the Allied ships.

Despo was rescued from the house on the Rue Franque by an
Italian neighbour who put on his Italian Army uniform and escorted
her to a French passenger ship. She paid for a cabin and was stowed
in the hold. She had only the clothes she stood up in.

> At first it was impossible to believe their personal lives could
> be reduced by a shuffle of history, which is what happened,
> momentarily at least, on the deck of the destroyer, after the sack

1 The Whites and their women assembled in 1913: *from left*, Arthur standing with dim Milly, James of Edinglassie with Emmy, Dick with Ruth. Frank of Saumarez seated with Margaret, H.L. with Maude, Ernest alone.

2 Belltrees looming over H.L.'s gardens.

3 *above* The valley at Belltrees looking east past the chapel to Mount Woolooma.

4 *right* Ruth and Dick on honeymoon with friends at Henley.

5 *below* Father and son.

Australian childhood

opposite
6 Sue as a dumpling in ballet shoes.
7 Lizzie Clark their Scottish nurse and Paddy's 'real mother';
8 The boy at twelve, with big ears and sharp eyes.
9 A motoring party at Withycombe.

10 *left* The sight that haunted White all his life: Ethel Kelly in 1923 dressed as the Primrose Pompadour.

11 *below left* Ruth at Lulworth in winter.

12 *below right* Lulworth: the original of all White's Harbour houses with buffalo lawns, palms and wild gardens.

13 'Striking a pose on Mount Wilson with Mariamne Wynne and Sue –
proud Ruth, glum Dick.'

14 Growing up in
Europe with Sue.

15 Clem Withycombe, the 'Hunter River
gent', at Barwon Vale.

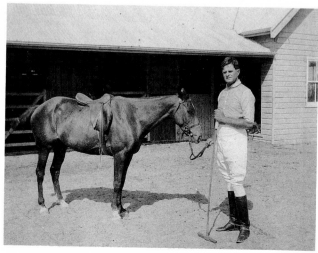

16 *above* Southwood on parade: Paddy in the back row behind Ronald Waterall. Immediately beneath them sits Priestley 'the jaw' beside Bishop the flogging housemaster.

19 *below* The three Withycombe sisters: Betty, Peggy and Joyce.

17 *above* A colonial in uniform.

18 *right* Ronald off the court.

20 *below* At the Schloss Hotel, New Year's Eve 1926. Dick in the centre in a dinner jacket above Ruth with her mouth set 'at twenty-past seven'; Ethel Kelly two along with a radiant smile; Paddy two more to the right as a spinster in lipstick and pearls.

Jackeroo

21 *above left* Tanned and healthy in *Twyborn* country: Paddy with his bulldog Soames on a bare hill at Bolaro. **22** *below left* Tea between sets out west at Walgett, White alone on the right with Loder 'the first of the reds' among the women. **23** *above right* Barwon Vale in its flat landscape of sheds and coolabahs.

24 Cambridge freshman with
moustache.

25 Ronald Waters, the young actor.

27 *opposite* London dandy as the undiscovered playwright of the late 1930s.

26 Patrick White and R, lovers in double exposure.

28, 29 *above, left and right*
Mentor and lover Roy de
Maistre with the 1939 portrait
White admired at first then
reviled for the rest of his life.

30 The Oertels on
their balcony above the
Holzgraben.

31 Dick's widow wintering in Switzerland.

32 The modern writer's room in Eccleston Street with the desk by Francis Bacon.

33 Theodora Goodman's *jardin exotique* found by White at the Hostellerie de Ciboure, summer 1937.

34 Franco's diplomat and White's lover: Pepe, Viscount Mamblas.

35 *opposite* First success: *Peter Plover's Party* performed in revue by Cyril Ritchard.

Found in America

36 *right* Spud Johnson of
Taos: 'Whenever I have
been in love before, it has
always seemed so one-sided'.
37 *below centre* The poet
Jean Starr Untermeyer,
his link to Ben Huebsch
of the Viking Press.
38 *below right* Huebsch:
the rock on which White's
career was built.

39 'Patrick White at war in Egypt.'

of their city. Because it had been personally theirs, which was now burning by bursts, and in long, funnelling socks of smoke, and reflexions of slow, oily light . . . None of the rabble of sufferers – wet, dry, singed, bleeding, deformed by the agony of their first historic situation – none of them *knew* any more, as they stood in their fashionable rags and watched their city burn.[46]

When she arrived in Alexandria she took off her shoes and said, 'Burn them. I had to step over corpses.'[47] Manoly was then eleven, and ships were arriving every day unloading refugees from Smyrna.

The Lascaris fortune had been shaken by the First World War – there was a lot of money in Austria and in Russian railways – but there were still the Anatolian estates and investments in America and England. Now the family lost the estates. The aunts sold the Alexandria house and they joined the flood of Anatolian refugees arriving in mainland Greece. Though they considered themselves ruined, their situation was infinitely better than most of the displaced Anatolians. They bought a house at 28 Academy Street in Athens and settled down to a frugal life in the care of a cook and three maids.

Despo and Elly never relaxed their standards. They were snobs, and Athens was full of people they knew but could not *know*. The children were related to some of the most prominent families in Greece. Their cousin Admiral Koundouriotis was President of Greece when they arrived from Alexandria, and Manoly and his little brother used to go to the royal palace – the King was in exile – to pick chrysanthemums.

In 1930 George Lascaris appeared from America and took his place at the head of the Academy Street household. Manoly was about to go to university, but his father ruled there was no point him wasting his time: there would always be a job for a Lascaris. He was sent back to Alexandria instead to work in the Bank of Athens, which was managed in Egypt by his uncle Mario. The bank was a family fief, and Mario Lascaris still lived on the family's extravagant old scale. For a couple of years Manoly had a room in the vast house his uncle had spent £40,000 rebuilding opposite the British Embassy in the Rue Mena.

At first his uncle paid him nothing and he survived on small sums sent by Elly from Athens. After six months Mario began to pay him a tiny wage. At the bank on the Rue Sherif he worked in English, French and Greek. One of his customers was the poet Cavafy, who lived close by in the quarter of the Greek brothels. Cavafy was then in the last years of his life, a rather squalid old man who appeared at the bank wrapped in a dirty overcoat. Lascaris was warned by a bank official to be careful. The poet and the young man met only over the counter.

After three years with the bank in Port Said, Lascaris returned to Alexandria and took a job in the Moya, the Alexandria Water Company.

He was twenty-two, played squash and tennis at the Sporting Club, and swam at Stanley Bay and Sidi Bischr, where the police kept Egyptians from the beach. In the last years of peace and the early years of war it was an extraordinary city for a young man with very little cash and very good connections.

'The parties were incredible. Those who really *were* rich had immense houses: forty or fifty rooms was nothing, and vast entertaining rooms. Parties of up to a thousand: mountains of caviar and champagne and dancing till the early morning then having breakfast and going home. People taking the wrong wife home, sometimes by mistake, and so on. Very, very loose city . . . After parties people would go to a whore show. That was quite normal. Young people would leave the parties and go to the brothel districts and see a whore show . . . as voyeurs because they were all native women, native performers. People would not participate, although one had the option if one wanted to.

'Anything was possible in Alexandria . . .

'Clothes! The women wore the most fabulous clothes. The women were all dressed in Paris – I mean the ones who *did* dress – in the most wonderful clothes. Jewellery. Incredible jewellery. They were idle people you see. Women had absolutely nothing to do. They'd get up in the morning and two or three maids would come and dress them and organise them for whatever it was they were going to – out to lunch – then they came back and had to dress again for the afternoon. They had absolutely nothing to do except a kind of social life and love affairs: who was going to commit adultery with whom and so on and so forth. Everybody knew about it but they were supposed not to: that kind of scandal.'

Servants were cheap. Foreigners paid no income tax: 'Tax was only for the natives.' The Greeks were the most powerful community in the city. 'It was very good if you had it good.' But Lascaris began to feel he no longer fitted into that sort of life. 'In fact I hated it. I hated those parties which were splendid, but distasteful. They somehow gave you gooseflesh . . . one felt for those Egyptians. One liked them. They were so kind . . . and one felt sorry for them. In fact one was conscious of being a parasite, living on the backs of those poor wretches. The country after all belonged to them.'[48]

When Greece fell to the Germans in 1941, Lascaris's father and aunts, his sisters and younger brother Mario (who had been about to make his début as a concert pianist) were trapped in Athens. One sister escaped. Lascaris continued at the Moya and waited to be called up into the Royal Greek Army. That summer at Charles de Menasce's afternoon tea, he met Patrick White.

Almost everything White wrote after that time bears traces of the history, ancient and modern, of the Lascaris family. Fragments of Byzantine genealogies, the sufferings of Smyrna, the squalor and magnificence of the Orthodox faith, the persistence of civilisations in exile – all became part of White's experience. In the weeks after they met White wrote a poem about the fall of Greece which appeared in September in *Australia*, a new glossy monthly edited by Sydney Ure Smith, which combined fine writing and art (nude) photography,

> The Goths have sat on the Acropolis
> Eating synthetic food, talking of mottled wives.
> The Poison-flower has dropped on Crete, and is
> Spreading its sickly, if defiant, roots in blood.
> But all these symptoms, like the fall of kings,
> And bricks and plaster and the sound of broken
>   glass,
> Are less substantial than remaining things,
> Events at most that serve to cauterise the soul.
>
> I have heard voices praising under fire,
> And death; the lovely sensual act of living,
> And guns are more spasmodic than desire,
> Or bread or earth or wind or hands outheld for
>   these.
> Much will remain when all the agonies
> Receive in time a shape and past. This is the way of
>   pain
> Carving and leaving the moments like a frieze,
> That half depicts a Persian massacre.[49]

In winter, when the Allies began their push into Libya, White was attached to the Thirteenth Army Corps HQ for the relief of Tobruk. The British issued him a Dodge truck and gave him an afternoon to learn to drive that 'gallant animal'.[50] After a lifetime of chauffeurs and taxis, White had never been behind the wheel. As they set out, the winter rains began and at first the wet was a welcome relief after months of summer sun.

At Sidi Omar, just inside the Libyan border, he came under fire for the first time in the war. Two Messerschmitts pounced on the 'soft and sprawling' Corps HQ. 'It was all very brief and emotional, the ack-ack bursting, and the rattle of machine guns, but more spectacular than effectual . . . this little operation succeeded in loosening up the Mess considerably. Even the more exquisite of the Army officers were now full of intimate anecdote.'[51]

White's companion in the Dodge was Flying Officer Atherley, 'a tall stork of a man, in shorts in the height of winter, with monocle and fly whisk, and guardee moustache'. They camped each night with the Corps HQ, where Lance-Corporal Truscott was in charge of the Mess. 'A direct descendent of the Elizabethan clown, one expected to hear his:- "Anon, anon, Sir," as he brought the last of the whisky ration in the last finger of our brackish water. Whether telling of his sex life at Penzance and the Elephant and Castle, or apostrophising his little yellow bitch "Ashenay", or persuading a reluctant officer to sign a chit with:- "Now come on, Sir, muscle in on the pencil, please," Truscott invariably suggested the earthier tradition, of Pistol and Falstaff; of green turf and wood fires; of bawdiness and beer. In the most unpleasant situation, the face of this guardian angel of the desert would rise like a big West Country moon from behind a tarpaulin or a truck, and whisper confidentially:- "It's 'ell, ain't it? Ow about a can of beer?"'52

White's job as 'Air Intelligence' was to trail the army along the coast, picking over the corpses of enemy dead for maps, letters and diaries. The worst were bodies washed up by the sea. 'Fish had been nibbling at them, they stank of watery putrefaction and the dope with which their crashed aircraft had been treated; any documents in their pockets, flight-notes, love letters and snapshots, were sodden and blurred almost out of existence.' He wondered if the bits and pieces he retrieved were much use in the campaign. 'Our activities were probably only of importance for the novelist in myself.'53

Once they crossed 'the Wire', Mussolini's ineffectual desert barrier, confusion set in. 'In the distance one could hear tank battles in progress, like a prolonged grinding of tin cans . . . we began to suspect that the tables had been turned; that we were surrounded, and so we moved on by stages up the wadi towards Sidi Rezegh. Preparing to strike camp one morning, we were unpleasantly surprised by the appearance of a number of German tanks, and the great dignified Corps H.Q. fled westward, scattering pyjamas, latrine seats and the remnants of a breakfast. The cold had increased too, and the rain. The wind drove across the soggy desert right down to the bone. At night one did not undress, in the morning one washed reluctantly, using the lack of water as an excuse, though glad to encourage the accumulating film of sweat and dirt as an additional protection against the cold.'54

A few nights later, they made their way into Tobruk. 'It was a black night. Crawling over hummocks and rocks, waiting for the first explosion of a mine, or the evidence of an enemy patrol, one had the sensation of being suspended in sleep somewhere between the living and the dead. Occasionally a figure would appear out of the darkness, to direct, and one heard the unmoved voice of a Northumberland Fusilier. Once we lost our link with the convoy, nosed into space and darkness, and breathed again on making contact. Once we heard the last of a truck on a mine. But the most dramatic climax to this nightmare drive was the loss of Atherley's surviving monocle. He sat in a kind of frozen horror, as if deprived of half his personality. Then, at dawn, in the wintry, watery, pale light, we drove down the muddy approaches to Tobruk.'[55]

The city had been under siege for months, and in the shattered streets men 'had that look in their eyes, a look of heavy waiting'.[56] White had nothing to do. He sat alone in the cabin of his Dodge with Everyman volumes of Dickens propped on the steering wheel and read. At Cheltenham he had hated Dickens, but now he saw him as 'the pulse, the intact jugular vein of a life which must continue, regardless of the destructive forces Dickens himself recognised'.[57] From this distance Cheltenham offered him odd comfort: 'When anything particularly awful was happening during the War, like the Blitz in London, or when one was being shot up or bombed in the Western Desert, or escaping into Tobruk in the dark, I used to tell myself: at least none of this is quite so bad as the years at Cheltenham, because the enemy is only trying to destroy one's body, not the part that matters.'[58] In the war he finally put his school years behind him, discarding in the rough camaraderie of squadron life the last of the shyness Cheltenham had inflicted on him. By the time White reached the Western Desert he was no longer the mouse.

After Tobruk, White and Atherley struck out on their own. 'It was legitimate enough. Landing grounds, old boy.' They headed south. 'Trundling over the potholed road, we patched our tubes every twenty miles. Tyres were butter to the fragments of shrapnel.' They saw Italian farmers with their possessions perched on barrows and carts; Arabs looting abandoned villages; gazelles scattering over red gravel; skeletons of German aircraft; a wheel of *parmigiana* lying in a ditch; the yellow corpses of soldiers on whom Maoris had exacted revenge; the honey-coloured ruins of Cyrene above an indigo winter sea. They were the first *Inglesi* into Cyrene, but their pride was shaken when an armoured car arrested them and they were made to explain themselves to a 'doubting' major.

'That night we spent at a café owned by a Mlle. Reine Ferry, who claimed to be Algerian-French, a rather hysterical old woman, who received us with clasped hands, and welcomed us as a shield against the Arabs. For the Senussi were making the most of the moment, paying off old scores in plunder, and sometimes also in blood. The hospitality of Mlle. Reine was stupendous after weeks of bully. A chicken, certainly stringy, but chicken; potatoes, Vermouth, Cognac and Vino. We sat down to this with our hostess and the Italian Curator of Antiquities, with a Berber in burnous, more ornament than slave, smoking cigarettes in the shadows. The rest of the night we slept in beds, only interrupted in the small hours by the whole household tumbling into the room to announce that the Arabs had come. But we let our tommy gun off through the window, and after that there was peace, broken only by the endless yelping of a dog.'[59]

The Dodge proceeded along the coast in triumph. Delegations of villagers turned out to wave as they passed. On Christmas Eve they drove into Benghazi – the first Allies to enter from the north – and celebrated with looted Italian cherry brandy at a vast party in the ruins of a hangar. After Christmas, when White and Atherley were again arrested – 'Somehow or other we never seemed to convince' – they rejoined the Corps HQ at Antelat. The winter rain was now pouring down. 'We lived like lake dwellers in our trucks.'[60] A formation of Stukas came over to strafe. White jumped into a ditch and tore a tendon in his ankle.

This was the ignominious end of the greatest adventure of White's war. After lying for six days in the back of the Dodge, he was driven home to Alexandria. A few days later Rommel counter-attacked and pushed the Allies back once more to the outskirts of Tobruk.

Lascaris had gone. He was issued with the uniform of the Royal Greek Army and put on a train for Palestine. At some point he made a pilgrimage to the Jordan, where an Orthodox priest took parties of infantrymen out on a raft and dribbled water over their heads. After this second baptism Lascaris was entitled to call himself, and have written on his grave, 'Emanuel the Pilgrim'. The soldiers were also issued with their shrouds but somewhere in the desert, moving backwards and forwards between Palestine, Syria and Egypt, Lascaris threw his shroud away. 'It was so cumbersome.'[61] For a time he was in a signals unit, then a machine-gun unit of the Greek Sacred Regiment, before becoming the company commander's aide on liaison duties with the British.

While White's ankle healed in the Rue Safîa Zaghloul, he wrote 'The Sewing Machine of Tobruk', a brief story of an Australian soldier sitting in the street of the battered city at a looted sewing machine. As he drinks chianti his mind wanders to scenes from home until he is killed by flying shrapnel. The story appeared in the January 1942 edition of Australia.

White was posted a few weeks later to the ops room beneath the sandhills at Mex on the western edge of Alexandria. 'It was a drowsy, horse-and-buggy version of Bentley Priory during the Blitz.'[62] An airstrip had been built at the head of the bay where Alexandrians once came to eat fish. Dunes ran parallel to the strip, and palms dotted the sand here and there like spectators at a slow game of cricket. White wrote reports on air activity. Occasionally he went out to scavenge documents from

German wrecks. Otherwise he drank tea, gossiped, censored the men's
letters and read. After Dickens he worked his way through the whole
of Trollope. Cyril Connolly's anthology *The Unquiet Grave* was 'my
Bible almost during the War'.[63]

Ruth sent Australian novels. Some he abandoned or never opened.
Joseph Furphy's *Such is Life* defeated him, and Ernestine Hill's tale of
Matthew Flinders' ordeals, *My Love must Wait*, stood unopened on
the shelves in the Rue Safîa Zaghloul. One of the Lascaris aunts later
saw it there and, knowing White was an Australian author, concluded
that he wrote under the name Ernestine Hill. But at Mex he read Eve
Langley's *The Pea Pickers*, a tale of two women disguised as men who go
fruit picking in Gippsland and travel through the apple country behind
Bolaro where White once lost and found himself on a journey down
to the Murray. He 'was filled with a longing for Australia, a country I
saw through a childhood glow . . . I could still grow drunk on visions
of its landscape.'[64]

He talked of books waiting to be written. In a letter to Spud
Johnson from Mex he spoke of saving seven novels and an account
of his adventures in the Cyrenaican campaign 'for the first opportunities of peace'.[65] Despite many empty days in the mess, he was
unable to write. He explained the problem to Huebsch: 'It is still
not quiet enough, or I should say, private enough for me to do the
things I want to do. I want to get started on my next book and that
must wait, perhaps too long for it to be anything but a period piece.
I envy people who are able to get a book off their chests with the
moment itself. I am always either forced, or inclined to keep mine
back till they risk appearing to be dated.'[66]

He was planning the explorer novel. White reached three decisions
about the project in North Africa: the explorer would be a megalomaniac
'at a time when all our lives were dominated by that greater German
megalomaniac' and it would involve 'his love affair with a woman of
equally strong will'. White's frustration at his isolation from Lascaris,
the voice of Vera Lynn on the wireless in the orderly tent, the poignant letters he was censoring, all fed the wish to tell 'the story of a
grand passion'. The third resolution was to write about Australia. 'As
Australia is the only country I really know in my bones, it had to be
set in Australia.'[67]

In his spare hours at Mex he adapted for the stage Henry James's
cautionary tale for biographers *The Aspern Papers*. White worked in an
exercise book, 'its pages gritty with sand, the text blurred by sweat'.
For the next couple of years he tried to get his agents to interest theatre
managements, but in late 1944 he confessed to Spud Johnson, 'Nobody
will touch it.'[68]

Three months after White came to Mex, Rommel began his advance into Egypt. Tobruk fell after only a day's resistance and the Germans moved rapidly across the desert until they reached a point only a few miles from Mex. On the evening of 3 July they broadcast in Arabic that they would be in Alexandria the next day. The British fleet disappeared from the harbour. Shops were shut. Bombs fell. 'Fever mounted in the unreal city.'[69] For a moment Alexandria and the Delta lay open to Rommel but his army was exhausted and could not take another step.

In the panic White was sent south to Helwan on the outskirts of Cairo to join a unit to defend upper Egypt if the Delta was overrun, but after a few days he managed to be posted back to Mex. 'I felt myself united more closely than ever, not only with the person who had become the centre of my world, but with a fragile decadent city suddenly compelled to face itself. Alexandria looked and felt like a blown eggshell.'[70] White heard the Greeks exaggerating wildly about the German forces outside the city. As an intelligence officer he knew fairly accurately the battle order of both sides, as the fighting raged around the railway siding at El Alamein. At the end of July the German armies, for the third and final time in the war, fell back into the Western Desert.

For the next eight months, White worked at Allied Headquarters in Alexandria and lived on the Rue Safîa Zaghloul in the care of Greek women who arrived each morning to cook, wash and clean. He began to take Greek lessons. In the desert his health had never been better, but that winter a bout of bronchitis turned to pneumonia and he spent some time in hospital. The Sacred Regiment returned to Alexandria and he had some time with Lascaris. The regiment was part of the force that put to sea as if to invade the Peloponnese, a charade designed to cover the American invasion of Sicily. The Sacred Regiment was much used for feints and diversions.

From the late summer of 1943 White was in Palestine quizzing refugees about bombing targets in the towns they had abandoned in Germany. He hated these nine months in Palestine, sleeping and eating in a kosher hotel in Haifa and working in a monastery on the slopes of Mount Carmel. Bakers, bus drivers, doctors, even the intendant of an opera house appeared in White's damp room. 'Probably nothing came out of my interrogations beyond insights of my own into the characters I came across, and sometimes friendship. But in one instance, the clues provided by one of my craziest and most persistent informants led to such a fruitful bombing raid that we received a letter of thanks and a senior officer in R.A.F. Intelligence was decorated for his pains.'[71] The intendant's tip that a glove factory in his *heimat* had been turned over to the production of armaments sent the RAF to

Holunderthal, the night Himmelfarb walked beneath the chariot of
the Blitz.

> 'They are belting hell out of the glove factory,' the man on duty
> informed the stranger. 'For God's sake! The glove factory!'[72]

White was a stranger surrounded by exiles. Among the Jews he
found remnants of the Germany he loved in the 1930s. Refugee cabaret
singers were singing the old numbers from Berlin and Vienna, but
new songs too, 'of true love, peace, permanence, an Israel visualised
by all the Jews, from the tragic European force settlers, the bloodiest
Stern Gangsters, to the tough new race of *sabras* born in the land of their
forebears'.[73] Refugees were still arriving from Europe. Some withered
in the hot Mediterranean sun.

> How their soft, parti-coloured souls lamented! Oh, the evenings at
> Kempinsky's, oh, the afternoons at Heringsdorf! Others who were
> thrown upon the stones of Zion, took root eventually and painful-
> ly, law of creation, as it were. Developing tough and bitter stems,
> they resisted the elements because, there, at last, it was natural to
> do so.[74]

That winter the fanatics of the Irgun began the fight to take
control of Palestine. In Haifa, time-bombs destroyed British police
vehicles, mines blew up the tax office. As the British deadline for
the cessation of Jewish immigration approached, violence intensified
and the city was placed under curfew. White loathed all this and
though his support for the Jewish state was unwavering for the next
thirty years, he thought Palestine at this time the most awful country
on earth. 'It makes one wonder where the few noble Jews one knows
really come from.'[75]

He made several journeys from his base in Haifa. He was on
Cyprus representing Air Force Intelligence the night the Allies made
a disastrous attempt to recover the island of Kos, and he went out
hunting for senior officers lost in the night-clubs of Nicosia as he had
once hunted for his South African pilots in the cabarets of Alexandria,
rounding them up to return to duty. That winter he went north with
troops taking part in an advance on Turkey. This was another feint,
to convince the Germans that the Allies might invade Europe through
Anatolia. He went as far as Aleppo, where 'the sky is white, above
the white town, like the dust from the cement works'. For a time
he was stationed there visiting advance units, 'listening to the grouses
of those who found themselves with nothing to do in a phoney
situation'. Back in Haifa he wrote a short story about cold, dusty

Aleppo, the tedium of the rail journey south, and the painful collapse of service marriages which he followed week by week in the letters of his men. He was the unit censor, reading everything but unable to offer sympathy. The situation was, after all, familiar. The letter of Lily to Fred in 'After Alep' is only a crude version of White's to Spud Johnson announcing his own defection,

> Dearest Fred, Something's happened that it's difficult to write, it's difficult to tell. I gone and done something you'll never forgive, as if I wanted you to forgive, I can take what I deserve. I been a fool . . .

One of the books which queued in his mind was a war novel based on the letters of RAF servicemen. This was never written, but the long-distance affair of Voss and Laura grew out of these censored letters between men and women who, it seemed, would never be together again.[76]

From Haifa White was able to meet Lascaris on leave. He would save a few free days and hitch-hike along the coast, 'determined not to lose the relationship I had found'.[77] They met in Tripoli when the Sacred Regiment was stationed in Syria, and several times in Beirut, a beautiful city even in wartime, with good food and good hotels. When the Greeks were posted to Palestine, White and Lascaris were able to keep in touch on the military telephone.

While Lascaris was at Nahariyya near the Lebanese border, he bought a schnauzer pup from a Jewish refugee. Franz was a hairy, black-faced, energetic and demanding dog. He came with no papers, a dog from nowhere. Lascaris adored him. In Sydney schnauzer circles it would be believed that Franz was the mascot of the Sacred Regiment and marched into Athens on the day of its liberation. Not quite. He was later with the troops on Samos and Chios, and a Greek princess tried to carry him off and Lascaris refused, but when the regiment was moving north from Nahariyya the order came 'No dogs will follow.' Lascaris was distraught, believing that Franz would have to be destroyed. He rang White, who came up to Nahariyya and rescued the dog, and when White returned to Alexandria in the spring of 1944 the dog went with him to the Rue Safîa Zaghloul. From that time Franz became a principal consideration in their lives.

Alexandria seemed unchanged but the time of the Greeks, Jews, British and French had begun to run out from the moment the fleet deserted the Eastern Harbour. The Europeans no longer seemed invincible. White had no affection for the almost invisible natives of the city. He thought them lying, bullying, blackmailing cowards, treacherous and apathetic, 'particularly during the bemusing feast of Ramadan'.[78]

He had, anyway, few dealings with them. Only with the *boab* on the door did he have to use a few words of Arabic.

He resumed his old life, living in the flat and working at Allied headquarters. Franz sat by his desk. More than ever White was fighting a writer's war: he compiled reports, collated clippings and observations for the HQ 'news rag', and briefed the press. So began his long and uneasy relations with journalism. He was now an acting Squadron Leader, but the rudeness of the headquarters hierarchy still rankled. He complained of feeling the butt of senior officers' frustrations: 'There is nothing so insulting as a senior R.A.F. officer who has not seen action. They had such terrible inferiority complexes. Those who had seen action were often as polite as Army and Navy officers.' Meeting Mollie McKie was a bright event in these dreary months at headquarters. She was a cheerful Australian WAAF who became one of his spinster friends, and their correspondence lasted for thirty years. McKie found this 'White of N.S.W.' bitter at first meeting but very entertaining.[79]

White claimed he could now 'read and write Greek and speak it in pidgin fashion'. He was trying to write fiction but managed no more than a few short pieces. The mood was not right. This double waste of time, the waste of hours as well as years, was the worst of war. 'After Alep' went to London and was accepted for an anthology of wartime writing. In a letter to Johnson – the first since 1942 – he wrote, 'I have written very little in the last couple of years. There has been time enough on and off, but one's mental state is not right in uniform. I have one short story supposed to be coming out, vaguely, in London, another one looking for a market (which it probably won't find as it satirises Palestinians), and I am working on a third at the moment . . . So on the whole I suppose I am a frustrated failure and would be very bitter indeed if it were not for one or two personal relationships, which are my anchor.'[80] His chief ambition was now to get to Greece.

Lascaris was on Chios with Franz when news reached the island that Athens was about to be liberated. He found a place on a small launch with a few fellow officers of the Sacred Regiment who were planning a private expedition to the capital, but before they embarked a gipsy told Lascaris his fortune. White assigned this scene to the distinguished refugee Monsieur Philippides in 'A Glass of Tea',

> 'In the end the gipsy said: "First you must pull a hair from your chest, and I shall take it, and dance, bare in front and bare behind, amongst the rocks at Ayia Moni."'
> Malliakis was listening to his own breathing.
> 'Did you?' he asked.

'In the end,' Philippides said. 'It was not easy. Because, as you see, I am rather smooth . . .'

'And what did the gipsy say?'

To Lascaris she said, 'A man with long legs will take you to a very distant country.'[81]

The launch took two days to reach Piraeus and arrived a few hours after the Germans withdrew from the city. Lascaris had no idea where his family was. He knew the house in Academy Street had been sold but jumped on to a truck heading in that direction. On impulse he stopped the truck a few blocks short of the old house. A man was standing at the door of a block of flats.

'Are you one of the liberating army?' he asked.

'Yes.'

'What is your name?'

'Lascaris, I am looking for my father George.'

'Well, he is on the third floor and your sister is on the second.'

It seemed a miracle. He went first to his sister's door. It was dark in the hallway. She was carrying a baby and said, in English, 'Come in,' for he was wearing what seemed a British uniform. Then she screamed, 'It's Manoly.'[82]

In the next hours he discovered how they had, and had not, survived the Occupation. He knew his formidable Aunt Elly was dead: now he learnt how she had refused to eat once the swastika was raised on the Parthenon. In hospital she resisted forcefeeding and died in Academy Street. At some point after the Occupation began, the house was sold. A party of Axis staff officers appeared at the flats to present the compliments of the Guistiniani chief of the Italian Imperial Military Command, father-in-law of one of their cousins. Was there anything they required? George Lascaris asked only that no soldiers be billeted on them. His sister Despo showed once again the practical side of her nature, raising money to keep the family fed by selling bits and pieces on the black market. They were lucky to have had a house full of things, icons, furniture and silver, sold piece by piece to buy food. Another winter under the Occupation would have seen them in great difficulty. When Manoly arrived they had only a few summer clothes and nothing to sell for food. Lascaris arranged for some gold sovereigns to be sent up from Alexandria and returned to his battalion on Chios.

Once the Germans were cleared from mainland Greece, the British determined to restore the monarchy and installed George Papandreou's team of hacks as a government of 'national unity' in Athens. The territory held by Papandreou's administration extended no further than the principal Greek cities. The resolution of the urgent political problem of Greece – the struggle between the Communist and

Republican guerrillas who actually held control of the country – was left to Civil War.

White was due to be shipped home to England, but he was pestering senior officers to give him a political or liaison job in Greece. 'If that is still possible and I am not put on a boat, I shall go that way,' he wrote to Peggy Garland in December. 'But it looks now as though the British will stink for many years to come as far as Greek noses are concerned. Still I think this is all the more reason for me to try to go there. I feel that individuals may do much to repair the damage that has been done – if our policy will allow sympathisers to go there. How I wish I could get out of this uniform and go my own way.'[83]

The pestering worked – a lesson he was to take into civilian life – and he was posted briefly to the outskirts of Naples where he caught bronchitis before flying on to Greece. The last lap of the journey, he told McKie, 'was like a beautiful, feverish dream with old maps coming to life underneath'. As soon as he reported for duty in Athens he was sent to hospital with pneumonia and lay there impatiently for ten days staring through the window at a fragment of landscape that seemed all he could desire. 'I . . . watched the snowflakes of melodrama scud past the windows and vanish at once on making contact with a barren hillside, on its summit a whitewashed chapel, that recurring symbol of Greek masochism. I was happy in the sense that I had reached my Promised Land.'[84]

This was February 1945 and in his ward were Greeks wounded in the savage fighting that had only just ended in the city. As he lay recuperating in hospital the Communist ELAS forces agreed to disarm, but they surrendered only their heavy old guns. The rest were stored underground. Some of the ELAS forces left for the mountains. The Civil War was not over, but in abeyance. White emerged from hospital to find Athens pocked with bullet holes. People were still hungry. The black market prospered.

He took a room on the upper slopes of the Lykavittos where he lived when he was off duty. This bare room in an ochre house was 'a great joy to one of a solitary disposition'. It was spring and the city was surrounded by blue sea and fields of stocks. One afternoon he walked up to the Acropolis, 'pure spirit for this last moment in time' and was alone on the marble summit. 'I saw the Parthenon as the symbol of everything I or any other solitary artist aspired to.'[85]

'As life seeped back into the bullet-scarred Athens its citizens were more joyous than I have known them in better times. There was singing in the streets. Food began to reappear in the tavernas. The smell of those days remains with me – the perfume of stocks in the Maroussi fields, chestnuts roasting at street corners, Kokkoretsi turning on spits in open doorways. And roses, the crimson roses ... As one who has always been stage-struck, I spent my evening when on leave at the theatre – seeing Kotopouli in the last years of her career, and [Melina Mercouri] then a little girl, playing the ingénue in an English piece with Katerina's company. I saw Miranda, who rode the white horse at the Battle of Kephissia, and later took the part of Theodora in the play about that empress by Dimitri Photiadis. The frivolous side of my nature rejoiced particularly in the popular theatre, those mercilessly satirical revues, with stars such as the Sisters Kalouta, Kakia Mendri, Hero Handa, and the Vempo (first seen in Beirut when that city was a haven of peace and beauty).'[86]

For a few weeks White was at the Kalamaki aerodrome near Athens training pilots of the Hellenic Air Force in operational intelligence. In April he was called suddenly and mysteriously to Florence, where he was asked to work on a translation of the surrender terms. 'I found that they had roped in all available German speakers, regardless of the state of their German.' White managed to sidestep the challenge. When he spoke of this in later years he said he was nervous of his German and declined to help. At the time he wrote to McKie, 'Fortunately they did not use us all, and after sitting about for a few days and seeing Florence, I came back to Greece.'[87]

The next months were spent at Air HQ in Athens writing speeches in Greek and English for the Air Officer Commanding. White persuaded him to accept the un-British sort of rhetoric that was essential in Greece, 'blue heavens and that sort of thing', but the two men did not see eye to eye on Greek politics. 'At times I forgot which country should have come first, and fell foul of my commanding officer for sympathising with the KKE.'[88] The KKE was communist and appeared then to represent more clearly than any of the other factions the interests of Greece as an independent nation.

The ordeal of his adopted country at the hands of the Germans and British made White reflect on unfamiliar issues of politics and religion. War, he told Peggy Garland, made democracy seem only a 'vague ghost' and he wondered if some combination of Communism and revived Christianity might not be the answer for Europe. 'Perhaps after all I am heading for Christianity myself! I don't know. But I do know that as far as my political views are concerned, the last few years have made me want to hear less theory and see more practice.'[89]

The Lascaris were republicans – all the best families and all the Smyrna people were republican – and White's republican loyalties were first engaged by Hellenic politics in 1945. These months were dramatic and absorbing. Greece, he told Spud Johnson, 'is an increasing obsession in spite of the fact that the people are frequently maddening and that one can see no real hope for them or ultimate solution to their problem. They have this terrible innate desire to destroy themselves, just as they have destroyed or attempted to destroy so many of their great men from Socrates down. But one continues to want to do all one can for them.'[90]

The great disappointment of the spring and early summer was Lascaris' absence from Athens. He was out in the Aegean with the Sacred Regiment mopping up the last German forces. But White met his family and heard their stories. He did not admire the father George. 'A charmer for a short spell, he dropped the charm on seeing you were there to stay, when he returned to being a glum, trivial old man whose selfishness had left him drought stricken. He tyrannised over Despo, the older sister with whom he was forced to live, and bullied his servants; yet continued to cast a spell over young girls, nurses, anybody who might serve his purpose.' By the time White met Despo she 'was an etiolated beauty of true distinction'. She showed him the fragment of a novel she had written in English after the last war. The third member of the family in George's flat was Manoly's younger brother Mario, the pianist, who was working once more to make his début on the concert platform.[91]

Manoly's sister Catina returned from exile in London. She was a courageous figure, a great gossip, rather a clown and a shrewd businesswoman. Catina was the child on whom all opportunities had been lavished. She was going to be a dancer or an actress but married, instead, a prosperous Left intellectual, Dimitri Photiades, son of another of the distinguished families of Smyrna. Catina had dedicated her life, as Manoly was to devote his, to the writer who was her spouse. Photiades had published an important periodical *Modern Greek Letters* before the war and since his return to Athens was producing its successor, *Free Letters*. He was a playwright – author of the 'terrible' play about Theodora – journalist and historian who wrote in the tough Greek which the Left affected but the Lascaris family found difficult to understand. The Photiades lived with a mob of cats in a flat on an Athenian rooftop. When Dimitri finally threw them out, Catina became 'The Woman Who Wasn't Allowed to Keep Cats'.

Of all the family, White was most attached to Manoly's younger sister Elly. She was poised and very *soignée* but had her brother's gentleness. Elly was married to a doctor, Elias Polymeropoulos, and they had a young son. 'Elly's crisp, rosy beauty as a young woman and mother was closely related to all that is admirable, all that is real, in the only country to which she could belong.'[92] Her fondness for White had none of the faint – sometimes more than faint – suspicion the Lascaris family felt towards this Australian friend. The nature of the relationship between the two men had not been grasped by the family. Absolutely nothing was said. An aunt suspected Manoly's RAF friend of falling in love with Elly. It was not so, Manoly told her. When he passed on her remarks White said, 'I would have under different circumstances.'[93]

Manoly had appeared at last in July. The two men took a caique to the island of Aiyina with Elly and her child. They read and swam and ate fish under the brushwood canopy of a little hotel on the shore. 'What might only be a pause in the endless upheaval we had learnt to expect, disguised itself as perpetual happiness.' One afternoon a newspaper arrived with the news that the bomb had dropped and the war with Japan was over. 'The future stretched ahead of us, purified and perfect, as it does apparently at the moment when any war ends, like the last shot in a bad film . . . We were modestly if incredulously happy at this happy ending.'[94]

TWELVE

Return to Abyssinia

WHITE AND LASCARIS had only a vague idea what peace would bring for them. It had been enough in the last four years to survive the war month by month. 'You didn't talk about long term plans; you didn't care; you were very used to death.'[1] They returned from the island to celebrate at wildly happy parties in Athens and then the two men began to sort out their future.

White had no doubt that Greece was where he wanted to live for the rest of his life. Greece was his chief obsession, here he saw perfection on every hand, 'not only the perfection of antiquity, but that of nature, and the warmth of human relationships expressed in daily living'.[2] Buried beneath his rich young man's existence in London had been a yearning for simplicity which war and a lover and Greece had exhumed. After five years in the Middle East he believed himself to be Levantine. Here in Greece, stripped bare of all superfluities, he could live a life of pure being, pure spirit.

On behalf of the country that was to be his new home, Flight-Lieutenant P. V. M. White wrote (via Ruth) to the Australian Prime Minister to ask for an experimental flock of merino sheep to help restore Greek agriculture. 'I am myself an Australian,' he explained to Ben Chifley. 'My father, Victor White, was part owner of the property Belltrees at Scone in New South Wales, of which my cousin Alfred White is now owner. I have had a little experience of sheep raising myself, and believe that parts of Greece resemble parts of Australia . . . It is my belief that Merino sheep might be bred profitably in Greece, and that the experiment would be worth the making.' Australia prohibited absolutely the export of its merinos and White's plea was met with official regrets.[3]

Lascaris, in the midst of the celebrations, was ordered to report to Greek Army headquarters. He knew what this meant: each side was gathering its forces for the 'third round' of the Civil War. As an 'overseas' Greek he was entitled to be discharged in Egypt and, within half an hour of his ominous summons to headquarters, he had his father's blessing to leave, packed his kit and found a British officer willing to order him back to Egypt. Outside the Grande Bretagne he joined a truckload of British officers on their way to catch a plane to Cairo. Safe in Egypt, Lascaris was posted for a while to Heliopolis, where he translated artillery lectures into English until he was demobbed and returned to Alexandria to take up his work on the Moya and live with Franz in the Rue Safîa Zaghloul.

White spent the next five months writing speeches and sparring with his commanding officer in Athens, oppressed by the atmosphere of abrasive bad manners that made service life not merely tedious but demeaning for him. He wrote to Spud Johnson, 'I can think of nothing more exhilarating and really unbelievable than escape from the Service and the automaton existence among uncongenial people one has led for so long.' Spud had been doing civilian war work in California, but however regimented that was, White told him, it could not match the 'esoteric nightmare of tradition, behaviour, procedure, or whatever you like to call it' of the RAF. 'This is something that has always horrified me. I suppose it is some kind of a colonial's complex or related to the anarchist hidden inside me.'[4]

When 'After Alep' appeared in the third *Bugle Blast* collection, he sent a copy to Huebsch, 'just to show you that I do occasionally put two words together'. Three years had passed since their last contact, and White told the publisher he had produced nothing in that time except half a dozen stories, 'a form in which I never feel at home'. He told Huebsch there were several novels coming, though it would still be some time before he was demobbed and could start work. He would be living and writing in Greece. 'Probably one will become engulfed in a Balkan chaos, but I mean to try.'[5]

His Greek plans were by this time far advanced: he would be demobbed in London, make a brief visit to Australia and then return to Greece. 'What I want to do is buy the agency for certain commodities to import into this country, have M. manage the business for me, and settle down to write all the things I have been prevented from writing during the War. No doubt it will be some time before all one's plans can materialise. I shall probably have to fight to get out of England again once I am inside it, and there will probably be difficulty attached to taking money out of the country. But again, one can achieve anything if one pesters long enough.'[6]

In October he managed to get down to Alexandria for a few days' leave – 'M will be at home when I arrive'[7] – then returned to work in Athens for about six weeks. His old pipe had had it; rather than break in another he gave up smoking. After Christmas, with great sadness but anticipating a quick return, he sailed from Piraeus,

> 'you should have seen the dove-coloured light, *chryso mou*, all the doves in the world huddling together on the shores of the Gulf. And the violet shadows. Athens is ashes and violets at dusk. Before it is burnt right out. Have you looked? Have you ever noticed?'[8]

He was dumped on a train in Italy, thrown off into the sinister prosperity of Milan, then taken through the snow-filled Switzerland of his childhood and across France, to find himself arriving once again at Victoria Station. On 10 January 1946, at Uxbridge on the outskirts of London, he was returned to civilian life with a handful of service medals, a hat, a pair of shoes, a suit, a raincoat and a cardboard suitcase.

The face that was sleek before the war was now craggy. His forehead was high and lined and the marks of a habitual grimace ran down each side of his thin mouth. He looked a decade older than his years, but it was to be another twenty before he seemed to age again. The RAF demobbed Patrick White with the indestructible face of an Australian grazier.

He was changed. The rich are able to choose the company they keep, but White had spent the war years thrown in with the crowd and discovered to his surprise that he could deal with mankind at random. The fear of being cut off from the human race no longer afflicted him with such intensity and his bond with Lascaris, the first affair of his life to endure for any time, had cured the self-pity that had haunted him since adolescence. He was in good health. 'From the letters he sent me from the Middle East, he was really on the whole more contented in that period than at any time I'd known him,' recalled Betty Withycombe. 'He was fit, never so fit in his life. And aloof. Before the War he was, if you like, constipated and moody. After he was demobbed he was moody and bad tempered.'[9]

White went down to Ebury Street and took a room in the house of his old landlady Inez Imhof for five guineas a week with breakfast. The only other lodger was a senile French spinster, 'fanged and bent, every child's idea of a witch'.[10] Next door was a bomb site. He bought a schnauzer bitch, Lottie, to keep him company as he plotted to escape England.

London came as a shock. In this battered, mean, haunted city he was cold and hungry again for the first time in years. Here were the ruins of a lost world he had no wish to re-enter and he looked back once more with distaste to his old life of first nights, meals at the Café Royal, broken affairs and little triumphs in revue. Worse than the physical discomfort of London was 'a kind of mental apathy and deadness' that got him down.[11] His friends seemed stuck in their old ruts. Everything was now expensive. 'The only thing one can still do at a reasonable outlay is to get squalidly drunk in a pub, though it takes longer as the beer is weak.'[12] He found an oasis in the West End, and one of the most exciting events in the theatre in his life was the night he saw *Oklahoma!* It seemed to him, demobbed in that drab city, that 'Oh What a Beautiful Morning' was the first song of peace.

Ronald Waters had left the stage to become an actors' agent – eventually one of the leading agents in London. Betty Withycombe was at the Commonwealth Forestry Bureau in Oxford after spending the war at the Admiralty working out train timetables in Europe in preparation for the invasion. Her *Oxford Dictionary of English Christian Names* was published in 1945 and has remained in print ever since. White's sister Suzanne and her husband Geoffrey Peck were in London. Peck, a diabetic, had remained with the BBC throughout the war. They had two children, Gillian and Alexandra, and White found himself enjoying the rituals of being an uncle.

A suitcase of belongings arrived from New York, sent over by Joe Rankin's brother. Among his own stuff were bits and pieces of Joe's. Picking through them, as he had picked over scraps taken from enemy corpses, White was able to piece together a little of what had happened to his lover. Joe had left New York to set up practice in Atlanta. White and Rankin never made contact again and when *The Living and the Dead* came to be republished, it appeared without its dedication to Joe.

White tried to reach the Oertels, not knowing that in January 1945 the apartment on the Holzgraben was destroyed in the raids that flattened Hanover. The Oertels survived but it was thirty years before they made contact with him again.

Roy de Maistre was still in Eccleston Street. Ten years before he had seemed an important figure in the British *avant-garde*, but he had not grown. De Maistre had paid a high price for living in London. His roots were in air. He was a warning of what might lie ahead should White change his mind and decide to stay in this spiritual graveyard: 'the prospect of ceasing to be an artist and turning instead into that most sterile of beings, a London intellectual'.[13] Roy was being kept afloat by a few patrons, who now included the Catholic Church. He was painting Stations of the Cross and being guided towards Rome by Father Alfonso de Zulveta, evangelist to the nobility. His baptism lay a few years ahead.

White found Roy in the grip of a genealogical delusion that his family was of royal blood. Since the 1880s the de Mestres had been tracking down ancestors in the hope of finding estates in France to replenish the fortunes lost on the Australian track. Roy had taken the family's passion to an odd extreme, and he wrote to his sister Melanie a little before Christmas 1945 with news of the most glorious ancestors: 'our great grandmother, the mother of Prosper de Mestre . . . became the morganatic wife of the Duke of Kent and lived with him in Canada and England for 25 years. The whole story is known to historians and the Royal Family. What is not generally known is that her first husband was Comte Jean Charles André de Mestre.' He claimed to have seen proofs of the story in the archives at Windsor. 'I have promised Queen Mary not to publish anything without *their* approval.'[14]

By Roy's calculations, his grandfather Prosper was Queen Victoria's half-brother. The remote origins of this balderdash appear to lie in the fictions Prosper put about after his arrival in Sydney in 1818: a Catholic of French parentage wanting to do business in a British colony a couple of years after Waterloo. Roy believed it all. At his baptism into the Roman Catholic church in 1949, the painter awarded himself the Christian name Laurent in honour of Kent's mistress. He did nothing to discourage stories that a black car came to the studio on occasional afternoons to take him round the corner to tea at the palace. In the studio he displayed with care Christmas cards from the Queen.

White loved and pitied the old man, and his admiration for the paintings was not dimmed by the 'wholly real or partly mythic' royal ancestry.[15] One of the new paintings he bought at this time was 'The Aunt', painted after Roy visited the ruins of Chelsea barracks where one of his relatives was killed by a buzz-bomb late in the war. On a heap of rubble he found a photograph of the dead woman's mother and from this grim souvenir he painted the portrait of a woman in full Edwardian dress but with a face entirely blank, as if her clothes were on a tailor's dummy.

The image of 'The Aunt' fused in White's mind with a long-planned novel about a wandering spinster going mad in a world on the brink of violence. The idea had come to him in 1939 after his admirable, plain godmother Gertrude Morrice appeared briefly in London. The title that fastened itself to this idea was *The Aunt's Story*. Shortly after buying Roy's painting, and within a month of his demobilisation, White was at work on the novel. 'My creative self, frozen into silence by the war years, began to thaw . . . I can't say it poured on to the paper after the years of drought; it was more like a foreign substance torn out by ugly handfuls.'[16]

The aunt began as a portrait of his godmother. She and Theodora Goodman were women who thought a great deal but said little; each was 'a distinguished creature in spite of her dowdiness and ugliness'. Theodora's appalling mother is a sharp likeness of Elizabeth Morrice, who had taken Paddy through *Hamlet* when he was a little boy. Mrs Goodman mostly sat on her sofa and was small and still. She rolled her hands into a tight small ivory ball, studded with diamond or emerald or garnet, just according, her hands were always hard with rings.

Meroë is drawn from White's childhood memories of the Morrices' pink brick Browley, but he shifted the little homestead from the creek flats near Moss Vale to Mount Ashby, the old volcano across the paddocks from Tudor House. White called the Goodmans' place Meroë after the Ethiopian city, 'because many Australian properties of that period had similar pretentious and semi-legendary names'.[17]

The novel grew from one of his jackerooing efforts, 'Sullen Moon', whose rudimentary plot – 'there were two sisters and a man, and the moon played a big part' – served the first section of the new book. And White drew on memories of Barwon Vale, where 'Sullen Moon' was written on the Withycombes' cedar table. Frank Parrott, the young bull who is drawn to Theodora Goodman but marries her silly sister Fanny, has Frank Loder's erotic red-gold hair and something of Clem Withycombe's dash. Roy used to taunt White by saying he was in love with Clem Withycombe.[18]

Memories of a country he had not seen for fourteen years poured on to the pages: the tussock flats and black hills of Moss Vale, the bunya bunya tree on the elbow of the drive at Lulworth, winter light splintering through pines, hawks in a white sky, brown creeks, the oak struck by lightning, the walk to Bong Bong church as magpies attacked his hat, nights lost in the high country, dry ham sandwiches on the New South Wales railways, skeleton trees in yellow paddocks, the sound of horses' hoofs steady as drums on a wooden bridge, bul-buls in palms, the red moon, bells across Rushcutters Bay, scandals in *Truth*, the great dumb organ brooding over the Town Hall, pines at Manly, the labyrinth of tramlines behind the Quay, bulls bellowing at the Easter Show.

White's response to Australia had changed. In *Happy Valley* he had recoiled from the landscape, but now he was seeing Australia in the light of his passion for Greece. He made the point through a character called Moraïtis, a cellist visiting Sydney, who explains: 'Greece, you see, is a bare country. It is all bones.'

'Like Meroë,' said Theodora.
'Please?' said Moraïtis.
'I too come from a country of bones.'
'That is good,' said Moraïtis solemnly. 'It is easier to see.'[19]

As he was working on *The Aunt's Story*, White had a letter

from Pepe Mamblas. For a couple of years during the war, Mamblas had been Minister Plenipotentiary at the Spanish Embassy in London. Now he was the Duke of Baena and Ambassador to The Hague. 'I have started on a new novel,' White told him. 'An alarming departure after writing R.A.F. prose for so long and not being free to think as I chose. But the despair and difficulties of writing one's own book are so much preferable to other despair and difficulties. And it is good to feel one can work away in a leisurely manner for so long as one likes.'

Pepe seemed to be asking White to join him in Holland. White mentioned in reply a 'Greek friend' and his plans to live in Greece. But he must first go to Egypt and then visit Australia, 'to see my mother, whom I have not seen for five years . . . I think it will take a miracle and great influence to get me away. So far I have not met the influence. You can't put me on to anyone, I suppose, who would make them give me a passage to Egypt?'[20] Ruth was trapped in Sydney. Keen as she was to resume her European existence, Mrs Victor White could not imagine life there on the £10 a week she would be allowed to draw from Australia. So for an uncertain time Ruth had to wait at home until these currency restrictions were lifted.

Her son was as anxious to get away from London as she was to reach the metropolis of her dreams. Hunger was the worst of marking time in that miserable city. White was ashamed of being so hungry every day, for his rations were soon finished and at night he waited impatiently for those cheap restaurants to open where he could fill his belly with goulash of horse and whale, the same sweet flesh he was feeding his dog. He hoarded a little chocolate to take to his nieces one day, but as the bus passed Constitution Hill, he tore open the wrapper and ate the block. 'And I thought, "Oh, let's go to Australia."'[21]

Neither influence nor miracles secured a passage to Egypt. After three months' work on the novel, in which he finished drafting the first section, White chartered a light plane to fly him and the dog, by slow stages, out to Alexandria. They arrived at the Rue Safîa Zaghloul in April, and White began to draft the central *jardin exotique* section of *The Aunt's Story*. He always liked writing in bed but Lascaris, a stickler for domestic routine, broke him of the habit in Alexandria. 'I said to Patrick you can't lie round in the bed till 10.30 because there are servants and we can't live like that in front of servants. He said, send them away. But I said no, you have to get up.' He wrote on the balcony of the flat, with the dogs playing in the garden, 'the pots of basil on the sill behind me, and the bookcase at the other end, as the radio in the café alongside churned out the Arab music'.[22]

Theodora Goodman, already a little mad, arrives on the Mediterranean coast of France. Her hotel is a version of the Hostellerie de

Ciboure, come down in the world since White was in St Jean polishing *Happy Valley*. The great cuisine is forgotten, the servants are insolent, and the garden is stripped of flowers to make way for beds of cacti. White shifted the hotel from the Atlantic to the Mediterranean coast to accommodate the cacti seen in public gardens near Monte Carlo. The Hôtel du Midi lies a morning's drive from Monte.[23]

In this odd garden, Theodora *becomes* the people she encounters. The writing shifts from the present to the past, from lives lived to lives imagined by the exiles in the hotel. Theodora Goodman discovers, invents and enters their lives, drawing on her small store of experience and a deep well of intuition. These are the hallucinations of a lonely traveller, but also a picture of White's technique as a writer. A name, a glance, a snatch of conversation overheard leads her into these vividly imagined existences. So it was with White, his imagination stimulated by a face in the street, tiny details of gossip, odd names discovered in a newspaper. 'How many of us', she asks, 'lead more than one of our several lives?'[24]

White drew into the *jardin exotique* the cross-currents of pre-war Europe. The German Lieselotte was a 'figment or facet' of himself born out of his experience in a world falling apart. 'I had lived in London through the 'Thirties, through the Spanish Civil War (certainly only at a distance), I discovered Spengler, and became fairly intimately involved with Hitler's War. All those experiences contributed to Lieselotte's remark, "We must destroy everything, everything, even ourselves. Then at last when there is nothing, perhaps we shall live."'[25]

The familiar world of Alexandria was dissolving around White as he wrote in the spring and early summer of 1946. Cars were stoned, trams attacked and grenades exploded in the garden of the British Army club as the Egyptians pressured the British to withdraw their troops. The foreign communities knew that once the British left they, too, must soon depart. But not yet! For as long as possible the rich of Alexandria put such thoughts out of their heads. Mobs poured from the slums of Kom-el-Dik down the Rue Safîa Zaghloul to riot through the city. 'Then we all closed and barred our shutters. It was snug enough inside . . . the noise did not detract from what I was doing. In fact it helped bring me closer to what was happening in Theodora Goodman's confused mind.'[26]

White's cast of refugees and expatriates sheltered against the coming storm in the *jardin exotique*. General Sokolnikov is the Russian admiral at 13 Eccleston Street 'set in aspic'. Both Russians were bores and crazy: 'Two of the most difficult literary feats are to make a virtuous woman interesting and a boring man bearable.' Miss Grigg is a portrait of the Cockney governess Miss Spink from Uncle Mario Lascaris'

household in Alexandria. Miss Spink was a little less refined than
Grigg, but otherwise so exactly her that White came to realise Grigg
had no life of her own. Grigg was a lesson not to rely on merely
reporting from life. Mrs Rapallo, the pantomime dame who often
strides across the stage of White's work, brings to the Hostellerie's
garden White's memories of Cape Cod – 'we shall walk in the lanes,
and gather blueberries, and feel the rain on us, and watch the emerald
beetles' – and her pet monkey is a final bow for the regimental mascot
White lost in the shunting yards of Egypt. The poet Wetherby is
White's version of the pre-war Auden,

> a thin young man in a tweed coat, of which the elbows had leather
> patches. Under the thick forelock of nondescript hair, which gave
> him the expression of a goat that prefers to consume tins, his face
> absorbed news, while remaining superior to events.

Theodora's advice to the radical ex-schoolteacher scribbler is to try
to discover his own flesh and blood: 'Perhaps you should forget to
think.'27

The *jardin exotique* cost White a good deal of pain and he confessed
he was so desperate at times as he worked on the novel that he was
once or twice on the point of tearing it up and throwing it away.28
More painful in these weeks was the death of his dream of Greece.
As he toiled over these pages of virtuoso prose, Lascaris forced him
to face the now very urgent question of their future.

Greece was impossible for him. In the background was always
his dread of embarrassing the family by setting up house in Athens
with White. But the more urgent problem was money. His family was
broke: they had lost their house and possessions, and the aunts had run
up colossal debts with money-lenders during the war. Manoly could not
land on their doorstep as they were working to re-establish themselves.
There was no prospect of him getting a job in Greece. 'Everyone was
rushing off to Germany and places to work.' At this time he was not
aware that White was rich – that only came out later in Australia – but
in any case it would not have been possible to live idly in Athens on
White's money while his own family was struggling.29

The Australian's 'great goal and object' was Greece, but the Greek
wanted Australia. 'It was his illusion,' White wrote. 'I suppose I sensed
it was better than mine.' Lascaris had been curious about the place for a
long time. As a little boy in Cairo he ate wonderful jam from Tasmania
and on the tin there was a map of the state. 'I asked about Tasmania
and was told it was an island owned by Australia.' Of course there
remained stumbling blocks. One was Ruth. 'It really wasn't possible
while Patrick's mother was living there.'30 But by October when White

left to join the boat at Port Said, the finished *jardin exotique* packed in
his luggage, he knew the brief visit home he had planned was now a
reconnaissance that would decide their future.

Fire destroys the Hôtel du Midi, and those of the exotic guests who
survive are dispersed. Katina Pavlou realises she is free to return home
from her wanderings. All she had to do is buy a ticket to recover the
lost world of her childhood.

> 'And what shall you do, Miss Goodman?' Katina Pavlou shivered.
> 'I? I shall go now,' Theodora said. 'I shall go too.'
> She touched the smooth, cold skin of a leaf of aloe.
> 'Where?' Katina Pavlou asked.
> 'I have not thought yet . . . But I shall go . . . I may even
> return to Abyssinia.'[31]

Critics have wondered if these references to Abyssinia in *The
Aunt's Story* are a sign that White was reworking in the novel
Johnson's fable *Rasselas*. White disclaimed such a purpose: 'I was
just fascinated by the idea of returning to one's origins after exploring
the "world" and finding in those origins the perfection for which one
had been looking.'[32]

The *Strathmore* was not a happy ship. The old high style of P&O
life was disturbed by two hundred east European immigrants packed
on board. White slept in a dormitory of a hundred men. Deputations
of Australians complained to the Captain that these people 'spat on
the decks, threw fruit peelings everywhere, and hung their washing
across the deck promenades'.[33] Sitting in a deckchair with his back to
this crowd White drafted the third part of *The Aunt's Story* in which
Theodora Goodman, too, is heading back to Australia. As they made
their separate journeys to the same destination, both feared to find there
was no place for them in this half-remembered, half-imagined home.

Half-way across America Theodora baulks. She leaves the train
one morning and walks into the dust and pink mountains of New
Mexico. In the forest above Taos she tears up her tickets and abandons
her name. 'This way perhaps she came a little closer to humility, to
anonymity, to pureness of being.' She walks to the Jacksons' farm
White remembered from his visit years before, and climbs higher to
the house like Brett's lantern house, where she finds peace with her
ghost companion Holstius.[34]

Why a black rose on her hat? The last section of *The Aunt's Story*
has inspired some of the most dogged symbol-searching ever carried
out on White's work. 'Because I see perfection in the rose, both of
the flesh, and of the spirit,' White answered. 'I think I gave Theodora
the black rose because it was at the point where she had been finally

reduced – charred and purified.' Is Holstius the Holy Ghost? No. 'He is a delusion arising out of Theodora's love for her father and forming at last when she is stranded in those mountains.' But why 'Holstius'? 'I knew a man called Holstius and I suppose I liked the suggestion of *Holz* (wood) for a sturdy, though non-existent character.'[35]

The *Strathmore* reached the coast of western Australia on the night of 15 October and berthed early next morning at shabby Fremantle. White stepped ashore after so many years away: Cambridge, London, America, Egypt, Greece, and now

> Fremantle, the first glimpse, the first whiff of a fate which can never be renounced, is enough to drive the pretensions out of any expatriate Australian.
>
> . . . I went down into the town. Rusted railway-lines are strips of red, solidified heat. Wharfies sweating round their hairy navels. I am the stranger of all time, for all such hairy bellies an object of contempt – a Pom, or worse, a suspected wonk. If only one had the courage to stick a finger in the outraged navel and await reactions. Nothing minces so daintily as an awakened male.
>
> Dream streets: the tiny houses in maroon or shit-coloured brick. Paint-blisters on brown woodwork. Festoons of iron doilies which suggest melting caramel. Blank, suetty faces . . .
>
> Oh, God, but I feel for them, *because I know exactly* – they are what I am, and I am they interchangeable.[36]

A week later he disembarked in Sydney carrying the finished draft of *The Aunt's Story* as a kind of shield against a 'familiar and at the same time hostile land'.[37]

Ruth had weathered the war on Darling Point. Though sixty-eight and grown quite grey, rather bent and occasionally vague, Mrs Victor White was imperious still. Her dogs had sustained her since she left London. That pack of fox terriers, her beautiful garden and work for the Red Cross had been her life. Every Thursday she held a working bee for the Red Cross shop in Rowe Street, and appeared behind the counter a couple of days a week selling bits of china and silver winkled out of friends to raise money for the war.

Fibrositis left her barely able to walk for a time but she battled her way back to health, determined to be fit for London when peace came. At one point in this crisis she had dabbled with Christian Science, but it was Withycombe determination rather than Mary Eddy's nostrums that got Ruth back on her feet. Throughout the hostilities she was a pillar of theatre and music in Sydney. Actors heard backstage before the curtain went up, 'Mrs Victor White is in tonight.' She was hard to miss in the stails for she always wore her jewels. In sympathy with modern times, Ruth now drank cocktails and wore lipstick.

'She was very kind, austere, stiff, awfully nice,' recalled Sheila Meekes, who stayed with Ruth on Darling Point towards the end of the war. 'One could chat away with her. Once I remember her saying to me about Patrick's novels, "Sue and I used to *scream* with laughter."' Ruth laughed at the writing but was proud of the writer. On her son's return to Sydney she introduced him to friends as a novelist. White sensed in these retired judges and stockbrokers curiosity, scepticism, fear and distaste.[38]

Mother and son started quarrelling almost at once. As their voices rose, White focused on a glass bird that stood on Ruth's table, the 'flawless crystal bird contemplating its own reflection in a pool of water' which would later come to Boo Hollingrake in *The Vivisector* as an heirloom from her mother. Lizzie Clark came down from the mountain and made this savage diagnosis of the trouble between mother and son: they both wanted to be the star. The old nurse was now a little country figure who had taken to half-singing, half-whistling to herself in her cottage. Her brother-in-law Tom Kirk, who had played with Paddy as a child, found him after the war very changed: 'He'd got himself right by then.'[39]

To defend himself from his mother, White retired to a dark room at the back of the house to type the final draft of *The Aunt's Story*. After working for two months, he posted the finished typescript to Ben Huebsch on 10 January 1947. As the novel left his hands he could only hope shyly that his publisher would approve. 'It has meant a lot to me in the writing, and has cost sweat and blood, as my first book after five years of inactivity. But I am still unable to judge it from the angle of a publisher or a public. So we shall see.'[40] A long silence followed.

The final decision to live in Sydney, which White took in these weeks, was the greatest gamble of his life. War had done little to soften Sydney's British smugness. Once the *Strathmore*'s holds were empty, offended passengers began complaining to the *Sydney Morning Herald* about peasants turning the ship into a 'floating tower of Babel'. Why, they asked, must British immigrants and Australians wait in London while these Jews, Czechs, Maltese and Poles were given a passage to Australia? The *Strathmore* controversy ran for some days in the paper until it was brought to an end by a magisterial letter from Patrick White urging Australians to consider the troubles of Europe. His advice was not entirely disinterested.

'To the north, our staunch allies, the Greeks, can barely support themselves in their own small and comparatively unproductive country, which, at the same time, is continually torn by domestic strife, and haunted by the likelihood of aggression. In Egypt, the whole European population, including many British Cypriots and Maltese, lives more or less anticipating its marching orders . . . Although I am myself a British national and an ex-Serviceman who shared a dormitory with nearly 100 foreign immigrants in the *Strathmore*, and although I argued for nine months to get a passage to Australia, I must still maintain the necessity for allotting a good percentage of passages to foreign immigrants . . . and that at once.'[41]

As White was deciding to return, Australian actors, journalists, painters, writers, dancers, photographers and musicians were waiting for boats to freedom. The export of talent had been interrupted by war but now the world – at least London and New York – was open to them again. Friends asked one another in the street, 'When are you off?' Farewell drinks were a Saturday night ritual before the sailing of every boat. Yet White had decided to come home. He wrote to Pepe Mamblas, 'I landed here after fourteen years absence, and immediately realised how Australian I have been all the time underneath. Even the uglier aspects of the place have their significance and rightness, to me, though I expect if you came here, a real European, you would be rightly appalled. But I am enjoying relaxing with my instinct after a long session with my reason.'[42]

He had found Bill Dobell painting in a warren of rooms above a bank in Darlinghurst, and the paintings bowled him over. Dobell had lived in Pimlico behind Ebury Street for years, painting the same blowsy women and pale men who turn up in White's London prose. But when he returned to Sydney in 1938, his work burst into life. True, a *cause célèbre* had erupted when the New South Wales Art Gallery was sued for giving him the Archibald Prize – detractors hired a barrister to argue that his painting was caricature not a portrait – but Dobell's cause had triumphed and he emerged a fashionable success. Dobell was to pay a price for this success, but in the late 1940s his work was gutsy, vivid and opulent. 'I have been impressed with a great many things,' White told Huebsch. 'The people are beginning to develop and take an interest in books and painting, and music, to an extent that surprises me, knowing them fourteen years ago. One gets the impression that a great deal is about to happen.'[43]

Dobell also demonstrated that homosexual artists could survive in Sydney. The rule was simple: society must be allowed to pretend that homosexuality did not exist, and a man must do nothing to disturb the pretence. One of the writers preparing to leave Sydney in these years was Sumner Locke Elliott. His version of the rule was this: 'So long as your fly was done up and you didn't make a pass at the husband as you left, you were all right.'[44]

Ruth still enjoyed the company of a few homosexual men, for

their taste if not their tastes. Some women, observed Marcia
Lushington to Eddie Twyborn, are *inveterate*,

> 'They adore to have queer men around. They find it amusing.
> A sort of court fool. I couldn't bear to touch one.'
> 'You must have touched a few,' he suggested, 'a few of
> your women friends' fools – if only in shaking hands.'
> She said, 'Oh, well – as a social formality one has to –
> don't you understand?
> 'Fortunately,' she added, 'most of them go away to Europe.
> They're too ashamed.'[45]

Men did not live together as lovers in Sydney unless they cut
hair or danced in the chorus of J. C. Williamson's musicals. Men
of some rank might 'share a flat' but they were expected to make
excuses, and they did, arriving at the theatre and dinners and public
events with women on their arms. Even as they entered their dotage,
these bachelors were called 'eligible' by the Sydney press. White had
the assurance of his upbringing and the experience of Alexandria to
help him avoid such pretences. It would be uncomfortable but not
impossible to live with Lascaris in Sydney, and easier on the fringe of
the city than in his mother's stamping ground in the Eastern Suburbs.
They could get by with little pretence and no advertisement.

Life in Sydney would be easier now, for the Whites had faded.
The family no longer loomed over the city; their town houses were
in other hands, and the ranks of relatives had thinned. Only the last
of the original Belltrees' partners, Arthur and Milly, survived in their
suite at the Australia. The old couple were worth a fortune but lived
with extreme frugality, endowing suburban churches, eating snacks,
washing their handkerchiefs in the basin and taking the tram to bowls.
Between the returning writer and his cousin Alfred at Belltrees there
was no prospect of more than occasional and polite contact. Patrick
often spoke of being shunned by his family after the war, but he
welcomed finding himself at this distance from Belltrees and Lulworth,
for it would make it all the easier to settle down 'to become an outcast
artist'.[46]

Ruth was determined to leave as soon as currency restrictions
allowed and she was able to plan for an exit at the end of the summer.
She wanted all her family around her when she settled in London but
now Patrick was proposing, quite unexpectedly, to thwart her. There
were violent rows, and the son believed his mother blamed Lascaris's
invisible presence for ruining her plans. But Ruth's response was more
complex and sympathetic than he would admit. He had lived abroad
too long to sponsor Lascaris's immigration to Australia, but she could

and she did. In late January White wrote to Pepe Mamblas, 'After many letters and a visit to Canberra, I have succeeded in getting the entry permit for my Greek friend, Manoly Lascaris, who is still in Egypt with our two schnauzers. The schnauzers unfortunately cannot come to Australia from a foreign country. So I am going back in March to take them . . . to England. After six months quarantine the schnauzers can pass as English dogs and come out here.'[47]

While he waited for his ship, White set to work researching the explorer novel. His uncle's great stamp cabinets had disappeared from their place of honour in the Mitchell Library but the room still smelt of varnish and rubber as it had when he was a child, and there were still 'all those brown ladies studying Australiana and crypto-journalists looking up their articles for the Saturday supplements'.[48] He joined them. The figure of the explorer, which had come to him first as he read Eyre's journals in the Blitz and was 'nourished by months spent traipsing backwards and forwards across the Egyptian and Cyrenaican deserts, influenced by the arch-megalomaniac of the day', began to take its final shape when he read Alec Chisholm's *Strange New World*, an account of the explorations of the Prussian Ludwig Leichhardt, who was lost without trace in the Australian desert in 1848. White responded to Leichhardt particularly 'because I know German and Germans fairly well'. He dug out old Leichhardt records, and read the accounts of the parties that went searching for him when he disappeared somewhere west of the Darling Downs. White read one or two of Leichhardt's letters, but most of what he knew of the Prussian came from the journals. He discovered a sponging, rash, half-blind, resolute, disloyal, ungrateful visionary. But Leichhardt was 'merely unusually unpleasant' and the man White called Voss would turn out to be mad.[49]

He made haphazard notes in an old notebook. It was a magpie's collection taken from letters, books and journals. He was hungry for detail, and wrote to Chisholm: 'You mention that Thompson of the Hume-O'Hea search party had been a piano tuner. The incongruity of it appealed to me immensely, but I have not been able to confirm the statement in any other source.' Chisholm did not reply until after *Voss* was published: he had only a newspaper cutting from the 1870s saying Thompson was a country traveller for a music firm. So that scrap was the source for Professor Topp, flautist and explorer *manqué*, who came to Australia hoping to 'bring nicety to barbarian minds'.[50]

He made an abortive return to the Hunter. Because he needed landscapes for the book he asked the other Ruth White, the eccentric benefactress of Muswellbrook, to put him up for a few days in her cottage and drive him round to see the White and Withycombe homesteads. He was already wheezy when they arrived at Piercefield on its windy spur overlooking the valley where his grandfather died of asthma. In one of the bedrooms a little boy was propped up having a terrible asthma attack. White wondered if coal under the ground might be to blame. (Though his mother had severed all other connections with Piercefield she still owned the coal rights.) White's own condition became rapidly worse, so bad that one of his cousins took him down that night by train to Sydney.

They shared a taxi from Central Station. The cousin was dropped first, and in the careful way of the Whites with small change he paid his share of the fare. But at the end of the journey the driver demanded the full fare from White outside Petty's Hotel. White refused and the driver began screaming, 'Go back to Germany! Go back to Germany!' In this ugly little incident in York Street Mordecai Himmelfarb was born. 'I think it was this more than anything which persuaded me to write the novel *Riders in the Chariot.*' Facing that tirade White sensed something of what it was like to be a refugee in Australia. Memories of Palestine, his admiration for Ben Huebsch and his sense of outcast sexuality also played their part in Himmelfarb's birth: 'As a homosexual I have always known what it is to be an outsider. It has given me added insight into the plight of the immigrant – the hate and contempt with which he is often received.'[51] Himmelfarb waited a decade to be put down on paper.

Ruth had a seat on the flying boat to London at the end of February. 'All the glorious antique furniture has gone on ahead,' reported the *Daily Mirror.*[52] Back to Belltrees went a couple of beds she had culled from the homestead in the early years of her marriage, and she tried to unload her old Christian Science texts on Lizzie Clark, who refused them because they were boring. Two hundred friends were invited to say goodbye. 'All social Sydney and many well-known country folk flocked to Mrs Victor White's huge and super cocktail party at the Royal Sydney Golf Club,' said the *Mirror.*[53] Her son was astonished: could she really have so many friends and must she invite ex-husbands and ex-wives to rub shoulders at the club? Ruth was unperturbed. As she set out for a new life at a great age she no longer had to worry about the opinions of the town she was leaving behind. She flew off two days later. 'Thank heaven,' she said to her son as she left for the air base at Rose Bay. 'No more westerlies. No more snakes.'[54]

London was suffering one of the worst winters of the century as John Wyse and friends turned a bombed cinema on the edge of Chelsea into the Boltons Theatre Club. Wyse had married, entered the army, caught polio in Italy and been invalided back to England. The Boltons was an idea that came to Wyse in the army: a theatre where new plays could run for a few weeks before being snapped up for the West End.

The Boltons opened on 15 January 1947. The first show was a dud. The second was William Douglas Home's *Now Barabbas,* which transferred and established Douglas Home's career. The third was White's *Return to Abyssinia*. 'I know it's not what you want to do,' Wyse had told his board, 'but I do have an obligation and it's very entertaining.'[55]

Françoise Rosay was now too famous and too old to come over to play Beauval. Old London actresses were plentiful, but Wyse could find no veteran to manage White's slabs of Racine. Though Barbara Shaw was only thirty her French was terrific, so good that she hid in a travelling Molière troupe in France for the duration of the war. From Australia White protested that Shaw was the wrong age, but *Return to Abyssinia* opened on 11 March with Shaw as Beauval. Wyse recalled: 'The audience enjoyed the spectacle, but it didn't do the play any good. It was received very pleasantly but if it had been an older woman it might have been taken up for the West End.'[56]

Shaw was praised for bearing up bravely in a role that called for 'the comedy of Marie Tempest and the tragedy of Bernhardt'. But the critics complained that she was too young, and a play set in the Spanish Civil War seemed to the press to come from the 'wildly remote past'. The writing was judged clever, light, ingenious, pointless, playful and awkward. The *Stage* rallied to White's side declaring, 'That the author can keep it going for three acts is a tribute to his skill in writing dialogue that avoids the obvious without being affected and is often brilliant.'[57]

Ruth saw the show. Queen Mary came to the matinée on 22 March 1947 and John Wyse unbolted a few seats in the front row to put the old monarch in a Louis Seize chair. She approved the play. Pepe Mamblas missed *Abyssinia*, but later that year 'the Dowager Queen Mary of England who honoured me with her friendship' asked him about a play by an unknown writer which had been performed for a few weeks in the suburbs, for 'During the entire performance she felt as though she were in touch with me, and that I was the character in question.' The Spanish diplomat was tremendously chuffed. 'I learned later that, in fact, it was I, incognito.'[58]

White, still waiting in Sydney, had reports from friends to help him judge *Abyssinia*'s success. Once more he was on the far side of the world when one of his plays was performed. Indeed, it was another fifteen years before he saw one on the stage. He was not entirely discouraged by what he heard of *Return to Abyssinia* from friends and critics. 'My general impression, picking dispassionately through what everyone has said, is that it must have been pretty bad, but that perhaps half of this was due to bad acting.'[59]

The *Asturias* sailed on the day of the Queen's visit to the Boltons. 'A foul voyage,' he told Huebsch. 'I was travelling steerage, sleeping in a dormitory with about 200 others, some of them very high, helping ourselves to our own pig swill, and washing up afterwards in buckets thick with grease. Still, it was the only way to come, and I expect I shall have similar experiences in the next year or two.'[60]

He was back with Lascaris on the Rue Safîa Zaghloul in mid-April and there he heard that *The Aunt's Story* had been accepted in London and New York. Huebsch's cable arrived via Sydney: 'CONGRATULATIONS ON ADMIRABLE BOOK. MAKING AGREEMENT.' In London Routledge was also extremely enthusiastic, though continuing paper shortages in England meant that publication would have to be delayed many months. Huebsch wrote: 'Those of us who have read your manuscript are keenly appreciative of its quality. The book will surely add to your reputation among the discerning.' But the publisher held out little hope of large sales, 'Our risk will be justified by books to come.' White asked Huebsch that the book be dedicated to Betty Withycombe. To Pepe Mamblas he wrote that the new book would appeal 'only to a few, though I cannot explain why, anymore than I know why a Picasso will sometimes appeal to a charwoman and not to a university don'.[61]

A litter of seven schnauzer pups appeared a few days after White arrived in Egypt and once they were weaned in early July he took Franz and Lottie to England. Lascaris decided to stay on at the Moya as long as he could before going out to Australia. Their cook Athena had broken down when she heard that they were both leaving Egypt, and it was decided that she would be kept on salary and then follow them out, but for the moment there was no prospect of Greeks in Egypt finding places on a ship.

The dogs went to their 'isolation cells' outside London and White bought a couple more schnauzers to keep him company. Solomon and Sheba pissed on the beds and tore up Mrs Imhof's new lino. White's smart Eccleston Street furniture appeared from store and there were dinner parties again. His agent Juliet O'Hea – a forthright Irish woman who was to represent Lawrence Durrell, Doris Lessing and Mary Renault among others at Curtis Brown – was nonplussed to be eating at a glass table and listening to 'a very pretentious conversation about a painting of a bit of barbed wire. It went on and on.'[62]

London life had seemed to suit Patrick White so well before the war that his friends were astonished by his decision to live in Australia. His public was in London and New York and his publishers were on that side of the world yet he was turning his back and retreating to Australia. O'Hea thought he would not stay long, certainly not for life: this was just a post-war impulse to get back to his roots for a while. But nothing White found on his return to London shook his resolution to settle in Australia. The city seemed '100% worse' in 1947 than it had in 1946. 'Most of the people one sees look ill, tired, hopeless, or just dull and apathetic. There seems to be a restriction on everything one attempts to do. And it is not as if one felt there was an end to it, and that one would get somewhere someday. I can see no future at all for England, and advise anyone I know to leave it.'[63]

Betty Withycombe found her cousin as vituperative now about London as he had been about Australia in the 1930s. 'Everything in England was bad.' Even worse was the discovery that the intense intimacy they had enjoyed in those years was gone never to be recovered. 'He had Manoly.' This was a decisive loss in Withycombe's life. White no longer confided in her; he told her nothing about writing *The Aunt's Story*; nor had he said that the new novel was dedicated to her.[64]

The Garlands were living on the edge of London at Hunton Bridge. Peggy had known White for as long as her sisters, but it was only after the war when he brought the dogs out to visit her and the children that the friendship between the cousins really began. The Garlands were leaving for New Zealand, for Tom had developed ulcers on his eyes and he had been ordered to move to a mild climate to save his sight. He was to establish a new post in the New Zealand Department of Health as chief of industrial medicine.

Manoly's younger brother Mario Lascaris was now pursuing the concert career delayed by the war. He had made his debut in Paris that winter, and White was planning to stage the London debut. 'He is a very brilliant pianist,' White told Mamblas, 'and a protégé of mine.'[65] He went over to Paris to see Lascaris and make the final arrangements for London. White hired the Wigmore Hall and tried to gather a crowd, but the event was not a great success. White thought for a time that Mario might become one of the great pianists, but in London he found him rather feckless, technically very good but not a professional.[66]

Huebsch, on his annual summer progress through Europe, appeared in White's bare room in Ebury Street. They strolled about London, White still in awe of the old man. On one of their walks they came across the shell of St Anne's Soho: to be there with Huebsch seemed to reconcile the ruins of White's old life in London and the determination, with this man's support, to realise his highest literary ambitions. 'I began to suspect one might return to the things that matter most.'[67]

He began a new play as he waited for the dogs to come out of quarantine. The conviction that he had failed with *Return to Abyssinia* – 'it is too slight, and has too little action for these times' – spurred him on to this fresh attempt. In Dobell's Sydney studio he had seen 'The Dead Landlord', painted in Pimlico before the war in one of those great, damp, crumbling houses down towards the river. White began to play with Dobell's story of how his landlord had died, how the landlady had taken down her hair, announcing there would be a 'ham funeral', and sent the young painter to fetch the relatives. 'Out of those original facts and my own self-searchings and experience as a young man in the house in Ebury Street, the play of *The Ham Funeral* developed.'[68] He wrote it as he prepared to go out to mess with life in Australia: it was his farewell to London and to the callow young man he had been before the war.

It was a kind of *tableau vivant*, like one of Ethel Kelly's Old Masters in the flesh, but with dialogue, poetry and music hall routines. White aimed for something universal and surreal, a mix of the hilarious and brutal. He feared the result was 'an act of indecent exposure',[69] for he was the prig on the first floor of the old house. When the play was eventually performed, White was asked about playwrights who had influenced him at this point. Brecht? The German Expressionists? 'I had read Wedekind.'[70]

The dramatic problem, as White saw it, was to project this pale introspective young man on the stage while allowing the play to move forward. He hoped he had overcome this, 'partly through the conflict between the Young Man and those human symbols Mr and Mrs Lusty, the figures in the basement with whom he wrestles in his attempt to come to terms with life, partly through the dialogues between the Young Man and his *anima*, the Girl in the room opposite'.[71]

The relatives who descend to flay Alma Lusty as they gorge themselves are meant to be expressions of conscience, 'with its multiple forebodings'. Once the ham is eaten and the mourners leave the Young Man is left alone with the monstrous landlady – 'there is nothing of Mrs Imhof herself (God rest her soul) in Mrs Lusty' – who begins a nightmare ritual to make the house snug for the Young Man who knows he must free himself or suffer the fate of becoming Alma Lusty's captive, part-son and part-lover. No man, she says, 'ever really leaves the breast. That's our weapon. The softest weapon in the world.'[72]

Ruth still wished her son would stay. There was not much contact between them in London in these months. 'We had a few rousing rows.'[73] He was holding fast to the independence from his mother he had reasserted in Sydney. The struggle with Ruth, still unresolved, was the fundamental drama of his life. He adored her but knew he had to break free and stay clear of her, as he broke free from the Whites, from the land, from friends, from lovers, from possessions, from obligations, from any ties which no longer served his purposes as an artist. In *The Ham Funeral* the struggle between the Young Man and Alma is humiliating and cruel. They wrestle on the iron bed until the man breaks out of her embrace to rush upstairs, where his anima is waiting to reproach but reassure him,

GIRL (*now tender and persuasive*). No. You are beginning . . . On many future occasions you'll wrestle with the figures in the basement . . . passion and compassion locked together. Sleepers are

stirring in other rooms to hear their dreams interpreted in words.
The hands are curled . . . waiting to open.[74]

He bursts into the anima's room which is empty except for a sprig of
lilac, White's symbol for his own lush romantic youthful work – the
'acts of abuse in an empty room' – which he is now leaving behind.
From the basement Mrs Lusty bids the Young Man farewell in the
voice of Hilda Richardson sending White off to America,

> Send us a pitcher post-card now and agen! Let's know you're alive
> and kickin'! But write plain . . .
> (*He leaves the house, goes into the street. As the door closes the whole
> of the back wall dissolves, so that the* YOUNG MAN *is seen walking into
> the distance through a luminous night.*)
> CURTAIN[75]

The *Orion* was to sail a few days after Christmas. The dogs had
already been shipped out to begin quarantine in Australia. De Maistre's
paintings were making the journey, but otherwise White shed his
possessions and sold or gave away all his furniture. One morning he
appeared at John Wyse's house with two 'perfectly hideous' moulded
glass door-stops in a haversack. The controversial glass table – cracked
in an air raid – the Butlers' stools, the great desk by Francis Bacon,
were all auctioned. White regretted the desk even then, but it seemed to
have no place in the almost monastic life he imagined himself leading in
Australia. A state of simplicity and humility was 'the only desirable one
for artist or for man', he declared, and though this might be impossible
to achieve, he meant to try, 'stripped of almost everything that I had
considered desirable and necessary'.[76]

While he was sailing out to Australia, *The Aunt's Story* appeared
in New York. White had been distressed to hear that Viking was
uneasy about the title. *Theo's Story* was thought more suitable. 'This
is very distressing to me personally, for it is the first of my titles to
please me. It fastened itself to the book when I first conceived it eight
years ago, and somehow I can't think of one without the other. So far
everyone else who has heard it has also expressed interest and pleasure.
These even include one American! You may know him. George Plank.
It was he who introduced me to Mrs Untermeyer, who introduced me
to you. However irrelevant that digression may be, I still hope you will
accept my title along with the book.'[77] He won the point.

This was only the first of the crises. Then came the Holstius
business. Viking saw a John Holstius on White's list of those to
be given advance notice of publication. They warned White of the
possibility of an intrusion of privacy charge under American law. 'I

can't think that any of the characters in *The Aunt's Story* would give
offence to any living person, though of course there is no accounting
for human vanity. Holstius certainly has no connexion with anyone
outside the book. I cannot change the name, because Holstius he is.
I am positive that the Holstius in San Francisco is not a person to
scent *invasion of privacy*. If he is, I quite understand that, after your
warning, I shall be responsible, and it would at least give me a certain
satisfaction to find the world even sillier than I think it to be.' Viking
was not reassured. Permission had to be obtained. White then wrote
to Holstius – at an old address – who assured the publishers he had
no objections and wished the new novel every success.[78]

The proofs had caused the worst crisis. At first none were offered
to White, and by the time he demanded and was given them, he was
warned it was already too late to make further corrections. From
London he sent a list of thirty-one meticulous corrections to spelling,
punctuation and his own French. He was appalled to find Viking had
a 'fiord' instead of a ford in the paddock at Meroë. 'I hate to think
of a book of mine going to Australia and talking of "fiords". The
other mistakes may quite well earn me the reputation for intellectual
bogusness, but that is not so hard to bear as ignorance of one's own
country.'[79] Viking tipped an errata slip into the first printing of the book,
and thereafter treated White with great care. 'We have learned our lesson
and next time you will unfailingly see proofs,' wrote Huebsch's assistant
Marshall Best. 'You have an eagle eye.'[80]

When the *Orion* arrived in Sydney in early February 1948, a batch
of press cuttings airmailed from New York was waiting. The major
reviews were good and the *New York Times Book Review* praised *The
Aunt's Story* without reservation. This was James Stern's first review
of White's work, and Stern was to play a key role in his success. Stern
found the novel brilliant, original, highly intelligent, gay, witty, tragic,
profound. He called on the ghosts of Virginia Woolf, Ronald Firbank,
Henry James and Flaubert to support his judgment. 'Is such affection
for a novel sufficient to sell it to the few, damn it for the many?' he
asked. 'While challenging anyone to call Theodora Goodman "dull,"
we will admit, and willingly, that her story is "hard to read" – fast.
For, like Flaubert, Mr White believes that good literature, like good
wine, should be sipped. The reader who drains the last drop from *The
Aunt's Story* will feel he's had a full bottle chosen by a connoisseur.'[81]

Viking had sold 6,000 copies in a few weeks and printed a second, corrected edition. White conceded this was 'pretty good' for
him, though he supposed his mother 'would be representative of the
reading public, i.e. those women who go to the library and get out
another novel, and her reaction was: "What a pity you didn't write
about a *cheery* aunt."'[82]

In Alexandria and later in London White had spoken to the writer Robert Liddell about his plans, and Liddell sensed he had at the back of his mind the notion of coming home as *the* Australian writer.[83] After this reception in New York, it looked as if such hopes were to be immediately fulfilled. The Routledge edition, with Roy's painting 'The Aunt' on the cover, was not due to appear in Britain and Australia until later in the year.

Lascaris had last seen White for a few hours at Port Said as the *Orion* entered the canal. Alexandrians with long memories had warned him against Australia, for hadn't Australians wrecked brothels, 'held respectable old ladies upside down in the main streets, and driven buggy horses into fashionable *pâtisseries*' during the First World War?[84] But Lascaris was determined. 'I was urging a lot of them to leave and they would not. They said, "Oh what a lot of nonsense you're talking: it will all settle down and be the same as it always was. But of course, it didn't . . . I had nothing to lose of course. I was young then and all I had to lose was a job, and I was coming out here to start all over again.'[85] But after a year he could still not get a berth on a ship.

He went up to Cairo to explain what he could of his predicament to the Australian High Commissioner. In an open-neck shirt and with his feet on the desk, the High Commissioner told Lascaris that a Yugoslav ship was about to come through the canal with 'non-essential' migrants on board. He offered to get him a berth by 'taking off a Jew'. Lascaris declined.[86]

He learnt that seats were available very occasionally on the BOAC flying boat when passengers died or fell ill. He had to go up to Cairo if he wanted to try for one of these seats, and wait perhaps for months, ready to leave at a few hours' notice. It was an uncertain and very expensive way of getting to Australia, for the ticket cost over 300 guineas. But he decided to try. He sold the Safîa Zaghloul lease to a rich Alexandrian wanting a *garçonnière*, and sent ahead his books and clothes and the Egyptian cotton for their house in Australia. Charles de Menasce had died and at the auction of his effects Lascaris tried to buy the cardinal's portrait. But the bidding reached £400 and he was unsure if this extravagant painting would fit the house White was planning in Sydney. He let it go.

He waited in Cairo. A Giustiniani cousin was married to Prince Goffredo Biondi Morra, secretary of the Italian Embassy in Cairo. Lascaris was living in their house in March 1948 when a call came from the airline at noon to say a woman had died over France. Could he be ready to take her seat at 3.30 that afternoon? Biondi Morra drove him down to the flying base on the Nile. A few days later, Lascaris'

flying boat landed on Rose Bay. White was waiting on the wharf in an
Akubra hat.

Lascaris liked Sydney at first sight. It looked beautiful, rather as he
imagined an English city would be, with handsome and polite faces in
the streets. They took a room at Petty's, an elegant colonial hotel in
York Street a block from the church where Ruth and Dick were
married. White invited Clem and Mag Withycombe, now living in
retirement in Sydney, and two White cousins, Pat and Morwenna, for
drinks. He introduced Lascaris to a few of his mother's friends, including the Kellys at their palazzo on Darling Point. A little later the
two men took the train to Muswellbrook to stay with Ruth White of
Edinglassie in her cottage by the hospital.

The trip served a double purpose. White was keen that Lascaris
see his family's home territory in the Hunter Valley, but he was also
resuming the interrupted search for the landscapes of the explorer novel. Ruth White drove them out one morning to Piercefield and back
to Edinglassie for morning tea on the lawn with Jim and Margaret
White. They were the last Whites on that stretch of the river. Merton
and Martindale were sold and most of what was left of Edinglassie
had been resumed by the government to give to soldiers coming back
from the war. The house and its gardens were neglected. Jim was back
there only very reluctantly, called down from his place in the Northern
Territory when his father died leaving him this rump of the old family
headquarters. They were curious to see their cousin again, though they
did not enjoy – and never finished – his books. They found him grim
and silent. He hardly looked around, but sat there on the lawn with his
face screwed up as if in distaste. 'Give me the Greek friend anytime,'
said Margaret White. 'He was interesting and much easier to talk to.'[87]

Ruth drove the two men over to Belltrees in the afternoon. Lascaris
was astonished. These black hills and khaki paddocks, the olive hedges
and shallow rivers seemed part of a Greek landscape. The place was in
perfect order, its lawns mown, roofs painted, sheds meticulously tidy.
On a veranda of the homestead stood rows of polished boots where
Alf dressed each morning before going out to work. Lascaris had not
suspected there might be a world in which the owners of such estates
actually worked. 'In another country they would have slaves.'[88]

That night at Ruth's cottage White had a massive asthma attack.
For the second time a return to the Hunter had plunged him into crisis.
After being given oxygen and morphine, he was put on the train for
Sydney where he recovered quickly in the reassuring isolation of Petty's
Hotel.

Since his return from London White had been looking for a little
farm on the outskirts of the city where he hoped to be settled and
ready to receive the dogs when they came out of quarantine. An estate

agent found a twenty-acre place at Kellyville to the west of Sydney. White was depressed by the sight of it. 'I know the smell of ducks need not prevail for ever, but it starts one with a prejudice. And then there is the bath on the end of the verandah, and the lavatory down the yard. However, my ambitions may grow humbler as the search is prolonged.'[89] On their return from the Hunter, the two men were shown six acres and an old piggery in a hollow behind Castle Hill. The house was in good order and came with everything down to the saucepans in the kitchen. It seemed just the thing though the owners were startled to hear Lascaris ask where the servants' quarters were. The Glen was on the market for £2,667 10s. They decided to buy. 'I am feeling very excited at the prospect,' White wrote to Huebsch. 'I suppose all this has been lying dormant in me all these years. Coming to think of it, I am almost the only renegade from the land my family has produced.'[90] The publisher wrote anxiously from New York to ask if this was going to interfere with his writing.

For a few weeks they shared the farm with the old owners, who showed them the ropes before disappearing. Then in mid-April the dogs arrived from quarantine. For a couple of months the two men had a housekeeper and suffered under 'her floods of gentility and pretentiousness'. Mrs Lumsden was a 'lidy' and never ceased to recommend the charms of her New Zealand homeland and the splendid marriages of her daughters. After she was fired, she grew in memory to become the detestable Mrs Jolley of Sarsaparilla.[91] That winter, for the first time in their lives, the two men cooked and cleaned entirely for themselves.

A Greek bootmaker in Parramatta told Lascaris where to buy pasta, olives, oil and coffee. Their kitchen was chaos, but it was a relief to eat the food they both craved after a hard day in the paddocks. In August White replied to Huebsch's anxious enquiries: 'Our acres are just beginning to come alive after a severe winter. I suppose that will mean *less* time for writing. And on top of it all, my favourite Schnauzer bitch has just had eleven pups, which I shall soon be handfeeding, each one separately, five times a day. And I am also about to take on a hundred day-old chickens. So you see.

'I may, however, start another novel in time, if my hand has not lost its shape, and if I can find the energy to root the junk out of an old outhouse to make a workroom.

'I don't know whether you heard that *Happy Valley* and *The Aunt's Story* are being published in French by Gallimard. I have not heard who will translate. Still no sign of the English edition of the latter. I should be filled with disgust if I had not lost interest, after being well satisfied by the results of your edition.'[92]

The day after writing his letter to Huebsch White found four bleak

paragraphs in the bottom corner of the *Sydney Morning Herald*'s literary page about *The Aunt's Story*. His novel rated the shortest,
coolest notice of the day beneath an Italian admiral's memoirs, the
new Graham Greene and a travel book on Mexico.[93] Supplies of the
book did not reach Australia for another four months when the
Melbourne *Age* dealt with it in three grim paragraphs. London reviews
were longer, respectful but for the most part unenthusiastic. Routledge
had printed an ambitious first edition of 4,000 copies, yet sales were
thin at home and abroad. White flicked through library copies and saw
by their pages where his readers' interest had run dry in the gravel
of the *jardin exotique*.

He felt the fate of *The Aunt's Story* as a crushing rejection. It
marked him for life, leaving a deep fissure of bitterness that ran to
the core of his character. Were he not a White, he might now have
upped sticks and returned to Europe, but he felt he had to stay. He
threw his energy into the farm and told his friends that the life of
a small farmer was all that sustained him. Huebsch's polite enquiries
from New York were deflected with accounts of chooks, dogs, goats,
vegetables and flowers.

'I am sure I have been right in returning to the land,' he told
Huebsch. 'Now I look with horror at the rootless, pointless years, for
they *were* pointless even at their most significant. What surprises me is
that so many people continue to miss the point. Do you own a small
piece of land as well as your perch on Manhattan rock? If you don't,
I beg you to acquire a few acres at once and see what I mean.'[94]

Once or twice he made jottings for a novel, but the impulse to
write was dying in him. A long, surreal poem was rejected from a
poetry competition in the *Sydney Morning Herald*.[95] Agents in London
and New York tried without success to find a producer to take *The
Ham Funeral*. He wrote to Peggy Garland in New Zealand, 'I feel I
shall never put pen to paper again, and can't much care.'[96]

PART THREE

Sarsaparilla

Because the void I had
to fill was so immense . . .

'The Prodigal Son'

THIRTEEN

Dogwoods

THEY WORKED THEIR acres like peasants, beginning at sunrise and returning to the house after nightfall, stamping mud off their boots. 'We plough, milk, wash, iron, weed, cook, make the butter and attempt to control the dogs all between 6 am and 11 pm . . . I have never felt happier than confined to this small piece of land.'[1] Lascaris was good with machines so he worked the rotary hoe in the paddock, mowed the orchard and drove the grey van in which they took the dogs about. He tried to teach White to drive, but it was useless and thereafter Lascaris was always the driver.

White took charge of the animals: young chicks in the brooder, layers in the fowl runs and a couple of cows in the paddock. He breathed

> the sleepy, morning smell of cows, the smell of warm milk-buckets waiting to be rinsed, and the feel of cows' teats, proud and rubbery at first, then dangling empty like a silly glove.[2]

He reflected, as he cranked the separator, that this work was in his blood: making cream and butter was a Withycombe vocation.[3] The only steady income the farm ever earned came from illicit cream at two shillings a jar. In those innocent days rich cream, eggs and bottled beer were the most valued contraband in Sydney.

A lawn shaded by a big jacaranda ran back from the house to a cluster of sheds where an old Russian lived when they first moved in. The name of this solitary figure was Mr Patchkoe and he earned his keep by doing odd jobs about the place. He ate boiled rabbits and eased his rumbling guts with mash. After a few months he left them to die in hospital and it was discovered that he owned a block of flats somewhere in Sydney. His niece rang the farm with the news of his death. 'He had asked her to do so because, she said, he liked us – which was about the most heartening news we had in our early life at Castle Hill.'[4]

Franz and Solomon slept in the house, but the rest of the schnauzers lived out in the old piggeries with their litters. Together the two men weaned, fed, wormed and stripped the dogs and took them about to shows. Horsemeat and offal for the schnauzers were kept in an ice chest out with Mr Patchkoe. The iceman called every few days with a great block of ice in iron tongs.

Beyond the sheds lay an orchard and the one big paddock that made up most of their six acres. The paddock ran back from the farm buildings for a few hundred yards, crossed a little clear-running creek and ended in a fringe of bush where the scrub and fallen timber was entangled with native sarsaparilla vine. A lane lined with great gum trees ran down the far side of the paddock and disappeared into the bush which hid the local Scout hall.

The house lay uncomfortably close to Showground Road. It was not really a country house but a bungalow, 'a bit of Strathfield in a paddock'[5] with bow windows each side of the front door. Gables jutted through the veranda roof, and over the front steps was a wooden porch where a builder had attempted something along the lines of a pediment. Such a half-hearted flourish was a common sight on cottages around Castle Hill and marked Waldo Brown's place as it lay rotting in long grass in Terminus Road.[6] The front was formal and rather cold for it faced south, so White and Lascaris found they lived at the back of the house on a sunny, closed veranda 'through which one tramps, and where one hangs about, reading papers and letters, and having tea in the last of the winter light'.[7]

They had no wireless and no washing machine. Laundry was sent out. A coke boiler which had to be stoked all day gave hot water. In winter the only heat came from two wood fires. Lascaris chopped the wood. 'One didn't mind doing all that. One was young.'[8] He kept those fires alight for eighteen years. On some nights of chaos, after the fires had died, possums climbed down the chimneys and fought with Franz and Solomon in a terrible uproar of soot and barking and possum piss.

The rooms filled with heavy furniture might have belonged to strangers but for the de Maistres on the walls. *Concert* hung over the sitting-room fireplace, a tangle of brilliant colours, flanked by the sombre *Aunt* on one side and the abstracted King and Mrs Simpson cruising the Mediterranean on the other. There was also a map of Alexandria, and in the dining room an ancient map of Crete 'to which the timid cling desperately on making their first entrance'.[9]

The first impression visitors had of the farm was discomfort. 'They were not used to making a meal,' recalled White's cousin Pat White, who came with her sister Morwenna in the early weeks. 'The kitchen was in turmoil. No washing up had been done. The house

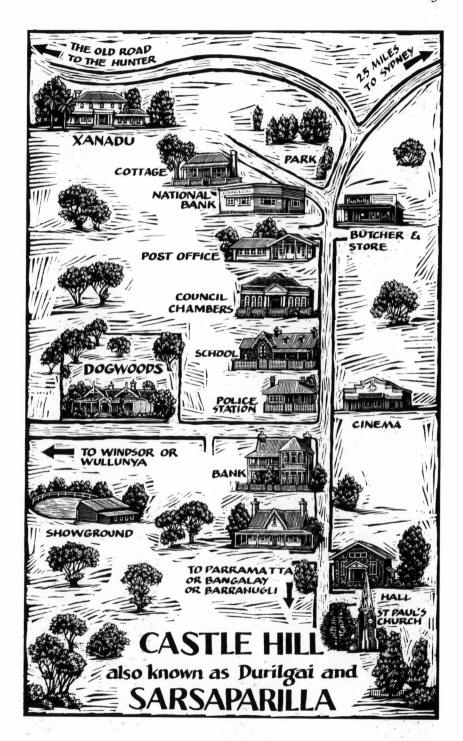

THE OLD ROAD TO THE HUNTER

25 MILES TO SYDNEY

XANADU

COTTAGE

PARK

NATIONAL BANK

Bushells

BUTCHER & STORE

POST OFFICE

COUNCIL CHAMBERS

SCHOOL

DOGWOODS

POLICE STATION

CINEMA

TO WINDSOR OR WULLUNYA

BANK

SHOWGROUND

TO PARRAMATTA OR BANGALAY OR BARRANUGLI

HALL

ST PAUL'S CHURCH

CASTLE HILL
also known as Durilgai and
SARSAPARILLA

was a cold, dreary place.'[10] But after a few months their Alexandrian cook Athena Borghese arrived, carrying a pillowslip of dried herbs. The relief, White reported to Peggy Garland, was immense and when Garland came over from New Zealand for their first Christmas on the farm she found the house in order, the food wonderful and everyone speaking Greek, even to the dogs. White explained that Greek was the only language the schnauzers understood.

In the New Year the two men set about planting the big paddock with cabbages, cauliflowers, egg plants and tomatoes, plus a few acres of Talisman roses, stocks and shasta daisies, 'because they do grow so big here and lahidies say "it's nice to have something white in the house at Christmastime" '.[11] The farm was hit by every imaginable disaster: 'powdery mildew in the cucurbits, a mysterious wilt amongst the egg plant, a few maggots in the tomatoes, as well as sunburn'.[12] The kerosene brooder burst into flames, distemper broke out among the dogs, and white wax scale appeared in the orchard. The two men laboriously sprayed the orange trees with white oil and washing soda, but the old peach and apricot trees were not worth saving, for fruit fly had reached Sydney and the crops were rotten. Lascaris strained his back grubbing out the old trees, and for a time he had to wear a corset. His back never quite recovered.

Whatever survived pest and catastrophe was taken by Lascaris to be sold at the markets. Very early in the morning he loaded the van with flowers and vegetables and disappeared down to the road to Sydney. But it seemed there was always a glut of whatever they grew, and they were left to sell what they could from the side of Showground Road. At weekends when cars drove past to the Hawkesbury River and the mountains beyond, Showground Road was a long market. At the gate of every farm stood a couple of buckets of oranges and flowers, duck eggs and potatoes, tomatoes and passion-fruit. In August that year, 1949, White wrote to Peggy Garland, 'We are going to plant more oranges and lemons. At weekends we are doing a roaring trade in citrus over the fence.'[13]

He found he had his mother's passion for gardening and assumed, at first, that he was living in the mock-European climate of Mount Wilson. He planted cherries, prunus, bouvardias, grevilleas, cistus, geum, thrift and fuchsias – 'But Franz has killed one of the best fuchsias by regularly lifting his leg on it'[14] – a Judas tree and a golden elm, rhus, japonicas and a white magnolia. By the front veranda there was a pink Cécile Brunner that grew into a great shaggy bush. White waited impatiently for the second winter so they could plant 'the arbutus, a crab apple, an English mulberry, and three Lombardy poplars on the boundary across the creek where the carobs have failed. Finally,' he told Peggy Garland, 'we have put in four dogwoods, and have just changed the name of the place to Dogwoods, as The Glen has always stuck in our throats, and this is more appropriate in more ways than one.'[15]

Autumn was the best time on the farm, a few quiet months of crisp days when all the work of summer was done and the two men waited for winter again. Autumn more than spring is the season of renewal in Australia. Energy returns. Landscapes that were hostile become benign. In the new garden at Dogwoods leaves hung in 'golden tatters' from the trees, and they woke on still mornings to see light lying 'in masses on the paddocks, which smoked and glistened'.[16]

Though mild by London standards, winters in Castle Hill were uncomfortably cold and damp in a house built to keep out the summer sun. Thick frosts covered the farm in the winter of 1949 and they lost many of the trees and shrubs they had planted. Between summer droughts and winter frosts the dogwoods never thrived; Mount Wilson was the place for dogwoods. 'From now on,' White told Peggy Garland, 'I am going to concentrate on growing what we know we can grow in this frost hollow. It is too depressing *trying* to grow shrubs that are shy of frost, and which die in spite of all one's determination.'[17]

Summer returned after a few weeks of blossom and mild days. Then for six months, from about November to April, the two men sweltered on the farm. This was not the steady Mediterranean heat Lascaris knew in Egypt, but a season of high drama. Summer in the hills behind Sydney meant floods, fires and storms. Each year seemed to bring the hottest, or wettest or driest summer on record. White found it an exhilarating ordeal,

> a time of white dust and yellow grit. In the glare of sky and iron, in the scent of dry eucalypt and crushed ant, men rounded their shoulders and screwed up their eyes as they leant against the veranda posts.[18]

Their neighbours told them stories of the fires that swept up through the bush along the creek to threaten the big houses on the ridge behind the farm. There were many times the two men stood waiting with hoses in case the flames reached Dogwoods. But the farm was spared. The only time White ever fought a bushfire was on Cape Cod.

'All day we lived in a furnace, with a westerly blowing, and the grass turning yellow under our eyes,' he wrote to Peggy Garland. 'In the evening a southerly came with a roaring like the sea. One watched the two winds meet like Kattegat and Skagerrak, the trees blowing inside out.'[19] Everyone waited for the southerly. Those with radios listened to reports of its progress up the coast. When the southerly hit

Wollongong, families in the hinterland of Sydney gathered on verandas waiting for the first breath of cool air.

> Dad jerked his head in the direction of the wind, and said: 'Just about the cheapest fulfilment of anybody's expectations.' It was the kind of remark which appealed to Mother. For touches like that she had Married Beneath Her. So the boys were taught to wait for the southerly.[20]

On nights of suffocating heat when no southerly appeared, the two men sometimes slept in the garden, 'the mown grass prickled against naked flesh as we lay this side of the sheet of moonlit shastas'.[21]

In one of their first summers at Castle Hill, the Hawkesbury flooded spectacularly and they watched the line of cars driving out along Showground Road to gawp at the disaster. White read of rowing boats in the streets of Windsor, drowned children, and houses filled with mud but it was a point of honour not to be a sightseer at the disaster. He imagined and remembered. The floods he never visited were raw material for novels yet to be written and once, years later, for a song:

> We pulled up and watched the river flowing
> From parts we didn't, and didn't want to know.
> It got cold down along the brown river.
> The water began turning up dead men's faces.
> Good job we didn't have to recognise the dead men.
> It was only part of the Sunday show.[22]

White had been protected nearly all his life from the last sticky months of Sydney's summer. Ruth and Dick had taken him up to the Southern Highlands when he was a baby and later they escaped to Mount Wilson. Now, in his mid-thirties, White found himself stuck in this tropical mire. For over ten years his asthma had been only a pale version of the terrible affliction of his childhood. There had been occasional attacks, some appalling, but he was virtually free of asthma in London and the Middle East. At Castle Hill his asthma returned. It was the worst of the plagues to hit the farm. All around Dogwoods lay neglected paddocks, the grass grew deep and rank, a haven of pollens and mould. After a first attack, White was warned by the local doctor to get out at once. Half his patients were asthmatics. 'But by this time we had fixed up the piggeries for the dogs and the trees were planted and we wanted to see them grow, so we stayed.'[23]

Castle Hill straggled along a hilltop on which four roads converged.

Here in what the locals called 'the village' stood a post office, a few shops with dusty verandas, a little public school, the granite war memorial, a couple of churches and halls. In one of those halls the Castle Hill Players, split into modern and classical factions, performed Greek tragedies and the comedies of Noël Coward under an iron roof. There was no castle.

Convicts were sent up here early on to farm a patch of good soil. Cotton and coffee failed, but the colony's first orange trees prospered. Irish convicts rebelled and marched on Parramatta, but the uprising was stopped by marines near Vinegar Hill in another of Australia's small slaughters. When the convicts and soldiers disappeared a few farmers remained and for the rest of the century five families bred and interbred in Castle Hill. Soldiers coming home in 1919 were given plots of land to go bankrupt growing passion-fruit and oranges. After the Second World War, when Sydney began to sprawl in all directions, a Green Belt was declared and Castle Hill found itself in a cordon of five-acre farms.

The road to Sydney ran through hills and patches of forest into the suburbs of the North Shore. The city was twenty-five miles from Dogwoods and the trip took Lascaris about forty-five minutes in the van. Parramatta was about eight miles away in the opposite direction. Once a 'spidery local train' ran beside the road, through orchards and farms, past the Church of England orphanages at Northmead, down to Parramatta. The little train was only a memory by the time the two men came to Dogwoods, but a bus made the journey to connect with the trains at Parramatta. Mrs Poulter and Mrs Dun took this 'flumping bus'.

> The bus became a comfort. Even when it jumped, which it did fairly frequently, all the young girls frowning, or giggling, the bolder of them knocking the ash off their cigarettes with their mother o' pearl finger nails, and the two ladies were not unpleasantly thrown against each other. Mrs Dun perhaps benefited from it more, though Mrs Poulter, it could not be denied, enjoyed the involuntary contact with her small, dry, decent friend.[24]

This was the journey White took to and from town: he walked to the village, took the bus to Parramatta and then the train into the city. On nights when he was returning tired to the farm, he took a taxi home from Parramatta station. This, by the standards of his neighbours, was an extravagance.

Dogwoods was about a mile from the village down the long, shallow hill of Showground Road which took its name from a dusty ring and cluster of iron sheds a few miles further out. The showground

came to life once a year in late summer when locals brought in their cows
and horses, chooks and cakes, goats and bottled fruit to be judged. The
schnauzers won their first ribbons at Castle Hill.

Fourth in the grid of roads that defined Castle Hill was the old
road to the Hunter Valley that ran along a ridge to the north. Here
in rambling gardens were a few big houses in stone, in weatherboard
with towers, and brick with walled courts and dormers in the manner
of Lutyens. The mansions on 'Millionaires' Ridge' looked out over the
Hawkesbury valley to the wall of the Blue Mountains beyond. This
was the Castle Hill of Miss Hare's opulent Xanadu, and the butcher's
Glastonbury. A red brick pile built by a tobacco magnate became, in
life, The Mowll Village and, in art, the Sundown Home for Old People
where Anglican widows went to die in the luxury of the Chinese Room.

Castle Hill did not divide itself neatly between rich and poor. It
was all one jumble of little farms, factories and bungalows. Behind
a row of cottages stood a ramshackle workshop of old iron, and
respectable homes survived among chicken farms and paddocks of
rank, sticky paspalum. Most of the families round Dogwoods did no
more than pick at their acres. They had other jobs. Their farms were
weekend hobbies or investments waiting for the day when the Green
Belt disappeared and the district could be cut up into building blocks.
In Castle Hill,

> It was really the grass that had control . . . deep and steaming
> masses of it, lolling yellow and enervated by the end of summer.
> As for the roads, with the exception of the highway, they almost
> all petered out, first in dust, then in paddock, with dollops of
> brown cow manure – or grey spinners – and the brittle spires of
> seeded thistles. [25]

In shacks round Dogwoods lived no-hopers and mad women, the
touched and eccentric, drunks and dying. White found himself among
the afflicted, for whom he had a mix of fascination, sympathy and
distaste. He was a good neighbour, and exercised thoughtful and
formal charity. To a family of eight living in a garage behind Dogwoods he gave eggs, milk and butter. He visited the sick. On the
lane lived an old man with cancer and White walked the dogs that
way each afternoon to stop and gossip on the veranda of the dying
man's cottage. Through such kindness White heard the stories of the
district.

No one paid much attention to the bachelors at Dogwoods, except
to shake their heads at the sight of them farming that patch of land so
seriously. In the village White attracted some attention by wearing a
beret, but in those days that suggested not an artist but someone who

had served in a tank regiment. 'He was not quite friendly, but a *bit* friendly.'[26] At night round the farm they heard him at the back door calling the dogs: always 'English' at first and then shouting hoarsely, 'Solomon, come here you bugger!'

As always, White felt more alien than others saw him: 'I had never felt such a foreigner.' That the postman was reluctant to stop and chat, White put down to a rumour that he and Lascaris were foreign Jews speculating in land, and 'I, if you please, was pretending to be an Australian.'[27] In fact, White's identity was Polichinelle's secret: everyone soon knew the man at Dogwoods was one of the Belltrees Whites who had written a couple of books. Castle Hill's early verdict was not so far from White's own in his gloomier moments: a failed writer and the black sheep of the Belltrees Whites.

Lascaris excited more attention and speculation in the district. White said: 'Australians are always amazed when they meet Manoly, simply because the only Greeks they have ever come across are fishmongers and milk-bar proprietors.' He introduced him as 'a Greek friend of the war years' and his partner in the business at Dogwoods.[28] White might come from the land, they said in Castle Hill, but it was the Greek who knew how to farm. Lascaris found himself called 'Mr Manoly' and toyed for a time with the idea of taking his mother's name. He decided, in the end, that White could not have stood having a Greek companion called Mayhew. Because he had served under British command in the war, he was allowed almost at once to take Australian citizenship. He went, alone, to the Court of Petty Sessions in Liverpool Street with a crowd of Greeks and Italians to swear allegiance to a King whose daughter had married one of the contemptible Greek royal family. The magistrate congratulated the New Australians, warned them not to speak foreign languages in public and urged them to read the poetry of Henry Lawson.

White had not cut himself off from his family. He wrote to Ruth every week, and was distressed if a letter did not appear every week from her. At these times Lascaris would point out that White always said he disliked his mother, 'So why be angry if there is no letter?' White replied, 'The bloody woman might write.' He invited his family to lunch at Dogwoods on Sundays, as was once the custom at Lulworth. Clem and Mag Withycombe came out to the farm. So did his cousins Pat and Morwenna White. Uncle Arthur, the last of the Belltrees brothers, had died in his suite at the Australia hotel – White put it down to malnutrition – and his widow, dim Milly, grew fond of her nephew and called at Dogwoods with her companion Miss Myles. Lascaris, who had still to recognise those flowers of Europe which were weeds in Australia, picked her a bunch of oxalis. Milly was charmed. 'Aren't they pretty, Miss Myles?' The two old girls were driven off in the Cadillac, Milly waving from the back seat like Queen Mary.

Lizzie came down from Mount Wilson. She was wizened and forty years in Australia had hardly touched her Scots accent. The Whites were her glory: she loved Patrick and that love was returned. Quietly, out of Patrick's earshot, she gave Lascaris the full story of the family and its fortunes. White had told him surprisingly little.

A cousin appeared from Italy. Eleanor (Nellie) Arrighi and her two young daughters were to play a vivid role in the lives of both men, who began by offering practical help in difficult circumstances: Lascaris said, this is where you buy coffee, this is where you buy oil. Eleanor Arrighi was a great beauty in her prime. She was tall, slim and voluptuous with the hazel eyes, straight back and dramatic streaks of white in jet black hair that came to distinguish Hurtle Duffield's friend and patron Boo Hollingrake.[29] Arrighi had put Mudgee behind her to work as a showgirl in J.C. Williamson's musicals before becoming a mannequin for Schiaparelli. In Paris in 1936 she met an Italian diplomat, Count Ernesto Arrighi, and they married after overcoming the objections of Mudgee Coxes and Mussolini's government. Her daughter Luciana was born in Rio de Janeiro and Niké was born in Nice. At the capitulation of Italy, the Count was taken prisoner by the Germans and never recovered his health after the treatment he had at their hands. His first posting after the war was to be Australia, so his wife and two daughters went on ahead. He died suddenly of a brain haemorrhage before he could join them on the far side of the world.

Eleanor Arrighi was broke. Her mother's cook Hess came down from Mudgee to take the girls in hand, and to pay the school bills Arrighi worked as a real estate agent. The title was there as a last resort to fend off tradesmen. When the Schiaparellis and Balenciagas wore out, Arrighi had 'couture' copies made up by an Italian dressmaker at the Cross. In these difficult times Dogwoods was an oasis for the Arrighis. White was a kind of surrogate parent to Luciana and she a kind of prodigal daughter to him.

Eleanor was the first Sydney hostess to invite the two men to dinner as a couple. When White was eating at the Arrighis' there was no need for Lascaris to kill time at the pictures. Indeed, it was in Manoly Lascaris that Eleanor Arrighi found the European link she missed so much in Sydney. She was never subdued by her cousin Patrick White – she was born Nellie Cox of Gunnegawah, Mudgee, and they had a Cox great-aunt in common – and there continued over the next twenty years the spats and shouting matches on which they thrived.[30]

Ethel Kelly's daughter Beatrice, an engraver, came out to lunch at Dogwoods and one of Roy's sisters, a fascinating gossip and snob, came over on visits from Parramatta. Dorothy Gordon, who wrote a column under the zappy by-line Andrea, was welcome for a time at Dogwoods. 'I would often motor out to visit them,' she wrote in her memoirs. 'Those were the days when Sunday motoring was a joy. Every time we went, we'd buy a bottle of cream which their cow had produced. I think what finished our friendship is that one day we left without paying for the cream.' She protested that this was done in error. 'I had no intention of chiselling Patrick, but from that day to this he has never spoken to me.'[31] White had a different view of the breach: her visits yielded no publicity for him, 'so I withdrew and let her get on with the nouveaux riches and visiting vaudeville'.[32]

The post brought fewer and fewer letters from America and England. 'Very few of my friends have survived my rustication,' he remarked to his New York agent Naomi Burton. 'It is something they just can't understand.'[33] Waters wrote, keeping White up to date with London theatrical gossip. Roy de Maistre stayed in contact, though the old painter found it an agony to write and his news was mostly distressing. Diabetes threatened the use of his legs. 'Roy is in a desperate state of impoverishment,' White reported to Peggy Garland. 'One doesn't know what to do about it (he is old and cannot be transplanted) except buy a picture. Then he insists on sending two.'[34] Huebsch lapsed into silence after White's advice that the Manhattan publisher should buy himself a farm.

He now drew very close to Peggy Garland. She was almost a sister, someone to whom he could open himself a little. In his letters to Wellington he gave a running account of the farm in good seasons and bad, the garden, the natives of Castle Hill, asthma attacks and asthma cures, religion and writing, books and music. Among these vivid passages are more sombre details: hints of dissatisfaction with life on the farm and pages of argument to stave off the disintegration of Peggy Garland's marriage.

She was so like her cousin: sharp, emphatic, quizzical, possessive, generous to anyone she trusted, cold to those who stimulated her Withycombe suspicion, curious about people and ideas, indifferent to the way the world saw her. But they had a fundamentally different view of the human race: she saw good and innocence where Patrick White suspected evil. He said of his cousin, 'Her great weakness is that she expects the good to spring naturally out of her young.'[35] She was slight, her face was small and grave, but lit by a sudden smile. Her long hair was coiled on her head in the style of the *Bunddeutsches Mädchen*. She no longer sculpted. White introduced her once as 'a sculptor exhausted by six children'. She accepted this verdict. The Garlands had a rambling house above Wellington and under her influence it became a meeting place for writers, artists, local grandees, Left-wing unionists, university people and hordes of children. Particularly exhausting for her was the care of her youngest child, Philip Wystan Garland, who was born brain-damaged.

The Garland marriage was unhappy even before the family arrived in New Zealand. Tom Garland was a beauty, a nomad, a man women adored. In the late 1930s, Auden had advised Peggy that his friend was perhaps one of those men who was not *meant* to be married. Though the marriage grew unhappier still in Wellington, White's advice was always that she should stick it out. He was, in a sense, addressing his own problems. 'What else can you do, anyway? Any manner of life is led in the cage, to pursue another is, as far as I can see, merely to exchange the cage. Not that one can't vary the monotony of the cage existence, until one accepts the illusion that one is *doing something*.'[36]

What mattered more than anything in their lives were the dogs. P.V.M. White and E.G. Lascaris reintroduced the schnauzer to Australia. Soon after they arrived at Castle Hill they registered the name Grauvolk Kennels, and from 1949 the *Breeders' Directory* carried advertisements for their Grauvolk schnauzers. Other kennels were soon established, but the Grauvolk dogs dominated Sydney shows for five years from 1949 when Solomon and Maggy each won a 'challenge' at the Royal Easter Show. White boasted to Mollie McKie after that first triumph that the English judge had insulted a great many of the exhibitors through a loudspeaker, 'However, he announced that Maggy had the makings of a great Schnauzer bitch, also through the loudspeaker.'[37]

Schnauzers are Austrian cattle dogs, hairy grey beasts with black snouts and a menacing growl. Those who love the breed say schnauzers are demanding, intelligent and so loyal that they haunt their owners' footsteps like pepper-and-salt ghosts. In the Australian world of dog intrigue, it mattered that Franz had come to Lascaris in Palestine without a pedigree. The problem was solved when local dog authorities were persuaded to declare Franz of pure blood. White gave the dog the pedigree name Ironsides of Erewhon and he became – and remains – a heroic animal in the memory of Australian schnauzer circles: smuggled out of central Europe by a Jewish refugee, saved from death by E.G. Lascaris to become the mascot of the Greek Sacred Regiment.

In Grauvolk's early days when litters were hard to sell White invited *Woman* magazine to visit the farm. 'An Author and his Dogs' records Dogwoods in spring, an old apple tree shimmering with blossom, the 'workmanlike' figure of Patrick White declaring he had written his last word, and a litter of schnauzer pups 'with satiny silk hair and the most appealing, bewhiskered faces'. When Lottie and Solomon were let out to be photographed they escaped across the paddock 'as if jet propelled.

Patrick tried desperately to bring them to heel. Obedient? "Oh, yes, usually very obedient," said their master, with a suddenly sweet smile, "but behaving like fiends today!" ' Male pups, reported *Woman*, sold for £20 and bitches for £15.[38]

At its height Grauvolk had ten permanent dogs and four litters each year. The dog calendar built to a climax after a series of local shows on the fringes of Sydney, at which the schnauzers qualified for the big event of the Royal Easter Show in late summer. 'We took seven dogs to Sydney for the Dalwood Show,' White reported to Molly McKie in late 1949. 'It caused quite a sensation, a team of seven Schnauzers but it was a great strain to me, especially when two young dogs slipped their collars in the traffic outside the Cricket Ground. We won masses of prizes of course, but all wrongly awarded.' Each Easter, as if by fixed routine, White had an attack of asthma/influenza/bronchitis and reached the Sydney ring in an exhausted trance. 'One stands for days beside the dogs' benches, looking out through the bars, sees human beings pushing, sweating, goggling and joking, and worse still, one has to answer the questions that they ask.'[39] Despite successes year after year, Grauvolk's great object was never achieved, to produce a schnauzer that was 'Best in Show (All Breeds)' in Sydney and Melbourne.

Grauvolk lost money hand over fist. When the pups developed scour from cows' milk, White bought Saanen goats and began to breed them as his uncle Clem had done out on Barwon Vale. He loved goats but they were expensive, litters sold unprofitably, and show victories earned them no more than five shillings and ribbons. 'We spent all our money on the dogs. Manoly spent all his savings.'[40] Lascaris earned no wages on the farm, and after the kennel catastrophes he was as poor as he had ever been in his life. The long road which began with Turkish expropriations in Anatolia, ended for this Lascaris at Grauvolk Kennels. He wanted to get a job but White insisted he stay with him on the farm.

No one was pressing Patrick White to write. Ben Huebsch had fallen silent. Routledge was remaindering *The Aunt's Story*. White received a royalty of £108 12s 5d from London the year after publication, but in the following year there was only £1 12s, and in 1951 a pitiful 6s 9d. Then the publishers remaindered nearly half the print run at ninepence a copy.[41] A few shillings came in from performances of *Peter Plover's Party* which was enjoying an afterlife in amateur revue. Hermione Gingold kept 'La Grande Amoureuse' in her repertoire, but refused to pay a royalty. She told White's agents he should be happy with the publicity.

He had no contact with Australian writers, nor did they seek him out in Castle Hill. He never had, never did, live in literary circles. In

London he preferred the company of actors, painters and musicians, and he felt no impulse now to find literary friends in Sydney. 'Literary circles are something to keep out of,' he told Mollie McKie. 'We seem to be worse here than anywhere else, or perhaps it is just that we are so provincial.'[42] Clinging to him still was something of the Lulworth view, that Australian writers were not of his class, but schoolteachers and public servants who scribbled at night. As well as that, Australian writers were absorbed by squabbles which held no interest whatever for White: the local scene was split between the social realists and radical nationalists, but he was a Modern, and hardly anyone but a few poets and painters shared that taste in Australia.

Those few Australians who admired his work had either not grasped that he was back home or had only the haziest notion of his whereabouts. In London, Juliet O'Hea at Curtis Brown urged an Englishman on his way out to Australia to get in touch with Patrick White. 'We put him in the Henry James class.' The Englishman read a couple of the novels and was bowled over. He asked for him in Sydney but without success until he met another White enthusiast at a dinner party. She told him, 'White has given up writing in disgust and gone to manage a sheep station in Queensland.'[43]

A little encouragement came from Paris. Gallimard engaged Marie Viton, Madame d'Estournelles de Constant, to translate *Happy Valley* and her enthusiasm for his work was so great that she persuaded the publisher to buy the rights to all three of his novels. *Happy Valley* was to appear under the title *Eden-ville*. Viton wrote 'long, interrogatory and autobiographical letters' and was inclined to sulk if White did not dash off immediate replies.[44] As well as reading and translating for Gallimard – Paul Bowles was another of her authors – Viton designed stage costumes and prepared abstracts of foreign news every morning for the Quai d'Orsay. She was also battling the tuberculosis that soon killed her. Viton's letters to White began in the winter of 1949 when he felt 'there was not much point in my continuing to write. Nobody read what I had to say. I was also up to my ears in the place at Castle Hill. However, d'Estournelles continued to pester me by correspondence.' He later claimed it was her efforts as much as anything else that decided him to embark on a novel.[45]

First he needed domestic order. In Ebury Street, on Cape Cod and in the Rue Safîa Zaghloul, domestic order was a key to his work. But Dogwoods was in turmoil. Athena Borghese, lonely at Castle Hill, had become possessed by grievances. When she was ill, she 'cries like a child, says she can't take her medicine because of the nasty taste, and goes about invoking God and muttering that her head is full of bells'.[46] The two men found her a job at Princes, a Greek-owned and very fashionable restaurant in the city. She flourished there for some time, appeared one day at Dogwoods with a new set of teeth and a fiancé, and disappeared from their lives.

After Athena came the Browns of Lancashire, who claimed to have run a restaurant in Blackpool. On close questioning this turned out to be a taxi drivers' café. White was appalled. Mrs Brown, 'with ends of greasy hair straying about, and a set of teeth from which several had come adrift from the purple gums . . . was intensely active from five in the morning until nine at night, during which time she got absolutely nowhere, but between nagging and nattering at her family and conducting long monologues on the theme of Old Brown, would contrive to smear everything she touched with grease, scatter tea and sugar everywhere, and let the blowflies in. I have never seen squalor take possession so quickly and completely. In a couple of days all one's standards were broken, and one couldn't quite see where it all might end.'

The Brown men were supposed to help about the farm, but the old man's memory was so shot he could not even feed the fowls. 'So he proceeded to sit in the kitchen amongst the sugar and the tea, while the useless little boy almost sent the cows dry, pulled the heads off the weeds and got ready for the pictures. Of Our Joyce, the granddaughter, we saw less, as she was learning to be "secretarial" at a "Business Ladies College" in Parramatta. We saw her arrive and depart, or sometimes seated at the dressing table trying on peasant handkerchiefs in ways she had learnt from Lana Turner and Linda Darnell.'[47]

The Browns lasted three weeks and the Kubiks arrived. White could not praise the couple enough in the early days. 'The floors shine, the cupboards glitter with glass and china, the beds are weeded and the fields ploughed. Really too much goodness to last. And the K.'s themselves, young, pleasant to look at, and agreeable to live with. The only thing is, we are not teaching them the Australian Way of Life, whatever *that* is.' The Kubiks helped them with the dogs, the farm and the house. In the domestic calm these Poles brought to Dogwoods, White began to write again. 'It is slow and painful, and not a bit what I want to say, but that is always the way, I'm afraid. Also the prospect of having it within me for months, if not years, disgusts me – until I begin to realise that when I am *not* in that state I really feel rather lost. It is a case of one misery or another.'[48] When he began, in January 1950, he thought of the novel as 'A Life Sentence on Earth'.

Had he been wise to come back to Abyssinia? At times he was convinced his life had taken a wrong turn when he came home, and in these bouts of despair he feared he might sink to the level of the worst around him. He and Lascaris had laughed at the sight of their neighbours 'wearing bags in the rain and watching their houses collapse into the paspalum'. But he began to see these signs of exhaustion and despair as a warning of what Australia might do to anyone.[49] Might it happen to him as a farmer or, worse still, as a writer?

Some part of him painfully grasped that he was not in the Australia of his childhood, the country which remained so vividly in his mind as a paradise of order and comfort, of freedom, primitive sensuality, well-run houses and beautiful gardens. Had he grown up in Australia, these early memories might have been overlaid by a truer picture of the country. Exile, instead, had preserved that country in all the colours of early morning. All his life Patrick White was to draw on these memories while raging at the reality around him.

Though he tried to isolate himself at Dogwoods, White could not altogether escape the impact of Australia's raw society. Books and films were cut and banned just as they were in his youth. In its passion for censorship, Australia was the Ireland of the South Pacific. Sidestepping this prudery was easy for those, like White, who had their books sent out from London shops. But the atmosphere in Australia was corrupted. Though the censorship laws were ridiculed, Australian newspapers and critics accommodated themselves, for the most part, to the norms of public decency. A sort of prudish tact became a necessary ingredient of Australian writing. It was understood certain truths could not be told. Nothing in the atmosphere encouraged White to confront his own tact or challenge the influence of Withycombe disapproval, and his agents' caution. 'Overtly homosexual novels weren't published,' declared Juliet O'Hea of this era.[50] Strictly speaking that was untrue, but Gore Vidal's *The City and the Pillar*, published in New York in the same weeks as *The Aunt's Story*, was banned in Australia until 1966.

Each week White's laconic postman delivered the *New Statesman* and the crackling, rice-paper edition of the London *Observer*. Nothing like these papers was published in Australia, and there were few local equivalents of that race of professional intellectuals who wrote for the quality press of London and New York. Local critics – some were writers themselves – were still debating the direction the Australian novel should take and the next step for Australian theatre, as if writing were a matter of state like opening up the hinterland or damming the Snowy River. Australian critics were still playing the mad game of declaring what was and was not 'Australian'. White's first three novels had each been declared un-Australian, and the accusation was to haunt him for years.

The definition of Australian had been narrowing since his childhood. Australia still aped the British, gave only British honours, and expected citizens to stand for the British national anthem even at the local pictures. But by the early 1950s Australia had lost its sense of being, at the same time, part of an international Empire. The experience of men like White, as at home in London as they were in Sydney, was once taken for granted as a privileged but Australian way of life. After the war, the country had turned in on itself, licking its wounds. White was of a generation and class brought up to despise the narrow loyalties now being demanded. To be torn between Australia and London as he always was, had come to seem in his homeland indecisive, even disloyal. Australia was growing chauvinistic in a way it had never been before. White never wavered from the view that 'Chauvinism is bad.'[51] Appeals to this chauvinism masked the second rate in writing, music and politics. And what place was there in 1950 for a poofter, ex-grazier's son and sometime Modernist in the official image of the Australian man?

In a famous essay 'Prodigal Son' he was to look back to Australia at the time he grew suddenly discontented with breeding dogs and growing vegetables, and began to write 'A Life Sentence on Earth'. 'Perhaps, in spite of Australian critics, writing novels was the only thing I could do with any degree of success; even my half-failures were some justification of an otherwise meaningless life. Returning sentimentally to a country I had left in my youth, what had I really found? Was there anything to prevent me packing my bag and leaving . . . like so many other artists? Bitterly I had to admit, no. In all directions stretched the Great Australian Emptiness, in which the mind is the least of possessions, in which the rich man is the important man, in which the schoolmaster and the journalist rule what intellectual roost there is, in which beautiful youths and girls stare at life through blind blue eyes, in which human teeth fall like autumn leaves, the buttocks of cars grow hourly glassier, food means steak and cake, muscles prevail, and the march of material ugliness does not raise a quiver from the average nerves. It was the exaltation of the "average" that made me panic most, and in this frame of mind, in spite of myself, I began to conceive another novel.'[52]

After working at the book for only two months, the domestic harmony of Dogwoods was again shattered. White and the Poles began to fight over wages. 'I doubt that they could do better,' White reported to Peggy Garland. 'They are making between them about £14 a week, with their food and somewhere to live.'[53] But a compromise had to be reached: Mrs Kubic would continue to look after the house while her husband took a job for four and a half days in a factory up the road while helping out on the farm at weekends. But when Jan Kubic left for the factory in early 1950, White left his desk. He explained to Huebsch, 'Now there is a crop of 4,000 stock plants to be rescued from the weeds. So I don't know what becomes of the novel.'[54]

The crisis triggered an asthma attack so severe that White thought he might die. It was a double blow, for after taking anti-allergy injections for a year, White hoped he was on the way to a permanent cure. Another miracle had failed. In despair he decided to sell Dogwoods in February 1950 only to withdraw it from the market a few weeks later. This would have been the moment for packing up and returning to Europe, but once again the dogs and the prospect of seeing their trees grow to maturity convinced him to stick it out. That was his White instinct.

There were no more servants now. The big paddock went to grass and they planted an olive grove. White wrote to Peggy Garland, 'I wish I could say I am writing. Too many things got in the way, and I gave up. I suppose if it had been anything *worth writing* I shouldn't have. So it is nothing to worry about.'[55]

White was feeling the pinch. Debt was not his problem for he never owed money to anyone in his life; Dogwoods was never mortgaged; and his investments were safe in the hands of the Perpetual Trustees whom he had inherited from his father. But after a couple of unremunerative years on the farm there was little ready cash, and the cash crisis grew worse. He was often in despair at this, but Lizzie Clark counselled Lascaris not to take White's worries too seriously. 'He *might* have spent the money,' she said. 'But I know he didn't, because I brought him up.' The crisis was at its height from 1950 to late 1951 after a brush with the Taxation Commissioner. 'I am now much poorer,' White told Peggy Garland for he had suddenly to pay two years' tax in one, with the prospect of the same the following year, 'to bring things up to date'.[56]

The two men lived very carefully. They drank cooking sherry. A vacuum cleaner was paid off by instalments over some years. A gramophone was out of the question. They bought no new clothes and got about the farm in khaki overalls. In winter they wore army surplus zip-up jackets and woollen caps knitted by Lascaris. It pleased White to believe he had purged the dandy in himself. He complained that life even as it was lived at Dogwoods was very expensive. 'So we grow all the vegetables we can, and yesterday we discovered a dish of garden snails is every bit as good as *escargots de Bourgogne*. While there are snails and dandelions, obviously one need not starve.'[57]

When their funds were at their lowest, Lascaris loaded a table into the van and went out stripping schnauzers. A dog took three hours and he charged ten shillings. He took the rotary hoe round the district, ploughing up paddocks, and mowed lawns of big houses along the ridge. 'Members of "old families" and a lady whose husband had made money out of saucepans treated him with condescension. On the other hand a widow fell in love and bicycled down regularly for cream and conversation.'[58]

One Monday early in the winter of 1951, Lascaris was on his way to Parramatta to do the shopping when he drove into a telegraph pole. One of their neighbours saw the smashed van and fetched White. All she could report was seeing Lascaris lying motionless beside the road. White was distraught, not knowing if his lover were alive or dead. He imagined the worst and panicked. 'Actually he broke three ribs and got a slight concussion, but it has been a painful business.'[59] These were the worst hours of a bad year.

White passed the rest of the winter in a state of accidie. In August he wrote to Peggy Garland, 'You say your wishes have always come true. Mine used to, I think, then stopped, or else I have nothing left to wish, apart from trivialities. Sometimes I feel: if only I could *wish* to write another book. But I don't. And of course that is why I don't begin. Have you ever been in this colourless state of wishing for nothing more? Not that it isn't very agreeable. "Colourless" is perhaps a wrong word.'[60]

They bought a radio and sat by the fire after work, 'drinking up music like a piece of blotting paper drinks ink . . . I can't have enough of music.' He found it hard to sit through radio plays, but they were something to hang on to in a city almost without a professional theatre. 'I was impressed by *Murder in the Cathedral* and thrilled by *The Family Reunion*, but there seems something dreadfully pretentious about *The Cocktail Party* and guaranteed to persuade the middlebrow that he is being highbrow, almost as if it were by Charles Morgan out of Shangri-La. And there is something so stale and old-worldly about a group of people revelling in their emotional and intellectual states in a vacuum. The shrink would claim them in fact before they got too far.'[61]

In a 'spasm of reading' in those aimless months he found Scott Fitzgerald ('I am still glowing from my discovery'), Kitto on the ancient Greeks and Henry Miller's *The Colossus of Maroussi* on the moderns ('crazy but true'). He reread Davidson's biography of Edward Lear and Symons's 'brilliant excavation of the nauseating Corvo'. Finally, he reread 'the two books that have meant more to me than anything else in the last ten years, George Moore's *Evelyn Innes* and *Sister Teresa*'.[62]

The garden was looking the worse for wear after the frosts of that winter, but the spring of 1951 brought 'clouds of prunus and cherry, and thickets of cerise and pink japonica. And I am particularly pleased with a bush of gorse, the yellowest of yellow in flowers, as if someone had taken a saucepan of scrambled egg and flung it at a bush of thorns. Some day, God willing, the garden will be a sight to see, and I look forward to that very definitely, even though we be in tatters ourselves and the house collapsed.'[63]

The great gamble of bringing Lascaris to the other end of the earth had produced nothing he valued but the schnauzers and a garden. At times he was so swept by the conviction of having gambled and lost, that he feared he would go mad: 'Nuthouse mad!'[64] In terrible rages at everything around him he blamed Lascaris for bringing him out to Australia, while tormenting himself for landing his lover in this predicament. In May 1952 he would turn forty. It seemed his life had run to a halt at Dogwoods. 'There are moments when I do take interest in a book I have in my head, of which I wrote a certain amount when the Poles were with us, then I succumb to the feeling of: What is the use? Since the War I cannot find any point, see any future, love my fellow men; I have gone quite sour – and it is not possible, in that condition, to be a novelist, for he does deal in human beings.'[65]

FOURTEEN

Life Sentence

TWICE THAT SUMMER the Blue Mountains were alight, and from Dogwoods the flames could be seen at night in the west. The sun rose through a curtain of smoke and cast a pallid, yellow light over the country. The heat was intense. Fires broke out along the Hawkesbury and only a late shift of wind saved Windsor from burning. Fires burnt through the bush valleys that lay between Castle Hill and the northern suburbs of the city, leaving in their wake a mess of blackened trees, lone chimneys and iron roofs reduced to twisted sheets of paper. A line of fires burned down the coast and, on one day of appalling heat and wind, fires threatened the fringes of Canberra. Between each bout of flames storms moved across the state with spectacular displays of lightning and occasional downpours of drenching rain.

In such a downpour, a few days before Christmas 1951, White was carrying bowls of slops to a litter of wormy pups. Somewhere between the jacaranda and the old piggery he slipped in the mud. Swearing and laughing he dragged himself to his feet. 'I stood in the rain, the water up to my ankles, and pouring off me, as I proceeded to curse God.' But how could he curse what did not exist? As he puzzled at this, he had an inkling of the presence of God. 'Faith began to come to me.'[1] Stan Parker experienced the same revelation

as the rain sluiced his lands, and the fork of the lightning entered the crests of his trees. The darkness was full of wonder. Standing there somewhat meekly, the man could have loved something, someone, if he could have penetrated beyond the wood, beyond the moving darkness. But he could not, and in his confusion he prayed to God, not in specific petition, wordlessly almost, for the sake of company. Till he began to know every corner of the darkness, as if it were daylight, and he were in love with the heaving world, down to the last blade of wet grass.[2]

White had once thought God lived in the garden at Lulworth, hiding in the upper branches of the great bunya bunya pine. When he discovered the simple and wild beauty of the gullies round Mount Wilson and the High Country beyond Bolaro, he wanted to consummate, somehow, the passion this country aroused in him. He longed to melt, to merge and disappear into the landscape. Now, after cursing God in the storm, he experienced that consummation in his own shabby paddock: a moment of ecstasy in which he apprehended God in all existence around him. It was the beginning of his faith and of a lifelong search for contact with that fleeting presence. This was 'the turning point'.[3]

Belief brought no revolutionary change to his life. White did not embrace the dogmas of sin and hell and the heave/n that lies beyond death. At the communion rail of the local church he toyed with these ideas, but they remained foreign to him. He sought illumination not forgiveness. White continued to drink, eat, desire, gossip and rage. He found no contradiction between his belief in God and homosexuality. He did not set out to become a do-gooder, a type he was to lacerate a few years later in the figure of the Cheery Soul. He would always believe Christian love should be 'administered in homeopathic doses . . . Minute doses to be really potent. Not get up and charge about, not be evangelical about it.'[4]

After the years of frustration and self-loathing belief brought White the courage to face himself. This was a gift of grace. Once he faced himself as a fallible man, he could begin once more to trust the kaleidoscopic jumble within himself from which he drew his inspiration. Released from the accidie that had almost overwhelmed him, White began to write again, taking up the manuscript of *A Life Sentence on Earth* which he now called *The Tree of Man*, a novel with 'no plot, except the only one of living and dying'.[5]

To a very sceptical Peggy Garland he tried to explain what had happened. 'I have not myself suffered any of the great injustices, such as hunger, or torture, or the devastations of war, to name a few, but I do feel by this time that all the minor injustices to which I have been submitted, and which at the time have seemed terribly unjust and unnecessary, even agonising, have in fact been necessary to my development. I do feel that every minute of my life has been necessary – though this conviction has only very recently come to me – and that the sum total can only be good, though how good one cannot presume to say.

'None of this is new. It is quite simple. You may even find it ludicrous. But it is better to say it, in case it may help simply by its

simplicity and obviousness. I think it is impossible to explain faith. It
is like trying to explain air, which one cannot do by dividing it into its
component parts and labelling them scientifically. It must be breathed
to be understood. But breathing is something that has been going on
all the time, and is almost imperceptible. I don't know when I began
to have faith, but it is only a short time since I admitted it.'[6]

White and Lascaris began to take communion at a church on
the road to Parramatta. The spiritual climate was discouraging, for
at St Paul's Castle Hill Anglicanism was at its lowest ebb: a bare
altar under a barn roof with Union Jacks hanging from the walls.
Yet the Evangelicals did not stand between a man and his God, and
White found communion peaceful and at times illuminating. The Rev.
Colin Craven-Sands was a big, earnest and rather dull clergyman with
beautiful blue eyes, on whom White came to build the figure of Mr
Purbrick, the Parkers' worthy man at Durilgai,

> He had scrubbed the face of religion till any nostalgia that might
> have answered the personal ones had fled out of it. He was rather
> a strong man, it would seem. His own muscles would not allow
> him to have doubts, anyway for a few years yet, as he wrestled
> with the evidence of indifference. The pores of this Laocoön were
> permanently exuding sweat, sometimes radiant, sometimes just
> sweat.[7]

To be among the twenty souls who gathered early each Sunday
at St Paul's was also an act of civic virtue for White, a way of
trying to draw closer to the community of Castle Hill. The same
impulse had propelled Ruth and Dick to church, to be well-dressed
presences in private pews with visiting cards attached. There were no
such formalities at Castle Hill. The two men drove a few neighbours
with them to church, but did not linger for long after the services, and
took no part in the general life of the parish. If the minister called at
Dogwoods, White found urgent chores in the yard while Lascaris was
left to make tea and conversation.

White's God was an Anglican, but the dogma of any religious
sect seemed to him 'ridiculous and presumptuous. Faith is something
between the person and God, and must vary in its forms accordingly.'[8]
White's upbringing had done more for his prose than his faith. At school
the Book of Common Prayer was drummed into him, and somewhere
in his memory were the Collects he recited to his cousin Ivy White,
née Voss, on cold Sundays at Mittabah. After his confirmation at
Cheltenham he found a spiritual excitement in communion, walking
down from the altar 'with a warm glow inside me, and downcast,
shriven eyes in imitation of my mother'.[9] But this was soon lost.

His was a typical Anglican childhood. 'I . . . went through my youth believing in nothing but my own ego, because I had to rebel against my family and imagine I was an intellectual. In the beginning, I suppose, I had "believed" only in the conventional, infantile sense.'[10]

In the war he discovered the Greek Orthodox church through Lascaris who was raised and remained in the Orthodox faith, a faith so ancient and fixed that it seemed almost a force of nature. This was part of the Greek experience that gave shape to White's own instincts. 'My inklings of God's presence are interwoven with my love of the one human being who never fails me,' White wrote many years later.[11] Narrow as it often is – there is a streak of passionate hatred of homosexuality in Orthodox teaching – the Greek church nevertheless accommodates a vast and contradictory world that is sublime and cruel, beautiful and squalid. The Christ of White's belief was the Christ beneath the domes of Byzantine chapels: Christ the judge, the man who penetrates truth. To images of the Orthodox Christ White gave the dazzling blue eyes of those figures of his imagination who have the uncomfortable power of staring into the inmost secrets of man. White the believer bolstered the courage of White the writer: worship and writing were both about the pursuit of truth, for the great truths could only be grasped intermittently, as 'the result of a daily wrestling match, and then only by glimmers, as through a veil'.[12]

Belief came as a democratic revelation. White believed *everyone* had faith, even those who could not admit it to themselves. He held that this personal connection to God, admitted or denied, was the sustaining force in all lives. Such faith humbled him. His old fear and ridicule of the rough lives lived around Dogwoods was overlaid by a sense of common humanity under God, 'I felt the life was, on the surface, so dreary, ugly, monotonous, there must be something hidden in it to give it a purpose, and so I set out to find a secret core, and *The Tree of Man* emerged.'[13] He saw the book as an expression of his new faith, but searched to find a new language in which to clothe this Christian impulse, 'to try to convey a religious faith through symbols and situations which can be accepted by people today'.[14]

White did not discuss his new faith with either of his mentors Ben Huebsch and Betty Withycombe. He had drifted a little apart from Withycombe, feeling that she was being deliberately uncommunicative about her own spiritual life. In 1950 she had joined the Anglican Franciscans as a Tertiary, living in the world but observing some of the discipline of monastic life with formal obligations of prayer and good works. White wondered if she was drifting towards Rome? 'That is one plunge I could not take. I suppose in my heart I am a bigoted Protestant.'[15]

To Huebsch the Jew he sent news more welcome than his conversion to Christianity: 'A short time ago I began painfully to write
another book, squeezing out an hour a day in which to do it, and then
not every day. Still, it is going ahead. I suppose I have written roughly
a quarter. But I shouldn't care to say when it may be finished. And of
course, with me there is always the chance of an abortion. However, it
gives me great pleasure to find I want to do it again. For a long time I
felt this is only a world for builders to build houses, farmers to grow
food, and priests to heal the spirit. Of course there is also the artist
with a message, but that is usually the artist without art. But lately
I began to think about it less and actually started to write. It may be
trash. I don't talk about it in case it is.'[16]

Writing, so easy for him in the past, was now painfully difficult. He
put aside the dazzling prose of The Aunt's Story, for the lives of Stan
Parker, a farmer of Durilgai, and his wife Amy could not be portrayed
in a 'perfectly literate' way. 'My aim was to keep things as primitive
as possible in writing about these people.'[17] He felt he had to learn
the language again, gossiping to his neighbours and shopkeepers, and
eavesdropping on the train to absorb the nuances of Australian speech.
This new beginning was the toughest creative struggle of his life. Each
of his novels had taken a year or less to write, but The Tree of Man
absorbed him for two and a half years from the moment he returned
to the abandoned manuscript.
    'Writing which had meant the practice of an art by a polished mind
in civilised surroundings, became a struggle to create completely fresh
forms out of the rocks and sticks of words. I began to see things for
the first time. Even the boredom and frustration presented avenues for
endless exploration; even the ugliness, the bags and iron of Australian
lives acquired a meaning.'[18]
    The novel put a terrible strain on his relationship with Lascaris.
Bad as his temper always was when he was writing, White's rages
during his struggle with The Tree of Man were demonic. He drank
heavily. A nightmare dogged him that he had lost, without knowing it, his absolute standards. So much depended on this book: the
sacrifices of exile, his broken affair with Greece and the loss of all he
loved in Europe could only be made good by a solid success, a New
York and London success. Once again he hoped this would be the book
that made his fortune 'instead of the usual miserable hundred pounds'.
Now that he was working once again he fretted over the wasted years.
His ambition was vast: 'Because the void I had to fill was so immense,
I wanted to try to suggest in this book every possible aspect of life,
through the lives of an ordinary man and a woman. But at the same
time I wanted to discover the extraordinary behind the ordinary, the

mystery and the poetry which alone could make bearable the lives of such people, and incidentally, my own life since my return.'[19]

After working on the farm all day, White came in about five and began to drink, self-absorbed and silent. He ate, and about nine collapsed into bed for a few hours. At midnight he got up and began to write. Lascaris rose too, lit a fire and made tea, keeping White company for a while before returning to bed. White finished writing about 4.30am. Not long after, Lascaris was stirring in his room, ready to start another day on the farm. More and more of the work at Dogwoods fell on his shoulders. White was often ill, scribbling in bed or sitting where he worked in a mess of papers at the kitchen table gasping for breath.

There were days White declared he could not bear to have Lascaris in the house, and nights of tantrums when he demanded Lascaris leave. White dragged suitcases from cupboards telling his lover to pack and be off. 'Go, go now.' Lascaris refused. 'It is 3am, Patrick, I cannot leave now. I will wait until morning.' But next day, White begged him to stay.[20] Battered as he was by these rages, Lascaris accepted them. 'He has a genius. Even he doesn't know where it comes from, but he obeys it. If he needs to rage, I am there, and he knows I will forgive him. It is very painful, but I do forgive him.'[21]

Most of the time White was depressed by the suspicion that no one could be interested in what he was writing. But after six months he confessed to Peggy Garland: 'I am lifted up at times to considerable heights, and that may be a sign. If it is another failure, I suppose the writing alone will have done something to one.'[22] Encouragement came, once again, from Paris. Gallimard sent him an early copy of *Eden-Ville*, the first of his works to be translated, and he thought it 'very well done'. An Italian translation was due to arrive at Dogwoods at any moment though he worried how it had turned out, for the publishers, Bompiani, had 'rushed it out without a single query on the part of the translator'.[23] Marie Viton was by this time at work on *The Aunt's Story* and as White struggled with *The Tree of Man* it was reassuring and stimulating to have her letters pestering him with questions about the text of his favourite novel, the neglected child to whom he then felt so close.

The Tree of Man is suffused with the life of Castle Hill, and the small but potent dramas of the two men's lives on Dogwoods: the shed demolished in a storm, the birth of a calf twisted in the womb, the death of a cow. The paddocks and farms of Durilgai are drawn on the map of Castle Hill. About where Dogwoods lay 'in a frosty, bloody hole' a mile from the village, Stan Parker clears a farm out of the bush and finds a wife to live in his hut.[24] They take root. Stan and Amy Parker milk cows and grow cabbages. Amy plants a garden. Neighbours join them along the road.

There was a man tilling the chocolate soil in between his orange trees. Outside a grey shack an old man sat beside his hollyhock. Children spilled from the doors of bursting cottages. Washing blew . . . Bright birds fell from the sky, and ascended. Voices could be heard where once the sound of the axe barely cut the silence, and your heart beat quicker for its company . . . Wire wound through the scrub. Many uses were found for bags and tin. And at night they sat around, the men with their shirts open on the hair of their chests, the women with their blouses easy, and drank whatever came to hand, as a comfort. If it was sometimes the kerosene, well, that too is drinkable. And more children were got to the tune of iron beds.[25]

The inhabitants of Castle Hill take on fresh names and destinies as the people of Durilgai. Mrs Gage, with a desperate face and brown-paper sleeves, was based on the local postmistress, always coming and going, trying to grapple people to her with conversations about the weather. The young Madeleine, 'godlike and remote' who rode by on a magnificent horse arousing dreams of different kinds in Stan and Amy Parker, was based on Anne Campbell, a handsome girl whom he watched riding along Showground Road. 'We knew the girl, finally. She wasn't really much like the character in the book except she rode up and down the road.'[26] Madeleine's married self, Mrs Fisher, was drawn on the rather pretentious original of Gwyneth Paul, one of the Lloyd Jones family, who came to lunch several times at Dogwoods. 'They used to visit to plunder the place: they got free cream, a free dog – which wouldn't eat, caused so much trouble – and flowers. After they'd left Manoly used to say the garden looked as though a goat had been loose in it.'[27]

Out along Showground Road lived Mrs Rispon, and on the ruins of this woman White built the drunken pile of Kathy O'Dowd. Mrs Rispon was bog Irish but Seventh Day Adventist. Her husband was dying of cancer. She saw doom round every corner. As Mrs Rispon drifted in and out of Dogwoods 'with her string bag and advice' a strange intimacy grew up between the farm and its Irish neighbours. 'I called on her a few days ago, and found her looking magnificent, her hair hanging down, a greenish grizzled brown, under a brown velvet cap in the Rembrandt manner. The poor thing has had out her teeth, by correspondence, I should think, and is now replete with some uneasy uppers in the shape of a shoebuckle, which fly out as she speaks, and which she hiccups back behind her hand with a: "Pardon me." ' Mrs O'Dowd inherited Mrs Rispon's enduring strength, her sense of doom and that shoebuckle set of teeth, 'a plate that I got by letter, an it is the bugger for poppun out'.[28] The O'Dowds' drunkenness came not from the Rispons who were teetotal, but from a wild Scottish couple who lived further out in the bush and were seen staggering drunk down Showground Road dragged by a couple of savage dogs on chains.

The O'Dowds are a triumph of love in squalor, of unearned devotion, of a marriage that persists against all reasonable objections. They live in a fantastically broken-down, nightmare version of the farmhouse White and Lascaris had not bought in the early days out at Kellyville. From the day it was built, the O'Dowds' place was in a state of collapse, smelling of duck shit and rot,

> The wind was torturing the roof. It took a leaf of iron and tore it off. The iron, tingling and tinkling with rust, flung across the yard and slapped a pig's arse fairly hard. This act committed, the iron sank into a pond or spill of brown water . . . There was such a quarking and groaning of animals, it was near murder, but unnoticed.[29]

Stan Parker, in contrast, is the sort of small farmer the Whites would admire. He keeps his sheds neat and his fences in repair. Neighbours seek his practical advice. Like Clem Withycombe, he is an adept, if amateur vet. White wrote with intimate understanding about the rhythm and habits of work on the Parkers' place and their intense satisfaction with work done,

> walking in the garden in the evening, after the children were fed, and the milk vessels scalded, and the dishes in the rack, then she came into her own. He liked to come along the path, and find her by accident at these times, and linger with her or put his arm awkwardly through hers, and stroll beside her, also awkwardly at first, till warmth and her acceptance made them part of each other.[30]

He gave Amy Parker something of his own possessive jealousy, and the longing for glamour he believed he had purged from himself. Amy is a practical woman, shy of the mysteries that absorb her husband, restless and greedy for love. She seduces and is seduced by a travelling salesman, who is another of White's ginger-haired lovers. The violation of marriage is terrible. White defended this incident to Peggy Garland: 'It is quite possible to be consumed by love for one individual and to be led to a fatal wallowing in something else at some point in one's life. A kind of desecration of the noble ideal one can't attain to. Amy Parker is led progressively and fatally to this, I feel, through her fleeting relationships with Madeleine, the Young Digger, Con the Greek, O'Dowd and finally the commercial traveller.'[31]

As he worked on *The Tree of Man*, White continued to advise his cousin to hang on to her deteriorating marriage. The Garlands' marriage was, by now, a most unhappy one but White argued they *must* stick together as a couple. The passion of this view seemed to grow from his own fears, for if men and women with children should break up, how much more vulnerable must the union of homosexuals be? 'My impulse is to say: Endure everything, because any other solution will be far worse for either of you. At this point in your lives, you cannot drift off from one another without each leaving such chunks of personality in the possession of the other, that you could not hope ever to be whole again. I am sorry you cannot work at your sculpture because I feel that if you got hold of the largest and hardest piece of marble you could find and bashed at it till something came out, you would probably resolve this drama of difficulty – from your side anyway. As for Tom's complaining that he is overpowered by your personality, then you must just humble yourself till he is not. You will still remain yourself to yourself. Humility, moreover, is a most catching picture and may work wonders.'[32]

The Parkers have this rocklike faith in union, and a wife who humbles herself to her husband. The Parkers' marriage is revealed with extraordinary intimacy as its passions build and die. Here is love in many guises even silence, fondness and habit; jealousy and betrayal, dependence and intractable frustration; the ascendancy of wife over husband and then in the next breath of husband over wife. The Parkers come to live the lives of intimate strangers but they endure, unflinchingly, as a couple.

Stan Parker is Patrick White's first good man. Simplicity is his only guide. The greatest technical difficulty White faced, one which drove him to rages and left him sitting, at times, 'three days over just one sentence'[33] was the challenge of making goodness live and breathe on the page. 'I am not a good person,' White often confessed to his friends. 'But I *know* goodness.' Parker is stubborn, erect and honourable. He has no plans. What happens to Stan Parker has to happen. This was as White had come to feel about his own life. He asked Ben Huebsch at this time: 'Do you feel that every step you have taken in your life, even the most stumbling one, has been inevitable? Or perhaps you don't stumble.'[34] Parker is strong, but the writer did not mean to make his strength unfailing. 'To me he is at many points weak and wavering. Certainly I wanted him to appear admirable as far as his human limitations would allow.'[35]

Parker is absorbed in the mystery of the God whose presence he senses in the shabby paddocks of the farm. He can express none of this in words – his notebook remains stubbornly blank – but the quest to find and know this God is Parker's real life. It is his *own* God, not

Amy's, nor his mother's, which was 'a pale-blue gentleness', the same
blue White remembered from the tin scroll above the altar at Bong
Bong claiming God was Love. White and Stan Parker share a God that
moves with the weather, a God of storms, floods, fire and disasters.
Lightning is his mark in the sky. Yet all Parker's attempts to see his
God face to face are near misses, and only at the very end, moments
before his death, he has a private and peculiar glimpse of the Almighty:

> He was illuminated.
> He pointed with his stick at the gob of spittle.
> 'That is God,' he said.[36]

The Parkers share the seasons that came to Dogwoods, the hot
summer days, nights of delicious coolness, frost in the hollow, paddocks
steaming on winter mornings. 'The seasons we experienced ran through
every cliché in the Australian climatic calendar: drought, fire, gales.'[37]
The same pests attack the cabbages. When times are hard, Parker goes
out to garden up at Glastonbury on the ridge, as Lascaris had when
the cash ran out at Dogwoods. Amy's great fleshy vulgar rose stands
by the veranda where the crisp pink bush of Cécile Brunner grew at
Dogwoods; both houses were soon overwhelmed by trees, for both
White and Amy Parker 'always have to plant another one somewhere.
In another ten years we shall be peering dottily out of the forest that
has swallowed us, if something more cosmic does not get us first.'[38]
    He drew on his own childhood. Rather late in life Stan and Amy
Parker have children, a son Ray and a daughter Thelma. The children
of White's fiction are, as he saw himself to be, a disappointment to their
parents. He gave Thelma his own asthma and waxy delicacy. She does
a secretarial course at a Business Ladies College. 'Everyone was going
to secretarial schools then.' She proves to be 'as cool as the bell on
the typewriter that rang at the end of the line'.[39] The horse trainer
Horrie Bourke with whom she boards in the city is an unblinking but
affectionate portrait of Dick's old trainer Harry England, a man who

> was never dolled up, though he approved of it in his wife,
> and in the rich, his patrons. He preferred his slippers. He would
> wear a collar but no tie. Just the brass stud that held together this
> slightly yellow starched collar. This way he went about his stable
> yard . . . Horrie, who was a decent cove.[40]

The Parkers' boy is beautiful, but hates the 'gentleness' in himself
and ruins his life. He goes to the pack. The boy shares familiar fascina-
tions and disloyalties. He sits with Con the Greek as Patrick sat with Sol
the Islander, going through the man's box of 'private and valuable and

interesting articles' that conjured up other worlds and other lives.[41] Ray
scales the ironbarks that grow around the farm, searching for magpies'
eggs,

> feeling the sweat behind his knees, he had reached the top, and
> was dipping and swaying, sheathed in a cold wind that brought
> the blood to his face. He was a beautiful little boy in his exaltation.[42]

For White it is axiomatic that humans betray. He still felt shame
at the betrayals committed in his childhood. He had joined the rabble
at Tudor House to mock old Skuse despite the affection he felt for that
troubled character, and among his earliest memories was seeing the
Germans in Cromer abused during the First World War. The Parkers'
kids fall in with the pack of Durilgai children who mock old Fritz when
that war breaks out. Like the Russian Mr Patchkoe, Fritz sleeps on bags
and helps with the milking on the Parkers' farm. Both men's guts rattled
'awful bad' as they dosed themselves with a porridge of mash.[43] Both
men are left to die in Parramatta, which White calls Bangalay. Yet Fritz
was

> a good old man, whom they had loved, they knew, but they
> resented the indignity he had imposed upon them. In their hot
> shame they began to hate him worse than anyone.[44]

The Tree of Man is free of hate, but there are evil presences
which White attacks in the writing, presences which threatened him
just as they threatened the Parkers. Dogwoods was White's oasis on the
edge of civilisation, but from the first he felt vulnerable. Farms along
the fringes of Sydney were being chopped up for cheap housing, and
the suburbs were creeping outwards. There were fortunes to be made
and the Green Belt could not protect him for ever. Already there were
a few streets of cheap council houses in Castle Hill,

> against which it was hoped the Council would revise its policy
> . . . It was in their favour, of course, that they could last only
> a little while . . . A child kicked a hole in one, for fun. And at
> night the fibro homes reverberated, changed their shape under the
> stress of love or strife, changed and returned, standing brittle in the
> moonlight, soluble in dreams.[45]

Most of the Parkers' land is taken for cheap houses. They lose their
farm. By the time they are old, the Parkers' hopes have failed them.
Their daughter has escaped into the middle classes. Their son is dead.
    Turning forty, as he worked on the first draft of *The Tree of*

Man, White felt for the first time that his own old age would 'inevitably happen . . . the fear of age grew'.[46] But he imagined great age would also have its benefits: peace, forgiveness, freedom from desire, and wisdom. The Parkers find this in their overgrown garden, but these gentle compensations would fail the man who conceived them at Castle Hill.

White and Lascaris were finding friends in this odd community. Over the next hill lived Helen Lloyd, a witty and beautiful woman whose husband was giving poultry farming a go. For a time Dogwoods and Jalna Farm shared a party line.

Freddie Glover lived out on the ridge in an old church hall with a wife who was crippled by polio. Freddie was one of the souls who took early communion at St Paul's. He had once directed shows for Doris Fitton's Independent Theatre; now he was the accountant at the Rural Bank in Parramatta. Even on the worst summer days, this frail little man was always formal, always neatly and sombrely dressed in a high stiff collar and tie. He wrote plays. White sent one to Curtis Brown in New York commending it as the sort of thing that 'might make a very successful vehicle for someone like Hepburn or Bette Davis'.[47] Nothing came of it.

Glover became an important minor figure in White's life. He led the classical faction of the Castle Hill Players, and directed their memorable, inaugural production of Euripides's *Trojan Women*. Nothing quite like it was ever seen in the hills. Helen was Helen Lloyd, and Hecuba was Myrtle Dunlop whom White had christened 'the Duse of Castle Hill'. He thought she moved like a sick duck, but she impressed the locals: 'Not much of a play,' remarked the grocer when Lascaris was doing the shopping next morning. 'But Myrtle was a wonderful Hecuba.'

Some time in 1952, at one of the dinner parties to which the two men were now invited in the district, they met Fritz and Ile Krieger. This was a decisive meeting for all four of them, for they found that night that they spoke the same language. 'We were foreigners,' recalled Ile Krieger. 'Patrick and Manoly were like foreigners too, also New Australians. It was wonderful to have friends out there at Castle Hill you didn't have to explain everything to.'[48] Their friendship, which began with a sense of relief, grew into a great intimacy. Ile Krieger called the two men *die Büben*, the lads. Though they met soon after White returned to work on *The Tree of Man*, the fact that he was writing remained a secret until he gave them an early copy of the book inscribed: 'To Fritz and Ilus who assisted at the birth.'

Ile Krieger was an intelligent and rather grand woman who lost her first husband on the Russian Front and came out to Melbourne after the war. Her family, the Fischers, had been landowners along the Austro-Hungarian border and one brother was already farming in Victoria. She married Fritz in 1951 and they came to live in Castle Hill to be close to his new factory at West Ryde. The Kriegers had moved into their severe, modern house on the Sydney side of the ridge only a few months before meeting White and Lascaris. She was a splendid talker and fond of giving small dinner parties. Ile protected her difficult husband.

Fritz Krieger came from a musical family that made bricks on the outskirts of Vienna. He had come out in the 1930s and tried to interest Sydney pits in the Krieger brick. He failed in this, but after the war he was one of three partners in CELCO, which made paper clips, drawing sets, torches and, later on, electric fans. Fritz was proud of CELCO's products: all metal, no plastic. They were modest staples of those booming years, requisites for schools and offices. CELCO and the Kriegers prospered.

Fritz was a quiet man, but very alert, sensitive and easily hurt. Though he seemed impassive much of the time, he registered every-thing about him and would break his silence to sum up people in a few, spare, sarcastic sentences. When roused, Fritz loved to argue and was a stubborn opponent. In his house, *die Büben* found an outpost of Europe where all the rules of polite Australian conversation were flouted. The crowd at the Kriegers talked religion, politics and money. When they discussed writing and music, the points of reference were not merely local. They read, as White and Lascaris did, in French and German. Politics at the Kriegers meant not only the anti-Communist campaigns of the new Australian Prime Minister Bob Menzies, but the crises of the Middle East, central Europe and North America. Fritz was a prolific letter writer and had first-hand news of the world from his family and their friends in Europe and the United States.

He had one peculiarity: he pretended not to be a Jew. Fritz Krieger was an Anglican and spoke about 'zees people' the Jews as though they were another race. Yet in White's judgment, 'he was so obviously a Jew he looked like a stage Jew'. White was to draw on Fritz Krieger's apostasy in the portrait of Haïm Rosenbaum, who becomes the Catholic Harry Rosetree, proprietor of Brighta Bicycle Lamps where the Jew Himmelfarb is crucified on a jacaranda tree in the factory yard.[49]

Fritz Krieger's great gift to White was to open the world of music to him. Krieger loved Richard Strauss, but his God was Mahler, and the years of his intimacy with White became White's Mahler years. Rows about music later drew the two men apart, but in the 1950s music was a bond between Dogwoods and the Kriegers. Under their influence White bought a gramophone. 'Do you know Bruckner's Ninth Symphony and Hindemith's *Harmonics of the World*?' he asked Peggy Garland. 'I intend to buy just one or two difficult works like those and play them over and over till I am saturated.'[50]

The Kriegers and *die Büben* began to go to concerts together, driving down every Thursday night to the Sydney Town Hall, scene of Ruth's crêpe-paper triumphs decades before. Australians were not cut off from music, for the best concert artists and chamber groups toured the country. Each state had its orchestra, and the Sydney Symphony was performing with distinction in these years under the composer and conductor Eugene Goossens. White was excited by the discoveries he made at the Town Hall and gave snapshot reports to Peggy Garland. Of the Greek contralto Elena Nikolaïdi: 'Such a slashing, dashing, dazzling, golden-skinned creature I have never seen, and a voice that must be the greatest in the world at present.'[51] And of Solomon a year later: 'I think his playing of the First Brahms Concerto the greatest musical experience I have known. He is really possessed by music to a most extraordinary degree. Rather an unpromising-looking man, carved out of a pumpkin, then the spirit starts to burn inside.'[52]

White met Klári Daniel through the Kriegers. Together they helped sustain him in his essential yet difficult exile. The romance of Klári and Patrick began at Castle Hill and lasted an intense, stimulating decade. She was the daughter of a great Budapest woolbroking family, the Diamants. By the time the Nazis began rounding up the Jews of Budapest, Daniel's father was dead; some of her siblings were safe in Switzerland; one had reached Sydney. But Klári, her mother and one brother were caught in Budapest. On their way to Auschwitz, on the railway platform as they were about to be loaded into the trucks, they managed to buy their freedom. The three made their way to Romania and arrived in Sydney after the war, where the family set up Klári and her mother in a flat in Elizabeth Bay. This tiny, dynamic woman had the task of looking after old Mrs Diamant until her death.

Klári was always performing. She had a small pugnacious face with jagged black eyebrows over deep black eyes. Around her neck hung a double string of pearls, and her hair was drawn into a severe chignon. Though she stood hardly five feet high, Klári had the voice and gestures of a commanding woman. Every door was an opportunity to make an entrance; when angry she was a whirlwind of fury. Klári was often exasperating, eccentric and ferociously dogmatic. She was also loyal, kind and warm-hearted. Her views of right and wrong were very formal. She believed her people should set an example and deplored the vast accumulation of wealth by Jews. 'Why do you go on?' she asked her nephew Peter Abeles. 'You have more than you need.' He replied, 'Tante Klári, you don't understand. You have to go on. You can't stop.'

So as not to feel entirely kept by her family, she gave French and English lessons. Her enthusiasms included gymnastics, diet and psychoanalysis. She read Freud and claimed a friendship with Alfred Adler from the coffee houses of Vienna. Klári read in English, French, German and Italian. She read day and night and slept very little, a habit assisted by drinking a great deal of very strong coffee. Coffee, she declared, was the essence of life and she travelled the world with a one-cup coffee pot and little spirit stove on which to brew coffee that must 'wake the dead'.

Few women White knew in life or conceived in fiction were so astonishingly *complete* as Klári Daniel. He was moved by her kindness and loyalty. In the early years of their friendship, their taste in books and music virtually coincided. They spoke almost every day on the telephone. She baked for him. They swapped books. She guarded her friendship with him jealously. During the years of their intimacy she came to see Patrick White as an Australian Thomas Mann, a great and civilised writer whose breaches of her own strict codes – the harshness, the rages against Lascaris – must be forgiven, for artists are holy monsters, possessed by demons.

By Christmas 1953 the first draft of *The Tree of Man* was almost finished. It was sprawling out he warned Peggy Garland. 'It is so long by this time, that I find myself suddenly remembering incidents I had forgotten, just as one remembers forgotten incidents in life, and derives a very fresh kind of pleasure from doing so. I don't think this is an unhappy book, as you suspect, because at present I am happy, and I think one's personal happiness must get into a book whatever the theme.

'There is still an awful lot of hard work to do, though, awful, boring desperate work. I am sure there is nothing similar to the drudgery of writing in any of the other arts. I hate writing intensely, and if I had the glimmering of anything else in me, would be off with that tomorrow.'[53]

An old yearning to paint returned as he worked on the tragic sub-plot of Durilgai's clandestine artist Mr Gage. At some point White bought oils and brushes but all that survived of this attempt was a painted rock that lay on his desk. White could not paint but he believed he knew how painters painted. Gage was his first: an outcast Modern whose work only comes to light after he hangs himself in the post office yard, 'something any creative artist in Australia is tempted to do on and off'.[54] To write Gage, he read the letters of Van Gogh to Emile Bernhard, and Douglas Cooper's study of the painter, which he told its author he found 'in a strange way helpful'.[55] He was disappointed on rereading *The Autobiography of Alice B. Toklas* to discover it now seemed 'not much more than a kind of intellectual gossip-writing. Though there are flashes of wisdom. And I do find the activities of all those painters – Picasso, Matisse, Braque *et cie* – stimulating, even when I cannot see the paintings.'[56]

Earlier in 1953 a travelling exhibition of recent French painting had arrived in Australia. White imagined it gave many Sydney people the shock of their lives, 'and liberated many more after shocking them. One forgets really that the average Australian has *seen* so little. He can have heard quite a lot, and read quite a lot, but on the visual side he is a complacent Victorian.'[57]

White kept an eye on painting in Sydney. Though his friendship with Dobell withered on Lascaris' arrival in Australia, he had kept up with Sydney galleries and was excited by what he found. For years he was too shy to make contact with painters, but by 1953 he had begun, rather tentatively, to meet and befriend them. He bought a few paintings at the Macquarie Galleries, usually at the annual sale of works for ten guineas.

The life of the farm went on. The Saanen goats became White's great passion as he worked at *The Tree of Man* though the animals were neither as easy to handle nor cheap to feed as he first imagined. White hoped to save the cost of repairing Dogwoods' tumbling fences by keeping his herd of goats on tethers, but the animals outwitted him and within months the two men were hard at work netting the big paddock to stop the goats ring-barking their new trees. Each goat had to be checked for ticks every night, for the country around Dogwoods was cursed with this pest. After a year the two men were making goat's cheese and eating their own olives. White now dreamed of keeping bees. 'One can't sit eating one's own olives and goat's cheese without adding one's own honey.'[58] By the end of that year their herd had grown to nine. White asked Huebsch: 'Do you know these civilised animals? One day I am going to write a novel about goats with human beings to make it appear more "moral" but only to enjoy the great luxury of writing about the goats.'[59]

The financial crisis having passed, Dogwoods was painted outside one year and inside the next. The scheme was Mediterranean: white with blue shutters, eaves and windows. Inside was also white because that is 'really the only background for pictures (though some insist this is red damask). The only startling piece of interior decoration is in the back veranda, which has bright yellow walls, a deep blue ceiling, and red curtains. Put thus crudely, it is rather crude. In fact, it is good and bright, just the thing for a back veranda . . . The kitchen is white again with the veranda yellow repeated in doors and windows.' The last of the furniture that came with the house was sold for depressing prices, some of it to a taxi driver who came in the middle of the night with a wife called Pet. In place of that 'heavy, black, suburban stuff' they bought light, severe modern furniture. The carpets were thrown out and the old floors polished. He told Huebsch, 'For the first time in six years the place has begun to look like mine.' Yet the old stuff had had its uses. White felt he knew intuitively by now 'about the sort of people who would buy and live with that kind of furniture'. Twenty years later he cited this as an instance of how his 'uneventful' life had allowed him to experience 'a lot that has not necessarily happened to me'.[60]

White found a carpenter in Parramatta to make a copy of the desk Francis Bacon had designed for the Eccleston Street flat. It was a crude version of the original but White was pleased. He had it painted 'a stone colour, outlined in white, with red linoleum inset in the top'. *The Tree of Man*, begun on the kitchen table, was finished on the new desk, its 'endless red linoleum top' usually hidden under a mess of paper.[61] In White's house everything was bare, orderly and polished except for the surface of his desk. Above it hung the new de Maistre which had just arrived from London, one of Roy's *Descents from the Cross*.

Early in the New Year, 1954, as he was revising the novel, White was struck down by asthma, bronchitis and then pneumonia. He continued to work, and by the time an autumn of unusually vivid colour had given way to winter, his health was restored. Looking back, he did not regret the two gloomy months spent in bed. 'I can't help feeling it was necessary. I see a lot of things more clearly than I did before.'[62] He typed all winter, unwilling to give up a working hour for anything else, and he killed Stan Parker in spring. It was a lovely spring at Dogwoods that year, 'all blossom and pregnant goats'.[63] White wept as he typed the last pages, and he took his tears to be a good omen, for he had come to believe that unless he cried as he finished writing a book he had failed.[64]

Stan Parker dies in a state of tenderness and understanding, having almost glimpsed God for a moment in that 'jewel of spittle'. Amy goes for help, a heavy woman in torn stockings running down the overgrown path,

> Whimpering a little for those remnants of love and habit that were clinging to her. Stan is dead. My husband. In the boundless garden.[65]

His death is not the end. Down the back of the Parkers' place one patch of bush survives, choked with sarsaparilla vine, where their grandson wanders on the morning of the funeral thinking of the poem he would one day write about

> all life, of what he did not know, but knew . . . So that in

the end there were the trees. The boy walking through them
with his head drooping as he increased in stature. Putting out
shoots of green thought. So that, in the end, there was no end.[66]

He dedicated the book 'To Manoly', but only when he had finished
did he allow Lascaris to begin to read the 715 single-spaced quarto
pages. Lascaris thought the book was wonderful. One copy was posted
to New York and another to London in the middle of August. Now
'the awful part' began: waiting for the publishers' verdicts.[67]

Underlying the nervous gloom of these weeks was the news
from Paris that Gallimard's ambitious edition of *Eden-Ville* had failed.
The publishers had gone on to treat the next two translations as 'less
urgent'[68] but Marie Viton, who was very ill with tuberculosis by this
time, had continued with her translation of *The Aunt's Story*. It was
never to appear. In May 1954, as White was working on the last revision
of *The Tree of Man*, Gallimard renounced its remaining translation rights
and Marie Viton died shortly afterwards in a sanatorium.

When White warned Ben Huebsch that a new book was on its
way, the publisher replied, 'I am indeed glad.'[69] Somewhat reassured
by this, White concentrated most of his nervous speculation on the
London response. This was a long book; and what market was there
for him any more in London? 'I expect Routledge will throw me out,
as they had to give away most of their copies of *The Aunt's Story*.'[70]
Huebsch was on his annual travels through Europe when the manuscript
arrived at Viking. He did not read it until his return to New York. White
waited seven, anxious weeks for Huebsch's thrilling verdict which came
by telegram on 11 November: VIKING CONGRATULATES YOU ON BEAUTIFUL
PROFOUNDLY IMPRESSIVE FULFILMENT OF EXPECTATIONS.[71] White was over-
joyed. Viking's response, he confessed to Peggy Garland, had brought
him the greatest elation of his life.[72]

Then came a gloomy letter from his London agent Juliet O'Hea,
at which he took to his bed with a foul attack of asthma. O'Hea
wrote wondering what the book was supposed to be about. When
the typescript had arrived in London she sent it to one of her readers
who was unable to finish it. O'Hea then tackled it herself, didn't like
it, but sent it on to Herbert Read, who by this time was a director of
Routledge's. She hoped he would be more enthusiastic. O'Hea then
wrote to White, frankly stating her misgivings. He reported to Peggy
Garland, 'If I had received the letters in the wrong order, and felt that
I had spent four years producing a pile of gibberish, I think I would
have cut my throat.'[73] To O'Hea's question, 'What is it about?' White
replied, 'It is about life.'[74]

After a week of misery – vital days, it would turn out – a letter
came from Huebsch expressing Viking's enthusiasm in full: 'we were

all bowled over by your performance, for, high as our expectations were, the result exceeds them. You have produced a rare and affecting book, one that confirms the wisdom of your withdrawal from Ebury Street and the hurly-burly to a life close to the earth. Surely the book could not be earthier, and your people might be out of the Scriptures. All of life and all of nature are implicit in the tale.'[75]

From his bed White confessed his excitement and relief to Huebsch: 'I don't know whether other authors experience what I do: a feeling that they may be writing a secret language that nobody else will be able to interpret. Consequently the strain is very great until one discovers it is intelligible to someone else. And this time the strain has been increasing over four years . . .

'I was knocked over like a ninepin about a week ago by an attack of asthma, and have been in bed ever since. My only consolation is that these attacks are a great help creatively. Yesterday I was seeing quite clearly whole stretches of a novel I am planning to start after Christmas, and which had remained misty until now.'[76] The novel was *Voss*.

FIFTEEN

Dead Centre

WHITE WAS IMPATIENT to write and filled with regret for the fallow years that lay behind him. 'Life is getting shorter,' he complained. 'I have at least four more to write, with a fifth if I can manage to spend several years in Greece before I die. It is shocking when one has to start calculating in years of life, and thinks of the waste – though there is so much that cannot be written before one has lived a fairly long time – at least I try to make that excuse.'[1]

He had been a long time pregnant with *Voss*. Conceived in Ebury Street during the Blitz, the explorer novel grew in his imagination in the Western Desert, found its true character in the Mitchell Library on his recce in Sydney but was then put aside in bitter apathy after the failure of *The Aunt's Story*. Now as White lay in the public wards of Sydney hospitals in the summer of 1954–5, battered by the most violent asthma attacks for nearly twenty years, the novel came back to life. The fevers of Voss and the hallucinations of Laura Trevelyan grew out of his own suffering that summer in the attacks first triggered by O'Hea's indifference to *The Tree of Man*. All summer these bouts returned as bad news about the book continued to arrive from London. Yet this hostility stimulated him profoundly and *The Tree of Man* crisis set a pattern for his life. White was driven by the need to *show* his detractors, to vindicate himself with the next novel, the next short story, the next play. Even in the midst of triumphs, White sought hostility as a spur to his art.

Ambulances rushed him down from Dogwoods to any hospital on the North Shore that had room for him in a public ward. Sometimes he lay with 'corpses falling out of bed and old men drinking from their urine bottles' and he came to dread one Catholic hospital where the nuns were too busy laying bets on the races to notice his bronchitis turning to pneumonia.[2] When aunts and cousins arrived to visit White they would take Lascaris aside and ask, 'Why don't you book him into a private room?' Lascaris replied they had no money. 'Nonsense!' said the Whites, and were driven off in their Cadillacs.

Despite Herbert Read's efforts, Routledge rejected *The Tree of Man*. Routledge was getting out of fiction and was giving its authors away: even the detective writer Georges Simenon was handed to Hamish Hamilton. The boom years for fiction ended with the war; the old commercial lending libraries were closing; and paper rationing was still in force in Britain. 'We don't really want another Patrick White, do we, Read?' asked the chairman Cecil Franklin. 'We aren't really fiction publishers.' *The Tree of Man* was returned to O'Hea. Later Read pointed out to the board that Routledge had turned down a bestseller.[3]

The Tree of Man earned perhaps as many as twenty rejection slips. The London verdict was that it had to be cut. 'It is all a matter of length, breadth and thickness with them,' White complained. 'What they want is *novellen* that they can get away with publishing disguised as novels.' But White's New York and London agents both argued the book would benefit from heavy cutting. Victor Gollancz was keen to publish *The Tree of Man* but only if it were chopped by a quarter. O'Hea put the idea to White, but he replied, 'Not a comma.' She was reaching the conclusion that the book was unsaleable in London.[4]

White's text was protected in New York by Huebsch's horror of tampering with manuscripts. Viking's copy-editors might politely point out inconsistencies, make grammatical quibbles and indicate errors of fact, but that was all Huebsch would allow. He was not worried that *The Tree of Man* would run to about 500 pages. It helped that North America had no paper rationing.

Back at Dogwoods, frail but breathing, White began a course of allergy injections. He fell ill again; blamed the injections; took antidotes; and by the New Year of 1955 was feeling restored. But when the next bout of asthma came in January, it was the worst he had ever suffered. After a fortnight gasping in bed at Dogwoods, he was taken down to Royal North Shore Hospital. 'In my half-drugged state the figures began moving in the desert landscape. I could hear snatches of conversation, I became in turn Voss and his anima Laura Trevelyan. On a night of crisis, with the asthma turning to pneumonia, I took hold of the hand of a resident doctor standing by my bed. He withdrew as though he had been burnt.'[5] The doctors warned Lascaris that White could only expect to live five years with his lungs in such a state. As he recovered in the ward, White began working on the skeleton of *Voss*.

On the map of world publishing Australia was a suburb of London. All White's novels reached the Australian market through London publishers. In February 1955 when it seemed no London publisher could be found for *The Tree of Man* White threatened to reverse the natural order of things: publish the book in Australia and ship copies to England. He warned both London and New York that he would probably try 'to work something along those lines' soon.[6] This alarmed both O'Hea and Huebsch. It had not crossed O'Hea's mind to place the book with an Australian publisher despite all the problems in London: 'That would have been a tremendous step down. Publication here was essential. Patrick wasn't regarded specifically as an Australian novelist. He was just one of our brilliant young novelists.'[7]

Huebsch's response to White's proposal was apparently sympathetic but, in the final analysis, as commercially tough as O'Hea's. 'In the course of time native authors will want to be published at home, and your country is developing good authors,' Huebsch replied. 'However, I have been told that your book would have suffered for lack of adequate distribution in England, for the publishers of that country are not yet ready to accept Australia on equal terms.'[8]

White was back in hospital. Huebsch took the London problem in his own hands. Frank Morley of Eyre & Spottiswoode was visiting New York, and Huebsch persuaded him to take White's novel. Morley had nothing to go on but Huebsch's high enthusiasm. He cabled his London office to buy *The Tree of Man*, which was lying once more on O'Hea's desk as she wondered where to send it next. The deal was done swiftly. When Morley read the book he became extremely enthusiastic. White was not only delighted the book had found a publisher but charmed to discover the Englishman was a goat breeder. 'It is the first time I have been able to relax with an English publisher as I have from the beginning with Ben Huebsch.'[9]

White had decided once again that Dogwoods had to be sold, for he could not see how they could keep the farm going if he were ill and writing. He planned to find a modern house in an acre of bush garden, which could be abandoned for a couple of months at a time if he were ill or they wanted to go away. He told Huebsch, 'I am . . . trying to find somewhere where I am free.' White was seized with a restless wish to travel, in particular to see Greece again. On one of his bouts in hospital, Lascaris cleared the farm. The cows and fowls were gone, all but three of the schnauzers were given away or destroyed. White planned to put Dogwoods on the market in the autumn. Huebsch protested from New York. 'Where is it, and in what occupation, that you expect to find the "freedom" that you seek? Illness or none, your successful completion of *The Tree of Man* appears to have had a generally good effect on you, to judge by the fact that you have been planning a new novel the writing of which you are about to undertake.'[10] Huebsch was a shrewd old publisher: the farm had produced all he could have wished from this man.

Hardly anybody came to inspect Dogwoods, for it seems White

put a high price on the place. He was rather relieved, for by early winter two events had brought a great change to his outlook: the deal with Eyre & Spottiswoode was signed, and he had found a Romanian doctor in the suburb of Stanmore to whom he gave the credit for the 'almost miraculous' good health he was suddenly enjoying. Dr Morgenstern gave him injections of calcium, and a course of therapy that involved staring at blue lights.

Two early copies of *The Tree of Man*, from the batch Viking sent to influential reviewers, booksellers and other makers of opinion to set the scene for publication, arrived at Dogwoods in April. Even in his excitement, White had a list of small complaints. Must it be 'such a Bible' of a volume? Why not thinner paper? The tree on the cover was not a gum tree! Australian critics might declare the book un-Australian, 'Just as I am condemned and accused of being un-Australian because I have spent half my life outside the country – that is how their minds work.' Where was the acknowledgment to Housman's poem from which he took the title? And on page 138 at line ten '(Mrs K.O'Dowd)' should read '(Mrs) K.O'Dowd' – but, 'It was very exciting to see *The Tree of Man*, and for the moment my life has no more to give.'[11]

Yet he was already hard at work on *Voss*. With his health restored, he worked swiftly that winter and was more than half-way through the first draft by August when the critical storm over *The Tree of Man* broke in New York.

Viking sent an advance copy of *The Tree of Man* to the critic James Stern in Dorset, hoping for a few kind lines to quote on the dust jacket. Stern replied: 'Very few things could be more exciting for me than the news of another novel by Patrick White. I had begun to accept as true the rumour I heard a long time ago that he had abandoned writing for sheep-farming in his native land. I cannot wait to read *The Tree of Man*.' Rather than give an endorsement, Stern offered to review the book for his old paper the *New York Times*. Viking was delighted: 'quite crassly . . . a *Times* review being of prime importance would be our choice'. A column of praise from Stern was worth a bundle of notices from lesser critics.[12]

At several points in its course, White's life was profoundly influenced by people who shared a background much like his own, all escapees from the world of sheep and horses. Roy de Maistre, the novelist George Moore, the painter Francis Bacon, the poet Geoffrey Dutton and critic James Stern all had childhoods so oddly similar to White's that they might have grown up in a single, prosperous corner of the Empire. A common past drew them together even as they made good their escape. Escape itself was another bond: they were all refugees, and by White's definition refugees are 'in contact with life'.[13]

Stern was born and brought up on his family's estates in Ireland. He came from what he called a mongrel family of Irish-German-Austrian-Jewish blood. The Sterns mapped out two careers for their son and he escaped both of them. First he gave life in the cavalry the slip and then eventually left the family bank to become a writer. Stern's high reputation as a critic in the 1950s was underpinned by a small body of short stories which earned him, in Auden's judgment, a place of permanent importance in fiction.[14]

Stern was living in New England in 1948, 'during a winter memorable for the ice and snow that reduced even New York City to silence. I was alone, and many miles from a friend. Left outside for a few minutes, the cream of the milk would rise stiff out of the bottle like the sprung neck of a jack-in-the-box. It was into this arctic bleakness that a book arrived one day for review. *The Aunt's Story* by Patrick White. The author's name was new to me. Within an hour my whole world had changed . . .

'I had never been to Australia, yet here was prose which, by its baroque richness, its plasticity and wealth of strange symbols, made an unknown landscape so real that I felt I could walk out into it as into country I had been brought up in. I could see the black volcanic hills, the dead skeleton trees . . . I could all but touch the rock, scrub, bones, the sheep's carcass, the ox's skull, as they lay bleached in Australia's eternal greyness . . . under the immense blue of its skies.'[15] Stern's review in the *New York Times* was essential to the success of the book in North America.

In the summer of 1955 he read *The Tree of Man* and was profoundly impressed. His review covered the front page of the *New York Times Book Review* on Sunday 14 August. He wrote: 'Almost all novels are transients, very few remain on, permanent residents of the mind. Of those that do, some cease to be books and become part of the reader's past, of an experience felt so deeply it is sometimes difficult to believe that the illusion has not been lived. From these rare works of literature characters emerge better known than our most intimate friends, for every human being has a secret life, one unknown to all but himself and which he takes with him to the grave. To reveal in a novel this life (which is that of the soul) in such a way that by the time the last page is reached all questions have been answered, while all the glory and mystery of the world remains, is not only the prime function of the novelist but the artist's greatest ambition – and surely his rarest achievement. Were I asked if I had read a book called *The Tree of Man*, I might hesitate. But if someone in my presence were to start speaking of Stan and Amy Parker, I would immediately wonder how he had come to be in a certain region of New South Wales, Australia, when I was there, how he knew this obscure and simple couple about whom I feel I know all there is to know.

'Only in retrospect is the magnitude of this feat fully realised. Not until, with a sense of wonder and profound satisfaction, the novel has been laid aside does it occur to the reader that some two hundred thousand words have been written about a man and a woman whose effective lives could be printed on the proverbial postcard. Perhaps this feat is related to the fact that Patrick White for the past seven years has been writing this book while working his farm in New South Wales, where he was raised. The novel grows a little the way nature grows.'

He had been praised in New York before, but Stern's review of *The Tree of Man* established Patrick White's reputation in the city and in North America. Stern was not alone, for that Sunday the *Post* and *Herald Tribune* also ran enthusiastic reviews of the book. That Monday, the official day of publication, Orville Prescott of the *New York Times* echoed Sunday's praise. He also had been a convert since reading *The Aunt's Story* seven years before. Now he wished the new book had been cut by a quarter, but even so declared *The Tree of Man* 'a majestic and impressive work of genuine art that digs more deeply into the universal experience of human living than all save a few great books'. Orville declared Stan Parker, 'one of the most perfectly characterised individuals in modern fiction'.[16]

His triumph was almost unalloyed. From their bureaux in New York, Australian journalists wired home the news: AUSTRALIAN'S NOVEL WINS HIGH PRAISE. These stories, appearing on page three across Australia in the following few days, were the first news his admirers had that he was alive and working in Australia. His friends in Castle Hill were astonished not only to find him suddenly acclaimed but to discover he had been writing.

'I could not have hoped for better,' White wrote of Stern's review, but in the midst of this success he picked bitterly at notices that did not ride as high as the tide mark of Stern's and Prescott's praise. 'Stupid, perhaps even drunk', he remarked of a complimentary but dull reviewer in the New York *Saturday Review*. The first full review of the book to reach Australia was in *Time*. This tart and jokey piece ended: 'Author White's literary unwisdom is worrying this theme for so long that his novel itself becomes a kind of endurance test.' This review stung White. 'In spite of the wonderful splash on the news page of the *Sydney Morning Herald* with extracts from the *N. Y. Times*, *Herald Tribune* etc. people go round saying to each other: "But have you seen *Time*?" I fear that *everybody* enjoys a bad notice unless, of course, they happen to be the subject of it.'[17] In the years ahead White rarely had *Time* on his side.

White was extremely sensitive to censure and his response to

praise was perverse. He could not shrug off hostile reviews, nor did
he have any straightforward way of enjoying the storm of praise now
breaking over *The Tree of Man*. Lizzie Clark had taught him so well
that he must never 'blow his own trumpet' that he was shy of simply
basking in glory. But if he could not boast his success, he could assert
it in another way by castigating hostile reviewers for their malice and
ignorance. Such was the perverse response to which he was condemned
by nature and a Presbyterian nurse. He seemed in this to be immune to
critical advice, but this was not so. Time would show that some critics
made their mark. Deep within him there was also the fear that praise
would be his ruin, and so the need to guard himself by turning inward
away from applause. Under this self-protective impulse he looked to
hostile critics for mortification, and the sense of being the object of
antagonisms and misunderstandings spurred him on to new efforts.
White had always viewed the world as hostile; it was necessary for
it to remain so. In time this very difficult, contradictory response to
his critics was to cast a shadow over the writer. No praise seemed to
satisfy him. In the midst of triumphs White seemed to be begging his
public for more.

Letters from unknown readers gave him the most straightforward
pleasure, and he could boast unselfconsciously of them arriving in great
bundles at Dogwoods. *The Tree of Man* was a book which seemed to
change many lives. White wrote to Huebsch, 'I am having wonderful
reactions here and there round the world. People are stealing copies.'
Later he was delighted to hear *The Tree of Man* was 'popular with truck
drivers'. When Australia seemed unbearable and he was tempted to find
somewhere more congenial to live, White found a reason for staying in
the letters from 'unknown Australians for whom my writing seems to
have opened a window'.[18] In a world White saw split into armed camps,
these men and women were his foot soldiers.

Ten thousand copies of *The Tree of Man* were sold in North America
in the first fortnight after publication. Considering the high praise, the
figures were a little disappointing, but Viking was confident the book
would continue to sell. For the first time, White had the prospect of
earning good money from his writing. Already he had spent part of his
$1,000 advance on three suits, 'as I have not had one for twenty years,
and I may not make another penny for another twenty', and he now
celebrated the early sales figures by buying a new gramophone and a
few 33 r.p.m. records: Schoenberg's *Verklärte Nacht*, which he found
unlikable, Berlioz's *Harold in Italy*, and Alban Berg's violin concerto,
which he played over and over again as he worked on *Voss*.[19]

He wrote the second draft of the novel very rapidly, and this was
almost finished in April 1956 when the Eyre & Spottiswoode edition of
The Tree of Man finally appeared in Britain and Australia. Frank Morley

had devoted himself to the book. He ordered a very large first run of 20,000 and hoped for an eventual sale of 40,000 copies.[20] No great splash was planned for the launch. At this time there was a strong convention in London and New York that publishers did not huckster a strong book. If a book was weak, then advertisements might be placed and stories about the author generated for the newspapers. But it was considered an admission of weakness for literary novels to be promoted in this way. When American sales of *The Tree of Man* slackened after a month, Stern urged Viking to waive good taste and 'give the book one of those great full-page "spreads" packed with "quotes" and if it *had* to be, a picture!'[21] But that was not the way.

This old-fashioned restraint, shared on each side of the Atlantic by Morley and Huebsch, was welcome also to White. It became a fixed prejudice against which publishers hammered in vain. White would never promote his novels with interviews, tours, or campus appearances. More subtle methods had to be employed.

In London Morley bent the ear of every literary acquaintance, every reviewer and editor who would listen to his praise for *The Tree of Man*. His forum was the Garrick Club, and drinks and lunches took a fearful toll. Morley had expected soon to be made chairman of Eyre & Spottiswoode, and *The Tree of Man* was to set the seal on his claim to the post, but in the course of its production Morley fell victim to the bottle.

The London reviews were enthusiastic, though without the excitement of New York's sense of discovery. They discussed and (for the most part) endorsed the New York verdict. Morley had sent copies of Stern's *New York Times* notice to 'all corners of the Commonwealth' and there was hardly a review that did not quote a chunk of Stern with approval. White acknowledged that the reviews were wonderful but the Australian reviews, he told an admirer, 'must really be the test of an Australian book'.[22]

A.D. Hope's gods were Yeats, Pope and Swift. He taught the virtues of crisp, direct English and wrote poetry in the Augustan manner. In the Australian literary landscape, which was then dominated by poets, Alec Hope was a large figure. He was Professor of English Literature at University College in Canberra and his first collection of poetry *The Wandering Islands* was about to be published. A man who shared many of Hope's tastes was John Douglas Pringle, editor of the *Sydney Morning Herald*. Pringle was a Scot of the sweater clan, who brought to his Sydney post a mind of Presbyterian clarity and an approach to newspapers learnt in fifteen years on the *Manchester Guardian*. When he arrived in 1952, Pringle had found the *Herald*'s book pages in the grip of old enthusiasms and old feuds, and set about reforming them.

He knew Hope slightly, admired his poetry and recruited him to review for the paper. He fell, he concedes, a little under Hope's influence.

Pringle was aware that *The Tree of Man* had been hailed in the United States as a great novel. 'It was obviously a serious work of some weight and importance. I glanced at it, of course, but did not try to read it myself and had reached absolutely no conclusions about it. I simply wanted to find a reviewer of equal status who could judge it from an Australian point of view. I chose Alec Hope because I admired his poetry, knew him slightly, and had liked the reviews he had done for me.'[23] Pringle sent the novel down in May, and Hope spent that month in Canberra working on his response.

White, meanwhile, had been hustling on his own behalf. With one of the early Viking copies under his arm, he had turned up at the Sydney shop of the bookseller and publisher Angus & Robertson. An Englishman, David Moore, was working there at the time, and the chief buyer came into his office to confess that he was unable to read past the first page of *The Tree of Man*. Would Moore try? Moore had read White's earlier books with great enthusiasm and had tried to track the writer down in Sydney. He was the fan who gave up the search on being told Patrick White had gone to Queensland grazing sheep.

Moore now read *The Tree of Man*, recommended the shop order it in bulk from London, and returned the book with a note of thanks to White who invited the Moores to lunch at Dogwoods a few days later. There began the only Australian friendships that survived all White's life. Moore had come to Australia with Ealing Films and met his wife Gwen in the Flinders Ranges on the set of *Bitter Springs*. She was a teacher from Western Australia whose task was to give the children in the film their school lessons. A common love of Delius, discovered in that unlikely desert setting, brought them together. They married. When Ealing's local studio folded, the Moores stayed on. David Moore worked as an editor for Angus & Robertson, helping to prepare a new edition of *The Australian Encyclopaedia*.

Moore mobilised the shop on White's behalf. A whole window was filled by a tree in the German Expressionist manner, and out of its cardboard branches stared photographs of the author. The effect was eye-catching but intimidating in drab Castlereagh Street. Axel Poignant had taken the photographs, and White dressed in severe black for the occasion, with Solomon by his side and a white cat on his knee. He stared unblinking at Poignant's camera. There was no sign of comfort. Every surface shone. One shot had him smiling, but this White suppressed. With de Maistre's uncompromising paintings appearing in every frame, White looked like a priest sitting in a spotless presbytery.

Australia's literary magazines made their plans for the launch according to the politics of the factions they represented. *Overland* was

Communist and decided, without seeing the book, to ignore this experimental, bourgeois and essentially diversionary writer whose work failed to reflect the reality of living.[24] *Quadrant*, as the upholder of Right-wing standards, arranged a single review. *Meanjin*, edited by the poet, asthmatic and former journalist Clem Christesen, was more eclectic and liberal. Christesen commissioned a full survey of Patrick White's work from the novelist Marjorie Barnard. She was co-author with Flora Eldershaw of *A House is Built*, which White was now using as a source for the early Sydney scenes in *Voss*.[25]

Barnard sent a draft of her essay to Dogwoods for White's comments. He made one or two suggestions: 'I don't like Theodora's "Kafka nightmare". Do you really feel there is any likeness to Kafka? I have only read one short thing of his (about a man who changed into a beetle) but after reading a lot about him, I found him most antipathetic. Also he is a kind of fetish of the English intellectual. He was always dragged in, willy nilly, everywhere.' On the whole, White was thrilled by what Barnard had written. 'A great many people have become excited over *The Tree of Man*, but it is the first time anyone has shown that I have been working towards it over the last twenty years.'[26]

When Alec Hope's piece arrived on Pringle's desk in early June, the editor was pleased. 'It was a venture which, from the journalistic point of view, came off perfectly. Any editor would have been delighted by Hope's review which was well written and controversial. I bunged it in without changing a word.'[27] It appeared under the headline, THE BUNYIP STAGES A COMEBACK. Hope's bunyip was the Great Australian Novel. 'From time to time we hear that it has appeared at last. Publishers hold a special corroboree. Rival novelists lock their doors and say their prayers. Critics reach for their shotguns. Very soon the excitement dies down, as it is perceived that this is, after all, just another novel.'

The complaint was familiar. White was first accused of not producing the Great Australian Novel with *Happy Valley* and the Melbourne *Age* had already reproached him for failing again with *The Tree of Man*. The 'unusual effect' this book had had on American and English critics was the result, said the man from the *Age*, of a mistake: had they known how imperfectly, how vaguely White had come to grips with Australia they might not have praised him so highly. 'He has nothing much in common with other Australian novelists, but a lot, I think, with such writers as Capote and McCullers. Perhaps that is why the seed he has sown has fallen on such fertile ground among the American critics.' White dismissed this review as a 'stinker'.[28]

Hope had deeper objections: for twenty years he had campaigned against what Joyce and Lawrence had 'done' to the English language. 'I set my face against the muck-about-with-style novels, and made fun of them.' From start to finish he loathed *The Tree of Man*'s 'fancy prose'.[29] Hope praised the work's memorable characters, mocked the familiar farms and fires and floods and comic Irishmen of Australian novels, and flayed White's style with memorable ferocity: 'When so few Australian novelists can write prose at all, it is a great pity to see Mr. White, who shows on every page some touch of the born writer, deliberately choose as his medium this pretentious and illiterate verbal sludge.'[30]

No shaft of criticism ever wounded White so deeply. He raged against Hope as a peacock, a dingo in a pack whose spite knew no bounds, and 'an embittered schoolmaster and a poet of a *certain* distinction'. He wrote, 'The only thing I enjoy about it, is the irony of having to come back to Sydney to be told I am illiterate.' A little of this pain can be explained by White's own doubts about the style of *The Tree of Man.* He had set out to be deliberately primitive in telling the story of an almost illiterate couple, yet he felt his writing, at times, was 'not nearly precise enough'.[31] In *Voss* he was trying to clarify his style, a process that continued thereafter novel by novel.

Hope's notice was a *cause célèbre* not only for the 'verbal sludge' rhetoric White found so wounding, but for the poet's eccentric decree that the novelist 'needs a plain style, a clear, easy stride, a good open texture of language to carry him to the end of his path'. Lawrence, Joyce, Proust, James, probably even Dickens would be swept away if such Puritan taste were put into law. In later life Hope said he felt ambivalent about the review when he saw the piece in print, and that he rang Pringle to say he regretted not taking more space to write a longer piece. '*The Tree of Man* deserved a fairer review.' In 1974 Hope republished the notice much changed in his collection *Native Companions.*[32]

White's suspicion of academics – including Hope's friend Leonie Kramer – now turned into set antagonism. He was never quite as hostile as he wished to appear. Over the years he patiently answered academics' questions and was pleased to correct the more far-fetched of their theories about his work. But the influence of the universities in the small world of Australian writing caused him profound anxiety. There was too little faith in intuition, too much faith in the intellect. A couple of years after the Hope crisis he remarked to the poet Nancy Keesing, 'I suppose we are largely façade and university degrees: perception still has to come.'[33]

To White's chagrin, the controversy over *The Tree of Man* ran for a fortnight before Eyre & Spottiswoode managed to get copies of the book into the shops. He complained his publishers delayed 'until everyone was thoroughly exasperated, booksellers thought they were being imposed upon, reviews came out too soon, and the public was bewildered'. Not until the last weeks of June 1956, nearly two years after White posted the typescript to his publishers, did *The Tree of*

Man go on sale in Australia. Sales in that small market were very large: about 8,000 copies in the first three months.[34] The Australian Literature Society awarded Patrick White a second gold medal.

He met the Australian press for the first time, and it proved a bizarre beginning. The novelist Kylie Tennant, working on the staff of the *Sydney Morning Herald*, thought Alec Hope's review a great piece of journalism until she read the book. She decided a terrible mistake had been made: 'This was a fine novel.' She asked her editor Sidney Baker if she could interview the writer.

Baker: 'I don't want any part of it.'

Tennant: 'Sidney you've got a yellow streak a mile wide. You'll send me out to interview Patrick White not only to make amends but to save your bacon.'[35] In recalling this, Tennant cast herself, typically, in a *Girl's Own* role, fearless and dashing. She got her way with Baker and a visit to Dogwoods was arranged. White was waiting for her in a blaze of daffodils and plum blossom at the gate.

'I dreamt about you last night,' she began. 'You had blue hair and it was quite terrifying.' Tennant had a way of disarming people with such baffling remarks. White said nothing. He was not disarmed. They stumbled on from there, and the piece she wrote captured perfectly the characteristic qualities of a Patrick White press interview: odd silences, abrupt answers, savage verdicts.

'Did you ever study the existentialists?'

'I find them revolting.'

He gave a bare account of his life, and did not hide his pain in speaking of *The Aunt's Story* and the difficulties of writing *The Tree of Man*. Of the reception of the new book he remarked, 'If it hadn't been for the Americans I would have felt like putting my head in a gas oven.'

'But the book is selling well?' Tennant asked.

'Yes. It's topping the lists.'

Two announcements he made to her were premature: that his asthma was cured, and that he had finished another novel.[36]

Suffering is a theme that runs through all White's work, but *Voss* is, more than any of his other novels, an account of its virtues. Mahatma Gandhi wrote, 'It is impossible to do away with the law of suffering, which is the one indispensable condition of our being. Progress is to be measured by the amount of suffering undergone . . . the purer the suffering, the greater the progress.' White had used those words as an epigraph for *Happy Valley*. Twenty years later they could have served as well for *Voss*.

White saw himself as a sufferer: as an asthmatic, homosexual, foreigner and artist. He was aware that his own sense of suffering was, at times, exaggerated; he knew that money had saved him from many of the ordinary miseries experienced by the human race; he clung to Lascaris as the man who saved him from the worst suffering of all, loneliness. Yet he saw suffering as a force in his life, making him what he was, making us as we are. For White, pain is a force of history, shaping men and events. 'I have always found in my own case that something positive, either creative or moral, has come out of anything I have experienced in the way of affliction.'[37]

Behind the sufferings of Johann Ulrich Voss in the Australian desert lay the pain White experienced writing *The Tree of Man*. Both men were explorers: Voss on horseback crossing the continent and White at his desk trying to fill the immense void of Australia. Writing of the two expeditions, White used the same rhetoric of men stripped bare of almost everything they once considered 'desirable and necessary' in order to realise their genius. 'Every man has a genius,' pronounced Voss,

> Though it is not always discoverable. Least of all when choked by the trivialities of daily existence. But in this disturbing country, so far as I have become acquainted with it already, it is possible more easily to discard the inessential and to attempt the infinite. You will be burnt up most likely . . . but you will realise that genius.[38]

Voss's expedition was not a failure, though he found no new pastoral Eden, made no maps, lost all the specimens his party collected, and failed to reach the sea on the far side of the continent. Through his suffering in the desert, Voss conquered his pride.

White's fear of pride appears to have intensified at the time of his conversion. Lizzie Clark had issued decent Presbyterian warnings to the boy but, after he fell in the rain and cursed God, White went further than anything she had encouraged. He spoke of searching for humility. 'Certainly the state of simplicity and humility is the only desirable one for artist or for man. While to reach it may be impossible, to attempt to do so is imperative.'[39] The Parkers on their farm at Durilgai were lucky, for they possessed all along the humility White was now seeking. It was in their blood.

This new imperative was all the more urgent in the face of the success of *The Tree of Man*, for he had an absolutely sure grasp of the dangers pride presented to an artist. He was proud – Withycombe assurance and White money had seen to that – and now he was afraid of his pride. Of all the failings he saw within himself, this was the one he was most determined to conquer. He never did. From the first it was an unequal struggle, yet he persisted. The struggle took many forms. In the early years of his faith he prayed. Then – and later – he sought to

mortify his pride through suffering. 'There is a greater humility than
that which simple souls are born with,' he wrote to Ronald Reagan in
1984. 'The humility which evolves after sophisticated intellects have
wrestled with their passions, self-hatred and despair in their search for
truth.'[40]

White put much the same grim warning in Laura Trevelyan's
mouth after she had attended the unveiling of a statue to the lost
explorer Voss. Knowledge, she says,

> was never a matter of geography. Quite the reverse, it overflows
> all maps that exist. Perhaps true knowledge only comes of death
> by torture in the country of the mind.[41]

White had been working on *Voss* for eighteen months through all
the dramas attending the publication of *The Tree of Man*. He was, as
usual, very secretive about his writing, though close friends like the
Kriegers knew this time that he was working on a new novel. The
second draft of *Voss* was finished soon after *The Tree of Man* appeared
in Australia. White then put the manuscript aside for a few weeks and
began the final typescript in the spring of 1956. Not until this was well
under way did he tell his publishers anything very much about the new
novel.

'As you know I hate talking about books before they are ready,' he
wrote to Huebsch in September. 'For one thing, if one tells, anybody
can see at once on reading the MS how far one has fallen short of one's
intentions. But perhaps I shall give you some idea.

'Some years ago I got the idea for a book about a megalomaniac
explorer. As Australia is the only country I really know in my bones,
it had to be set in Australia, and as there is practically nothing left to
explore, I had to go back to the middle of the last century. When I
returned here after the War and began to look up old records, my idea
seemed to fit the character of Leichhardt. But as I did not want to limit
myself to a historical reconstruction (too difficult and too boring), I
only *based* my explorer on Leichhardt. The latter was, besides, merely
unusually unpleasant, whereas Voss is mad as well.

'I also wanted to write the story of a *grand passion* – don't jump. So
this is at the same time the story of a girl called Laura Trevelyan, the
niece of a Sydney merchant, one of the patrons of Voss's expedition. It
is different from other grand passions in that it grows in the minds of the
two people concerned more through the stimulus of their surroundings
and through almost irrelevant incidents. Voss and Laura only meet three
or four times before the expedition sets out. They even find each other
partly antipathetic. Yet, Voss writes proposing to the girl on one of the
early stages of the journey, partly out of vanity, and partly because he

realises he is already lost; she accepts, partly out of a desire to save him
from his delusions of divinity; partly out of a longing for religious faith,
to which she feels she can only return to through love . . .

'As the two characters are separated by events and distances,
their stories have to be developed alternately, but they do also fuse, in
dreams, in memories, and in delirium – most closely, for instance, when
Voss is lying half-dead of thirst and starvation, and Laura is suffering
from delusions as the result of a psychic disturbance diagnosed as the
inevitable "brain fever". Voss is finally dragged from his golden throne,
humbled in the dust, and accepts the principles Laura would have liked
him to accept before he is murdered by the blacks. Laura recovers. She
becomes a headmistress, and figure of some respect in the community,
if also one that nobody really understands, because of some mysterious
past.

'You will see that there is a lot that has to be *made* convincing.
I want to include the crimson plush and organ peals, while making
them acceptable to the age of reason by a certain dryness of style. To
a certain extent the style is based on that of records of the day (it may
even make the Australian critics feel I am saved from illiteracy) but I
have also left some loopholes through which to get my own effects.

'Two of the practical difficulties have been to try to make an
unpleasant, mad, basically unattractive hero, sufficiently attractive, and
to show how a heroine with a strong strain of priggishness can at the
same time appeal.

'As for the look and the sound of the thing, I have tried to marry
Delacroix to Blake, and Liszt to Mahler. Now I really am committed
to my own shortcomings! And on reading over what I have written,
I see I have failed to convey that there are *lots* of subsidiary characters,
minor alarms and excursions, deaths by thirst, a suicide, an illegitimate
child, picnics, balls and weddings.'[42]

The essence of Voss was White himself: 'bits of Leichhardt . . .
bits of Eyre, and I suppose, some of the others, but there is more of
my own character than anybody else's'. He gave him the 'gabled town'
of Hanover as his birthplace, and his first explorations were conducted
on the sandy heath – *Die Heide* – that surrounds the city White knew
best in Germany.[43]

White's heroine Laura Trevelyan and her cousin Belle Bonner
grew from his memories of the Ebsworth children. The Ebsworth
family appear in many guises in his writing. Charles Ebsworth, the
tall, stuffy solicitor who looked after the affairs of his parents and
H.L. and Belltrees, had already appeared as Dudley Forsdyke in *The
Tree of Man*. He is the lawyer the Parkers' daughter marries: 'a dry
man, but a true man'. The Ebsworths had three daughters. When the
high-spirited, mischievous, inseparable twins Mary and Elaine came to

Lulworth they ragged the boy they called 'poor old Paddy', for they felt he was a misfit and rather pathetic. These two – always on the run, plaits flying, undisciplined and haughty – he merged into the figure of Belle Bonner.[44]

From their older sister Isabelle, the boy sensed a measure of intuitive sympathy. This became the core of Laura Trevelyan's character. Isabelle Ebsworth was years older than the twins, intense, and with a face of great interest. She had a dramatic jaw and wide green eyes cut at a slant. The Ebsworths held her out to be the brainy one of the family, but she was not at all cold. Even when White last saw her – she was twenty and he was about to leave for Cheltenham – Isabelle showed an almost provocative self-possession. She attracted idealistic suitors.[45] By the time White was working on *Voss* she had divorced, moved to Scotland and married a Glasgow psychiatrist. Once in later years she and White arranged to meet in Scotland but the plan fell through. They never met again.

As he was writing *Voss*, White drew deeply for the first time on the history of his own family. Mr Bonner, patron to the expedition, lives in a house with Lulworth's dark gardens overlooking a rushy marsh on the edge of the Harbour. There is a bunya bunya on the drive. The house is a wilderness of mahogany and Bonner's study, like Dick's room at the end of the veranda, was somewhere 'all is disposed for work except the owner'.[46]

The first stage of Voss's journey takes the party by sea to Newcastle and overland through the 'gentle, healing landscape' of the Hunter to Rhine Towers, a picture of Belltrees in the early, more innocent years before the great house was built.[47] In the care of the Sandersons – the name belonged to one of Clem Withycombe's friends out at Walgett – Rhine Towers is a place of simplicity and perfection, an Eden in the bush. Memories of Belltrees are strong in the book. In the boy's imagination there was always a connection between the property and explorers. From Belltrees H.L. sent the naturalist Sidney Jackson to unexplored corners of Australia searching for birds and eggs. When White was a boy he was taken to meet Jackson in Sydney and watched him sorting through the skins and corpses of his finds. The Christ-like ornithologist Palfreyman who accompanies Voss is not Sidney Jackson – for one thing, he was astonishingly fat for a tree-climber and Palfreyman very thin – but the ornithologist and his German leader were conceived by a man with this childhood link to explorers and exploration.

Voss leads the party from that sublime valley across New England to the flat coolabah country of White's jackerooing days. Jildra is the last outpost before the wilderness. For the portrait of Jildra White drew on his memory of Brenda, the station over the Queensland border to which he had driven with his uncle, where they woke at dawn to the

sound of birds and black servants padding about on bare feet. But the
squalor of Jildra comes from a half-remembered newspaper story from
that time: a story about 'a real bastard on an isolated station pumping
up bungs'.[48] West of Jildra lay the desert. White had never seen, never
saw, the dead heart of Australia. All he had to draw on were his
memories of Africa, and books and paintings. Once the expedition left
Jildra, Voss was on an expedition to the outer limits of his imagination.

White had a guide. On the seventh floor of the David Jones Elizabeth
Street store, he had seen the great exhibitions of Sidney Nolan's outback
paintings in March 1949 and March 1950. These made Nolan's name in
Australia. 'When you enter the gallery', wrote the critic of the Sydney
Daily Telegraph, 'the blaze of reddish-brown hits you like a ton or
two of real red earth.'[49] White came to the Australian desert through
Nolan's eyes. Nolan had seen the gold mines in Queensland, flown for
weeks over the centre in the back seat of a Beechcraft of Connellan's
Mail Services delivering to stations and missions from Alice Springs,
travelled through the Gulf country and down the coast to Perth. About
the time White was first researching Leichhardt, Nolan was reading
the diaries of the doomed explorers Burke and Wills. His paintings of
their ludicrous journey to the Gulf were those that particularly stirred
White: men and camels tramping across the grey-green country of the
Gulf, incongruous historical figures in a hostile landscape. Years after
these exhibitions, he told the painter how he felt they had both been
exploring the same territory, and expressed what they found in the
same way. So he asked Nolan to do the jacket for *Voss*.[50]

In his magpie fashion White searched for the historical details
he needed for the book. He found accounts of Aboriginal painting
and ritual in the Mitchell Library. For life in early Sydney he drew
on 'M. Barnard Eldershaw's' *A House is Built* and Ruth Bedford's
Think of Stephen, an account of the family of Sir Alfred Stephen.
He was Chief Justice of New South Wales in the 1840s when Voss
made his journey into the hinterland. 'I feel these chronicles are of
great importance,' White wrote to Bedford. 'All the data on the early
rabble is already there, but there is not so much to hand on the more
respectable classes. You must help fill the gap.'[51]

In the end there was little he took directly from Leichhardt's
papers. White accepted Alec Chisholm's often mocking attitude to
the explorer set out in *Strange New World*, the book in which White
had first discovered Leichhardt nearly ten years before. One detail does
come straight from the explorer. White was struck by his description of
the great comet which, in *Voss*, hovers over Laura on Potts Point and
the rump of Voss's party in the desert: that 'unearthly phenomenon . . .
that quick wanderer, almost transfixed by distance in that immeasurable
sky'.[52]

The affair of Voss and Laura was the greatest technical challenge he faced in the novel. Though they were not 'seen to copulate' their passion was intended as an answer to the passionless life White saw around him in Australia. 'Intellectual passion seems to me to rise no higher than the snarling of a mongrel pack in the correspondence columns of the fortnightlies and weeklies. As for physical passion, I sense on the one hand sparrow-fucks, and on the other the weekly grind. Surely Voss and Laura were passionate individuals.' Nor was the long-distance courtship meant entirely as a literary device, for White believed in such communication of the spirit as a fact. From Cape Cod he had written to Spud Johnson half a continent away in Taos, 'you have been extraordinarily close. I could almost put out a hand'. In his bronchial fevers he had seen the figures of Voss and Laura together, just as they were to meet in their own fevers; and he came to have a guarded belief in the existence of extra-sensory perception: 'I am continually receiving evidence of it myself.'[53]

Critics would later spend a good deal of time guessing which writers had influenced White as he worked on *Voss*. 'Most of the time, I'm afraid, it leads up the wrong tree!' T.S. Eliot's *Four Quartets* were cited but White had not yet read them, nor *The Golden Bough*, nor Dante except a little in the translation by Dorothy Sayers. All these were said to have influenced *Voss*. In correcting these misapprehensions White acknowledged he may have 'arrived at certain conclusions *via other writers* who had read' these works. He rather regretted not having read some of those whose influence was detected in his work – André Malraux, for instance, whose *La Condition humaine* he had read about twenty years before, 'when I did not care enough to follow him in his career; Conrad, several books in my teens when I could not understand what all his conflicts were about, and consequently did not like him. (The one Conrad I do like, and which I read just at the end of the War on the advice of Robert Liddell, is *Under Western Eyes*.) Of Nietzsche I read *Also sprach Zarathustra* when I was an undergraduate without being drawn to it.'[54]

One important influence at the time of *Voss* was Rimbaud. Frank Le Mesurier, the poet on Voss's expedition, a man with dark thin lips, dark eyes and proud nose, emerged from White's passion for Rimbaud. He had grown drunk on the poetry when he first discovered it, and read Enid Starkie's study of the poet several times. By the time he wrote *Voss* he was 'soaked in Rimbaud'. Le Mesurier, though he is 'a comparatively undeveloped character in the novel . . . just *had to be there*'.[55]

White was conscious of being influenced more by music and painting than writing. 'In the last ten years I think music has taught me a lot about writing,' he told Huebsch. 'That may sound pretentious, and I would not know how to go into it *rationally*, but I feel that listening

constantly to music helps one to develop a book more logically.' To get
into the mood for work, he played the gramophone until he was 'quite
drunk' with music. 'Always something of a frustrated painter, and a
composer *manqué*, I wanted to give my book the textures of music,
the sensuousness of paint, to convey through the theme and characters
of *Voss* what Delacroix and Blake might have seen, what Mahler and
Liszt might have heard.' The music of Mahler meant most to him as he
was writing *Voss*. Liszt was not a composer he liked much, 'only that his
bravura and a certain formal side helped me in conveying some of the
more worldly, superficial passages of *Voss*. The same with Delacroix.
The latter is a painter I admire, but for whom I have no affection.' He felt
very close to Alban Berg – an affection strengthened when he discovered
Berg was a bronchial asthmatic – and he played Berg's Violin Concerto
all through the 'illness' of Laura Trevelyan. It took Bartok to finish off
the explorer. 'I couldn't get the death of Voss right, and I was in bed
with bronchitis feeling like death. I suddenly got out and put on the
Bartok Violin Concerto, and everything began to come right. I suppose
there was not much connection between that scene and the concerto,
but it liberated me.'[56]

White was working on the last pages of *Voss* when British and
French troops entered Egypt to seize the Suez Canal. The preceding
months of diplomatic manœuvring – in which the Australian Prime
Minister's delegation to Cairo was humiliated by Nasser – had filled
him with apprehension and disgust. He told Huebsch, 'It is difficult
to concentrate for the stink of history just at present.'[57] Megalomaniacs
were loose again in the world. His loyalties were mixed: he loathed the
Egyptians, but yet the 'Rabid Rabbit' Anthony Eden seemed determined
to provoke war with Russia. Preying on his mind was the danger to his
mother and sister.

     For some time he had wanted them to leave London. 'Why they
can't come out here too, I don't know. Or I do. They are that type
of Australian who have developed enough sophistication to feel they
must live within reach of the West End, and not enough to have
realised their mistake.' Now as war threatened White urgently wanted
them back in Sydney. Ruth refused to budge. 'One needs perhaps
the atomic bomb itself,' White remarked grimly to Peggy Garland.
'You have really missed something never having had a peep into my
mother's mentality. So far she has made not one remark on what
has been happening in the world in the last few weeks.'[58]

     Ruth was enjoying her quiet London existence. Though her energy,
at the age of seventy-eight, was remarkable, she cut nothing like the
figure she had in Sydney. The London life of Mrs Victor White meant
small social engagements on the formal English calendar of opera,

theatre, the palace garden party and Chelsea Flower Show. Ruth was a woman with season tickets. She was devoted to Glyndebourne, and poured a little of the White fortune into the opera: her gifts each year of one hundred guineas earned her the unique status of Glyndebourne's 'only individual corporate member'.[59] Ruth was a generous but rather intimidating grandmother, giving Suzanne's children lunch in the roof-garden at Derry & Toms or taking them to Covent Garden. When they visited her Rutland House flat overlooking Kensington, the children preferred to slip away and play in the kitchen with the cook.

Everything was done perfectly at Rutland House under Ruth's direction. Australian visitors recall the loot from Lulworth crowded into the big apartment, the buhl and porcelain artichokes, rugs and silver, the green china with its gold monogram W and Ruth always beautifully dressed in black with pearls and high heels, like a bright, elegant, sharp-eyed blackbird.

White's friends were surprised to find her less intimidating, more sophisticated and far more interested in his work than they expected. There seemed to be two passions in her life at this time: Glyndebourne and Patrick. She was thrilled by the success of *The Tree of Man*, and showed great pride in her son's achievement, relaying any scraps of news about him that came through from Australia. Certainly, she dominated events as they had been warned she would: if you invited Ruth out to dinner, she whisked you off to *her* restaurant and ordered the bottle of wine you *had* to have, and usually paid for the meal. She welcomed stray Australians using the Rutland House flat as their English base, and she was generous to her son's friends.

Suzanne was now a widow. Geoffrey Peck had a stroke at the wheel of his car one night after taking his mother home from the theatre. A policeman found him slumped in the driver's seat and helped him up to the flat. Peck was dead when he arrived at the hospital. A few weeks later Suzanne found she was pregnant with her third daughter Frances. At the time of Suez, the baby was one, Alexandra was thirteen and Gillian seventeen. White was very curious about his nieces. He wrote to David and Gwen Moore when they were on their way to London, 'My sister is the kind of mother who talks about her children. The only thing she ever reads is a best seller with a tinge of pornography. It is really the children I would like you to inspect and report on.'[60]

Suzanne was keen to return home, but she could not leave London without her mother, and Ruth would not budge. If there was to be another war, the old woman was determined to see it out in London. White continued to appeal to her to come out to safety. For a time she broke off contact with him in a huff.

All this was in the air as he finished *Voss*. He was exhausted and nervous, genuinely apprehensive of another world war, locked once more in conflict with his mother and, as always, deeply worried about his writing. Sydney had also been hit by drought and, as it was forbidden to use hoses in the garden, he was spending hours each day carting water to his shrubs.

Voss was finished in early December 1956 and he gave Lascaris one copy of the typescript to read. This developed into a set routine. Unless there was some Greek to be checked, Lascaris saw nothing of a book until it was written. He then read the typescript slowly and very carefully without making any comment until he had finished. These silent days always brought White to a pitch of apprehension. But Lascaris was very pleased with *Voss*. White dedicated it to Marie Viton, the translator whose work had encouraged him to begin writing again in the early years at Dogwoods. On 17 December Lascaris drove him down to Martin Place in the new Rover they had bought with American royalties, and from the GPO White posted copies of *Voss* by registered airmail to London and New York.

Christmas at Dogwoods was uneasy. His mother was still not speaking to him. He was living in limbo, weathering a bout of summer flu as he waited for Huebsch's response. Naomi Burton wrote from New York in mid-January extremely enthusiastically about the book, but it was not until sometime later in the month that Huebsch cabled and wrote accepting *Voss* and making a few minor suggestions about White's German. Huebsch asked what Australians would make of the book. White replied: 'Quite a lot of them are beginning to look for works of art, and will accept *Voss*, and even exalt it, but there will be the usual outcry from those who expect a novel to be a string of pedestrian facts, and from the critics, themselves mostly writers, or worse still, "professors".'[61]

He sent Huebsch a detail from Breughel's *Triumph of Death* clipped from a newspaper. In a landscape of gibbets and corpses, a praying figure is about to be beheaded with a sword. Bodies rot on poles. Prisoners are broken on the wheel. 'It seemed to me to convey something of the climax of *Voss*, although the latter is certainly not a "Triumph of Death". Perhaps Breughel and the artist who does the jacket for Viking may get together in some way.' Huebsch dismissed the idea, promising to hold the clipping in reserve 'against the need of an illustrated edition of *Mein Kampf*'.[62]

The writing of *Voss* had taken its toll on Lascaris. At least he was able to talk about his trials with Ile Krieger, for the fact that White was writing was no longer a secret. 'We discussed the business of handling our difficult men. Patrick was sitting alone, very nervy, getting very drunk and not talking to Manoly. I gave Manoly wifely advice: how to humour him, what to forgive. I said, that if this was the way Patrick wrote, then he had to accept it.'[63]

Lascaris had decided to return to Greece for a few months once *Voss* was finished, and booked a passage on the *Oceania* sailing via Cape Town in late February 1957. He did not know if White wanted him to return. At first White offered only a one-way ticket to Athens with the promise of a return if Lascaris wished to come back. Lascaris insisted on the return: even if he did not rejoin White he would come back to Australia and find a job. He had spent all his money: no more now than in 1946 could he land on his family's doorstep like a beggar. Both men believed that his departure for Greece might mark a permanent breach.

White came home from the ship desperately miserable. Fritz Krieger drove over to see him but drew back in the face of White's awful distress. Thirty years later he thanked Krieger for his tact. 'In the evening I ran down out of the house where the Cécile Brunner rosebush grew against the veranda. I saw through my tears that you were standing at the front gate. You melted away on seeing what the situation was. Whenever I remember this incident I feel most grateful for your kindness and consideration.'[64]

White was quite lost. 'Once in the middle of the night I found myself about to piss in the bathroom waste-paper basket. I grabbed at food, I guzzled drink. The dogs were my only comfort, Solomon sleeping at my feet, Lottie snuggled into one armpit.'[65] His chest was a mess again. Morgenstern ordered fresh X-rays and diagnosed cancer or tuberculosis. The more horrifying possibility was soon discounted, but twice a week through the next few months he took the long journey to town by bus and train to attend a TB clinic. Not until spring was this second TB scare of his life officially over. Its shadow hung over the year.

Lascaris reported from the ship that elderly ladies sailing to an audience with the Pope rubbed up against him like cats in season. There were a number of *Tree of Man* enthusiasts on board, which gave him, as the dedicatee, a sort of position during the voyage. White told his friends: 'Manoly . . . is followed round the ship by a group of young Australians as if he were a phenomenon.'[66]

The proofs of *Voss* arrived by air in March. Huebsch had retired from the day-to-day routine at Viking though remaining White's editor in name. His successor Marshall Best had the task of producing *Voss* and wanted to clean up some points of grammar and punctuation. Best had three objections which remained a persistent worry at Viking for the next twenty years: first, White's 'dangling modifiers', those participial phrases at the far ends of sentences left with nothing to cling to; second, the mixed use of both 'that' and 'which' in linked clauses; and third, excessive punctuation.

Viking had purged the *Voss* proofs of commas. 'We realise that fashions change in this regard and that Mr White has a perfect right to punctuate in what will seem a somewhat old-fashioned way if he feels that that adds to the colour he wants in his book. For most readers, however, this is apt to call attention to itself and to slow up the reading.' White rejected all changes, but allowed Best to thin out a few of the commas, acknowledging that his punctuation was 'rather laboured'.[67] White still had Huebsch in the background insisting that his prose not be touched.

The omens for *Voss* were excellent. *Harper's Bazaar* wanted a short story to coincide with its appearance and offered a fee of $300. White had not written a short story for ten years, but had a few left from a batch finished in Athens after the War. 'On the Balcony' is the tale of a failed courtship in a city of women anxious to find husbands. It was the first of his Greek stories to be published and the first appearance of the Catastrophe of Smyrna in his writing. Mrs Papaioannou, 'like a big downy Smyrna peach . . . had fallen on the stones of Attica and bruised'.[68]

Also from New York came news that *Voss* would be Book of the Month Club selection for August. It meant a minimum advance to White of $20,000. This magnificent windfall came with only one hitch: one of the selectors complained about the title. White insisted it remain *Voss*. 'A book grows with its title. If one starts to mess around with the latter afterwards, the whole thing begins to look a bit like a bad Hollywood film. Besides, I have recently remembered how, some years ago, before I had started to get anywhere with my writing, one of my aunts dreamed that I had a big success with "a book with a funny foreign name". So that is another very good reason why the title must remain.'[69]

London planned to publish *Voss* eight months after New York. White was exasperated by this leisurely approach, but the Book Society came to his rescue by choosing *Voss* as its December selection. Eyre & Spottiswoode did what they could to impress on them the inconvenience of such haste, but after sending astonishing letters of complaint to White, the firm finally accepted the society's offer and brought forward the date of publication. The society was to take an extra 11,000 copies.

Morley, who had drunk his way out of the job, had been replaced by Maurice Temple Smith, who was summoned unexpectedly at the age of thirty to take over the firm's fiction list after biding his time editing works on farm maintenance and irrigation. Eyre & Spottiswoode was well on the way to bankruptcy then and this odd appointment may have been meant as a stop-gap, but under Temple Smith the firm's fiction list prospered once again. The mainstay of Eyre & Spottiswoode remained the Bible, for the firm was one of the licensed publishers of the King James Version. Temple Smith admired White's work and feared White. Reading the back files he found copies of the furious correspondence with Viking over the errors in the first American edition of *The Aunt's Story*. Most of White's complaints struck him as trivial, but he took them as a shot across the bows: 'Alteration was impertinence.' He touched nothing in *Voss* except a few spelling mistakes.[70]

For the jacket of *The Tree of Man*, Eyre & Spottiswoode had commissioned some gum trees from an amateur painter who worked in Australia House. The result was a drab mess. White took the *Voss* jacket in hand, persuading the firm to accept Sidney Nolan, and persuading Nolan to accept the commission. The artist sent White a preliminary sketch on a postcard. 'It got the character to perfection – thin and prickly.' But Voss in the final version, which White approved despite his disappointment, turned into 'that fat amiable botanist'.[71]

He waited anxiously for *Voss* and for news of whether Lascaris would return. He felt himself slowing down. 'It is intolerably dreary here on my own,' he told the Moores. 'It is not the work, just the slow passage of time. At night I wash up, and drink, and play Mahler and Bruckner, till my head thunders – and I shall probably be ready for Alcoholics Anonymous at the end of it all.'[72] The drought continued all winter, and he was still watering the garden by hand, lugging buckets to the shrubs. There were two heifers in the paddock, three cats and five dogs to feed. A new bathroom was built, the roof was repaired and the house painted once again inside and out. Dogwoods emerged Mediterranean pink, with woodwork and gutters of deep blue. The house became a landmark.

During these upheavals White began to cull his papers. 'It is dreadful to think . . . that one's letters still exist. I am always burning and burning, and must go out to-morrow to the incinerator with a wartime diary I discovered at the back of a wardrobe the other day.'[73]

He poured his nervous frustration into a brawl with Heinrich Böll over the German translation of *The Tree of Man*. Böll, who was working for the publishers Kiepenheuer & Witsch, gave the book the astonishing title *Zur Ruhe kam der Baum des Menschen nie*: the tree of man never came to rest. Though White read and spoke German with ease, his literary German was not up to the task of answering Böll's queries, so he turned to Ile Krieger for help. Part, at least, of the translation arrived at Dogwoods in midwinter, but White suspected it came too late for his corrections to be incorporated. He found a number of mistakes, such as 'Goldgräber' for 'digger', i.e. soldier. Böll's letters struck him as arrogant.

By June he was so exasperated he declared his translator 'an

insufferable kind of German. I think he is really trying to work it
so that his translation will appear without my having looked at it.'
White did not see the second half of the text in translation, but
when the book appeared later that year, Ile Krieger reassured him that
apart from mistakes over Australian details, it seemed to be excellent.
Unmollified, White wrote to Huebsch: 'I shall always remember him
as an intolerable person and arrogant German, and if K.&.W. want to
do *Voss*, they will have to find another translator.'[74] Böll's *Zur Ruhe
kam der Baum des Menschen nie* won the Wupperthal Prize for translation in 1957. The book has the odd distinction of being one of few
novels by one winner of the Nobel Prize to be translated by another.

White had warned Huebsch that he could not see himself writing
for a long time to come. He wrote nothing that winter, but figures in
a new novel were moving in his imagination. The German megalomaniac had led him to the Holocaust, and even as he was writing *Voss*
White began to study Judaism and the history of the Jews in Europe.
Honegger's 'stupendous' *Liturgical Symphony* broadcast that year from
Salzburg seemed to be saying a lot of what he wanted to say in the
novel, which was forming 'a kind of cantata for four voices' in his
mind. 'I am still a long way from starting,' he told Peggy Garland.
'But enjoy brooding over it. I shall be forced to eke out that luxury
for some time.' Huebsch was admitted to the secret but warned, 'My
Jewish novel will take a lot more thought and reading. Even then I
may not have the courage to embark on anything so esoteric. Time
and other powers will decide.'[75]

Lascaris wrote before setting out from Athens to say he would
return to Dogwoods. 'His trip was very necessary, and had to take
place when it did,' White told Peggy Garland, trying to put the best
face on the situation. 'Now I can tell he wants honestly to come
back. Before, I could always sense he felt something of an exile
from Greece. He says he finds he really does not have much in
common with his family any longer, or indeed, with anyone over
there. The country was as beautiful as ever, but the poverty of
the majority of the inhabitants so miserable that he could only
feel ashamed.'[76]

White's miserable three months alone confirmed Lascaris' authority
in their relationship. White could not do without him. He had planned
a long trip of his own in 1958 to Europe and America, but realised he
would prefer to stay at Dogwoods now if there was not the money for
Lascaris to go with him. 'Since I know what it is like to stay here alone
for months, I would not bring the same thing upon anyone else.'[77]

Their reunion was not easy, but in making plans to travel the
following year the two men sealed their compact: they would stay
together. At Easter they would leave for Greece and go on around

the world. Both had old mothers to face. Lascaris had not seen his since she left Egypt after the First World War, though they had been writing to one another since Lascaris left school. 'No matter what she has done,' said his aunt Elly, giving him her address in America, 'she is your mother.' Now Mrs Randolph Bronson of St Petersburg, Florida, she had a son Randy – Lascaris' half-brother – in New York.

Ruth had fallen in Kensington High Street and broken her hip. At first it was thought she would not walk again, but she was soon out of hospital walking on crutches which she exchanged almost immediately for sticks. That summer she began taking taxis on the fifty-mile journey to Glyndebourne. White heard she was 'doing all of what she wants to do, almost as if the accident had not happened'.[78] But there was now no prospect of her making the journey out to Australia. If he were to see her again, he would have to go to the mountain.

Voss appeared in New York on 19 August 1957. Enthusiastic as critics were, they betrayed a faint sense of disappointment. They rather put *Voss* to one side, gave *The Tree of Man* a fresh round of applause, and predicted a distinguished future for Patrick White. The *New Yorker* captured this mood of hesitant enthusiasm: 'His prose . . . tends to set up an obstinate and exasperating barrier between his subject matter and the reader. Nonetheless, this is a heroic and sometimes brilliant novel.'[79]

On the whole White was pleased by the American response, but the *New Yorker*'s reservations puzzled him. Wasn't the reviewer contradicting himself? 'I feel that my style, which he deplores, gives him the effects that he admires. But cleverness does cause a great many reviewers to contradict themselves. And I suppose one should not complain too much about this one, who has let fall a few quite juicy plums for a publisher to pick up.'[80] *Voss* sold rather poorly, not matching the figures for *The Tree of Man*.

Voss appeared in London in early December after a publisher's launch which White boasted was 'the biggest of all time'.[81] Reviews had that exhilarating note of discovery which was absent in New York. Of course, there were dissenters. James Stern, not this time leading the New York pack, used his long piece in the *London Magazine* more to consolidate White's general position than applaud the new novel. But the end result of the appearance of *Voss* was to establish White for the first time as a literary celebrity in London.[82] In their excitement the critics offered Patrick White a place in the company of Lawrence, Hardy, Conrad, George Eliot, Ivy Compton-Burnett, Austen, Malraux, Faulkner and – in a moment of delirious enthusiasm at the *Observer* – Tolstoy.

Voss was a bestseller, and on the strength of its success both

Viking and Eyre & Spottiswoode decided to reissue *The Aunt's Story*. White was delighted, for he was still confident the book would make its mark.

The Australian critics did not have their say until the New Year, for Eyre & Spottiswoode was unable to get *Voss* into the shops for the Christmas rush. White boiled with rage. He had a shrewd eye for lost business, and an author's incredulity at the ways of publishing. By the early New Year he was bristling with hostility before a major review had appeared. 'I can feel the critics poised for ritual murder,' he told the Moores. 'All the Sydney papers have been very careful to keep the British opinions dark, so this time a good time should be had by the jackals.'[83]

Voss was immediately a bestseller at home, but the Australian press turned its attention to the book with a kind of weariness. The rather brief reviews by mostly undistinguished reviewers which appeared not very conspicuously over the next few weeks, suggest a general editorial opinion that it was a publishing event of no local importance, despite what was happening in London and New York. It was as if they were trying by this deliberate lack of excitement to contain a fuss which they had neither provoked nor sanctioned. Foreign flatterers were reproved. 'One thing is certain,' wrote the poet Douglas Stewart, 'overseas praise does tend to be excessive, and . . . lacking in the fundamental knowledge of the subject which alone can give real authority.'[84]

There survived here and there an artless yearning for a different man with some of White's talents who would provide 'more Australian' novels. The *Age* thought this pessimistic book came undone because the German was a poor explorer: 'It is still permissible to yearn for writers with some faith and hope, backed by Patrick White's imaginative power and the verbal clarity of, say, Robert Louis Stevenson.'[85] Certainly, Australian critics spoke of White with new respect, and he was now taken seriously by all the little factions of the local literary world – even the far Left – but Australian critics offered him no place in the pantheon. The *Bulletin* observed that Patrick White had yet to match the achievement of William Gosse Hay, author of the nineteenth-century historical romance *The Escape of the Notorious Sir William Heans*. He meant this as abuse – though it was a novel White greatly admired.[86]

The critics were not compelled to praise *Voss*. They had every right to dislike the book and say so bluntly. That it was greeted at first with a general air of reproach was a source of great anger to White, especially as the critical verdict in Australia was reversed after a few years and the explorer novel came to be revered almost to the point of tedium. But time had to pass. The great ambition of the provincial critic is to have the detached intelligence to puncture a false reputation. The great nightmare is to be fooled by a hasty enthusiasm. On balance, they find it safer to be wrong than swept away.

As he waited for the Australian reviews, White found the Jewish novel was growing in his mind, 'shaping and altering, and the four voices of what I still like to think of as a kind of cantata are beginning to sing in the way that, finally, they must'. He was afraid it would boil over before he and Lascaris left on their travels. 'I . . . don't know whether to let it or suppress it. I think probably I should not begin yet, and should read and think for a bit longer.' The reviews of *Voss* broke in on his absorption. 'There are times when I become quite desperate about my fellow countrymen,' he complained to Huebsch. 'Sentimental realism is still about all that most of them can follow in fiction. If you don't trundle along by way of that same dreary rut, they accuse you of *not being Australian* . . . If I were not going away, I think I might start *Riders in the Chariot* at this point. Always when I meet with lack of understanding in Australian critics, I feel like sitting down and starting another of the novels they deplore, to give them further cause for complaint. But perhaps it is a good thing in this case that I am being restrained by circumstances.'[87]

Lying in bed ill with bronchitis, wounded by a review he found particularly vicious, he took out a notebook and wrote a few paragraphs in the character of Himmelfarb the Jew on his terrible journey across the suburbs of Sydney on Seder night, a journey 'expressive of hopelessness and despair, both for what has happened to him, and for the ugliness and awfulness with which he is surrounded'. The first words of *Riders in the Chariot* were put down on paper at a moment when hate, White admitted, had got the better of him.

As the darkness spat sparks, and asphalt sinews ran with salt sweat, the fuddled trams would be tunnelling farther into the furry air, over the bottle-tops, through the smell of squashed pennies, and not omitting from time to time to tear an arm out of its screeching socket. But would arrive at last under the frangipani, the breezes sucking with the mouths of sponges. Sodom had not been softer, silkier at night than the sea gardens of Sydney. The streets of Nineveh had not clanged with such metal. The waters of Babylon had not sounded sadder than the sea, ending on a crumpled beach, in a scum of French letters.[88]

A new literary magazine, *Australian Letters* edited in Adelaide by the poets Geoffrey Dutton and Max Harris, had asked White to answer a piece from Alister Kershaw praising expatriate life in Paris. White now agreed. The result was the extraordinary 'Prodigal Son': the first public explanation of his aims, the first defence against

the critics, and the most devastating attack he ever launched against
Australia. He wrote nothing like it again, and nothing he has written
is so often quoted as this.

At one level, 'Prodigal Son' was written to defend *Voss*: 'I was
determined to prove that the Australian novel is not necessarily the
dreary, dun-coloured offspring of journalistic realism. On the whole,
the world has been convinced, only here, at the present moment, the
dingoes are howling unmercifully.' But White's deeper purpose was to
make the painful admission that for all he hated about his country –
with reasons set out in coruscating prose – he was bound to Australia
for life.

'What then have been the rewards of this returned expatriate? I
remember when, in the flush of success after my first novel, an old
and wise Australian journalist called Guy Innes came to interview me
in my London flat. He asked me whether I wanted to go back. I had
just "arrived"; who was I to want to go back? "Ah, but when you do,"
he persisted, "the colours will come flooding back onto your palette."
This gentle criticism of my first novel only occurred to me as such in
recent years. But I think perhaps Guy Innes has been right.

'So, amongst the rewards, there is the refreshed landscape, which
even in its shabbier, remembered versions, has always made a background to my life. The worlds of plants and music may never have
revealed themselves had I sat talking brilliantly to Alister Kershaw over a
Pernod on the Left Bank. Possibly all art flowers more readily in silence.'
Australia had stripped him bare, allowed him to begin again, challenged
him to create 'fresh forms out of the rocks and sticks of words. I began
to see things for the first time.'[89]

White would rail against both his country and his fate for the
rest of his life, driven by deep love and blasts of disappointment, by
the frustration of finding himself tied to the scenes of his childhood,
'after all, the purest well from which the creative artist draws'. As he
suffered blows from the critics of *Voss* and drafted his reply for *Australian Letters*, he wrote to the Moores: 'How sick I am of the bloody
word AUSTRALIA. What a pity I am part of it; if I were not, I would
get out tomorrow. As it is, they will have me with them till my bitter
end, and there are about six more of my un–Australian novels to fling
in their faces.'[90]

Only days before the two men were due to fly to Europe – boats
now seemed far too slow – it was announced that *Voss* had won the
first Miles Franklin Literary Award for a novel of 'the highest literary
merit which must present Australian life in any of its phases'. The
£500 prize was then one of the most generous literary awards in the
world. The judges' choice was unanimous. Huebsch heard the news

in New York and cabled: TRUTH IS GREAT AND SHALL PREVAIL. White
was thrilled to have the cash but even more to be so vindicated. He
confessed to Huebsch: 'I suppose, at heart, I am really as malicious as
my Australian critics.'[91]

On the way to the ceremony he called at his doctor's surgery for
something to get him through the ordeal. Morgenstern gave him an
injection and dropped him at the Rural Bank in Martin Place where
the Prime Minister Bob Menzies and the bedraggled Dr Bert Evatt,
Leader of the Opposition, were waiting. Television recorded the scene.
The Prime Minister complimented the Australian novel on its new
maturity, and handed over the cheque. White, braced by whatever
Morgenstern had provided, stood there and said a few dry words. He
had survived to the age of forty-six without ever speaking in public.
Photographers posed him between the two politicians. A journalist
asked what he planned to do with the money. 'I am going to buy
a hi-fi set,' he replied, then added after a moment's reflection, 'and
a kitchen stove.'[92]

SIXTEEN

Letters and Cards

White to Naomi Burton   *19.viii.1957*

$5,000 seems a very large sum for our few weeks in the States, but
if you think that is necessary, better hold that back, and send the rest
to the Bank of New South Wales, Sydney. If we find we don't have
enough money for the European part of the trip, we shall just have
to draw some of the dollars, and live on hamburger while we are in
the States. (I suppose, as I am a foreigner, there is no possibility of
my investing the dollars in something safe in the States, and making
something out of them, for we shall not arrive there till early Fall 1958?)

To Peggy Garland   *13.xi.1957*

I can produce tears almost any time for Greece, and nearly cried
my head off reading *Bitter Lemons*. It is the Mediterranean really.
Everything on earth that matters is concentrated there as far as I
am concerned – and when I say earth, I mean space too.

To Douglas Cooper   *6.ii.1958*

I will only start off if we can leave in April and spend the Spring
in Greece, wander up through Italy during June, to Vienna, where
we must look up a couple of old Jews who lived for years out here;
then, across to Toulouse, where Manoly has some Italian cousins in a
diplomatic job, England in August, New York in the Fall, and home.
Perhaps we could look in on you for a couple of days on the way to
Toulouse? The whole trip must be very brief – only about six months
in all – as we shall be leaving five aged Schnauzers in boarding kennels,
five breeding cats at home, and we can't expect anybody else to go on
living at Dogwoods once the season of growth begins; it would become
a jungle . . .

I suppose it *is* time I emerged from the Bush, but I am actually happy in it, so why not stay? Of course, the human beings can be maddening, but I now take a great interest in plants, and by the time I have attended to those I possess, scrubbed, dug, cooked, mown, even baked the bread, there is little time left over for people. Certainly I am fortunate in having had Manoly with me all these years; my need for anyone else is reduced. And I listen to a lot of music.

To Ben Huebsch   11.ii.1958

I would like first to go to Jerusalem and speak to one or two people. I am never altogether happy if I do not know about past stages in the lives of my characters. And my 'hidden zaddik' – because that is how he appears to be developing – did pass through Jerusalem.

Oh dear, it is going to be a very trying book to write, but I am living with it all the time now . . .

To Mollie McKie   5.iii.*1958*

There never was such red tape. It is harder to get into Jerusalem now than it was into Tobruk during the siege. Duplicate passports are the order of the day for Israel. And on top of it all I was told by the travel agency that technically I am English, as I was born in London, my parents had never bothered to have me registered as an Australian, and I had acquired an English passport when I needed one of my own. So, to prove my father was Australian, and that I would be eligible for an Australian passport, I have had to trace the registration of his birth at Muswellbrook ninety-one years ago.

Ben Huebsch to White   2.iv.*1958*

Your plan to spend a few days in Jerusalem prompts me to suggest that you should see Schocken, the publisher, over there. I take it that he is still active and engaged in bringing out books, and perhaps a newspaper, in Hebrew. Mr Schocken was a wealthy department store owner in Germany but with a soul above shoe leather . . . He was in the ideal position to publish what he thought ought to be perpetuated in print, and to hell with the public.

White to Fritz and Ile Krieger   20.iv.*1958*

I did decide to bring the Olivetti. (Incidentally, we had a big blow from excess baggage right in the beginning; they made us pay £51 overweight as far as London, and that was without the typewriter. Our big cases and the overnight bags were in order, but we had not

reckoned that the little Orbit bags would be weighed, and into those
we had stuffed a lot of medicine bottles, dictionaries, papers and things.
Now we have learnt from a travel-seasoned Jewess to carry an Orbit
bag under the coat one is wearing, although this does make one look
as though one is possessed of a third buttock.)

. . . From our experience so far, Qantas is easily the best air
company. As soon as we parted with them we started running into
irritations. At Bangkok we were told that we should have to wait
24 hrs to catch the Air France plane, as this had 'broke' on the way
from Tokyo. In the heat of the moment this was very distressing,
and a great wailing broke out amongst the Jewish pilgrims to Israel. I
suppose I must have done my share of wailing, for in the middle of it
all they asked me if I wasn't 'Mr Winkel'. At the height of the crisis,
too, the skirt fell off the elderly *Blaustrumpf*, Mrs Cohen, who was
trying to lead her flock, and she was left standing on Bangkok airport
in a flesh-coloured slip. Finally, we were all disposed of in hotels, and
Manoly and I at least were glad of the delay as we were able to look
at some wonderful Buddhist temples the following morning – all glass,
and porcelain, and marble, with bells tinkling, incense rising, crowds
praying – it happened that that day of all days was their New Year.
For twenty-four hours I became, I think, a Buddhist.

Air France arrived fairly late that night . . . At Tehran next morning
we found we had emerged from the steam baths of Thailand, and were
now surrounded by snowy peaks on a vast, bare, wind-swept plain. For
our stay at the airport, we were herded into a small, square, sinister
room, like something at a lesser Arab railway station, by a kind of
female Commissar, with a very bad temper, and food-spots down her
front. Doors were slammed. We were commanded. We were given
cups of cold tea with egg-stained tea-spoons, all in the Arab tradition,
while Persians stood around looking, drinking little coffees, and, one
of the Jewesses insisted, talking a kind of bastard Russian . . .

Later that afternoon, after flying over the snows of Southern Turkey,
and turning at Cyprus, we began to approach the Promised Land. The
Pilgrims, who had been putting on their best in the lavatories for the
last hour in preparation for the reunion with *Verwandten*, now began
to jump from side to side of the plane, and finally weigh it down, one
feared, on the side of Tel Aviv.

It was a relief to get down, and soon be on our own again,
although there were first many formalities at the airport, incredible
efficiency, very agreeable and helpful hostesses, and civilised customs
officials. Israel is really most impressive . . . everywhere something
positive and constructive seems to be happening, the young Israelis are
most stirring, and everyone looks happy – which was an impression I
never had when I was there fifteen years ago.

Unfortunately the dusk became darkness as we drove towards Jerusalem and we were not able to approach it by daylight as I had hoped. In spite of being told we should never find accommodation during the Celebrations, we were accepted by the first hotel at which we asked, very clean, and reasonable – a co-operative – with good food and excellent service. Soon we were swallowed up in a comic mixture of Diaspora – American Orthodox eating in caps, but accompanied by elegant social wives, discreetly disguised English Jews, correct Germans, and a terrible Johannesburg couple, she like a Black Orpington, and he like a dinkum Australian mite, taking his teeth out for comfort after dinner.

We took a couple of motor trips while in Jerusalem, which did give us a general impression of the Jewish side of the city, only a very general one, however, and it was most disappointing not to be able to visit the Holy Places, which are all in Arab hands. Although we went to the British Consul, the most he could offer was to get us a permit to pass into Jordan; from there the Arabs would not have allowed us to return . . .

We spent a very interesting evening with a friend of Klari's, a Dr Spitzer, who had worked for Schocken, the publisher in Germany, and who is now employed by the publishing house of the Jewish Agency. At one time also he worked with Martin Buber, who is at present in New York. We sat up with Dr S. till about 2 a.m., drinking brandy, looking at prints, and talking about everything under the sun. The following day we lunched with him at an oriental restaurant, after which he took us to see one of the old quarters, and into a Yemenite synagogue, where I found an air of peace and perfection such as one seldom finds in a church.

. . . Approaching Greece a couple of days ago, we were every bit as bad as the Jewish Pilgrims arriving at the Promised Land, jumping from side to side in the same way, as we identified islands in the incredible Aegean. Athens is much changed – it has lost a lot of the village atmosphere which I so much liked but it has still got the ability to squeeze my stomach into a ball, and to make me sing as I walk through the streets. I know of no other place in the world which does this sort of thing for me.

So far we have been much taken up with relations. Manoly is staying at the above address, which is that of his youngest sister, Elly, and I have a very pleasant room and bathroom in an empty flat belonging to a friend, in a house directly opposite. In a few days we shall start moving about . . .

To Gwen and David Moore   *23.iv.1958*

But the fish . . . ! That is really something, and we have more or less decided to eat nothing else while we are in Greece. To think that

Australians believe they know about fish; it is pathetic. Last night we went to a place near the water in Piraeus and feasted with many cousins on clams on the shell, fried baby kalamaria, prawns about six inches long, little red rock cod, of tender, melting flesh (these are perhaps the best of all), and an enormous fish, I don't know what, grilled in the piece, with crisp, salty black and golden skin. All this with plenty of retsina, of course, and raw salads.

The weather has been a bit disappointing up to date, quite cold, and at times even grey and drizzly. So that, on the day we decided to revisit the Acropolis, the Parthenon appeared to be made out of dirty washstands, and the whole impression was rather a melancholy one. I shall have to go up again to correct it on one of the hot, blue days. Because the Parthenon *is* the sight of sights, as close to perfection as it is possible to come.

The latest book news is that *Voss* will become a Penguin towards the end of '59, by which time the sales of the E&S edition will have died. I am very pleased about the Penguins; it adds to one's respectability. I forget whether I told you I am fiddling with a play written some time ago. I have almost got it into shape for typing, but the distractions are many of course, not the least of them being endless tangoes sung with the same dying fall by a builder's labourer, outside my window, every morning . . .

Must go out now, about various bits of small business. It feels very strange to be almost free, to have to think about nothing but buying carbons or a copy of *The Times*, and at moments it seems ridiculous that one should have tied oneself up in a ball of habits, when there was really no need. I shall be interested to see whether this dangerous sensation persists in other countries.

Lascaris to Fritz and Ile Krieger   *8.v.1958*

P. is very comfortably installed just across the street . . . He has been all the time of a very happy disposition and carried out none of his threats to be nasty to my father, my younger brother and a number of my cousins whom he has always professed to dislike. In fact he now appears to like them all, sends flowers to the women and takes them out to meals. As a result my nerves are quite relaxed and I feel very happy and free of strain.

We have done a very pleasant tour of the south . . . Ideal weather and magnificent landscapes. The Spring this year might have been to order for us, everything green and lush, piles of wildflowers in the valleys and snow still on the mountain tops.

White to Gwen and David Moore   *15.v.1958*

We are only now on Mikonos . . .

For me the landscape means much more than the antiquities, as I did not have more than a very rough classical education, and besides, I am a romantic at heart. For that reason Delphi leaves the greatest impression. It is such a stupendous panorama, and the same goes for all the country between Delphi and the Ionian Sea, where we took a ferry to get to Patras. I don't think I shall ever see anything to equal what we saw in those two days, and quite untouched by tourists, officials, politicians, and all the decadent, parasitic life of Athens . . .

Sparta again was a wonderful landscape that one had to bow down to, though the town itself shows no apparent traces of antiquity. Just near it we clambered up a mountain in the dusk and drizzle to the Byzantine city of Mistra, with a church perched every few hundred yards. The topmost church was of particular interest as an ancestor of Manoly's, another Emanuel Lascaris, founded it. His tomb is there, and a fresco portrait from which the Turks scratched the eyes during the Occupation. The Abbess entertained us with ouzo in a very stovey little room, and sold us embroidery when the heat and drink had broken down our resistance. (Very beautiful embroidery, too.)

. . . A very emotional situation has just blown up on the waterfront at Mikonos as the result of a lattice erected by two Americans to hide the goings-on in an old house they rent, and which they run as a bar. The Prefect of the Cyclades arrived the last day of our visit, and proposed to ban the lattice as something that spoils the uniformity of the waterfront. One of the Americans has now rushed to Athens to enlist the sympathies of a Minister, and thus save the lattice. The Americans claim they are being persecuted (probably rightly) as foreigners, while the Islanders claim (rightly also, I should think) that their bar is a homosexual brothel and that the proprietors are seducing all the boys, and even the husbands on the Island! The delightful part is that, in their rage, the Islanders are practically accusing America of introducing homosexuality *into Greece*, whereas, if they want to go no farther back in history than today, the Abbot of a monastery on the far side of the Island is keeping a harem of twenty boy-orphans! (We met him while we were there, a crafty piece of work with his hair done up in a net, but all he offered us was a piece of Turkish delight.) I don't know what will come of the Lattice of Mikonos. It is a lovely plot, I think and might well end up in the fall of governments, and diplomatic incidents, for the uncle of one of the Americans is said to control Aid-to-Greece.

I have wasted a lot of time on that, and must now say something about Delos, which we visited from Mikonos, and which was a perfect idyll. A long rocky barren island covered with yellow grass and thistles, but at the same time masses of pink convolvulus, purple statice, yellow sea-poppies and the common field red, as well as a little flower resembling the gentian. The air full of a sound of what could have been deafening larks. Cisterns full of green water and enormous, green, coupling frogs. Crimson dragonflies above the water, intent on the same game. And all through it, the remains of what must have been a great city, columns, temples, mosaics (fabulously beautiful ones that one wants at once for a house of one's own), with down, by the sea, propped up against stones, the marble torso of a giant Apollo, worn down by the weather to a texture of cuttlefish. We came back to Mikonos, suitably pricked by thistles and burnt by the sun, over a classic sea.

To Geoffrey Dutton   *30.v.1958*

. . . it is very difficult to write letters travelling about as I have been lately, from island to island, and through some of the remoter mainland, with the German translation of *Voss* to correct at night . . .

Even after all that has been said about expatriates, I find myself tempted to become one over again! But I shall not, or anyway, not until I am much older, and have said almost all I still have to say. I can imagine spending a few years in Rhodes, say, at the end of my life, and doing a book I have long thought of writing about Greece, not of great consequence, a kind of impressionist sunset, chiefly for my own pleasure.

To Fritz and Ile Krieger   *4.vi.1958*

Greece is the paradise of the official, and home of the rubber stamp. Where one man and one stamp is enough in most countries, five men and as many stamps are necessary in Greece. The day I leave I am thinking of posting a letter to one of the papers on the subject of officials, officers, and priests. As much as anything else I feel that these three bodies contribute to keep the country down. On the poorest island one sees a swarm of officers of at least two of the services, strolling with brief-cases containing what one would like to know, or sitting down to a long, livery meal of the best the village can offer. In the same way provincial priests seem to spend most of their day sitting over coffee at a café, playing with a string of amber, or just staring. Wherever poverty abounds, they almost always remain plump. And the dirt is not quite credible – that they could have spilled so much down their fronts, or accumulated so much grease at the back of the neck . . .

Idleness also has begun to get me down. There are even times when I wish I could rush into our own kitchen and wash a batch of dishes, or cook a meal for half a dozen people. It is sad and humiliating to see the slaves of Athens still drudging at eleven o'clock at night.

Manoly will have told you about our dog troubles. I think Evchen can only have committed suicide. Lottie is our greatest worry, and I only hope she will last till we get back. They say she is better and that the tumour is only benign, but I never believe implicitly in the benignity of tumours . . .

It is a long time since I listened to any music, and I must say that with so many things to look at I have not felt the need for it lately. Probably if I had stayed in Greece, I would never have 'discovered' music, nor written any more novels; I was driven to both in an effort to fill the Australian vacuum.

To Peggy Garland   *4.vi.1958*

I am now quite ready to go home, and can't think how I shall last till October.

To James Stern   *6.vi.1958*

Thanks for your letter. I nearly wrote to you after your review of *The Tree of Man*, one of the most understanding I have ever had, and again after your enthusiastic article in *The London Magazine*. Then I thought: Let it never be said that I am a collector of critics.

However, now that you have set the ball rolling, I would like to meet you, and perhaps that will be possible while I am in England in August. I shall make a note of your address, and drop you a line after I arrive.

Incidentally, there are one or two mistakes in your essay on the books . . .

To Douglas Cooper   *13.vi.1958*

I'm afraid it won't be possible to get down to Argilliers. Manoly's relations are taking up rather a lot of our time, and since my mother lost her sight I shall have to make a point of paying her a more conscientious visit than I might have otherwise.

Huebsch to White   *17.vi.1958*

The season has grown late, and I am now at the point of crossing the Atlantic again . . . except for something unforeseen I will sail on the *Queen Elizabeth* on June 25th; destination undetermined at the moment, but I have a mind to proceed to Switzerland or northern Italy, to loaf for a while before making gestures of usefulness.

According to your itinerary we might meet in Italy or Zurich . . .

It seems better to return the Australian reviews of *Voss* herewith than to post them to your home. How grudging they are! And often unconsciously amusing, as when one picks the 'male moon' to disclose how badly you write and another picks it to praise your style. A couple of them mean to be honest, but their sphere is limited and they are fearful.

White to Douglas Cooper   *25.vi.1958*

I am a little more reconciled to Italy after arriving in Perugia to-day. Rome is definitely not for me. I find both the buildings and the people disappointing, to say nothing of those soggy-gingerbread ruins. There is perhaps one church which suggests sanctity – Santa Maria in Cosmedin – and one place where I would like to live – the Villa Giulia – behind walls. In Perugia at least, there seem to be few tourists, and less priests, and the air and the light are immediately amiable.

To Fritz and Ile Krieger   *11.vii.1958*

I refuse to go in a gondola, as they are now almost the exclusive property of elderly American ladies, they look so funereal (much more than Liszt suggested), and in the smaller canals they keep so close to the water and move so slowly one would be asphyxiated by the smells. Everything must go into those canals – kittens, corpses, abortions, to say nothing of the more obvious forms of refuse. When we arrived here and found our room looked onto a narrow street (the Calle Goldoni, incidentally), we were very disappointed, but after the first twenty-four hours we realised how kind the management had been to spare us a canal . . .

Perhaps another drawback is the number of German tourists. These Goths pour down into Northern Italy in thousands. We came across them first in any numbers in Ravenna, now in Venice they even swamp the Americans. Except at the Lido, where the fabulously expensive Excelsior seems to be inhabited exclusively by Germans, they appear to be doing it all on the cheap – the kind that wander round with shapeless bags full of *Wurst* which they gnaw in their rooms at the pensione at night. There are the clear-golden ones, the men a kind of ageing *Heldentenor* with *Bauch* and wedding-ring, the women of quite agreeable texture, but with those hypocritical fish's eyes. Then there is the grey-skinned variety, made out of lumps joined together, both sexes inclined to B.O., the men in *Lederhosen* with all the stains of the *Italienische Reise*, the women in what are supposed to be 'gay' dresses, but which by any other standards are a screaming jangle of bad taste. The women are all so sweet and innocent. When occasionally I cannot resist giving them a look to suggest that I know exactly what evil their wombs have conceived, there is no sign that anything has ever happened; if anything, they grow sweeter and even more innocent.

We are leaving here tomorrow and going straight to Milan, cutting out Verona which we had intended seeing, because Huebsch has turned up at Milan, and I gather is hanging on there in order to see me . . .

Ile will be pleased to know there are three orchestras on the Piazza of San Marco of which at least one is playing *My Fair Lady* during the day or night. They seem to have come to an arrangement whereby one takes over when the other stops. I must say I hope never to hear another note of 'I Could Have Danced All Night' since the half-dozen of which it is composed have been dinned into me so mercilessly.

To the Grolier Club   *November 1964*

Ben much older, walking with a stick, but no less tough in spirit or agile of mind. I had travelled across Italy to meet him in Milan – perhaps the least rewarding Italian city. But there was the perfect day, eating trout in the sunshine on the edge of Maggiore. Afterwards we took the little steamer to the Borromean Isles. It will remain one of my great pleasures, to have seen the white peacocks and the rock crystals of Isola Bella in Ben Huebsch's company on that gently perfect day.

To Fritz and Ile Krieger   *21.vii.1958*

Grüssen aus Wien! We are staying within a stone's throw of the Belvedere, and we have seen where Bruckner lived and died. Sunday we walked in the Wälder between Cahlenberg (?) and Leopoldberg. Many Schnauzers in the streets.

To Gwen and David Moore   *12.viii.1958*

Manoly and I . . . are by now in the thick of London life. It has been wonderfully pleasant to meet old friends again, and find we can slip back into friendship without any effort. That has been the best part of it. London itself not so good. I wonder how I succeeded in living in it for so long, overlooking so much, for it is so terribly dirty, ugly, the people so drab – also ugly and dirty – the women like uncooked dough, the men so often suggestive of raw veal. Manoly thinks it becomes beautiful at night, and that it is only saved in the daytime by its trees, and I think he is right. Certainly an awful daytime skyline of black or red brick can wear a lovely purple bloom at night; even the telly aerials grow mysterious and right; and the trees make perfect oases in squares and parks, particularly after this drizzly summer.

I have been seeing a lot of my family, and so far have had no rows with my mother. She is now very pathetic, half-blind, going deaf, and walking very slowly with her two sticks. Suzanne is quite remarkable in the midst of the very dreary life she has to lead. It always amazes me to think I am related to her – she is so cheerful, and nice – whereas I am every bit of my mother, which is one of the reasons why we have never been able to get on together . . .

Since I began this, I have lunched with Eyre & Spottiswoode. Douglas Jerrold, the Chairman, is a kind of Grey Eminence, with beaky nose, withered arm, and habit of chewing his words in the best English manner – as if they were a difficult and unpleasant meat. One hears hair-raising stories about him – how he literally drives others to drink, crushes all personality out of those around him, and how he once reduced Laski to gibberish in an unscripted radio discussion. He is a rabid Roman Catholic, and clashed badly with Graham Greene when the latter was a member of the firm. After he had dislodged Greene, he once said: 'I was a Catholic before it was *fashionable* to be one. Greene pops in and out of the Church just as he pops in and out of bed.' However, today at lunch, he spoke very kindly of his Great Hate, saying: 'Greene is perhaps the only real novelist writing in England today.'

Also at lunch was Temple Smith, the junior partner of the firm, with whom I have been corresponding for some time now. From his letters I always took him to be a dry, dusty individual, probably at least ten years older than myself, but I found a glamorous young man still in his twenties, with rather sunken blue eyes, and a full under lip, who spoke very intelligently, and bridged some of the gulfs between the Grey Eminence and myself. On the whole we all got on fairly well, except that I have had to scotch a horrible plan of theirs to give a party so that people can satisfy their curiosity . . .

We shall be in New York c/o Curtis Brown . . . for about ten days, then for about a fortnight with Manoly's sister, Mrs W. Reagan . . . Fort Lauderdale, Florida, arriving back some time at the beginning of October. How I look forward to it – to feel the dogs' wet noses again, and to smell the evening air in our own back garden – that really will be returning.

Ruth White to Gwen and David Moore   *4.ix.1958*

I do find difficulty writing now as my sight is no better and much of my time has been taken up with almost daily visits from Patrick – we have all been so happy and he has been most kind and delightful to us all – He looks so well and young for one 'middle aged' as he describes himself. I think he looks younger and decidedly happier than when I last saw him years ago. His visit has been wonderful . . . we have all taken Manoly to our hearts. He is a very sweet natured man.

Patrick White to Peggy Garland   *26.ix.1958*

. . . we did not have a single row, although I went to see her nearly every day. Perhaps whatever it was has been exorcised . . . I expect being forced in on herself as a result of this last misfortune, has made her discover some inner resources that she was not aware of in the past. She still tries to keep up physical appearances, wears jewellery and make-up, which only serves to make her look like a corpse, at least in the early stages, by the time the lipstick has worn off she begins to look more human. And she certainly *is* more human than she used to be . . .

Had something of a reunion with Francis Bacon, who has matured as a person, and of course, Roy de Maistre. I have bought a crucifixion by Roy, quite small, very beautiful . . .

To Fritz Krieger   17.viii.1958

Some of the shops here are very impressive, particularly those for men's clothes, which are comparatively cheap, and make one feel one would like to start wearing clothes again. Trains are absolutely filthy. Trees and flowers without rivals.

To James Stern   19.viii.1958

Thank you for your electrifying letter. I had always felt that *Voss*, even *The Tree of Man*, could be made into a film by the right person. I do know Zachary Scott as an actor. I was even a fan of his years ago, on the strength of a film called, I think, *The Southerner*, about a family of poor cotton-croppers. I went to several of his other pictures, all very mediocre, lost sight of him, presumed he had been killed by bad parts, and was very glad to hear of him again in connection with *Requiem for a Nun*, and to see that he was occupied with something worthwhile. Perhaps he *is* the right person to handle *Voss*. Anyway, I shall be sure to look him up in New York. We used to take an additional interest in him because we read somewhere that he was half-Greek, but perhaps you are better informed on that point, and he is not Greek but Mexican . . .

To Peggy Garland   26.ix.1958

We had an exhilarating week in New York, thanks mostly to a number of cosmopolitan, intellectual Jews. It is really the Jews of that type who make life in the States bearable. Otherwise, it is a horrifying kind of sub-civilisation, full of sudden gusts of fascism. The routine of living has been made so easy that the average person has lost touch with life, its primary forms and substances. I shall be glad to get out of it, even more glad that I am Australian . . .

How I long to find myself at Dogwoods again.

To Fritz Krieger   13.ix.1958

. . . we went to visit your family, and spent a very agreeable evening

there. The journey was not very heartening, first through those horrifying up-town slums of New York, with even a real corpse on the line
at one of the stations, and cops cutting his pockets open, then all those
Tudor mansions at Bronxville, which I find quite as horrifying in their
different ways. We were met by your sister and brother-in-law. Nana
is really very pretty! . . . We found your mother very sympathetic –
young, and gay. In some ways I should think she is a lot like you, and
you have a definite physical likeness to one another. The young people
we took to at once, Eva so warm and pleasant, and the young men
handsome and intelligent. After dinner we were shown the paintings
. . . During the exhibition of paintings, your mother went off to her
room, and was sitting there playing patience, with a cigarette hanging
out of her mouth, and a terrific smoker's cough. I think probably, like
you, she is more for music than for the visual arts.

We were entertained a lot in New York. The first night one of
the directors of the Viking took us to dinner at the Plaza, in a horrific
oaken room, but we ate and drank and talked in spite of the decoration.
On another occasion about four other members of the Viking took us
out to lunch, so they really gave us the treatment, though I refused the
publicity trimmings that were hinted at at one stage . . .

New York was most stimulating. Just to walk down Park Avenue
and look at those new, wonderful buildings. The last morning we
went over the United Nations Building, which I think must be the
most beautiful thing since the Parthenon was built.

We also saw one of the most exciting plays – *The Visit*, in which
the Lunts are appearing, by a young Swiss called Dürrenmatt. Really
creative theatre at last. By comparison, *Look Homeward, Angel*, from
Thomas Wolfe's book, was stale and boring, and we had to walk out
of *West Side Story*, the musical we were told we must see at all cost – a
story of rival gangs of hoodlums, 90% ballet, with some lame dialogue,
and pathetic musical numbers thrown in.

To James Stern   *24.ix.1958*

. . . we had a couple of sessions with Zachary Scott. The first time
we went to a drink at their apartment, and also met Ruth Ford. It
was all very New York, slightly brittle, but pleasant to experience
again as a social game. I can't say I appreciate most of the pictures;
the tea-tray school of painters has never appealed to me, especially
those with surrealist overtones. The second occasion we met Z. was
at a lunch, at which we discussed his movie project in more detail. I
think his enthusiasm seems real, but it is very difficult to make sure
with Americans, or rather, their enthusiasm can often be real enough,
but that does not mean it will last. Z. speaks as though he wants to

go to Australia in 1960 and start shooting either *Voss* or *The Tree of Man* . . .

He has all sorts of contacts in Australia to advise on sites and geographic and climatic questions, and was asking me about composers, script writers etc. The thing that pleased me most was his announcement that the director he wants to interest in my work is Jean Renoir – the only man I have always felt might translate it into film. Z. suggested that I should write the script, which I refused, as that is something I would not know how to go about. Then he asked me whether I would be willing to come to the States for six months to work with a professional scriptwriter, but I had to refuse that too . . . I want to start on a new book when I get home, and I cannot let anything else interfere with it. After all, I am 46, and still have five or six books left to write.

To Fritz Krieger   *13.ix.1958*

Yesterday we came to Florida, and are now with Manoly's sister Anna, who M. finds has aged a lot, and he can't sleep in consequence. In New York we also saw his half-brother whom he had never met. Although he can't be more than 39 he looks older than both Manoly and Mario so perhaps there is something life in the States does to one. It seems to be hair-raisingly expensive. A serious illness would be enough to set one back for ever by the time one had paid for it . . .

Must stop now. Sidney Nolan, the painter, who did the jackets for *Voss* and the new *Aunt's Story*, is passing through Florida with his wife, and they are stopping off in Fort Lauderdale to see me.

Sidney Nolan to Brian Adams   *June 1986*

Patrick sent me another book, *The Aunt's Story*, to do a jacket . . . Up to this point we hadn't met. But I did this woman's face, as much as I could get a likeness to the book, because the book is rather a complicated book in three parts, and the woman was a shadowy and strange woman, so it was quite difficult to find an image for the face, but I arranged to meet Patrick in Florida – we were both going to be a long way from home – in an orange grove. Anyway we met first of all under a big tree with long beans hanging on underneath about two feet long. A tall, rather gaunt man met us and we went into a little tea place and I unpacked my little cover and he said, 'Oh damn!' I'd got the wrong character. And that was the beginning of our relationship.[1]

White to David Moore   *15.ix.1958*

We spent most of yesterday together, driving through Florida, and also lunched the day before . . . I found Cynthia forthright and intelligent,

perhaps a little ambitious (a fortunate quality in an artist's wife), perhaps
also a bit jealous, but she is the wife who is slightly older than a very
attractive husband, and she says that other women are always offering
to mend his shirts and trying to put their hands up under his coat to
massage his shoulders. Sidney N. seems to be completely honest and
without nonsense. He is of simple Australian-Irish stock and makes
no bones about it. In fact, I can't think when I have met a man so
much Himself, which of course is why his work is so much his own.
Physically he is medium, fresh in colouring, or rather brick-coloured,
and with eyes of a blue that I can imagine might suck the unwary
right under . . .

Tomorrow Mom is due to arrive from St Petersburg, and we are
prepared for drama, as she has not seen Manoly for forty years. I feel
anything may happen, from the awful to the disappointing.

Florida itself I can't say I like one little bit. The climate makes
one feel like a beachcomber, a tropical wreck, with green whiskers on
one's lungs, and a grey-purple bloom upon one's cheeks. Most of the
state seems to be swamp, but swamp would certainly be preferable to
this re-claimed coastal strip, which is a shambles of motels, hamburger
joints, gas stations, super-markets, and girlie girlie shows. One good
bit yesterday when we discovered a botanic garden full of peacocks and
exotic fruits. But I can really only say: Roll on the plane to San Francisco.

To Ben Huebsch   *17.xii.1958*

. . . I felt I was going quite mad, what with the general atmosphere
of steamy Southern ignorance, Madame Chiang on TV, integration,
dynamite in synagogues. It was a relief to get away and wind up with
a couple of days in San Francisco, which remains one of my favourite
cities. I can't feel that time or history really touches it, and it is com-
forting to think there is one such place. Incidentally, I was not molested
by either of the two journalists your publicity girl wanted me to meet.
I did not mind.

To Nellie Sukerman, Curtis Brown, New York   *2.xi.1958*

The Pacific flight just endless and dreary, and I finished up falling
down and bashing my ribs in a concrete shower in Fiji.

To Ben Huebsch   *17.xii.1958*

. . . arrived back here on October 1st with cracked ribs . . . then went
off on a short spell of my usual bronchitis. After that there was all the
business of getting settled again, breaking our way through the jungle
of a garden, finding out what had happened in the house, looking for
lost cats. Then – a few improvements to the house, with all the exas-

peration that workmen provide: we have had air conditioning installed in three of the rooms, fly screens on the other windows, and finally a new stove, which is a great pleasure to use.

In addition I have started on my new book – I don't like using the titles of unfinished books, but I think I did mention this one once – and have written how much it is difficult to say, perhaps a third, perhaps not so much, but I can see it will take some time, and perhaps need as many as three writings. I shall want somebody here to check the Jewish parts after a second writing. I feel I may have given myself away a good deal, although passages I have been able to check for myself, seem to have come through by instinct or good luck, so perhaps I shall survive. After all, I did survive the deserts of *Voss*.

SEVENTEEN

Public View

AFTER *VOSS* PATRICK WHITE was famous and determined to keep fame at arm's length. 'Adulation is the most insidious form of death the world can inflict on artists of any kind.'[1] Yet the attention of the literary world was deeply satisfying. He complained about the fuss that was made in England and America – all those journalists to avoid and would-be hosts he had to rebuff – but by these signs he knew he had found his place. White was forty-six and had triumphed in his fight for recognition.

The publication of *Voss* in Germany at this time was an event in European writing. In Britain and Australia the novel was about to appear as a Penguin 'Modern Classic'. Another film offer was on the table to challenge the faltering proposal of Zachary Scott: the Australian actor Keith Michell was offering £3,000 for the rights, with himself as the explorer – he had demonstrated his German accent to White in London – and Ingmar Bergman's cameraman as cinematographer. White turned to Ronald Waters for advice: 'Of course, I have no idea what to ask, but do not want to throw away a nest egg for my old age,' White wrote. 'After all, "unfilmable" Faulkner novels are sold in the end for thousands. On the other hand I would not want to see the book turned into some American monstrosity with Ava Gardner and Gregory Peck.' Though Scott's and Michell's offers both collapsed, there was always someone, now, offering to film *Voss*. White came to wonder in the end if the difficulties of turning the book into a film were not 'Leichhardt's revenge for something I should never have done'.[2]

White's response to success was perverse but entirely in keeping with the man. Frank enjoyment eluded him. He could not forget old slights, and his gratitude always had an edge of rebuke. He was not a writer who thanked his readers for his success, nor did he make the public feel it had any stake in his discovery. White felt and expressed intense gratitude to those who offered support over the years, but the general message he had when success arrived was this: about time.

The republication of *The Aunt's Story* at Christmas 1958 was a modest commercial and strong critical success. White's pleasure was heightened by a sharp sense of vindication. He made this clear: today's praise was proof of early neglect.

Those who loved his work tolerated the sight of him reliving these old quarrels, but there were others who found evidence here of meanness and pride. *Voss*, coming hard on the heels of *The Tree of Man*, won Patrick White new admirers in the world, but these fresh successes and his prickly response to fame confirmed in the public a strong streak of distaste for the man.

White so feared what might happen to him now if he led the life of a literary celebrity that he welcomed and in a sense provoked this hostility so that he might deliberately turn his back on the public. He believed all that should matter to him now was the novel in hand. Early in the New Year of 1959 he was able to report to Peggy Garland that he had written 'a mountain of words' already, and welcomed the quiet years that lay ahead of him writing and rewriting *Riders in the Chariot*. 'I shall not mind sitting withdrawn in my burrow for some time to come.'[3]

He gave very few interviews, refused to appear on radio and television, and turned down all requests to speak in public. He insisted, 'I am in no way a public figure.' So he honoured Lizzie Clark's ban on blowing his own trumpet, but there was also the worry that he might make a hash of these appearances. Some time in the 1950s he heard a recording of himself and decided he had 'a monotonous, maddening delivery . . . I know how disgusted I should be to listen to it coming from anybody else'.[4]

He refused to teach, and the prospect of talking to university students left him cold. 'Those who will understand my books will do so intuitively; I don't want to waste time on the others.' Once he was tempted to break his rule and lecture at Booloominbah, 'a vast, impossible' house built by his great-uncle and given by the Whites to start off the University of New England. He had never seen the place, but mastered his curiosity and, with regret, turned the invitation down. 'I could not give a lecture in any circumstances.'[5]

PEN, the world association of writers, wanted Patrick White as guest of honour at its international congress in Germany. He shied away. The Australian National University offered him an honorary doctorate of philosophy, but he declined. He turned down all the honorary doctorates offered over the years. An invitation came from London to become an honorary fellow of the Royal Society of Literature. He declined. 'I thought it would be a bit unreal belonging to such a body while living at the opposite end of the earth,' he told Geoffrey Dutton. 'They sent me a list of Fellows and Members and I thought I'd look through to see whether there was anybody else from Australia. What did I turn up but – Morris West! Ever so literary.'6

He refused to write for the press. The *Sydney Morning Herald* asked him to review Greek novels. He declined. New York's *Sports Illustrated* offered a large fee for a 'deeply felt Australian story by the writer who probably means most to Australians, about the athlete who probably means most to Australians'. The odd couple in mind were Patrick White and the runner Herb Elliott. White suggested they try Gwen Meredith, writer of the radio epic *Blue Hills*: 'She is the Household Word.'7

He could now have taken the helm of Australian letters, but his distaste for literary politics was fixed. The only point of being a writer, he believed, was to write, and if he were to steer a course for local literature then he would do so from his desk. When a fund was raised for the first university chair in Australian Literature, White declined both to contribute and to attend the public meeting in the Sydney Town Hall at which poets and mayors, scholars and politicians gathered to inaugurate this patriotic project.

Frankly he found most local writing drab. If he discovered Australian novels that excited him, he urged them on his publishers, not to promote a cause but to help the writers break into the big market. One of the first novels he recommended (unsuccessfully) to Viking was Marjorie Barnard and Flora Eldershaw's apocalyptic *Tomorrow and Tomorrow and Tomorrow*. 'I . . . am amazed it is not better known,' he told Huebsch. 'It is one of the few mature Australian novels, and at the same time it is of universal interest. The shell is, admittedly, a little tough, but do get inside it, and I think you will be surprised. It is full of passion and truth.'8

He dealt with the literary factions of Australia with even-handed care. The little magazines were on side. White established cordial relations with Clem Christesen the editor of *Meanjin*, Stephen Murray-Smith of the Left's *Overland*, Geoffrey Dutton and Max Harris of *Australian Letters*, Professor Gerry Wilkes of *Southerly*, and the poet James McAuley, who set the literary agenda for the anti-Communist *Quadrant* funded (covertly) by the CIA. On the strength of McAuley's admiring review of *The Aunt's Story*, the two men had some contact for a time, and White consulted the poet on points of Roman Catholic doctrine while researching *Riders in the Chariot*. So ordered were White's links with the factions and their little magazines that he made a practice of writing to the editors at the same sitting. To each, in turn, he gave excerpts from the novels and, later, short stories. Usually they paid him nothing for his work. Sometimes he asked for a nominal fee. When his New York agent complained about the Australian magazines, White replied, 'they *must* be helped occasionally'.9

Only once was he persuaded to appear at a book fair to sign copies of his work. This was in 1957 just before *Voss* appeared. Such mortification had not come his way since he sat with the schnauzers in the dog pavilion at the Royal Easter Show. For two afternoons he stood at a counter in David Jones dealing with customers, and the memory of those hours remained with him as an awful warning. 'Australia was at its most provincial,' he told Huebsch. 'I have come to the conclusion that pointless speech-making is one of our worst national diseases, and that lady writers are the worst sufferers. They will spring up and clutch at the mike with the very slightest encouragement, and spend the most time conveying the least. I did autograph a few copies of *The Tree of Man*, even at this late date, which was gratifying, but on the whole the experience was in the same category as a bad dream I have regularly, in which I am expected to conduct an orchestra, with no warning, and without being able to read music.'[10]

White did accept prizes. A crown was set on his success when *Voss* was chosen as 'the most outstanding recent contribution to English literature' by the judges of the first W.H. Smith & Son Literary Award. He was warned in August 1959 that he would be declared the winner in a ceremony at the Savoy in December. Smith's begged White to fly to London at their expense, but he refused for he had been suffering from bronchitis that winter as he worked on *Riders in the Chariot* and feared what would happen if he flew into one of London's December fogs. 'It was a heaven sent excuse,' he confessed to Peggy Garland. 'They had told me I should have to appear on television, give radio interviews, and that, of course, then there would have been the nightmare of the dinner itself.' He knew he was disappointing Smith's by staying away, for they 'must have been anticipating a big advertising coup'.[11]

On the stage of the Lancaster Room of the Savoy sat the three judges – Harold Nicolson, the historian C.V. Wedgwood and the poet William Plomer – and among the three hundred dining below were Juliet O'Hea, all the London publishers, agents, booksellers, journalists and a knot of writers who hoped – until the curtains opened on a montage of Nolan's drawings and Poignant's photographs – that they might be the winner. White's cheque for £1,000 (tax free) was accepted by the Australian High Commissioner to London, Sir Eric Harrison. Safe at home the winner reflected, 'It was one in the eye for the Australian Professors of English who continue to accuse me of illiteracy.'[12]

White was so shy of hearing his voice on tape that he refused to send a recorded message or speak to the ceremony by telephone. But he answered a questionnaire for Smith's, and a few brief lines were published: 'I don't write for love, but because my writing seems to be a disease for which there is no cure. I am fortunate in having a small inherited income, on which I have been able to live while writing. I am no longer a farmer. While I did attempt to farm, it interfered with my writing and the latter prevented me from being anything but an amateurish and unsuccessful farmer. My so-called farm has now been swallowed up by suburbia. It is only 25 miles from Sydney, where I sometimes go to concerts. Friends come out from Sydney on Sundays, when I cook lunch myself – usually for six . . .

'Whatever happens I sit down at my desk for at least four hours a day. The morning, as soon as possible after getting up is the best time creatively. But it is rather pleasant to revise a manuscript late at night. For some time now I have devoted myself entirely to writing. In fact, I have always been entirely devoted to it – or it has been devoted to me – even when I have been fiddling about with other things.'[13]

Despite what he told W.H. Smith & Sons, Dogwoods still lay in the Green Belt, surrounded by shabby paddocks and bush. But by now the village of Castle Hill had grown into a suburban shopping centre, and there was talk of Woolworth's opening a supermarket. Houses had begun to edge down the hill, and every time a paddock on Showground Road was cut up for building blocks White saw Dogwoods in peril. About the time of the Smith award, he had heard that the Housing Commission had bought the land at the back of Dogwoods. 'Of course we don't know how much of their horrible boxes will be visible through the trees,' he told James Stern. 'But usually when they start to destroy in Australia, they do things very thoroughly. The national genius is for ugliness. I should hate to leave here, and wouldn't know where to go next.'[14] Nothing came of this, but the two men knew they were living in an oasis under threat. This was absorbed into *Riders in the Chariot*. On the last pages of the novel, the chariot itself, like a golden sunset, passes over the fibro houses, ugly yet full of life, standing on the ruins of Xanadu.

Behind a hedge of scarlet-flowering pomegranates, the gardens at Dogwoods were very beautiful. A forest had grown up around the pink and blue house. Sheets of violets flowered under the cherry trees in spring. Where the afternoon sun fell through the branches of the jacaranda Lascaris had built a Mediterranean courtyard of pots and vines, where the two men sat in the afternoons under a wisteria, drinking jasmine tea. A white cat slept in the bronze slats of Clem Meadmore's sculpture *Silence*. In the orchard the old trees were heavy with oranges all winter, though the olive trees, now grown into a handsome grove, stubbornly refused to bear. Lascaris' latest project was to turn the big paddock into a kind of Kew in Castle Hill, and he was planting exotic trees from all over the world.

After lunch on Sundays White took his guests on a tour of Dog-woods inside and out. There was nothing remarkable about the interior of the house, except the paintings that covered every wall. As his guests wandered through, trailed by the last of the old schnauzers, White spoke of modern art and/or the propagation of fuchsias, the role of garlic in a fish stew, Bartok's violin music, divorces, Roy's old age. Cuttings were given from the garden. Tests were set: what did so-and-so think of Eric Smith? or *Virgilia capensis*? or Rumer Godden's *The River*?

He was not a recluse. 'A constant stream of people rolls through this house,' he told Mollie McKie, but he rather welcomed the reputation of leading a hermit's life because it helped him decide who should come through his gate. Few came to Dogwoods uninvited and those who did, even friends, were turned away with a couple of words and a basilisk stare. Kylie Tennant, calling *en passant*, brought White to the half-opened door. He said, 'I have been eating garlic, and the Brissendens are coming.'[15] She fled.

His friends were kept in compartments: there were neighbours, the central Europeans, painters, old family connections, and one or two actors. But not all the painters met one another at his table, nor all his neighbours, nor all the Jews, for he kept the compartments as tight as they had been in London from a stubborn notion of who went with whom, and to protect the weak from the strong at his table. An invitation to Dogwoods carried a whiff of fear. Those who came back often knew to expect superb food, good gossip, sudden tensions, hair-raising arguments and, occasionally, famous faces. White would not play the distinguished man in public, but the farm was becoming a point on the map for travelling celebrities.

White was a keen and eccentric host. Guests arrived to find him stoked with a few whiskies, sweating under his eyes, almost wordless with tension. After a moment he disappeared into the kitchen to deal with the food. No one followed. Out in the sitting room, Lascaris kept things on an even keel until it was time to eat. He shepherded people to the table. If he was slow off the mark pouring wine, White would snap, 'Well! Aren't we having any wine tonight?' Soup was eaten to scattered remarks and silence. White never felt compelled to fill the gaps in conversations. Those who rose to help with the plates were frowned back into their seats. If there was a joint to be carved, he put on carving gloves. These rituals were done perfectly. Only when the main course was served – and only if it was a success – did he relax.

Then it was wonderful to be at his table. He had a big shouting laugh, and fresh morsels of gossip set him laughing uproariously. His memory was astonishing, and on the best days at Dogwoods his own reminiscences provoked his friends to lay their lives bare. 'He could remember gesture, intonation, colour, smell, the light, nuances,' recalled Gwen Moore. 'He once said that he remembered every single detail of his miserable childhood. What made him a great novelist was being interested in everything about people: clothes, cooking, children, their animals.' It rather thrilled White's guests that some detail they provided, even a *faux pas* committed over lunch, might turn up in the next novel. He said, 'I think one really has to be a bitch and a gossip to succeed at fiction.'[16]

Maria Prerauer came to Dogwoods at this time with her husband the opera critic Curt Prerauer. She was a singer about to embark on a career in journalism. 'Looking back over those years I have the oddest feeling that it was all one long dinner with Patrick.' She found the talk at his table unexpectedly lightweight. 'The conversations one expected to have with him on deep and difficult topics never happened, because he was far more interested in the latest gossip. It was surprising and a little distressing at first, but we went along with it because we realised it was his way of relaxing. But it was really quite peculiar: he would not be drawn into conversations of any depth. He almost always dictated the course of conversation. If he didn't like the way it was going, he set off at a different tangent, and one followed him for fear of the consequences.'[17]

He was eager to meet new people and he swept them into Dogwoods with enthusiasm. At this time, while he was working on *Riders in the Chariot*, he was particularly keen to meet Jews. They found it odd that White would not speak about his own time in Germany before the war. Germany was not a topic of conversation at Dogwoods and he rarely spoke about the war. Later when the novel appeared, these escapees from the Holocaust wondered why he had not asked them about their own experiences. They could have told him so much. One day at lunch White had produced a photograph of himself and said, 'It makes me look like somebody who's gone mad in a Nazi concentration camp.' A woman at the table interrupted him. 'You don't go mad in a concentration camp. That is a luxury you cannot afford. You have to survive. If you go mad you get put in the gas.' White asked how she knew this. 'I was in Auschwitz.' She never mentioned this again. White asked nothing more.

He preferred to talk about paintings rather than books. Literature was sometimes discussed, but he never made more than a throw-away remark about progress on his own work. He rebuffed discussion about his published novels and coldly cut short any enquiries about work in hand. Homosexuality was never mentioned at his table.

White's friendship was prized despite its hazards. For a few hours in his company, friends saw the world through his eyes. White was stimulating and sharp-tongued, very funny and wise. There was a lot to learn at his table. Through the gossip and laughter, they saw, by flashes, the core of what mattered to the writer. Nothing was more intriguing than the contradictions of the man himself. His friends were left to puzzle out how one man could be so worldly and naïve, cruel and beguiling, so much older than his years yet still at times a child, so complex yet essentially simple. The source of White's simplicity was his writing, which brought all these contradictions into a single focus. He embraced whatever he needed for his work. Nothing in himself or the world around him was off-limits. People, ideas, gossip, rows were all grist to his mill. Behind his many faces White lived one, writer's, life. He spoke of living his *real* life inside his skull; he wrote that artists only experience pure being in their art. 'My flawed self has only ever felt intensely alive in the fictions I create.'[18]

His friendship was subject to sudden shifts of weather. As it was with Ruth, so with Patrick: the threat of storms was present even in a clear sky. He delivered sudden, blunt reproaches. He had his mother's taste for laying down the law about money, marriages and manners. The prophet was a connoisseur, the sage was also a governess. He believed in good behaviour: 'In some ways I suppose I am very Victorian.' Profound insight into the human condition sat with a fussy, bourgeois insistence on good form. And he did insist. It was self-evident to him that disapproval *had* to be expressed and rage vented. Looking back on these years Barry Humphries remarked that Patrick White 'was more Kensington than any man I know in Australia'.[19]

On a night of peculiar tension at Dogwoods, the Moores were eating with Kylie Tennant and Marshall Best of Viking Press. The conversation veered round to the state of 'young people today' and White was laying down the law about the shocking way that kids who were not from 'good homes' behaved. As a teacher, Gwen Moore's sympathies were with the children he was attacking, and she defended them. As she tangled with White she began to weep and could not stop. She was saying, 'I am sorry. I am sorry.' Best reached over and took her hand and said, 'The first time I've seen real tears in years.' She left the table and went to the other end of the room. Kylie Tennant came over as she composed herself. White disappeared. In the morning she rang to say how sorry she was to upset the dinner party. 'It is for me to apologise,' he said. 'I am a failure as a human being.'[20]

His self-hatred was shocking. Terrible as he could be to others, he was worse on himself. There were times he seemed to be a man at war, the victim of a battle always going on within himself. He spoke darkly to his friends of suffering a 'disease' and wishing to be rid of it. He made no explicit confessions, but over the years he named several of these 'diseases' from which he saw himself suffering without hope of cure: the disease of foreignness, which made him a stranger everywhere; the disease of memory, which did not allow him to forget wounds and slights; the disease of writing, which gave him no rest. To this list must be added the deeper afflictions of a bad chest and homosexuality. It was not that he wished to be cured of his sexuality, but it was another source of the sufferings to which life had fated him. From such a sense of frailty, there were many who shied away almost in disgust. But others – women more often than men – drew closer to the man, anxious to comfort White in this struggle with himself.

The historian Manning Clark met Patrick White for the first time in the years after *Voss*. Clark was walking down George Street with James McAuley when White appeared in the distance, dressed as he always was for town in a suit and beret, carrying his shopping, notebooks and nose spray in a large, shapeless dillybag. White was quite indifferent to his eccentric appearance. When they all drew abreast, McAuley introduced Clark and they spoke briefly before passing on. Even in those few moments Clark was struck by the hunger in White's face. 'It is the face of a man who wants something he is never going to get . . . something possibly no human being can give him.' What, Clark wondered, could this be? Perhaps it was simply a hunger for ordinary communion with the human race: to enjoy in life what could only be lived by White on the page. Perhaps it was deeper: 'a hunger for forgiveness in a man who places himself, through his pride and pessimism, beyond the reach of forgiveness'.[21]

Success had changed White: the reins had slipped a little. He was more sardonic, more wary, more dogmatic. Now more than ever he felt justified in obeying the imperatives of his art. In the past few years he had read a lot of biography, and mulled over the careers of Goya, Van Gogh, Rimbaud, Bartok and Mahler. As he worked on *Riders in the Chariot*, he read George Painter's *Proust* and Richard Ellmann's *Joyce* – a writer he now found 'fascinating to read about but not to read'. Out of these lives and his own life, White built an image of the artist as a truth-teller and betrayer, a man by nature misunderstood and often despised, a destroyer where needs be, perhaps 'diseased and degraded as a human being' yet vindicated by creative genius.[22] He was turning this image into flesh and blood in *Riders in the Chariot*.

The painter Alf Dubbo, a half-caste Aboriginal and one of the four riders in White's chariot, is sick and degraded. When James Stern later complained about the squalor of Dubbo, White defended his invention: 'Dubbo does some very squalid things. One reason is that the Australian aboriginal in contact with civilisation is a very squalid creature. I have even read an account of aboriginals in their normal state in the last century eating maggots, and the lice on one another's heads. I also wanted a contrast between Dubbo's physical squalor and depravity, and his devotion to his gift. I feel his gift would have been the less if he had not experienced the depths. (I am convinced of that in my own case.)'[23]

In Dubbo White exaggerated the failings he saw in himself. His

painter does not suffer from asthma, but TB and the pox. His disease
and his gift are 'the two poles, the negative and positive of his being: the
furtive, destroying sickness, and the almost as furtive but regenerating,
creative act'.[24] Dubbo's failings are – as White believed his own to be –
the source and spur to his genius. What might not otherwise be forgiven
the man must be forgiven the artist: his art vindicates the flaws.

Now that he had overcome his shyness with painters, White was
happiest in their company. As he sat at his desk pouring out grey words,
he envied them at work with colour. Though he and Lascaris were rarely
lured to a publisher's cocktail party or a first night at the theatre, they
sometimes went to gallery bashes and on to dinner afterwards with a
noisy crowd of painters and wives. White listened to painters.

Gerald and Margo Lewers were his friends. He was a sculptor
with a gravel-carting fortune; she was a painter and potter. The Lewers
lived on the river west of Castle Hill, and White spoke of their house
and its beautiful garden as if it were another Dogwoods, where 'ideas
hurtled, arguments flared, voices shouted, sparks flew. It was a place
in which people gathered . . . to eat, drink and discuss, and I shall
remember the mass of friends surging out to welcome the New Year
festooned with coloured lights. Along with the paintings and the
sculpture, the mosaics and the watergarden, an ephemeral dish of food
wore the expression of a work of art.' The Lewers's place on the river
'provided one of the focus points of our still tentative civilisation'.[25]

Lady disciples appeared at Dogwoods with their unwanted and
often unwilling husbands. Gretel and Stephen Feher established the
pattern of the *Riders in the Chariot* years. They were Viennese Jews.
He was a heart surgeon, and she had a brand of slashing energy White
admired. Both loved his work. When they first invited him to lunch
at their flat on the water at Kirribilli he asked, 'Can I bring a
friend?'

'By all means bring her.'

'It's a he.'

So began an intense friendship. White and Lascaris came down
to dinner every few weeks bearing gifts of oranges, flowers and fresh
eggs with dates pencilled on the shell. The Fehers came to Dogwoods
to listen to music, for White had a wonderful collection of records by
this time. Conversation stopped while they listened. When he bought
Lotte Lenya's new recording of the *Threepenny Opera*, they sat one night
and listened to it right through. But White's warmth was directed to
her not him. Stephen Feher found a streak of cruelty in White which
he could not excuse. White called Stephen 'the magazine reader' when
he was gossiping on the telephone to Gretel. The joke wore thin, but
White persisted. He was testing her as he tested all his friends' loyalties

to *their* friends, to writers and composers, even to their spouses.

As these new, unlikely people were swept into Dogwoods, White's old friends began to wonder how good a judge of people he was. Certainly some of those he cultivated were needed for his work. But at times his imagination seemed to outstrip his remarkable intuition, as if he were inventing these people like figures in his books. When he found what they were really like – not worse, perhaps, just not as he imagined them to be – he felt let down, sometimes even betrayed. A mask of reserve hid this change of heart until, out of the blue and apparently provoked by some trivial cause, came harsh words and a cutting-off. For those whose self-esteem had come to depend on White's approval and friendship, the rejection was crushing, and the pain was remembered for decades. One day in the garden at Dogwoods, at the height of Gretel Feher's friendship with White, Lascaris warned her, 'You'll get it in the neck yet.'[26]

For the first time in his life, White began to have a number of writers among his friends. For some, like Kylie Tennant, friendship grew out of gratitude. She had written that bizarre early profile in the *Sydney Morning Herald* and later reviewed *Voss* affectionately. Tennant, her husband the devout Anglo-Catholic Lewis Rodd, and their children were part of the Dogwoods years. White turned out to have a great knack for finding the right gifts for young children. It was a mark of his intuition.

Thea Astley invented an excuse one day to introduce herself at the door. 'Patrick looked at me with those eyes like mooncraters and I thought, "He knows I'm lying." '[27] But their friendship grew up over the next few years – more on the telephone than face to face – as he wrote *Riders in the Chariot* and she was working on her novel *Descant for Gossips*. The first time White and Lascaris came to dinner at Astley's new, very bare house in Epping, they pulled from the back of their car a big red-and-white striped drugget and carried it up the path. 'His kindness was melting.'[28]

For old friends and new there remained the puzzle of Lascaris. They loved him, depended on him to ease the strains that White brought with him into their lives, and they worried for him. On some nights they felt such tension in the air at Dogwoods that it was hard to sit and eat. They heard White's cruel words and saw Lascaris holding his ground as if his existence was at stake. They sensed pain in Lascaris and exasperation in White. Yet it seemed impossible to imagine the two men apart. Nothing was disguised at Dogwoods, but nothing was discussed. It was as if, by the immense force of his personality, White convinced them all that this was an unremarkable union: an obviously volatile but intensely respectable marriage.

In fact no one who knew the pair stopped speculating about the dynamics of their relationship. One night at Dogwoods when Thea Astley had had a few drinks and the air was charged with the electricity of a big row, she asked Lascaris, 'If you had married, what sort of woman would you choose?' There was a stunned silence. After a little consideration Lascaris replied, 'I would have married her for her brains and lived very unhappily thereafter.'[29] With such rueful self-deprecation, Lascaris masked his role: he served White.

He had all his partner's determination and was without illusions. Having once given his word that he would stay, he stayed through thick and thin. That might not have been possible if Lascaris were not convinced of the bond between them. 'I know he does love me.' He defended White against those who would condemn the man for bad manners, bad temper, bad behaviour. 'Patrick can't be judged as others are, you can't use the same weights and measures, because out of this comes his work.' What made suffering in this service worthwhile for Lascaris was the conviction that White was a great novelist and that he had a part in his success. He kept White on his course, and restored him to his course when he faltered. 'It is the pleasure of the disciple', he explained, 'to serve Christ.'[30]

The two men no longer took communion. Their trip around the world had broken the habit of formal worship, a habit badly frayed by years in the bleak evangelical atmosphere of St Paul's, Castle Hill. As ministers came and went, the drift of the parish was always down towards the lower depths. The prudery of St Paul's became comic. Pat-the-balloon was introduced on Fellowship nights to fight the profane temptation of dancing, and at the annual fête guess the number of beans in the jar contests were forbidden as gambling. Ludicrous as this was, the cause of White's breach lay deeper. He had worshipped there for six years, hoping to stimulate that ecstatic apprehension of God which had first come to him when he fell cursing in the rain, but the bleak evangelism and wretched music eventually failed him.

For a time, 'looking for a church in which to worship after the barren Low-church deserts of Castle Hill', the two men drove down to Christ Church St Laurence in the city, an Anglican parish so high it seemed Roman Catholic. The music was wonderful, the bells and smells appealed to White's sense of theatre and the acolytes were handsome. He wondered if he should take the plunge and go over to Rome. Catholics were very interested in his work; nuns were writing theses on *Voss*. Though he toyed with the idea of Rome, he could not forget Ruth lowering her voice as she broke the news of Ethel Kelly's conversion. He retreated from Christ Church: it seemed too showy and he never really worked out what was going on. 'I did not return to orthodox

Anglicanism, but the Anglican church is a feeble organisation compared with the Jewish faith.'[31]

Judaism attracted him more than any branches of Christianity, but in the end he thought that it would be absurd 'for someone not a Jew to bundle into it'. He had believed ever since his brush with Franco as a young man that we are what we are: he was not a Jew. When the American evangelist Billy Graham appeared in Sydney, White was tempted to join the crowds but pulled out at the last minute: 'we suddenly felt the traffic would be too much of a good thing – fortunately, as that was the night it poured, and the electric light bulbs exploded (perfect touch) in the rain'. Graham's arrival was the biggest event in the Sydney diocese since the war. His Baptist rhetoric heard on the radio helped White to define his own faith while arousing his novelist's interest in the behaviour of some of Sydney's society figures. 'I am afraid he made me writhe more every day he was here, with the result that I find I am not a Christian, but some kind of eclectic.' He noted several figures in Sydney society had made 'decisions' for Christ including the newspaper proprietor Warwick Fairfax and the woman who was about to be his third wife. 'Mrs Marcel Dekyvere has started holding prayer meetings. Incidentally two words I never want to hear again are "decision" and "challenge".'[32]

Throughout White's wanderings Lascaris remained the Orthodox Greek he had always been, a man who lived by plain notions of holiness. Through him White absorbed the superstitions of the Orthodox faith. Icons hung at Dogwoods; they believed in saints and holy places. They celebrated Greek Easter not on their knees but with a binge of cooking. Greek friends in Sydney like Alexander Cambitoglou, the Professor of Classical Archaeology at Sydney University, came to Dogwoods to eat sheep soup. Finding heads and brains was no problem, but White complained, 'I can't get hold of the intestines in this decadent world in which we live.'[33]

White was left to explore his faith at his desk. He told Stern that after abandoning the church because churches 'destroy the mystery of God', he set to work to 'evolve symbols of my own through which to worship'.[34] These were the symbols familiar to his four riders in the chariot. He saw the novel as 'an expression (rather than profession) of faith by four different people, connected more by a similarity of aim than by the intertwining of their lives. One of the characters hardly makes sufficient contact with the other three to communicate with them in words. But all four are spiritually united in one shattering final incident. Possibly the whole thing will be a colossal flop in 200,000 words!'[35]

EIGHTEEN

Diaspora

WHITE FIRST CAUGHT sight of the chariot in a Bond Street gallery when he was a young man. He was walking along one day and there in the window was a fey painting by Odilon Redon of Apollo's chariot. It rose

> behind the wooden horses, along the pathway of the sun. The god's arm – for the text implied it was a god – lit the faces of the four figures, so stiff, in the body of the tinny chariot. The rather ineffectual torch trailed its streamers of material light . . .

In the town of Numburra, perched on a riverbank as Walgett stands on the Barwon, the half-caste boy Alf Dubbo came across this image in one of the Rev. Timothy Calderon's picture books. Dubbo would always remember his first glimpse of the chariot, and criticise it and wish to improve it:

> 'The arm is not painted good. I could do the arm better. And horses. My horses,' the boy claimed, 'would have the fire flowing from their tails. And dropping sparks. Or stars. Moving. Everything would move in my picture because that is the way it ought to be.'[1]

This was the chariot familiar to Blake, Ovid, the more apocalyptic contributors to the Bible, and to Redon. In White's chariot the riders are those who have known illumination as he had experienced it in mystical ecstasy, in creation, in music, in landscape, in formal worship, in books and abstruse study, even illumination as he experienced it one night in Eccleston Street under a rain of German bombs. White's riders share, too, his own frustrating failure to seize the vision that illuminates: more often than not it stays half-seen, just apprehended, always a little out of sight.

As he was wrestling with the first draft of the novel, White wrote to Huebsch, 'What I want to emphasise through my four "Riders" – an orthodox refugee intellectual Jew, a mad *Erdgeist* of an Australian spinster, an evangelical laundress, and a half-caste Aboriginal painter – is that all faiths, whether religious, humanistic, instinctive, or the creative artist's act of praise, are in fact one.'[2]

Dubbo the black painter is entirely White's invention. At Walgett he had had no more than distant contact with the Aboriginals who lived along the river. He had never *met* one. For the portrait of Dubbo he drew on books, newspapers and the Withycombes' grim stories of the blacks round Barwon Vale. In Australian fiction the Aboriginal had been shown as artist/mystic or squalid fringe dweller. Dubbo was both.

The laundress Ruth Godbold, born in the Fens, discovers the chariot in the Evangelical hymns she sang as a child and later in the music of Bach, heard on a winter afternoon in Ely Cathedral. Ruth Godbold is the portrait of a perfect servant: massive, big-breasted, waxy-skinned but yet 'the most positive evidence of good'. She is drawn from all the devoted servants whom White had known since leaving Lulworth, but is especially a memorial to Hilda Richardson of Ebury and Eccleston Streets. In Australia the chariot is revealed once more to her in the great sunsets that fall over Castle Hill which now, and henceforth, Patrick White calls Sarsaparilla.[3]

Miss Hare of Xanadu, the big house on the ridge, sees the chariot in fevers and madness. Hare is an earth spirit. 'The earth is wonderful,' she says. 'It is all we have. It has brought me back, when, otherwise, I should have died.' White had known such a woman, who looked at people 'in the way the simple do, and seems to intercept one's thoughts'. This was Mag Withycombe's sister Mattie Keys, a spinster from the Hunter Valley. Miss Hare has White's own ability to enter other lives and his refusal to love the human race *en masse*. White took her name from *The Lady and the Hare*, John Layard's study of hares as sacrificial creatures in many mythologies. Layard was a friend of Peggy Garland's, who had sent the book out to Alexandria during the war. This was the first Jungian text White read, and he was impressed.[4]

Mordecai Himmelfarb finds himself in the presence of the chariot as he walks through the bombs falling from the bellies of RAF planes on to the town of Holunderthal. He had searched through recondite books for the secret of the ecstasy he now experienced, 'an ecstasy so cool and green his own desert would drink' but found it in the revelation of man's bestiality in war.[5] The Jew escapes the death camps and makes his way to Australia along the route White had known during the war: from central Europe to Romania, thence to Istanbul and Palestine, before moving to the other end of the earth. In Sarsaparilla, Himmelfarb follows the rituals of his faith and works in a factory. 'The intellect', he says, 'has failed us.'[6]

Riders in the Chariot is a study of these good people pitted against evil. The underlying evil is the persecution of the weak by the strong, epitomised here in the Holocaust. Though White was writing fifteen years after the revelations of Belsen and Auschwitz, he was one of the first novelists to come to grips with this century's innovations in horror. The massacre of the European Jews was not yet the major preoccupation of writers that it was to become. Guilt and gratitude both provoked White to tackle the task: guilt that he had been so indifferent to the fate of the Jews as he roamed round Germany in the late 1930s, guilt also for the traces of anti-semitism he recognised in his own nature, and gratitude for the friendship of those Jews who were now his lifeline to a wider world.

Himmelfarb the outcast also grew from his own sense of being always a stranger: 'first a child with what kind of a strange gift nobody quite knew; then a despised colonial boy in an English public school; finally an artist in horrified Australia'. A crucial memory was the taxi driver shouting in York Street in 1947: 'Go back to Germany.' 'Then I knew what it was like to be a reffo in Australia. I think it was this more than anything which persuaded me to write the novel *Riders in the Chariot*.' The Jew is strung up on a jacaranda tree in the yard of Brighta Bicycle Lamps to shouts of 'Go Home to Germany.' White's sexuality strengthened his identification with Himmelfarb: 'As a homosexual I have always known what it is to be an outsider. It has given me added insight into the plight of the immigrant – the hate and contempt with which he is often received.' And Himmelfarb's spiritual journey from apostasy back to belief White modelled on his own rejection and rediscovery of God.[7]

To recast his own experience in the figure of a Jew required the most intense research White had yet undertaken for one of his novels. Even before finishing *Voss* he was reading Jewish philosophers. He pressed on his neighbours copies of *The Scourge of the Swastika*, Lord Russell of Liverpool's history of Nazi war crimes. 'It seems to me the last word on Nazism.'[8] As he read about Jews, Judaism and the Holocaust, he worried about the errors there might be in his own work. It had to be right. He wrote to Huebsch: 'Sometimes I wonder whether I didn't make a colossal mistake in attempting to portray a Jew at any depth. In the beginning he had me petrified, with the result that the writing suffered, but as the book developed my blood began to circulate again, and the other characters seem in a curious way to have helped me understand Himmelfarb.'[9]

Memories of Hanover and the Oertel family – with whom he had had no contact for twenty years – are strong in the text. White settled

Himmelfarb on the Holzgraben in the town he calls Holunderthal, shifting statues and rearranging the streets of Hanover to suit the book's purposes. The park opposite the Jew's house contains both the forest of the Eilenriede and the baroque gardens of Herrenhausen.[10] The eccentric military man who lived beneath the Oertels' apartment is here called Jürgen Stauffer and becomes one of Himmelfarb's friends.[11] White honoured the Oertels by giving their name to the mathematician who first offered to help Himmelfarb leave Germany. The Jew refused. 'He had become, of course, more than a little crazy, Oertel added in telling of Himmelfarb's refusal.'[12]

Had White been able to turn to the Kriegers for help, the difficulties of researching *Riders in the Chariot* might have been relieved considerably; however, they would not acknowledge they were Jewish, nor would Fritz concede that he had left Austria to escape the approaching Holocaust. To add to the complications, White had decided to turn this difficulty into an element of the novel itself. Coarsened and stripped of his culture, Fritz Krieger becomes Harry Rosetree, proprietor of the Brighta Bicycle Lamps factory. Brighta shares a few of CELCO's lines, but the factory is not Fritz's new, neat, orange-brick factory which White often visited in Ryde, but the sort of galvanised-iron dump found in paddocks round Dogwoods.[13]

White could rely, however, on their friend Klári Daniel, 'a blue stocking and militantly Jewish', who had escaped the train to Auschwitz.[14] They spoke on the telephone every day. Daniel's father the wool merchant, long dead in Budapest, was a monster of meticulous traditional observances, and even as she rebelled against him Klári had absorbed his learning. Now she put at White's disposal her great knowledge of Jewish belief and ritual. What she did not know she asked her brothers or dug out of libraries.[15] But, as a woman, Daniel had not had a thorough education in the Talmud which Himmelfarb, as a *zaddic* or a hidden prophet, had to have absorbed completely. White still needed to find 'a male Jew with sufficient knowledge, as she really has not been introduced to the core of the matter being a woman'. He told Huebsch the search was proving difficult: 'Male Jews in Sydney seem to be either completely materialistic, or assimilated, or else the devout ones are suspicious of the motives of anybody who is taking an interest. But I do grow more and more interested. At the moment, I am up to my ears in an abridgment of the Talmud, which I find most rewarding, and that is leading to other reading.'[16]

A few days after writing this to Huebsch, White left for Casino on the north coast of New South Wales to see the Glovers. His friend had taken his passion for the theatre into the bush, and in whatever country town the Rural Bank posted him over the next few years Freddie Glover discovered young men who might be the next Gielgud

if only they would abandon everything and leave for London. A few
lives were ruined. But White found Freddie Glover very useful, for it
was due to him that he 'got the lowdown on the Australian (or N.S.W.)
country town by going to stay with them at his various posts'.[17] White
wanted to see Casino in the winter of 1959 because he was on the point
of drafting Alf Dubbo's journey from Numburra to Mungindribble –
where the outcast lived for a time on the lip of a rubbish tip – on his
way down to Sydney to paint and to work at Brighta Bicycle Lamps.

After a depressing week in the bank residence, White was forced
back to Sydney by an attack of pleurisy. When he failed to respond
to treatment, he consulted a new physician, Sydney's leading chest
specialist Maurice Joseph who lived, by chance, on the ridge at Castle
Hill. Fresh X-rays of White's lungs indicated the possibility of cancer,
TB, pneumonia, pleurisy and a collapsed lobe. Joseph determined it was
neither of the first two, though the ominous shadows on the lungs were
so like TB that thereafter he used these X-rays in his lectures. Patrick
White's lungs were a familiar, though anonymous, sight to generations
of Sydney medical students.

Joseph identified the problem for the first time with the help of
White's graphic description of the muck he coughed up from his chest –
'grey pellets . . . spaghetti'. Superimposed on White's asthma was
an allergy to mould spores in the bronchi. The shadows on his lungs
were clotted mucus, and the blood he had been coughing intermittently
for years was a symptom not of TB but of this rare condition: allergic
bronchopulmonory aspergillosis. His first coughing blood in London
before the war suggested this problem had been with White undiagnosed
for over twenty years.

Joseph prescribed cortisone. This new wonder drug – and its
synthetic equivalent prednisone – was to keep White out of hospital for
years at a time, but it did not cure the underlying condition. His asthma
remained chronic with occasional acute attacks; episodes of bronchitis
and pleurisy continued; but cortisone kept them in check. In time the
drug was to take its awful toll.

White turned to Joseph for help with the book. The physician,
a grave and reflective Jew, was the first person to hear the story
of Himmelfarb. But he was only able to take his patient a certain
distance, for though Joseph had studied the Talmud keenly as a young
man, he had left the practice of Judaism behind. Now he passed White
to Abe Rothfield, headmaster of the Hebrew Education Department at
the Great Synagogue, and through the Synagogue White found Joseph
Luvis, a Bessarabian taxi driver, the Hebrew scholar and guide he
needed. At New Year that October White saw his first Jewish service.
'It was strange to sit in one's hat,' he wrote to Peggy Garland. 'And
I felt rather naked as I was the only man in hundreds not wearing a

shawl. Apart from these formalities, everything was very informal. The members of the congregation made endless conversation during the service, and children ran up and down between the body of the Synagogue and the gallery where the women sat, carrying messages between parents and relations. At one point the buzz rose to such a pitch, the Chief Rabbi had to make a speech about the difficulties of carrying on a service at the same time. When it was all over, everybody scuttled about shaking hands with everybody else, wishing each other a happy New Year, and looking much happier than Christians usually do after a Church service.' He returned to the Great Synagogue for Yom Kippur and Succoth. A couple of old schnauzer customers invited him to the Bar Mitzvah of their son. 'They still don't know how useful their invitation was.'[18]

The music of Bloch helped him to write Himmelfarb. White believed he had only to listen to the second sonata for violin and piano 'to know inside me what it means to be a Jew'. Music remained immensely important to his writing. Mahler gave him the background music for *Voss*; for *Riders in the Chariot* it was Bach. Karajan conducting the B Minor Mass seemed 'the peak of music' at this time, and the Christmas Oratorio was a 'wonderful and consoling' work. 'I think now there is nothing in life that I love more than the music of Bach. But it can be grim, of course, in the hands of the worthy mediocrity.' Bartok remained an inspiration, and White told friends he had worn out a set of records of the string quartets. Most of the bitter dialogues between the various women in the book were worked out to Bartok. Berg's Violin Concerto was important again in the early stages of the writing, as was his Concerto for Wind Instruments. The final 'orchestrated' passages leading up to the apotheosis of Mrs Godbold were helped by the symphonies of Bruckner, 'for whom I shall always have a weakness'.[19]

White loved detail, 'the accumulation of down-to-earth detail. All my novels are accumulations of detail. I am a bit of a bower-bird.' His memory was a repository so vast it could furnish the Himmelfarbs' bourgeois establishment on the Holzgraben, the schloss in the Herrenwaldau, the Godbolds' shed of children like the garage in the bush at the back of Dogwoods, the Rosetrees' suburban box and the Chalmers-Robinson place on the Harbour. He confessed, 'I enjoy decoration.'[20] White's passion for these houses turns them into characters in their own right. Miss Hare's crumbling dream mansion Xanadu is furnished down to the last chandelier and mixing bowl. Here are the little parasols from Belltrees' gardens, Ruth's buhl, the flamingo fan of White's elderly cousin in Cheltenham and the fabulously beautiful mosaics of Delos.

White remembered everything, but only in *Riders in the Chariot* did he begin to draw on his memories of Ruth's and Dick's Sydney. The Chalmers-Robinsons' mansion on the Harbour, where Ruth Godbold first works in Sydney, is Lulworth as if ruined in the Depression, and Mrs Chalmers-Robinson is a portrait of Ruth stripped of her fortune, dabbling in Christian Science and torturing herself at the mirror.[21] White was beginning, cautiously, to disinter fragments of experience hitherto buried in his memory.

In mid-November 1959 after a little over a year's work, the first draft of the novel was finished. Early on he had thought it might run to 120,000 words, but it had ended up twice that length. White reported his progress to Huebsch and various friends, then put the manuscript away in a drawer and spent a month reading and pulling weeds.

He lost Solomon. A malignant growth appeared on the dog's head and nothing could be done. 'So far he shows no sign of suffering, and we are letting him keep on until he does,' White told Peggy Garland. 'I still hope the vet may be wrong, and that a grass-seed or some other foreign body may drop out of place.' But only a few days later, it was evident that Solomon was in pain. He was destroyed, held in their arms so he suffered no anxiety while the injection took effect. After having Solomon at his heels for twelve years, White felt he was suddenly 'without a shadow'.[22]

It was a time of losses. That winter saw the final quarrel with Betty Withycombe, his cousin and mentor to whom he had dedicated *The Aunt's Story*. The links between them had survived many differences over thirty years. Religion had lately come between these two Christians, for Betty Withycombe remained an Anglican, living as a Tertiary of the Franciscan Order, as White was moving away from Anglicanism to less orthodox beliefs. He never discussed his faith with Betty Withycombe and referred to her rather scornfully as the 'Nun of Oxford'. When the dust of this quarrel had settled years later, White acknowledged this difference between them: 'I am not good. I only know what good is. That is probably what is wrong with Betty. She knows what it is, and would like to be good, but remains an exercise in goodness.'[23]

Mentors made White fret after a time, but he had continued to value his cousin's literary judgment despite the sharp differences in their taste. After *The Tree of Man* there was an uncomfortable exchange: White replied to her letter of congratulations by accusing her of not liking the book. She had, but she insisted 'fulsome praise' was not her style.[24] She still thought *The Aunt's Story* the best and most concise of his novels, and so disliked *Voss* that she found herself stuck in the desert and unable to read on. She wrote to report this. 'Your style which always bordered on the precious has toppled right over. It reminds me of a custard that has cooked too long and curdled.' White dismissed this at the time as 'rather bitchy', and a few weeks later, when *The Times* published a hostile and anonymous review of the novel, White remarked to Peggy Garland, 'The cold, six-line dismissal . . . could have been by Betty.'[25]

Lascaris and Betty Withycombe met for the first time in London in 1958. She did not take Lascaris' offered hand, nor did she address more than a few words to him over lunch. Lascaris was puzzled, but White defended his cousin, saying this was just English behaviour. They all went down to Kew. It was a wonderful summer day but White, already morose, was plunged deeper in gloom as they strolled through the gardens. She put this down to the sight of so many trees flourishing in Kew that had failed him at Dogwoods. But White was gloomy and nervous as he listened to Lascaris chatting politely to his cousin, who seemed possessive and disapproving.

'How many children does your sister Joyce have?'

'None.'

'Why?'

'Because her husband is a homosexual. I doubt whether the marriage has ever been consummated.' To White that sounded 'like the firing of a gun'.[26]

One of his own casual remarks detonated the final charge. When he had not heard from Peggy Garland for some months after his return to Australia, he speculated in a letter to Catina Photiades that something might be 'wrong with one of the girls'. As his quip was transmitted along a chain of gossip from Athens to Oxford it became an accusation that one of Peggy's unmarried daughters was pregnant. This was not the case. When the slur reached Betty Withycombe she passed it on to her sister in an angry letter calling White 'this unnatural person'. Very annoyed with White, Peggy Garland then forwarded her sister's letter to Australia with one of her own demanding an explanation.[27]

White was stung by Betty Withycombe's language. 'Of course I was wrong to make the remark in the first place,' he told Peggy Garland. 'But who doesn't let such things fall . . . As for the demi-nun of Oxford I am writing to let her have a piece of my mind, as perhaps you intended me to. She has been bitchy enough about you in her day, and even since the Christian metamorphosis. She is really lousy with her miserable religiosity and self-sacrifice. If anybody wanted their knots untied by a "free Jungian analysis" it is Betty (poor Joyce we know has been luxuriating in masochism for years) but Betty, this super half veiled thing . . .'[28]

They exchanged several cold letters. From White's response it appears his cousin was mounting a formidable assault on many fronts. His self-esteem was at stake. This contest came in the bronchial weeks in which White feared, once again, he was the victim of lung cancer or TB. He had a great deal of frustration and rage to vent. In July he decided to stop writing, though he thought his cousin's last letter 'was so Jesuitical in tone and full of misunderstanding, that I think I shall be tempted to have one last fling'. He told her sister Peggy, 'If I were the heartless monster she professes to find me, I doubt whether I should have a friend, and I do have quite a number, nor are they by any means sycophantic, superficial ones. It is also dreadful to think that she has endured with Christian fortitude all these years what she describes as the "deformity" of my nature. The trouble is, I feel, I have never been impressed by her exhibitions of hysterical intensity, nor wanted to be swallowed up in her possessive cloud. Hence, I lack feeling. Admittedly there is a great deal in life that I find grotesque, but that does not mean that I do not also find it tragic, sometimes, or at least pathetic.'[29]

White and Betty Withycombe met and corresponded occasionally after that, but there was no reconciliation. With their breach there disappeared from White's writing those severe women who stand outside the turmoil of life and yet are passionately engaged by it. There are no more Theodora Goodmans or Laura Trevelyans. In each of them was a little of Betty Withycombe.

On Christmas morning 1959 red and black swastikas were found painted on the walls of the new synagogue in Cologne. A memorial that stood nearby to the men and women of the German Resistance was smeared with black paint. Police arrested a clerk and a baker's boy, both members of the neo-Nazi Reichspartei. Anti-semitism, it seemed, had risen from the ashes of Auschwitz and Treblinka. The Cologne desecrations were followed by outrage and imitation around the world. Slogans and swastikas were daubed in German cities, in Paris, in London and in towns across the deep south of the United States.

The 'swastika plague' spread to Australia in the first days of 1960; on Beth Weizmann's fence in Melbourne three swastikas and KILL JEWS in red paint: on a wall in Hawthorn, GAS JEWS; swastikas on a house in Toorak and in the halls of Moriah College; mud smeared on the gates of the Sir Moses Montefiore Home in Hunters Hill; in the Sydney synagogue, EXTERMINATE THE JEWS in chalk; and on a baker's shop in Canberra the primal, ominous call, JUDEN RAUS.

Australian Jews were divided. Some saw the daubings as merely the work of larrikins, but the Boards of Deputies spoke of organised anti-semitic plotting, perhaps encouraged by the Russians. White was of their grim opinion. He and Lascaris came down to the Town Hall for a meeting of protest on 20 January. 'As I watched the Jews pouring in before the meeting, and a sprinkling of Gentiles beginning to arrive as time was up, I began to have a suspicion that the Foolish Virgins were probably Gentile. The speeches, by politicians and the representatives of religious bodies, were mostly abysmal – ignorant and innocent, which only added to my depression. It made me wonder who is going to save this country from the wolves, especially when the proceedings were rounded off by a woman exhorting us six times over to remain *just ordinary Australians*. That hateful religion of *ordinariness*.'[30]

His own response to these flickerings of anti-semitism was to send each of Sydney's thirty-five municipal libraries a copy of *The Scourge of the Swastika*. 'Whether anybody reads them, is, of course, another matter.'[31] The swastika plague and its aftermath confirmed in White's mind the plausibility of the climax of his novel: the mock crucifixion of the Jew in the yard of Brighta Bicycle Lamps. Himmelfarb is led to the tree by ordinary Australians reassuring one another they are only playing a larrikin Australian joke. In White's hostile world crucifixions happen all the time. White's cross is not an image of salvation but of the good and evil in men and women: at once tormentors and victims, cruel and innocent, crucifiers and the crucified.

He had returned to the manuscript in these weeks both appalled and delighted by what he read. He found it 'vast and frightening', with patches of terrible writing, but it had the design he wanted. 'If you can imagine', he wrote to Huebsch, 'a section of castle wall with four merlons (that is the correct word for the raised parts; I have just looked it up in the dictionary!), that is the kind of shape it is: the four merlons being the "lives" of the four Riders set at regular intervals. The reviewer . . . on coming to the second merlon, will certainly think: What is all this? He has gone off his head, throwing everything away in such a digression. But we *hope* the right kind of reader will carry on, and realise in the end that all is balance and intention.'[32]

February was a wretched month. Despite the new drugs, he spent three weeks in bed with chest infections. Despairing of orthodox medicine's failure to eliminate the underlying causes of his distress, he turned to a naturopath. After a couple of months of short-wave, comfrey and diet, he declared he felt 'a hundred times better'.[33] Cortisone was still called on in major crises, but for the next few years he devoted himself to the sacrifices and rituals of the naturopath's diet: he was allowed only a dash of milk in his coffee, no sugar, no starch and absolutely no citrus. Every morning since moving to Dogwoods he had drunk a great glass of orange juice. Now this was forbidden and he insisted Lascaris join him in the sacrifice. 'I am supposed to concentrate on red meat and green leaf vegetables (with the exception of spinach). At breakfast, even, I eat a green salad – with plenty of garlic! Half an hour before breakfast, I drink two glasses of warm water, with a little salt, then eat eight prunes, then drink a third glass of water. How disgustingly faddy it all sounds! But it has had results, and I had grown desperate.'[34]

The illness of late summer, once again, had the effect of accelerating his work. The second draft of *Riders in the Chariot*, written in 'elation and raging despair', was quickly finished and shown to Lascaris and Klári Daniel by July. Daniel flew into ecstasies and announced that White was 'the first *Goy* to have understood the Jewish mind'. But Lascaris was more reserved: 'always a sober judge', he worried that the book would offend a great many Australians. 'Manoly says too much hate has got into it.'[35] White admitted he was sometimes overwhelmed by hatred as he was writing the book, but argued that he acknowledged this in the writing. Himmelfarb, returning from the nightmare journey of Seder night, touches the Mezuzah at his door and admits hatred has got the better of him. There was also, White countered, love in *Riders in the Chariot*. He was writing a book in which good and evil, love and hate collide.[36]

White had always been a hater, but the open expression of hatred was a new element in his work which corresponded to that slipping of the reins that came with fame. He had changed. But he was also now writing about the present day, and he believed the innocent wonder that fills *The Tree of Man* was not applicable. 'Stan and Amy are like characters out of my childhood or from recollections of my parents. I was always fascinated hearing them talk about the last century. It had a glow of morning. But only the saints, the Mrs Godbolds, are innocent today.'[37]

The targets of White's hatred in *Riders in the Chariot* are oddly mixed, some high and some low: the brick and fibro houses closing in on Dogwoods, Iceland poppies, vulgar bedspreads, the body beautiful (Himmelfarb's chief persecutor Blue 'had always been primarily a torso, an Antinous of the suburbs'),[38] restlessness (an old worry of the Whites) and migrants who slough off their old culture in a new land.

Ile Krieger's niece in Melbourne was refusing to eat chives because she 'wanted to be an Australian'. White was working on the second draft of the novel when he heard this, and he sent the young girl a little book on herbs. 'The chives in themselves are an unimportant detail (though I consider them one of the minor pleasures of life); it is the attitude which horrifies because it is so false and mistaken. I know that a great many ignorant native-born Australians (and nothing can be more ignorant than certain native-born Australians) go out of their way to encourage New Australians to drop their own standards in favour of the dreary semi-culture which exists here at present. However, there are also a great number of civilised Old Australians who are hoping that the migrants from European countries will bring something of their own cultures with them, so that we can incorporate them into what will some day be a true civilisation of our own.' Shirl Rosetree's kids hated the *Beinfleisch* she sometimes served instead of chops. 'Who wants bloody foreign food!'[39]

Mrs Jolley and her companion in evil Mrs Flack are creations of pure hate. These two devils, as White described them to Huebsch, had been a long time in his mind. When he was in the United States in 1939 newspapers were reporting the case of a couple of respectable Philadelphian widows who poisoned their husbands to collect the life insurance. At the time White had tried and failed to work this up into a short story called 'Duet for Harpies'. The American idiom defeated him, 'but the idea clung on, and came out finally as Mrs Jolley and Mrs Flack, each of whom had been the death of her husband, if not by poison'. As Miss Hare's housekeeper, Mrs Jolley showed the relentless snobbery of Mrs Lumsden, the first housekeeper at Dogwoods, who never ceased commending the charms of New Zealand and the excellent marriages her daughters had made, one to an American, the other to an aristocrat, neither of whom it seemed could bear to have their mother-in-law around.[40] Mrs Flack wears on her right hand the deceivers' ruby ring.

'Are you bitter, Mrs Jolley?'
'Bitter, no. I am just remembering.'
'One thing I never was, was bitter.'[41]

In *Riders in the Chariot* colloquial obscenities appear for the first time in his writing. From old admirers like James Stern, this development drew protests. White defended himself in musical terms: if discords can be used in music, why not in prose? 'I don't think I have used them recklessly . . . I have deliberately used the word "shit" in a couple of places to produce a shock discord: the smell of it to emphasise the "slime of despair" as the Jewish mother wipes her sick child when they are waiting in the shed for the train which will cart them off; again where Miss Hare is chasing Mrs Jolley through the house and the "brown word" shoots out of her memory as she tries to defend her dear, her good Jew, and for the first time she begins to accept the Christian image which Peg had always offered without success.'[42]

Music gave him the form of the last pages of the novel, and inspired the bizarre scene of the hatted ladies at lunch. 'I wanted something grotesque, brutally comic, as a relief from some of the tensions that had come before, and it does lead up to Mrs Chalmers-Robinson's moment of near-revelation as they sit in the darkened restaurant, and that in turn leads to the apotheosis of Mrs Godbold, which might have sounded too sweet, too much like "heavenly choirs" if there had not been a break of a discordant nature.' For those who refused to believe a woman would wear a smoking hat to lunch, White recalled another incident from his

American years: Gloria Swanson in 1939 drawing attention to herself at the Colony by wearing a volcano hat.[43]

The spring of 1960 was wonderful at Dogwoods, 'bursting with prunus, almond blossom, daffodils, anemones, magnolias, and the first cherries. Really a bit too much.' White had locked the novel away for two months, happy with what he had achieved so far. Some of the language had to be clarified and perhaps a greater fluidity achieved, but it seemed the final draft would not cause him much trouble.[44]

He spent the time digging, cooking and catching up on accumulated reading, for he had come to find it very hard to read novels as he was writing them. He dreamed of travelling again: to Sinai and Petra, to Christian Jerusalem, Constantinople, through the Greek islands once more, to Spain and Russia. 'Pasternak's landscapes are haunting me.' *Dr Zhivago* had held him spellbound. 'There was hardly a page which did not leave me wanting to shout and sing. I also finished the Durrell quartet of which the brilliance has begun to appear slightly meretricious after Pasternak's more mature wisdom. Still, I am thankful for Durrell too.'[45]

That spring the Duttons came into their lives. Geoffrey Dutton had been commissioned by Lansdowne Press to write a little book about White in the series 'Australian Writers and Their Work'. White was glad it was Dutton: 'One could have fared rather badly.' He had already sent some clippings over to Adelaide – V.S. Pritchett's review of *Happy Valley* and Edwin Muir's essay on *The Living and the Dead* which was one of his 'most cherished possessions' – but he urged Dutton to come to stay for a few days at Dogwoods while he was resting between drafts of the new novel. 'It is very difficult to tell you things at long distance.'[46]

The omens were good from the start. Dutton was the first Australian White knew who shattered Ruth's old rule that local writers were not of their class. The Duttons of Anlaby had been grazing in South Australia as long as the Whites in New South Wales. The two writers believed they were distantly related. White recalled a couple of Whites somewhere up in New England – 'Archie and I think Jack (or Fred?)' – who married Dutton sisters.[47] As it turned out, they were other Duttons, but for years White believed Geoffrey Dutton had a perch on some far branch of his family tree. Family connections predisposed White to both curiosity and trust.

Dutton was thirty-eight: a poet, critic, editor and historian. After flying with the Australian Air Force in the war, he studied at Oxford and came home to Adelaide to live with his wife Ninette (known as Nin – pronounced Neen) at their house Nonesuch in the Hills. They were a beautiful couple: intelligent, rich and dashing. Heaven seemed to have favoured them lavishly. Nonesuch was handsome enough, but only their base while Dutton's mother remained as the chatelaine of Anlaby, a great, low house standing on 8,000 acres sixty miles from town. Old Mrs Dutton was a beauty who had spent years of triumph in London as a young widow before the war. King George II of Greece was her admirer and every birthday and Christmas there were gifts and telegrams from Athens. Even now at a great age, like Ursula Polkinghorn of 'The Letters', Mrs Dutton stole the show:

> Whenever she had made her entrance, at weddings, for instance, smoothing the long kid gloves, or hand barely passing through the faint effulgence of her pale hair, everybody forgot the bride.[48]

Dutton and White had been writing to one another for nearly three years since the coup of 'Prodigal Son' in Dutton's magazine *Australian Letters*. White sent him news of the progress of *Riders in the Chariot*; a place was found at Anlaby for a couple of old Lascaris retainers washed up in Adelaide with no English: copies of Dutton's work arrived at Dogwoods. White admired some of the poetry and found himself unexpectedly fascinated by Dutton's biography of Colonel William Light, the military surveyor who laid out the city of Adelaide. 'I had no idea there was any character in Australian history of such charming and noble simplicity.'[49] That, roughly speaking, was White's first impression of Dutton himself when Lascaris drove him up from the airport in October 1960.

White cooked *bouillabaisse* and wore his beret for the occasion. Lascaris served drinks. Dutton was surprised to find White gentler and funnier in the flesh than he had expected. And Lascaris turned out to have 'an often Rabelaisian' sense of humour. 'He told some very funny stories about his experiences with Australians. I particularly liked the one about an odd-job man who had come in to the house and said to Patrick and Manoly: "The gentleman who drives the shitcart would like a cup of tea – not for himself but his fiancée who's taking a ride with him and is feeling crook." '

Dutton kept notes. 'Next day, when we were about to start talking over the material for the monograph, Patrick was down with the flu and a temperature of 101 degrees. Manoly drove him off to the herb-doctor. When they returned Patrick went to bed and Manoly was deputed to take me for a long scenic drive. I was disturbed that I had come at a bad time. "Don't worry," said Manoly, "it's only because he's nervous about talking about himself and his work with you. He'll be all right in the morning." And so he was. I sat by his bed and we drank tea and talked about everything from music to cooking, theatre to his relations, bitches (human and canine) to religion: "I am a believer. God is in anything, any religion, any art." '50

So the friendship of Geoff Dutton and Patrick White began. Dutton became like a son to White: a shining boy, to be loved, encouraged and occasionally reproved. He expected him to achieve great things as a writer, and before the stubborn disappointment of later years set in, was kind in private about Dutton's work and promoted it in public.

Nin Dutton and their three children were swept up in this family friendship with White and Lascaris. Within two years of meeting the Duttons, White included them among his 'best friends'.51 They spoke the same language, and knew the rituals of visits and gifts – a case of red, a small piece of pottery, a cookbook, some cuttings from their garden – by which friendships in the world of Lulworth and Anlaby are maintained. A happy bond between them all was their intimacy with Sid and Cynthia Nolan. Dutton had known the painter since the late 1940s when they were both contributing to the *avant-garde Angry Penguins*, and Nolan designed the cover of Dutton's first book of verse.

Between White and the poet there was also a shared and snobbish delight in the silly names they found reading the *Herald* and the *Adelaide Advertiser*. The deaths column turned up gems: Hilma, Iffla, Lurline . . . Dutton sent a couple of discoveries every few months and White put them on the lists of names kept in his desk drawer. This was more than a joke for White: 'names can be the first step towards a novel'.52

A few days after Dutton left Dogwoods, White began the final draft of *Riders in the Chariot*. His 'inconvenient and a-social' routine was to go to bed after dinner and then 'get up and use the middle and small hours. They are the best for writing letters and cooking, also for revising, though not creating novels; first thing in the morning is best, I find, for that.'53

He had long settled into a routine of writing only three drafts of each novel. The first draft was impressionistic, sketchy in places, and very private. Here he established the shape of the book, said roughly what he wanted to say, but pointed to ends yet to be reached. The first draft was a kind of childbirth, always the most painful and took the longest to write, 'dragged out, by tongs, a bloody mess'. In these months he found himself 'at loggerheads with everyone and every-thing'. He drank for 'the flashes' and used alcohol 'to cut the knots' in his writing. He only ever abandoned a novel towards the end of the first draft. If he finished this draft he finished the novel. During the first draft White most gave vent to the self-pity of writing. 'I hate it at present,' he told Dutton in the early stages of *Riders in the Chariot*. 'But on the whole I get very little pleasure out of writing; it is just something that comes over me like a recurring disease.'54

He wrote with a fountain pen – later a biro – in a clear hand on bundles of lined foolscap paper. Most of the time he maintained a strong forward momentum, drafting not on the page but in his head. Though Lascaris reported White spending weeks wrestling with a single phrase, his output in these years suggests such tussles happened only at moments of exceptional difficulty.[55]

Second drafts were a pleasure to write. 'Getting the first down on paper is sheer agony, and the third has something too irrevocable about it, not to say boring; but the second can make one feel quite godlike at times, with right words slipping into one's head, and shapes forming out of chaos.'[56] This was not childbirth but engineering: White always spoke of second drafts as oxywelding.

The final draft was typed on his portable Olivetti, overhauled to meet the challenge of *Riders in the Chariot*. Before he began he reread the second draft from beginning to end: 'a very slovenly piece of writing . . . some of my pages have shocked me on going over them for the last time. I am wondering whether, even now, I have found the right words, and clarified the obscurities without creating fresh ones.' Typing out the text created an entirely fresh perspective. 'One suddenly sees how to unknot situations which eluded one in a handwritten MS; yet one could not have launched into a typescript in the beginning – or I couldn't have.'[57]

White typed with two fingers, single-spaced, keeping only very narrow margins on flimsy, almost transparent paper. These crowded pages drove his publishers to distraction, but White was worried about the price of stamps. 'It was really meanness on my part. I thought that if I did not try to reduce the bulk it would cost about £25 to send the parcel by air, remembering my experience with *The Tree of Man*, and that was many years ago when postal costs had not soared to what they are today.'[58]

As usual he worked far more quickly on the final draft than he first expected; and as usual he suffered a terrible crisis of confidence as he neared the end. Would anyone be interested? Was he speaking a private language? Should he, even at this late stage, throw it away? Yet in the final moments, even as those doubts gathered, he was entirely swept up in the writing. As Alf Dubbo died of TB, having at last painted his image of the chariot blazing across the sky, White found himself coughing blood.[59] He wept as he finished, and that was always an omen of success.

For the last time he read the book through, making tiny corrections. It seemed 'a mess with some bright patches' but he knew that by now he was too close to see the book whole. On 4 January 1961 Lascaris drove him into town, and he posted one carbon to New York and another to London. 'The parcels crashed down into the bowels of the G.P.O., making me feel they had probably burst open at the start, and even if they hadn't, they were probably setting out on an ominous career.'[60]

Waiting for the publishers' verdict was the awful part of the process, but this time he only had to fret for a fortnight. Huebsch was in New York when the manuscript arrived. He read it swiftly and telegraphed White: 'RIDERS IS A GREAT BOOK YOUR BEST CONGRATULATIONS.'[61] The letter that followed invited White, for the first time, to call him Ben. 'Your letter and cable were a great relief,' White replied. 'Of course I realise it has to be read and accepted by other people too, but you have been the true judge over so many decades, and true judgment is what interests me most.' White asked if he could dedicate the book to him with Klári Daniel. 'I wanted to see how you reacted to the book first, otherwise it would have been too much like holding a gun at your head! Even now, perhaps, you would not like to be associated with it to that extent. I leave it to you. If you agree, let the dedication be simply:

FOR

KLARI DANIEL

AND

BEN HUEBSCH.'[62]

In London, Temple Smith at Eyre & Spottiswoode read eighty pages of the typescript and was very impressed, but then had to lend it to Sidney Nolan, who was to do the cover before leaving for Egypt. Back to Dogwoods came a chaotic letter from Cynthia Nolan saying how excited they were, and that Sid had almost decided what the jacket was to be. White found their enthusiasm most gratifying. 'They are the first Australians to read it.'[63]

The Garland marriage had broken up after twenty difficult years and Peggy was soon to return to England. For some time she had been trying to persuade her cousin to visit New Zealand. If he were ever to make the trip it had to be now.

White flew over to Wellington in March 1961 and found himself, against all his expectations, in a country both beautiful and mysterious: 'it makes Australia seem like a rubbish dump, and yet with all this unspoiled material beauty there are the most astonishing outbreaks of human violence and youthful degeneracy'.[64] The hills and harbour of Wellington reminded him of Greece with a dash of Norway. Once again he was in Katherine Mansfield country.

At the Garlands' he met a number of interesting people, 'more . . . in a short time than I have in years'. Fred Wood, who had coached him for Cambridge, was now Professor of History at the city's Victoria University. White was delighted to see him again: 'His wife said I ruined their honeymoon because he was always having to break off to give me tuition.' Living as a lodger in the Garlands' house was Katherine Mansfield's biographer Antony Alpers, who drove White out to the bays of her stories and let him handle Mansfield's letters and notebooks.[65] As a reader of Mansfield he was fascinated by these relics; but as a writer they disturbed him.

'Letters are the devil,' he wrote to Best. 'I always hope that any I have written have been destroyed, excepting those which for business reasons have to go on file. Somerset Maugham had the right idea when he appealed to anybody possessing letters he had written to destroy them when he dies. Katherine Mansfield is a good example of the letter-writer traduced . . . her original letters and notebooks . . . have lingered on to accuse her as a monster of sensibility and egotism. I would prefer to remember her by her stories, although I confess to being tremendously intrigued by the private, sometimes automatic outpourings.'[66]

Alpers gave White a paper knife which had been Mansfield's. He was very touched. It remained among his most valued possessions.

None of Peggy's civilised friends made so much impact on White in that fortnight as her youngest son, Philip. Peggy never knew precisely what damage had been done to the child at birth. He was simple but not dumb. Against all predictions, she had taught him to walk and talk and read. He had a good ear and he chattered away so easily that it puzzled her to think how he picked up his vocabulary. He read newspapers aloud with great fluency but almost no understanding. There was one brand of children's book, Reindeer Books, which he loved and would wander off to the library to read. He was fond of a bag of glass marbles. The sight of loneliness and suffering hurt him.

At ten the boy had stopped growing and stayed a very fat, clumsy child who shied away from being touched and could not bear to be kissed or embraced. Only out walking would he hold hands, sometimes breaking away to talk to strangers. He made people laugh. Strangers told him their troubles. Then the boy began to suffer fits of anger and destructiveness. He knew when these attacks were approaching, and begged his mother to save him from them. She realised that he would soon have to be placed in an institution, but for the moment he was restrained by doses of Largactyl. He was fourteen when White came to Wellington.

White played with the child and listened to his conversations for hours, delighting in the unexpected turns of his behaviour. He reported to Huebsch how Philip, sitting in a dentist's waiting room, had reproved a bishop for saying it was 'fun' to go to church. 'The boy maintaining that as one went to church to get help in combating one's sins, it was a matter that could only be taken seriously.'[67] Above

40 Manoly Lascaris: 'this small Greek of immense moral strength'.

41 On leave together in Beirut.

42 Abandoned children: Anna, Manoly, Mario, Aristo, Katina and Elly Lascaris.

43 *top* Carlton, the Lascaris'
summer house in Alexandria.

44 *above* On Aiyina when
the war in Europe ended:
White and Elly with her son
Notis.

45 *right* Before the
Catastrophe: Aunt Despo
aboard the family's yacht on
the Bosphorus.

48 *above* Gertrude
Morris, the aunt of
The Aunt's Story.

49 *above* Early days at Dogwoods with White weeding.

46 *opposite*, Walking the schnauzers in London.

47 *opposite, below left* After the car crash in *Return to Abyssinia*: Barbara Shaw on the right posing as Beauval.

50 *below* The paddock with an unprofitable crop of roses.

Scenes from life at Dogwoods

51 Lascaris with a litter of pups.
52 White milking the Dream of Penrith II.
53 Parading Grauvolk's best before the press.

54 Old Clem Withycombe, adviser to White as novelist and farmer.

55 The Kubics, who brought order to the farm so White could write again.

56 Reading *The Tree of Man* in manuscript beneath de Maistre's
Descent from the Cross. In the photograph beside him are his nieces
Gillian and Alexandra.

Friends: intimate and estranged

57 *above* His 'lady disciple' Margery Williams: politics wrecked their twelve-year friendship. **58** *right* Nin Dutton on the beach at Kangaroo Island: rows with Geoff ended twenty-two years of intimacy. **59** *below* Klari Daniel: the most intense friendship of all came to grief over a salad. **60** *below right* Fritz and Ile Krieger: dogs and Mozart ended their lives with *'die Büben'*.

61 Sidney Nolan whose friendship White valued above all others:
'I feel I have known him all my life . . .'

62 Prize night for *Voss* with the Prime Minister Bob Menzies and
Labor's Bert Evatt.

63 *below* Canberra
vicereine: Maie
Casey.

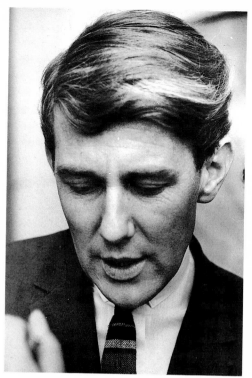

64 Producer, protégé and Geminian, John Tasker.

65 Zoe Caldwell as *The Ham Funeral*'s pale girl.

66 Fuss over Patrick White in New York, 1968, with Arthur Miller and publisher Marshall Best.

67 *above* An afternoon of mutual admiration with Barry Humphries in Sydney.

68 *left* The Nobel summer of 1973: playing with the pugs in the garden at Martin Road.

The Jim Sharman crowd

opposite, from top left
69 Kerry Walker, leading lady. 70 Neil Armfield, the next director in White's life. 71 Sharman: 'a perfect example of fruitful sublimation'.
72 Luciana Arrighi, cousin and designer.
73 Brian Thomson, designer.
74 Elizabeth Knight, the producer.

75 Marching for peace.

Patrick and Manoly

76 *below* The *Signal Driver*
version with John Wood and
Melissa Jaffer as Theo and Ivy
Vokes, Kerry Walker and Peter
Cummins as the Beings.
77 *right* And in life: a couple of
old men on the terrace at Martin
Road.

78 *opposite, below* The Cheery
Soul heads home against a bitter
wind: Robyn Nevin in
Sharman's 1979 production.

79 Back in hospital in 1985 facing his uncertain future.

the Garlands' house, on the far side of a pine forest, was the Wellington zoo. Philip walked up there alone to keep the gibbon company. He told his mother, 'I will be his friend. He probably won't know I'm his friend, but I will be.' One day he took White by the hand and led him up through the forest to see his friend the gibbon.

From Dogwoods, where White arrived in late March, he wrote to Philip about cats and chooks and guinea-pigs and music and his plans to sail up the coast to Queensland. 'Now you will have to write back, as you promised, and tell me everything. I shall always be interested to hear what you have to say.' He never did. But the 'expedition over the mountain to the zoo, and Philip hanging over the gramophone listening to Schubert' were images that returned to White as he was writing *The Solid Mandala*. A lot of Philip was to emerge in Arthur Brown, the simple man of unexpected gifts living in Terminus Road, Sarsaparilla.[68]

White paused at Dogwoods for a few weeks working on proofs of *Riders in the Chariot*. He found it terrible to be going through it again, and grumbled that correcting proofs 'kills my eyes and my equanimity'. The copy editors at Viking were again complaining about 'dangling modifiers' and punctuation. He appealed to Marshall Best: 'We have that argument every time I write a book, and I still don't altogether understand what they mean. In the circumstances, as they seem to be so much part of me and my peculiar style, don't you think they can stay? I agree that my punctuation gets a bit out of hand, and that it can well be tidied up by an expert. Anxiety drives me to an excess of commas.'[69]

Best promised his prose would not be touched. 'You have a right to re-form the language to your purposes regardless of what former re-formers have done to it.'[70] This penultimate effort to edit Patrick White ended in yet another defeat.

The last of the coastal steamers, the sturdy *Manoora*, sailed from Sydney Harbour in June with Patrick White on board. Gretel and Stephen Feher were at the wharf with Lascaris to say goodbye, and they left White with a good bottle of whisky for the two-day voyage to Brisbane.

He was not making the trip for love of ocean travel – he asked Dutton afterwards, 'Is its formlessness the thing about the sea that always dismays me?'[71] – but to research the book he was now anxious to begin. This was to be based on the ordeal of Eliza Fraser after the shipwreck of the *Stirling Castle* in 1836. White wanted to sail along the Australia coast and explore Fraser Island off Queensland, where all the survivors of the wreck were killed by the blacks, except for the captain's wife who was kept by them as a slave. She was stripped of everything, until she was reduced to wearing a vine round her waist – the 'fringe of leaves' – in which she hid her wedding ring. At a corroboree she found an escaped convict who took her back to civilisation.

White first heard this story in Florida. Sid Nolan had hitch-hiked up to the island in 1947 with the poet Barrett Reid, who had discovered in a Brisbane library the old blood-and-guts account of Mrs Fraser's ordeal, *The Shipwreck of the Stirling Castle*. Nolan talked their way on to a timber barge for the trip out to the island – Nolan's charm was irresistible – and for a few weeks they lived among the timber cutters with Nolan sketching, photographing and painting his first Mrs Fraser paintings on scraps of hardboard scavenged from the camp. They are some of Nolan's finest works. Years after he left the island the theme still pursued him, and in London he painted another thirty Eliza Fraser paintings to hang in the Whitechapel Gallery's 1957 retrospective of his work. The following year in Florida he saw the Everglades, which reminded him of the swamps of Fraser Island, and soon after White joined them at Fort Lauderdale, Nolan told him about the wreck and the island and Mrs Fraser's rescue. White found, 'We had so much to say, as often happens when we meet those who have been saved up for us.'[72]

The whole span of White's intense friendship with Nolan lay between that Florida meeting and the publication nearly twenty years later of *A Fringe of Leaves*. A few weeks after it appeared Cynthia committed suicide. White's feeling for the painter changed and the friendship he valued above any other ended in an ugly public feud. The patron of this friendship, from first meeting to final wreckage, was Eliza Fraser.

Nolan had sprung from a rough Melbourne suburb on the bay, where his father was a tram driver and illegal bookmaker. The boy grew up in a world of football, swimming baths and respectable crime. He had fresh eyes, talent, beauty and an air of innocence that won the support of men and protection of women. But underneath his charm, Nolan never lost the cunning and resilience bred in that St Kilda childhood. He was the one who did the deals, while his wife Cynthia kept the world at bay. They had settled far from Australia, in a house on the Thames at Putney.

Cynthia was a difficult woman: dark, dramatic, intransigent, original and wilfully possessive. White observed that she was capable of happiness 'in its most limpid forms' but yet she was a tormented creature.[73] Her torments sprang from familiar territory. She was another refugee from the world of sheep, and looked back on her childhood as a nightmare, a source of black rage. Her family, the Reeds, were graziers in northern Tasmania and divided their time between that island and their English headquarters, a large and hideous house outside Bath. A decade before White's time, Cynthia's brother John was condemned to Cheltenham. She escaped into bohemia and had a daughter, Jinx.

Marriage to Nolan had given her a role which suited her perfectly in those years: the jealous protector of her husband's genius, for which she was both despised and admired. It was Cynthia who always answered the telephone. Life with Nolan allowed her to exercise a great flair for houses, art, clothes, food, gardens, entertaining. She wrote books – awkward when the subject was Nolan, penetrating when she wrote about herself. White called her, 'A kingfisher of a spirit'.[74] Sid was always promising to write and sending his love, but Cynthia wrote the letters – crammed aerograms, every flap covered in her difficult handwriting – through which their intimacy prospered.

White and the Nolans had not met since Florida, but in those three years their friendship had been sustained, indeed deepened, by this correspondence. White was already learning something of Nolan's charming but vagrant ways. The jackets for *Voss* and *The Aunt's Story* were disappointing, but White's regard for Nolan was so high that he accepted them both. Now, as the *Manoora* headed up the coast to Queensland, Nolan was leaving London for Egypt without giving Eyre & Spottiswoode something for the cover of *Riders in the Chariot*. White was baffled. 'He is the one to do a jacket if he would only get down to it. I know he would understand the book. I know from his wife that it appealed to them. But he has been committed to so many things at once, including sets for a play, and now I feel too many Egyptian images will get in the way. However, there is just a faint hope. Things have a habit of rising up out of a painter's unconscious suddenly and without warning.'[75]

Cables and airletters flew between London, Cairo, New York and Sydney. Finally Nolan asked Temple Smith to go to Putney and find anything that might convey the spirit of the book. Cynthia insisted he pick from a couple of sketches she had chosen, but quite accidentally Temple Smith came across a series of ten or twenty works clearly painted in response to *Riders in the Chariot*. He took one over Cynthia's objections, and it turned out to be the finest of Sid Nolan's jackets for Patrick White.[76]

The *Manoora* reached Brisbane on 16 June. The city surprised him. It was his first visit: 'full of interesting ramshackle latticed houses built on stilts, and the people, just to meet them in the streets, an amiable, extrovert race'.[77] On his way through he wanted to meet the reclusive painter Ian Fairweather, whose haunting *Gethsemane* covered his bedroom wall at Dogwoods. 'I don't know whether he will want to see me,' White had written to Philip Garland, 'but I shall have a try.'[78] Fairweather lived absolutely White's dream of the artist stripped bare: at the age of seventy-three he lived and painted in an open hut in the bush. Brisbane was only a ferry ride away, but it seemed Fairweather had not left Bribie for eight years. White took the ferry to the island and found the painter working in his hut. The place was squalid. Fairweather was 'tall, rather frail, with a wonderful face – perfect brow, nose and mouth – and he is one of the few people who can wear a beard today without looking self-conscious. When he is not painting – he paints at night by the light of a hurricane lamp – he is translating from the Chinese.'[79]

They had not much to say to one another. White suspected the painter was bored with life on Bribie and, compared with the glamorous photographs of Fairweather as an officer in the war, he was now a scabby and unattractive old man.[80] The two men wandered down to the store by the jetty and waited in silence for the ferry.

White took the train north to Maryborough, where his plans hit a snag. The price of a place on the boat to Fraser Island was £25. White was furious. 'I didn't have enough money with me, and didn't want to pay so much in any case.'[81] Just as he was about to head back in defeat to Brisbane, White found a young pilot who was to make his weekly food drop next morning to the timber-getters. White could join him for £10. They left early and circled the island for an hour so that White could see the forests dotted with lakes on the high dunes, and the great sweep of Seventy Mile Beach along the island's ocean flank.

The plane landed on a strip of grey sand near the swamps that fringe the island's western side. Pilot and passenger walked for several miles into the forest until they met a timber truck, 'a kind of Emmett bomb, held together by wire and string, with a fuel tank tied to the roof – which rushed us into the interior, a magnificent jungle of tallow wood, box, satinay and blackbutt, and vines strung from trunk to trunk'. Brumbies lived in the forest, the wild offspring of horses brought over in the early days. Parrots flashed across shafts of light. White's few hours on the truck made such a profound impression on him that ten years later he was able to imagine in precise detail,

> the columns so moss-upholstered or lichen-encrusted, the vines suspended from them so intricately rigged, the light barely slithered down, and then a dark watery green, though in rare gaps where the sassafras had been thinned out, and once where a giant blackbutt had crashed, the intruders might have been reminded of actual light if this had not flittered, again like moss, but dry, crumbled, white to golden.

Back in Maryborough he wrote to Peggy Garland, 'I now know what I want to know.'[82]

An Aboriginal story-teller Wilf Reeves lived in Maryborough and White was taken to meet him. Reeves's father was a timber-getter on the island and his mother was the daughter of a white missionary. The man of God had found his daughter with the black, forced them to marry and turned them out to live in the blacks' camp. Reeves was one of many sons of this Christian union. He yarned, wrote poetry and published his father's stories of the Butchulla People of Fraser Island.[83] White and Reeves talked in a house on the edge of town. Patrick White was a 49-year-old Australian, and this was the first time he had sat down with an Aboriginal. Reeves's life reminded him strangely of his own creation Alf Dubbo, a first sign of the alarming way life had of imitating his art.

Reeves urged White to be sceptical about the official accounts of Mrs Fraser's ordeal. She had created a sensation with her tales of the indignities foisted on her by the natives, and her tales of woe were the basis of *The Shipwreck of the Stirling Castle*. But the Aboriginals passed down a different story of white men who were welcomed at first as reincarnated spirits, and a white woman who survived and was absorbed into the life of the tribe until more whites appeared to take her away. Mrs Fraser had brought back reports of hell, but White was putting together the picture of a savage paradise.

Now he was anxious to get home. He ended his letter to his cousin, 'All the time I have been on this present journey I don't think I have seen one person who would understand a word of what I write. So it is very depressing . . . I am itching to get back to peace, and one's own oasis. Except for the day I was on Fraser Island the radio hasn't stopped drooling in my ears – in hotels, in buses, in the streets, even in trains there has been the transistor in the next compartment. Now I must go down and take a good stiff brandy before my last meal with the commercial travellers.'[84]

Intense enthusiasm was building at Viking Press as advance orders for *Riders in the Chariot* poured in. The figures were 'staggeringly good'[85] and the publishers were sure the excitement generated by the novel would reverse the slide in White's North American sales. Viking sold 16,000 copies of *The Tree of Man*, but *Voss* – apart from book club sales – sold only 9,000 in hardback. This had surprised and disappointed Huebsch, but now the omens suggested a major success for the new book.

Once again Stern would be leading the critical pack with a notice in the *New York Times Book Review*. The London *Observer* and *Time* had sent photographers to Dogwoods. Curt and Maria Prerauer were to translate it for the Germans. The Swedish translation was already under way. 'It is all very exciting and oppressive waiting for the day,' White wrote to Peggy Garland. 'Something like having a baby, I imagine. All so slow.'[86]

Riders in the Chariot appeared in New York in October, but the reviews did not lead the book sections. Critics praised White warmly for the most part, but the editors had made their own tough, commercial judgment. The failure of *Voss* to reach a mass market relegated Patrick White to the status of a literary author. Stern's extremely enthusiastic notice was short and appeared on page four of the *Review*. The *New Yorker* took for granted that White was the prisoner of a coterie and warned him of the perils facing those in his position. 'Their worshippers coddle them, over celebrate their virtues, shush their faults, and frighten away prospective and perhaps skeptical readers with an apologist's fervour.' *Time* reworked White's history to deny his past triumphs, declared he had never really impressed American reviewers, while eliciting from the English only 'little civil cries of educated pleasure'. The Viking edition of *Riders in the Chariot* sold about 8,000 copies in North America.[87]

Across the Atlantic, the big guns spoke for Patrick White. Notices for *Riders in the Chariot* led the book sections, and the novel entered London's bestseller lists where it stayed for thirteen weeks. Eyre & Spottiswoode sold over 24,000 copies: more than 9,000 in England, another 9,500 out in Australia, and the remaining 6,000 or so through the rest of the English-speaking world.

The new novel was not only a commercial success in Australia's tiny market, but was met for the first time by an almost unanimously enthusiastic press. Some critics, hostile in the past, began cautiously to revise their opinions. The book won White a second Miles Franklin award, but he asked Kylie Tennant to go to the ceremony in his place. The *Sydney Morning Herald* rang Dogwoods to discover why: 'A friend, Mr E. Lascaris, who was looking after him said Mr White had been in bed for a week and would remain there for another week.'[88] Tennant thought this 'a typical piece of male scrimshanking' but went along happily to join the 'teachers, publishers reps and people out for a free feed. I gave a moving speech about how ill Patrick was and then, straight after the ceremony, drove out to Castle Hill. As I drove over the rise, there was the hollow covered in mist. Patrick was up and about and seized the award with both hands. I told him that night. "You've got to get out of here, coughing and wheezing in Frog Hollow." '[89]

At Viking a disappointed Marshall Best mulled over the last paragraph of Orville Prescott's review in the *New York Times*. Prescott had praised the book warmly yet ended with these words, 'It desperately needs editing.' Best took all his courage in his hands and made a final appeal to White: 'As an aside, may I say that Orville Prescott's . . . sentence reflects the American attitude, so different from the English, that the publisher's editor has a real responsibility. We certainly don't want to shirk that responsibility if at any time you think our opinions might be useful to you. But we are glad to publish your books as you write them, even though we might have minor reservations.' White replied: 'The editing of novels – it sounds about as horrible as a packaged dinner.'[90]

By the time *Riders in the Chariot* appeared in October 1961, White's life had taken a new course and he was dispersing his Jewish friends. Relations between *die Büben* and the Kriegers had been under strain for some time, and their friendship was no longer as intense or sustaining as it had been in the middle of the 1950s. 'When he became famous we began to worry about him. He changed very much. He was very cynical. He got the wrong view of people. We did not want to hear these things.' The Kriegers disapproved of the new theatrical friends who were becoming the centre of White's attention at Dogwoods.[91]

Fritz Krieger had never discussed business affairs with White, but these were bad times for CELCO in the aftermath of the 1960 credit squeeze, and it began to embitter Fritz that his friend seemed indifferent to the hard times he was having at the factory. They quarrelled. 'Neither had the patience to listen to the other and they began to have terrible arguments.' Each was stubborn, each dogmatic, each passionate. White wrote to Ile Krieger's sister-in-law, Elly Fisher. 'As Fritz grows more and more intolerant and remote from life I found our meetings too much of a strain. He really doesn't want to see anybody who doesn't hold the same opinions.'[92]

Their battleground was music. White had moved beyond their shared devotion to Bruckner and Mahler, but Fritz did not approve of Bach or Bartok or White's growing enthusiasm for Mozart, whose music Krieger dismissed as 'a stream of lemonade'.[93] White now knew enough to challenge these prejudices and they fought. On one side was a cultured refugee reassured by the familiar, and on the other an artist compelled to keep exploring.

Fritz returned from visiting his family in New York and Mexico at this time and declared that Australia might be the most boring country in the world, but he was happy to live in it as it was. White disagreed. 'We *are* a boring race, and the constant realisation of it makes me desperate. I do feel, however, that the change is taking place, only very, very slowly: there is so much dead wood keeping the live growth back. The heads of Establishments are still telling us what is good for Australians. English throw-outs still flock here to teach us, and there is a dreadful atmosphere of Adult Education in which no art can flourish. One had hopes of the Jews who came here after the Troubles, but on the whole they have been a disappointment. They have given us doctors, handbags and *Torten*. But in the arts, they lurk in a thicket of Brahms and Richard Strauss; visually, wild horses wouldn't drag them farther than Kokoschka.'[94]

Several grim incidents marked the path towards the final split. One night Ile Krieger was alone and heard a strange dog prowling in her garden. She rang White for help. He suggested she bring the animal in and give it a feed. She was frightened and protested. White flared into an extraordinary rage. 'You have been homeless, give it a home. You are heartless.' *Riders in the Chariot* appeared, and it seemed to White the Kriegers were hurt by the portrait of Harry Rosetree. Ile Krieger denies this. 'That was Patrick's view of Fritz, not mine. The final row began when Fritz Krieger disputed a scrap of political gossip. White shouted, "When *I* say that, you have to accept it." The terrible argument that followed was the end of ten years' wonderful friendship.'[95]

Several attempts were made to patch things up, but each meeting ended with one of the men feeling wounded. It was no use. For some years there was no contact between them. The Kriegers left Castle Hill and eventually moved to Melbourne. There, in about 1967, they received out of the blue a copy of *The Tree of Man* in Hungarian. White did not write to them again until 1982 when Fritz was dying.

He sloughed off Gretel Feher. On the telephone one morning she begged him to stop calling her husband 'the magazine reader' and 'the fan of Morris West'. To her surprise White exploded and the call ended in an acrimonious shambles. She rang back and tried without success to patch things up. That week the publishers delivered an advance copy of *Riders in the Chariot* to Kirribilli with the author's compliments. She rang White to ask if he now wanted this gift back. He refused and that was their last contact. Her wounds are unhealed.

Thea Astley's friendship also came to grief on the telephone. She remarked, after reading one or two poems, 'Of course, Geoff Dutton can't write.' White replied, without pause, 'You fucking malicious bitch.' Astley was shocked. One did not hear such language then. She said, rather dazed, 'Well, I'm sorry, but that's how I feel.' A few days later White rang to say he regretted they could no longer be friends. They did not meet again for fifteen years.

White spoke of these old friends as millstones and complained especially that his Jewish friends were possessive and suffocating.[96] When he broke with them he broke brutally. It was the only way he knew and allowed him at some level to share the pain he was inflicting. As an artist he felt this was justified, indeed that he was compelled to take this course because he needed the freedom to pursue an old ambition which was reasserting itself in his life. He was back in the theatre. White complained this was destroying his peace of mind and poisoning his life; he protested that he was being dragged back against his will; and he confessed to Margery Williams, one of his new and devoted friends, 'It will bring out the very worst in me.'[97] He was having an exhilarating time.

NINETEEN

Stage Struck

RUTH HAD TAKEN her boy even before he could read to Sydney's magic, dusty theatres. Theatre was her passion, and she left her son stage-struck. Among the first pieces White wrote were little melodramas to fill empty afternoons at Tudor House; at Cheltenham he dreamed of being an actor; in London it was as a playwright that he first tried, and failed, to make his mark. Nothing much had come of this passion apart from a brief success in revue, but these sketches from his Eccleston Street years, the respectable failure of *Return to Abyssinia*, and the unperformed *Ham Funeral* left him wondering still if he could 'pull it off, just once, to show myself'. Ronald Waters always thought his old friend wanted to write 'one great play' more than all the novels.[1]

When this ambition rose to the surface in the late 1950s, White wondered if he had the technical flair for theatre: 'That does rankle. Particularly as I know when someone else has done something wrong.' This uncertainty did not deter him. Even as he paused on the brink of committing himself to the stage once more, he wondered if drama itself was possible in Australia, 'because we are un-dramatic, too *boring*. The average Australian can't tell one anything without making it sound pointless. Such a chronic shapelessness can build novels, but the drama will hardly flourish in it.'[2]

The Ham Funeral, White was fond of saying, lay undiscovered in a drawer for years. In truth, the script lay in many drawers for many years before White rediscovered and reworked it. His agents had failed to sell the play in the late 1940s on either side of the Atlantic. A report commissioned by Curtis Brown in New York concluded, 'The whole play suffers from an intolerable attitudinising on the part of the author, and its lack of body and substance is frustrating and irritating. Furthermore, this type of impressionistic morality play is extremely tedious, dated and boring even when well done, and certainly this script is not. Absolutely no possibilities.'

Scrawled in pencil on the report are the words, 'Return . . . write kindly.'[3]

When White returned to Australia that year, 1948, he found Beryl Bryant had disappeared, assumed bodily into the ranks of Moral Rearmament. What was left of serious theatre in Sydney was dominated by Doris Fitton, an imperious woman with more pluck than talent. Her casts were amateurs, students and radio actors. No one was paid. Amateur taste lay like a curse on the Sydney stage. Fitton's new Independent Theatre was founded the day White arrived back in Australia after the war. He gave her a copy of *The Ham Funeral* and she hung on to it, never quite able to make up her mind. He did nothing more with it. 'Of course I should have persevered in between instead of letting it lie those nine years in bloody Doris Fitton's drawer. But I went through a depressed phase after returning to live in Australia and could not make the effort.'[4]

The idea of a national theatre in Australia had been in the wind for decades. Tyrone Guthrie was brought out to advise the Labor government of Ben Chifley, but when the mandate of the suburbs shifted to Bob Menzies in 1949, Guthrie's report was buried. The banker Nugget Coombs revived the idea after the Royal Tour of 1954. Taking advantage of the idea that the young Queen would bring a second Elizabethan age to the British world, Coombs established the Elizabethan Theatre Trust (known as the Trust) with private money and promises of public support to foster indigenous drama, opera and ballet in Australia.

White was among those who were soon disappointed. Hugh Hunt, an Englishman, was imported to direct the Trust. He brought out an English staff and opened the Trust's theatre in Sydney with Terence Rattigan's *Separate Tables*, starring Ralph Richardson, Sybil Thorndike and Lewis Casson. White admired all three actors – he had lunch with Thorndike on one of her later tours, 'and was burnt up by that wonderful personality. Even at that age, she is ablaze with everything that is vital, and so beautiful' – but nothing new had been achieved. English stars and English shows were already familiar on the Australian circuit. There was clearly not enough public or private money in the Trust to 'foster' Australian theatre. Some cash was doled out to help local writers, but in effect the Trust became a subsidised entrepreneur of mainly British theatre in Australia: 'a dreadful set-up, of about the same standard as the Hull Repertory'.[5]

The Summer of the Seventeenth Doll, the Trust's one great success in these years, left White dissatisfied, but cautious of admitting his disappointment for fear of being lynched by fellow Australians.[6] He saw Ray Lawler's play at the Elizabethan Theatre in Sydney on a night of intense heat with everyone 'sweating to death' on both sides of the curtain. Later he read the play and thought, perhaps, the heat had something to do with his response. 'As acted it seemed to me an occasion of lost opportunities, both for humour, and poetry. (I am right off *realism* anyway. I read the other day that somebody had referred to it as "reality in degeneracy", and that is perhaps what I feel about it.)' From theatre he expected 'imagination, wit and mystery'. Why, he wondered, are Australian writers expected to shout at audiences 'in the accents of canecutters, and show them everything in terms of photographic realism'?[7]

Some time in 1956, after being 'bowled over' by *The Tree of Man*, the Australian actor Keith Michell wrote from London asking White for a play. White fobbed him off in the New Year, but Michell had struck a spark. White now retrieved *The Ham Funeral* from Doris Fitton's drawer, and sent it to Grafton for Freddie Glover to read. Glover urged him to 'refurbish it a little' and find a producer.[8] White agreed it needed 'writing up a bit here and there, and perhaps one complete new scene substituted for one of those already in existence'. He put it aside until the world tour of 1958. As he explained to Huebsch, 'It is the sort of thing I can scribble at on bits of paper in aeroplanes, type out in Athens, and thrust at a certain young Australian star in London, as he is very keen to have a play of mine. If nothing happens, I don't mind; plays don't really mean anything to me. However, I *would* like to have a theatrical success in New York just to make the Australian press die finally of apoplexy.'[9]

White tinkered with *The Ham Funeral* in Greece and gave Michell a slightly revised script in London that summer. The actor was disappointed: 'It had a splendid and shining new opening soliloquy for an actor. The rest of the play was not for me. I suspected – and said so – that it was not new material. I did give it to George Devine who was director at the Royal Court.'[10] London managements were curious, in the aftermath of the great success of *Voss*, to see what Patrick White could do for the stage. Fame earned *The Ham Funeral* another reading. Copies were called for, and White spent much of that London summer selling the play. Several producers were polite; George Devine seemed interested. In New York Zachary Scott, whose first ambition was to film one of the novels, also took an option on *The Ham Funeral*, and by the time White flew home to Australia it seemed London and Broadway productions were in his grasp.

The existence of *The Ham Funeral* was almost unknown in Australia. Dutton knew nothing about it until January 1959 when White mentioned these international negotiations and remarked that Hunt at the Trust had also 'taken a fancy to it'. Yet Hunt warned White that if the play were first produced in London, 'the Great Australian Audience might be more willing to accept it, or less inclined to wonder whether it

is having its leg pulled'. Hunt offered to encourage Devine to stage the
première in London.[11] Hunt's response was sad but shrewd, for when
the Trust produced an Australian play for the first time, the taste and
morals of the citizens on its board were put in public question. But
by some odd magic, a London season would relieve the bankers and
industrialists on the Trust from any personal responsibility for a play's
novelty, bad language and doubtful taste.

White's hopes for the play fell away as he worked on *Riders in the
Chariot* and the London and New York options expired unexercised.
Among his friends, White insisted he no longer cared about the theatre
or this play, and comforted himself with the reflection that *The Ham
Funeral* was once 'a precursor without anybody's realising. When I
hawked it round London in the beginning everybody said it was
meaningless. Now it is too late.' Only when his London and New
York hopes were over, did he send a copy to Geoffrey Dutton in
Adelaide. Dutton had been trying to get hold of a copy of the play for
nearly two years. It arrived with a letter: 'I finally unearthed the
copy of *The Ham Funeral*. I send it with diffidence, as it seems to
me more of a private matter than the novels, almost an act of indecent
exposure . . . I have just been reading about Joyce's play *Exiles*, which
hung fire for years, then was a flop in Munich, and, one suspects, in
London too. I think perhaps *The Ham Funeral* is the same kind of piece,
and should be discreetly forgotten.'[12]

At this point White was about to send the typescript of *Riders in
the Chariot* to his publishers, and the drama that followed in Australia
over *The Ham Funeral* was played out against the background of intense
excitement in Manhattan and London as the new novel was prepared for
publication. The trouble began when Geoffrey Dutton and his friends,
who were very excited when they read the script, suggested *The Ham
Funeral* be performed at the next Adelaide Festival.

Adelaide stands almost isolated from the rest of Australia on a tongue
of land pointing south into the Great Australian Bight. The city basks
in a perfect Mediterranean climate. To the north are the deserts and
salt lakes that baffled Eyre and to the south the ocean that White had
crossed and recrossed on P & O liners since childhood. Built between
these extremes, Adelaide was committed to notions of civilised moderation and shelter from the harsher elements. Green parks surround the
centre of the city, and vineyards at this time flourished in the suburbs.
The city was compact, rational and smug. Benign neglect and modest
prosperity preserved monuments of its early wealth. Adelaide was a
city of corrugated iron roofs and Palladian façades; avenues fit for a
German spa ran to the foot of Australian hills.

The city was in the hands of a few families of brewers, bankers, graziers, newspapermen and stockbrokers who had decided to hold a festival every couple of years along the lines of Edinburgh, Bath and Stratford, Ontario. The Queen Mother was enlisted as patron. Public celebrations of this sort in Australia were usually marked by a patriotic play on a historical theme – the life of an early governor, or perhaps one of the disasters of desert exploration. The Drama Advisory Committee was determined to rise above this, and for the first festival they chose a new play by Alan Seymour, *The One Day of the Year*, about a battle between a father and son over the place of war and the commemoration of war in their lives. The governors of the festival rejected the play as a slur on those Australians who had fought and died for their country. The ban caused anger and ridicule across the country, but the governors stood firm, their resolve stiffened by a military man in the machine of the festival, Major-General Ron Hopkins, who was once commandant of Duntroon, the national Military College in Canberra.

By the winter of that year, the Drama Committee was in despair once more, for an Australian play could not be found for the 1962 festival. Then in October Dutton showed his friends on the committee *The Ham Funeral* and they were, in Hopkins' words, 'scone hot' for the play.[13] The artistic director of the festival, Professor John Bishop, flew over to Dogwoods to discuss a production. White shilly-shallied in the next weeks, afraid of being burnt again and reluctant to give up the faint hopes he had of persuading Hugh Hunt to back a national tour. 'After feeling bitter all these years because nobody wanted to do it, I now find I am horrified when somebody gets excited about it, and am doing everything possible to stave off giving a definite answer,' he told Peggy Garland. 'Anyway, the producer, like all producers, says that this and that would have to be done to the play first, and even if I had the inclination, I certainly shall not have the time until February or March. But how would you feel about starting to fiddle about with something you had finished fourteen years ago?'[14]

Meanwhile, the governors of the festival had turned their eyes in other directions. At their request the Australian Ambassador to Washington Sir Howard Beale was investigating Archibald McLeish's Broadway hit *JB*, a verse drama about the trials of a modern Job.[15] These enquiries were still afoot in the New Year when the drama committee made its formal recommendation of *The Ham Funeral*. The governors deferred a decision; the few who had read White's play were nervous; the brewer Rolly Jacobs objected vehemently to its filth, for the young man of the play finds an abortion in a garbage bin. Scripts were distributed to all the governors, and the drama committee was asked to give the matter further consideration. Fundamental to the ugly farce that followed were two propositions: the governors had another play in mind, and these men were used always to having their way in Adelaide.

Among the governors were two brothers, Clive and Ewen Water-man who owned the Ozone chain of outback picture shows and the Adelaide Mercedes-Benz franchise. As businessmen with theatre inter-ests they were listened to very carefully. As always, the Watermans turned for advice to their manager, a canny, cheerful, dry little man called Glen McBride, who once ran variety acts on the old Tivoli circuit. McBride reported that White's play was 'not up to much' and filthy. McBride was then imposed on the drama committee, and when the committee reaffirmed its support for The Ham Funeral, McBride was the lone dissenter. The governors then rejected the play 'as a result of reports being received from reliable sources that box office receipts would be poor and also because the recommendation from the Drama Committee was not unanimous'.[16]

None of this had yet reached the press, but the uproar behind the scenes was such that the governors now invited the drama committee 'to advance concrete reasons' for The Ham Funeral. Two more men were imposed on the committee to bolster McBride's lone dissent, but one of these defected to the pro-White faction and wrote passionately on behalf of the play, warning the governors to 'think very seriously before turning down the opportunity of a world-première of a work of this class'.[17]

One member of the committee was absent through all this and his opinion was now crucial. Neil Hutchison was another of those Englishmen who had come to command the arts in Australia. The BBC had sent him out to Sydney, where he transferred to the ABC as Director of Drama and Features. Hutchison had declined to mark the publication of The Tree of Man with a radio feature on Patrick White. 'Why should we do one on him', he asked David Moore, 'when we haven't done one on Henry Handel Richardson?'[18] Hutchison then took over the Trust after Hugh Hunt returned to England. He must be given credit for picking up The One Day of the Year after its rejection by Adelaide. When the (revised) play opened in Sydney it was a huge success for Alan Seymour and the Trust.

Both sides in the Ham Funeral fracas hoped for Hutchison's support. When he finally read White's script he sent a damning report in time for the governors' meeting on 14 April: 'a piece of work which quite fails to reconcile poetry with social realism. I think it would be very tedious in production. There is practically no character development and the dialogue is insufferably mannered. As for the abortion in the dustbin . . . Really, words fail me!'[19] Heartened by this, armed with a long minority report from McBride, stiffened for the coming uproar by General Hopkins, the governors reaffirmed their rejection of The Ham Funeral. It was announced that the 1962 festival would present Bernard Shaw's Saint Joan – directed by an American academic with the young

Melbourne actress Zoe Caldwell as Joan – and McLeish's *JB*.

News of White's rejection went round the world. The minority and majority reports of the drama committee were leaked to the press. The one was high praise; the other condemned the play as 'unappetising fare'. While he was on the job, McBride attacked White's novels: 'In an interview with Mr Ryan of the Adelaide Circulating Library, the question was asked "Do many people read Patrick White's books?" The answer was "No-one will read them. Each comes out in a blaze of publicity. In the case of *Voss* the library purchased twenty two copies. We got rid of some of them for 5/– a copy, and the last was reduced to 2/– a copy.'[20]

White maintained the pose that things had turned out just as he expected. To Charles Wicks at the festival he wrote, 'Of course it will cause me much less trouble if the play is not put on! I am only sorry for those who have given me their support in the battle with the Philistines.' He urged Geoffrey Dutton not to worry. 'I am not worried at all.'[21]

In fact, White was roused to such a fury by the governors, that he sat down on May Day and began to draft the play which had been germinating in his mind for some time. To the task he brought all his White contempt for the coy pretences of respectable Australia. The pack of dogs that roam the suburb of Sarsaparilla in this 'suburban and vulgar' play, tell the truth for those who can face it: our lives are governed by desire. He told Peggy Garland, 'The new one is called *The Season at Sarsaparilla*, and is about the effect a bitch in season has on a certain suburban street. It has allowed me to blow off a lot of what I have been feeling about Australia.'[22]

The play poured out in a way that almost alarmed him. The first draft was done in only three weeks despite a bad chest – 'not that that interferes with writing, rather it seems to help'. He warned Dutton that *Sarsaparilla* was probably more shocking than *The Ham Funeral*: 'This one is purely Australian, and at the same time has burst right out of the prescribed four walls of Australian social realism. If I don't get this one on, and twist the tails of all the Adelaide aldermen, Elizabethan hack producers, and old maids dabbling in the Sydney theatre, I shall just about bust.'[23]

After the first draft he paused to correct the London proofs of *Riders in the Chariot* and then returned to the play. He was pleased. 'It seems more fluid somehow, more like music, whereas in *The Ham Funeral* I suspect myself of trying to push around troublesome groups of statuary.'[24] He worked at *Sarsaparilla* in the writing room of the *Manoora* on the voyage to Brisbane in June and finished the second draft a few days later in Maryborough. Back at Dogwoods he typed it up and sent copies to London and New York – and to his supporters in Adelaide who were preparing to bring off a coup: the première of *The Ham Funeral* by an amateur theatre at Adelaide University.

This was as far as could be imagined from the West End splash White had wanted to make with the play. But it was also the end of the line. No one else was interested. Harry Medlin, a bearded scientist at the university, had stepped in when the governors rejected the play, and offered White a production by the University Guild in the Union Hall in November. Both Dutton and Max Harris backed Medlin's plan. White accepted the offer, took a £25 advance against royalties and nominated the director. His choice was John Tasker. 'He is a young man who is sensitive to what is going on in theatre today.' Pale, flirtatious, caustic, beautiful, obstinate, John Tasker brought the excitement of theatre back into Patrick White's life. Lascaris remarked, 'Tasker was the virus.'[25]

Tasker made the first contact. The son of a coal-miner, he was rescued from the Hunter Valley at the age of eighteen by a lover who took him to London to study at the Central School of Speech and Drama. Four obscure years were spent in Vienna avoiding National Service, and then Tasker arrived back in Australia in 1959 full of energy and European ideas. White fobbed the young man off when he wrote out of the blue asking for a play, but he kept an eye on Tasker's work. A masked *Oedipus Rex* at the Cell Block in 1960 convinced White that this newcomer was the most promising director in Sydney. They met and liked one another. It mattered a great deal to White that Tasker was a Geminian: their birthdays were only days apart. When the question of finding a director for the Guild production arose, White named Tasker at once.

Tasker used his students at the National Institute of Dramatic Art to stage a reading of the play in early August 1961. For the first time White saw a performance – of a kind – of one of his plays. It needed work. He picked at the text for a month, 'loosened some congested passages, clarified the language generally, added a few effective lines, and expanded three main scenes: the ding-dong between the Landlord and the Landlady, the funeral feast, and the Landlady's attempted seduction of the Young Man'. His confidence waned towards the end and he sent off the final version to Adelaide rather nervously. The Guild was delighted, but asked him to drop some barbed lines in the prologue about the festival governors. White agreed under protest: 'I thought this production was by way of being an Anti-Festival, and so my hit at the governors was permissible. I have never been one to sit and smile sweetly when there was an offending eye to spit in, and there is, besides, a tradition of satiric rejoinder in English literature and drama.' He gave notice: he had never agreed to cut his novels and this would be the last cut made to his plays.[26]

White was involved directly in all the principal decisions taken by Tasker and the Guild in these weeks. He complained about the demands this made on his time and creativity, but he felt uniquely equipped for the task and could not have borne being left out. The Guild had very little cash. Most of the cast was amateur and only Joan Bruce was paid. She was not White's first choice as Mrs Lusty the landlady, but he was relieved that an actress of her stature was secured for the role. Despite Neil Hutchison's earlier vituperation, the Trust was persuaded to put £140 towards Tasker's fee. Having taken part in all of this, White was then shocked to be barred from rehearsals when the cast met in Adelaide in October. He conceded Tasker could be right: 'I might put too many spokes in his wheel.'[27]

The rehearsal weeks were an exciting time for White, for *Riders in the Chariot* was published in New York as the cast was working on the play, and the publication in London and Australia followed a few weeks later. At this time the Guild bought the rights to *Sarsaparilla* and in America a Houston theatre was asking for *The Ham Funeral*. Reports from Adelaide left White apprehensive at first, but by the end of the month he wrote to Tasker, 'For the first time since all the controversy over the *Ham Funeral* began, I feel it is going to be a success. You seem to have hatched the thing out, as it were. Even if it remains a bit of a curiosity as a play, I hope it is going to sweep you . . . to where you ought to be – in spite of all the little nonentities who try to apply the brake to everything one does . . .

'*Riders in the Chariot* keeps exploding at every letter delivery. I have now all the important American reviews, most of them very good. I have even had, for the first time ever, a remarkably good review in the *Sydney Morning Herald* . . . One of the most exciting recent bits of news is that Manès Sperber, a reader for Calmann-Levy, and himself a novelist, essayist, and philosopher, wants the option for all my available novels for that house. The French have been very cold since the failure of *Happy Valley* when published by Gallimard ten years ago. Now it looks as though I may get a hearing . . .

'Had a very nice letter from Sid Nolan, and the original of the *Riders* jacket so my collection of Nolans is growing without my ever having bought one! This painting is so much subtler and to the point when you actually see it; one would say it had actually been designed for the book, which in fact was not the case. I do hope the Nolans will come back here. His painting gives me such a lot in my work, and he claims I do the same for him . . .

'Must stop. There's a whole kitchenful of washing up. Looking forward to seeing you all next week, not only to escape these depressing duties, but because I feel you are really making something happen. (Have taken a ticket in the Opera House Lottery to float my New Venture Players in Chekov, Ibsen, Dürrenmatt, Ghelderode, Genet, Brecht – and even – you must allow the impresario one touch of vanity – Patrick White. Direction, of course: John Tasker.)'[28]

White left Lascaris to look after the animals – he would come over, alone, later – and flew to Adelaide on 10 November. Arriving that night at the Duttons' house in the Hills, he caused a flurry by remarking, 'I have a simple breakfast: lettuce and molasses.' The local chemist was woken for molasses. The Duttons were bemused by the sight of White standing every morning at the marble table in their kitchen mixing a green salad with garlic and molasses and oil. Despite the indignities the city had foisted on him, Adelaide struck White as a wonderful place to live. 'The vibrations are right,' he told the Kriegers. 'It is peaceful and civilised. A wonderful market full of *würst*, cheeses, herbs, *fresh* fruit and vegetables . . . I am living in the bush only twenty minutes from the centre. Rehearsals going well.'[29]

The literary world's attention was hardly focused on this première at the far end of the earth. But its curiosity was roused: the *Observer* and *New Statesman* would be represented on the opening night. Among Australians, the controversy over the play had dragged in many who were hardly interested in the theatre. *The Ham Funeral* had become a rallying point for those who were unhappy with the boring, official culture of Australia in the late 1950s and early 1960s, and hated the philistine power of the Establishment – the power, especially, to determine what was written and read in a country where books, films and plays continued to be censored and banned. By the time it opened in Adelaide on 15 November 1961, *The Ham Funeral* was an old play written, for the most part, in another country half a generation earlier, yet the fact of it being staged was like the waving of a banner of revolt.[30] Dutton wrote: 'Perhaps there was among the audience the thought that a reactionary Establishment was being beaten on its own ground, that the evening was going to be a triumph of the imagination over mediocrity. So it was.'[31]

White stood in the shadows at the back of the theatre. Apart from an attack of hiccups, he showed little sign of strain. The lights died. The young poet came forward, yawning,

> I have just woken, it seems. It is about . . . well, the time doesn't matter. The same applies to my origins. It could be that I was born in Birmingham . . . or Brooklyn . . . or Murwillumbah. What *is* important is that, thanks to a succession of meat pies (the gristle-and-gravy, cardboard kind) and many cups of pink tea, I am *alive*! Therefore . . . and this is the rather painful point . . . I

must go in soon and take part in the play, which, as usual, is a piece about eels. As I am also a poet . . . though, to be perfectly honest, I have not yet found out for sure . . . my dilemma in the play is how to take part in the conflict of eels, and survive at the same time . . . becoming a kind of Roman candle . . . fizzing for ever in the dark. (*Somewhat stern.*) Probably quite a number of you are wondering by now whether this is your kind of play. I'm sorry to have to announce the management won't refund any money. You must simply sit it out.[32]

The night was a triumph. White's verdict was, 'It turned out just about as well as it possibly could.' He won a great supporter in Harry Kippax, the country's leading critic, who found that night what he had been waiting years to find: a play by an Australian that broke free from the confines of Australian working-class characters and speech. 'Mr White can write bigger and probably better plays than this,' wrote Kippax, but *The Ham Funeral* 'brilliantly suggests a way out of the impasse in which the Australian drama finds itself . . . Mr White, at one blow, has demonstrated something that still needs to be learned in England and America – that drama's richest resource is language.'[33]

White was back in Sydney a few nights later at a British Council cocktail party for John Betjeman ('a *most* amiable old thing') when Neil Hutchison walked over looking, Lascaris observed, like a poodle that had wet the best carpet. 'Are you going to let the Trust do something about it?' Hutchison asked. White enjoyed being cold as Hutchison scribbled down telephone numbers to set up a lunch the following week.[34] There they struck an extraordinary deal: the Trust would mount a fully professional season of *The Ham Funeral* in Sydney but leave White the power to veto director, cast and even the theatre in which the play was to appear. He quickly did so, refusing to put the play into a university theatre with some untried Australian works, 'one about bodgies and widgies, and one about alcoholics at the Cross'. White insisted *The Ham Funeral* go into a city theatre, where it could be done 'with a flourish'.[35] A theatre was not found until winter.

The Sydney opening at the Palace in July 1962 was a second triumph for the play and White. 'I was well bricked up in a pillar of alcohol, and watched from the back row of the circle,' he told Dutton. 'I don't think I have ever been in such a full theatre in Sydney, and the audience was with the play.' There had been a torrent of publicity for White and Tasker. The set was redesigned, Zoe Caldwell had joined the cast as the phantom Girl. Harry Kippax wrote, 'I am not going to mince words or hedge against the future. I believe the professional performance of *The Ham Funeral* at the Palace . . . is an epoch-making event.'[36]

Roaming the foyers at the interval that night, White had taken grim pleasure in refusing to be photographed with a society newspaper columnist, Mrs Marcel Dekyvere, who was on the Trust board. 'I didn't see why I should so I refused.' What followed was reported on the front page of a Sydney paper under the block headline SOCIETY FEUD. Mrs Dekyvere – pictured with three poodles: 'All wearing our new sweaters' – gave vent to her disappointment in her column. 'I was so hoping the play would be a success, partly because I knew Mr White's mother Mrs Victor White many years ago. She and my mother worked together in the Red Cross shop in Rowe Street during the war. But despite this association, I couldn't bring myself to like Mr White's strange play. In fact I hated it. To my mind, the play was in very bad taste, with its sordidness and bad language.'[37]

By chance White and Dekyvere found themselves at a gallery that week. White strolled across. 'So you didn't like my play?'

'No, Mr White. I didn't.'

'Well, in my bad taste that you wrote about, I've just bought that painting you're admiring.'

She assured him, it was not his but his play's bad taste she disliked: the filth and bad language.

'But that's life.'

'Not my life.'

'You've been very lucky.'

She agreed. White suggested she stop writing about her Bible class in the column. He was very religious, too, he pointed out, but didn't publicise the fact. Mrs Dekyvere reminded him that we are all taught to be public witnesses for God.[38]

The Ham Funeral had only a two-and-a-half week slot at the Palace. The box office was slow for the first week, but in the second there was standing room only. On the last night Kippax watched the most vehement demonstration of applause he could remember in a Sydney theatre, 'a stamping tumult of enthusiasm which brought Patrick White, most retiring of men, onto the stage to thank all concerned'.[39] John Tasker threw a party afterwards, a terrific party, and there were those who saw White that night happier than they saw the man before or after.

The Adelaide and Sydney openings of *The Ham Funeral* were peaks separated by frustrating terrain. White was aware something had gone wrong in those months, but was unable to identify the problem. He turned fifty and talked of being on the brink of old age. 'My eyes and ears seem to be celebrating it by going off.' He suffered savage bouts of hay fever and asthma, brought on by rain and lush grass in the Castle Hill paddocks. A new naturopath was consulted. White confessed to

Huebsch, 'I am definitely one who needs a bit of magic.'[40] Milk and cream disappeared from his diet. The last of the schnauzers had to be destroyed. He was dispersing his unwanted friends.

Barred from rehearsals and waiting to go over to Adelaide, he had begun work on the Mrs Fraser novel. 'The characters would give me no rest.' To plunge in this way into new work as he faced the opening of a play became a pattern in his life, a way of shouting at the world to stay clear and leave him to 'burrow into something positive and forget the chaos'. He began in a familiar state of hope and frustration, afraid of forgetting 'those admirable small touches which flood through one's mind' before he could get them down on paper. 'I can never decide whether to rush at it, or go cautiously. Well, there it is, the same awful muddle as usual, which somehow, one prays, will turn into a novel.'[41]

Friends were quizzed for details. He was mastering the language of the sea to give the text authenticity. 'I have managed worse in the past.' As Mrs Fraser performed in the theatre of his mind, she merged in his imagination with the figure of Vivien Leigh. 'I can't stop seeing her as the woman in the novel,' he told Tasker. 'It would make a good film if it weren't for the fact that she and her leading man – Burt Lancaster for preference – would have to go through most of the action practically stark naked.'[42]

After writing from midnight until dawn for a few weeks, the flow of words was choked off. This he blamed on the opening looming in Adelaide and the critical hullabaloo over *Riders in the Chariot*.[43] With Adelaide behind him he got back to work on the manuscript, but then with about a third of the first draft written he embroiled himself in a public squabble over who was to take credit for *The Ham Funeral* appearing in Adelaide. White defended Dutton and Max Harris against the claims of the Trust. Letters poured out of Dogwoods. 'It is more important to me to stand by those who supported me in the beginning, and forced the play into the light. My conscience would not allow me to take any other line.' He added ruefully to Medlin, 'I wonder whether I shall ever be able to get down to creative work again. All these arguments and wranglings have sickened me, and driven everything else out of my head.'[44] He returned to the manuscript, but then paused for Christmas.

This was always an event. The son had inherited his mother's love of giving presents but, unlike her, he had an instinct for the perfect gift. Shopping began weeks before Christmas, but at the last moment White usually found himself up to his elbows at Dogwoods in string ends and scraps of wrapping paper and late cards and cooking. This year he cooked two huge meals for six people: one for Christmas Eve and the other for Boxing Day. He knew he would reach the New Year exhausted – he often did – but in the early weeks of 1962 he found himself unable to return to his work.

The notion of writing a nineteenth-century novel seemed suddenly unsatisfying, so conventional and so remote from his own life. He was tired. He could not whip himself back to the book. After *The Ham Funeral* and *Riders in the Chariot* his real and phantom enemies were in retreat, and there was no immediate need to vindicate himself. The pleasures of his solitary life at the desk had palled after the theatre. A world of new friends had come to him through Tasker. Where once he had hung about on the fringe, now he had a theatre crowd of his own, another family. This was delightful and diverting. And with Tasker around, said Zoe Caldwell, 'It was always Geisha time.'45

Lascaris stood apart from this theatre life, not excluded but at an inner distance. He did not speak showbiz; he did not share White's fascination with actresses; he disapproved of Tasker. But life was calmer at Dogwoods when White was writing plays: there were no outbursts of rage with plays, not like the novels. He looked on White's absorption in the lives and gossip and intrigues of the theatricals as the curiosity of a novelist at work.

In this confused time White opened himself a little to Ben Huebsch: 'I have begun to feel the five or six novels I still have inside me might just be novels, and that I must do quite a lot of stocktaking before I start anything else of that nature. I think perhaps when I do write a novel it will be something I have never contemplated writing before. I don't yet quite understand what has happened, but something has, both inside and out. I have just celebrated these suspicions by having the worst asthmatic blow-out I have experienced in ten years, and still feel rather groggy, while at the same time, stimulated! I suppose it all amounts to this: if I went on as I have been doing I should find myself a comfortable mediocrity, whereas I am looking for an unopened door, through which I can step and find myself rejuvenated.'46

He was in great demand at Sydney parties that summer. Patrick White was a name, a presence even to those who found his work impenetrable. Stories of his awkward remarks and eccentric habits did the rounds of the city's society. White was sought and feared at a dinner table. He was at a Macquarie Galleries' celebration – 'much shouting, warm beer, and searing sherry' – when the painter John Olsen, just back from Majorca, gave him a message from Robert Graves. ' "Tell Patrick White when you go back to Australia that I think he is the greatest novelist writing in English today". And here I am,' added Olsen, 'like the carrier pigeon.' White was astonished.47

Through his devoted admirer Margery Williams, White found himself on the British Council circuit, and lunch at Dogwoods was often the most stimulating event on the Australian tours of English writers and actors. When Hayley Mills came to lunch White pressed on her a script of *The Ham Funeral* to take to Joan Littlewood at Stratford East. The day Sir John Gielgud was at Dogwoods the *coq au vin* fell on the kitchen floor. The actor was surprised to find that the novelist he admired 'seemed so very stage struck'. [48]

White had seen none of Barry Humphries' shows when Margery Williams persuaded him, rather against his will, to go to *A Nice Night's Entertainment* at the Macquarie Auditorium in Phillip Street. He emerged very excited. Unknown to him, as he worked away in Sarsaparilla, Humphries had been exploring the same vein of suburban satire in Melbourne's Moonee Ponds. That night White saw for the first time the dowdy (in those days) and opinionated housewife Edna Everage. On the phone to Margery Williams next morning, he declared Humphries a 'potential genius'. [49] When they met later in Melbourne, White began to write for Humphries. He became, for many years, the man's friend, protector and promoter.

Sydney's greatest scalp-hunter was Hannah Lloyd Jones, the Ethel Kelly of the Menzies years. She was a friend of the Victor Whites in the days when hardly anyone in society opened their doors to her. Time and money had seen her triumph. When Stravinsky conducted in Sydney that summer White went to dinner afterwards at Rosemont, the Lloyd Jones' place in Woollahra. White and the composer sat together. 'He was quite different from what I expected – which was something tall, cold, and cerebral. In reality he is a dear old thing, but very old, tiny and arthritic. His wife is a kind of St Bernard: one imagines her carrying him about the house in her teeth. Robert Craft the young American conductor, who is the Boswell to Stravinsky's Johnson, and chief interpreter of his music, seemed somewhat peevish at dinner last night. Perhaps not enough attention. Stravinsky and I sat together at dinner. He told me: "I am a professional drunkard. All the time I drink whisky, whisky, whisky!" I must say he held it very well. During dessert he passed me shelled walnuts on the palm of his very soft hand. Lots of rings.' [50]

Craft made his own record of that evening. White was 'a rugged figure with a craggy jaw and a hard stare . . . he prefers to talk about ballet, books, the music of Mahler. When he talks at all, that is, for he is a man of silent temperament – the only nonbuoyant Australian so far.' [51]

White was suddenly writing short stories, the first since those few finished in Athens in 1945. Three or four came into his head at once, and he put them down in short bursts, finding it was usually possible to knock one off before the next 'onrush of exasperation from outside developments'. He had not thought his style was suitable, but saw them now as a way of working through his confusion to get back to novels. He reflected: 'I think probably I have come to it now, apart from the emotional reasons, through the artificiality of the theatre. There is something a bit dishonest about the short story, just as there is about a play.'[52]

The first story was 'Willy-Wagtails by Moonlight', the tale of a fornicating birdwatcher called Arch Mackenzie. The adulterer is a savage portrait of Margery Williams' husband Norman. White's friendship with the Williams of the British Council fell into a familiar pattern: he liked the wife and loathed her spouse. Her devotion somehow survived White's contempt for a husband she also loved. Margery Williams was the most devoted disciple for years, one of those who sensed pain in the writer's existence and was drawn to comfort him. White said to her once, 'My life is unbearable.' If he was cruel, then she saw this as evidence of his stature. 'His is a great spirit, and that enters all aspects of the man. If he is nasty, then he is going to be very, very nasty.' She knew what 'Willy-Wagtails' was about. She told him part of the story, and it was written, in part, to avenge her. Several of the stories began with her and she was proud of him telling her once, 'You are my eyes and ears'.[53]

She told – or perhaps reminded – White of the painter Bill Dobell's strange fear of opening his mail. This became the phobia of the young man in 'The Letters', but the man sprang not from the painter but a sweet, rich queen called George Blackwood, who was dragged off the London stage by his mother and brought back to Sydney before the war to manage the family engineering works. Mother and son lived at Mareeba, their 'Tudor' mansion in a forest of gum trees on the road to Castle Hill. The mother of the story has a dash of Ruth in her, but she is really a portrait of Geoffrey Dutton's mother, the fabulous and ancient beauty of Anlaby who died at this time.[54] Sybil Thorndike is said to have remarked, waving from her car as she left a lunch with Mrs Dutton at Anlaby, 'I wish I could play that role.'

'Being Kind to Titina' was a sketch for a few fragments of an enormous novel White imagined himself writing at the very end of his career. 'My Athenian Family' would be a trilogy tracing the vicissitudes of the Lascaris family in this century, beginning in Smyrna with 'The Sweet Waters of Asia', then a volume set in Alexandria, and a third in Athens which would end at the invasion in 1941 with a 'Greek version of a Turner sunset with a lot of brown Byzantine figures in the foreground – at least the closing scenes, with the Germans approaching Athens, and refugees leaving'.[55] 'Being Kind to Titina' covers only a few years in the upbringing of a young man very like Manoly Lascaris, raised by snobbish but remarkable aunts in Alexandria and Athens. When White writes about Greeks, his fear of being lush and sentimental does not weigh so heavily on him. The deliberate harshness he adopts as a countermeasure is less in evidence. Greece refreshed his imagination, as if it were drawing not only on his memories of the Mediterranean, but also on the innocence, peasant devotion, the pure and spare landscape of his own childhood.

When *Harper's* bought 'Titina' for $300, White began to have high hopes for selling the stories in America. These hopes came to nothing in the end. 'Miss Slattery and her Demon Lover' first entered his head as a screenplay – for Marilyn Monroe or Shirley MacLaine – but he wrote it out as a short story and sent it off to *Esquire*. White was astonished when his agent warned him that this tale of a woman whose flair with a stockwhip turns her Hungarian lover from an ogre to a poodle might be 'too far out for the rather prudish American magazines'. He took the point as magazine after magazine turned it down. Finally he sent it to the *New Yorker*. 'I'd like to appear just once in that glossy deceiver.'[56]

White was paradoxically keen to keep out of American magazines the story he judged his best, 'The Woman Who Wasn't Allowed to Keep Cats', for he feared if it reached Athens – via the Lascaris of Florida – it might cause mortal offence to Manoly's sister Catina and her husband the writer Dimitri Photiades. They are the originals of Kikitsa and her somnolent Anatolian intellectual husband Aleko Alexiou. White told his agent, 'Of course if the story appears eventually in a volume I shall have to face the music.' Meanwhile the magazine *Meanjin* rejected the story. White explained this surprising rebuff as a response to the story's send-up of a certain kind of dated Left-wing intellectual. 'It also has a slight Lesbian flavour which might offend, but I had hoped it would jazz things up a bit at *Meanjin*. Australian literature is inclined to become unbearably solemn.'[57]

Meanjin did accept 'Down at the Dump', but then the printers refused to set the swear words. The editor, Clem Christesen, offered half-heartedly to make a test case of this, but begged White to make changes to save them embarrassment. White replied, 'The whole point of the story is that here are purity and incorruptibility germinating on the rubbish dump.' But he put up only token resistance and offered to change 'fuckun' to 'flickin' ' and 'shit' to 'dung'. When the story appeared in *Meanjin*, White was plagued by complaints and wrote in exasperation to Christesen: 'Surely I have shown over and over again that the point I am trying to make is the distinction between rich, ripe, fertile vulgarity and sour trash which silts up, chokes and kills?'[58]

Writing these stories did not bring him back to the novel as he had hoped it would. The manuscript of *A Fringe of Leaves* remained obstinately in his drawer.

The relationship between White and Tasker had taken on a peculiar complexity. White was still delighted with the young man but, as preparations went ahead for the opening of *The Season at Sarsaparilla* in September, they began to quarrel. Tasker wanted changes. He accused White of getting laughs at the expense of people he did not understand. White found this insulting, and their bickering left him depressed and doubtful. In March 1962 he wrote to Dutton, 'It seems to me we are in a state of deadlock, for although lines can be altered, and even whole scenes, an author can't alter his "slant" if a producer doesn't have faith in a play. Nor can I think of anyone else who would produce the play as I want it produced. Don't know what will come of this situation.'[59]

White set his 'charade of suburbia' in Mildred Street, Sarsaparilla in the summer of 1960. This is one of those jumbled Castle Hill streets where a sanitary man, a businessman and a chap in men's wear might live in houses side by side. That summer the families in the street see birth and death, love and betrayal. The background music to their lives is the sound of randy dogs roaming about after a bitch on heat. 'Those dogs!' Girlie Pogson wails. 'It shouldn't be allowed.'[60]

Girlie is one of White's great inventions, and her terrible refinement is the butt of *Sarsaparilla*. She rose from his uncomfortable recollections of the woman with daughters who lived next to Barwon Vale: 'very hard headed, a shrewd bookkeeper, thin and wiry, with the tight perm that I always see Girlie Pogson as having'. The pretentious Girlie has suffered the fate of marriage to a businessman on the lower rungs of the ladder, troubled, as Fritz Krieger was, by the credit squeeze.[61] Girlie is initiating her little daughter Pippy in the respectable lies that rule her existence. But the Pogsons' efforts to protect their 'impressionable' daughter are undone by Nola Boyle, the wife of the sanitary man next door. Nola Boyle is motherly, candid and sexually charged. Pippy learns from this 'suburban nymphomaniac' what the dogs are up to and watches, half-comprehending, Nola's adultery with Digger Masson.[62] From the stories Digger tells of the Western Desert, it seems Digger and Ernie Boyle and Patrick White fought side by side in the Cyrenaican campaign.

Sarsaparilla has a pregnant wife, a corrupt alderman, a post office clerk in love, and another of White's self-conscious young men struggling to break free and start a life of his own. The play inhabits the same territory as *The Tree of Man*: the same patch of country on the edge of Sydney and the same ordinary lives. With immense seriousness in the novel, and now as comedy in the play, White was searching for the mystery and poetry that might make a few of these lives bearable. *Sarsaparilla* has some of the stature of *The Tree of Man*. 'A kind of folk piece,' White called it, 'with overtones'.[63]

GIRLIE. It's peaceful enough in Mildred Street. Nowadays, at

least. Remember all those dogs? How disgraceful! I'll never forget. Anyway, it's finished.
PIPPY. But it's gunna begin again.
GIRLIE. When?
PIPPY. In six months time.
GIRLIE. But it shouldn't be allowed!
PIPPY. Every six months. For ever and ever.[64]

After stormy beginnings the two men settled down to work on the play, each unable to relinquish a single detail of the production. 'We have terrible rows along the way which from time to time threaten to wreck everything,' White told Waters. There was an early row when Tasker's designer produced two sets which White disliked. The playwright asked Desmond Digby to 'walk round the streets of Sarsaparilla' to get an idea of what he was after. Digby produced a simple design of three adjoining box houses and three attached backyards. White was delighted: 'He has managed to catch the essence of Australian suburbia for *The Season*.'[65]

White and Digby met over dinner at Eleanor Arrighi's, for Digby was sharing a studio in Darlinghurst with Arrighi's daughter Luciana, who was beginning her own distinguished career as a designer. Digby had left New Zealand to study set design at the Slade, worked at Glyndebourne and came back out to Australia, where he exhibited his paintings very successfully and made a career designing opera sets for the Trust. On the surface Digby was an unlikely choice for *Sarsaparilla* – 'baroque glamour is his real line'[66] – but White saw that beneath this frou-frou lay a sharp satiric instinct. At first meeting he found Digby sharp, stage-struck and camp in the Ronald Waters style. The *Sarsaparilla* set was the beginning of their enduring friendship.

Over supper after a terrible performance of *St Joan* in Sydney, Zoe Caldwell declared she wanted to play Nola Boyle more than any other part she had ever read. White hesitated: 'not a part of her' was anything like the sanitary man's wife. 'Zoe is minute, with a sharp, rather fine face, whereas Nola Boyle is a big blowsy overflowing blonde about ten years older.' But White fell in love with this engaging and candid actress who seemed twenty women in one. They had lunch and she won White over. 'I hope we gave each other the courage to face certain aspects of *The Season*. I find we look at many things through the same eyes.'[67] First she took the role of the Girl in *The Ham Funeral* at the Palace, then returned home to Melbourne, where her mother got to work building her a body out of an old corset. That winter the hair she had cropped for St Joan grew into a lion's mane.

White could not remember a better season for sarsaparilla at Castle Hill. The vine was smothering shrubs all along Showground Road, but this year he had a superstitious dread of tearing it out. As he left for his last meeting with Tasker before the director's departure for Adelaide, a dog was trying to rape a bitch outside the Dogwoods gate. 'So all the right omens are there!'[68]

White flew over only a few days before opening night, an event which drew a swathe of Adelaide society, including the Governor. The etiquette of such vice-regal occasions demanded black ties and long white gloves, but White refused to dig out the dinner jacket he had packed away at the outbreak of the war: 'has probably turned to lace by now; I daren't look at it . . . I don't want to wear a dinner jacket again in my lifetime.'[69] In a plain black suit he hung back once again in the shadows. The audience stood for 'God Save the Queen' as the Governor arrived, but wafting over their heads as they settled down in their seats came the theme from the radio soap opera *Blue Hills*. There was a roar of recognition, and the night that began on this note of pleasure ended in triumph. At its heart was Zoe Caldwell's Nola. Kippax called her 'tawny-headed, a proud slattern . . . the childless Nola, the trapped Nola struggling in the throbbing insistent flesh, mother of men and lover of men – in slack shuffle, in taut and ugly stance, in wide, generous movements of love and desire and regret, in sidelong hooded glance or in blazing candour'.[70]

The Adelaide season sold out at once. White was thrilled with the figures: 'Far more important than the first night was the second, when people actually paid to stand!' He wrote all over the world to tell friends, editors and agents that 4,226 people came to eight performances and one hastily arranged extra matinée. The show made a profit of £1,200, a third of which went to the Trust for paying the salaries of Tasker and Caldwell. 'It's all becoming very vulgar but I shall be glad when some vulgar money starts coming in.'[71]

Sarsaparilla closed in Adelaide on 22 September and opened in Melbourne a month later. Caldwell was Nola Boyle once again, but this was a new production by the Union Theatre Repertory Company directed by John Sumner. Sumner was then best known for having directed the first productions in Australia and London of *The Summer of the Seventeenth Doll*. White toyed with the idea of withdrawing the rights from Sumner in favour of Tasker. Sumner was appalled. He had never met White, and this capricious action confirmed all he had heard of the difficulties of dealing with him. Knowing he had nothing to lose, Sumner wrote to White pointing out that much work had been done and many actors had given up other commitments to be in his production. White relented.

He did not appear in Melbourne until a few days before opening night and the cast awaited his arrival with apprehension. After sitting silently through a run of the play he announced laconically, 'It's fine.'

The cast warmed to the sight of this stiff man hanging about backstage breathing the atmosphere of the theatre. He was not the abrasive figure they expected, nor quite the 'darling' Zoe Caldwell promised. He was very fast at the dressing room sport of finding the perfect nickname to skewer a person. He stayed with Zoe Caldwell. 'Zoe drove me about madly. When things get particularly depressing at a rehearsal you have swigs out of the whisky bottle at the red lights on the way home. Anyway, it was all beaut, and I loved it.' He liked Sumner and reported to Tasker that Sumner's production 'has a strain of appealing mellowness running through it, but it lacks the style and brilliance of yours. I shall ask for you to do the Trust production, because I have always felt it was your play despite the quarrels.'[72]

In these hectic days, White had his first real contact with the 'puritanical, stiff and forbidding' city of Melbourne. With old friends and new faces he enjoyed himself very much. 'There was a lot of lunching out.' He met Barry Humphries for the first time and began the story 'Clay' with the idea of turning it later into a short film for Humphries and Caldwell. Clay is a peculiar young man who writes a novel that springs to life, so ruining his own mundane existence. This twist took even White by surprise. 'It has turned out very peculiar and surrealist.' Humphries waited with White in a sordid lane to read the *Age* review of *Sarsaparilla* as it came off the press. Clutching the paper to his breast, Humphries intoned the headline: 'PATRICK WHITE IS A BORN PLAYWRIGHT'. Later notices were not so complimentary. There were complaints that this was a trivial comedy. 'No flowers there,' White remarked, 'only fury.' Yet business boomed at the Union Theatre and *The Season at Sarsaparilla* took over £5,000 in four weeks. White declared to Dutton, 'I am pocketing my triviality with no more than a grim smile.'[73]

Melbourne was the high point. By the time *Sarsaparilla* closed in November 1962, White had enjoyed popular and critical success with his plays in three cities. The old ambition had been achieved: now he was a playwright and novelist. The lesson he drew from the last years was that if he fought to get his plays on to the stage, crowds would come. He had already written a third play, *A Cheery Soul*, and a fourth was kicking around in his head: 'Everybody talking in the right context. I think the time will soon be ripe.'[74]

Before returning to Sydney, White sat down on the terrace of Sumner's little house in Toorak and read *A Cheery Soul* to him from beginning to end. Sumner had seen the script already and not liked it. White read in his asthmatic baritone, giving the name of each character before every speech. It took hours. Sumner felt defeated before he began. He reflected that it was Patrick White after all, 'So we must have a go.' White wrote afterwards to Tasker, 'he seemed genuinely impressed. But of course Adelaide must have it if they want it first'.[75]

The sight of Patrick White pouring his energy into the theatre distressed many of his admirers. Few had the courage to say so to his face. His friends the Tildesley sisters, the twin pillars of the British Drama League, held a party after the Sydney opening of *The Ham Funeral* at which Beatrice Tildesley declared, 'We must all get together and save Patrick from himself. No more plays!' Her remarks got back to him, and a coolness came between them for years. Back in Sydney after the opening of *Sarsaparilla*, White was confronted by the bookseller Alec Sheppard, who told him he was wasting himself and added, 'Of course the trouble with you is that you are in love with Tasker and Zoe.' White was stung: 'I can assure everybody that John T. is the last person who would lead me astray, and that I have been many times on the verge of wringing his bloody neck. I shan't deny that I am a bit in love with Zoe, but then everybody is.'[76]

Huebsch looked on White's 'flights in other fields' with misgivings. Though the old man said nothing, White sensed his objections and tried to explain himself: 'I have been so drained by theatre politics, and sometimes wonder whether I shouldn't ease myself gently out of that world and back to the quieter one in which novels are written. But the theatre does fascinate me, especially in this country where it hardly exists in native form; I feel I want to be in at its creation.' From the first, Huebsch's colleague Marshall Best had not held back: after *The Ham Funeral* opened in Adelaide he told White cheerfully that he hoped the experience would poison him against the theatre, 'as I want you to go on using your best talents for your novels'.[77]

White responded to these hints with tirades against the theatre and theatricals. To Stern: 'Theatrical life in Australia is full of traps and bitchery.' To Christesen of *Meanjin*, whom he met for the first time in Melbourne: 'I shall have no peace for a long time to come . . . I hate the theatre.' To Dutton: 'It poisons one's life.' White was personally entangled once more in negotiations with managements in London and New York: 'There are so many business details which an agent is not capable of dealing with.' He was not blind to the role of his own character in the multiple frustrations of theatre: 'The right kind of dramatist probably loves to *collaborate* in putting a play on the stage, whereas I am quite unsuited to this sort of thing temperamentally. I have always been used to doing everything on my own.' But yet he was driven inexorably on. 'I do regret all this entanglement with the theatre. On the other hand I mean to have my way.'[78]

All these theatrical scenes were coloured by White's volatile relationship with John Tasker. White did not doubt his talent, but by late 1962 his affection for the young man was souring. 'His life is one long card game, with a stacked pack. I don't really feel I can go along any more.' But White did, for he found himself in the galling position of *needing* this man. Tasker was headstrong and tactless in his dealings with White and he had an odd quality that showed often in his career: he was a protégé born to antagonise his patrons. The biggest problem between them was White's refusal to countenance changes to his scripts. When Tasker was unable to persuade him face to face, he began to scheme. In those schemes White sensed betrayal. All this came to a head over *A Cheery Soul*. White gave him the script after lunch one day at Dogwoods. Tasker rose from the sofa some hours later and in what White called 'his most loutish manner', declared the play unstageable. He suggested cuts. White adamantly refused. He let Tasker know that he rated this play above *Voss* and *Riders in the Chariot*. Tasker thought it needed 'a hell of a lot of work'.[79]

A Cheery Soul began as a short story, based on the life of Alex Scott, a much-loved bore in Castle Hill who had come a day a week to help in the garden at Dogwoods.[80] She was fifteen stone of tough old lady with a crew cut, an army hat and a pair of flapping shorts worn in all weathers. Though she was a good worker she had a taste for beer and could not shut up. Out of her mouth poured handy hints, maxims, stray facts, anecdotes, recipes, new theories, and frank observations. After a few meetings she gave the sort of blunt advice old friends would hesitate to offer after a lifetime's intimacy. 'I am praying', she told White one day as they pulled weeds together, 'that someday you will write something good.' Her legs were her glory, and there was a shoe-box of photographs somewhere to prove how wonderful they once were. She had danced with the Prince of Wales, or perhaps the story went that the prince put a two shilling piece between her perfect thighs. Scottie suffered a breakdown while working behind the counter at David Jones and outdoor work was prescribed as a cure. So she gardened and babysat round Castle Hill. As a result of her ordeal she fancied herself as an expert on mental illness. She told White, 'You're borderline.' She was also a Christian, converted after reading the Bible cover to cover in a wet fortnight. 'Before that I was pagan. But suddenly I saw.' She taught at St Paul's Sunday School and outsang the choir. She was one of the reasons worship became impossible in Castle Hill. Somehow, she came into a bit of money, put on lipstick and disappeared for a few months overseas. On her return she retired to the Mowll Memorial Village, a Church of England home set up in one of the biggest houses on the ridge. She and White had a showdown over roses pruned back to the stump: 'What? You're not one of those who're *afraid* to prune?'[81] Something went wrong at the Mowll: Scottie claimed she pulled out of her own accord because they didn't treat her properly. Perhaps she was thrown out. From a cottage in the bush she continued to rain down on her old families gauzy pink birthday cards and little Christmas presents she could not afford. Scottie never forgot the children she 'sat' and spread a haze of guilt over the district.

White called his cheery soul Miss Docker: 'a wrecker, who first of all almost destroys two private lives, then a home for old people, and finally the Church, by her obsession that what she is doing for other people is for their own good. Only at the end for a moment she gets a glimpse of the truth when a dog lifts his leg on her in the street.'[82] White's Miss Docker is Scottie with a dash of Marjorie Barnard's companion Vera Murdoch, a worthy woman but a great talker whom White found 'One of the most crashing Philistines I have ever met.'[83] The cheery soul is darker, more splendidly awful and more decayed than either woman. The same impulse transformed the Chinese Room of the Mowll: in place of the innocent souvenirs, the tea-sets and lanterns gathered on Archbishop and Mrs Mowll's missionary expeditions to China, are the enormous *cloisonné* vases, threadbare rugs and black shadows of the Chinese Room of the Sundown Home.

As White wrote the short story, he began to hear Miss Docker speaking in the voice of Nita Pannell, a short, plump and dynamic actress who had made her name as the mother in *The One Day of the Year*. White met Pannell during the Sydney season of Seymour's play and was so impressed that he wanted her to be the first Mrs Lusty, but she was then carried off to the London season of *The One Day of the Year*. Now he sent her the galleys of the Miss Docker story – it was to appear in the *London Magazine* in September 1962 – and asked if she would like to create the part on stage. 'If it comes off as I hope it will, it will put you in the position you should be in as an actress. It will require a virtuoso performance, from comedy to tragedy, but you can give that.' Pannell was rather appalled: 'I read the short story again and again and finally accepted, knowing full well the enormity of the undertaking – a completely *unloved* woman.'[84]

He wrote the play in the winter of 1962, happy to feel he was suggesting 'inwardness' for the first time, 'the way one can in a novel, but now without clogging the dramatic action'. It was probably August when he showed the script to Tasker and sent a copy to Harry Medlin at the Guild. Medlin was very unhappy with what he read. He thought *A Cheery Soul* too poetic and the poetry not translated into drama: 'More like the dramas of Shelley and Keats.' And it called for a cast of thirty. The Guild prevaricated for a few weeks and then rejected it. Tasker encouraged them in this and may have been hoping to force White to make changes. If so, the tactic did not work. White wrote scornfully to Peggy Garland: 'The university scientists who usually take the first plunge with my plays seem to have been shocked by the fact that God plays a certain part in this one: a randy slut and a bitch in season were different matters. But I mean to see *A Cheery Soul* on the stage if I bust, because I think it is by far my best play so far.'[85]

Once it was sold to John Sumner, Tasker began to show fresh enthusiasm for the play and spoke of a première in Perth in early 1963 to be directed by him. But White felt it was too late. He wrote to Charles Osborne, who had published the short story in the *London Magazine*: 'It is a great pity, because he is the most brilliant director in Australia – perhaps I should say the only brilliant one – but I can't submit to any more of what gets dished out. He is about to depart for Perth in a pale tremble to produce *Bartholomew Fair* with 50 actors and 20 monkeys, or 20 actors and 50 monkeys, I forget which. Perhaps a monkey will be the solution to his problem. Has been appearing in Sydney in pale blue lined with cherry silk, a cornflower in the buttonhole. Poor thing, ought to have been out of that ten years ago. But speaking sincerely, all this business has been a great disappointment to me. I had hoped he would produce *all* my plays, but he would have to be different. He is a destroyer at heart.'[86]

Though he railed against Tasker, White urged his friends not to spread these angry remarks. 'I don't want to prejudice his career in any way.' He still wanted Tasker to direct any London productions, and Tasker was his choice for the new play which he had started writing after coming home from the Melbourne season of *Sarsaparilla*. The new play was *A Night on Bald Mountain*: 'The title deliberately pinched from Moussorgsky. If it comes off, it will be the first Australian tragedy.'[87] He saw Michael Redgrave playing the lead and, with such a name in his cast, the governors would be forced to accept him and Tasker and the play for the 1964 Adelaide Festival.

Every summer Geoff and Nin Dutton took a party over to their house on Kangaroo Island. White had refused a couple of invitations, but in 1962 he and Lascaris flew over to Adelaide and reached the island a few days before Christmas.

Life there was simple and generous in an old house perched above a deserted bay. On hot, still mornings they swam early and trooped back, fourteen adults and children, for long breakfasts of eggs and fish. They learnt to beat White to the sink, for he sprang to the washing up and took hours over it. 'Very meticulous: all the knives were just so; all the plates rinsed three times,' Nin Dutton recalled. 'This not only took a long time when people would prefer to be out swimming or fishing or whatever was on that day, but there was very little water.' Water was drawn from deep tanks, and at night kerosene lamps were lit through the house. They spent the week reading, swimming, eating and fishing on rocks standing knee deep in surf. White found it fascinating, though he was no fisherman. 'Fortunately there were so many fish they just couldn't help coming my way,' he told Stern. 'Our hosts were the Geoffrey Duttons . . . he is one of our better poets and a historian in his own right. He and his wife are two of the people with whom I feel completely happy.'[88]

White obeyed the Duttons' rule that on the island there was no writing; but once back in Sydney he wrote *about* Rocky Point and the house party – with Christian names – in the novella 'Dead Roses'. The Duttons are barely disguised as Val and Gil Tulloch. Some in the Kangaroo Island party were outraged to see themselves in print and urged the Duttons to break with White over this betrayal. They defended him: 'Artists don't operate like that. You have to allow.'[89]

Waiting for White at home were the proofs of 'Being Kind to Titina'. To his astonishment he found *Harper's* had made deep cuts to the text, bowdlerised the story and ironed out White's prose into 'a kind of, well, "magazinese" to coin a sufficiently awful word. I cannot believe their readers are as stupid or puritanical as they would like to think . . . it is a sad, even a terrifying thought.'[90] The magazine replied with the usual excuses about 'length' and asked White to make his own cuts. He refused, withdrew the story, and with gritted teeth repaid *Harper's* fee. He told his agent to withdraw all his pieces still on offer to American magazines. 'Miss Slattery and her Demon Lover' was retrieved from *New Yorker*. White never after placed a story in America.

Despite this ugly curtain-raiser, he faced 1963 in a mood of almost sunny optimism. The break on the island had done him good and there was much good news for him on his return. It seemed *A Night on Bald Mountain*, which he had finished before Christmas, would be accepted for the next festival, and a Sydney theatre had at last been found for *Sarsaparilla* which would open in the coming winter. His pleasure in both these developments was a little overshadowed by Zoe Caldwell's departure for America. His star would be out of reach. 'How shattering these airport departures are,' he told the Duttons. 'Made me remember with longing the nostalgic days of shipside farewells.' He and Lascaris were themselves shortly to leave on another world tour and would spend about six months away. They began to invite friends to farewell dinners. Chicken was large on the menu. 'The worst part of leaving', White confessed to Dutton, 'is having to kill off our old hens. I must commit murder twice a week every week before we go, and they come racing towards me, wings outstretched, asking for it!'[91]

Standing on the roof of a grim new block of flats, the Queen looked down on the terrace houses of Sydney and remarked, 'You have a lot more slum clearance to do here.' On that busy March morning, Her Majesty had already opened a medical school, and ahead lay a lunch for prominent citizens on the royal yacht *Britannia*. The sun was shining after days of rain, and seventy-nine people collapsed at Circular Quay waiting for the Queen and Prince Philip to return to the yacht.

White was in the crowd. He had hesitated for only a moment before accepting the invitation to lunch. He explained to his friends, 'One might use little bits of it later on.'[92] Lascaris had driven him, after a night of bronchial complications and vomiting, to Parramatta station. He felt as he sat on the train in his new black summer suit like a waiter going on duty. After steadying himself with a couple of vodkas at the Newcastle Hotel, he took his position near the gangway. A rolling roar down George Street announced the royal progress. The faint straightened, eyes brightened, flags wagged as she drove in sight. The Queen was in blue and the Prince wore tweed. At the top of the gangway, they waved and disappeared. Then the guests followed them up the red carpet.

Sailors were slapping rifle butts and equerries strolled forward to shake hands and marshal the guests in the saloon for introductions. An Australian who was the army equerry appeared to have read some of White's books, and confessed that the copy of *Voss* had disappeared mysteriously from the ship. White wondered, silently, if the Prince had thrown it out of the porthole 'after reading half of Chapter 1'. Once assembled the guests seemed a very odd bunch. There were admirals and generals, a few industrialists, Warwick Fairfax, the proprietor of the *Sydney Morning Herald* and the remarkable Mary who was now his wife, the swimmer Murray Rose, Joern Utzon, the architect of the Opera House, and Doris Fitton. White reported to Desmond Digby that Doris was in her element, 'doing all that *grande dame* stuff she'd learnt in rep, tremendous curtsy while Lady This and Lady That were tottering and nearly falling under their chiffon hats.

'Lunch was really very good – rolls of smoked salmon with scrambled egg at the side (it's worth remembering), tournedos on foie gras with a salad, and *profiterolles* with chocolate sauce. I have never sat at such a long mahogany table. There were some rather ugly gold urns down the centre, and vases of yellow and white flowers. *They* sat on either side, and I was at the lower end, so could look right down and observe. I was between Murray Rose, who is a most civilised young man, able to talk about things, and a Mrs Parbury, a youngish woman with heavily loaded eyelashes, who is a niece of the Duchess of Gloucester. She came out here originally to be with her auntie, and fell for Parbury, a tall dark handsome Australian of family . . . My mother used to know the Parburys in her youth on the Hunter and I can remember her telling me in shocked tones that whenever the Parburys wanted to go for another trip they sold off a paddock. I used that in connection with the Goodmans in *The Aunt's Story*. However, I couldn't tell the Hon. Mrs Parbury any of that . . .

'After lunch we stood about in the saloon again for coffee, and I spoke to Admiral McNicoll and his wife. He is the brother of the bastard on the *Telegraph* who is one of the leaders of the opposition to my books. I think the admirals would show themselves to be of the opposition also if the politenesses were down, but we were soon led up to Ma'am, who began to discuss with McNicoll the oiling of stabilisers. She is fed up because the stabilisers in *Britannia* are apparently of an old-fashioned variety, which have to be taken out for oiling, while the latest can be oiled in position. After they had been through all this another lady who had been led up, all coffee lice and chiffon hat, spoke about the Barrier Reef, so I thought I had better put in a word as obviously a word wasn't going to be put to me. I told Ma'am she must make a point of seeing Fraser Island one day, and about the interesting wreck which had taken place there, and of the Nolan paintings which no doubt she had seen. At which she gave a shriek, or as close to a shriek as she could come, and said: "Ohhh, yurss! the Naked Lehdy! We saw one in Adelaide."

'Poor girl, she might loosen up if one took her in hand, but as it was she struck me as being quite without charm, except of a perfectly stereotyped English county kind, and hard as nails under the Little-thing-in-Blew appearance. I suppose it's just as well that she's tough. One wasn't led up to the Jokey Juke – he approached, and I think he made up his mind early on that he was going to keep well away from anything that might be an intellectual or an artist. When all this was over I went up to the Cross and had a long gin session with Jack Lee, the English film director.'[93]

Utzon promised over lunch to show White and Lascaris the Opera House. A few days later they were clambering up the great tiers of concrete rising on Bennelong Point. White was exhilarated. 'It has made me feel glad I am alive in Australia today. At last we are going to have something worth having . . . Funnily enough as we were walking up and down all those steps in such a very contemporary setting I kept thinking of Phaestos, Mycenae and Tiryns. It occurred to Manoly too, without our having discussed it.' White took the building to be a symbol of the wonderful changes already happening in Sydney. A new professional theatre, the Old Tote, had opened with a fine performance of *The Cherry Orchard* and this venture had an 'aura of success' about it.[94] The first graduates of the National Institute of Dramatic Art, NIDA, were entering the theatre. The amateur age was over. A new man, Stefan Haag, was at the helm of the Trust. He was a boy in the Vienna Boys' Choir trapped in Australia at the outbreak of the war. Now he was full of ideas and plans which he laid out to White, taking him into his confidence as none of his predecessors had before.

Haag thought White the only writer in Australia with 'a sense of music' and asked him to write the libretto for an opera to open the Opera House. White agreed – if he could find the right composer. In England he planned to pursue Benjamin Britten, the only composer who might do justice to an opera about the naked lady. From the abandoned manuscript of *A Fringe of Leaves* White had already roughed out a brief synopsis. He wanted Nolan to do the sets: 'One can no longer imagine Mrs Fraser apart from the Nolan paintings.' Beneath the cranes on Bennelong Point he already imagined himself 'at the opening of the Britten-Nolan-White opera with Marie Collier singing Mrs Fraser'.[95]

TWENTY

Greece Again

White to the Moores   31.iii.1963

A very smooth, but exhausting journey. Manoly developed dysentery
from a Singapore sandwich, and now 'flu. I have had a streaming cold.
Arrived to find the aunt* had died the week before. So all we could
do was take flowers to the cemetery. Everyone fortunately very calm.
Athens much altered. Only the light is the same and the Acropolis.

Lascaris to the Moores   11.iv.1963

Up to yesterday we were both in bed, being, I'm afraid a lot of
trouble to my poor sister Ellie, who has had to come up and down
with trays and remedies ever since we've been here. Anyway it's all
over now we hope and to-morrow we are off to Mykonos for Easter.
Ellie has a little house there and I feel we shall both have a peaceful time
away from so many relations. As Patrick put it, they keep coming here
like tidal waves!

White to John Tasker   26.iv.1963

We have just returned from a fortnight of island-hopping – Mykonos-
Delos-Samos-Patmos – during which we were completely cut off from
the world, particularly mail, so that it was very good to find practically
a mailbagful of letters, including yours waiting here in Athens. I must
take your word for the casting of *The Season* as most of the actors are unknown to me. I do think one star attraction would have been a practical
asset, which is why I tried hard to make them bring out Coral Browne,
but it is obvious they are going to skimp as much as possible . . .

    Since we arrived in Greece I have written the second and third of

*Despo. She was ninety-two.

the three short films, *Clay* and *Down at the Dump*, for my triple bill *Triple Sec.*★ The story versions of these two should be in the current *Overland* and *Meanjin*. As soon as I have typed the last of the three, I am going to start on the play 'Don Juan and Don Joan' for Zoe and Les Dayman. The other day a Greek introduced me as Kyrios Juan.

To the Moores   *27.iv.1963*

These islands of Greece are really only for a couple of nights or a couple of years: anything in between is futile . . .

From Samos we went to Patmos as we discovered a little boat, unknown to Athens, plys between the two islands once a week. It was very small, the sea very rough, and our fellow passengers, mostly theological students bound for Patmos, spouting over the side like whales. In addition one was distressed by the sight of country cheeses standing exposed on top of the hold round which all these seasick youths were milling, and a pathetic lamb tied to a stanchion by a string, being taken from one rock to be slaughtered on another . . .

Everybody has his island, and I think Patmos will remain ours. There is a small and comparatively modern port, where we stayed, right on the quay, with people expecting boats and screaming at each other all through the night. But the main village is on the top of a mountain which rises behind, a warren of narrow white streets winding round an enormous grey monastery with crenellations like a fortress in *Apocalypse*. Two very charming novices led us to the cave,† and afterwards presented us with wallflowers picked from outside, which I feel we shall have to keep pressed between the appropriate pages and bring out to show to bored and sceptical visitors.

. . . The last day we discovered a most wonderful 18th Century house, which will be comparatively cheap to buy, although one will have to spend a fair amount on doing it up. But I felt it was *our* house the moment we went inside. There are twelve rooms, including a long glassed-in veranda-place at the back, paved with brick, a courtyard paved with flint in a formal pattern, three wells, one of them inside the house, and a walled garden full of almond trees, pomegranates, and quinces. The last owner spent some years in Odessa before the Revolution, and the house does have a great deal of the Chekov atmosphere. It would make just the right set for *The Cherry Orchard*, for instance. We are going to *try* to buy the house, although we can't really afford it after this trip and paying my latest income tax, and then there will

---

★*Willy-Wagtails* made up the set. White had picked the young Australian Bruce Beresford to direct *Triple Sec*. Les Dayman played Digger Masson in the Adelaide and Sydney productions of *The Season at Sarsaparilla*.

†Of St John the Divine, where the apostle in exile dictated *The Apocalypse*.

be the expense of trying to live on two sides of the world, the problem
of where to keep the animals, and so forth. But it is just one of those
crazy things one has to do every now and again.

To Geoffrey Dutton   *8.v.1963*

The house itself would cost only about £A2,000, but one would have
to spend as much again in doing it up . . . The woman who owns it,
and who prefers to live with her children in Athens, said she couldn't
take less when we said we couldn't give so much. However, she is
going to discuss the matter with her children, and if they have climbed
down by the time we return we shall have the agony of decision all over
again. I hope not. It would be crazy to be landed with that house, and
we might have to end up living exclusively at Patmos.

We only spent a week in Athens before setting out again, for the
north this time. Every fresh direction in Greece makes me feel that this
is Greece at last, and that I haven't seen anything beautiful until now.
We are on Pelion at present, making very exhausting expeditions up
and down the mountain, through forests of chestnut, and straggling
slate-roofed villages, down paths cobbled with chunks of marble which
seem to have dislocated every bone in my feet and sent shooting pains
up my shins. Yesterday we decided to engage a couple of mules to
bring us up to the top again, and I must say that mule's back was the
greatest luxury I have ever experienced.

This will be mild, I expect, to what we are going to find on
Mt Athos . . .

I have finished typing *Triple Sec.* I think *Down at the Dump*, which
you haven't yet read, will turn out to be the best of the three stories,
at least on the screen. Now I'm hoping Zoe will unearth a Minnesotan
millionaire who will put up the money for an Australian film, although
if she doesn't I have another possible string in Douglas Fairbanks Jr, for
whom one of my nieces has begun to work. She, poor girl, will be
horrified at the suggestion, but nothing will stop her old uncle from
having a try . . .*

Oh – something that will interest you – while we were in Samos
we discovered that Katsimbilis was staying in our hotel! We didn't meet
him, but often used to look at him. He is not a bit Colossal† – rather
like one of those large, grey, shiny ticks filled with borrowed blood.
He has a wife with a peacock's voice and an ugly face who was much
more interesting. She had a clever technique of dropping the peacock-
voice and tearing strips off the maids in sweet, affectionate tones. But

---

*Alexandra Peck was then working for Fairbanks International Development
Co. in London, but in the end White made no approach.

†Katsimbilis appears in Henry Miller's *The Colossus of Maroussi.*

Robert Liddell says everybody likes her, and that he has known two people dying of cancer who couldn't bear to have anybody else at their bedside.

To Margery Williams from Mount Athos   15.v.1963

The Monastic Life is one of those exploded myths, like the Noble Bedouin. For there is nothing so dirty, spiteful, crazy, useless as a monk, anyway a Greek Orthodox one. There is one enormous monastery outside Karyès in which five old Russians are dying off. Manoly feels that when they do, the whole tribe of monks on the Holy Mountain should be rounded up and put in it. Then the other monasteries can be run as museums which one will be able to visit without a struggle. Because one becomes involved in endless struggles as it is, in all the monasteries, to put one's nose inside a church or library. The day we attempted the Russian monastery at Karyès a crazy old abbott came screaming out at us, saying he wasn't going to waste his time, he had the wine to bottle, and so he did, in spite of the answering screams of another old monk, our ally, who could at least speak Greek as well as Russian, and who took us aside to say the abbott was really a Communist and should be reported to the police. In other places we did not meet with quite such a display of emotion, but were obstructed as much as possible.* The argument is that the foreigners steal the monastery treasures, but when we got back to Salonica we were told there are frequent cases of monks stealing and selling their own property, then coming to Salonica to paint the town. On one occasion a monk killed another over a woman.

The only time we encountered any Christian spirit on Mount Athos was in the laymen who slave for the monks and in one or two of our fellow pilgrims. The nicest of these was a man who plays the trumpet and vibraphone in an Athens night club called the *Flamingo*, and who came to the Holy Mountain to beg some miraculous raisins which would ensure the safe delivery of his pregnant wife. The craziest was a man who tottered along, rather frail, with 'Apostle of Christ' embroidered on his beret, and whose chief concern was the Day of Judgment. All the people one met on the Mountain kept on bobbing up again, and one night at the Grand Lavra I had the misfortune to be pinned in between others at the refectory table, after we had finished our corn mush, while the Apostle of Christ delivered a sermon lasting three-quarters of an hour, in the course of which six fat merchants from Livadhiá took him up on points of heresy . . . At the Lavra we shared a room with a policeman from Sparta, who started off being as

---

*Most galling of all: they were unable to see a gold chalice given to one of the houses by a Lascaris Emperor of Nicaea.

awful as all Spartans are, so many of them policemen too – suspicious, arrogant, cross-questioning incessantly – but who came good in the end and helped us escape from the Lavra when the regular caïque failed to turn up – and another man connected with the timber from which the monks made a tidy penny for themselves, who wanted Manoly to stop off at his village on our way back to Salonica, and choose one of his five sisters as a bride.

It is all good fun to look back on, but the atmosphere was full of hatred and spite while we were there. One particular monk used to fly into tantrums I'm sure only Callas could equal. His victims would scuttle away pale and trembling. On the last night at the Lavra as we waited for our overdue means of escape to arrive in the rocky little harbour below, the surly, scruffy old door-keeping monk slammed the door at my back without a word, and tried to shut me out – the rule is that everybody must be in by sunset. The caïque did arrive but fled in the night because a storm arose, and the captain would not risk a morning exit through the rocks . . .

The maddening thing about it all was that there are so many wonderful things to see if one can afford to spend twenty-four hours in each monastery and court a handful of surly monks. The church at Vatopédi is a fabulous sight – all the gold and saints in the world, but with a taste that one doesn't often encounter in Byzantine church interiors. The only thing I would have had different was a rusty screw on which a priceless icon was hanging. Everything, in fact, was fabulous at Vatopédi, but it may have seemed so because there we also encountered infinite peace – even a civilised monk. The interesting part was that this man came from Smyrna, from which all good Greeks, including the Lascaris family, are sprung, and that he had been three times a refugee, or in other words he has been in contact with life.

To Denis and Alice Halmagyi   *2.vi.1963*

Constantinople is one of the most squalid places I know – it makes Cairo seem hygienic – but then there is the Bosporus, just to drive along it washes one clean, and Ayia Sophia, which I think must be the most noble building on earth. You can keep all the mosques, and even the Seraglio, wonderful though it is, but I shall take the several excellent restaurants in which we ate, particularly fish, and always cooked by Greeks. We had a tremendous drive from Constantinople to Smyrna fifteen hours of it in a bus, with Turkish music blaring all the way, and a hostess to squirt cheap eau de cologne into our hands and offer us chewing gum. Again one felt very squalid but the landscape is on the grand scale, if too nostalgic – one is reminded continually of the rightful owners.

Almost the whole of Smyrna was destroyed when the Turks set fire to it and drove out the Greeks, but along the waterfront there are a number of old houses, mostly foreign consulates and mansions of rich Levantines at the time of the Catastrophe, façades of white, and rose, and creamy marble, with iron doors and shutters, which show one what Smyrna must have been like at the turn of the century when it was still in Greek hands. We looked for Manoly's grandparents' house, but there is no longer any trace of it.

To Geoffrey Dutton   *26.v.1963*

This place is full of personal ghosts, rather uneasy.

To Geoffrey Dutton   *8.vi.1963*

We finished our travels in a blaze of excitement on Lesbos, the most beautiful and varied island so far. (By now I realise the only way to live in Greece would be on a large and comfortably adapted caïque, cruising round to all one's favourite places, living on board, and cooking all the wonderful things one finds in the markets ashore.) But Lesbos is really exciting, in places very savage, grey, distorted rock formation and combed-out trees, in one place a monastery sitting on top of an extinct volcano, here and there gently bucolic, very fertile valleys with trees and streams, reminiscent of Ionia. The most beautiful place of all is Molivos, one of those villages rising up to a fortress beside the sea . . .

The only disappointing thing about Lesbos is Mitilini, where we were staying. It has the squalor and bourgeois pretensions of most of the island capitals. But it was some compensation to stay at the Lesbian Hotel, with the Sappho in opposition next door, and to find a statue of Sappho looking terribly like Marjorie Barnard. It has given me an idea for a play. Can't you see the opening? Lesbos at night, a starlit court, one of the followers reading from those deathless, palpitating, passionate poems to celebrate the arrival of the poetess in their midst, then – enter Margaret Rutherford. I remember reading Forster's guidebook to Alexandria in which he says, roughly, 'At the time of her death Hypatia was not the glamorous slavegirl of fiction, but an elderly lady with a gift for mathematics.' In the same way I expect Sappho was a blowsy bluestocking with a gift for exciting that semi-intellectual semi-sexual frenzy in which Lesbians thrive.

. . . You need have no real fear about my living permanently in Greece. It is a wonderful temptation, but I realise it wouldn't work – too many irritations, complications, and then, I am far too deeply rooted in Australia. I think the real reason I have always kept dogs is that the dogs will always force me back, being of a sentimental nature where animals are concerned. And a couple of weeks ago I ordered a dozen advanced pullets for our return in October, as I don't feel life is quite right without a fowlyard. If we sell Dogwoods and move to Sydney, the place we have our eye on should allow us to keep a disguised pen for a few fowls.

The *Season* opened in Sydney with a great bang – shouts of joy and screams of rage intermingled. But I gather some of the cast are far from good enough, and the whole thing was thrown onto the stage after only a fortnight's rehearsal. The Tasker is now trying madly to cover up by letter, praising in particular those actors everybody else has picked on as bad, and in general doing a Tasker. He left Sydney for Europe a few days after the play opened, which alarmed me exceedingly, both that he shouldn't be there to watch over the production, and because we shall probably have him dogging our footsteps . . . He has made a proper fool of himself again in the Sydney press, and was photographed in the foyer on the first night with a kiss-curl plastered on his forehead.

To the Moores   *5.vi.1963*

We are in Athens till the end of the month so that M. can run from relation to relation. I am writing a play . . .

To John Tasker   *7.vi.1963*

I have written nearly an act of 'Don Juan and Don Joan'. It involves great technical difficulties, such as conveying the activities of two characters in bed together without showing them and shocking the stalls, and keeping interest alive in what is practically a duet throughout. I am hating it and enjoying it at the same time.

To the Moores   *28.vi.1963*

I almost wish we were back at the beginning with everything still before us . . .

Lots of people have written enthusiastically about [*Sarsaparilla*], and I have had masses of cuttings, some of them including the most nauseating and defamatory crap. I have been forced to answer one particularly childish piece in the *Sunday Telegraph*, in which they ask how could a rich bachelor know anything about suburbia (they hadn't even waited to see the play). I have had to point out that it isn't necessary to commit a murder in order to write about one, and that in any case I have spent the last seventeen years in Sarsaparilla.

We have been twice to Epidauros. The journey itself is something of a triumph, I mean when one has overcome it. Add to that two hours on ancient stone seats, and one rises full of admiration for one's own stamina, understanding at last about the purge of ancient Greek tragedy. Actually, of the two plays we saw, Aristophanes' *The Wasps* pleased us the more – a riotous, bawdy pantomime with the enormous chorus of elderly male wasps dressed in black and gold frockcoats, cellophane wings, bowler hats, horn-rimmed glasses, their stings concealed in walking-sticks. Philocleion was played by Nezer, one of the great comics of this world, who can draw laughter out of the air just by raising his hand . . .

Delphi is where one should really see *Prometheus*, in those rocky, supernatural surroundings with hawks circling overhead. We went there the other day, and found that it could survive all the other wonderful things we have seen lately. Unfortunately I brought back a violent attack of dysentery, either from the moussaká at lunch or from drinking of the Castalian waters . . .

In the end we haven't bought the house on Patmos, though I have been sorely tempted. It would be far too expensive and complicated a life, with the result that we should probably have to withdraw to Patmos altogether. Much as I should like that I am not going to give in to the Australian devils.

I am not in the mood for writing letters at the moment. There is too much to tie up in Athens in the next three days. I am half-way through my new play, but there again I am stuck – I hope only stuck – there are moments when I feel it shouldn't be written at all. It is something which has to be very crude and very subtle at the same time, and will probably have to be written and re-written over the years.

To Margery Williams   *28.vi.1963*

Only three more days and we shall be leaving Athens. Everything is in rather a muddle at present – too many farewells – and I begin to feel sorry for all the irritations I have experienced, and to wonder whether they were irritations at all . . .

We reach London on July 18, or rather, I shall, as Manoly will have to go to Geneva for a few days to see his Italian relations who will be unable to fit in with us in Rome.

I expect a lot that will be trying in London. My mother has called for her black hat with feathers, because she has heard the King is dead and there is going to be a Black Ascot.

TWENTY-ONE

Ruth, Death and the Afterlife

DIMINISHED AS SHE was by illness and great age, a victim of strokes and falls, Mrs Victor White refused to die. From her bed in Rutland House, where she lay in paint and jewels, Ruth ruled her London world with all that survived of her old imperious energy. She was eighty-five and only left her bed to be wheeled into the kitchen for lunch. Suzanne, still devoted and fearful of her mother's disapproval, came to the flat every day. Her youngest daughter, Frances, often came with Suzanne but was too overawed to stay in her grandmother's bedroom. She slipped away to the kitchen where the cook let her see her wooden leg.

Ruth was lingering in immense comfort: as well as two nurses who attended her during the day, she had a night nurse, a house-keeper and a woman who came a few days every week to clean the flat and sew. The last of these was said to play tennis and dance the twist. 'You can imagine the fortune which is being drained away by all this,' White wrote to the Moores. 'Her mind is now half gone, and it would really be easier if it would go altogether so that we could get her into a nursing home without hurting her feelings.'[1] He visited her every other day. Her mind drifted in and out of focus.

As Ruth's powers failed, her son had been drawn into the management of her affairs. To his chagrin, he discovered she was far richer than he supposed. Her own holdings, plus the income from his father's estate, had yielded a large surplus that accumulated through the 1950s and early 1960s. He had come to London partly with the purpose of persuading Ruth to begin tidying up her estate, and to make a settlement of capital on himself and Suzanne. He had not looked forward to facing his mother with this, 'All those halting, crazy conversations with the octogenarian!'[2]

He wanted Ruth placed in the care of an order of nuns. Suzanne was sceptical of this plan, nor was she entirely convinced by her brother's claim that in his own old age he would rather be looked after by nuns than live at home. He found a suitable order, the Blue Nuns of Holland Park. But Ruth refused to budge. This was the last victory she enjoyed over her son. Years later he wondered if this abortive attempt to send Ruth to die among Roman Catholics might be retaliation for the years of purgatory to which she condemned him at Cheltenham. 'I hope not, but it could be so.' He left her to the care of her devoted women, but persuaded her to begin dividing her jewels, furs and furniture among her daughter and granddaughters. 'All this should have started happening some time ago, but she clings to the possessions she no longer uses and can barely see.' To him and his sister, Ruth also made gifts of cash. It came to White, as he was crossing Kensington High Street, that these events would make a novel he must write one day. But it must be set in Sydney not London, 'because Sydney is what I have in my blood'.[3]

He spent his first weeks back in London 'in a whirl' – eating, drinking, fending off journalists, talking to publishers and agents, negotiating with theatres, and seeing old friends. W.H. Smith and Sons gave 'a quaint but rather appealing' lunch to celebrate his winning their prize for *Voss*.[4] The Duttons and Nolans were in town. Tasker was due. Huebsch appeared, and their meetings were happy, memorable occasions. But sad, too. 'When Ben was preparing to leave on some incredible but typically Huebschian journey across Spain, we were planning our next meeting – But only superficially, humanly planning. I felt, as he closed the door, we had been telling each other that this would be the last time.'[5]

Roy de Maistre was pursuing an elderly existence in Eccleston Street. He was seventy. Little had changed in the studio. The painter's treasures were carefully arranged: a missal on a little table with an opera hat, Francis Bacon's yellow sofa, a parchment hedge of old invitations along the mantelpiece, a few bits of beautiful china which he hinted were of royal lineage like himself. 'Roy's studio', wrote John Rothenstein, 'was a work of art, and, like Courbet's, a repertory of his whole life.'[6] Roy's own appearance was as carefully contrived as the studio's. He wore ochre make-up carefully applied to his face, but it stopped at his ears, leaving the back of his neck a ghastly white. Visitors were entertained to meagre lunches of sherry and curried eggs, though knives and forks (engraved with fresh coronets) spread across the cloth as if the painter were about to serve a banquet. De Maistre offered to leave White the studio in his will. He declined.

White's chief ambition in London was to sell the plays with – if possible – Tasker as their director. When Tasker arrived in London, White took the young man to lunch with backers and producers. It soon seemed he had sold *The Season at Sarsaparilla* to the Mermaid. 'Even though it won't be till September next year, it is something to throw *now* in the faces of the Australian opposition,' he told Huebsch and released the news to the Australian press.[7]

The state of the opposition was this: in Sydney, the *Sarsaparilla* season earned a shower of abuse from the tabloids. Banner headlines on the front page of the *Mirror* read,

A PLAY THAT STINKS!

EVERYTHING BUT THE KITCHEN SINK

CUT THE CACKLE, MR TASKER!

The *Mirror*, which was then training the pool of talent that put Rupert Murdoch's stamp on the journalism of the world, complained about White's filthy language. The comic journalist Ron Saw was assigned to cover the play's opening night and reported that the actors hawked up 'cusses like rotten oysters'. But his night was not entirely wasted. 'By a happy mischance, a door in the scenery fell slightly open, presenting the unforgettable sight of Nola Boyle (Miss Doreen Warburton) changing from a chenille dressing-gown into an orange blouse. For those of us in the front stalls who could see it, it was bloody good value.'[8]

Sarsaparilla limped through a season of five weeks, despite the enthusiasm of critics like Harry Kippax, who declared this 'rich, relevant, accessible play is one of the two best yet written by an Australian, being equalled in its confident trajectory through comedy to compassion only by *The Doll'*.[9] White had won the critics but not the crowds in Sydney.

Meanwhile in Adelaide the city fathers once more embroiled themselves in the matter of Patrick White the playwright. A production of *Night on Bald Mountain* at the 1964 festival had seemed almost certain, but while White was in Greece, the Governors once more dug in their heels. The chief opponent was Glen McBride, who fought the new play with all the unyielding hostility he had shown towards *The Ham Funeral*. Behind the closed doors of the Town Hall there raged 'terrifying' arguments. The Governors had their way once more and threw *Bald Mountain* out. 'All very ridiculous,' White wrote to Margery Williams, 'but I do not like the idea of playing the part of the intellectual and social pariah of Adelaide for the third time.'[10]

Harry Medlin and the Guild then refused to give up their theatre for the weeks of the festival, and decided to go ahead with the play. The festival needed the theatre. The Governors brought great pressure on the University to force the Guild to hand it over, but the Guild and the University refused. Medlin was then summoned to the Lord Mayor's rooms at the Town Hall to confront Lloyd Dumas, the rotund and clever newspaper proprietor who was chief of the Governors. Medlin recalls Dumas saying, 'Give us the hall for the Festival, and you can put on *Bald Mountain* some other time and rub our noses in it.' He replied, 'We've done that twice already.'

Dumas' eyes filled with tears and his mouth was quivering as he pleaded for the theatre. 'He was a wily man and used every wile.'[11] But the Guild held out: *Bald Mountain* would go on during the festival. The Governors then resolved to deny the play even the status of a fringe event. Without the festival's financial backing, more locals and more amateurs would have to be cast. That made White's task of securing Michael Redgrave for the lead all the more difficult. It was a step forward – and sweet revenge – to announce from London that Michael Codron had taken an option to put *Night on Bald Mountain* into the West End.

Then these London plans fell apart. The Mermaid withdrew from *Sarsaparilla*, pleading indecency. This was despite the high decadence White discovered in the London theatre that summer. 'Australia would have a fit at all the incest, abortion, adultery and language which gets let loose over here on the stage . . .' And after Tasker staged a rehearsed reading of *Bald Mountain* at the Embassy Theatre in Swiss Cottage with Madge Ryan as the goat woman, Codron dropped the play 'like a hot brick'.[12] Through that London summer White approached Peter Finch, Keith Michell and Paul Scofield. Each turned him down.

White's greatest pleasure in London was to be with the Nolans again. 'Although we meet very seldom, I feel I have known him all my life, and we always begin again just where we left off.' The Nolans took the two men to the ballet and opera, drove them about, introduced them to theatre managers and entertained them in Putney, where Cynthia was making a beautiful garden on the river. This was the Putney garden of Jack Chance in *A Fringe of Leaves*, 'the prettiest little place you could imagine' with an arbour by the river,

> And the river allus appealed to me – right from when I was a boy down from Arfordsheer. There's times when the river gets to be the colour of pigeons – both sky an' water. I love that river.[13]

The Nolans were White's collaborators in the pursuit of Benjamin Britten. They had contacts. His talent, their charm, her austere elegance had opened doors in England. Nolan sent the composer a copy of the synopsis of the Mrs Fraser opera in August. Britten, White reported, was 'rather guarded. Naturally, he has things planned, like anybody else, for some time ahead.' Nolan was 'working hard' on the composer over the next few weeks, but when there was no response, he took White to Suffolk to meet him at a concert in Sir Richard and Lady Hyde Parker's Melford Hall.[14] The two Australians had seats behind a silk rope, which divided them from the three-guinea crowd at the front entitled to a champagne supper.

Nolan called Britten over to the rope at the interval. Two versions have survived of the awkward exchange that followed. Nolan says Britten was listing the commitments which made it impossible for him to compose the Mrs Fraser opera, when White asked bluntly, 'Don't you have control of your own life?' And that was that. But White recalls Britten refusing to engage him in conversation at all, not even looking at him, while discussing a local painter with Nolan: 'Poor Mary,' said Britten. 'She's so tahd.' After the Melford Hall incident, White abandoned his hope of Britten composing for the Opera House. All that remains of his pursuit are the unhappy figures in his novels who are tahd, terribly tahd.[15]

As White and Lascaris were preparing to return to Australia, Ruth collapsed and seemed on the point of death. 'Although I shall not be able to assume emotions I can't feel,' White told Margery Williams, 'I may be involved in the practical side of death – arranging a funeral and going to it. So one is living in a very queer, fragmentary world indeed.' But Ruth rallied on a diet of egg and brandy and began to take notice of the small world around her. 'My mother lingers on, quite brightly at times,' White wrote to the Duttons who had returned. 'We had a good session the other day when I thought of going through all the cooks and maids who had ever worked for us. She enjoyed that, and when I had exhausted them kept asking: "Haven't you any more reminiscences?" I don't know whether to let her know we are going back to Australia, or just to disappear. In that case she will probably think I haven't called today.'[16]

They left for home on 1 October. Nolan's last service to the travellers was to save the day at Heathrow when the airline tried to charge £27 for overweight luggage. White was incensed, but Sid Nolan 'threw his weight about' and they were allowed on the plane without paying.[17] They did not stop at Athens, but flew straight through to Sydney, where Gwen and David Moore were waiting to drive them out to Castle Hill. White and Lascaris began at once to prepare Dogwoods for sale. White was now determined to get rid of the farm and planned to spend a little of the fortune which would soon be coming to him to buy a house in the city. The Sarsaparilla years would end with his mother's death.

As they were working on the house a telegram came with the expected news. Ruth was dead. Details of the scene took a while to reach White in Sydney and then they began to work in his imagination. One morning Ruth was lifted on to the commode beside her bed and was sitting there quite peacefully with one of the nurses chatting away when she

slipped sideways on her throne while still hooked to the mahogany
rails. One buttock, though withered, was made to shine like ivory
where the rose brocade was rucked up. The eyes were mooning.

White did not appear to mourn. That he and his mother had reached
a kind of understanding in their often childish conversations after her
collapse pleased him. Death, when it came, was fortunate. He wrote
rather woodenly to Peggy Garland, 'It is certainly the end of something when one's mother dies, even when it has been a mother one
has disagreed with all through life.'[18] Ruth's death was indeed the end
of a long struggle, a lifetime of passionate engagement, yet death could
not entirely release him from this woman. Three more of his novels
were to reflect the affection, antagonisms, dependence, betrayals and
guilt that ebbed and flowed between mother and son for fifty years.

Except for a few small legacies, Ruth left all her shares, furniture,
silver and pictures to her daughter and grandchildren. But her death
also released Dick's fortune, which now passed to his son and daughter
in equal shares after twenty-five years.

Purgatory followed. White flew to Melbourne for the rehearsals of
A Cheery Soul and took a room in an unfinished motel where the
management offered a discount for theatricals. Sumner was now steeped
in the play and found it very satisfying: 'It was so fluid – poetry, tragedy,
comedy, farce and a lot of revue – and Patrick was not interested in the
barriers. He stepped through them as if they weren't there.' The days
passed pleasantly: there were no tantrums with Sumner. White strolled
with Nita Pannell through the Fitzroy Gardens, talking over the interpretation of Miss Docker. As a devout Catholic, she was reluctant to
deliver a line in the play about the Virgin Mary. Pannell had written
to White about this. Pannell recalls him replying, 'Why does everyone
believe that no one *else* believes?' He told her that if she visited his house
she would find a statuette of the Virgin before which he placed fresh
flowers every day. She persisted and White changed a few words of
the script. It was a notable triumph. Pannell had combed Melbourne's
old clothes shops for cardigans for Miss Docker, but White thought she
could do with just one more. Lascaris was phoned to send to Melbourne
the cardigan wrapped round the end of a broom at Dogwoods. White
wished he might always be as involved in productions of his plays.
Perhaps Sumner was not as 'brilliant' as Tasker, but almost always he
seemed to know what White was trying to say, and when he didn't
White found him 'willing to accept my explanations'.[19]

White felt entirely confident by the opening night, 19 November
1963. He was sure this was his best play; the direction was fine; the sets
were the best Desmond Digby had ever done; the cast was devoted. 'I

was in every way pleased with it – I *know* it was right.' But as Miss
Docker pursued her course of do-good destruction through Sarsaparilla, an awful silence settled on the first-night audience. White had never
sensed such hostility to his plays. 'There were people stamping up and
down in the intervals saying the theatre should be locked to keep such
stuff out of it.' After the show White and Digby roamed the streets
together for hours, staring in shop windows, gossiping, bitching,
aimlessly killing time. At 2am they were in the lane at the back of the
Age as the papers were loaded on to the trucks. The *Age*'s review was
terrible. 'Almost all the Melbourne critics condemned it (one of them
in one line) saying that I am without wit, humour, love or even liking
for human beings, in fact what so many Australian critics said of my
novels in the past.' Harry Kippax was not there. The Sydney *Sunday
Telegraph* suggested that instead of bringing the play to Sydney, one
plane should be chartered to take White's admirers to Melbourne. Box
office was diabolical: less than half the income earned by *Sarsaparilla*,
leaving the company with a loss of over £4,000. White confessed to
Sumner that he was bruised by all this. And he knew he faced another
'trial by theatre' in the New Year.[20]

Tasker was not due home in Australia until the end of January,
but the two men were already quarrelling. From the safety of Europe,
the director suggested setting *Night on Bald Mountain* between the wars.
White replied by return post, 'I will NOT ON ANY ACCOUNT (repeat)
NOT ON ANY ACCOUNT set the play in any time but the present.'
Tasker had already suggested so many changes that White suspected
he wanted 'a different play from what I have written. And now this
time change. I'm sorry my bandwagon creaks so badly – a pity it was
the only one offering.'[21]

Night on Bald Mountain has at its heart a subject that worried both
men: booze. Professor Hugo Sword has imprisoned his alcoholic wife
Miriam in a kind of Mount Wilson retreat. The contest between the
Swords is a familiar one in White's work – and in White himself. Sword
is 'an inhibited ascetic, a believer, with a strain of repressed sensuality.
One of his tragedies is that he is not creative. It has made him jealous of
those who are. He is a secret writer of pornographic verses. His wife is
not of the same intellectual level, but far more intuitive – an additional
source of strife between them. She too is a believer, but in a feverish,
mystical way; she has persuaded herself that she comes closer to God
'at the bottom of the glass'.[22] Mrs Sword evades her nurse, the virginal
Miss Summerhayes, and goes on a bender with booze supplied by the
local grocer in exchange for jewellery – this was a Castle Hill detail.
The Professor tries to rape the nurse, who then flings herself over a
cliff. The Swords are left to cope with the remainder of their lives, not
in tranquillity but facing round after round of the same conflict. The

animal emblem of *Bald Mountain* is not the rutting dog, but the goat. The play opens and closes with the goat woman Miss Quodling – a role written for Nita Pannell – releasing these most rational creatures to forage in the bush.

Tasker was a drinker, and early in the writing of *Bald Mountain* he took White to an Alcoholics Anonymous meeting at St Canice's at the Cross. White wanted to know about AA. The upshot was that he gave up drink himself for a time and got one or two details of alcoholic guile for Miriam Sword. White also turned to his own doctor, Alice Halmagyi, for professional advice on keeping Miriam Sword on her feet. 'Where you come in, Alice, is in helping me keep Miriam Sword sufficiently mobile to do all she has to do, and to say all she has to say. *Semi-coherence* in the later stages are what I am trying to aim at. In that way I shall be able to convey much more than through sober, natural speech.' Could the nurse administer something to rally Mrs Sword? Halmagyi recommended White cut down her drinks.[23]

Tasker was all for removing Miss Quodling and the outer frame of the play. Nor was he convinced the nurse would be so overwhelmed when she realises 'her love for her father might be an incestuous one' that she would throw herself off a cliff. White refused to make any changes to accommodate those objections. All he would do for Tasker was rewrite the final reconciliation between the Swords to make it explicitly sour, 'because you did not seem able to see your way to making it anything but sweet'.[24]

Tasker suggested they meet for lunch soon after his return to Sydney in January 1964. The meal at the Rex Hotel ended in a shouting match. 'I keep asking him why he condescended to direct the fucking thing. But he harps on telling me "my cast is most unhappy about it" – other people are always enlisted now . . . It is all part of the Tasker technique – to bash everybody to pulp in the preliminaries, and then when he has reduced them to doubt and despondency, keep them where he wants them. By now I know enough about it to be anything but a stone wall to his treatment. He started shouting at me: "You don't trust me! You have no faith in me like you did during *The Ham Funeral*." I could only reply: "In those days I didn't know so much about you." There was much repetition. "How can I give my actors confidence if you don't have faith in me?" A possibility, of course, and a sad one. "If what I see at rehearsals gives me faith, I shall have it." "Ah, no, but I must have it *now*!" Already I can see efforts ahead to discourage me from coming to all those rehearsals at which *meaning* is discussed, and to have me at the run-throughs, by which time the thing will have set, and any call for alteration can be brushed aside.' White confessed he had come to hate Tasker.[25]

The Adelaide Festival had relented sufficiently to list *Night on*

Bald Mountain among the fringe events of the fortnight. White had never seen a festival, and he explored the event with aloof curiosity. The bar of the old South Australia Hotel was the field of his command, a meeting place for the Duttons, Haag of the Trust, and the Nolans. The painter was in town to show his African paintings. Of the moments of 'pure fright' White suffered that week, the worst came at the Nolan opening. 'I couldn't get away fast enough from that.' He kept clear of all writers' gatherings for they sounded 'quite pathetic'. He indulged in a triumph of sorts by accepting an invitation to lunch at the Adelaide Club, a colonial institution which was the stronghold of those leading citizens who had opposed his plays with such passion. As he ate, 'a number of dying elephants looked on'.[26]

On the opening night, 9 March 1964, White and Tasker managed a last row over dinner before going down to the theatre. Pannell was the goat woman, Joan Bruce the unfortunate Miriam Sword, and Alexander Archdale took the Michael Redgrave role of the sterile Dr Hugo Sword. The sets by Wendy Dickson were mountainsides and sitting rooms. But for the mountain rock, stuck in mid-air over the sitting room for some time in Act One, the opening night went well. *Bald Mountain* did good business over the next fortnight, and the Guild extended the season for a week to cope with the crowds. The critics divided: Melbourne's were hostile but Sydney's were warm – except for Kippax, who set out his deep reservations in a long and careful essay in *Nation*. He had come to the view that what White was trying to say at this point in his career was inherently unsuitable for the stage. Kippax wrote: 'I do wonder whether a philosophy which appears to be distrustful of intellectual communication, and suspicious of emotional and physical relationships between human beings can fruitfully use the drama as a medium of expression.'[27]

White was shocked and put Kippax's response down to the fact that the critic was about to announce his engagement: 'Such an examination of failure as *Bald Mountain* must have jolted him.'[28] Curt and Maria Prerauer, fearing a breach between the two men, asked if each would agree to be present at a dinner with the other. The dinner, held at the Prerauers' a few days after the review appeared in *Nation*, was one of the most uncomfortable those present ever endured. White and Kippax were silent all through the meal. The Prerauers and Lascaris set up a triangular conversation and once the food was cleared away they disappeared, leaving the writer and critic alone with a bottle of cognac. Out of his pocket White drew a copy of the review heavily underscored in pencil.

White worked his way through, defending himself paragraph by paragraph: 'You say here . . .' Kippax argued in his own defence for a while, but as it seemed White was hardly listening, he sat back and let

the storm rage. He knew it would blow itself out, and he recognised
that much of what White was saying was fair enough from the playwright's point of view. White finished, folded the magazine and put
it back in his coat pocket. He said, 'So you see I don't think much of
your review.' Kippax replied, 'I didn't think you would like it.' For
many years thereafter relations between the two were civil. White told
Dutton: 'Harry is a serious critic and an honest man.'[29] *Bald Mountain*
has never been performed in Australia since.

Tasker and White parted company. Tasker had made his reputation
with White's plays, but the high promise he showed in the early 1960s
was not realised. Appointed the first director of the South Australian
Theatre Company, he fell out with the board and was sacked. He
found it extremely hard to get on with authority. His talent was
real but too many feuds, too many unhappy actors, too much booze
counted against the man despite some fine productions. Tasker was
always arriving, always making a comeback. Whenever he had a show
opening in Sydney he rang White to invite him. The invitation and
White's refusal became a ritual: 'I won't come. You know I don't like
you.'[30]

White now had enough stories to make up a volume which he
planned to dedicate to Nin and Geoffrey Dutton. The collection
would begin with the Duttons' story 'Dead Roses', in which he
welded to the house party on Kangaroo Island a Castle Hill romance
between a man of notorious meanness and a woman many years his
junior. The originals were neighbours of the Kriegers, who laughed
to see this pair heaving horse manure up the steep garden from the
paddock below, the old husband pushing and the young wife pulling
the wheelbarrow in a harness.[31]

With 'Dead Roses' White returned to a theme as old as *Happy
Valley*: that couples must endure. The Mortlocks' marriage was awful,
but White saw it as the only 'real' part of the young woman's life. 'Then
she solidifies. When she leaves him, if for very good reasons, she loses
her *raison d'être* and goes to pieces again. Finally she becomes like so
many rich, aimless, though complacent widows . . . there is nothing
exactly wrong with her, but nothing right. Her sexual delusion – the
attempted rape by the non–existent Greek – make her blur once more,
and, I had hoped, something of a tragic figure.'[32]

Two Greek stories completed the volume. He had finished 'A
Glass of Tea' the previous summer in London, and now he wrote
'The Evening at Sissy Kamara's'. As always, he tried out the names
and 'all the details' on Lascaris first. White was proud that his Greeks
were not those that foreign writers usually took as their subjects. 'Mystification sets in when aristocratic or intellectual Greeks are produced,

to say nothing of Anatolian Greeks, who are very different from the metropolitan ones.' The spur to both stories was his recent visit to Smyrna. 'A Glass of Tea' draws on the courtship of Lascaris's Athenogenes grandmother in the old house on the Rue Franque, and the stories he had heard from Aunt Despo about the sack of the city.

> None of that rabble of sufferers – wet, dry, singed, bleeding, deformed by the agony of their first historic situation – none of them *knew* any more, as they stood in their fashionable rags and watched the city burn.[33]

Patrick White had so absorbed the Catastrophe into his own experience that he sacrificed friendships to the loyalties of 1922. Alan Seymour spent some time teaching English in Smyrna – he called it Izmir – and sent White a Christmas card saying how delighted he was by the city, the Anatolian coast and the Turks. A friendship had sprung up between the two writers during the season of *The One Day of the Year*. They met at a camp party at Tasker's flat, where a handsome student from NIDA was playing butler. Seymour was touched when White punctured this atmosphere by arriving with a string bag of fresh eggs and oranges. 'There was a warmth, humour, generosity and directness of response one had not expected. The impression of an intellect and an imagination ceaselessly at work in the observation of his fellow-creatures was also present in some force.' But White's reply to the Christmas card was shattering: did Seymour not realise that this was the city from which Manoly's family had been ejected by ignorant, barbaric savages who had wiped out the Greek Christians of Asia Minor and terrorised Greece itself for centuries? 'In his long, ranting attack he allowed to the Turks no redeeming features at all . . . I'd never thought to read such banal generalisations and bigoted vituperation from such a source. Grieved, I wrote back in what I hoped was a mood of dignified regret, saying, for my part, I could speak only as I found. The Turks were obviously not angels but they did not seem to me *now* to be the villains he was depicting . . . No answer came from Patrick and we have not been in touch since.'[34]

As a title for the volume of stories White took the perfunctory Greek cry, OI KAYMENOI, 'the poor unfortunates' or, literally, *The Burnt Ones*. He explained to Huebsch, 'The Greeks come out with this so frequently. It is an expression of formal pity. One realises they aren't prepared to do anything about the objects of their pity because nothing can be done.'[35]

Viking was worried about the 'local low-life Aussie lingo' in the stories. Nothing was said to White but when a hint of these fears reached him in Sydney he exploded, first in a letter to Juliet O'Hea and then in more diplomatic language to Marshall Best. 'There is a lot in the American language I have had to puzzle out for myself, and am none the worse for doing so. Why can't the American do the same when it comes to ours?' White never had a satisfactory answer. His lingo became a serious bar to his American sales over the years as his writing grew more laconic and satirical. When *The Burnt Ones* appeared in November 1964 sales and reviews were strong in England and Australia – 'the whole Sydney stock . . . sold out within twenty-four hours' – but the book failed in America where Viking sold fewer than 1,700 copies.[36]

Rebuffed by Benjamin Britten, White cast about for a local composer for his opera and was led to Peter Sculthorpe, whom he declared 'the first Australian composer whose music I have found in any way exciting'. There was much in the young man's work to appeal to White. It was native, brooding and elegant – yet it hardly suited the project they had in mind. The voice is essentially contemplative; Sculthorpe is inspired less by the play of human passion than the beauty of landscape; his impulse is to search for tranquillity. That such a man should wish to write an opera on the wreck and sufferings of Mrs Fraser was surprising, but at thirty-five Sculthorpe was flattered by the invitation to collaborate and in awe of White. White roused him with the cry: 'Let us set out to give them something for the best opera house in the world.'[37] They met for the first time over lunch at Dogwoods after White got back from Melbourne in late 1963. The auguries were terrible. White spent all morning cooking an elaborate dish of chickens, for no one had warned him Sculthorpe was a vegetarian.

A few days before this, White and Lascaris had driven up to see Lizzie Kirk and eat one of her meals of boiled mince and beetroot. These trips to Mount Wilson were journeys back to White's childhood. Lizzie was now very old, living with her husband Sid in a spotless cottage on the mountain. They were survivors of a time and place which still glowed in White's memory and against which life in modern Sydney seemed cheap. On the trip White found himself thinking of a song cycle. 'All Sunday as we drove to Mount Wilson and back it wouldn't leave me alone, and I wrote it down on Sunday night after we got back; it is called "Six Urban Songs". I suppose really they arise from my disappointment at the inability of most people to understand *Cheery Soul*. There is more than a little spleen in them.' When Sculthorpe mentioned at lunch that he wanted to compose a song cycle, White was able to say he had the words. As White was not able to get to work on the libretto for a time, the song cycle would be something 'to help us to approach the opera'.[38]

The ironic, bitter lines of the 'Urban Songs' pit childhood memories of the city,

> In the days of trams and dreams
> When the frangipani was ground against the ox-blood wall

against images of a city White was now convinced was the ugliest thing about Australia. A housewife rhapsodises over

> The Bendix, the Dishlex,
> The Mixmaster and the Holden Special . . .

A Pole goes berserk in a theatre. This had actually happened in a Sydney picture theatre, and the image of the crazed immigrant axing people to death

> At the five o'clock session
> At the Magnifico-Splendid

persisted in White's work for years. He marked the Pole's song to be sung 'sourly matter-of-fact over depths of loneliness and pathos'. All is cheap: the image at the centre of the cycle is the sight of Sydney at night, seen from the mountains when the ugly new suburbs become a sheet of glittering lights,

> The pretty rhinestones
> On Sydney's neck[39]

White gave Sculthorpe a broad hint that Maria Prerauer might use the 'Urban Songs' to make her return to the concert platform. Sculthorpe acquiesced. He suggested scoring them for soprano and piano, but White countered with the notion of soprano, baritone and orchestra. It was as if he were to compose them himself. 'I think one soprano could do "Song of the Housewives" if the music helps her with the right chattery-nattery, twittery-jittery tones. Perhaps here and there a rumble from the baritone would help – to introduce *Angst*. (However, please disregard any of this if you don't like it, or find it corny. The composer is the one who matters.) "Night and Dreams" and "To Watch the River" are obviously for the baritone, but perhaps the soprano could help with odd phrases.'[40] Sculthorpe noticed White was particularly scathing at this time about the music of Britten, while showing great enthusiasm for the work of Messiaen and Richard Strauss.

Sculthorpe was dismayed when he received the first pages of the libretto in late March 1964. He expected poetry, but this was prose; White had promised *A Fringe of Leaves* would be about contemporary 'states of mind', but the opening scene read like the historical opera Sculthorpe had feared from the first. White's detestation of Sydney had reached such intensity – Sculthorpe put this down to Kippax's review of *Bald Mountain* – that he had the opera opening with one soldier singing to another: 'I caught the fuckin' pox in Sydney.'[41]

When they met for dinner at Dogwoods in early April, all their differences were revealed. White realised Sculthorpe was not the composer he wanted, and felt he had failed to grasp what Mrs Fraser – called Ellen Roxburgh in the libretto – was all about. Sculthorpe saw that White was not going to compromise on the shape of the scenes he had already written. The night ended badly. Next morning White wrote to apologise: 'I am sorry about last night. Of course it was fatal to try to discuss such things after I had been cooking a meal, by which time I am always at my worst. But I should have felt shattered in any circumstances to find you had gathered *nothing* about Mrs Roxburgh from the synopsis . . . You must have a mind the complete antithesis of mine – analytical, whereas I approach everything intuitively. Perhaps in the long run this may be a good thing – if it is not a complete disaster!'[42]

White thought to withdraw at this point, but Nolan and the Trust urged the two men forward. 'I am doing nothing for the moment', White told Peggy Garland in April, 'except send the composer a biography of the character he doesn't understand. There is this curious business of "understanding" with Australians. What they really crave for is factual journalism.' A fortnight later he reflected more calmly to O'Hea: 'I think perhaps we got together too late, and by that time the idea had got set too rigidly in my mind to be able to alter it to satisfy a collaborator.'[43]

Both men took a few months to realise that the blow-up in March had sunk the project. Sculthorpe tried a few times to raise the opera from the ocean floor, but White refused to have anything more to do with it. He conceived a passionate disapproval for Sculthorpe which time did nothing to soften. By October he was asking for the return of the 'Six Urban Songs' in order to destroy them. He explained, 'they belong to a period in my life which I no longer care for'.[44] Sculthorpe prevaricated. White finally appeared one day on his doorstep demanding the songs. Sculthorpe, anxious to guarantee their survival, feigned an attack of diarrhoea to make a hasty copy on the lavatory.

The Mrs Fraser project died a slow death. Sculthorpe worked with two more librettists: the historian Alan Moorehead and then the critic Roger Covell. He then abandoned hope of the opera, but years later two works emerged from his aborted collaboration with Patrick

White: the theatre piece *Mrs Fraser Sings* and the evocative orchestral suite *Mangrove*. The Opera House opened with Prokofiev's *War and Peace*.

So much had been wasted since White finished *Riders in the Chariot*. There was the Mrs Fraser novel abandoned, the play 'Don Juan and Don Joan' left unfinished in Athens, the screenplay *Triple Sec* unfilmed for want of backers – 'rich people', he remarked to Zoe Caldwell, 'are never as rich as they are supposed to be' – and the plays unproduced in the West End. O'Hea thought they were almost unsaleable, and laid some of the blame at White's door: 'He is not easy to deal with on the play side because he always gums up the works by insisting that he has control of the cast and then deciding that he must have an all-Australian cast.'[45] In fact White was willing to compromise in order to get London productions, but his concessions clinched no deals.

White and Lascaris had been fighting. White was very fond of one of his Melbourne actors and Lascaris saw this as an infidelity. There were terrible rows in which White claimed the *right* to infidelities: 'I have enough love for two or three.' Lascaris considered quitting but stayed because he had sworn to stay. White drew back. The crisis passed, but fed his general exhaustion and bewilderment. White was exhausted. 'Everything which has been written and said in Australia over the years about all my work, by all the hack journalists, prize academics, knowing amateurs and anonymous letter writers, has suddenly made me feel rather confused, and one wonders whether it has all been worth it. Of course there have been wonderfully encouraging things said too, but Eugene O'Neill once wrote: "We have to keep diaries to remember what is pleasant; it is the unpleasant things which stick in the mind." And I don't keep a diary.'[46]

March 1964 was a low point. He had not found in theatre the door through which he might stride rejuvenated. *Night on Bald Mountain* was immediately behind him and the *Fringe of Leaves* opera was dying within him. Dogwoods was on the market but there were no customers. White now feared the move to town almost as much as he craved being rid of the farm and living in the heart of a city again. 'I am in the doldrums at the moment,' he told Peggy Garland. 'Theatrical productions take it out of one more than anything I know . . . I wish I could see where to go next.'[47]

That winter he vowed to put the stage behind him. He told Huebsch he was the wrong kind of writer for collaborations. 'For me even a comma is a piece of sculpture. If I put it, I mean it to be there.' He refused to allow his plays to be performed in Australia, but went on hoping for success before 'sophisticated audiences in other countries, just to find out what the plays are really like. Here – never!' The Germans took up rights to translations by the Prerauers; the BBC produced a television version of *A Cheery Soul* which they transposed to an English setting. 'What the hell,' White wrote to Nita Pannell, 'the Australians hated it when it was done Australian, there is no reason why it shouldn't be done as a universal fable.'[48] It was not a success. He earned not much more than £600 from stage performances,[49] and when his *Four Plays* appeared – dedicated to his old friend Freddie Glover – sales were modest. In the United States, Viking produced only a tiny edition of 500 copies.

Money was never less a worry in his life – except that he feared being plagued by distractions now that he was coming into his father's fortune. He expressed these fears characteristically by reproaching one who faced a somewhat similar danger. The Duttons had moved out to the family's house on Anlaby and White hoped this change would bring new depth to Geoff's work: 'I am sure life at Anlaby will help you burrow even farther into whatever you happen to be interested in.'[50] But in the autumn and early winter of 1964 he saw Dutton's busy life proceed unchanged, a hectic schedule of lectures and conferences all over the country. 'How is it going to affect your work, the work which really matters?' White asked. 'It is very difficult to write this sort of thing without sounding pompous and awful, but I feel that you and I can quite easily get sucked back into something from which we thought we had escaped. I know I have to sit down to a serious stocktaking. I feel just about clapped out creatively partly through the recent critical battering, partly through the temptation to become a kind of social flibberty gibbet. I've got to humble myself, and more or less start painfully all over again.'[51]

In these doldrums *The Solid Mandala* had begun 'stirring maddeningly' in White's head. He wrote to Huebsch in mid-June hinting that he was about to write 'the last of the Sarsaparilla novels'. Then an attack of bronchitis landed him in hospital for the first time in years. Large doses of cortisone fixed his chest but left him with a long and depressing hangover. He recovered slowly, plodding about Dogwoods like a zombie. Once his energy returned he began to put down on paper the story of Arthur and Waldo Brown, the twins of Terminus Road, Sarsaparilla. He found the work 'very peaceful and gentlemanly after plays' and returned to his old routine of sleeping in the evening and writing through the early hours of the morning. Though *The Solid Mandala* was conceived as a novella, it rapidly developed into something far longer and more complex as details accumulated and side roads opened up. He buried himself in the book.[52]

As he was hesitating to write more definite news of the book to Huebsch, he heard that his publisher had died in a London hotel. Huebsch was eighty-eight, some years older than he had ever admitted.

White did not need the old man any more, but in the early days he had been his only lifeline in publishing, and in the years after it had been a source of confidence for White to know he was one of Huebsch's authors. Whatever anyone might say of his writing, White knew he had the blessing of the man who had brought Joyce and Lawrence to America. The five novels written since their meeting in 1940 were written, in some ways, *for* Huebsch. After the publisher's death, the tone of White's writing shifted. The painful theatre years had a good deal to do with this change, but a quality of formal grandeur that now faded from White's writing had reflected Huebsch himself.

'Living at opposite ends of the earth we met rarely, but each meeting when it happened had something rare and memorable about it,' White wrote in a public valediction for the old man. 'Such qualities as were united in Ben Huebsch, of warm heart and worldly wit, of subtle perception and simple directness, of immense steadfastness and intellectual renewal, are never more than partially withdrawn into the core of truth.'[53]

The Whites of New South Wales had always done business on the principle that family gives the best service. White's friend and cousin Eleanor Arrighi was now a real estate agent in Double Bay and he turned to her to find him a house in town. White had toyed with the idea of buying one of the beautiful city houses of Adelaide, but Lascaris warned him there were not enough people to quarrel with in Adelaide. It had to be Sydney: 'It is a case of the pit from which one was dug.'[54]

Lascaris had hoped they might live on at Castle Hill despite all the old objections to the place – frosts, asthma, encroaching houses, the tedious drives to and from town – so that it could be left to the public, in the end, as a park and gallery. The thought of abandoning his garden was distressing, for as they farmed less over the years he had gardened more. The hedges and trees were his work. But White, who had baulked on four or five occasions in the past, was now determined to move on. He was breaking free of Sarsaparilla in order to write the Sydney novels queuing in his mind. He had first to *live* what he was to write. The move was imperative. In these months he wrote sadly to his friends about the coming upheaval, he buried himself in his writing, he spoke of the *Cherry Orchard* atmosphere at Dogwoods, but in his heart he faced the departure with grim exhilaration.

There was a rambling place in North Sydney that seemed perfect, but a deal could not be struck with a couple of ancient sisters, 'hard as nails underneath all their vagueness'.[55] Then Arrighi found a terrace in Queen Street, Woollahra, but there was no yard for the dogs and their needs were crucial.

Dogs were the two men's passion, and on them they lavished their love and care. There runs through all the letters he wrote in these years – even letters to London agents and New York publishers – a stream of pure domestic comedy: the story of Lucy and Fanny. Lucy was a miniature pinscher who arrived as the last of the schnauzers was, in Miss Docker's words, gathered to God. 'She is very elegant,' White reported to Ronald Waters when the pup arrived. 'Wears rhinestones in the evening, green jade for afternoon receptions, and red leather *pour le sport*.' Fanny came a few months later. She was a pug. 'You should have a pug before you die,' White advised his old friend. 'They are so like so many of one's friends.'[56] He found them game and athletic.

When the decision was taken to do the right thing by Fanny, White arranged an assignation in Strathfield with a dog of the noble name Teng Wah Lo-Sze. Of the difficulties that followed, Dutton received a full account: 'Unfortunately Fanny has so far been terrified and Lo-Sze not all that interested. I wish you could see the house in which all this takes place. It is a real Home Beautiful in the right kind of brick, with pixies, storks, and toadstools on the lawn, dog ornaments inside – literally hundreds of them, from small china ones to enormous cloth Dismal Desmonds, the size of a man, standing in corners. Quite eerie. The matings take place in what the pug-lady refers to as the "dogs' TV lounge". Certainly there is a TV working madly all the time, which is perhaps what puts the dogs off. On the last occasion there was some dreadful musical, with a number, the chorus of which went: "Sit down! Sit down! Sit down!" Teng Wah Lo-Sze obediently did, and that was the end of the mating for that evening. We are also learning "terms", such as "showing colour" for bloody discharge, "tied", and "a slip mating" – all too Dekyvere.'[57]

News of the litter born just before Christmas was widely broadcast. What gripped White at any moment went into his letters: 'Fanny gave birth to a litter of seven three days ago, refuses to do anything for them and we live now by the alarm clock, feeding, and wiping the bottoms of pups. A pug is something to get ready-made.' Four pups survived. Two were sold, one was given to Doris Fitton, and the last remained at Dogwoods. She grew into the Divine Ethel. White wrote to Charles Osborne at the *London Magazine*, 'Pugs are probably going to be the vice of my old age.'[58]

With the dogs in mind, Arrighi explored the territory round Centennial Park and found a house for sale at 20 Martin Road. It stood on the spine of a sandy hill and looked out over the park, which ran up to iron railings on the other side of the street. Centennial Park was a suburb White had never had much to do with. To people like the Whites it seemed it was somehow Catholic, an address for bookmakers and dentists with big families. The fate of the big places round the park seemed to be to end up as boarding houses. Migrants threatened the suburb. Already a few Greeks had moved in. They had the money but not the style to spend it on something smaller at a better address. And surely it was hot in Centennial Park? Ruth's old crowd had a settled prejudice that sea breezes never reached unfashionable streets.

White saw 20 Martin Road and decided to buy. He broke the news to Peggy Garland. 'The address is unfashionable and the house of the wrong period – it must have been built some time during the first decade of the century – but it has the makings of what we want, and it will be like living in the country while only ten minutes' drive from the GPO. There is a forty-foot living room with wonderful wall space for paintings, and another large room which I shall use as a workroom. Both the kitchen and laundry are large compared with what one usually finds, an excellent, if very pastel bathroom, two spare rooms on the ground floor, and the bedrooms which we shall use are large interesting atticky, with glassed-in balconies looking out over the parks. There are two garages, when you rarely find one in Sydney – one of these we shall be able to use for tools and luggage and things – the garden is enough to keep us happy, and already wired to receive dogs. Perhaps the greatest advantage is that very little will have to be done beyond altering some ceilings, architraves or doorways, and painting, before the place will be habitable.'[59]

No buyer appeared at Dogwoods. The march of the suburbs which engulfed the Parkers' farm and shaved Xanadu 'right down to a bald, red, rudimentary hill' had, ironically, stopped short of their farm which lay protected still from the developers' axe just within the Green Belt. The property market was slow, White decided, reluctantly, to lease Dogwoods and buy the new house by borrowing against his mother's estate. This violated White principles, but 'I am determined to move and start building the shell for my last years while I am still young enough to do it. This may sound over-pessimistic, but I only consider it realistic. From experience I know that it takes years to make the shell, and I suppose I can reasonably expect another twenty years before senility sets in – or the chopper descends.'[60]

Martin Road was bought for £17,500 in May 1964, and workmen began alterations the following month. They stripped the house bare. The autumn-tone carpets were pulled out and heavy plaster reliefs were scraped from the ceilings. They ripped out door frames built like the architraves on Egyptian tombs. And after those years of chopping wood at Castle Hill it was decided to brick up all the fireplaces. Almost at once, White was complaining, 'I expect the work is going to cost a whole lot more, as the basic wage for New South Wales went up by £1 only last week.' The renovations took far longer than they expected.

At Dogwoods White was working steadily on the novel, putting down 10,000 words a week. Writing was a godsend in the frustrations of dealing with the architect and builders, 'a complete escape from what might otherwise have sent me crazy. Instead I think the craziness has gone into the novel.'[61]

By late September, 20 Martin Road 'was starting to look spacious and civilised, so beautifully clean and white I shall hardly dare live in it for some time. On the other hand I shall only want to close my door and never go out.' He wanted to arrive, as he had reached Australia after the war, free of superfluous baggage. 'I have accumulated far too many possessions,' he told Manning Clark. Apart from a houseful of furniture, there were over fifty paintings, a sculpture, a fountain, three dogs and four cats to move down to Centennial Park. 'We discarded two-thirds of what we possessed – not nearly enough.'[62]

A fire was lit in the garden a few days before the move and White heaped box after box of papers beside the pit. Twice since moving to Castle Hill he had culled his papers; now he planned the most thorough purging of his past, an act of renewal by fire. Lascaris fed the flames as White fetched more fuel from the house. Into this little inferno Lascaris threw the last surviving copies of *Return to Abyssinia* and the last copy (so White thought) of his novel 'Nightside', which no publisher had ever seen. Into the flames went the American journal he once hoped to dedicate to Spud Johnson. More wartime notes and diaries from the Middle East followed into the fire. Waiting for this occasion was a small suitcase full of copies of *The Ploughman*, collected over the years by the Sydney book dealer Isidoor Berkelouw under a standing order from White. 'They should never have been published.'[63] All were burnt. He had kept few letters, but among them were all those from Betty Withycombe over the thirty-five years of their friendship. He had stored them in a chest on the back veranda. Now they were burnt. Stan Parker believed,

> It doesn't do to keep old letters . . . It's morbid. You start reading back, and forget that you have moved on. Mother was a great one for that. She had a drawerful of old letters. They had changed colour.[64]

Now Lascaris fed into the pit the manuscripts of *The Tree of Man* and *Voss*. 'I stood there at the fire feeding the manuscripts in, bundle by bundle, thinking perhaps I could keep out just this little bundle. It was all handwritten and in those days Patrick had a most beautiful hand, it was very easy to read. But I couldn't because I had promised to burn them. And if I make a promise I must keep it.'[65] Lascaris turned the heaps of smouldering paper so that every sheet burnt to a fine ash.

Smoke from the bonfire drifted through the garden and into the pages of *The Solid Mandala*, where Waldo Brown stands by the pit in slippers and dressing-gown,

> He began to throw his papers by handfuls, or would hold one down with his slippered foot, when the wind threatened to carry too far, with his slippered foot from which the blue veins and smoke wreathed upward.
>
> It was both a sowing and a scattering of seed. When he had finished he felt lighter, but always had been, he suspected while walking away.
>
> Now at least he was free of practically everything . . . [66]

Early on the morning of 12 October David Moore drove White down to the new house with the icons and dogs (two in season) to wait for the carriers who were bringing the paintings. He sat on the low, broad windowsill of the dining room with the manuscript of the novel on his knee, wondering if the book would survive this break in the routine of his life. He had hoped to finish the first draft before the move, and had 115,000 words on paper, but there was still a little way to go. The first words written in the deserted house were 'pure, if fearful, bliss'.[67] He sat writing for most of the day while the work went on around him.

Their friend the physiologist John Young drove his Volkswagen up and back all day loaded to the running boards. Klári Daniel brought a picnic lunch over to Martin Road. In the afternoon Grace Brothers came with the furniture in a pantechnicon, while Lascaris stayed behind to do a last sweep through the old house. Young brought him down in the evening with a last load of pot plants and cats.[68]

PART FOUR

The Pavement and the Crowd

Everything comes out of the mess you're in.

PW

TWENTY-TWO

Twins

WHITE FINISHED THE first draft of *The Solid Mandala* a fortnight after moving to Martin Road and put the manuscript away while he worked on the house. 'We still have lots of jobs to do,' he reported to Dutton after a month. 'Two days ago we got the painters back, and half the house had to be dismantled. You've never seen anything like the mess the furniture movers made of the stairway on the day of the move, and a clot of a plumber, who did almost everything wrong, excelled himself by turning on the main before connecting up the upstairs lavatory, and flooding the diningroom ceiling just after it had been painted. Now all this has been made good at last.

'I must say painters are the most amiable, the most house-trained of all the tradesmen. They insisted on putting back all the curtains and paintings we had to take down for them, and some of the paintings give one a rupture just to think about moving them . . . The Finnish light fittings and curtains are the greatest success. It is strange that that little country, with such stodgy and rather unpleasant inhabitants (at least the few I have met) can produce things in such infallibly good taste.'[1]

At first sight 20 Martin Road seemed more like a gallery than a house. The dining room and sitting room, opening each side of the entrance hall, made one long space hung with paintings dominated by Nolan's huge blue canvas called *Galaxy*. This was a birthday present from the painter and White saw it as convincing proof that his friend was 'our greatest *creative* painter'.[2] The most familiar photograph of Patrick White from these years – it first appeared on the jacket of *The Burnt Ones* – shows him sitting in a sports coat and tie in front of Nolan's swirls, the ghost of a smile on his proud face.

The hall was hung with icons above shelves of Greek books. The rugs were Greek, Anatolian and Persian. Levantine instinct encouraged Lascaris to buy rugs in times of inflation. 'Our Greek rugs, or some of them, are about to arrive from Alexandroupolis,' White wrote a few weeks after moving into the house. 'We are also expecting the icon of Manoly's sainted ancestor, Christodoulos, which we commissioned Kondoglou to paint. We are told he had it blessed by the Church when finished, so now we shall have to get Ezekiel to decontaminate the house when the icon arrives.'[3]

A green sofa in the shape of a crescent moon stood on one side of the sitting room. A low table stood in front of this with books and a square of old embroidered silk brought back from China by Peggy Garland. A photograph of Roy de Maistre stood on a shelf near the carriage clock from Smyrna, and in an alcove overlooking the garden was one of two revolving bookcases White bought after seeing these strange but practical devices in Steven Runciman's tower on the Scottish borders. Doors opened on to a veranda that looked across the garden and Centennial Park.

His workroom, a darker version of the sitting room, opened on to the same veranda. Fairweather's great *Gethsemane* hung over his desk, the Parramatta copy of the Francis Bacon desk, its red lino top heaped with envelopes, piles of foolscap, string, papers and dictionaries was the only patch of chaos in a neat house. A few rugs lay on the polished boards; a rocking chair stood in the alcove beneath an air-conditioner. Paintings filled the room rather than books, but a low bookcase by the door held a copy of each English edition of his work and, by the time of the move to Martin Road, editions in German, Italian, Portuguese, French, Turkish, Polish, Norwegian, Finnish, Spanish and Czech. The bronze figure of a dancer by Peggy Garland stood on the bookcase beside an old apothecary's jar with letters in gold: SARSAPARILL.

The track White beat between his desk and the stove took him along a passage behind the dining room, past a second bathroom and the spare bedrooms. The kitchen was a big plain room almost cut in half by a bench. On the far side of the bench were sink, cupboards and stove; on the near side was a low table and chairs. White's lifeline to the outside world, the telephone, stood on this kitchen table. The Martin Road number was always unlisted. On the door of the refrigerator the two men stuck notes in Greek to remind one another when to buy the dogs' meat. Doors led from the kitchen to the dining room, a pantry and the laundry where the dogs slept on litters. Beyond the laundry lay the back garden where Lascaris had brought the pots of herbs and geraniums from Dogwoods.

Out the back over the garages they built a Greek terrace with a 'pergola which will be covered in vines' where they drank tea in the mornings. From their terrace they looked across a few roofs to the grass fields of Moore Park and beyond that to the city which was almost hidden beneath the trees. White had the same view from his attic bedroom, and standing at his window at night he liked to imagine himself in Paris. Dawn brought its inevitable disappointment: 'what has been the Champs Elysées by night is turned back into Anzac Parade'.[4]

He had taken the larger of the two bedrooms under the roof. The walls were low, but there was room for bookshelves and small paintings. An air-conditioner in the window worked for a few years, failed, and was never repaired. On still summer nights the room was like an oven. Lying on the dressing table were the monogrammed ivory brushes Dick had left him in 1937, those tokens of a prosperous past he shared with Theodora Goodman, Madeleine the horsewoman of Durilgai, Sir Basil Hunter and Eddie Twyborn.

Lascaris slept on the other side of the landing. His room had a monastic simplicity with a small neat bed, a rug and framed family photographs standing neatly on a chest of drawers. Those mute, appealing faces from Smyrna and Alexandria were proof that Lascaris was truly the foreigner in the house. Life for him was essentially unchanged by the move from Castle Hill. All the driving, most of the shopping and most of the outdoor work was still done by Lascaris. He was rarely still. White liked to say there were sitting Greeks and running Greeks. Lascaris was a runner.

Only a few big trees stood on their sandy hill when they came to Martin Road. Lascaris began their second garden from scratch. Even the top-soil was the work of many years and many compost heaps. They planted all the things they couldn't grow at Castle Hill. 'A hibiscus was never happy there till autumn, and as soon as it got into its stride the frost would catch it.' Hannah Lloyd Jones presented them with four white azaleas and a white camellia 'which we now have round the house in tubs. I'm afraid we shall look rather self-consciously white, with white cats for good measure.' The azaleas stood up well to the winds which were the main problem at Martin Road. White called the house Wuthering Heights, for there was 'a gale raging almost every day from one direction or another'. The Duttons sent clippings of white sarsaparilla, and the vine grew into such a wonderful sight White wondered if he had 'misused the name'.[5]

Briefly they had a cleaning woman. White at first found her pleasant, 'a Jewess from Harbin, whose grandfather came from Minsk – a family of printers. However, after doing everything in the way of house-cleaning ourselves over the last fifteen years, I find it a great strain having somebody else about, and I am always relieved when those mornings are over.'[6] She did not last. White explained that she was a poor sort of Russian who liked Tchaikovsky and hadn't read Tolstoy. Once again, he took up the broom and Hoover himself.

Not since Alexandria had they had close neighbours. In a big bare house on one side of No. 20 lived a barrister and his family. Their twelve-year-old son assumed at first that Lascaris was the butler. The little boy became very formal when that was corrected, and said: 'Well, I hope you are enjoying the comforts of your new home.' He went on to reveal that his mother was reading *Riders in the Chariot*. 'But she finds it so heavy she has to take a rest after every couple of lines.' White found the father, an Australian-born Greek, a tremendously profitable gossip and he foresaw 'happy talks ahead'.[7]

White grizzled for years about the distractions of life 'on the wild side' but he kept a close eye on the action and in letters to friends gave a soap opera account, episode by episode, of life next door. When the new paling fence was attacked with a tomahawk, White called the police. 'But of course police will do nothing until you are a corpse.' The fence feud was resolved. In time White grew fond of the children, and the mother knitted him jumpers for Christmas – one year she brought over two for him to choose from and he kept both – but in these early days he had nothing but scorn for the 'dreadful' neighbours. They kept a Shetland pony in the house which White blamed for a plague of flies. At first he kept a fly swat at hand to protect his clean white walls. 'I expect we shall forget about all this after a month or two and simply relax.'[8]

Six weeks after moving in White was able to report he was resting and enjoying a read 'such as I haven't had for years. I have just finished *The Brothers Karamazov* for the third time in my life. Each reading has given me a little more. I hope I have the opportunity of reading it again in twenty years time. By then I should be able to get into every corner of it. The sad part of the book is that one realises one hasn't, and never will arrive anywhere very much in one's own writing. Now I am re-reading *Varieties of Religious Experience*, and mopped up a funny, sour, bankrupt little novel of Edna O'Brien's, *Girls in Their Married Bliss*. I finally got hold of *Notre dame des fleurs* – in English though . . . it sailed in without a hitch.'[9]

He returned to *The Solid Mandala* after a busy Christmas of cooking, cleaning, dealing with a litter of pups, talking to 'symbol chasers' from the university and showing off the new house. He was rather surprised when he reread the first draft of the novel. 'It must have written itself.'[10]

The Browns of Sarsaparilla seemed two halves of his own nature: it was as if he had taken a scalpel to himself and excised the innocent Arthur, leaving the monster Waldo behind.[11] Memory and imagination gave him all he needed to make the twins real and separate characters, but at heart they are Patrick White: an expression of the best hopes and worst fears he held for himself.

He made Arthur the sort of man his cousin Philip Garland might have been if the boy's 'childish wisdom' had matured. Philip's direct simplicity, his intuition and sympathy, his openness to strangers, his way of provoking kindness and affection, were all part of Arthur Brown. 'You *must* be kind to him,' Mrs Poulter explains. 'Kindness is something he understands.' White was haunted by the memory of walking through the woods to the Wellington zoo hand in hand with this fat odd child. Walking is important in *The Solid Mandala*: Arthur and Waldo are locked together as they drag themselves round the streets of Sarsaparilla.[12]

The mother of each of these simple boys believed there was some genius in them. White allowed it to be true for Arthur Brown, the perceptive one and 'keeper of the mandalas'.[13] He gave Arthur an *idiot savant*'s talent for numbers and a precocious taste for literature. Philip Garland had managed to wander down to the local library to read children's books, but Arthur Brown catches the train to the Mitchell Library and discovers *The Brothers Karamazov*. White spared Arthur the drugs and rages that dogged Philip Garland's young life, but both of the boys ended in asylums. As White was writing the novel, Philip Garland was in a Rudolf Steiner school in Scotland. Soon he was moved to an asylum in Wales where he lived for the rest of his life, the last years in self-imposed silence. He died in 1986.

Waldo is White's idea of what he might be if all traces of love and intuition were cut away: a spiteful intellectual with a nose for failure, timid, fragile and unforgiving. 'I *am* unforgiving,' he confessed to Dutton. 'It is one of my worst faults – too much Waldo in me.' Waldo's unforgiving hatred is directed against his brother, his colleagues, his neighbours in Sarsaparilla, dogs, his writing, his father and himself. He dies of spite, bursting like a boil filled with pent-up hatred of all living things. Waldo is also another of White's fearful portraits of closeted homosexuals: he is 'a veiled bride'.[14]

The name was an act of revenge. 'Waldo . . . was based on an actual Waldo (name and all) the friend of a friend I had at Cambridge.' He was the man who introduced R to sex. White was not ungrateful for this – 'on the basis of that affair, we had ours' – but while he was away on one of his trips to Cornwall Waldo appeared in Cambridge and R later confessed a minor betrayal. Waldo and White never met, but 'a rather nasty, thin character' and an odd name lodged in his jealous imagination to re-emerge thirty years later in Sydney. The *look* of the man White found from an entirely different source: 'Physically, Waldo Brown at all stages is, for me, Joyce at all stages.' And White noted that James Joyce, whom he could no longer read but loved to read about, had 'the face of the arch-masturbator'.[15]

Waldo is a local writer, one of those public servant scribblers

Ruth taught her son to despise. To Juliet O'Hea he remarked as he was drafting *The Solid Mandala*, 'When I hear the phrase "Australian writers" a heavy brown curtain always seems to descend before my eyes.' Waldo is White's complaint against a particular species: he is afraid to live and determined to be respectable, he dreams of writing but barely lifts a pen, he has no interest in painting or music and he so lacks intuition that faces in the street reflect only his own sentiments back to him. Waldo can never remember faces. The 'vast corrosive satire on the public service' inspired by the malice he bears his superiors in the Mitchell Library is never begun. Of Waldo's great plans, only a fragment of *Tiresias a Youngish Man* is ever realised – but it is Arthur who grasps the meaning of the blind prophet who has lived as both man and woman.[16]

For the first few weeks of the New Year, 1965, all went well with the book, but then he entered a very rough patch in which the manuscript turned grey and stodgy. He stopped writing and read it all through again. 'I think half the trouble was I had become too obsessed with words and textures and had forgotten what I was trying to build up into a whole.' In February he had a bad bout of asthma which may have been brought on by these struggles, 'or perhaps the asthma has been making the novel seem more desperately bad than it is. I do know that two doctors have told me all their asthma patients have started up.' But illness once more came to his aid:

> Arthur said: 'You know when you are ill, really ill, not diphtheria, which we haven't had, but anything, pneumonia – you can't say we haven't had pneumonia – you can get, you can get much farther in.'
>   'Into what?'
>   It tired Waldo.
>   'Into anything.'

By the end of the month the bad patch was behind him. 'I have my moments of despair and revulsion,' he told Dutton. 'But on the whole I am obsessed by it, which I like to think a promising sign.'[17]

He wrote from midnight till dawn. The dark was full of strange noises, odd cries and the honking of wildfowl from the lakes. His reward for a night's work was the sight of Centennial Park at dawn: 'a Corot full of mists and flooded trees'. Only a few acres were civilised with statues and palms. The rest of the park was left much as it was when this stretch of country was fenced off in 1888 to commemorate a century of white settlement in Australia. Here were half a dozen lakes, acres of sandhills and wild heath, a few rough playing fields marked with whitewashed lines, a soft track for riders and banks of coral trees that

put out scarlet flowers on bare winter branches. Tramps slept in caves.
From time to time a body surfaced on one of the lakes. White found
the park full of unexpected pleasures in the first weeks of exploration.
'All sorts of wild life, including on one occasion a porcupine, and a
strange solitary duck with bearded pouch.'[18] Every afternoon he and
Lascaris walked the dogs for a few miles round the lakes as far as the
magnificent paperbarks near the Paddington gates. Then they turned
for home.

That first summer at Centennial Park was very dry. On a day of
high wind a grass fire burnt to the edge of Martin Road with 'little
flames trickling through the railings. Fortunately a fire engine arrived
and a hose was played round the pine tree directly opposite before
it could begin to throw torches at this house.' The two men were
reassured to have professional protection after the 'horse-and-buggy
volunteer brigade' of Castle Hill.[19]

As White was working on the second draft of *The Solid Mandala*
the summer drought broke and the lakes filled with water. 'I went down
with a bagful of stale bread the evening the rain cleared. I had ducks
flying and swimming at me from all corners, a wonderful pattern of
converging wakes on silver water, but quite a solid wall of cold. I
also found a Queensland wheel-tree in flower. Do you know it? Very
Jungian. I have had to bring one into my novel.'[20]

White was now a believer without any formal faith. He could not
accept 'the sterility, the vulgarity, in many cases the bigotry of the
Christian churches in Australia' and more than ever doubted his capacity
to forgive, which he knew was at the core of orthodox Christianity.
Unable and unwilling to call himself a Christian, White nevertheless
recognised Christ as one of the means by which 'God reveals Himself'.[21]

White's unshackled spiritual curiosity had led him in the early
1960s towards the occult. He was a figure of his time. He discovered
the tarot in London in 1963 when the Duttons introduced him to the
painter Lawrence Daws. White already had a vast abstract by Daws
called 'Song of the Edda' and he was fascinated to see the silk screens
Daws was then making of the juggler, the emperor, the hierophant and
the chariot from the tarot. When he was told over lunch that he could
buy a tarot pack at Foyle's for two guineas, he announced, 'I am going
to have a try.'[22]

Daws recalled them discussing these images, 'and the possibility that
they were archetypal images that we carried around and that, loosely,
the images they evoked were common to all people. We talked about
mandalas and the mandala paintings I had exhibited at the Matthiesen
Gallery the year before. Then onto Jung. The idea of making oneself
whole, of making *a mandala of one's life* . . . appealed strongly to Patrick

. . . I think Jung clarified for Patrick the idea of the *whole* and the attempting to arrive at it as the real purpose of our lives.' They remained in contact. White became enthusiastic about horoscopes and the *I Ching*: 'he behaved at times in a fairly vulnerable way, sometimes seizing on the slightest reference as a divine message and giving it significance in shaping his life. In a way, the Jungian mandala concept gave him . . . a structure on which to hang all those things that were separately shaping his being.'[23]

White found confirmation in Jung of ideas he had long held: 'Symmetry appeals to me, and life I find symmetrical, when I used to think it haphazard, without design.'[24] Those circular images of perfection Jung called mandalas had always cropped up in White's writing, as jewels, birds' eggs, lakes, bays, trees, stones and the whirling patterns of dance. He recognised mandalas as signs of the divine pattern of the world for which he had searched, following one map or another, since he fell in the rain at Dogwoods. But his search for wholeness predated even that conversion, for he always saw himself as a shattered personality – not one man but a cast of characters – and Jung offered him fresh hope of making sense of this jumble.

White had gone some distance with *The Solid Mandala* when he turned to Daws for help. In answer to his appeal, Daws arranged for a copy of Jung's *Psychology and Alchemy* to be sent to White along with a little volume by Jung on psychology and religion. White was excited to find '*all* the symbols which came to me spontaneously in connection with [the novel] are meaningful and recognised ones now that I am investigating them in Jung'. Among the books he read in the pause between writing the first and second versions of the novel were more volumes of Jung. 'He seems to me to have a lot of the answers.'[25]

White did not absorb influences of this kind systematically. He took on board not the whole cargo but only what was needed for the voyage. More books and essays seem to have been written about the role of Jung in his writing than any other aspect of his work, but White grew exasperated with Jungian commentators. Against one who sent him an essay in the early 1980s, White railed: 'Like all such obsessed characters, he tries to tie his subject down in the straitjacket of his system and finds I don't fit. Of course I'm no expert on Jung, only picked a few bits which suited my purpose, just as I've picked a few bits from Christian theology and the Jewish mystics.'[26]

White's search for serenity was all the more urgent for the hate that was pouring out of him into the pages of *The Solid Mandala*. He was gloomier than ever about the human race, and the bitter frustrations of the theatre years just past had left him with a darker, more pessimistic view of his fellow countrymen. When James Stern later rebuked him for the hate in the novel White replied: 'Unfortunately, we live in black times with less and less that may be called good, and I suppose I must reflect the blackness of those times. I tried to write a book about saints, but saints are few and far between. If I were a saint myself I could project my saintliness, perhaps, endlessly in what I write. But I am a sensual and irritable human being. Certainly the longer I live the less I see to like in the human beings of whom I am one.'27

The theatre had blackened his outlook but clarified his prose. He found he was writing in quite a different style, simplifying and abbreviating to save his theme from coming to grief 'in a lush labyrinth of poetic prose . . . I have tried to develop more of a throw-away technique.' But he was unsure that his writing would survive the departure from Castle Hill and the severing of the 'spiritual roots' he had put down in that uncongenial soil. His anxiety gave the new novel an edge of ambivalence and unease, fatality and foreboding. *The Solid Mandala* was emerging as a book of 'transitoriness': he had only returned to the landscape of Sarsaparilla to get it out of his system.28

The oxywelding of the second draft took only three months. 'I find things go more quickly than they did at Castle Hill, I suppose because one has so much less ground to cover, and there is no longer the long and exhausting drive to get anywhere.' The last days were very tense, and he put the manuscript aside in autumn in a state of acute constipation. 'Now I have taken a Brooklax and hope to function normally for the next month. After that the final round.'29

He endured his first Easter Show in Martin Road. 'The world of chestnut bulls with mattress rumps, and jet trotters, and towers of golden corn' was familiar from childhood. Here in a side alley Theodora Goodman had taken up a gun and shattered all the clay ducks. Grauvolk had had its triumphs in the show ring, and before moving down to the new house White thought he might take Ethel over in a basket and carry off the Bitches' Challenge. But the whole thing was a different proposition once he found himself in Martin Road with the showground at the end of the block. Easter was ten days of hell. Martin Road filled with floats, trailers, trucks, caravans and people. White and Lascaris could not escape, indeed the neighbours urged them to stay home for this was the break-and-enter season. 'Of course it brings a lot of life to the neighbourhood, and some of the inhabitants obviously flourish in it: ladies who normally stroll listlessly down the street and back start spanking twice round the block.' Up the street he observed a woman sitting on her terrace, 'at an iron table in her pastel bubble-nightie, I suspect when her husband (to whom she isn't speaking) is out. One starts speaking to neighbours one had never addressed before, and I wonder whether one will speak to them again before the next Show. It's all probably like the War in London.'30

White resented the show more each year. By the 1970s he declared

Martin Road off-limits to the world for those ten days. 'Yesterday
– Saturday – was the most hideous Arab bedlam I have ever had
to endure,' he reported to Dutton one year. 'The final frenzy of
fireworks, loudspeakers, and screams made me long for a downpour
on Easter Monday to wash the whole thing away.' But early on he
detected a most curious phenomenon: a large number of babies were
born in the neighbourhood every Christmas. He gave the show credit:
'I think everyone is so relieved when the Show is over in April, they
throw the pills into Centennial Park and fuck solid.'[31]

He typed the final draft of *The Solid Mandala* in May and June. The book
was shorter than he thought it would be, because his handwriting seemed
to have developed a spread with age. 'I am still too close to the book to
be able to get much idea how good or bad it is,' he told Marshall Best. 'I
like to think my own involvement means the involvement of my future
readers, and the writing of this one has certainly torn me to shreds.' The
dogs that tore Waldo's corpse to pieces in the final pages of the book
were the offspring of some beasts from Castle Hill. A drunken Scottish
couple used to stagger down Showground Road with these animals on
leads. As White was finishing *The Solid Mandala* he heard that one of
the dogs had broken free and torn a piece out of the woman's arm –
or was it her leg?[32]

Copies of the typescript left for New York and London at the end
of June. Gwen and David Moore were overwhelmed to hear White was
dedicating the book to them. 'You won't be too pleased by the time the
critics get stuck into it,' he said. When Marshall Best cabled and wrote
enthusiastically in July – 'I think it is the most concentrated and most
intensely felt of all your books' – White handed the letter to the Moores
and told them to keep it. 'It's your book.' The London advance was
the best Eyre & Spottiswoode had ever given him: £1,500. They did
try to change the title, but White would not budge: 'The title is the
book and the book the title.' He arranged for the London publishers
to commission Desmond Digby to do the cover, and one afternoon the
two men returned to Sarsaparilla to find the sort of house the Browns
would have lived in. They never found the one White had in mind.
Digby recalled a very pleasant day, 'but I have seen much better Greek
fronts since'.[33]

As was now a settled ritual, the world at large first heard of the
new Patrick White from a hostile review in *Time*. White rated this
effort 'about the dirtiest and most personal attack so far'. *The Solid
Mandala* appeared in New York in February 1966, and in Australia and
London a couple of months later. Viking had scaled down both print
run and promotion, and Best admitted to O'Hea after a few weeks
that the reviews in New York 'were only so-so and our sales have

been disappointing'.[34] London and Australia were more enthusiastic, but sales everywhere sagged from the heights of *Riders in the Chariot*.

As one of the last acts of a friendship that had seemed indestructible, White asked Viking to send a complimentary copy of the new book to Klári Daniel. She was as energetic, intense and demanding as ever. She lived through him still, and her role in *Riders in the Chariot* was her glory. Klári's conversation was always about Patrick. But White had tired of her. She had survived the general scattering of his central European friends, but he had begun to level against her all the complaints he brought against the others: that their intellectual life was set fast fifty years in the past, and nothing would drag them forward. White may have sensed her disappointment with *The Solid Mandala*, for she could not bear its violent climax. That baring of the soul contradicted her image of White as the lofty, assured Thomas Mann of the Antipodes. As White withdrew from her intellectually, she made the mistake of trying to draw him back by mothering him.

The breach came, as it usually did with White, over a triviality. One day Daniel refused a new cauliflower salad he had made for lunch. 'You never want to *try* anything,' White snapped. The row that followed seemed routine, but Daniel was appalled to find that this little quarrel marked a final breach. It almost destroyed her, but she was a resilient woman and bore the humiliation with dignity. 'I don't hold it against him,' she told Maria Prerauer. 'I was there at the right time. I did it gladly. He squeezes you out like a lemon and when it is dry he turns to someone else.'[35]

Once *The Solid Mandala* was behind him White flew over to Anlaby, where the Duttons were living in disordered splendour while Geoff maintained his hectic career as an entrepreneur of Australian writing: lecturing and editing while grabbing time here and there to work on his own books. Duttons' *Literature of Australia* had been published in 1964, and his latest venture was a new paperback publishing house called Sun Books. White's writing plans were now shaped by the wish to help Dutton get Sun Books off the ground.

White recommended verse by Peter Porter, quotations by Huxley, Genet's *Our Lady of the Flowers* and a book of soups, 'full of hints that thousands of lazy Australian housewives have been waiting for'. Of these only the Porter appeared, with illustrations by Desmond Digby. 'Patrick did try to help,' Dutton recalled, 'but of course he had no idea what would sell.' As the new editions appeared White registered approval and disapproval: why had they republished David Martin's *The Young Wife*, 'that miserable little piece of unreadable journalism'? And why Henry Handel Richardson's *Maurice Guest*, 'the most appalling and unreadable novelette'? White wrote a blurb for some novellas by the young Australian writer David Foster, but his great service to Sun Books was to secure, by treading on a number of toes in London, the paperback rights to *Four Plays*.[36]

Another novel was boiling up in him but he was reluctant to start so soon after the last, and on his return from Anlaby he began a long, light story which he saw as the first of three that would make up a little volume called *Presences*. He thought he would be free to offer this to Dutton despite his contracts with Viking and Eyre & Spottiswoode. 'I don't feel the three short novels will be trivial,' he told Peggy Garland. 'But it is necessary to live one's literary life on several planes to stay the right side of sanity.' The first was called 'A Woman's Hand'.[37]

Lascaris, at this point, suffered what seemed a heart attack and in the nightmare hours that followed White was unable to find a doctor. Eventually he called an ambulance and Lascaris was taken to St Vincent's Hospital at the Cross. By the time they arrived, he 'looked like a corpse, terribly yellow, and he felt cold and lifeless – after some time the experts decided it might be a coronary but with peculiar symptoms. They also let me know in a tactful way that it was going to be touch and go.' After twenty-four hours the trouble was diagnosed as acute pericarditis, an inflammation of the membrane round the heart. White was relieved. 'His life won't be altered by pericarditis.'[38] Lascaris was in hospital for three weeks, only surviving, White believed, on the food he brought each night in a vacuum flask. White was left alone at Martin Road while Lascaris went over to Anlaby to rest for a couple of weeks.

White crawled through the first draft of 'A Woman's Hand': a study of sexual ambiguity presided over by 'one of those women who are 100% conceit'. Once that was down, he began the medical research for the next novella, which involved the theatre and cocaine. A psychiatrist at the big Sydney lunatic asylum, Callan Park, gave him some instruction on cocaine addiction but, he told Dutton, 'I expect in the end I shall have to go gingerly hand in hand with my intuition and my own schizoid nature.' After a month he abandoned 'Dolly Formosa's Last Stand', for he found that writing about theatre people forced him to stay on a trivial level, 'or else lose touch with the ground in developing their abnormalities. Perhaps, on the other hand, there is something wrong with me at the moment. I may have embarked too soon. The whole thing smells a bit of carpentry and book-making.'[39] He gave Dutton 'A Woman's Hand' to publish in *Australian Letters*. The third novella was never begun.

White began to blame 'a surfeit of Australia' for his frustrations and toyed with the idea of following Eleanor Arrighi to live in Rome. Lascaris was very sceptical about this plan to abandon Sydney, and White's enthusiasm waned as he thought of what it would cost. 'Also when it came to the point, I shouldn't want to leave my friends who alone make all the gimcrackery and hot air of Australia bearable.' There was more to it than that, but White was reluctant to give his reasons for staying in a country he spent so much time railing against. He spoke of it as his fate but that was a formula to mask a more difficult admission that Australia was what he *needed* as an artist. To Peter Beatson he once confessed that coming home had often been unpleasant but 'the right thing to do . . . I'd only have been a beachcomber in Greece, a curiosity, a freak. Here I'm often not much better, but it's what I come from and what I can write about. From time to time I have to protest against various awful aspects of Australian life; even those serve a purpose, I think, providing the kind of irritant I need creatively.'[40]

After a break at Kangaroo Island with the Duttons, White began to draft a long novel that had been working in his mind for years. Perhaps he put off writing 'The Binoculars and Helen Nell' too long. He might have begun before *The Solid Mandala* but felt he must first get Sarsaparilla out of his system. Then he put the novel off again to write the novellas for Geoffrey Dutton. Now in the New Year of 1966 he settled down to the task. He imagined that years of demanding and satisfying work lay ahead.

He had not forgotten Sun Books. Dutton had lured the Russian poet Yevgeny Yevtushenko away from Penguin, and White half-agreed to write an introduction to the new edition, but quickly began to back-pedal. 'More and more embarrassing! . . . much as I love "Zhima Junction", which I can see, touch, and smell, I can't admire "Bratsk Hydroelectric" at all. Certainly the translation is repulsive, but I suspect the substance would not be much subtler if less crudely treated. Little could be done about such rhetoric, sentimentality, and copybook patriotism. It may provoke orgasms in the youth of every Bratsk in Siberia, but to me it is the kind of stuff which is not for export.'[41] With regret, he refused. The Russian was the star of that year's Adelaide Festival and when he came back through Sydney, White organised a big party of 'young artists' to meet him. It was the most celebrated of White's Martin Road parties. He cooked for days beforehand, and the tension was raised to new heights that night, for White's preparations included a plan to rush the poet into hiding 'if there should be any hint of his wanting asylum'.[42]

Yevtushenko arrived with his 'interpreter' Oxana Krugerskaya and a local Communist novelist, Frank Hardy, whom White could never bear. Yevtushenko was charming. Lascaris worked with easy efficiency to get the party moving. White hovered grimly over the food. By the standards of Martin Road, things were going splendidly when Frank Hardy opened the front door to a man carrying a television set. Yevtushenko apologised profusely to White: he, too, had no television in Russia as a matter of principle, and he was sorry for inflicting his shame on the gathering but a recital he had given in Adelaide was to be broadcast. The set was put in a corner and Yevtushenko knelt a few feet away, mouthing the words and re-enacting in miniature his own performance on the screen. White bolted for the kitchen.

After the meal, which the thirty guests ate standing, Yevtushenko called for silence and made a speech. Krugerskaya translated. Reading *Voss* had been a traumatic experience, said the poet: 'It is like using an iron crow-bar at minus sixty-five degrees centigrade in Siberia: when you let go, part of the skin adheres to it. Part of me went to *Voss* and blood too.' White sat thunderstruck. The poet declared the guests had kind eyes. He could see no hostility. He turned to a young woman in green, and said, 'Especially your eyes are kind.' She blew him a kiss. Yevtushenko then launched, in the words of the host, 'into an embarrassing tirade of hate' against America. White sat grim and unflinching as the poet and his translator pursued their 'operatic duet-cum-ballet'. The Russian hoped that eventually 'We will all be working for all people, the whole world.'[43] There was no applause. White left for the kitchen clutching his head.

The night ended with an exchange of books. White presented Yevtushenko with paperbacks of his novels – and had the impression the Russian wanted to make sure his wife beat Krugerskaya to the job of translating them – and the poet presented White with an edition of his poems inscribed, 'Too great writer Patrick Wait from all may russian Learto Ev Yevtushenko.' They parted, White told Dutton, 'with tremendous love arias . . . and invitations to Russia. A nice little touch at the end, when Oxana was laying it on extra thick: "Frank Hardy was the first to get to love you" – whereupon Frank looked very grave, and murmured: "Your books." '[44]

When he settled at Martin Road Patrick White reclaimed the place that was always waiting for him in Sydney society. He knew these people. He was fond of them. Their names and faces were familiar from his childhood. For a time he hoped to enlist them and their money in the cause of art. He cultivated the eccentric, brash Mary Fairfax in the hope that she would fund his Mrs Fraser opera. She proved a grave disappointment. He tried to interest 'some of the rich' in giving to a new theatre in Sydney, 'along the lines of Guthrie's theatre in Minneapolis'.[45] Over dinners at Martin Road he renewed his links with Hannah Lloyd Jones, and came to know James Fairfax. The fund-raising soon petered out, but the money was never what mattered. He needed these people because he was going to write about them and their kind.

Old Hannah Lloyd Jones was chaotic and snobbish and nights at Rosemont could be 'bloody awful', but White liked her particularly 'when she stops having the social jitters, and one can get down to talking about a few new lines for the shop'. She was eating at Martin Road one night when she remarked that her son Charles and three or four friends had hired a boat to see the Isles of Greece. ' "Oh," said Manoly, visualising a caïque, or perhaps some kind of plushy yacht, "what kind of boat?" "A Lloyd Triestino," Hannah replied. Don't you think it has the germ of a film – Charles Lloyd Jones and Friends drifting round the Greek Islands in an empty Lloyd Triestino with much taxed crew and stewardry.'[46]

There were nights White found himself among the survivors of old White society. They knew his cousins or *were* his cousins or remembered Lulworth in the old days. Those who had known White as a child, still called him Paddy. His painter Hurtle Duffield came across this crowd on his exploration of Sydney:

> an old, slow, swollen-veined, heavily tactical train of tortoises, moving their arthritic necks in the direction of the conversation they were making: some of them relatives – revered, theoretically loved – old barristers, doctors, heaviest of all, the graziers, and old lipstuck ladies who forgot what they had begun to tell, but continued bravely throwing in Galsworthy, Asprey, and Our Pioneer Families. All of them tortoises, when not elephants, sometimes a stiff flamingo, but old: some of them on sticks, some with signet rings eating into skin-cancered hands.[47]

They had passed to their children and grandchildren the sort of tales he himself once heard about Roy de Maistre. And these generations were now pleased, curious and unsurprised to meet Patrick White.

James Fairfax's grandmother had struggled through *The Tree of Man* out of friendship for Ruth, and alerted her grandson to White's writing. Fairfax was an amiable man in his early thirties, an art collector and director of the family firm that published the *Sydney Morning Herald*. He and White first met in the art world, but came to know each other well only after White moved to Martin Road. White was fond of James Fairfax in a rather puzzled way. 'There is much more in him than he cares to admit, but I expect he gets so outrageously flattered because he is a millionaire and a Fairfax, and he has withdrawn into himself in embarrassment.'[48]

In October 1965, White went to the state dinner to welcome the new Governor-General Lord Casey to Sydney. He had almost refused the invitation – he had been to a Government House bash a few weeks before that turned into a 'rout of human pigs'[49] – but he had a new dinner jacket now and felt there was something civilised and sympathetic about the Caseys. At the Town Hall that night he sat with graziers, flanked on each side by members of the War Widows' Guild. Opposite was the painter Bill Dobell, whom he had not seen for years. Towards the end of the dinner a man came and hissed in White's ear: ' "Lady Casey specially wants to have a word with you afterwards. Somebody will come and take you to where the meeting will take place." Quite the Dumas touch, in fact, and I must admit it gave me a thrill. When everybody got up, a minion did appear and Bill Dobell, who had been hissed at also, and I, were whisked away into a private room. There we had a long and fairly uninterrupted conversation with the Caseys.

'He is rather like a British statesman of another era, but a great relief after the Australian politician. (I expect really I am a True-Blue Peg at heart.) Maie Casey I felt at once was a person I could see a lot of, and it is a pity to think I have discovered this too late, although she did say, as though she meant it, "I hope we shall be able to see something of each other later on." She may like to come out here and spend a few peaceful hours. At one stage she made the remark, "Before we became involved in this silly business . . ." then stopped herself.'[50]

The Caseys were almost the last survivors in public life of an Anglo-Australian ideal: their money was Australian, their connections British and their field of action imperial. Casey had returned after the war from governing Bengal to discover he lacked the brains and bloodlust to become Prime Minister of Australia. Ever since he had been taking all the consolation prizes with such style that they seemed accolades: he was Minister for External Affairs, created Baron Casey of Berwick and Westminster, and took his seat in the House of Lords. To be Governor-General of Australia, wrote his biographer, 'was Bengal all over again, but better'.[51]

Maie was the dynamo. She was never a beauty and photographs of her and Dick on their wedding day in London – they were both thirty-six – show a woman with a saucer jaw and the eager carriage of a pony about to bolt. She was rich, ambitious and a tremendous snob. It mattered a great deal to Maie that the marriage of an aunt to the brother of the Duke of Buccleuch gave her a distant connection to royalty. Yet there was also a streak of bohemian independence in her. She had many faces – vicereine, aviatrix, writer, art collector, illustrator, even mother – and knew which face to show the world at any time. She bought paintings and Herbert Read declared her a woman of taste. Cecil Beaton helped arrange the furniture in Calcutta before he collapsed there with dengue fever. Though she was now in her seventies, Maie Casey was in the throes of a new friendship, with Princess Marthe Bibesco, whose memoir *Au Bal avec Marcel Proust* Maie pressed on her Australian friends. When the time came, White told her bluntly that Bibesco did not add much to the world's understanding of Proust.[52]

White began by sending a copy of *The Solid Mandala* and she replied with her new book *Tides and Eddies*. He invited her to see his paintings. She arrived at Martin Road in June 1966 with a lady-in-waiting and a paper knife made of pearl shell from New Guinea. They found they shared a passion for cooking, and she sent a recipe for ratatouille. When the Bibesco arrived White replied with Christina Stead's *The Man Who Loved Children*, which he confessed he had discovered 'late in the day and regret my neglect'. She was to interrupt a day of official engagements to come to lunch at Martin Road. White wanted to cook a hare. 'Canberra must be hellishly cold. Do you ever come across hares? I mean to eat.' She sent two and White cooked them the Cephalonian way in the juice of twelve lemons and twenty-four cloves of garlic. 'We had chlorophyll pills for her to take, to kill the garlic, in case it was thought our lunch was part of a republican plot. However, she said nothing would induce her to take the pills; she didn't mind whether she smelled.'[53]

Maie Casey was a stylish monster, forthright yet discreetly flattering, one of those rich figures White admired for breaking free and making lives of their own. He felt Maie Casey made sense of his own estrangement from Australia at a time when he was bitterly despondent about the country of his fate. Shortly before they met, Sun Books republished her family history, *An Australian Story*, and White was delighted by this account of an Anglo-Irish family in the Australian bush. He told Dutton, 'She is full of wisdom . . . the book has solved something of my own puzzle. It is not that I am not Australian, I am an anachronism, something left over from that period when people were no longer English and not yet indigenous.' Dutton protested. White insisted: 'I am an anachronism in Australia – not intellectually, intellectually I think I am thirty years ahead of most Australians, but spiritually, and to me there is a very great difference between the intellectual and the unfashionable spiritual.'[54]

'The Binoculars and Helen Nell' followed the many lives of a Sydney woman who was at one time on the musical stage, at another a cook, and was later burgling houses with a man who worked as a lawyer by day and thief by night. She was to suffer from dropsy in her old age and die in a nursing home, attached by rubber tube to an enamel bucket. The binoculars of the title were a pair through which she looked at life, staring through both ends.[55] White thought 'The Far and the Near' would be a good subtitle, or 'The Varieties of Sexual Experience'.

He needed to research Sydney from the turn of the century onwards, and found himself again in the Mitchell Library, described so cruelly and accurately in *The Solid Mandala* as 'smelling of varnish and rubber'.[56] Once more he was quizzing his friends: an abandoned weatherboard

'Palais de Danse' stood on the Harbour when he came back from school in 1930, but did it exist in 1919? 'About that time I can remember the nurse of some children we used to play with getting into evening dresses and going to dance at a "Pally" somewhere, I think it was the one at Clifton Gardens . . . I want my fictitious characters to go across by ferry and dance in that old ramshackle weatherboard.'[57]

Maie Casey was, from the first, an excellent source of detail, and after knowing the vicereine only a few months White was quizzing her. First about fast cars: 'In the book I am writing there is a flashy and rather hysterical new-rich woman called Ethel Taylour who owns several cars for different occasions. There are those she shares with her husband, and which are driven by the chauffeur. But she has something fast and exotic which she jumps into and drives herself when she wants to blow off steam. The period is 1928. Would an Isotto Fraschini (spelling?) have been owned by somebody rich and capricious in Australia at that time? How large, how open would it have been? I want her to go on rather a damp, windswept drive down the coast taking with her Ellen her cook (Helen Nell at this phase of the story). If the car could not have been an Isotto – what? . . . Can one refer to a "glove box" in a car by then? The drive in question takes place in the early hours of the morning after a disastrous formal dinner party. There is a point where Ethel Taylour stops the car and takes off her jewels for greater freedom. She has to put them somewhere.' They settled on a Bentley.[58]

A bout of flu in May 1966 was followed by a bronchial fever that produced 'a splendidly obscene rabble to populate some of the more shadowy areas' of the book.[59] But as winter continued he became disgruntled, and after getting about 100,000 words of the first draft on paper, he put the novel aside to write another Athenian short story. 'The Full Belly' was based on the struggle of the Lascaris family to survive in Athens during the Occupation. Though the story had been in his mind for some time, it had chosen this inconvenient time to rise to the surface. He spent six weeks on 'The Full Belly' and when he returned to the novel it seemed 'very fresh and alive'. He was determined to take it slowly: 'Haste is disastrous to fiction and cookery.'[60]

Ever since Ruth's death, White had been urging his sister to bring her children out to live in Australia. A short recce in 1964 – about the time of the move to Martin Road – had been a great success. All her old friends were waiting. Everyone was glad to see her. Suzanne had not set foot in the country for thirty years, but it seemed she had hardly been away. White was delighted. In August 1966 she returned with two of her daughters to settle in Sydney. White volunteered to take the older of the two, Gillian, while Suzanne found a house. He was a little nervous about this, but excited by the prospect of being a father to his niece for a few months. 'It will change our lives a bit,' he remarked to Marshall

Best. 'Less alcohol and farts, more shaves and edifying conversation.
Or perhaps it will end by her teaching us a thing or two about life
and squalor, the way the young seem able to now.'[61]

Gillian Peck was twenty-four and had made the move to Sydney
reluctantly, leaving behind a job at the BBC and the man she was to
marry. Life at Martin Road was rather daunting. It was as strange for
her to be in a house with two middle-aged men as it was for them to
be living with a shy young woman. White set about 'doing something'
for Gillian – introducing her to friends, trying to organise a job – and as
the weeks went by he grew impatient with her just as Ruth had once
been impatient with his refusal to be moulded. He began to complain
that Gillian did not show initiative, spent too long washing her hair,
would not pursue the openings he found for her, was making too many
calls to London to a man who was, to White's dismay, divorced. In a
rage of disappointment he wrote to Juliet O'Hea, 'I realise I have been
spared a lot in life, not having to push children of my own in directions
they didn't want to go.'[62] Gillian decided to return to London. There
was a 'dust-up' between uncle and niece, and she left to stay with her
great-aunt, Clem Withycombe's widow Mag, until the ship sailed for
England.

White worked at 'Helen Nell' all through these months despite
vituperative complaints that the crisis at Martin Road was sapping his
vitality. In mid-November he reported to Dutton, 'The flow has set
in, perhaps because I have got amongst the whores; it is always easy
to write about prostitutes.' A few weeks later he was telling Stern, 'All
sorts of repulsive things are coming up in it, and I hate it most of the
time. Writing is so difficult too, more difficult the longer one keeps
at it.' He put the novel aside for Christmas. The family ate a goose
on Boxing Night and twenty came for 'a welter' on New Year's Eve.
When he returned to the manuscript in the first week of January 1967,
he expected to finish the first draft at a canter, but three weeks later, after
writing 160,000 words, he abandoned the novel altogether in disgust. 'I
think I have been indulging in too many fantasies. It is an overblown
mass, of too much flesh, and not enough bone.' He grumbled that he
had lost his way in the crisis with Gillian. From time to time he dug
out the manuscript and found it full of life and interest. He often felt
he might return to finish it. He never did.[63]

White began 1967 with two resolutions. He gave up drink again, and
after a few weeks of this he confessed life was 'a bit grey' but he was
determined to make an effort 'to keep the right side of austerity'.[64] He
was drinking whisky again in February.

The second resolution was to accept no more prizes for his novels.
The *Encyclopaedia Britannica* had begun to give generous awards for local

achievements in literature, science and the arts. On the literature committee were Geoff Dutton and ABC executive and critic Clem
Semmler, who was given the job of telling White that *The Solid Mandala*
had won the Britannica Award for 1966. Semmler's diary recorded the
fiasco of his visit to Martin Road. 'Nice place. Wonderful paintings.
Was reasonably amiable and offered us a drink. I told him the good
news. But he refused point-blank to accept the prize. Would give no
reason. Furthermore said if we publicly gave it to him he'd publicly
refuse. Wouldn't reconsider.' After putting his foot through a fly-wire
door, Semmler left. The *Britannica* people could not believe anyone
could turn down $10,000.*

White thought his point had been made, but in early April 1967 he
had a call from Sir Oliver Crosthwaite Eyre of Eyre & Spottiswoode,
congratulating him on his latest award.

'Which award?' White asked.

'The Miles Franklin.'

White told him he had not entered the book.

'Oh, but I think my colleagues have.'

White told Eyre it must be withdrawn. Eyre 'blathered off', saying
nothing could be done because he was racing for his plane. White rang
the trustees of the prize, who asked him to accept the money and donate
it back to the fund. He refused. He telegraphed Beatrice Davis, one of
the judges: 'Must emphasise cannot accept award for book submitted
without my knowledge.' He suggested they divide the prize between
Elizabeth Harrower's *The Watchtower* and Peter Mather's *Trap*. 'Then
there was a silence,' he told O'Hea, 'and when they came out of it they
announced that *Trap* had won the prize. I was very glad. I had read it a
short time before and felt it was one of the few creative novels about
Australia.'[65]

The Miles Franklin fiasco was the last straw. For years publishers
had been trying to poach White from Eyre & Spottiswoode, but he
had refused to budge despite his long list of complaints against the
firm. Eyre & Spottiswoode had shown a deep affection for delay
that culminated in a plan to hold publication of *The Solid Mandala*
for a year. White and O'Hea forced them to follow as soon as
possible after New York, but at this point White began to think of
finding a new publisher. His loyalty to Eyre & Spottiswoode had been
eroded further by the departure of Maurice Temple Smith for Secker
& Warburg. O'Hea was keen for change. She had been investigating
the publisher's accounts and discovered records in such confusion that
White's royalties had been miscalculated. She was also 'horrified' to

---

*Australia changed its currency in February 1966: one pound became two dollars.
All sums are in Australian dollars unless otherwise stated.

see the drop in sales: the London edition of *Riders in the Chariot* had sold 15,681 copies at home and abroad in its first four months, but *The Solid Mandala* had sold only 11,608 copies in that time.[66] White heard nothing from Eyre & Spottiswoode to explain the Miles Franklin mess. He wrote to O'Hea, 'I already refer to them as my ex-publishers, but until I have another book to offer I'm not going to bother thinking about someone else.'[67]

He was under way. As 'Helen Nell' died, an old fascination returned. The figure of the painter was one of the permanent members of the repertory of White's imagination. He had made his first appearance as the postmaster of Durilgai, and then in the role of the wandering Aborigine of Sarsaparilla. Now White imagined him centre stage as Hurtle Duffield of *The Vivisector*, a novel set in the same city circles and same era as 'Helen Nell'. He told Dutton, 'I am trying to be a painter.'[68]

TWENTY-THREE

Working with Paint

THE EMPTY WALLS at Martin Road sent White back to the galleries again, for at Castle Hill he had bought paintings until Dogwoods could hold no more. The de Maistres brought out from London were the core of his collection still, but he had been buying more paintings ever since his books began to make money. In his euphoria after finishing *Voss*, White declared the only reason he would like to become rich 'would be so that I might descend on artists with commissions and largesse'.[1] At Centennial Park he was no longer restrained by the walls or his wallet and he began collecting on a Belltrees scale. The impulse was in his blood.

When his brooding figure appeared in their galleries, an old shopping bag in his hand and a look of grim dissatisfaction on his face, dealers looked up with a mix of alarm and excitement. They knew to keep back for a while and let White circle the exhibition a couple of times alone. If artists came in sight, he brushed them off. 'I hate looking at paintings with the painter on my heels.'[2]

White was not searching for beauty. Raw creative ideas excited him, and a blare of colour filled him with pleasure. He liked to see the pain and struggle of creation in a painting. Menace caught his eye. He was stimulated by the prospect of a long tussle to make a difficult work yield up its meaning. Here, too, a little suffering was important. Abstract art was White's first love, but he was excited by paintings with a sharp satiric edge, or those in which he discovered some private omen or images with links to his childhood – like Max Watters' Hunter River sheds, and the iron windmills Charles Blackman loved. White bought to shake up the collection. 'I have just bought a sledge-hammer of a painting by Kevin Connor,' he told Dutton soon after the move to Martin Road. 'A large portrait of a woman after the style of Mrs Rapallo in *The Aunt's Story*. I am going to hang it at the end of the dining room, over the table – just what was needed. I could feel an air of complacency creeping in.'[3]

White often bought a painting simply because he liked the painter, sometimes buying to help them out and sometimes hoping his patronage would push them in the right direction. He wished Desmond Digby would cut himself free from the theatre and concentrate on painting. 'He could reach the level of Daumier.' When he saw Digby's multiple portrait of the art collector Margaret Carnegie he knew he would buy it if the subject did not take it herself. 'Now, as I suspected, she doesn't want it. She says "the girls don't like it", that she couldn't hang it in the house if she got it, and complains that he has given her "a melon chest". "Which," Desmond says, "is exactly what she has." (Ladies' chests must have strained a lot of painter-client relationships.)'[4] White hung it by his desk.

Painting, he declared, was the only art that flourished in Sydney, but often for the wrong reasons. He despised 'the name game' in Sydney. 'Certainly we have some pretty good painters, but I'm sure they wouldn't be doing so well if a number of vulgarians hadn't decided paintings were an investment and collected them. Good for the painters, but as a writer I sometimes grow resentful.' Most of all he was a patron of the new and deserving. He liked taking risks. As painters favoured in their early careers became established, he lost his enthusiasm. Men like Charles Blackman and Bob Dickerson did not need White then – and their prices shot up. White's collection had more works of early promise than late mastery. Yet he was proud of his collector's acumen. Visitors to Dogwoods recall how pleased he was to point out that works like his big Fairweather which cost £100 had multiplied many times in value since he bought them.[5]

White enlisted his friends to help deserving painters and galleries. He thanked Maie Casey for her vice-regal visit to the Macquarie Galleries: 'the mink locusts will decide they ought to descend'. But the tastes of the rich in the mid-1960s baffled and rather disgusted White. 'Nowadays the mink smarties expect at least a full French letter or a girl's bloodstained pants stuck to the canvas. (The pants did actually occur in a recent show, in a painting called 'The Nineteenth Hole at Pymble Golf Course': it was bought too.) I had thought French letters might be old world in these days of the pill, but I am told they are considered "more Catholic".'[6]

White's pithy verdicts were subject to change at short notice as painters, paintings, galleries and dealers fell in and out of favour. He was willing to admit mistakes, willing to be persuaded, but once cast out a painting was never readmitted. Those that began to 'recede into the wall' were rehung in the passageway or (worse) the second guest bedroom or (much worse) buried with a pithy epitaph in the garage. His private criticism was funny and tough. Arthur Boyd was ridiculed for his 'pubic hair in the bush'; Bob Dickerson was painting 'foetuses

with a social grudge'; the fashionable John Olsen's work was 'a kind
of brown knitting. I cannot share the raptures of the disciples, because
I just cannot get excited about brown, even, I have to confess, when
Rembrandt uses it.'[7]

From time to time magazines asked him to write about painting, but
he always refused. 'When literary people write on the subject of painting
I find it altogether unconvincing and literary,' he told Charles Osborne
at the *London Magazine*. Of course he had written about painters in his
novels, 'but that is fiction – rather different'.[8] He was confident he
understood the act of painting, and painters had been a potent source
of inspiration in his writing. Plays and novels had begun with paintings.
He had brought to life, rather like the *tableaux vivants* of his childhood,
the work of de Maistre, Dobell, Blake, Delacroix, Redon and Nolan.
There was a time – now past – when he tried to write as a painter used
paint, laying down prose in impasto or thin wash or skeins of abstract
colour. White frankly envied painters the luxury of working with
colour: 'we don't have such a lovely sensuous material to play about
with in expressing ourselves. I do loathe sitting at my desk day after
day week after week year after year grinding out novels greyly.' He
believed – perhaps only on the example of Sid Nolan – that they worked
wonderfully quickly, 'able to produce an exhibition in a fortnight and
then enjoy themselves for months, it seems very unfair'.[9]

The commercial galleries that mattered at this time in Sydney were
the old Macquarie and the Komon. They are part of the landscape of
The Vivisector. For years White had a strange but engrossing relationship with the two women who ran the Macquarie. Treania Smith he
admired, but the forthright Lucy Swanton intimidated him in the early
days and he decided he could not endure her. In the novel they became
Ailsa Harkness, 'the steel eagle', and her partner Biddy Prickett: 'There
was more of the red ferret in Biddy.' The years in which he worked
on *The Vivisector* saw the full flowering of his ritual animosity with
Swanton, and when they met at galleries they snapped insults at one
another.

> 'I adore Hurtle.'
> 'With your dried-up peanut of a tasteful spinster's mind.'
> 'If you want me to tell you why you're a misfit, Patrick,
> it's because you hate everybody.'
> 'Because I don't love peanuts, Biddy, it doesn't mean I don't
> love.'
> 'I'm going home. You've upset me too much. You've made
> me feel ill.'[10]

White hated having to ask the price of a painting, and pursued a campaign to persuade Sydney galleries to print their price lists. The toughest of the 'priceless' dealers was Rudi Komon, and White tried to organise a boycott of that 'Viennese spiv' to make him change his ways. Duffield's dealer Benny Loebel is a tribute to the skill and oleaginous drive of Rudi Komon.

> 'Zese faht you see are all early lyrical veuorks. Zere is greater Kraft
> – depth – later; but *purity* – ze lyrical purity of youss hess its appeal,
> I sink you vill agree.' He lowered his voice still lower. 'I heff one
> early *fah*bulous Duffield – little – very small – if the maestro isn't
> personally interested in selling any zet you here see.'[11]

Komon conducted his own, successful, campaign to seduce White. The dealer asked White to lunch at his apparently decrepit villa on the waterfront at Watson's Bay. 'Inside there are paintings to make a thief's eyes fall out. Dobell miniatures and drawings by the dozen, things one didn't know existed. A Conder in a frame made by Conder himself out of what looks like the woodwork from a stable. Little masterpieces by several painters I had always tended to dismiss. One of the best of Williams's abstract landscapes. A most unusual Blackman of a schoolgirl looking like Thea Astley surrounded by phallic arums on a very yellow beach . . . We ate a mass of delicatessen and drank several bottles of wine, but it was the paintings which made me drunk.'[12]

The Vivisector was to be dedicated to the Nolans. The painter was now a client of Marlborough Fine Art, exhibiting and travelling everywhere: the Antarctic in 1964, New Guinea and China in 1965, New York in 1966, Morocco and Mexico in 1967 – with a few weeks each year in Australia. The Queen bought from his African series. He was rich, honoured and famous. Paintings poured out of him, but the reviewers had begun to savage his exhibitions. White was not uncritical: 'I think Sid is going through the worries of an artist of a certain age and standing, but he has what will bring him out of them. Of course they continue to attack him here, even those who borrow from him most assiduously.'[13]

Nolan's visits to Australia were complicated by Cynthia's refusal to go anywhere near Melbourne in case she should encounter her brother John Reed and his wife Sunday. Cynthia's fears were black and deep. White knew the story – or a jaundiced version of it as told by Cynthia. John and Sunday were the painter's first patrons, and the three had lived in a *ménage* at Heide, the Reeds' farm on the Yarra outside Melbourne. Nolan painted the first Ned Kelly series on their dining-room table. The Reeds were the great patrons of Modernism, and for a time it seemed the future of art in Australia would be decided at Heide. Then the blows began to fall. They were caught in the brilliant snare of the

Ern Malley hoax when their magazine *Angry Penguins* published some concocted poems as the work of an undiscovered Modern master; the painters Joy Hester and Albert Tucker split up and fled Melbourne: Cynthia wrenched Sid away.

The passions aroused by these failures and defections had not cooled in twenty years, and Cynthia's refusal to have anything to do with Heide was absolute. Nolan was painting a mural at the Rural Bank in Melbourne in 1966, but Cynthia insisted they make their headquarters in Sydney. 'Poor Sid had to fly backwards and forwards,' White told Geoffrey Dutton. 'I think he found it pretty exhausting, what with the directors' hostility to the mural, and sessions with his mother, who, since the father died, sleeps with his hat and his pipe on the pillow. Some of the Gallipoli drawings and the big Anzac head are magnificent . . .' These foibles of Cynthia Nolan's did nothing to diminish White's admiration. 'Of all the people I know I think Cynthia is the one who reacts to people and things most like I do.'[14]

Roy de Maistre, unhonoured except by a few friends and connoisseurs, was still playing the role of the Catholic, demi-royal artist. But at the age of seventy-five, he was very poor and frail. Diabetes was sending him blind. Australian curators went to Eccleston Street not to buy Roy's paintings, but to interview him about the early years of those lesser painters who had stayed behind and enjoyed success. There was no market for de Maistre's paintings in his homeland. Roy was 'another who didn't blow his own trumpet enough', thought White. 'But I think in time his best painting will be appreciated for what it is.'[15]

White bought a painting every so often – he would pay for one and Roy would send two – and sent visitors to the studio to cheer him. White urged Maie Casey to call on their next vice-regal visit to London, but warned her to tread carefully. 'If Roy asks you about the portrait he painted of me years ago, pretend you have seen it, and I'll show it to you one day. I suppose it flattered my vanity in my youth, but I got to hate it as I grew older, and for a long time it has been "under the stairs". I believe Roy started asking James Fairfax about it once, and James had to get out of it somehow. It's difficult to know what to do with it. I have a vague plan for giving it to James, who will present it to the Gallery of NSW, because one can't very well present a portrait oneself. Yet for Roy's sake I feel perhaps it ought to go there.'[16]

Roy never wrote, but in January 1967 White had a sad letter from him. 'I don't think he will be able to communicate very much longer,' he told Ronald Waters. 'I owe him so much; it was Roy, through his painting, who taught me to write.'[17] The idea for *The Vivisector* came to White in the days after the painter's note arrived at

Martin Road. The name White took for his painter is a link to Roy, whose horse-trainer brother was Hurtle de Mestre. After reading and thinking about the new project for a month, White bought a heap of lined, foolscap paper and began work on 14 February.

By now it was the established pattern of his career that he would suffer an asthmatic blow-out at some point early in the first draft. This time he was struck down by a foul attack after only one day and was rushed off to Prince Alfred Hospital. He blamed the attack on the frustrations of the months just passed: the death of 'Helen Nell', the difficulties of life with his niece Gillian, and the row over the Miles Franklin Prize. He was in hospital for a fortnight, sharing a room with an amiable old man from the country: 'We have long nostalgic dialogues about NSW earlier in the century.' Once home, but still full of cortisone, he plunged into the book and worked rapidly. After six weeks he let Marshall Best know a new novel was under way. 'I am enjoying constant dialogues while not at it and the characters are developing as many skins as onions . . . I have had the shits for weeks, some kind of intestinal infection, perhaps it is helping bring the novel out so easily.'[18]

The Vivisector is the life of a 'genius at work'. The genius is a painter, but the novel is a writer's profound exercise in self-justification. Lady Gordon, walking among the raspberry canes at Browns river, wondered if the Victor Whites' strange little boy was a changeling. That barbed remark had come to offer White comfort over the years. He saw writing as a cruel business, but the changeling/artist is free of those loyalties and obligations of kindness that make difficult truths so hard to tell. He is the intimate stranger, the one who is free to watch and remember and tell. 'I think you're an artist, aren't you?' Rhoda Courtney asks Duffield. 'What I meant was *sans famille*.'[19]

Duffield is bought by the Courtneys for £500 from a poor family in the slums of Surry Hills. Here White drew on a 'vague parallel' in the history of Heide, but kept very quiet about this, anxious not to stir up the Reeds. 'They sound such vicious bastards they might get up to anything in retaliation.'[20] Joy Hester had a boy called Sweeney – named after T.S. Eliot's Sweeney – and left the baby behind at Heide when she and Albert Tucker split up in 1947. Hester settled in Sydney, Tucker went off to paint in Paris and little Sweeney was brought up as the Reeds' son. They did not buy him, as White appeared to believe, but they continued to pay stipends to both his artist parents. A little later they adopted the boy and raised him to be a genius. Sweeney grew into a very pretty, troubled and violent young man. As White was writing *The Vivisector*, Sweeney Reed was in his early twenties. He was to cut a path through the Reed fortune, run an art gallery, try painting and then commit suicide.

Who is Hurtle Duffield? No other character in White's novels so provokes the search for the *actual* man. But there was no one child, artist, recluse, lover or celebrity. Hurtle Duffield is one of the great works of White's imagination, a synthesis of many lives beginning with White's own. The painter's early years are saturated with details from White's rich childhood. White believed he was writing the most detailed portrait of Sydney's plutocracy ever attempted. 'Australian writers don't seem to have considered it aesthetically desirable to write about the rich. (There is an exception in Martin Boyd, but he came from Victoria and concentrated on Melbourne society.) At least with the rich, who are usually slightly more cosmopolitan, one can get away from what is referred to as "the Australian image", which no longer interests me.'[21]

The Courtneys' house in Rushcutters Bay is another Lulworth, and the Courtneys – Alfreda (Birdie) and her husband Harry – are Ruth and Dick in light disguise. The disfiguring hump on their daughter Rhoda is another – but exaggerated – detail from White family history. 'Suzanne had a suspicion of a hump. My mother had one in old age. Uncle Clem told me of my grandmother Cobb's hump that nobody talked about. There were a lot of humps about.'[22]

His mother is Hurtle's first subject:

'Oh, darling, how clever of you! But I shouldn't have taken it for me, exactly. Do you see me like that? You've given me a melon chest.'

But Hurtle Duffield's eye is true. Rather than argue, he keeps on working, 'any possible answers were enclosed by the lines of his drawing'.[23] Alfreda's complaint echoes through Duffield's career. Are you a perv? 'I am an artist.' Is it honest to make paintings by lumping many real people into a single figure? 'Only the painting can answer that – when it is finished.' Was it not cruel to paint Rhoda naked with her hump? 'How can you say it's cruel? It's the truth!' Why must he paint disgusting images? 'I was trying to find some formal order behind a moment of chaos and unreason. Otherwise it would have been too horrible and terrifying.'[24]

The formal order is God's: White was trying once more in *The Vivisector* to show 'unbelievers' the faith buried inside them. Duffield's belief follows the pattern of White's loss and rediscovery of faith. 'As an old man he realises that his belief in God has been there all the time "like a secret relationship".' This God is fallible – 'everyone can make mistakes, including God' – and man is one of God's blunders, a kind of Frankenstein monster. This God is also cruel: 'Otherwise, how would men come by their cruelty – and their brilliance?' Where White believed the churches went wrong was in rejecting so much that is sordid and shocking, 'which can still be related to religious experience'. An artist who celebrates the world by depicting it in all its squalor and beauty, draws close to God. The pursuit of truth is an act of worship.[25]

White loves to disguise the passage of time in his writing, and the age of a character is often the last mystery to be revealed. Duffield was born about 1900 and at sixteen plunges into the First World War to escape his mother. He lives in Paris for a few years after the Armistice, studying while washing dishes at *Le Rat à l'Oeil* and is back in Sydney painting in a studio near the Quay by the mid-1920s. He saw the adult Duffield as 'physically a kind of David Campbell'. White met the poet through the Duttons in 1966 and found him 'a great charmer and very witty'. Campbell was a stocky, handsome, rather battered figure; a grazier from near Canberra, a boxer in his youth at Cambridge, a man who was as much at ease in filthy overalls as a Bond Street suit. 'I was glad to find I liked him so much,' White told Maie Casey. 'He is one of the few Australian poets I can read with pleasure.'[26]

Two eccentric Sydney artists, John Passmore and Godfrey Miller, are the principal sources for Hurtle Duffield's life. Duffield's studios and his voluntary poverty owe a great deal to Godfrey Miller, who lived and worked in such squalor that it seemed he didn't have two pennies to rub together. Rich clients like Mary Fairfax supported him with food parcels, but Miller had inherited part of a New Zealand shipping fortune. Once he flew to Paris for the weekend to see a Picasso exhibition. White courted the painter with eggs and oranges brought down from Castle Hill, in the hope of being allowed to buy a painting called *Nude with Moon*. It was as hard to prise a painting from Miller as it was from Duffield, but Miller ruined many of his best paintings because he could not leave them alone. White saw everything he loved in *Nude with Moon* painted out, and gave up the pursuit.[27]

Hurtle Duffield lived in Miller's territory, first at the Quay and then in Paddington, but Duffield's is a far grander and more dilapidated house than Miller's in Sutherland Street. Duffield's place had urns, a ruined conservatory, a great tree in the garden and a view over the roofs to the Harbour. Out the back, however, the two painters shared the same Paddington world of cat-infested lanes, sagging fences and shabby back yards.[28]

John Passmore was self-absorbed and full of terrible doubts. When this 'very complicated number' first appeared at Dogwoods, he seemed affronted by the presence of others at lunch and hardly uttered. White thought to calm him by saying how much he liked his painting *The Quarrel*. Passmore replied, 'If I could lay hands on that, I'd burn it.' Passmore asked if he could come back another time and see White alone. He agreed. 'Seems to have some theory he wants to expound,' White speculated to Dutton. 'Or perhaps it is that he wants to talk uninterruptedly about himself. There are lots of ideas, but they just fail to surface. Perhaps they will when we are alone.' An almost illegible letter in green ink arrived asking for the second meeting. Passmore talked endlessly that day, only about himself, wiping his nose with scraps from a roll of lavatory paper. The food hung on his fork as he talked. He left early to be home before dark, for he said he was apprehensive about the Paddington Slasher. White politely remarked at the gate that he must come again. 'I've got what I wanted,' said Passmore. White never knew what he meant by this. Later there was a night at James Fairfax's house on Darling Point, when White and Passmore came to dinner, and Fairfax had hung all the Passmores he owned around the room. Passmore was cast into deep gloom. 'They just show what a terrible painter I am.'[29]

White drew on these lives for his painter's life, but Duffield's paintings are more than anyone's the paintings of Francis Bacon. By the time White was writing *The Vivisector*, his once unknown friend was such a potent influence in the international art world that White could identify a whole school of Bacon imitators in Sydney. Duffield has Bacon's love of paint – 'the most bearable part of his act of painting' – the passion for destroying his canvases, and Bacon's delight in the 'random arabesques' he used to find on walls and hoardings. White had seen Bacon again in London in 1958, and on the next trip saw his 1963 exhibition at Marlborough Fine Art. Bacon was painting figures like half-dismembered medical specimens laid out on slabs for inspection. At the time White said he had not liked them, but when *The Vivisector* was done, he praised his London publishers for commissioning a jacket with just the 'right touch of Bacon-ish horror'.[30]

De Maistre has only a shadowy presence in *The Vivisector*. White loved the old man too much to put his foibles and pretensions into a novel, for he feared fiction would reduce him to a joke. But deep in *The Vivisector* is a superb speech of thanks which White might have delivered to Roy, but here he gives to the young pianist Kathy Volkov after her brief erotic entanglement with the old painter,

> It was you who taught me how to see, to be, to know instinctively. When I used to come to your house in Flint Street, melting with excitement and terror, wondering whether I would dare go through with it again, or whether I would turn to wood, or dough, or say something so stupid and tactless you would chuck me out into the street, it wasn't simply thought of the delicious kisses and all the other lovely play which forced the courage into me. It was

the paintings I used to look at sideways whenever I got a chance. I wouldn't have let on, because I was afraid you might have been amused, and made me talk about them, and been even more amused when I couldn't discuss them at your level. But I was drinking them in through the pores of my skin.[31]

In September 1967 the Art Gallery of New South Wales held a great retrospective to mark Sid Nolan's fiftieth birthday. Nolan came to believe that he and he alone was Hurtle Duffield, and has in his library in Herefordshire a copy of *The Vivisector* closely annotated to demonstrate all the many links between the two lives. When White was asked if his old friend was his inspiration, he replied, 'Not in the least.' But the retrospective was an event in both painters' lives. White and Lascaris were there the night before the opening, as Nolan drifted through the deserted courts looking at his life's work,

all these paintings along the walls, the windows to your actual, willed, life, your every iridescent tremor and transparent thought.

White told Luciana Arrighi: 'It was staggering to see all the imaginative and painting genius that has poured out of one man. It has made the retrospective of other Australian painters seem quite trivial and pathetic – and yet there are still people here who will not admit that he can paint. To me this has been the greatest event – not just in painting – in Australia in my lifetime. It has made up for a lot if not all the bitterness for having been dug out of this pit.'[32]

The painter's solo journey across the 'blaze of parquet' and the official opening the following night both entered *The Vivisector*. White made the usual grumbling noises about going to an opening night: 'I suppose I shall have to go, but I'm afraid I may be rude to some of those who will be there smiling and gushing, after going round trying to destroy him behind his back.' Five hundred people, described by the *Sydney Morning Herald* as 'old friends and art enthusiasts', drank champagne as they waited for the Lord Mayor to speak. The caterer paid tribute to the painter by dressing his waitresses in 'mini-skirts and blouses in hot oranges, reds and browns – the colours depicted in so many of Mr Nolan's outback paintings'. The painter arrived trailed by television lights, for the ABC was filming every move Nolan made on this Australian visit. Cynthia Nolan had decided to stay in her hotel room, but Sid was enjoying himself.[33]

Duffield enjoyed the fuss a good deal less than Sid Nolan. One of the themes of *The Vivisector* is the perils of celebrity. When he believed he was despised and overlooked, White created the outcast painters Gage and Dubbo; now Hurtle Duffield has White's fame and White's fear of being turned into 'a national monument'. The night of the retrospective becomes an occasion of pretentious mayhem in *The Vivisector*. To recapture the mood of the night as he wrote, White played a record of Stockhausen's *Momente*, a piece of concrete music with scraps of conversation. Sid Nolan did all that was expected of him on this great public occasion, but Duffield escapes into the night, pausing to piss under a fig tree in the Domain before hailing a taxi to take him home, 'into that silence where he had spent half a lifetime begetting, and giving birth'.[34]

Hurtle Duffield lives on the page because the half a dozen lives on which White drew were all fused in his own character. Later he admitted to Stern: '*The Vivisector* is more about myself than any other – my unfortunate character at least – though in very different circumstances.' This was White as he saw himself,

> turning his back and distorting truth to get at an effect, which he did, he knew, better than anybody else – well, almost anybody. But there were the days when he himself was operated on, half-drunk sometimes, shitting himself with agony, when out of the tortures of knife and mind, he was suddenly carried, without choice, on the wings of his exhaustion, to the point of intellectual and – dare he begin to say it? – spiritual self-justification.[35]

White set himself a year to write the first draft, and then planned to take a long break in Europe and America before beginning to oxyweld. He complained cheerfully enough that writing was as terrifying as ever. 'Still, there are moments when things slip out of their own accord, and one wonders: how on earth did I think of that?' It was a pleasure to find fragments of the abandoned 'Helen Nell' surfacing in the work, 'so perhaps I was trying myself out in that, and it won't be wasted'.[36]

Questionnaires went down to Yarralumla: what did Maie Casey know about Australian art schools between the turn of the century and 1914? 'I want to get some idea of the kind of teaching there was at that period and the kind of atmosphere that prevailed.' Were portraits by Sargent hanging in public galleries in London in 1914? Were Toulouse-Lautrecs in Parisian public collections by then? Could she remember telephones in Sydney in 1914? His earliest memory of a telephone was at Cromer in 1915. Did people use toothpaste or toothpowder in 1907? Was the word 'smoodge' in use before the First World War, 'Or was it only born during the War? I can remember hearing it about 1918, when we were forbidden to use it.' Could she bring back some anti-vivisectionist literature from London? 'I visualised a pamphlet, not a tome, for which I shall pay you of course. I see 25/–

on the jacket but only twelve and something on an account. Was it a remainder?'[37]

He read Herbert Read on Henry Moore and Enid Starkie on Flaubert. Starkie was very consoling. 'I had never realised how very similar in mind and temperament F. and I are.' The painters in Noel Barber's *Conversations with Painters* were illuminating, even if the book was presented like 'one of those dreadful telly interviews, all sweet smarm and Christian names'. Casey's *An Australian Story* helped him with plutocratic details.[38]

He trudged the streets to reacquaint himself with Sydney, for *The Vivisector* was to be a portrait of his city, half-dream and half-reality, still the sunlit town of his youth yet also the parvenu bastard it was becoming in the booming 1960s. The landscape of the town is strong in the novel, though White deliberately obscured some key locations. One is Rushcutters Bay Park, his childhood stamping ground, where he was warned not to speak to strangers. Duffield meets his prostitute muse Nance Lightfoot by the wall on Rushcutters Bay. The Gash where the furtive Cecil Cutbush accosts the painter is the deep cleft of Cooper Park in Bellevue Hill. The grocer's shop is over the road and his seat is perched on the edge of the drop; the lantana comes and goes; at dusk the houses across the valley in Woollahra fade to pink and grey shapes that might look for a few minutes as Duffield imagined them, like 'unlit gas fires'.[39]

White was also writing the portrait of Sydney society for which he had been preparing since he came down to Martin Road. More than any other part of his books, this was a *roman à clef* – though White strenuously denied that fact if caught by people like the music critic Julian Russell. 'Now tell me, I *am* Hal Shuard aren't I?' he asked. Mumbling a few words about characters never being taken directly from life, White made his escape. 'But he was dead right.' The critic's sexual tastes were White's invention, but the rest was Russell. The 'jolly-extrovert' Honeysett is a portrait of Hal Missingham, the director of the New South Wales Art Gallery: 'I must say he grows on one.' The mild and refined figure of Maurice Caldicott is a version of an art and book collector who drifted out of White's life at about this time. White mocked his taste for reading poems in exquisite editions. 'They would be just the same in a paperback.'[40]

Kathy Volkov was 'a kind of Zoe at the piano'. White turned to his GP Alice Halmagyi here for technical advice. She was surprised by his question: 'Would a man know if a girl was innocent, I mean a virgin?'

'If he had experience. Is this man experienced?'

'Yes.'

'Then he would.'

The affair of the young girl and the old painter also owed something to Vladimir Nabokov's *Lolita*, which White thought a great novel.[41]

Boo Hollingrake/Lopez/Davenport is a version of his cousin Eleanor Arrighi. 'The Boo of the book is a fairly close physical resemblance to the real Nellie,' recalled her daughter Luciana. 'The distinguishing white streak or "horns" in the jet black hair came naturally and very easily – the eyes were hazel, but just as Hurtle discovered they changed colour with the light. She was tall and always slim though voluptuous, and hardly aged so she never reached the old Boo stage. The red talons and the utterly straight back are accurate and she always dressed with great chic. Our own house (at Vaucluse looking not out to sea but over the Harbour) was rather as described in the book re the garden and the chessboard floor – there was a Buddha in the stair niche where Boo tripped and there was much tussore silk and Japanese wallpapers . . .

'Emily, "the survivor parlourmaid tough as aspidistra" is partly our Hess . . . From cooking shearers' meals, she graduated under my mother's tutelage, to producing the exquisite Italian dinners and to handling the social evenings *very* like [Boo's parties]. She once replied to Patrick's query as to what pudding she might be producing that evening – "Wait-and-see pudding, Mr White." The guests at that party are also fairly accurate. P. was always derogatory re our relations – "the Santa Gertrudis bull" (our Queensland cousins) and "the old Tortoises" (the old Cox aunts).' White invented Boo Hollingrake's Lesbian flirtations: 'Nellie's tastes were strictly for the chaps.'[42]

Margery Williams makes an appearance in Duffield's life as the stocky hostess Mrs Mortimer, 'scratching herself, slowly and thoughtfully, with an index finger, between her breasts'. Since Klári Daniel's exile from Martin Road, Margery Williams had taken her place as the principal lady disciple in White's life. It was for her sake – and to satisfy his own curiosity – that White continued to receive the English celebrities delivered to his 'densely populated ivory tower' by the despised Norman. White wrote brief portraits of his visitors: Iris Murdoch and her husband John Bayley turned out to be very appealing in their odd way, 'she in her velveteens and brown amber and he looking as though he were held together by pipe cleaners and grubby string'. John Gielgud asked him to see Osbert Sitwell, and White went down to the *Orsova* to find a 'pathetic old man . . . trembling with Parkinson's disease, although at the same time, one feels, very much alive inside his shell'. Why, he asked Dutton, did the Sitwells 'all wait till they are almost corpses before coming to Australia, when there was never a country which so demanded all one's life's-blood'?[43]

Norman Williams died while White was working on *The Vivisector*, and he was surprised by Margery's grief. In White's mind, Norman had betrayed her and made matters worse by leaving her with no money.

From being a hostess of some repute, Margery Williams was reduced like Peggy Mortimer to minding other people's flats. She

> had suffered from her husband's good looks and roving eye. He had also left her hard up . . . Perhaps this was why she was now blushing all the way up her goitrous throat: her flat cried her poverty in accents of discreet luxury.[44]

To friends in distress there was no one who could offer such intuitive comfort as White, but he expected them to pull themselves together fairly rapidly. His sympathy was intense, but his patience was limited and he grew irritated as Margery remained so long in the doldrums after Norman's death. White wrote urging her to take a grip on her future. 'My experience has always been that nothing has ever come my way without pushing, fighting, manoeuvring, exploding. Nor does it happen any easier now: not the things I really want, anyway.'[45]

Taking a few weeks' break from the novel during the Nolan celebrations, White wrote the most anthologised of all his short stories. He had noticed a man in a little car driving down Martin Road every afternoon at 5.20 and the story was sparked by him speculating how the watcher and passer-by might meet. 'Five Twenty' grew from there into an essay on marriage and widowhood that drew on Clem Withycombe's querulous, bed-ridden old age attended by his devoted wife.[46] White offered the story to *Southerly* in gratitude for its support over the years, but wondered if it had 'too much despair and too little grammar for the kids'. It was accepted and later appeared in the Australian anthology *Coast to Coast* and also in V.S. Pritchett's *Oxford Book of Short Stories*.[47]

After this break he returned, refreshed, to *The Vivisector* and reread all he had written. He was happy with what he found. 'It begins to fall into place, thank God. But it will need a terrific re-writing. Some of it is very good, some so bad it makes my hair stand on end. It has to begin this way because part of it is a descent into the abyss.' In late November he reported, 'The end of *The Vivisector* is in sight. That is, I have come out of the jungle, but it doesn't mean there won't be a long and arduous march till one reaches the sea.'[48]

That year saw the severing of their last ties with Dogwoods. The farm had been leased since they moved to Martin Road, but a buyer appeared in the winter of 1967, and after a few months 'telephoning, haggling, and near ulcers' Dogwoods was sold. White eased his regrets with the reflection that their ghosts, at least, would haunt the place. 'It certainly made us suffer enough at times, and I think all the suffering that went into those books must come out in some way.'[49] Lascaris invested his share of the $40,000, and they bought a new car and more paintings.

White did a few literary chores for the first time. For years he had protected himself from committees and seminars by declaring a writer's job was to write. But now the Australian Society of Authors, which had some public money to award a fellowship in 1967, asked White to join the panel to choose the writer. It was all very amiable, and they gave the fellowship to David Ireland, whose novels White thought remarkable. He urged his editors at Viking to read them.[50] Encouraged by White's participation, the authors offered him the presidency of their Society, but he drew back from this: 'I still maintain that all a writer needs in the way of protection is an experienced agent. The rest is waste of time.'[51]

Late in the day White was discovering Australian writers whom he might have come across years before had he grown up in Australia. The 'pretty shattering' stories of Barbara Baynton, for instance, were not on the syllabus at Cheltenham. 'It is extraordinary the way she tells one so little and one sees everything. I wonder whether the Australians who call me "crool" have ever read Barbara Baynton. She's a prolonged knife job.' White found the 'brown curtain of Aust. Lit.' beginning to lift. Manning Clark sent White the first volume of his *History of Australia*. White opened it only very reluctantly. 'I have always tended to be blind to Australian history,' he confessed to Clark. But he discovered there one of the few Australian books he could 'admire without reservation'. He read each of the volumes as they appeared over the next twenty years: 'Interesting to see how we have remained the same pack of snarling mongrel dogs.'[52]

White's great discovery was Christina Stead and he grew to admire her as 'one of the most interesting living novelists'. None of her books had quite the mighty impact of *The Man Who Loved Children* which was the first he read, but he was elated even by the lesser novels. One night at this time he had dinner with an American refugee from the Vietnam War who was working at Sydney University. 'Tell me, Mr White,' the American asked, 'who is the most important living Australian author?' Those at the table were paralysed with embarrassment. White replied without hesitation, 'Christina Stead.'[53]

The Britannica Award's literary committee recommended Stead for its $10,000 prize in 1967, but this was disallowed on the ground that Stead had lived too long away – nearly forty years – to be called an Australian. White erupted at this 'disgusting piece of literary injustice' and denounced the 'Higher Junta of Australian Intellect' for taking the prize away from Stead. He wrote to the *Sydney Morning Herald*, 'It helps explain to me why, for some time past, I have felt a foreigner in this pathetically chauvinistic parish.'[54] White did not give a damn where Stead was born or how long she had been out of Australia. She was a great writer. She deserved and needed such a prize.

He, like Hurtle Duffield, had returned after the war 'to renew himself'; perhaps it did all artists good to go away for a while; but there were no rules that determined when and if they should come home. That was only a matter for them. He knew he *had* to live in Australia – and railed against this fate – but he never condemned the expatriate life outright. In his polemic *Prodigal Son*, he argued only that life in London or Paris was not for him. He envied the Nolans. A few weeks after the retrospective, he saw them off at the airport. 'They are the wise ones. They fly in to be renewed, but get out before they are chewed up.' When the Britannica business erupted he raged to Dutton, 'This incredible country! Thank God I no longer feel I am much to do with it.'[55]

In the New Year, 1968, White and Lascaris flew over to Kangaroo Island to spend a week fishing, swimming, sleeping and reading. These were extrovert, happy days in a house full of children, good food and conversation. 'The Duttons' vitality is unquenched at 45, while Manoly and I, at 55, creep rather sluggishly in and out of boats, nursing our incipient arthritis and too audible wheezes.'[56]

The sea was running strongly one evening when four of them went fishing. Dutton saw a rogue wave approaching, and the four managed to link arms as it swept across the rocks at chest height. The Duttons' rule was to wear sandshoes on the rocks, but White had insisted on his gumboots. These filled with water and he was swept back into a narrow blowhole. 'I will never forget the look in his eyes as he was washed down,' Nin Dutton recalled. 'Those eyes are strange enough as it is, but they looked awful.' As the water sucked him down, she threw herself by the hole and grabbed him. Had he gone under he would have been battered to death beneath the rock shelf. She held him for a moment before the others could grab hold and pull him clear. White stood on the rocks, drenched and in shock like 'a clown with lead feet'.[57] White was all for going over to Adelaide next day to replace the lost rod, but he was persuaded to wait. This brush with destruction became, in *The Vivisector*, another of his unpleasant metaphors for sex: Duffield and his whore-patroness Nance Lightfoot 'were swept together into the blowhole, themselves boiling and lashing'.[58]

Back at Martin Road he settled down to finish the draft. All seemed to be going well, though he was never sure: 'I wish I could "see" what I'm writing while I am writing it.' He finished at 3am on 20 February. Ahead lay two years of oxywelding, 'but oxywelding is nothing compared with a series of caesareans without anaesthetics. That part of the procedure I can't believe any writer enjoys; it wrecks me every time. Now it is over and since Tuesday I have been floating like a cloud, reading other people's books, and accepting hospitality I had staved off for months.' When he read the draft he discovered the opening was chaotic and would have to be entirely rewritten. There were too many voices, for he had thought to make the book richer by presenting it through the minds of several of the characters, 'but as it developed it all started coming out through the mind of the one. Of course, I really started too soon after coming out of hospital last year, when I was still full of the drugs they had been giving me, and I hadn't yet got my nerve back.'[59]

They had seats booked to Athens on 1 May. White spent the weeks before departure fixing the muddled opening, but as he worked the whole second version 'boiled up very fiercely' and he was reluctant to leave the book behind. Yet it was far too cumbersome to drag along on the trip. He warned Marshall Best that *The Vivisector* was going to be longer than *The Tree of Man*: 'Don't blench – it is roughly 224,000.'[60] Before flying out, Lascaris drove White into Martin Place in the new Rover, and he left the book in a safe deposit box in the head office of the Bank of New South Wales.

Athens under the Colonels was dismal. 'Life had gone out of the Greece we knew.' Lascaris divided his time between the last of his aunts, who had prepared a list of suitable brides, and his father George, who suffered a mild heart attack while they were there. White rather wished it had carried the old man off. 'As he is stone deaf, no longer able to read, half senile and pretty helpless.' White had never liked the Lascaris father.[61]

They drove across Thessaly to the monasteries of Metéora perched on needles of rock, and spent happy days driving once again through the mountains round Métsovo before crossing to Corfu. After a few days back in Athens recovering from coughs and wheezes, they set out for the islands: to Mykonos, Skyros, Sciathos and Skopelos. *The Vivisector* had not been left entirely behind. White told the Duttons, 'I keep getting maddening insights into the novel.'[62]

All their island journeys went into Hurtle Duffield's expedition to the Aegean with his mistress Hero Pavloussi: thyme and dust, bare fields and shabby villages, fragments of marble cutting their feet, gold in the chapels and greed in the monasteries. The island of 'Perialos' where Hero hopes to find grace is a portrait of Patmos remembered from five years before, when the two men climbed to the shrine of St John the Divine and visited the convent of the Assumption where the abbess fed them ouzo and sold embroideries. From the heights of the island they watched 'the scaly sea, like a huge, live fish, rejoicing in its evening play'. Both couples saw the same peasant funeral, the

stream of kerchiefed women through the streets and the body lying on
an open bier, the old head with its leather mouth, 'intent on guarding
its secrets as closely as a Greek village will allow'.[63]

Lascaris said goodbye to his family at the end of June and the two
men left Athens for Rome, where Eleanor Arrighi had found them a
hotel on the Piazza Minerva. It gave White great pleasure that Stendhal
had lived there when it was still a palazzo. The heat was terrible. In the
evenings they sat on the terraces of Arrighi's flat in the via del Foro
Piscario gossiping and squabbling. They left for Bologna on 10 July
and after eating heavily for a few days went on to Parma, Lyons and
Rouen. The Flaubert museum was closed which no doubt contributed
to White's sour verdict on Rouen: 'rather a depressing town . . . very
good sole normande, however, and stuffed sheep's foot'.[64]

Paris was calm. White's interest in the tumultuous events of that
European spring had extended no further than de Gaulle's difficulties. 'I
must say I am enjoying the idea of de Gaulle having to cope with chaos at
home after meddling in everybody else's affairs.' The great joy of Paris
was an orgy of paintings, especially little intimate Vuillards 'of people
sitting over the remains of a meal, women sewing, and nursemaids
looking after children in parks. Although he is so very French he is
also related to the best 19th century Russian writers in his ability to
make domestic detail come alive.' At this time, he was enthralled by
Henri Troyat's biography of Tolstoy. 'I can read endlessly about that
old abomination.'[65]

The orgy continued in London where Sid Nolan took them
to the Matisse and Henry Moore exhibitions. Matisse disappointed
White. 'Perhaps he is still too "modern" for one to form a true
opinion. Paintings one thought rich and seductive in the past have
gone flat, and the later ones are too close to contemporary imitators.
At the moment I should say he comes miles behind Picasso, and Braque
though attempting less is a better painter.'[66] After spending nearly every
day with the Nolans for a week, they took them to catch a plane to
Australia, where the painter was to collect an honorary doctorate at the
Australian National University. They arranged to meet in the autumn
in San Francisco.

The two men had as their base in London a small hotel in Chesham
Place which was in walking distance of the West End. 'One needn't
worry when the trains and buses give out, or depend on blackmailing
taxi-drivers in the middle of the night.'[67] They had a kitchen, bathroom
and a bed-sitting-room that looked on to a leafy square where a black
pug exercised every day. Busy as they were in these weeks, White spent
some time here at the hotel making a rough first draft of a story he called
The Night the Prowler. There was no time for polishing.

Among the chores that faced him in London was a visit to Roy's studio. The painter had died a few weeks before they set out for Europe, and there was a painting to collect from Eccleston Street, and a few bits and pieces Roy wanted him to have. The whole street, he told the Moores, 'looks cold and foreign now that Roy is no longer there'. White was jolted to find among the painter's things a manuscript copy of his unpublished novel 'Nightside'. 'I thought I had destroyed the remaining copies before we left Castle Hill,' he told Dutton. 'Now I wonder what else may be lying around waiting for the wrong hands.'[68]

They saw the Sterns in Wiltshire, Steven Runciman in his tower on the Scottish border, Angus Wilson in East Anglia – 'the part of England which appeals to me most' – and Edna O'Brien in Putney. O'Brien promised a family dinner and turned on a formal affair for twenty at which there was so much Irish whiskey that White couldn't afterwards recall the conversation. 'We only seem to meet Edna in a mob of people, so I have never been able to find out what she is like, how much is innocence, and how much calculation. The other night, in black velvet from the 'Thirties and a pair of silver shoes, she had rather the manner of a kindly landlady.' Cecil Beaton took his picture and the session went off amiably enough, though White decided the photographs made him look like a stuffed sea-lion. 'Perhaps that is the truth.'[69]

The three Withycombe sisters had converged on a corner of Oxfordshire, where Joyce and Betty were living on a small farm at South Leigh. Joyce and her husband Richard Ward had parted, and she was teaching in a private mental hospital near the farm. Peggy was alone now that Philip was in an asylum and she had moved down to the village of Eynsham to be near her sisters. White could never understand this English habit of retiring to villages: so damp, so dull. One Sunday he came down alone for lunch with Peggy and afterwards she drove him over to the farm to see Betty for the first time since their breach. The two cousins walked round the rather wild cottage garden at South Leigh. White was polite but unreconciled.

Swinging London of 1968 was utterly uncongenial to White. Everything about the city seemed so squalid that it might have endured another war since they were there in 1963. It rained continually. Here was 'filth almost to equal that of Istanbul, most of the older affluent looking down-at-heel and desperate, most of the young dressed to take part in some shoddy and unattractive carnival . . . at least the whole thing has made me feel I shan't complain any more about living in Australia! (Manoly says: for another six months.)'[70]

The Viking Press had proposed a heavy round of engagements in New York. White accepted a reception, refused to see the press and declined to be guest of honour at a PEN conference on Russian matters. Marshall Best drove the two men through Vermont and

New Hampshire to see the woods in fall, out to Tanglewood and
Emily Dickinson's house at Amherst and to the writers' colony at
Yaddo – 'Ugh!' White's New York agent John Cushman wrote to
Juliet O'Hea after lunch with their client: 'He does have very fixed,
if vague ideas about all his affairs.'[71] White was still hoping Cushman
could do something for the plays in New York.

Zoe Caldwell became a Broadway star that year in *The Prime of Miss
Jean Brodie*. White and Lascaris saw the show and had supper with her
afterwards in a restaurant above Times Square. The problem White had
with Zoe – and it drove him to exasperation – was that she never wrote,
and her friendships, sincere and intimate as they were, broke off when
she was out of the room. You had to *be* with her as White was now.
'It was wonderful to see her enthroned there with Broadway flowing
underneath. As herself she is just the same.'[72] They met and approved
of her husband, the show's producer, Robert Whitehead. Caldwell said
she wanted a child; White recommended wheatgerm and when she had
a son nine months later White claimed a share of the credit.

The plane to 'fetid Florida' stopped at Atlanta. While waiting in the
transit lounge, White looked up Joe Rankin's number in the telephone
book and was about to ring his old lover 'to tell him what a cunt he
was' when he thought better of the plan. He might miss the plane while
he was having a row – and what would happen then? Florida was no
less depressing now than it had been ten years before. He reported, 'I
haven't heard such fascist talk since Germany before the War.'[73]

Lascaris had a second reunion with his mother. Mrs Bronson was
now eighty-one, stout and lived in a cottage surrounded by flowers.
The approaching death of her Lascaris husband was to admit her, once
again, to Mass and she was to be very grateful for this comfort. Mother
and son got on well enough when they were together, but they never
discussed the troubles of the distant past.

Martin Road was burgled while the two men lingered in America.
Four icons were taken, a record player and the house minder's jewellery.
It was the first of the Martin Road break ins, and White was anxious
to be home. The Nolans met them in San Francisco as planned, and
they spent a few days 'mucking round together v. pleasantly'. One
wonderful expedition they took was to Lake Tahoe. White was worried
about Nolan. He seemed lost. 'He . . . didn't quite know where to go
next. I had to try to tell him I was altogether lost and just intended to
go where I was led by whatever leads me (God, of course, though it
hardly does to go round saying it directly.)'[74]

They were home in early November, and White was back at *The
Vivisector* by the end of the month. His routine had changed: he now
abandoned midnight-to-dawn in favour of five-till-noon, for he felt too
old to be getting up to work in the middle of the night. He wrote to

Peggy Garland, 'It is wonderful to be home again and leading a real life – I mean working, which is the only thing that makes life real.'[75] He worked fast and reached the half-way point in the second draft in the first days of the New Year, 1969.

'Fortunately it interests me more and more: I am finding all sorts of things I didn't realise were there, which link up along the way, and I must have put down unconsciously. I expect a lot of people will be furious and disgusted, but it has to come out the way it is coming. I feel more and more that creative activity in the arts is very closely connected with sexual activity, and that an awful lot of the insights I have had have come from that source. It isn't necessary to "sleep around" but to investigate the variety of regularity.' Never had the business of writing been more satisfying. He confessed at times to feeling Godlike.[76]

Suzanne Peck, fashionably slim for the first time in her life, had set out for London to see her new grandchildren. Tax problems had kept her from visiting them until this European midwinter. Travelling with her was her youngest daughter Frances, who was now twelve. After a few days of London fog, Suzanne went to hospital with asthma. She recovered from that and seemed all right, except that she emerged weighing only six stone. She was expected home in Sydney in early February.

White was at his desk on 2 February when his niece Alexandra rang from London to say that Suzanne had died after a short bout of flu. She had no strength to resist the virus. White told Waters, 'When she left here she was already far too thin because her blood pressure had gone wrong as the result of being on too strong a dose of prednisone. It's the same drug which I have been taking on and off, and I know how careful you have to be. But she would never look after herself . . . I mustn't continue harping on it. I shall miss S. very much in spite of our not having interests in common. She was the only close relation I ever cared about; she was so sane, and one could always "have a laugh" together.'[77] Suzanne was fifty-four.

Lizzie Clark was hard hit. Suzanne had kept in close contact with her old nurse, closer than Patrick had been in the last years. Lizzie treated Suzanne's children almost as if they were her own grandchildren. Before leaving for England, Suzanne had brought Frances up to Mount Wilson to say goodbye. White's telegram announcing the death was shattering, and Lizzie cried for days. 'It was the end of her,' recalled her brother-in-law Tom Kirk. 'She went downhill bang. She lost her memory and went senile.'[78]

Deaths, feuds and marriages had now almost entirely dispersed White's Australian family. Clem Withycombe's widow Mag was eighty-three and survived in a flat in Double Bay. She, too, was shattered by the death for Suzanne was the one who rang each morning to see that she had survived the night. Of the Withycombes in Australia, White only had contact with his cousin Geoffrey, a dentist with rooms in Macquarie Street. In the ranks of the Whites, Patrick's only friend was his distant cousin Pat, who worked at the Royal Sydney Golf Club. Alf White had died at Belltrees the year White moved to Centennial Park, and the property was now being run by his son Michael. They found themselves face to face in Martin Place soon after the funeral. Patrick said: 'Now your father is dead perhaps we'll see more of you.' But his hat was on his head and he kept walking.[79] Many years had passed since Patrick White had seen Belltrees, but he sent young Hurtle Duffield along the road into the valley, half-asleep in the buggy at dawn, as the darkness

> turned into silver paddocks. The silver light was trickling down out of the trees, down the hillside; the rocks themselves were for a second liquid. There were rabbits humped in the white grass, then scuttering away.[80]

White threw himself into his work. He felt suddenly mortal, afraid of what might happen if he died before finishing the book. 'When we are both eighty we shall probably laugh at these preoccupations, but one has to be prepared for the worst in case it happens,' he told Waters. Something of the same determination drove Duffield on, afraid he might die 'before he had dared light the fireworks still inside him'.[81] The second draft of *The Vivisector* was finished on Good Friday.

He put the manuscript aside for a month to read and sort out some problems with Suzanne's estate. For the third time in his life he tackled *Madame Bovary*. He found it still 'one of the most wonderful novels' and he finished 'feeling cold as death. Shan't be able to read any fiction for a long time after this, except that I have to face my own. And what a lot of Emmas one knows. A few months ago I heard of a group of unappreciated wives bringing significance into their lives by studying *Madame Bovary*. I think I may work that up into something.' The great literary passion in the last lap of *The Vivisector* was Pushkin, 'the most wonderful writer I have been left to discover in my old age'. He began with the stories, one or two of which 'suddenly develop the tempo of silent films', paused to read Berlioz's *Memoirs*, and returned to finish Pushkin's letters. His immediate sense of being in tune with the Russian was explained when he discovered Pushkin was a fellow Geminian. He envied the Russian: 'How easy it must have been to write a novel in those days, in the classical style, and from the outside.'[82]

He turned fifty-seven. 'The day was rather cold and nasty,' he told Dutton. 'We wormed the dogs early (always something of a wrestling match), and for the rest of the day I worked as usual. At night Desmond and James gave us a very good dinner.'[83]

He complained of spending whole days typing and retyping the same page, but the final draft took him only twelve weeks to finish, single-spaced with two fingers. His moods veered. 'Why did it look so good on previous readings, and finally so awful? I'd like to know whether the lights go on and off in other people the way they do in my-self.' In July he told Maie Casey, 'The Vivisector is lugging me along. I am a bit frightened of it: it's a kind of Frankenstein's monster.' A month later he wrote to her, 'I have been working at great pressure, till I now have left what may take me only another week if all goes well. One can never predict, though: sometimes ideas which have seemed perfectly simple and straightforward all along, suddenly turn into something false and ruinous, and there one sits, trying to repair the damage.'[84]

Duffield dies in his studio, as Stan Parker died in his garden, illuminated by an image of God: for the painter this was the never-yet attainable 'blessed' blue.[85] Blue had been the colour of God ever since White sat at Bong Bong in front of the tin scroll that announced God was Love. Duffield collapsed at the foot of his canvas in the last days of August 1969, and White put the typescript away for a week before reading it through and making a few last corrections. The Vivisector was 562 closely typed pages. He posted it to his agents in New York and London on 8 September after a thumping row at the counter of the GPO. 'Apparently MSS addressed to publishers can go Second Class Air, but those to a literary agent must go First Class. In the end, after a scene and a lot of emotion, they told me I could send it as an insured air parcel for only a few cents more. Now the next phase begins: waiting to hear what publishers think: Manoly thinks it is my best book, but he may be prejudiced, having survived the writing of it.'[86]

When rumours spread that Patrick White was looking for a new publisher, suitors began sending him kind letters and gifts of new books. Harold Macmillan, in Australia on family business, came for tea at Martin Road and the two men spent about an hour talking about Mount Athos. For a while, Macmillan's firm was a favoured contender.

London was the scene of the search which O'Hea conducted on ground rules laid down by White. He did not want to deal with publishers that had rejected The Tree of Man – this proved impossible: most of the best had – nor any that employed vulgar advertising. He would rather not be involved with those London houses that also published in Australia: 'they expect you to appear at dreadful launching parties and to submit to all sorts of publicity which

I won't stand for'. For nearly seven years now, White had absolutely refused to give press interviews. 'I notice that when their books come out the Mailers and Bellows of this world rush to London and jump on the telly. Edna O'Brien starts telling how she wants to become a nun and so forth . . . but I find it all nauseating; and in any case my life is not the least bit spectacular: it is humdrum. I expect that is one of the reasons I write novels.'[87]

O'Hea had one stipulation of her own: the new publisher had to have good salesmen: 'Until Patrick was really famous he needed a good sales force.' Her choice was Jonathan Cape and she guided White firmly in that direction. About the time Macmillan called at Martin Road, O'Hea took the managing director of Cape, Tom Maschler, to lunch. Maschler wrote to her next day: 'I can't think of a living author I would rather publish than Patrick White; for example, if you gave me the choice between publishing Graham Greene and publishing Patrick White, I would choose Patrick White any day – and then the statement is almost an insult to White.'[88]

In London that summer White had been wooed by almost every publisher in town, but warned them he was making no decision until *The Vivisector* was finished. The man who forgot nothing enjoyed being courted by these men, for the mortifications endured over *The Tree of Man* were still fresh in his memory. He met Maschler and found him 'very much alive to contemporary fiction'. The following year, Maschler's joint managing director Graham C. Greene – a nephew of the novelist – was to make one of his annual visits to Cape's distribution arm in Sydney. Maschler sent White a new edition of the poems of George Seferis, and asked if he would see Greene in October: 'I think you would like him.'[89] White agreed.

The Governor-General Sir Paul Hasluck – the Caseys had retired from public life by now – was enlisted by the old firm of Angus & Robertson to help snare Patrick White. They were offering an open cheque. 'Poor things, I wish one wanted them more,' White remarked to Dutton. Hasluck was to host a dinner for White at Admiralty House. White was reluctant: 'I don't want to become a collector of Governors-General.'[90] But Maie persuaded him to go. He was sat among the directors of Angus & Robertson. Across the table was Leonie Kramer, an academic critic he had been at pains to avoid for years. Her presence on this vice-regal occasion did not advance the publisher's cause. A & R was willing, in the end, to top any other offered advance by $2,000 and start royalties at fifteen per cent. O'Hea was very frosty.

Greene left Martin Road after dinner there in October 1969 convinced he had failed. 'It was an austere occasion,' he reported to Maschler. 'If I had written to you immediately after the dinner I would

have described it as a pretty unsuccessful occasion and unlikely to lead
to Patrick White joining us.' But Greene had never experienced one of
White's dinners, and in the days afterwards the other guests reassured
him that the night had gone well. This was so. White liked the Englishman, though there had not been much chance to speak, 'what with my
having to get the dinner and feeling exhausted after it'.[91] White decided
to go with Cape. They had not mentioned money.

The Vivisector had been in London by this time for some weeks.
After a long and puzzling silence, Eyre & Spottiswoode made what
O'Hea thought was a 'fairly spectacular' offer, but when she rang White
in Sydney he confirmed his decision to go to Cape.[92] The typescript
was then sent round to Bedford Square for Greene and Maschler to
see for the first time. White spent a nervous month waiting for their
verdict. He typed a final version of The Night the Prowler and as he
worked on this, a new novel boiled up in his mind. This was The Eye
of the Storm, the novel of his mother's death. He was anxious to begin
work at once. 'I suppose it is old age spurring me on: can't waste too
much time at fifty-eight.'[93]

He faced, also, the faint but real possibility that he might be arrested
at any moment. In the first public political gesture of his life, he appeared
in Chifley Square on the morning of 9 December, in a raincoat and beret,
to sign a declaration urging young men not to register for service in the
Vietnam War. This was a clear breach of the Crimes Act, designed to
provoke arrests. That night he went to bed rather drunk and woke at
1.30am to hear the doorbell ringing violently. A van was parked in
the street. 'I wondered whether I wasn't being arrested already – after
all, a VAN – when it suddenly occurred to me it was the PMG, and I
rushed down to grab the urgent cable.'[94]

'CAPE ENTHUSIASM TREMENDOUS,' cabled O'Hea. She had accepted a
£5,000 advance with royalties that began at fifteen per cent. Next morning, rested and much relieved, White wired in reply: 'DELIGHTED. SPLENDID
NEWS.'[95]

TWENTY-FOUR

Storms

WHITE CAME TO think politics were in his blood because his grand-father Honest Frank had taken himself into the Parliament of New South Wales. But Frank was dead long before his grandson was born, and the boy was raised in a house where politics were hardly discussed. The Victor Whites were happy so long as Labor was out of power. Their friends were not politicians but representatives of the continuing interests of old money in Australia.

Their son absorbed their loyalties. Though he wondered for a while if Europe might be better off for a Communist or Christian revolution after the war, and sided in Greece with Republican nationalists against the royalists, he returned home as if none of this had any application in Australia. At each election he cast his vote for the conservative Liberal-Country Party coalition of Bob Menzies which had been in power since late 1949.

'My political convictions do not burn,' White admitted in his first decade home. He had little grasp of economics and the mechanics of political power bored him. He worried that politics were a threat to art, and maintained that those races like the Greeks who could not detach themselves from politics could not be artists. 'Art is art, and politics is politics – I am afraid,' he told Peggy Garland at the time of her enthusiasm for the new China of Mao Tse-tung. 'I am trying to think *who* has brought them together convincingly, and I cannot: I am sure Picasso's Guernica will turn out to be the least satisfactory Picasso.'[1]

White had opinions and expressed some of them in magisterial letters to the editor of the *Sydney Morning Herald*. He saw Russia's hand behind most international crises; he was elated by Israel's triumphs over the Arabs; he sided with the Greeks over Cyprus; he condemned South Africa as a police state; and he feared Australia becoming a colony of the United States.[2] This suspicion of America was one of the few clear political convictions he absorbed from his parents and it turned out to be important. At Lulworth the decline of Britain was felt as a blow to the family of which they were part. America was certainly friendly, but this was the rise of another empire and another family to which rich Australia had little connection. The Whites and their friends voiced something of this anxiety in the amused distaste they had for American vulgarity, but Patrick could also remember his parents in the early 1930s pressing on people copies of a tract called *Honour or Dollars* which argued the need for Britain to be forgiven the immense war debts it owed the United States. This was the Victor Whites' only political enthusiasm and their son was impressed. Thirty-five years later the transformation of this private conservative into a public radical began with his initially cautious and later vociferous disapproval of America's role in Vietnam.

Australia had begun sending troops to Saigon in 1962 and fed its war machine by conscripting a few thousand young men each year, drawing their birthdays out of a barrel in a lottery where the prize was two years in the army. Despite this, the war was a popular cause in Australia and a new conservative Prime Minister, Harold Holt, faced general elections in November 1966 confident of victory. His Labor opponent – 'That imbecile!' White called him – was a working-class, anti-Communist Irishman with a voice like a cement mixer.[3] Labor was divided about the war. White was unworried.

A few weeks before the election Geoffrey Dutton sent White a copy of the *Vietnam Primer* published by the radical American *Ramparts* magazine. He was sceptical before he began but convinced by what he read. The *Primer* told him a lot he did not know, especially about the origins of the war. The first-hand testimony of those who had fought in Vietnam struck him as sincere. In reply to Dutton he wrote, 'I . . . see I have been wrong, chiefly through ignorance. I am writing to *Ramparts* for more copies.' Nevertheless, a few days later White contributed his vote to Harold Holt's handsome victory at the polls.[4]

Marshall Best tried to persuade White that the *Ramparts* crowd were irresponsible, men and women disgruntled 'because they have not quite made it with the Establishment'. White was not impressed and when a bundle of copies of the *Primer* eventually arrived at Martin Road, he sent copies to friends, churchmen and to the Prime Minister. 'I have always voted Liberal,' he told Holt, 'but can't go along with the war-in-Vietnam policy, nor can I stomach the invasion of Australia by the United States, although I have nothing against Americans in their own milieu.'[5]

Canberra took some trouble with its reply to Patrick White. Officers of the Prime Minister's Department and External Affairs worked on the draft. But when it came to be signed, Holt was away in the United States assuring President Lyndon Johnson that Australia would go 'All the way with LBJ' in the war. Holt's deputy, John (Black Jack) McEwen, pencilled on the draft: 'I don't see any need to acknowledge the letter.' Holt only signed and posted it on his return in June 1967.[6]

'Of course each side is right and each side is wrong and only God will decide,' White remarked to Margery Williams. 'But I who am not God can't help feeling that the Americans are more immoral than the Communists for resurrecting fascism (how could they help it – they're so Germanic) to combat Communism. Democracy is every-day more firmly nailed in its coffin.' White's mind was finally made up when he read newspaper reports of Holt's behaviour at a barbecue in California urging the Americans to keep bombing North Vietnam. 'It is all very gloomy,' White wrote to Dutton. 'Not the least gloomy part is the impression that awful little Holt makes the minute he is let out of Australia. He's definitely not for export. Never again shall I vote for him if he's foolish enough to expect us to.'[7]

Holt drowned swimming in the Melbourne surf and his place was taken by John Gorton, a grapefruit farmer and former air ace who called fresh elections in the spring of 1969. Labor was now led by a middle-class lawyer, Gough Whitlam, but White was unimpressed. Still, he felt he had no choice: 'I shall have to vote for Whitlam whom I don't like much more than Gorton.'[8] Labor lost.

Sometime soon after those elections White agreed to help the Committee in Defiance of the National Service Act. Already 115 of the committee's recruits had been convicted of breaching the Crimes Act by calling on young men not to register for conscription. White was to be the star of a new, distinguished cast of protesters whose call to dis-obedience would provoke the government into action. 'One can pay a fine,' he told O'Hea. 'But I think that would be pointless: help the cause not at all; and from another point of view a term in jail might be quite a useful experience.' She replied by return post urging him to think of his health.[9]

On the late afternoon of 9 December 1969, forty-four writers, actors, politicians and academics had gathered in Chifley Square. A dozen faint hearts failed to appear. This was the first sight the Australian public had had of White for seven or eight years. He signed three forms: the statement of defiance, an expression of willingness to be prosecuted and an instruction to a firm of solicitors to enter a guilty plea. He was photographed and said a few words to reporters: 'I am ready to go to jail because it is useless saying the same things over and over about a war I believe to be futile and immoral. Anyone who has been in a war, and who thinks, will know that it has been the most horrifying and wasteful period of their lives.'[10]

The campaign failed in its immediate aim – the government re-mained resolutely inert: no more fines were levied, those already fined were never jailed, and the courts were closed to the protesters – but a point of political importance was established in Chifley Square. The government's incessant rhetoric of law and order was seen for what it was: not an appeal to the evenhandedness of the law, but a euphemism for the machinery that sent young men to fight. Only those who refused to go into the army were now pursued, fined and imprisoned. For the size of its forces in Vietnam Australia was suffering high casualties: four hundred men had been killed so far and another hundred were to die.

The Eye of the Storm was working in White's mind all this time. There was never a novel he knew so much about before he put it on paper. Even as Ruth lay in Rutland House six years before, he knew he would write about her death, attended by acolytes and besieged by heirs who wished this opulent convalescence would end, either with death or a bare room at the Blue Nuns. He saw that the core of the novel would be the struggle between himself and that almost senile woman of immense will. He might have called it *Death and Corruption* or perhaps *Darker Purposes*. 'The novel tends to stress the darker purposes in the lives of the main characters, one of whom is an actor who has failed as Lear, like most actors, and who returns to Australia with his sister to persuade their aged mother to die.'[11]

He began to write on the Australia Day weekend at the end of January, 'to give myself a kind of excuse for not going to the Premier's party'. This time no first-draft attacks of asthma interrupted the flow, and the words poured out almost effortlessly for months. The cast began to grow: Elizabeth Hunter dying in her great house on Centennial Park, her son Sir Basil the London actor, and daughter Dorothy de Lascabanes surviving the wreck of her marriage to Hubert de Lascabanes by clinging to a few jewels and a title. There were nurses and their lovers, the housekeeper and her crowded past, the lawyer and his family, the tenants past and present of the property Kudjeri. The number of characters was giving him trouble by June when he told Ronald Waters, 'While I am involved with one in particular, I have to leave the others for long stretches, then work myself back into the right frame of mind when I return to them. I imagine Esmé Berenger must have felt something the same when she played all the parts in *Hamlet*.'[12]

Had White been able to act, he might not have written a word. He still dreamed of *his* Lear, *his* Hedda and the vaudeville routines he would perform – if he had the knack. His imagination was essentially theatrical, and the best of White's characters are not only astonishing inventions but great performances. At his desk he acted all the roles. When he spoke of the creative process, he used the language of the theatre. Characters wandered across the stage of his imagination for years – the spinster, the artist, the dame, the boy, the laundress – but not until a couple of them came face to face and began to speak did a novel begin. They put on costume; the air smelt of hot lights and greasepaint. 'There are moments when you have *no* control over it, it takes control of you. One's characters are part of one's unconscious but they do take control and you haven't much say in the matter.'[13] His writing life was dotted with complaints of his characters keeping him awake at night. When he could not stop their dialogues, it was time to put them down on paper. The performance continued until the last words were written, with White as cast, director and audience in this theatre of the mind.

In Basil Hunter, White came close to laying bare his own creative machinery. Hunter is not 'stuffed with theories and "taste" ' but builds his roles from flashes of intuition. 'Perhaps you were, after all, the man of inspired mistakes.' At the same time there was nobody like Hunter for doing his homework,

> Given a part which interested him, yes, he would ferret out the last refinement of lust in a Bosola, say, or just to show them, wrap up a homosexual bread–carter in all the oblique motivation required by the Royal Court . . .[14]

But his performances remained intuitive. White's early research for *The Eye of the Storm* led him to a remark of John Gielgud's: 'The joke is that people think of me as a cerebral actor when I am not in the least bit intellectual. Everything I do is through my intuition and emotions.' White approved. 'I never stop repeating this of myself to Australian academics and intellectuals who stare at me in bemused disbelief.'[15]

Sir Basil was to be a ham actor of the Sir Donald Wolfit type preparing to play Lear. A new biography of Wolfit had just been published, and White devoured it when it arrived from London. The old actor was 'a fascinating, though in many ways awful character'. White reread *Lear*, and read all he could about the great Lears. He wished he had seen Wolfit's: 'I suspect his of being the Lear of our lifetime – anyway, so far. To read about other good actors in the part one doesn't get the impression they got anywhere near what it ought to be . . . How I should love to see a great Lear, but I don't expect I ever shall.' He relied on Ronald Waters to help work up details of the actor's career. 'What should my ageing actor use to take his make-up off? I'm sure I can remember them using coconut butter in my youth, and I don't go back to Kean's day.'[16] John Gielgud also gave him advice on the actor's life.

Hunter's mother Elizabeth is one of White's great roles, an opulent monster searching for illumination in a death scene that lasts six hundred pages. The core of Elizabeth Hunter was Ruth, 'one of those domineering, dominating characters who couldn't help having power over people. There are always the people who enslave . . . and the ones who want to be enslaved.' But Elizabeth Hunter is a more theatrical and more beautiful version of his mother, 'the same kind of dazzling beauty as Glad[ys Cooper] in her heyday'. Ruth never, according to her son, committed Elizabeth Hunter's adulteries. For this performance White also drew on the lives of two other matriarchs: Geoffrey Dutton's mother, the favourite of King George of Greece, and Lady Sackville, the flamboyant and dirt-mean friend of his friend George Plank and mother of Vita Sackville-West. Yet, from first to last, Elizabeth Hunter is Patrick White in costume: 'I shall always be a sucker for jewels and furs: if I were a woman I expect I should have become the most rapacious kind of cocotte, and probably would have got stoned for wearing bird-of-paradise plumes on top of everything else.'[17]

Australians never traded their daughters to European aristocrats on a transatlantic scale, but many exotic marriages were made on the prospect of a wool fortune and the lure of a title. Elizabeth Hunter's daughter Dorothy, a cold young woman with the thin lips that always signal the more censorious side of White's nature, goes through a conversion to Catholicism to marry Prince Hubert de Lascabanes. The match is a feather in the mother's cap, and purgatory for the daughter on a foreign shore. White was always very careful to get aristocratic details right. He turned to James Fairfax for help. Fairfax's mother had divorced old Warwick Fairfax, the newspaper magnate, in 1945 and married Pierre Gilly, a French naval officer and diplomat. Gilly came from the sort of French family 'with houses in the country and shooting parties and that sort of thing' to which White was condemning Dorothy de Lascabanes. Several times White rang to question Fairfax: how had his mother found French society; how had Gilly's friends accepted her?[18]

The last of White's Jews is Elizabeth Hunter's housekeeper Lotte Lippman, 'a steamy, devoted, often tiresome Jewess' who escapes the Holocaust to dance in one of the cabarets he watched during the war in Haifa. She makes her way to Australia to work as a cook: 'that too is an art – a creative one, I tell myself', and her coffee is 'strong enough to blow a safe'. Lippman knows Elizabeth Hunter well: yes, she is evil, brutal, destructive, 'but understands more of the truth than most others'. Such is Lippman's love for her mistress that she ends by committing suicide in the bath after Hunter's death. In the figure of Lotte Lippman White was addressing an old debt of affection: 'There is a lot of Klári in Mrs Hunter's housekeeper.'[19]

White is a rare novelist for holding lawyers in high regard. Lawyers in English fiction have always been rogues and pedants. They fare no better in French. But in the world Patrick White grew up in, lawyers were sorted among the faithful servants. Arnold Wyburd in *The Eye of the Storm* is a portrait of the family's solicitor Charles Ebsworth, whom White had earlier sketched in the figure of Dudley Forsdyke in *The Tree of Man*. Ebsworth was a 'splendid, slender' young man with the head of a pedigree gun dog. He lived at the beck and call of old H.L. at Belltrees, and grew into a precise and reserved old man, dull company but understanding. Ebsworth never showed emotion. He always acquiesced. He was never heard to utter a critical comment about anyone. The Whites of Belltrees and Lulworth were the most distinguished clients in the 'restricted but respectable practice' of the firm Ebsworth and Ebsworth.[20] Their files were kept apart in his office, for he thought it beneath the Whites' dignity to put their papers in the common run of alphabetical order. For Ebsworth to have committed adultery with a client was an unthinkable violation. Wyburd did: that is a measure of Elizabeth Hunter's seductive powers.

In the theatre of his imagination, White had three or four basic sets, 'all of them linked to the actual past, which can be dismantled and re-constructed to accommodate the illusion of reality'. Elizabeth Hunter is dying in a more theatrical version of 20 Martin Road, which had given him something of the Feinsteins' Sarsaparilla house in *The Solid Mandala*, and the stairs and attics for Duffield's Paddington studio. Later the house would be Alex Demirjian Gray's last bolthole beside the park. Another of the three or four basic sets gave White the Hunters' country place: 'Kudjeri in *The Eye* grew out of my memories of Belltrees,' and he drew also on his impressions of Havilah, the Whites' property at Mudgee which he had never visited but knew from family photographs. Belltrees' landscape had been used before – Voss and Duffield each rode along the river into that extraordinary valley – but only in *The Eye of the Storm* does White use a version of H.L.'s opulent house. 'Our family station', as he called it in a letter to Tom Maschler at this time, was as alive as ever in his imagination, though he had not been there for over twenty years.[21]

Elizabeth Hunter's children had been away from Kudjeri so long that they remembered it 'only by flashes or in dreams' yet as they loiter there waiting for their mother to die they discover the potency of the place as the source of their family myths. They love those 'mineral hills' but know they must leave, for the seeds of exile are within themselves,

> 'You've got to admit it's beautiful.' It was her brother looking over her shoulder at the landscape at 'Kudjeri'.
> 'Oh, God, yes, we know that!' she had to agree; 'beautiful – but sterile.'

'That's what it isn't in other circumstances.'
'Other circumstances aren't ours.'[22]

After writing for six months, and with two-thirds of the first draft on paper, White found the novel drying up in the unpleasantness over *Voss*.[23] Film deals had been talked for ten years without ever coming to anything. Options were taken and expired unexercised. In 1968 the Sydney promoter Harry M. Miller had decided to try to put *Voss* on the screen. He had never made a film. The biggest coup of Miller's career had been Judy Garland's farewell tour of Australia when the troubled singer performed in the boxing ring of the Sydney Stadium. Ahead of him lay enormously successful musicals and a short stint in prison.

He arrived at Martin Road in a state of some foreboding. As the ghost-writer of his memoirs recalled, 'White's house put me in mind of a miniaturised version of Wuthering Heights. It . . . evoked a strangely metaphysical feeling. Inside, a brace of small dogs yapped as I knocked at the door. Patrick White, tall and stern, bade me come in.' White mixed gins and tonic. They sat. Miller detailed his desire to turn *Voss* into a great motion picture. 'He just sat there looking at me with his arms contoured to the arms of his chair. I held his stare, thinking, "This man really has got a great sense of theatre." When at last he spoke it was almost as if he was trying to break my nerve. "And what makes you think you will be able to make a film of this book over and above anyone else?" '[24]

The deal they struck locked these two men in a strange commercial embrace for the next decade. Miller came out of the New Zealand rag trade. After selling nylon socks and Maybelle Lingerie, he began promoting rock bands and club acts on the south-east Asian circuit. He left New Zealand for Sydney in the early 1960s and talked his way into society. His handsome face was always in the papers. Harry was a promoter of genius and his finest product was himself.

Their deal gave White the final say on the director. Within weeks Miller was trying to work around this difficulty. 'Now, according to Harry, Universal Pictures are prepared to invest millions of dollars, and send a scriptwriter ("a very gentle young man") all the way to Australia to do research and consult my every wish, provided I give up that veto on the director. So we are stuck,' White told Dutton in early 1969. 'Universal won't give a clue to the kind of director they would choose . . . When I brought up [Satyajit] Ray, Harry said: "He hasn't even a track record! He makes *art* films! Aren't you interested in money?" So I had to say – yes, to give away, but that I have enough to be happy on, and all I am really interested in is art. Still, I like Harry Miller, and I think we shall get on together in spite of this.'[25]

Silence descended on the project. A review in the *Observer*, which still arrived by air every week at Martin Road, prompted White to watch Ken Russell's *Delius* on a friend's television when it went to air in Australia. Impressed by the 'wonderfully real characterisation', he put Russell's name to Miller.[26] At first the promoter was unimpressed, but when Russell's *Women in Love* began to make money, Miller flew to London, knocked on Russell's door, handed him a copy of *Voss* and pestered him with telephone calls. Russell turned to his collaborator John McGrath, the scriptwriter and playwright, for advice. McGrath told Russell this was one of the greatest novels he had read and it should be filmed. Russell and Miller struck a deal.

The unpleasantness began when McGrath flew out to Australia in July 1970. At the airport he walked into an aggressive press conference. Had he actually *read* the book? How did writing scripts for *Z Cars* qualify him to do *Voss*? How could an Irishman living in Scotland write a film about Australia? Why weren't the leads going to be played by Australian actors? White was appalled by the reports next morning in the papers. 'The Australian press has never behaved so odiously, trying to make mischief between everybody concerned, because the film hasn't been handed over holus bolus to Australian amateurs. One monstrous little vulgarian of a columnist has even accused Harry Miller of engaging an "aesthetically pretentious" director. So I have had to give my first press interview in ten years to say it was I who thought of the director . . . I only pray this film is a tremendous success artistically so that we can throw it in the faces of all these foul Australians.' He kept these fears from McGrath, who was surprised to find him so calm in the face of this hostility. 'He was working extremely hard and very obsessively, very isolated, marooned in this sea of racist sharks – and amazingly dedicated to Australia.' McGrath left to explore the outback of South Australia, and White put *The Eye of the Storm* aside. The book had dried up, he told Waters, 'but it will come back in time'.[27]

McGrath returned from the wilds of Oodnadatta to scout locations in Sydney. He persuaded White to show him Lulworth. 'Patrick was very nervous of going there. He had to be dragged. We only got into the grounds and peered through the windows. He was very silent, less communicative than usual. The place was broken down, overrun.' Early on White imagined filming in the old house, with the explorer's cavalcade 'riding down the Bonners' stairs and across the desert of their mahogany drawing room'.[28] Having done its work as a maternity hospital, Lulworth was standing empty waiting to be converted into a geriatric nursing home. The wild garden was untouched and dank: the great bunya bunya still stood at the elbow of the drive.

McGrath returned to Britain to start work. White reread *The Eye of the Storm*, laughing a lot which he always took to be a good sign, and was back at work on the manuscript in September. He had set himself

the goal of finishing in about six months, which would allow him to put
the book in the bank and take another break overseas before starting to
oxyweld. 'I've almost got the First Version of my new novel down on
paper,' he told Stern in November. 'But the best rushes always come
when I am in bed, in the bus, at the sink, or anywhere inconvenient.
The sessions at my desk are the usual agony.'[29]

One day in November they drove to Mount Wilson, stopping on
their way past Dogwoods to pinch some slips of winter buddleia. 'The
garden is now a jungle, quite awe-inspiring to see trees we planted as
threads twenty-four years ago, but from the brief glimpse I got of the
house I didn't want to look any more: it is tumbling down.' Up on
the mountain, Matt Davies was now so crippled with arthritis he could
only crawl about with sticks attached to his arms. Flo was still a Good
Plain Cook. After lunch the two men went over to see Lizzie and Sid
Kirk. 'He still has his wits about him to some extent,' White wrote.
'But she doesn't know what she is doing and saying half the time; she
kept telling Manoly and me how we had grown since she saw us last
(a year ago). She and her house used to be spotless, but now there are
little heaps of dust she has forgotten to sweep away, and she is rather
grimy, and done up with safety pins instead of the cairngorm brooch I
remember. I expect she will go before long: she is as frail as a deformed
sparrow.'[30]

Hectic preparations for Christmas kept White away from his desk
for a fortnight buying presents and cooking. Into the middle of the
celebrations staggered the figure of Barry Humphries. After battling the
bottle for some years, Humphries had gone into a Melbourne hospital
to dry out. He had seemed on the mend. The spectacular backsliding
of these weeks appears to have begun when the *Age* sacked him for
writing a column sending up the rich Melbourne Jews who celebrate
Christmas. Humphries fled the hospital and appeared in Sydney to try to
persuade Harry Miller to become his manager. He burst into Miller's flat
in Woollahra and alarmed the housekeeper by raging about the paintings
and furniture. 'According to Barry he was confused by his first day of
freedom after a year of hospital. According to the housekeeper, he was
drunk. Next day he rang up the secretary and insulted her too, according
to Harry; amongst other things he said, "I'm trying to get in touch with
a friend who's become an acquaintance: a Christian writer called Patrick
White." '[31]

When Humphries rang begging White to make his peace with Miller,
he was invited to lunch at Martin Road. 'He arrived an hour late, after
two more telephone calls announcing himself, and a taxi driver at the
door to ask whether I still expected to see Barry Humphries. Barry,
in a grazier's hat and monocle, was looking rather strange. He says he
has been "weaned off one or two toxic breasts" but I felt he must have

got on to at least one of them again on his way to Martin Road. I'd be most interested to see his medical report. He still has flashes of great brilliance, but moments of despair, one feels. Very difficult to assess. He is such an actor one can't decide when the acting has stopped.' White spoke to Miller. 'I . . . told him he ought to see Barry: although he's crazy, he's a genius, and one can't dismiss him just like that.'[32] Miller arrived home to find Humphries had strewn the flights of stairs to his flat with thousands of gladioli. Miller took him on; Humphries took the pledge and his remarkable career was reborn.

The first draft of *The Eye of the Storm* was finished in January 1971 and a few weeks later White tied the manuscript into a flat parcel and put it in the bank, where it would stay while they made their trip around the world. After despairing of finding anyone to look after the house, they discovered two young women who would move in when they left for America in April. The normal order of things was to be reversed: this time the travellers would see America in spring and Greece in autumn. But before White was free to leave Sydney, he had first to reappear in the criminal trial of Philip Roth's novel *Portnoy's Complaint*.

While the liberating winds of the 1960s swept the rest of the world Australia continued to censor books and films. Censorship was a national habit. Customs officers were busy at airports searching travellers' bags for copies of *Peyton Place* and *The Carpetbaggers* hidden in the underwear. The works of Henry Miller and William Burroughs, were all banned. T. E. Lawrence's memoir *The Mint*, Norman Mailer's *An American Dream* and his anti-war tract *Why Are We in Vietnam?* were forbidden imports. Regularly-updated departmental bulletins detailed the erotic manuals that must be kept out of Australia's hands. The list of the banned had changed a little in White's lifetime, but was still what it had always been: an official index of Australia's innocence.

White thought *Portnoy* was one of the funniest books he had ever read: 'on the other hand there are a great many people I'd hesitate to recommend it to'. His copy arrived in a pile of books from America. Tom Maschler consulted him about Jonathan Cape's plans to export the novel to Australia. Should it be launched in Adelaide? White was doubtful. 'One is inclined to think of the Adelaide-ians as being advanced because of a handful of progressive intellectuals one knows, but the majority are terribly starchy and reactionary. Sydney is the most emancipated city in Australia: I'm not saying that because I come from it; there is much that I detest about it. On the other hand, I'd like to see Portnoy come in the Adelaide Establishment's eye!'[33]

Portnoy was banned and Cape's plans foundered. But the book could still be printed inside Australia and its fate decided by the criminal courts in each state. In great secrecy Penguin Books printed

75,000 copies, which reached the shops in August 1970 and sold out within a couple of days. Police brought prosecutions in all states – except in South Australia, where a Labor government had come to power for the first time in decades – and White agreed to give evidence as a literary expert at trials in Melbourne and Sydney.

Peter Beatson was staying at Martin Road at this time. He was a young scholar from New Zealand via Cambridge, beautiful and going blind. Beatson later wrote a study of White's religious beliefs called *The Eye in the Mandala*. Patrick White was his idol. For many nights they sat up late drinking brandy and talking about music, mothers and writing. The night before White was to fly down to Melbourne he staged a pantomime of his evidence. Beatson cannot recall every word of the performance, but it went along these lines.

White as witness: 'Your Honour, similar charges of pornography were laid against *Lady Chatterley's Lover*. I felt that Lawrence's novel might well be considered pornographic since when I read it I developed a cockstand. Judged by this criterion, *Portnoy's Complaint* cannot be considered pornographic since I read it from start to finish without once developing a cockstand.'

As judge: 'But Mr White – at your age do you think you are capable of manifesting such a physical alteration?'

Beaming around the courtroom: 'Shall the court go *in camera* while we find out?'[34]

White found the real thing conducted with great solemnity, but the actor in him enjoyed the performance once it was under way. 'But I couldn't resist saying what a funny book I think *Portnoy* is,' he told Maschler. 'I hope I didn't put my foot in it.'[35] A long line of literary figures spoke for the book, but the magistrate declared it an obscene article and fined Penguin $100. This was a setback for the cause, but for a ban to be effective in Australia another conviction was needed in Sydney. Between the two trials the Federal Government released forty-eight books from its banned list. *Portnoy* was not among them, but this was a signal of sorts to the Sydney jury that the long winter of censorship might be drawing to an end.

The climax of the Sydney trial was White's appearance on a 'deadly steaming' morning at the old court-house in Taylor Square. He stepped into the box in a Prince-of-Wales check suit, eased his teeth, swore on the Bible and faced Penguin's barrister. Could he list the criteria of literary merit?

'I can define what I look for in a novel.'

'What is that?'

'Well, I expect to have my sense of reality heightened in reading the novel. I expect it to be written with style. When I say "style" that can be anything from the most limpid simplicity to elaborate ornamentation.

I also expect the book to be durable.' Roth's book, he said, had great literary merit. 'I feel personally it could become a minor classic.'

'In *Portnoy's Complaint* the words "fuck", "cunt", "prick" and that type of word are frequently used?'

White agreed.

'In your view does the use of those words in any way detract from the literary merit?'

'They are the kinds of words that man would use.'

'There is a page where the Monkey watches while a negress defecates on a glass table with the Monkey's husband's face underneath, and the Monkey on this occasion drinks cognac. Do you recall that passage?'

'Yes, now that you bring it up.'

'What in your view is the effect of passages such as that on the literary merit?'

'Well, if you take a passage out like that it does seem very crude, but I think you have got to take the picture as a whole, not certain passages.'

The Crown prosecutor was an Irish-Australian with a nasal delivery that cut sharply across White's bronchial sing-song. He jabbed an old, long, crooked index finger at the witness as he put his questions.

'I take it from your observation a few moments ago, it is the sort of incident you would soon forget about?'

'No,' White replied. 'I just had forgotten about it. I had heard of worse in Sydney actually. It is a part of life which the book reflects.'

It seemed the prosecutor wanted White to stumble over dirty words, reach for euphemisms, perhaps blush. But he stood in the box with patrician nonchalance.

'Any incident that takes place in real life can be reproduced in detail in a book?'

'It depends.'

'It depends on what?'

'I think it was quite relevant to introduce it there.'

'Introduce what?'

'That incident.'

'Which one?' The finger jabbed across the court.

'Of the negress shitting on the table.'

Which incident? Calmly, as if describing a traffic accident, White replied, 'I told you, shitting on the table.'[36]

White had not enjoyed this. That night he wrote to Dutton, 'The prosecutor I can only describe as a cunt.'[37] The jury deliberated for hours in a room off Taylor Square, but was unable to reach a verdict. A second trial was held while White was abroad in May 1971, and when the jury again refused to convict or acquit, the book was released for sale. This tactical victory was made complete a few months later when the federal government removed Roth's little masterpiece from its index of banned imports.

The trial did not end censorship in Australia – films are still cut and occasionally banned, and magazines are restricted – but after *Portnoy* the apparatus of book censorship was dismantled and the nation began to enjoy new intellectual freedom as police and Irish senators lost their say in literary affairs. Of course, these victories are never complete. As soon as schools began to set White's own books for study, a campaign began and still continues to keep them out of the hands of the innocent.

White wheezed his way across America feeling aimless and out of love with the country. The only prospect that pleased was the Grand Canyon. 'Nowhere does one see a soul who might share one's thoughts and opinions. I can see why my books don't sell in the States: what is surprising is that any book should sell.' Neither *The Solid Mandala* nor *The Burnt Ones* had earned their advance in America, and White only broke even on *The Vivisector* when it appeared in the States in July 1970. The critics had sorted Patrick White among the interesting exotics; *Time* did not strike; of Viking's edition of 13,000, only 4,000 were sold. Returns were still coming in. These were White's worst figures in America since *The Living and the Dead*. 'It seems to be the direst flop.'[38] Viking asked him to help by making some personal appearances as he crossed America. He refused.

They spent five days in St Petersburg with Lascaris's mother and sister Anna. 'M. has a daily session with his Mom, who is still very lively (in her eighties) but as unreal as ever.' New York brought on 'a certain *nostalgie de la boue*' and a doctor cleared White's lungs by bumping up the dose of prednisone. On their last night in New York they had dinner with Zoe Caldwell and Robert Whitehead, who appeared at the last moment from Barbados. 'They want another child, and are hoping it will begin from now, because the last one started after our last visit!'[39] Once again, White recommended wheatgerm.

London was cleaner and more cheerful now, and White had a sense of homecoming he had not felt on their last visit. The two men grew so fat on London hospitality over the next six weeks that they had to buy new clothes. 'We lunched with the Charles Johnstons . . . and in addition to the Princess Bagration had Princess Aly Khan and Diana Duff Cooper! The latter still has a very blue stare, but by now is rather crippled and wafty: she told us a long and tangled story about a pair of gorillas having sex in a private zoo for the entertainment of a number of Bright Old Things.' The Nolans took them to concerts and exhibitions; Margery Williams invited them out to see her new flat on the edge of Maida Vale. The older nieces Gillian and Alexandra had both given birth to boys a few weeks before White arrived in London.

His relations with Gillian and her husband had been strained since the débâcle of her stay at Martin Road, but now White decided that husband and wife were 'much improved by marriage and parenthood, so I have to admit I am wrong'. The youngest of Suzanne's girls, Frances, took a mid-term holiday from her boarding school to see the rock opera *Catch My Soul* with them. She seemed 'the heaviest of silent adolescents' and reminded White unhappily of himself at that awful age.[40]

Nothing mattered so much to him in England as his meeting with Ken Russell. It loomed as 'a life-or-death occasion' but he half-hoped it might turn into comedy. 'At least it will be best to keep it that way if I can manage it, otherwise one would suffer too much.' On the way across America, he had reread *Voss* for the first time in fourteen years and thought it stood up well, though he would like 'to alter much of the punctuation and many a phrase'. When he arrived in London he read John McGrath's script, and was respectful but a little disappointed. 'Naturally he has had to leave out an awful lot and do one or two things for the sake of compression which the author of the novel cannot like.'[41] Together they went down to Portsmouth, where Russell was filming *The Boy Friend*, and White was delighted to find himself once again in the old Southsea theatre to which Mrs Courtney Mitchell had brought him on holidays from Cheltenham. He met Twiggy.

Relations between scriptwriter and director had soured when McGrath had refused to write *The Devils* and urged Russell to have nothing to do with it. After that he had trouble getting to Russell with drafts of *Voss*, and he wondered if the director was really interested in the project. 'The only suggestion he made was that Voss should be seen trudging through the desert and the camera would go up and over a ridge to see a pool of fresh water full of naked aboriginal women.' McGrath's suspicions deepened in Portsmouth. He felt the director was treating White 'like a supplicant commercial traveller'. After they had waited for some hours, Russell put them into a vintage Rolls-Royce and drove a hundred yards around the corner to a Chinese restaurant. White found the man affable enough, and Russell agreed to fly out to Australia after Christmas to look around, and then begin filming in July. They disagreed on the man to play Voss. 'It makes one feel that other people are completely incapable of visualising characters as the author saw them in the beginning.'[42]

Disturbing news reached the travellers from Sydney: 20 Martin Road had been burgled and the neighbours reported that the young women were holding wild parties. Lascaris was so distressed he came out in a rash which was diagnosed in Paris as diabetes. 'I suppose we shall get used to this new situation in time,' White remarked to Greene at Jonathan Cape. 'But it is a strain to travel through Europe on a diet.'[43]

That summer in Paris there was a great exhibition to mark

the centenary of Proust's birth. White was not passionately fond
of Proust, respectful rather than keen, and willing to admit he
had often been bored reading *A la Recherche*. He never imagined
he would tackle it again, 'unless I dry up, and I don't want that to
happen'. But there were mysteries in Proust's life close to his own.
Not least of these was disease: 'Proust may not have been Proust if
he had not had asthma.' The exhibition proved rather comic: 'All his
beau monde looked so second-rate, at least in the second-rate portraits
and posturing photographs. What did astonish me was the Bed: still
so full of life! Perhaps that is why most of the public seemed to be
turning their backs on it while we were there. I am more shameless,
so I couldn't help staring.'[44]

They spent a happy fortnight exploring the Dordogne by taxi,
and left for Spain to battle with crowds, lost luggage, missed trains
and locked churches. 'I can only think somebody has put the Eye on
us in spite of the fact that we are laden with holy medals to take to
our Maltese ironing woman, and even splinters from Santa Teresa's
staircase given us by a little nun in Salamanca.' There were moments
of delight, marvellous paintings, the sight of Avila and the discovery
of Teresa's tambourine, but White was pleased to fly to Sicily. A sore
tooth began to nag him, 'one of the key teeth of course, to which my
false ones are hitched'.[45] After only a few days they abandoned Palermo
to find a dentist in Rome, but it seemed the dentists had all fled to the
hills to escape the heat.

The two travellers ate delicate meals to suit Lascaris's diabetes
and White's teeth, spent happy hours on Eleanor Arrighi's terrace, and
wandered about the city. When the heat was too fierce they cooled off
in churches and lit candles for the cure of their ailments. 'I can see one
might easily be converted to Catholicism during a Roman August,' he
told Maie Casey. 'Strictly no *sightseeing* in the real sense. And I am
reading *Clarissa*, a duty I have been keeping for my old age.'[46]

Living alone at a great age in the Pensione Alto Adige was the
novelist Martin Boyd. White was concerned for the old man and set
out one day to find him. They had never met. Boyd was the homosexual child of an Australian dynasty whose novels of Anglo–Australian
life were only just beginning to make their mark. He was the writer
Patrick White might have become if he had chosen such a timid life
of exile in Europe. Neither man was a fan of the other – White found
Boyd 'a bit watercolour' – yet White was one of a small band asking
that some recognition and assistance be given to 'one of our most distinguished writers'. In his seventies, Boyd was surviving in Rome on
his meagre royalties and help from the painter Arthur Boyd who was
his nephew. White called at the Alto Adige. Boyd was out. He made
no further effort to find him, but snooped around, later talked to friends

and wrote to the Commonwealth Literary Fund, 'Martin Boyd . . . is having difficulty making ends meet in his old age, particularly since a major operation in Rome cost him a large sum of money, and left him . . . with only partial use of his legs.' White's intervention in Australia was decisive, and within a fortnight the fund had granted Boyd $1,000 and a weekly pension for life.[47]

Athens was defaced by yet more filth, television aerials, cranes and apartment blocks, but from their roof-top flat the travellers could still see the Parthenon in the distance, 'like a fragile toy made of matchsticks'. White began to draft a story that had come to him after his attack of toothache in Palermo. Work on 'Sicilian Vespers' was very painful, he reported. 'I don't yet know whether it has turned out an abortion; what I really want now is to start work on the second version of the novel I left in the bank.'[48] Lascaris was told by his brother-in-law Dr Elias Polymeropoulos that the diabetes scare was much exaggerated. The travellers ate potatoes again and had drinks before dinner.

They revisited Pelion at apple harvest, and the forests of Metsovo which was one of White's favourite places on earth. They sailed to new islands: to Naxos, Paros and Santorini, which the ferry reached at dusk. 'The view as one approaches is stupendous: one sails into what is almost a lake, the two "Burnt Ones" in the middle (both thrown up by volcanic eruption), and the razorback of the main island, with its white villages apparently in the sky.' The island, devastated by a recent earthquake, seemed barren and spent. One day, standing on a dusty ledge, they smelled the wind blowing out of Egypt. Their departure was such a shambles of donkeys, late boats and foul weather that White vowed this would be the last bout of island hopping. It was a vow made to be broken. To James Stern he wrote: 'Greece is only for Greeks and masochists.'[49]

Terrible reports of life at Martin Road had followed the travellers for months, and they flew home in mid-October expecting the worst. Piecing the evidence together they came to the wild conclusion their house had suffered most of the horrors of hippydom: motorbikes, drugs, drink and fornication. They searched the place for wine stains. Plates and glasses were missing; the record player was on the blink; a leg of White's bed was crudely repaired; saucepan lids no longer seemed to fit; there was hair – pubic? – in blankets. Solicitors wrote letters. White told Waters he tried not to think about it any more, 'but over and over again my rage boils up against that pretentious Bellevue Hill trash. Three times before we've had decent honest people looking after the house and nothing to complain about.'[50] The telephone number – never listed in the directory – was changed again.

'To counteract all this a bit, I got my novel out of pawn immediately I came back. Have been hard at it: by now I have written about a quarter of the second version. This doesn't mean the book will be ready before a couple of years, as it is a fairly long one and I shall have to do a third version. I think this will be different: more dialogue certainly, less stylistic. I find as time goes on that I am more obsessed by trying to get precise meanings, which means that style is inclined to go overboard. Whether this is good or bad I can't tell.'[51]

At New Year White struck a bargain: he would give up alcohol again if Lascaris gave up cigarettes. Lascaris never smoked again. 'Alcohol has become too exhausting,' White explained. 'I need all my strength for my book during these three humid Sydney months.'[52] Perhaps as a result of this abstinence, work on *The Eye of the Storm* proceeded far more rapidly than he imagined it would. He was nearly two-thirds of the way through the second draft when 'the Blow' fell on Martin Road.

There had been rumours for some time that Sydney would stage the Olympic Games in 1988 to celebrate two hundred years of white settlement in Australia. At breakfast on the morning of 16 March 1972 White opened the *Sydney Morning Herald* to read the headline: $76 MILLION PLAN TO CREATE STATE SPORTS CENTRE. Moore Park and the lower reaches of Centennial Park would be covered in concrete. His own house and thirty-five others along the spine between the two parks would be bulldozed to make way for the Olympic stadium.

He was appalled. 'Apart from the personal aspect, fancy contemplating funding such a vast project in the centre of a large city, and spending such a fortune on SPORT (they say it would cost $76 million, but an architect tells us more like $250) when we haven't enough hospitals, schools, poverty is increasing every month, we have done hardly anything for the Aborigines, and our art gallery and museum are miserable makeshift affairs.'[53] The doorbell rang and there was a reporter asking if he would appear on television. White disappeared upstairs for a few minutes and returned dressed for his début in a corduroy coat and paisley scarf. A camera was set up in the garden. Somewhere in the distance bagpipes were playing. White was affable but tense. He was never really convinced by the conventions of a television interview, and every line on his face expressed surprise that Mike Carlton bothered to ask him these questions. Surely this young man knew the answers himself?

'I thought it would be too gruesome to watch, but various people told me it came over all right. However, the *Herald* reported the interview leaving out certain key words, which made it look as though my concern is only for myself. From now on I am afraid an awful lot of time and emotion will have to go into defeating this move.'[54]

White put it about that he would abandon Australia if the Olympic plan went ahead. The *New York Times* carried the news. Friends had rather self-pitying accounts of 'the Blow' in letters: 'If the worst happens, and we are bulldozed out, we shall bundle in just anywhere, provided there is a good back yard, and wait till the last of our aged dogs has died, then leave this country for ever. But I hope it won't come to that, much as I should like to spend the rest of my life going to the theatre and listening to music in London. Better perhaps to live it up hectically till my bronchial tubes perish, than eke out a careful, boring old age in some Australian backwater. What I should be sorry about is this house, which we love, and where the vibrations have been just right from the beginning.'[55]

He turned his back on the brouhaha to get on with the second draft of the novel. Misfortune, as always, helped him work at great speed. 'In a way the book is a kind of parallel of what has begun to happen round here, though perhaps only I could see it!' The progress of ugliness and greed is a pulse that beats through *The Eye of the Storm*. Corrupt Sydney, more corrupt than ever, was booming and half the city seemed to have been torn down to make way for cheap apartments and glass office blocks: 'a most horrifying wave of vulgarity is sweeping the land'. Centennial Park was an oasis in this ugly world for White and the cast of his novel. At dawn it was strung with skeins of mist and, as the light faded in the evening, the lakes turned to silver and the pines disappeared into acres of dark until all that was visible from Martin Road was the 'cut-out of convents' along the Randwick skyline.[56]

The oxywelded manuscript went to the bank in May, and White threw himself into the campaign against the stadium. He haunted the park with a petition in his hand, hiding in thickets to pounce on innocent citizens. Most willing were people with dogs and children. 'Hippies also respond very quickly and want to sign; the respectable long hairs are also a safe bet.' Knocking on his neighbours' doors for cash, he learnt the old political truth that the poor give better than the rich. 'To ask the well-laced industrialists and doctors for a miserable $100 is like asking them to cut off their right hand. I think far less of human beings since all this began, and not because of the enemy.'[57] He gave a number of small dinner parties for the editors of Sydney's newspapers who had been generally in favour of the Olympic plans at first, but ended by giving sympathetic coverage to the opposition campaign.

In June, standing on the back of a truck in Centennial Park, White made his début as a public speaker. He had hoped Edna Everage in full drag would join him on the tray, but he was supported in her absence by an ornithologist, a Communist union official and Harry Miller. He braced himself from a hip-flask, and read from a sheet of paper that shook in his hand. 'Your parks are your breathing spaces,' he told the crowd. 'Guard them, cherish them.'[58] With a flower in his lapel, and his glasses perched half-way down his nose, he looked like a grazier at the races studying the form. When the speeches were over, he put on his beret and led a thousand of the crowd down to the Town Hall, where he had a second speech to deliver to a rally of citizens, suburban mayors and athletes.

'I must have stood in this Town Hall for the first time in 1917. I would have been five years old. I was brought here to a fancy dress ball, dressed as the Mad Hatter from *Alice in Wonderland*. Sometimes in 1972 . . . waiting to plunge on towards the city, where so much has been torn down . . . I feel there is some kind of Mad Hatter's party going on – in the name of progress. What, I wonder, constitutes this progress we are urged to believe in?' He spoke of his passion for Sydney, his fears for those living in the new suburbs ('years ago this used to be goat country; I used to take my own goats to the buck at Fairfield . . .') and he pleaded for good sense and candour in the planning of the city. It was a curious and personal speech, drafted and rehearsed very carefully. White ended by recalling a young woman at the ball in 1917, 'wearing nothing but a few sheets of newspaper round her middle and a pair of high-heeled shoes. She represented *The Naked Truth*. Today the truth is a good deal nakeder than she was. If, paradoxically, she is even more elusive, that does not mean we must ever relax in our truthful pursuit of her.'[59]

Jack Mundey announced that a Green Ban had been placed on Centennial Park by his union, the Builders' Labourers' Federation. He and the BLF had perfected a tactic to frustrate developers in Sydney: at the request of local residents, the union refused to supply labour to tear down old buildings or dig up parks. Whole districts of Sydney and acres of bush were being protected by Mundey's BLF. Though this was not clear for some months, his announcement at the Town Hall doomed the Olympic plan. White became a great admirer of this compelling and beefy Communist, 'the first citizen of our increasingly benighted, shark-infested city of Sydney who succeeded effectively in calling the bluff of those who had begun tearing us to bits'. He was to appear on television to praise Mundey's work, stand in rowdy and sometimes dangerous rallies to support the Green Bans and, when Mundey had been thrown out of his union and the bans broken, White paid his respects to the man in the figure of Terry Legge, the union official in *Big Toys* who resists the blandishments of his corrupt city.[60]

White griped about making public appearances, and complained of the peculiar people who cornered him at meetings: 'the usual intense ladies of course, but also some of the scruffiest young men, who seem to have liked *The Vivisector* in particular; Brett Whiteley must have been right when he said the acid people are all with me.' But in truth he was heartened by the response to his speeches and pleased

to find he could do it after a lifetime of thinking it impossible. 'Now
I can see that unexpected avenues have opened for me, and that I have
found other ways of communicating with people.'[61]

A few days after his Town Hall adventure, White collected *The Eye
of the Storm* from the bank and began to type the final version. The
storm of the novel is a cyclone sweeping over Brumby Island, in
which Elizabeth Hunter finds 'peace and spiritual awareness'. White
had appealed to the elderly aviatrix Maie Casey to tell him all she knew
about hurricanes. 'I am particularly interested in how far up they reach,
and how they would affect flying; also the *eye* of the hurricane: whether
a ship can sail along within the eye and miss most of the storm.'[62]

Hunter's journey to Brumby follows White's own to Fraser Island
ten years before, when he was exploring for the abandoned *Fringe of
Leaves*. Mrs Hunter and her daughter land on the same grey strip, to
be driven through the dark rain forest in a wreck of a car, past a loggers'
camp and on to the immense beach with the 'ocean perpetually unrolling
out of an indeterminate east'. But Brumby Island is not Fraser renamed.
The visitors have come to stay with hosts in the Dutton mould, living
in a Queensland version of the house on Rocky Point. White explained
to the Duttons, 'the skeleton is Kangaroo Island behind a façade of
Fraser'.[63] Deserted on Brumby, Elizabeth Hunter waits for the cyclone
to strike.

The Eye of the Storm follows the fundamental plot of all the books
White wrote since falling in the storm at Castle Hill: the erratic, often
unconscious search for God. In the eye of the cyclone Elizabeth Hunter
experiences 'a moment of sublimity which she had always been grasping
for in her rather self-obsessed materialistic life. She has had glimmers
of it before . . . even when she was in her youth riding round Kudjeri.
She was trying to arrive at something that she suspected was there . . .
it had to be a tremendous upheaval to daunt such a dominant character.
She remained a bitch because there was that side of her nature too. But
she did have, I think, more insights after the storm.'[64]

God and love are the two great mysteries of White's world. Love
has a peculiar place in his work, for White is not much interested in
the central drama of most Western novels: the hazards of passion. Few
of his lives are shaped by the search for pleasure: his men and women
sacrifice very little for desire; and more often than not his characters
are haunted by their inability to love *enough*. The Hunters are all
troubled by this fear: Elizabeth Hunter shocks her saintly night nurse
by confessing, 'I wanted very badly to love my husband, Sister, even
after I knew I didn't – or couldn't enough.'[65]

Sex is not what matters here. Robert Hughes, reviewing *Night
on Bald Mountain* in 1964, wrote that sensuality could have saved the

Swords' marriage. This idea White dismissed as an undergraduate mis-
conception: 'sensuality won't save anybody's marriage, although it is a
very agreeable side dish'. Sex is necessary in White's world. Sex offers
relief from lust. It is a service offered and taken. The many whores of
White's fiction are saints who pursue in bed and on street corners their
vocation: they are the nuns of relief. Nance Lightfoot is there whenever
Hurtle Duffield comes down from the bush for a screw,

> It was a relief, though, finally. When he had come, and the
> acid was no longer eating him, he lay caressing her hair with a
> hand which seemed to be recovering its normal function after a
> long period of feverish stress, such as an illness, or some creative
> activity . . . [66]

Love makes sex bearable. Without love White's men and women
are left prey to the great hazard of self-disgust. Intransigent, frigid
Dorothy de Lascabanes comes to suspect on Brumby Island that 'Lust
and disgust are one . . . the same shooting pain in both mind and
body. Love: she must learn love.' White was to rebuke one of his
friends: 'Personally I find sex without love so boring.' But what is this
love? Nothing White experienced as a man displaced Lizzie Clark's
example from his child's heart. Her love was the selfless devotion of a
servant for her charge. She was demanding, but her love endured any
demand Paddy White could place on it. Love is service. Elizabeth
Hunter's night nurse Sister Maria de Santis, raised above a corner shop
in Sydney by refugees from Smyrna, expresses something of White's
own idea,

> 'Love is a kind of supernatural state to which I must give myself
> entirely, and be used up, particularly my imperfections – till I am
> nothing.'[67]

White saw an intimate connection between love and disease, a link
he explored most deeply in *The Eye of the Storm*. This is a novel
about sickness and nursing written by a man with a lifetime's experience
of the subject. In White's world, the way we fulfil our obligations to the
sick is a mark of our capacity to love. Cleaning up vomit is a sure sign
of a loving heart. Elizabeth Hunter is estranged from her husband, but
returns to Kudjeri to nurse him as he dies of cancer. White's account of
her loving service, of love without desire between a man and woman,
of the understanding bond between patient and nurse, is one of the
finest passages in his novels.

Alfred (Bill) Hunter is another of the versions of Dick White
in his son's novels. Stan Furlow of Glen Marsh, Harry Courtney of

Sunningdale and Seven Oaks, and Bill Hunter of Kudjeri are figures
of kindness, wealth and modest understanding who love their children
in a tongue-tied fashion. Their children fail them: Basil is too busy
rehearsing *Macbeth* in the West End, and Dorothy too involved with
her own role as the Princess de Lascabanes, to return home to see him
before he dies. Freudians have spent a great deal of energy showing how
Patrick White has revenged himself in his novels on his mother. But
there is a parallel and perhaps overlooked ambition in White's work,
to seek an accommodation with the memory of Dick: 'as I remember
you, the kindest and most generous of human beings'.[68]

So tough is old Elizabeth Hunter that her death presented technical
difficulties. White considered suicide. 'Could Elizabeth Hunter when
she is blind and hardly able to move, swallow enough sleeping pills to
die?' he asked his doctor Alice Halmagyi. Halmagyi advised not. 'She
wouldn't have been able to swallow so many pills and so much water.
If the pills were left within reach, then that would mean a court case for
the nurse.' White did not want a court case, so Mrs Hunter's plea to the
day nurse to leave the box of 'little capsules' within reach is refused.

'It wouldn't be ethical.' She was genuinely shaken.

'Love is above ethics. And you love me. You said.'

'That's unfair, Mrs Hunter. How would I stand if anything
happened?'

'If you love me.' Her eyes still screwed up.

The end White chose for Elizabeth Hunter was the death he
feared he had wished on Ruth. He asked Halmagyi if the old
woman could die simply because her children want her money and
want her to die. 'Sue and I wanted my mother to die.' Halmagyi said
she might. So Elizabeth Hunter performed her death from life in the
final scene as White imagined it was played in the old flat in Rutland
House. The make-up and jewels Mrs Hunter wore for the occasion
were an exaggerated, theatrical touch but paint and jewels had been a
passion of Ruth's to the end. Seated on her commode, in full regalia,
Elizabeth Hunter gathers her last strength to *will* her heart – 'a fleshy fist
to love and fight with' – to stop beating and allow her to enter the
calm centre of the surrounding storm. Her ashes are to be scattered, as
White wished his own to be, on one of the little lakes in the park.[69]

'Still working away at my book,' White told Peggy Garland in
late October. 'I have got past the worst part, which has been so hellish
to write. I wonder whether everyone will find it too hellish to read.'
These last weeks were complicated by the crisis of Fanny's prolapsed
vagina – 'blood all over the yard and the laundry' – but he soldiered
on, even forcing the pace a little towards the end because Tom Maschler

was arriving from London and wanted to read the manuscript while he was in Sydney. 'Knowing all about the visits of English publishers to Australia I can't see him doing this. But perhaps what he really wants is to re-assure himself it is not unbearable. I still have no idea.'[70]

To his despair, White discovered in these final days a book on the guerrillas of Angola just published by Longman under the title *In the Eye of the Storm*. Must he change his own title? He canvassed his friends: should he use *Darker Purposes* instead, the words taken from the speech Lear delivers as he divides up his kingdom,

> Meanwhile we shall express our darker purpose.
> Give me the map there. Know that we have divided
> In three our kingdom; and 'tis our fast intent
> To shake all cares and business from our age,
> Conferring them on younger strengths, while we
> Unburdened crawl toward death . . .

Maschler reassured him that the original title should stand. The book was finished on 14 November and White gave his publishers the corrected typescript over lunch three weeks later. Greene was also in Australia. Maschler read the book rapidly and before flying home to London declared it White's best. White also sent a copy to Maie Casey, to whom he wished it dedicated. 'I wanted her to read it first because there are things in it which might start a certain kind of person saying, "Fancy Lady Casey having anything to do with him and his dirty books!" '[71] She accepted the dedication, a brilliant late feather in Maie Casey's cap.

White delayed sending the book to New York. At Christmas he told Viking he was too busy tying up parcels to get round to sending the typescript. He knew the excuse was lame, but he was stalling to make sure the book appeared first in London where good reviews might 'give a lead to those incompetent Americans'. Indeed, he wondered if Viking wanted him after the poor showing of *The Vivisector*. 'I can't help feeling Viking continues to publish my long and financially profitless novels only because I was a protegé of Ben's.' Now Huebsch's successor Marshall Best had all but retired, and White was dealing with a new man, Alan Williams. He felt his contact with the firm slipping. Only after O'Hea made soundings – 'everyone at Viking would be totally desolate if you were ever to leave them' – did White send them *The Eye of the Storm*. Alan Williams read the typescript and telegraphed: 'HAVE JUST EMERGED SHAKEN AND AWED FROM THE VORTEX THAT IS ELIZABETH HUNTER. HEARTFELT CONGRATULATIONS.'[72]

White had switched his vote only reluctantly as a protest against the

Vietnam War but, by the time the watershed elections of December 1972 came, he was a committed supporter of the Labor Party. 'I realised we had reached the stage where a change had to be made – that we must cure ourselves of mentally constipated attitudes, heave ourselves out of that terrible stagnation . . .'[73]

New friends had made Labor palatable. Senator (Diamond) Jim McClelland was a worldly lawyer almost untouched by the Tory pessimism that passes for wisdom among Sydney's barristers. They had met in 1971. McClelland admired White's steadfastness, the lack of vanity, the meticulous curiosity, and the malice. 'He has a greater gift for malice than anyone I know.'[74] White admired and trusted Diamond Jim, but loved his beautiful and subtle wife Freda. The McClellands' apartment on Darling Point was a salon for young people of promise. She collected protégés, enjoyed her rich life and ignored the political barriers of those years, moving as easily among squatters as socialists.

In the first dramatic days after Labor won office on 2 December 1972, Gough Whitlam released all conscripts from the army and brought home Australia's last few troops from Vietnam. White was encouraged by these signs of profound change, but his excitement was kept in check by congenital pessimism and the exhaustion that had settled on him after finishing work on the novel. Christmas was quiet. On New Year's Eve he was asleep by 9.30 but woke by chance at midnight and watched from his balcony some half-hearted fireworks exploding over the Harbour. 'I hope next year will be better than this when I had to do so many things which don't come naturally to me,' he wrote to the critic Ingmar Björkstén in Sweden. 'We have probably staved off the stadium. We have also changed the Government – a very necessary move. And I finished my novel *The Eye of the Storm*.'[75]

TWENTY-FIVE

The Prize

AT SIXTY WHITE'S hair was silver and his face had softened, falling in folds and creases round his Withycombe jaw. Walking the dogs kept him fit, but cortisone and whisky were giving him the look of one of those 'pursy' men who inhabit his novels: a face of soft skin and a belly under his shirt. His eyes were still remarkable, blazing eyes in an impassive face. No one forgot them, but few could say what colour they were for people flinched from his stare. He was as healthy now as he had been at any time since the war, though his teeth were dropping out and he imagined he walked a little more slowly. The fires of asthma were burning low and his chest was free of muck. He took vitamins E and a lot of C every day and wondered if he would end up blind like his mother. 'In a press photograph yesterday I came out looking like Vaughan Williams at the age of eighty,' he told Luciana Arrighi. But White was still a large, handsome man.[1]

Desmond Digby gave a dinner on his birthday. 'There was no *Virginia Woolf*. Desmond thinks everybody was too exhausted.' No public fuss was made of the event and White was pleased, for the sort of public carnival held on Nolan's fiftieth birthday seemed mechanical and pointless: why celebrate age? He had already refused most of the honours that might have come to him at sixty. He was offered a knighthood eighteen months earlier but turned it down. 'The only kind of artist who can safely accept a title is the actor,' he told Dutton. 'Actors can blow it out in a series of histrionic farts, but painters, writers and composers seem to bottle it up and become museum objects.'[2] Embarrassing rumours about the Nobel had been around for a couple of years, but they had come to nothing. He claimed to be glad.

Reuters and a few local papers were allowed to conduct birthday interviews only in order, White said, to carry on the fight to save Centennial Park and show the state government 'we are not sitting here like a lot of turkeys waiting to be slaughtered for their political Christmas'.[3] He told the press that birthdays meant nothing to him.

'If I live to seventy-five it means I have fifteen years left in which to do what I have planned,' he told the *Australian Financial Review*. 'There are ideas for books. A collection of short stories and novellas to be published shortly.' He mentioned the novel he was working on. 'It is about old age, death, and mortality. Old age I am afraid of, but not death.'

'Do you think much about death?'

'Yes I do. What will death hold for me? Will there be a giant unravelling at the last moment? Will I be able to pass on what I see? Will there be a great uplift, a surging of light and power? Will death be a beginning or an end?'

The future?

'Who can foretell? Who knows? I may drop dead in the gutter tomorrow, then what? I just hope I can finish what I want to finish.'[4]

Life at Martin Road was lived to an inflexible timetable which had grown from the useful pattern Lascaris was taught as a child by his Smyrna aunts. And routine was White's guarantee that he was living that 'normal life' every serious artist must lead. He was at his desk about 5am and took a break for coffee at 8am. He finished in time for the ABC radio news at 12.30. Lunch was usually leftovers. Afterwards came the siesta. The dogs were fed at 3.30 and taken across to the park. He cooked and wrote some more before dinner. There was no television and the two men went up to their beds about 9pm. Monday was the day for going to town to do the banking or post or see his trustees. Tuesday was shopping day. Friday was cleaning – no one came near the house on Fridays – and Saturday was washing day, rain or shine. Sunday morning was spent on the telephone. His friends had slots: 8am for Desmond Digby, 9am for Elizabeth Harrower. On Monday the cycle began again. Cooking and cleaning were White's responsibility; Lascaris handled most of the shopping and all the gardening. 'He does too much, however, is an obsessive gardener, never out of the garden,' White wrote to James Stern. 'When there is nothing left to do, sweeps up every fallen leaf. The bitches say that is the way he escapes from me.'[5]

Except in the last weeks of a novel, when White went into retreat, the two men went out two or three times a week to eat with friends or see a film. The Orchid Terrace in Brisbane Street was their favourite restaurant: 'It didn't invite you in, but had the most marvellous food.' They saw hardly any theatre now – though a little more than White admitted – and went to few concerts. The Sydney Symphony Orchestra and Musica Viva's chamber music seemed stodgy, and they had given up their subscription tickets. White's taste was changing. Mahler, the

great passion of the 1950s and 1960s, was now the incongruous enthusiasm of Mrs Hunter's pharmacist Col Pardoe in *The Eye of the Storm*.
They turned out for concerts of experimental music at the Cell Block
– indeed, White financed some of them – and each summer went to one
or two prom concerts to hear some big modern piece, two old men and
hordes of kids on sweltering nights in the Town Hall. Otherwise they
waited until they were abroad for 'orgies' of theatre and music.

He wished he had two lives: one for work and another for travel
and reading. 'A third would come in handy.'[6] Books piled up at
Martin Road waiting for a break between drafts of his own novels,
for when he was writing he could only manage to read for about half
an hour a day. During the years he spent on *The Eye of the Storm* he
discovered Yasunari Kawabata and thought his haunting novella *Snow
Country* one of the best novels he had ever read. He went on to read
Kawabata's *The Sound of the Mountain* and Junichiro Tanizaki's *Some
Prefer Nettles*. 'Discovering the Japanese novelists in my old age is as
exciting as plunging into the nineteenth century Russians in my youth,'
he told the translator Magnus Lindberg.[7] As one of the epigraphs for *The
Eye of the Storm* White chose a line from Kawabata: 'He felt what could have
been a tremor of heaven's own perverse love.'

Dealing with translators was always a happy chore, for White
wondered darkly what 'dreadful mistakes' were being made when
translators did not bother to ask him questions.[8] His precise, patient
explanations are little manuals of Australian life and language. To
Ingegärd Martinell's queries as she translated *The Solid Mandala* into
Swedish, White replied,

> p.128   boiler = an old and tough fowl which can only be made
> eatable by boiling.
>
> p.160   lamb's fry = lamb's liver.
>
> p.172   shower teas = Australian suburban brides are given tea
> parties by their friends before the wedding, to which the
> friends bring perhaps something for the kitchen, sometimes
> at more modest functions just a recipe. C.'s daughters are
> always giving such teas, but as they never catch a husband
> they are never showered upon themselves.
>
> p.183   gross business minotaur = a certain type of business man
> with an eye for girls, they often look rather like bulls.
>
> p.211   stuff a mutton flap = an economical and not very pleasant
> dish because breast of mutton is so fatty and there isn't much
> lean. A stuffing is made out of moistened breadcrumbs
> and herbs bound with an egg. The flap is rolled up with
> the stuffing inside, skewers are stuck through the roll to
> keep it in place, and it is then baked in the oven. Only

very primitive cooks in very poor families would eat this nowadays.

p.216 Primrose Pompadour: there is a portrait of Mme de Pompadour by I forget which French painter of the period. I remember when I was a child a rather pretentious Sydney society lady went to a fancy dress ball as the Primrose Pompadour.

p.292 mere claws or rain-scurries = sounds on an iron roof at night can be frightening in old houses in the country. "mere claws etc" is an attempt to exorcise these fears . . .[9]

Though Martin Road was chock full of paintings he was still buying more. For some time he had resisted Brett Whiteley's work, for it was lush and beautiful and the painter was already rather fashionable. But Whiteley's big show in Paddington in March 1972 convinced White that this man was one of the 'creative geniuses' of Australian painting. The other, of course, was Sid Nolan. 'This exhibition brought me alive again, wanting to do things myself as I only ever feel when in contact with a great artist in whatever medium.'[10]

Whiteley came to Martin Road and they found he spoke almost a whole new language. Sometimes he was lucid but there were moments when White thought it was just 'a fizzing of fireworks. I expect he is used to most people looking blank.' The painter brought a record by the singer Van Morrison who had announced that Patrick White was one of the greatest influences on his life. 'I find this sort of thing quite alarming. Also according to Brett, many of my followers belong to the acid world because I see things the way they do. He couldn't believe I had never been on acid; actually I have come across this before from people who are on it. Again mysterious and somewhat alarming, though I suppose it ought to be consoling to realise that they are no different from the very ordinary self one knows too well. Brett is all for pushing acid and grass on to us ("mescalin is a must") but I said if we took to that at our age we would show up like the parents in *Taking Off*. Before he left he made us touch his hair, which is a mop of tight little corkscrew curls which look silky, but feel as though they have been rubbed with resin. Manoly thinks it was like touching some strange animal one has never touched before.'[11]

White had been giving paintings to the Art Gallery of New South Wales for years, and had promised them the lot when he died. These gifts began after the 1968 world trip when Roy's estate, Lascaris' sister Elly in Athens and Sid Nolan each gave him paintings. 'Have to start easing out a few to the Gallery of N.S.W.'[12] The following year, shortly after finishing *The Vivisector*, White invited Daniel Thomas to lunch and afterwards they went through the house making an inventory and

photographing the whole collection on the walls. Thomas, Curator of
the gallery, was particularly keen to have White's de Maistres in the
public collection. They saw eye to eye on de Maistre. White continued
to give individual paintings to the gallery, sometimes to make space on
the walls, but he often arranged for canvases to be trucked directly from
exhibitions to the gallery. Not all his gifts were welcome, for the Trustees were least keen about those difficult works by new painters which
most excited White. Most of his gifts were stored in the basements, but
White was not deterred. He looked to the day when his paintings would
rise like Lazarus, and take life on the walls upstairs.

Shortly before his sixtieth birthday, he offered the gallery the
White family portraits. 'I should like if possible to keep the trio of
portraits together,' he told his niece Alexandra Bishop. 'Not only are
they excellent as paintings, they will be of historical interest later on in
Sydney.'[13] He bought de Maistre's paintings of Ruth and Suzanne from
his sister's estate. White was embarrassed by the notion of presenting
the portrait of himself, so the gallery was told all three were the gifts
of his nieces. Only Ruth is hung in public, a familiar sight in Sydney
once again, striking a sour pose in a flowered hat.

Life on the scale it was lived at Martin Road would not have been
possible on White's royalties alone. Writing had not made him rich.
Patrick White was a literary author: his novels sold a few tens of
thousands when they first appeared in hardback, then steadily by
thousands in paperback. In the 1960s – the decade that began with
Riders in the Chariot and ended with *The Vivisector* – White's hardbacks
earned him about $40,000 before tax and commissions.[14] His paperback
sales were climbing to impressive heights and were to climb more
steeply still when his books began to appear on school syllabuses. *Riders
in the Chariot* had sold, in the Penguin edition alone, 30,000 copies
by 1970. Over the length of his career, White's paperback earnings ran
in the ratio of 60:40 to hardbacks. On this basis, his paperback brought
him roughly $60,000 in the 1960s. The plays contributed only about
$1,400, but Harry Miller paid $30,000 for the film rights to *Voss*.
Short stories earned, in effect, nothing. Curtis Brown continued to sell
new translation rights, though foreign royalties were not always
available to him. A heap of zlotys was trapped in a bank in Warsaw, and
he eventually gave them to the families of political internees. From these
sources, his exact income is impossible to calculate. But it is possible
to say that writing earned White a gross income in the decade of about
$150,000.

Only the Belltrees inheritance made it possible for White to live
and write as he did. He was 'hardly a gold mine', he told Dutton. 'I
think a lot of people imagine I am a successful Author because I was
fortunate enough to inherit some money, and am able to live and write

on that, using it with care, and doing most of the work ourselves.' They had no servants, did not gamble, nor did White play the stock market: 'I . . . would be in the gutter if it weren't for the Perpetual Trustees whom I inherited from my father.' The Rover was getting old and so were their clothes. In these inflationary times, White worried about the cost of birdseed, postage, toothbrushes and paste ('probably the reason I lost my teeth') and underclothes. 'I can never bear to buy new ones till the old ones are in rags.' He was not exactly mean, he said, but had 'cautious blood in my veins. That, and not feeling attracted to the kind of life one can live in Australia, has kept me anchored to my work.'15

His only luxuries were paintings and travel. He was determined to escape Australia every few years – 'otherwise I should go mad'16 – and he was as easy with money abroad as he was tight with it at home. After exercising little sacrifices at Martin Road for two or three years, White and Lascaris flew round the world staying at comfortable hotels and eating the best food. Once they were home again, they resumed their careful regimen: good old clothes, wonderful cooking, the leftovers for lunch – 'Manoly makes such a fuss if I throw anything out' – and the Orchid Terrace once a week.17

White lived to exercise mastery over his own fortune. He was not afraid the money would run out, but that it might take control of his life. 'I wish somebody could work out for me the point beyond which money becomes a burden,' he wrote in the late 1960s to Maie Casey. 'Of course the point would vary with the person, and some seem happy to go on accumulating it endlessly, but I could easily draw the line somewhere if only I knew roughly where.'18 For the next twenty years he was the most generous supporter of the Smith Family, which helps to feed and clothe the poor in Sydney. He began with the biggest single donation the Smith Family had then received, and after that gave what he had to spare: between $10,000 and $50,000 each year. How the money was spent he left entirely to the charity. In 1971 he put $5,000 into a scholarship fund for Aboriginal school students. Help to Aboriginal students and Aboriginal medical services continued through the 1970s and 1980s. He gave more than $30,000 to the Aboriginal and Islander Dance Company. When the *Sydney Morning Herald* reported the outbreak of another war, White took a taxi to Red Cross headquarters with a cheque for a few thousand dollars. He gave to new theatre companies as they appeared, to conservative campaigns, to Greenpeace and later to new political parties. Almost none of these gifts were publicly known. There were friends who, in absolute secrecy, received kindnesses from him: one woman left alone to raise several small children had a monthly cheque for years. Favours he would never have solicited for himself, White asked for his friends and for their children who were now growing up and looking for jobs.

These friends were changing. The last of the graziers disappeared from Martin Road. Of the few literary friends who survived, Kylie Tennant was growing more eccentric every year and took her daughter to live on an apple farm on the Blue Mountains. Elizabeth Harrower, whom he had met in the early 1960s, was no longer writing. He tried to interest his American publishers in her novels and never ceased badgering her to get back to work. She was devoted to him and they were drawn closer by their shared enthusiasm for the new Labor Government. In the early 1970s Harrower was looking for somewhere to live, and for weeks White sent her pages torn from the real estate section of the *Herald* with flats near Martin Road circled in green pencil.

Penny Coleing loved dogs, cooking, gardens, paintings and the two men of Martin Road. White had known her all her life, for she was the daughter of Shirley Horn, one of the distinguished Eastern Suburbs' bluestockings who read and loved his work in the early days. Shirley Horn took courses; the Horns had the Boudin of bathers on a seashore that caught young Hurtle Duffield's eye. Their Boudin, alas, turned out to be a fake – 'so obviously fake' – but it now hung among the new Australian paintings their daughter Penny collected passionately. White advised and chided her over the years, often with astonishing bluntness. Lascaris loved her small children. They walked their dogs together. Later Coleing was to be White's link with the anti-nuclear movement. He often turned to her for help. Once as he was writing *The Eye of the Storm* he rang wanting a 'low-class' expression for menstruation. Her suggestions were rejected: 'I don't want your Frensham euphemisms!' Her husband, the artist Tony Coleing, offered 'to have the painters in', and that is how Nurse Manhood finds herself the night of her reconciliation with Col Pardoe: 'she had the painters in and there was nothing doing'.[19]

One happy outcome of the *Voss* business was White's friendship with Elizabeth Riddell, for it was this forthright and sensible woman who came to interview him when he wanted to save McGrath and Russell from the hounds of the Australian press in 1970. Riddell was a poet as well as a distinguished journalist and a shrewd judge of writing. White valued her for her 'judgment, taste and worldliness'.[20] Riddell became the fence-mender in his life.

Meals at Martin Road were now, more than ever, high-adrenalin occasions, with any combination of tears, laughter, smashed plates, rows, vaudeville, confessions, gossip and wonderful food. Frank Watters, whose gallery White particularly admired for its young painters, came to dinner at Martin Road in these years for the first time. 'Patrick was getting the guests. Women were in floods of tears; men were stamping out the door. An incredible scene, and he sat there lapping it all up. When all the other guests had been dealt with in one way or another, Patrick took me for a tour of the house to see the paintings. We got to a room full of Lawrence Daws, and I said, "I've never really liked Daws." He turned away and left me there and I had to make my own way back to the table, where the other guests were waiting eagerly to see my own discomfiture at his hands.'[21]

White was still moving about society, and among his friends was a knot of Eastern Suburbs ladies. There was a fashionable photographer he liked called Laurie le Guay, who was married to one of these women. One day they came to lunch. Anne le Guay was on White's right. 'Suddenly he asked a question, then a second and a third question and it began to get nasty and difficult. I don't know what provoked it. Perhaps I said something flippant – I was young, I didn't have opinions – but he had me pinned to the table like a butterfly. Some of the others thought it was a shriek. Manoly tried to interrupt and help. No way. I was fighting for my life; struggling to keep calm. I don't think I've ever fought so hard for myself. Then I remembered seeing his de Maistres and I said, "Patrick, let's stop all this. Tell me about the de Mestres. I knew them." He said, "How?" I told him about riding my pony over to Biddy de Mestre's when I was eight and seeing interesting paintings on the walls, instead of the hunting prints we had at home, and how Biddy explained about her famous brother. That saved me.'[22] She never went back to Martin Road.

His rages were shocking. Within hours of arriving on his first visit to Martin Road, Peter Beatson found himself having a terrible row over the Jewish question. This was late 1970. He had remarked on the irony that the Jews were giving Palestine just the kind of treatment they themselves had received down through history. 'Patrick exploded with wrath. I sit crouched miserably over my plate as he towers and rumbles. He interprets my remarks as being anti-semitic, and he implies that I am on Hitler's side. My stay with my idol has not started well. Somehow the situation is defused, cordial relations are resumed and for the rest of my time at Martin Road relations remain friendly. But I have learned quickly that Patrick is extremely direct and uninhibited in expressing his viewpoint and making his feelings on subjects known. It is unnerving to be in the company of someone who communicates, without prophylactic, his precise, honest and sometimes pugnacious opinion of you. The corollary, however, is that if he is relaxed and friendly with you, you can be sure it is not just a social façade.'[23] But not entirely sure.

White was troubled when his friends were friends with his enemies. He tested loyalties. When he asked, 'How *is* your friend?' there was never much doubt what he meant. Fay Gosse had known and admired Hal Porter for many years. Porter had met White once, embarrassed him, and the two thereafter loathed one another. 'How *is* your friend?'

White would ask Fay Gosse when he heard Hal Porter was in town.

'Patrick, I do wish you'd stop needling me about Hal.'

'A detestable man.'

'I like Hal very much.'

She forgave White this for years. 'One felt sorry for Patrick. He was raw. He didn't take anything through the shutters we all have, and he could never forget anything.'[24]

The counterpart to White's hunger for undivided loyalty was the loyalty he showed his own friends. He was a lion on their behalf, and in their company he was funny, capricious, original, difficult, charming, taunting and extraordinarily kind. It might be hell to be with him at times but it was never boring. Peggy Garland remembers him then as 'the best company and nicest companion I have ever known. He never seemed to be in a hurry or flap; there always seemed all the time in the world. He spoke as he does still – with a sort of drawling hesitation – picking his words carefully and exactly – he had the air, I think, of a great actor or grandee. He was extremely attractive to men and women, I thought platonically. I trusted him as I have trusted few other men. No other man, come to think of it. I knew he would say things about me behind my back but I felt that they would be true, so I didn't mind that.'[25]

The Duttons were still his closest friends, and the two or three letters he sent every month to Anlaby give the most vivid running account of his life and writing. He also peppered them with reproaches, for after ten years' friendship he was more than ever worried that Geoff Dutton was wasting his money and talent in fast books, frantic travel and boring seminars. Where were the books planned and never started, begun and never finished, done but falling far short of what they might have been? 'This would be none of my business,' he wrote in early 1971, 'if your every other letter didn't come up with the cry of poverty and what-will-become-of-Anlaby-and-the-children? I should have thought if you dug yourself in at Anlaby for two or three years you might improve the situation. When the pre-Revolutionary Russians were hard up they retired to their estates. Certainly they drove themselves mad with boredom in most cases, but you, like Pushkin, have your "embroidery".'[26]

The intimacy of the two couples continued uninterrupted. 'He was always extending you,' Nin Dutton recalled. 'He knew what people were writing, what was about to be published, and what people were painting. His antennae are so good that you can go out with him in the morning, buy some coffee, go to a couple of galleries, get the bus home, and he has accumulated enough material for a week.' But she found him a hard man to comfort. 'I remember one night when he was hammering away at himself at the table. I was sitting next to him and didn't know what to do to comfort him. So I just put my hand over his, and I could feel it in his hand.' To explain this, she clenched her fist tight. Pain and hunger still dogged him, and even now he suffered bouts of relentless self-dissatisfaction. He spoke of suffering from self-disgust so powerful at times that it made him 'ashamed to go amongst people who have completely different and exalted ideas of what I am'.[27]

Deep into the brandy one night at Martin Road he raged to Peter Beatson that he would give anything to be cured of his affliction and lead a normal life. Beatson hesitated to ask precisely what he meant, but later put it to White that if he felt so spiritually afflicted he should see a psychotherapist. White replied, that if he lost his 'disease' he would also have lost his gift and he was not prepared to make the sacrifice. When White talked of being a writer, he frequently used the rhetoric of affliction. He spoke of the disease of memory; the disease of foreignness; the disease of writing. Rodney Wetherell observed that Hurtle Duffield seemed to regard his vocation as a terrible burden. 'It is a burden,' White replied. 'It's hell. I'd far rather not have been any kind of artist.' But he paused. 'No perhaps that's wrong. But in another life I wouldn't like to be an artist.'[28]

He worried about drink. In these years he was drinking about half a bottle of spirits a day and then wine with meals. He made sour jokes about being an alcoholic. He quizzed doctors: *am* I an alcoholic? It was as if he wished to be one officially so that he was not held personally responsible for his drinking. He carried booze well, never fell about, never entirely lost control, but feared the way drink exacerbated his temper. He drank and raged. It left him exhausted. By the early 1970s he had given the bottle up two or three times, but only for a few months at a stretch.

Marihuana might have been an alternative, but he decided it was impossible because of his lungs. Mescalin sounded 'just the thing' in Aldous Huxley's accounts. 'Everything one has ever been trying to bring off achieved in a few moments. One arrives at the chairness of the chair, of which Van Gogh's is only an emblem. All my life I have been knocking off only the emblems of things.' But he did not try. He was urged to experiment with LSD. Again he declined. 'I am sure I know all about it from my dreams and most despairing moments. So I don't think the temptation will be a lasting one: I have too much to cope with without that.'[29] He stuck to alcohol.

White confessed to being frivolous, a bitch, possessive, unforgiving and jealous. 'I was terribly jealous in my youth. Sexually jealous more than anything else, but also jealous of writers who I knew were inferior but who were accepted when I was seen as a freak.' Traces of that jealousy remained. He found it galling that a writer like Alan Moorehead, whom he had met in Egypt during the Cyrenaican campaign, should be paid huge advances to write books on the Nile and the Pacific. 'I am even told that Moorehead is not very good, but of course journalism is what the world wants to lap up.'[30] He was still upset when pulp novelists sold huge numbers of books. His refusal to promote sales of his own novels seemed to strengthen in response. Huebsch's dictum still held: that good books will find their own readers.

He began to suspect that a jealous Australian was behind one or two hostile notices in London. His suspicions were aroused by an unsigned review of *The Vivisector* in the *Times Literary Supplement* which seemed the work of the art critic Bob Hughes: 'that ingrown type of Irish R.C.-cum intellectual playboy'. White found he was wrong and shifted the blame to the expatriate television critic Clive James. Thereafter he held 'that thug' to be working against him behind the scenes in London. When Paul Bailey wrote a bad review of *The Eye of the Storm* in the *Observer* it was because 'she is a jealous bitch under the influence of the expatriate Australian Clive James'. When Bailey used the word 'sludge' in his review it seemed more than coincidental. 'I believe he got it from an Australian, and who more likely than Clive James of the *Observer*, an admirer of A.D. Hope's . . . ?'[31]

How baffling it was for his friends to see a man who had almost all he could expect from the world still pitting himself against these adversaries. His universe was hostile. Enemies were out there waiting. At the age of sixty, with five or six great novels to his credit, with his name known throughout the literate world, White still spoke of the battles and tough times that lay ahead.

White would not come out. A few men in the late 1960s, taking their cue from the Gay Rights movement in America, had begun to declare their homosexuality in public in order to campaign for the reform of laws which nearly everywhere in Australia made sex between men a crime. The notion of coming out struck White as preposterous. He declined to add his name to those homosexuals, churchmen, anarchists, lawyers and politicians appealing for reform. The first demonstrations for homosexual rights began in Australia in 1971. White never marched. His advice to those who suggested he take part was to get off the streets and get on with their lives.

Homosexuality was lived not debated by him. At lunch one day in 1972 White remarked that a poison-pen letter had come in the morning post. 'Just the usual sort of thing,' he said, refusing to give details. Lascaris cheerfully volunteered: 'It said: you are living with a man, presumably white' (laughter) 'in an uncertain sexual relationship . . .' They were all old acquaintances around the table, but this openness seemed to distress White. He sat looking into his plate as Lascaris rattled off the letter. He did not share the joke. Lascaris finished and White said flatly, 'Yes, that was it.'[32]

White was contemptuous of those who pretended not to be homosexual. He made no secret of it, nor did he make declarations. As he
gossiped about everyone in the most precise detail, so he gossiped about
homosexuals, but his own sexuality was not a topic for general discussion at Martin Road. His house was never a homosexual enclave and he
scorned those who lived in a coterie of queens. Yet for all this he and
Manoly Lascaris were the best-known homosexual couple in the country.
Australians took it on the chin. For homosexuals this long marriage
was an emblem – at least from a distance – of stability and happiness.

'Manoly fortunately seems well,' White wrote in one of his
New Year letters to Ronald Waters. 'I am so lucky to have found
him, and that it has lasted twenty-six years in spite of me.' Lascaris
survived this life like a reef in a difficult stretch of sea. Visitors saw
terrible storms at Martin Road. White snarled and raged. Grim things
were said. Drink exaggerated it all, and in fury and self-disgust White
wondered how Lascaris could love him – and this, in turn, made the
rages worse. He who sought to possess all he loved found this man
was not to be possessed. So the storms continued, blowing up out of a
calm sea and dying away again. Living together, White once explained,
'means endless sacrifices . . . endless disappointments and patching up. I
imagine only vegetables live happily ever after, and then only in a vague,
vegetable way.' White's recipe for staying together was this: 'Laughter,
love and now and then a really blistering row to clear the air.' David
Moore watched one of these rows, familiar to him now after knowing
them for so many years, and wrote in his diary: 'M. took off his glasses
and his eyes seemed to show unbearable sadness.'[33]

Yet White would say that the only good thing he had done in his
life was to find Manoly; that his existence was inconceivable without
him; that his only loyalty was to Manoly; that Manoly was the source
of any virtue in his own life. He once gave Margery Williams a list
of the worst that could happen to him. It began, 'if Manoly should
die' and continued, 'if I should lose all my money, suffer a stroke,
go blind, dry up as a writer, experience a foreign occupation'. He
defended Lascaris ferociously. One night Douglas Carnegie, a grazier
married to a great art collector, turned to Lascaris and asked, 'And
what do you do?' There was a volcanic eruption from White. When
Time wrote that Patrick White lived in Sydney 'with several dogs
and a male housekeeper', he drew the magazine's attention to 'an
incorrect, and I should have thought gratuitous, biographical detail.
The distinguished, and universally respected man who has given me
his friendship and moral support over a period of thirty-four years,
has never been a housekeeper. I am that, and shall continue playing
the role at least till I am paralysed: it keeps me in touch with reality . . .' Time did not publish the rest of the sentence: 'often remote from

those who dish up their superficial, slovenly pieces for *Time Magazine*'.[34]

They were still lovers. People sometimes assumed in a muddled way that the two men had entered some elderly celibate phase of existence. White corrected them sharply. A couple of years before his sixtieth birthday, he was joking with Ronald Waters about some friend who only found happiness when he became impotent. 'I'm sure I never shall,' White wrote. 'So here's to unhappiness. Of course that is only deep down amongst the fantasies, whereas in actual fact I am happier than most people have been.'[35]

So dry were the early months of 1973 that flocks of sulphur-crested cockatoos flew in from the bush to plunder city gardens. When they first appeared on the lawn outside his window White stopped typing, but soon they were so at ease that Ethel sat with them and they preened and squabbled around her on the grass. Six, then twelve, then fourteen birds flew down each day. 'Manoly puts out sunflower seed and I suppose word has got round that the food is good,' White told David Campbell. 'I can't think where they've come from. The only time I've seen them in mobs was when I was at Bolaro and they used to pull down the oats as soon as we had stooked them up at harvest. A wave of white cockatoos is the most beautiful, clumsy sight.'[36] Campbell replied with a poem,

> cornstalks
> Down for the Show,
> Boasting of nuts they've cracked,
> Crops they've wrecked;
>
> And passing the word:
> Good pickings at Martin Road[37]

White was tidying up the stories he had written in the last six years, and correcting proofs of *The Eye of the Storm*. The two tasks proceeded together. He was oxywelding 'Sicilian Vespers' as he answered publishers' queries on the novel. Should the Princess de Lascabanes hear 'rust rubbing against rust' as she flies on Air France? Cape cautioned that airlines were particularly sensitive after recent crashes. The words were dropped. Did ecologists and private helicopters exist in the 1950s? Yes. Would he substitute 'dark brown' for 'nigger' in the Viking edition? He was surprised. 'By all means if you feel unhappy about it. "Dark brown" sounds a bit feeble. I'd prefer "burnt umber".' Are princes so rare in France that he should explain the Lascabanes' title? No. 'Princes are, indeed, rare in France, and usually rather parvenu, being descended from the royalty created by Napoleon

. . . But I can't very well go into a dissertation, can I? in a novel, any more than I could have given the recipes from Greek dishes referred to in my Greek stories in *The Burnt Ones*, as was more or less suggested. Mrs Hunter, in a conversation with Dorothy, does refer to Hubert de Lascabanes as "that upstart prince". Perhaps if I substitute "*parvenu*" for "upstart" it will demonstrate more emphatically that he is not of the best.' More play should be made, he thought, of princes and knights in the publishers' blurb: 'I think it might help sales in Australia, where so many are social snobs at heart in spite of all the talk of democracy.'[38]

For 'Sicilian Vespers' he needed to check some Catholic details, so he returned to mass a couple of times at Christ Church, St Laurence 'to get a bit of religious feeling into me. I found drag queens with sequins on their eyelids screaming their heads off.' Once the second version of the story was finished he started to rework 'A Woman's Hand'. Even in the stories already published he found a lot he wanted to alter: not the general drift but many 'words and meanings'. As he revised, a new story came 'fully fledged' to him and he broke off to get a first version down on paper. 'The latest story is called "The Cockatoos",' he told Maschler, and that would be the title of the collection. 'I can see a beautiful jacket.' The day he finished the first draft, David Campbell's poem arrived. It was something to add to the book of coincidences he always meant to keep. 'My life is made up of them.'[39] He quizzed the poet on Air Force jargon and the lethal possibilities of double-barrelled shot guns.

Swapping back and forth from late to early versions of the six stories was relaxing work, and the only minor irritation was a stuck 'm' on his Olivetti. In July the typescript of the book was finished and despatched to his agent with a dedication: 'To Ronald Waters for having survived forty-eight years of friendship.' Waters was surprised and flattered by this, though he discovered he liked *The Cockatoos* least of all White's books. 'So gloomy. Everyone in it died.'[40]

A spirit of creative housekeeping hovered over White. *A Fringe of Leaves* had been lying ten years in his drawer for Mrs Fraser to recover, he said, from the mauling of librettists and composers. Now it seemed time to go back to her. White was still uncertain, and wanted to see the Barrier Reef for the first time, and be 'immersed in the seascapes and light before embarking on the Mrs Fraser novel – if I do'. In August, once the stories were cleared from his desk, he and Lascaris flew north and joined a cruise ship that took them through the Whitsunday Islands. This was school holiday time, and the decks were so crowded they thought themselves lucky to get 'one buttock on the seat'.[41]

From Happy Bay he wrote to Alice Halmagyi: 'This is the place we have liked most for fortunately it doesn't seem to appeal to the average tourist – because it has simplicity. I'd like to go back some time and spend a couple of weeks. The real nightmare is Daydream Island which has everything vulgar, including mature Hungarian whores stretched on banana-lounges. (One of them was having her thighs kissed as we passed.) Over everything hangs a stench of sewage. Swarms of tourists everywhere.' But the light and scenery of the reef confirmed the decision to return to the novel. 'It is every bit as beautiful as the Aegean, though with no human life of any interest – none of those cubist villages and chapels and monasteries.'[42]

After a week they flew south, planning to stop at Gladstone for a few days, but the airline refused to land for only two passengers. In Brisbane offers were made to fly them back but White said, Home![43] They came down the coast over ports blocked by boom-time shipping. Somewhere in a hold lay *The Eye of the Storm*. The book was launched in London a few days after they returned to Sydney in late August. White now waited impatiently until October for the book to clear the wharves and reach the shops in Australia as the storm he both feared and longed for broke over Martin Road.

They had gone to their beds early on the night of 18 October after a hard day's housework. About 9pm a loud knocking began on the door. The message was clearer than words. Lascaris went down to investigate and found journalists on the path and television crews setting up on the lawn. They were demanding to see Patrick White at once. He'd won.

Artur Lundkvist gave *Happy Valley* an admiring notice in Stockholm before the Second World War and forgot all about Patrick White. He was only one of hundreds of new writers the Swede came across as he read in Spanish, German, French, Portuguese, English and the Scandinavian languages. But by chance Lundkvist found himself without a book on holidays in Spain in 1962 and bought a paperback of *The Tree of Man*. He was swept away by 'the remarkably clear and living story' of Stan and Amy Parker.[44] The Swede now read everything White wrote. When Lundkvist was offered a place in the Swedish Academy a few years later, he accepted this long-delayed honour in order to secure the Nobel for three writers: Pablo Neruda, Vicente Aleixandre and Patrick White.

Lundkvist is an original. He was born before the First World War on a farm in the south of Sweden, a lanky boy, strong, but lazy in the fields, and determined from an early age to be a writer. A sympathetic father gave him a typewriter and by the age of eighteen the young man had published about thirty articles in local newspapers. He lived as a poet and literary journalist. His criticism, travelogues and interviews were collected over the years into more than eighty books. Lundkvist did not go to university and taught himself languages and literature. He never lost the enthusiasm of the self-taught nor did he bother to refine a southern accent many city colleagues find coarse. The publishers Bonniers employed him as a spotter, and Lundkvist was one of the gates by which new writing from the outside world reached Sweden. It was for *Bonniers Litterära Magasin* in 1939 that he read *Happy Valley* and praised that 'decidedly modern' new novel about life in a little country town in New South Wales which 'can be observed from any part of the world with largely undiminished interest'.[45]

Once he rediscovered White in the 1960s, Lundkvist reviewed each of the novels as they appeared. His excitement was, perhaps, sharpened by knowing almost nothing else of Australian writing. 'As far as one can judge from a distance, Patrick White has done something unique for Australian literature. He has given it a style, a flexible and characteristic form of expression, in short, something of a language of its own. For Australia has long been one of the relatively voiceless countries unable to articulate its innermost problems, its own outlook on life. In this respect, the effects of British colonisation have been prolonged. Emptiness, desolation, banality, robust extroversion and stagnant welfare – these are the main things one associates with Australia, this "white" continent awkwardly situated between Asia and Oceania. Patrick White does not contradict this impression, but gives it sharpness, depth, light and shade in a single-mindedly critical way. It is for this purpose he has shaped that sharp and sensitive instrument, his style.'[46]

On Lundkvist's fiftieth birthday, T.S. Eliot sent fraternal greetings, 'as from one European man of letters to another', but this regard was not shared in the small world of Swedish literature.[47] The energy of the man was admired, his grasp of foreign literature was acknowledged, but he was charged with failures of moderation. Lundkvist hated and loved passionately. His politics were not as tame as they might be in neutral Sweden and in the 1950s his poetry had expressed radical sympathies. Winning the Lenin Prize in 1958 earned Lundkvist few friends in Stockholm, even though he declined to travel to Moscow for the celebrations and then put the money into a fund for the translation of Swedish writing into foreign languages.

At the age of sixty-two, Lundkvist was finally offered a place in the Academy. He hesitated to accept, deterred by the intricate formalities of membership. Even from outside the Academy he had managed to secure the Nobel for William Faulkner in 1949 and Miguel Asturias in 1967. But he decided it was worth entering that world of tails and starched waistcoats essentially to advance the cause of Pablo Neruda. On his arrival, Lundkvist persuaded the Nobel Committee of the Academy to place Neruda, Aleixandre and White on their short list for the 1969 Nobel.

Patrick White was unknown to them, and barely known in Sweden. Five years before, Bonniers had published a translation of *Riders in the Chariot* – the only one of White's novels Lundkvist expressed serious doubts about – but it had sold a mere 1,900 copies in the years since. Nevertheless, at this point Bonniers was pressing ahead with a translation of *The Solid Mandala* and the eighteen members of the Academy appear to have had advance copies of the translation in the summer of 1969, when they considered Patrick White for the first time. Only a few of the academicians tackled him in English; others read *Voss* and *The Tree of Man* in German. On the eve of the 1969 award Stockholm's evening papers reported that White was a candidate for the prize. *Aftonbladet* described him as an Australian who had lived for long periods in Italy and wrote novels with a Catholic twist. 'The fact that one of them, *Shoes of the Fisherman*, was made into an unsuccessful film is not likely to influence the Academy.'[48] The prize was given a couple of days later to Samuel Beckett.

The critics of Stockholm tend to see their city as the Rome of world literature, and they stake out territories for themselves – keeping an eye on trends in India, pinpointing new talent in Central America – as if responsible for these provinces to mother Church. When Ingmar Björkstén set out to be a literary journalist in the early 1960s he found the East had already been seized, so he chose Australia. Björkstén read *Voss* on his first expedition to the far side of the world and, though he struggled with White's English, declared this his greatest reading experience. He had tea at Dogwoods and returned home to promote White's writing on the radio, in Swedish newspapers and magazines, and in his book *Australian Diary*.

After Beckett's win, Björkstén wrote a letter of condolence to Sydney. White replied, 'We heard some of the awful rumours in Australia and I had to make some quick plans for going into hiding if there was any truth in them. But of course there wasn't, so one felt rather embarrassed and humiliated. I saw a photograph of poor Beckett looking quite crazed after he had fled to Tunisia.'[49] Björkstén persuaded White to see Lundkvist, who was travelling out to Australia in the New Year. All three knew this meeting was about the Nobel.

White's attitude was deeply ambivalent. For over a decade he had refused every award and decoration offered to him, but he wanted this prize. None of the praise heaped on him over the years could offer the absolute vindication of the Nobel. Yet he could not allow himself to be seen wanting it. From 1969 when his name was first on the short list he forbade his publishers to mention that he was a contender for the Nobel, deflected any questions about his chances of winning and, for fear of being thought to be courting the Swedes, refused to visit Sweden. White had to guard himself from the pain of being a contender who misses out, and from the old spectre of destruction by fame if he should win. He wondered about Swedes – 'very well-behaved, well-spoken, clean, rational . . . but shadowless' – and outlaid a little pre-emptive spite, observing from time to time that it would 'only be humiliating' to have what was not given to Tolstoy, Henry James, Proust and Joyce.[50]

Lundkvist came to dinner at Martin Road with his wife, the poet Maria Wine, in late March 1970. Everyone was stiff. White knew he was under scrutiny and Lundkvist found himself awkward in the presence of the writer he admired so much. They skirted the subject of the prize for some time. When Lundkvist mentioned it, White burst out, 'I'm so damned tired of this. Over and over I figure as a likely candidate and nothing comes of it.'

Lundkvist replied, 'Many would offer their lives to be considered likely candidates.' White fell silent and the Nobel was not mentioned again that night. In letters to friends afterwards White remarked that he found the Lundkvists polite, earnest and Swedish. 'I don't think we made much contact.'[51]

Each year the members of the Academy agree on a short list and then disperse to their cottages to read. White was in a strong position in 1970, and his position strengthened during that summer when the new Swedish edition of *The Tree of Man* became available. But much of his support came from those academicians nervous about awarding the prize to Alexander Solzhenitsin, the other principal contender. By autumn the Academy found the courage to brave Soviet hostility and they gave the Nobel to the Russian. 'Reservations don't occur in the Swedish Academy,' Lundkvist told the Stockholm paper *Expressen*. 'You either say that the Academy made a good choice, or you refuse to comment. I choose the second alternative.'[52]

Lundkvist put aside his ambitions for White in 1971 and secured the prize for Pablo Neruda. Officials of the Academy continued to take soundings about the Australian. Professor Ragnar Christophersen was a peculiarly useful source of advice for the Swedes for he was at Southwood with White, his wife was Australian, he taught English literature in Oslo and he was related by marriage to Stig Ramel, who was about to become President of the Nobel Foundation. In late 1971 or early 1972 Christophersen was sitting in his office at the University of Oslo, 'and some geyser was asking me all sorts of questions about Paddy White . . . I put two and two together.' Christophersen warned White what was happening and back came a letter in which 'he more or less said to hell with the Nobel Prize'.[53]

When the Academy met in 1972 there was an immediate majority for White, but opposition was mounted by Karl Ragnar Gierow, secretary to the Academy. He was a formidable opponent, a tragedian in

blank verse and director of the Royal Dramatic Theatre in Stockholm.
American writing was Gierow's passion, and in his time at the theatre
some of Eugene O'Neill's unperformed plays were given their world
premières. Gierow was implacably hostile to Patrick White.

But the omens were good. The press once more tipped White
as the winner and in early September a team of Swedish journalists
appeared at Martin Road. 'I was cleaning the house and without my
teeth,' White explained to Geoffrey Dutton. 'I refused to see them. But
as Manoly said one of them was terribly crippled, I felt I had to make a
later date. They arrived with trunks full of cameras, microphones, and
tape recorders, and I suddenly realised I was in for the full works. The
two young men were very agreeable, but I have spent sleepless nights
since, going over what I had said; if the Australian ambassador to
Stockholm happens to hear it I shall probably be run out of Australia.'[54]
In Sweden that summer Bonniers' translation of *The Vivisector* became
available, and Gierow attacked White for demeaning the image of the
artist. He argued that White depicted the painter as a user and consumer
of human beings. A number of academicians were swayed by Gierow
and a bare majority formed against White. The prize went to Heinrich
Böll.

The height to which White's hopes had been raised may be gauged
by the scorn he poured on 'the dreary' Böll, the man who had turned
The Tree of Man into *Zur Ruhe kam der Baum des Menschen nie*. 'No
doubt it helps to be International President of PEN. If Mailer is even
the faintest possibility the whole thing is a farce. And to pass over
Borges and Nabokov!' To Björkstén's annual letter of commiseration
White replied, 'I no longer believe in the Nobel Prize. I think it should
be discontinued and the money used to feed the hungry.'[55]

Lundkvist considered White had only one more chance: it would be
1973 or never. The Swede was now a member of the inner committee
of six which decided the short list on which Patrick White's name was,
once again, secure. Also on the list were Saul Bellow, Norman Mailer,
V.S. Naipaul, Nadine Gordimer and the Nigerians Wole Soyinka and
Chinua Achebe. The academicians dispersed to their summer cottages.
Jonathan Cape rushed four advance copies of *The Eye of the Storm* to
Lundkvist, who distributed them to English-reading friends in the
Academy. As the academicians returned to Stockholm, Lundkvist's
review of the new novel appeared in *Dagens Nyheter*, almost the
first notice to appear anywhere in the world: 'a universally valid
enquiry into the terms of human existence . . . sombre and free
from illusion . . . devastating in his satire . . . he never loses his
feeling for the wonder of life in the midst of degradation . . . we
are almost entirely spared the elements of obscurantism that have
at times been present in White's work . . . he further heightens the

power of his language . . . articulating the well-nigh inexpressible, the fleeting and the quintessential . . . a pioneer, breaking new ground in contemporary literature.'[56]

Again the Academy was divided. Gierow fought for Saul Bellow, but Lundkvist was able to win over a few more colleagues by arguing that *The Eye of the Storm* presented a more moral view of the artist than White had shown in *The Vivisector*. This brought the Academy to a deadlock. One member, Harry Martinson, was ill and unable to be at the final meeting. Martinson was a lyric poet, a writer of memoirs and fables. In his life there was an odd echo of Hurtle Duffield's career, for Martinson was sold for adoption when he was a child. He worked in the merchant navy before breaking free to write. The academicians decided to let Martinson make the final choice. He was telephoned. Martinson said he did not wish to choose between White and Bellow, but why not award the prize to the new land of Australia? So it was settled and the academicians drafted a citation along the lines suggested by Martinson: 'To Patrick White for an epic and psychological narrative art which has introduced a new continent into literature.'

The Swedish Academy shares a little palace with the stock exchange in the old town of Stockholm. At 1pm on a Thursday in the middle of October every year, the press assembles in a salon on the upper floor of the palace. The eighteen members of the Academy meet nearby to confirm their choice made the week before. The only stumbling block that remained in 1973 was the form of the invitation to White to attend the King's award ceremony in December. Lundkvist argued that Manoly Lascaris be invited as White's companion for life, but the Academy would not agree to this. Why not, it was suggested, ask Patrick White and 'secretary'? Lundkvist assured them neither man would then come. They settled on an invitation 'to you and your family'.[57] As permanent secretary, Gierow had the task of announcing the name of the laureate and reading the citation. His anger at the result was unabated. He crossed the palace to face the press, gave White's name and read the citation. The Academy's decision was repeated in English, German and French. An Australian translator broke with precedent and applauded. Then the television lights were switched off and the press dispersed.

It was nine at night in Sydney. The Swedish Ambassador to Australia, Per Anger, had been trying for some hours to find White's telephone number. Anger could not explain why he needed it and none of White's friends would break the absolute rule against giving it out. While Anger was still searching, the press, alerted by calls from Stockholm, began to arrive at Martin Road expecting to find celebrations in full swing. The house was in darkness and the dogs were barking wildly. A face was seen peering out through the curtains. Neighbours were quizzed and one reported seeing a light upstairs before the journalists arrived, so they trouped back to knock at the door again. It was not opened.

'Come back in the morning,' called Lascaris.

'We can't wait,' replied an anxious photographer. 'We have to do the Queen in the morning.'[58] She was in Sydney to open the Opera House that weekend. White had not been invited to the ceremonies. The knocking continued for about an hour, but Lascaris calmed the journalists with shouted promises that they would be up and about at six in the morning as usual. The Ambassador had the number by now, but the telephone was unanswered. He sent friends around with flowers. They reported seeing a light in the house, but it went out when they rang the bell. From the upstairs windows White counted twenty people camped on the lawn and more on the terrace out the back. Very carefully he groped his way downstairs to get a whisky.[59]

He sat in a cane chair on the lawn next morning to receive six television teams, three radio stations, all the local newspapers, *Newsweek* and a woman from Finland. White seemed neither overwhelmed nor particularly grateful. His response to the award? 'Bewilderment, alarm and cynicism.'

Telegram boys climbed the path. Among the first messages was the official notification from the Academy, signed by Gierow. Flowers arrived. A nun called asking for money. White posed on the path for photographers. His blue shirt flapped over his trousers, he chewed his teeth, worked his tongue, smiled only from time to time, and gave the press few of the reassuring lines they expected to hear from an honoured Australian.

'I feel what I am, I don't feel particularly Australian. I live here and work here. A Londoner is what I think I am at heart but my blood is Australian and that's what gets me going.'

'I'm not for nationalism at all – not for flag-wagging and drum thumping.'

'There have been plenty of authentic voices before mine and many Australians will say that mine is not authentic.'[60]

White found it hard to admit his delight, but it was evident to those who knew him well. Visitors to the house over the next few days found him as happy as they had ever seen him. He spent much of the time at the stove. That weekend he made his first visit to the Opera House since the building was finished – 'extraordinary . . . like some place of pagan pilgrimage' – and strangers were walking up to shake his hand. White was happy and bemused. He autographed programmes. Next day he wrote to Maschler, 'I am amazed at the way Australians have reacted, in a way they usually behave only for swimmers and athletes. I am very touched, and have been feeling guilty for some of the things I have said in the past.'[61]

The Prime Minister, having swayed a reluctant Speaker, invited White to take a seat on the floor of the House of Representatives to receive the congratulations of Parliament. Such gestures were usually reserved for visiting royalty and Heads of State. The only civilian ever given this accolade before was the aviator Bert Hinkler who made the first solo flight from London to Australia in 1928. White declined the honour. 'Unfortunately, this is the kind of situation to which my nature does not easily adapt itself.' He was, he wrote, moved that so many people had already expressed their enthusiasm. 'So may we, please, leave it at that?'[62]

He refused to travel to Stockholm. 'My sister died of such an expedition,' he explained to Maschler. Nor did he want to go, and was pleased to have an irreproachable excuse for avoiding the ceremonies. He pleaded his 'chest condition' first to Gierow and then in a later letter to King Carl XVI Gustav.[63] He declined to give the traditional oration. Through the Australian Embassy in Stockholm, White announced that Sidney Nolan would receive the prize on his behalf in December.

From the first he had made it clear he would keep none of the money, and after a few days he announced he would use the $81,862 to set up a fund for older Australian writers who had not received due recognition for their work. The first winner would be chosen in 1974, and the award would be made each year without conditions of any kind. It was the most generous gift ever made by an individual to Australian writers. White had acted before to help save men and women from the vacuum of indifference in which he had written in his early years, but the reasons for setting up the prize were more complex than that. For his own mortification, and in order not to be hobbled by obligations, he had decided years before that if he were to win the Nobel he would give the money away. 'I thought', he later confessed, 'that would get me out of any further trouble, but it didn't.'[64]

Juliet O'Hea, cool and professional as ever, despatched White the least frothy letter of congratulations: 'What does give me untold pleasure is that it will surely regain for you the American market which has been so dismal lately.' Viking had yet to publish *The Eye of the Storm*. The print run was more than doubled to 18,000 before publication; the Literary Guild asked to take 6,000; paperback rights were sold for $US12,500, the largest advance by far White had ever had from North America.

For the next eighteen months there was a worldwide upsurge in White's sales. Now for the first time in his career, White earned a substantial income from his writing. Viking decided to reissue six of his novels in hardback with new jackets. O'Hea reported from

London that Penguin was selling what they regarded as two years' stock of some titles in two weeks. Reprints were going ahead in Britain and Australia. Tom Maschler had a grand plan to publish a uniform edition of the novels, one or two a year, with prefaces by White. He refused. Maschler pursued the plan for months, but White would neither reread the books nor write about himself. 'It will only give the vultures of the trendy literary world an additional opportunity for attack. It is bad enough putting up with that as new books appear, without having old books which were praised when they first appeared, torn to shreds one by one. Better wait till I am dead, and time will sort things out.'[65]

Translation sales were swift. There is a rule of thumb in publishing that a Nobel creates such an appetite for translations that they alone can yield as much cash as the prize. White was already published in French, German, Swedish, Italian, Dutch, Polish, Norwegian, Portuguese, Romanian, Czech and Hungarian. Old translations were hurried back into the shops, and publishing houses which had only ever translated one or two of his titles now set out to fill the gaps. Greece joined the list for the first time, buying the novels but not yet his superb Greek short stories. Pirate editions appeared in the East. He reported 'Mysterious goings-on in Russia.' Shortly after the prize, O'Hea told White's New York agent that translation sales were 'very impressive . . . something over £50,000 – of which of course Patrick gets half'.[66]

The Oertels wrote from Hanover. They had seen his face on television – 'Aber das ist unser Pat!' – and restored the contact interrupted by the war. Madame Jacquet, now retired from the Hostellerie de Ciboure, sent her congratulations from Biarritz. Pepe Mamblas, Duke of Baena, wrote a sentimental memoir for the local newspaper *Sud-Ouest*: 'Just as I am about to turn eighty, I have received a very lovely, and unexpected present . . .' An announcement was made to the assembled boys of Cheltenham College and the *Cheltonian* offered warm congratulations to the school's first Nobel laureate. Tudor House 'basked a little in some reflected glory'. R took up his pen to write for the first time in nearly forty years, but he put it down again. It seemed an impertinence to be making contact now, for he had been flying to Sydney for years on business and never tried to get in touch before.[67] A.D. Hope sent a telegram making peace and the two men corresponded a little for a few years. Out at Castle Hill Dogwoods' acres were only now being cut up into building blocks. The house and a few Greek pines survived. Two of the streets on the subdivision were called Patrick Place and Nobel Avenue.

White and Lascaris escaped to Tasmania. White wanted to look around before getting back to work on *A Fringe of Leaves* and the trip had been planned for some time but they were both glad to be away from the fuss. Almost. Every morning and evening White crouched over motel dressing tables answering letters and telegrams sorted before he left Sydney into three grocery bags marked PRIORITY, OFFICIAL and PERSONAL. A fourth bag, NO HURRY, had been left behind at Martin Road. 'Quite apart from friends and acquaintances, I've had letters from the unknown from Saskatchewan to Bengal (floods from Bengal) mostly begging. They want me to buy them houses, farms, trucks, caravans, save them from having glaucoma, paralysed husbands (or wives) asthmatic children – it all comes from my having said that I wasn't going to keep the money.'[68]

White and Lascaris were driven up and down Tasmania by a companionable taxi driver who wore a hair-piece. Lascaris was seeing for the first time the island he discovered as a child eating jam in Cairo. At about the same age Paddy White was playing at Browns River, and he had often thought of coming back to this 'kind of paradise lost which I might some day regain'. He remembered walking with Lizzie to see the convict chains and the stuffed heads of guard dogs hanging on the wall. Nowhere in Australia has such a settled literary landscape as Tasmania, or Van Diemen's Land as it was known until it was rechristened to help it shed the stench of convicts and Aboriginal slaughter. William Gosse Hay gave an account of those times in *The Escape of the Notorious Sir William Heans*, which White rated one of the best Australian novels. He used to wonder why he neglected Tasmania: 'I only have to read about it to become fascinated.'[69]

The scenery was 'bland rural and grand Wagnerian'. He could hear the rattle of the chains, and the novel's characters were talking incessantly in his head. Ellen Roxburgh – his version of the Eliza Fraser of history – would visit Van Diemen's Land to see her husband's brother, and she would cross this landscape,

> by turns cultivated and wild. An occasional stone cottage or hut built of wattle-and-daub looked the meaner for the tiered forests towering above them. The roads were consistently execrable . . .

> They toiled on. The drizzle was blown past and behind them. Above an uneven crop of oats, through a gap in darkling trees, hung the faintest smudge of rainbow. She could feel her cheeks glowing, not only from the chill, but from the veiled surprises the country had to offer at every turn.

In one of the little towns in the centre of the island, White was taken by an old house. 'I could have worked in it, but I said, "What else would we do?" Manoly replied, "Sit by the fire and eat scones" which about sums it up. I'd rather risk bursting a blood vessel every week in Sydney.'[70]

Life at Martin Road 'returned to abnormal' when they reached home in mid-November. *Le Figaro littéraire*, German television and Ingmar Björkstén were waiting for him. Björkstén's critical study of White's work had just appeared in Stockholm. He and a Swedish television crew trailed around with White for a couple of days. Björkstén was a little put out that the laureate knew the taxi driver ('he asks about his holidays') and was puzzled that no one knew White's face in the fish shop at Double Bay when they went down to get a kilo of prawns to feed Yevtushenko. At a gallery in east Sydney, the Swede watched White circle an exhibition by Imants Tillers and then return for a second look with the gallery's owner Frank Watters. 'They talk about this and that, then suddenly White says in his quiet, measured way: "I'll take the whole series – if the NSW Gallery will have them." '[71]

The *Overland* crowd was a little surprised when White turned up in Melbourne. Stephen Murray-Smith had asked him, some months before the Nobel was announced, to be guest of honour at the magazine's annual dinner at the university in December. White accepted on the one condition that there be no speeches. But then he won the prize and it seemed to *Overland* that the dinner might be forgotten in all the fuss. This was not so. White flew down alone on 10 December and stayed with the director John Sumner. None of *Overland*'s dozen guests realised that the King of Sweden that day was handing out the Nobel prizes.

All went well until White remarked over pudding that Lindsay Anderson's film *O Lucky Man* was a work of genius – indeed as good as any novel in the last ten years.

'Come off it,' interjected Barrett Reid.

White was gripped by a sudden paroxysm of rage. 'I said it and I meant it!' he shouted. Reid was Sid Nolan's old companion who had stayed behind at Heide, the last survivor of the disciples and still an intimate of the Nolans' adversary Sunday Reed. White knew all this. 'You', he thundered, 'would be the one person in Australia I would disagree with everything about.'

To try to calm things down, the critic and historian Ian Turner asked if White had ever published in John and Sunday Reed's magazine *Angry Penguins* in the early days.

'Certainly not. But I would like to write a novel about *her*.'

'About Sunday?' Reid asked. 'Have you ever met her?'

'That woman! That woman! I don't need to meet her to write about her.'

Reid issued an invitation for him to come to Heide next day to have tea with John and Sunday. White refused point blank. 'Well in that case your novel will be based on muddled mythology like your other novels.' There was a terrible silence. Conversation became general.

When Murray-Smith apologised for the brawling over dinner, the guest of honour insisted he had enjoyed himself very much, 'It wasn't nearly as noisy as some in my house, which is sometimes referred to as Monkey Hill.'[72] But neither was it, frankly, a match for the Nobel ceremony that day in Stockholm. The scene in the grand auditorium of the Concert Hall might have come from the pages of one of the great Russians who never won the prize.

The King's party faced a line of laureates in black across a stage bare but for a large N on the pale blue carpet. Nolan, who had taken advantage of his visit to Stockholm to clinch a major exhibition of paintings at the Moderna Museet, wore the rose pink and pearl grey ribbon of a Commander of the British Empire. Carl Gustav in evening dress and decorations stood in a little knot of Swedish nobility. Diamonds in swags on pale silk and bare throats drew fire from the arc lights. The royal party spilled over the stage into the first rows of the auditorium, a scene of confused hand-kissing and bowing. Across the back of the stage, academicians sat in tiers like schoolboys about to be photographed around the bust of Alfred Nobel. The inventor of dynamite was bathed in a pool of pale blue light. Wreaths of spring flowers lay at his feet.

Lundkvist came forward to read the official discourse on Patrick White. Traditionally this was the task of the secretary of the Swedish Academy, but Gierow was still so angry about the award that he refused. Lundkvist took over the role, quoting Gierow the old Swedish maxim: 'He who lets the Devil in the boat should row him ashore.' Lundkvist spoke for a few minutes in Swedish and then English. Nolan crossed the stage, shook the King's hand, and took the box containing the medal. To mark each award the Stockholm Philharmonic in a gallery above the stage played an interlude of appropriate music. To honour Patrick White for introducing 'a new continent to literature' the band played Percy Grainger's *In an English Country Garden*.

TWENTY-SIX

The Biggest Sandbank in the World

WRITING *A Fringe of Leaves* was a discipline, a kind of penance, the only way White knew of 'returning to a normal life'. Usually he kept his publishers in the dark for months, throwing out only a few hints until he felt sure of a new novel. But this time, as if to bind himself to the task, he announced the book to Tom Maschler as he began. 'Today I started on *A Fringe of Leaves* which I want to finish before I am finished.'[1]

He had the abandoned manuscript from twelve years before, but he began writing once again from scratch. The strategy had not changed: to turn to his own purposes the story of the wreck of the *Stirling Castle* and the ordeal of one survivor, Eliza Fraser. 'I feel historical reconstructions are too limiting,' he told Alan Williams, 'so I did not stick to the original facts.' The Mrs Fraser of history was born in the Orkneys, but White gave his heroine Ellen Gluyas a Cornish background, for 'I know something of Cornwall and nothing of the Orkneys.' The name Ellen was another tribute to his old love, Ellen Withycombe. His Ellen is a farmer's daughter from the cliff country round Zennor, familiar to him from his undergraduate literary pilgrimages. He had not seen Cornwall for forty years, but Jonathan Cape reissued A.L. Rowse's *A Cornish Childhood* as he began work on the novel, and White ordered a copy to be sent out urgently by air.[2]

He gave Ellen his own odd fascination with unmade journeys. She longed to see – but never reached – Tintagel a few miles from her farm where, her father assured her, the lovers Sir Tristram and Lady Iseult reached Cornwall.

> Her mind's eye watched the ship's prow entering the narrow cove, in a moment of evening sunlight, through a fuzz of hectic summer green.

A Fringe of Leaves is full of echoes of this legend, and as he worked on the book he dug out some old Tristram romances. In 1971 the Nolans had taken him to Wagner's opera at Covent Garden. 'It was a wonderful evening in every way.' Wagner had never gripped him before – *Die Walküre* was a bore, *Die Meistersinger* was loathsome – but this was a great experience. Georg Solti was making his farewell appearance at the Royal Opera House; Jess Thomas was Tristan and Ludmilla Dvorakova Isolde; the director Peter Hall had Tristan rise from the dead in the final moments. *Tristan und Isolde* was *the* opera for White after this. He felt, were he born a singer, he would have been a great Isolde.[3]

So that he could make Ellen Gluyas function at more than one level, 'and turn something which would otherwise have been a mere adventure story into a novel of psychological interest', he married his farm girl to an invalid gentleman whose family had moved to Gloucestershire, 'in the hopes that Mr Austin's health might benefit by the mild climate and polite society of Cheltenham'.[4] This was the first time White had drawn on the landscape where he lived and suffered as a boy. Even so, the sense of place is not strong. Cornwall, which he saw only briefly, seems more alive in his writing than the country round Cheltenham.

On his first attempt at *A Fringe of Leaves*, White had boned up on sailing ships and the sea. 'Nobody could be less nautical than I,' he had told Ben Huebsch back in 1961. 'It is as though I now have to learn a new language – not that I want to submerge the thing in "terms" – but to give it authenticity.'[5] He mocked himself now in the portrait of Roxburgh fussing over nautical details on the voyage of *The Kestrel* to Van Diemen's Land. After their dramatic months on the island they sail to Sydney and then continue up the coast to an appointment with a jagged outcrop of the Great Barrier Reef.

'Half the crew attempted to reach Moreton Bay (Brisbane) in one of the boats,' White explained to Huebsch. 'The other finally landed on a large island off the coast, where the men were gradually killed off by the blacks, and the captain's wife kept as a slave. This Victorian lady was stripped of everything, until she was reduced to wearing a vine round her waist – hence the "fringe of leaves" – to hide her wedding ring and anything else she had. In the course of her duties she was made to shin up trees to fetch possums and wild honey, and when she objected a fire stick was simply held under her behind. She became quite skilled at climbing. Then at a big Aboriginal corroboree she happened to meet an escaped convict who had been living for years with the blacks as one of themselves. In fact it took him some time to remember his English after coming across the white woman. However, he decided to rescue her, and they set out to walk the 160 miles or so to Moreton Bay both stark naked, in return for which she was to get him a pardon.'[6]

The story of the wreck and ordeal was essentially to be as White drafted it years before, but now he saw the possibility of a quite different relationship developing between the woman and the convict. This was a crucial change in the novel, and a mark of the new freedom that appears in White's writing after the Nobel.

The prize was not behind him. He had been back at his desk only a week when a brigadier knocked at the door to warn him he had been chosen Australian of the Year, and was expected to lunch in Melbourne on the eve of Australia Day with the Lord Mayor, Premier and other notables, to receive a plaque from the Governor. 'I was horrified – and so was the brigadier to find he wasn't received with gladness and joy. I tried to fob them off, then to think of somebody who could do it for me, but everybody suitable is having holidays.' But he saw an opportunity here 'to tell them a few things about themselves' and decided to go. The occasion was more difficult than he feared, though he stoked up his courage at the Duke of Wellington before reaching the Town Hall. More drinks were served in the lobby, where he found himself so en- raged by the Governor's wife that he bit hard through a savoury boat and broke a few teeth from his lower plate. 'I had to decide whether to risk letting them lie on my gums and perhaps swallowing them while trying to eat the lunch, or worse, spitting them out while making my speech afterwards. I finished by putting them in my handkerchief just before lunch began, then hissed my way through the speech, which offended a lot of people anyway.'[7]

He thanked no one. In the accents of an Anglican divine he declared Australia Day 'a day of self-searching rather than trumpet-blowing' and told the assembled Establishment that the nation's future lay with those men and women who saw and articulated Australia's faults. Three such mavericks had a right to be standing in his place on this day: Manning Clark, whose huge *History of Australia* was showing us that 'what we were is what we are'. And Barry Humphries, 'one of the most original, scintillating minds we have produced . . . if the mirror is sometimes a distorting one, isn't distortion the prerogative of art?' And Jack Mundey, the Communist champion of Green Bans. 'I want to take this opportunity to salute Jack, the farm boy from Northern Queensland, who became an exceptional Australian, and incidentally that other phenomenon, a man whose sincerity has survived his rise to a position of influence.'[8] White's audience was baffled and disappointed.

The Melbourne visit was more important than this civic narrative suggests. White killed a few spare hours that day wandering through the Victorian National Gallery with an energetic polymath and Labor

Member of Parliament called Barry Jones. They were standing in front of a pretty Edwardian study of figures reading in an arbour when Jones remarked that there was an interesting story behind the painting, for the fragile figure wearing a white dress and carrying a white parasol was a man. White was interested. Jones told him something of the history of Herbert Dyce-Murphy, whom he had met as a very old man living out on Mornington Peninsula. White returned to the subject later as they drank at the Duke of Wellington and walked together in the Botanical Gardens. One detail he heard that day, an exchange between Dyce-Murphy and his mother, sowed the seed of *The Twyborn Affair*.

'Are you my son, Herbert?' Mrs Murphy had asked this familiar figure in a dress.

'No, but I am your daughter, Edith.'

'I'm so glad. I always wanted a daughter.'[9]

The Swedish Ambassador, Per Anger, invited him to dinner in Canberra 'with dinner jacket and Prime Minister' to receive the Nobel plaque and diploma, but White preferred to cook for the Ambassador at Martin Road. 'I shall keep ceremony to a minimum,' he told the Duttons, 'though Manoly unwisely went out and bought champagne and new glasses.' The Nolans came, with Cynthia wearing the same dress and jewels she wore at the royal banquet in Stockholm. 'We had a pleasant evening, though I spent three days sweating over the dinner,' White told Waters. 'Really very little news. I am working as much as possible on my new novel . . . Have been invited to fly to New York to address PEN International at a dinner in June. Imagine all those vultures of the media! They said in their cable that I should be "protected" but that is no longer possible unless you stay at home and don't open the door.'[10]

He chipped away at the heaps of mail that arrived at Martin Road, and refused to use a secretary to cope with an ordeal from which he would now never be free. 'I am asked to go here, go there, do this, do that, save a minority, a landscape, an individual, give endless opinions.' Sunday became his correspondence day. He began to fear his signature was growing, and set about 'reducing, reducing'. Hardly a letter, now, went out to friends without a routine complaint about the prize. To Björkstén: '*Between ourselves*, the Nobel Prize is a terrifying and destructive experience, though it mightn't be to somebody else. (I'm sure Heinrich Böll was able to take it in his stride, and it was a shot of life to the unfortunate Solzhenitsin.) But the backwash is too much, for me at least.'[11] Yet in ways he could never confess, White found he enjoyed being a great man. The Nobel gave him freedom, power and money. He used them all.

The Eye of the Storm was on the lists of bestsellers in America for the first three months of 1974. The press coverage was astounding,

Thomas Guinzburg at Viking told Juliet O'Hea. 'Every major news-paper and syndicate has covered the book and many of them are doing follow-up pieces on his entire career. *The Eye of the Storm* continues to find its audience.'[12] The critics were by no means unanimous, but now neither the low-life lingo nor the old division between enthusiasts and detractors were standing in the way of American sales. By mid-March Viking had placed 25,000 copies and another reprint was under way.

In the aftermath of the prize, White allowed *Happy Valley* to be republished in French and published for the first time in Italian. Tom Maschler was curious about the book, and O'Hea found him one of the rare copies of the first edition. 'If you think well of it then let us by all means tackle Patrick.' White had already, years before, stopped Eyre & Spottiswoode republishing the novel, and even forbade microfilm copies being made for universities. He complained of its derivative style – too much Lawrence and Joyce – but the true cause of his reluctance to see *Happy Valley* on the market again was the fear of being sued if it ever re-appeared in Australia. 'I had used the first names of a whole family without realising what I was doing. As the characters in the book behave very much like the members of the actual family, trouble might blow up if their descendants realised. I don't want this generally known.' Kylie Tennant had put the fear of libel in him when she told him once how she was sued during the war by a man she named in her novel *Ride on Stranger*. Tennant's publishers lost a couple of hundred pounds, but White feared far worse from the Yens of Adaminaby if they ever recognised themselves as the Quongs of Happy Valley.[13]

Maschler wanted to republish *Happy Valley*. White again refused, but without explaining his fear of libel to the publishers. So the question was not tested by lawyers, nor were enquiries made in the Monaro where the danger of a successful action had long passed. Old Frank Yen who went on mad sprees pissing in the streets of Cooma had died in 1955. His wife Minnie, who in the book (but not in life) conceived a child before marriage, was also dead. Patrick White and his novel were now forgotten in Cooma, except by Norris King his fellow-jackeroo, living in an elegant slab homestead in the mountains. The Cooma papers made no mention of the Nobel. Adaminaby in that week was celebrating the completion of a giant concrete trout to lure tourists off the highway.

By May, despite an ominous bout of bronchial troubles in late summer, White was more than half-way through the first draft of *A Fringe of Leaves* when the political crisis of 1974 took him from his desk. Gough Whitlam's victory at the polls eighteen months before had left the Senate still in the hands of the conservative parties. In April 1974 they threatened to destroy the government from above by cutting off its revenue. The blocking of Supply had never been threatened in Canberra before, but the men of the old coalition were true revolutionaries in their own interest. Whitlam called a general election. He faced a difficult task, for the electorate was disappointed with Labor. Over the past year strikes and shortages had become commonplace. Inflation was rising sharply. White shared this general disillusionment, yet he could not bear the thought of the old parties returning to power. 'We have a nerve-wracking election hanging over us,' he told Alan Williams. 'If the Government doesn't get back, Australia will return to being a very dreary place indeed. Perhaps I shall go and live in Samoa.'[14]

Over a few bottles at the Bistro in Sydney towards the end of the campaign, Jim McClelland had the idea that a rally of writers and artists at the Opera House might mobilise support for Whitlam. There had never been a political rally at the Opera House before. To enlist the speakers he had to have a name. 'That was Patrick's. I went home and rang Patrick and asked him. I waited what seemed an age before he said, "One would be prepared to do that." '[15] Freda McClelland then recruited painters, poets, actors and playwrights for the platform. On the day of the meeting, the hall was full, and five thousand people stood outside listening to the speeches. White spoke directly to those who, like him, had grown disenchanted.

'I was a friend and supporter of the architect who conceived this noble building, who was driven away by Those Who Know Better before he had a chance of finishing his work. Today I am here in support of a man with similar aims whom we must not *allow* to be sacrificed as Utzon was.' The hall cheered him. 'Today I am not talking to artists, rather to those who are not creative themselves, thousands of thoughtful people throughout Australia for whom the life of the imagination – books, painting, music, theatre – plays a very important part, and without which, existence would be drab indeed.' There had been disappointments, but Whitlam's government had to be supported as it tried to come to grips with the complex problems of poverty and Aborigines, guide the nation through 'the labyrinth' of foreign affairs and end the terrible stagnation of Australia by creating 'an intellectual climate from which artists would no longer feel the need to flee'.[16]

White spoke for seven exhilarating minutes and knew for the first time what it was to have the feel of an enormous audience. 'I could move them and also make them laugh.'[17] The mood of the crowd even survived Whitlam's drab speech about the evils of tax evasion, and the rally was credited with dragging back a few thousand crucial votes. On 18 May the Labor government won a second but very narrow victory.

White's next crowd gathered in Grenfell, an old gold mining town west of the Blue Mountains, to hear him open the Henry Lawson Festival

of the Arts. The festival had honoured Patrick White in the old days and
now he was showing his gratitude by opening the 1974 festival from
a truck parked on Main Street. The *Grenfell Record* reported gloriously
sunny winter weather for the big event on Grenfell's calendar. White
had known almost nothing about Henry Lawson except a few 'un-
mentionable' poems and a sickening myth about a drunken writer of
the people. Most Australian schoolchildren read Lawson's superb stories
at school, but these were not on the Cheltenham syllabus. White read
a few of the stories and some biographies before the ordeal in Grenfell
and discovered a man who seemed almost his twin. 'It backs up my
belief in astrological characteristics,' he told Clem Semmler. 'We are
both Geminian.'[18]

White confessed to the country crowd gathered on Main Street that
an artist's soul was fragmented, lonely and manic depressive. 'Believe
me, the creative artist does live under enormous stress, which drives
many of us to drink or drugs in order to wring out the ultimate meaning,
and I cannot see that it will be otherwise unless the arts die an unnatural
death.' He spoke in the tones of an Anglican bishop, perhaps a bishop
who knew the rhetoric of AA. The meeting heard that Lawson was a
man whose immense popularity had not brought spiritual contentment.
'Henry had personal friends, too – often injudiciously chosen – those
phoney bohemians and bad poets of the day, chasing after Pan at Lane
Cove with artificial vine leaves in their hair (they lived before the age of
plastic). Sometimes Henry fell, and sometimes his friends picked him up
– but not always. (Personally I divide friends into two categories: those
who would pick me up when they find me lying in the gutter and those
who would step over the body, pretending it wasn't there.)'[19]

On this uncertain note, White declared the festival open, and the
procession moved off towards the sports ground. On his return to
Sydney he reported to Waters, 'It was all very rustic, except that Barry
Humphries was there to receive the award for Artist of the Year. I had
also to present the awards that evening at the bowling club; they
wanted me to crown the Festival and Charity Queens, but I got out of
that, and thankful I was when I saw somebody else struggling to get
the glass tiaras over those hair-dos.'[20]

Despite these excursions into public life, White was hard at work
on the book. He planned a research trip to Fraser Island in midwinter,
but before they set out White took an extraordinary step. He stripped
the house of its great paintings. Fourteen de Maistres, eight Nolans
and the Fairweather went to the Art Gallery of New South Wales. He
spoke of protecting these now very valuable works from burglars; he
said he looked forward to filling the blank spaces with new works by
young painters; but essentially this was an act of self-mortification. 'It
was a terrible wrench,' he told Ronald Waters. 'But I felt it had to

happen.' The Nobel medal and diploma, and the originals of some of the book jackets went to the Mitchell Library, that brown linoleum cavern which had swallowed his uncle's stamp collection in the First World War. When it was all done he wrote to Dutton to say he was sad but relieved. 'Some of those paintings have been through half my life with me.'[21]

Three headlands almost smothered by sand anchor the dunes of Fraser Island. Against these rocks, the wind and sea have built the biggest sandbank in the world. Rain forests grow here in pure sand. Lakes of fresh water perch in the high dunes, and clear fresh streams flow over sand into the sea. The dunes along the surf coast are overhung in places by cliffs of sand in garish red and orange strips. Ellen Roxburgh's party landed on a version of this ever-shifting beach:

> Round them shimmered the light, the sand, and farther back, the darker, proprietary trees. Where the beach rose higher, to encroach on the forest, great mattresses of sand, far removed from the attentions of the tides, were quilted and buttoned down by vines, a variety of convolvulus, its furled trumpets of a pale mauve.[22]

The sand is useful. The dunes have deposits of heavy black rutile, for which there are a hundred profitable applications. Since lead went out of favour, rutile has been a prime ingredient in the world's paint. A mine at the south of the island had stripped six miles of dunes by the time White returned in July 1974, and a string of leases had been granted that would allow almost the entire ninety miles of surf coast to be mined for rutile. The miners were being fought and so far these dunes remained untouched.

A hotel had been built on the surf shore since White's last visit, but exploration was still a challenge for visitors. 'One's feet get one nowhere.' For a couple of days they wandered around the pub on Orchid Point, and then found a tractor to take them 'along the fantastic ocean beach and into the rain forest. Apart from half-a-dozen fishermen here and there we were the only people on earth.' For the rest of the week they took tractors round the lakes in the high dunes, through the mangroves along the inland coast, and into the forests of sassafras and vines and flowers. Every evening a little before sunset they went into the forest and lay listening to the birds. 'I enjoyed this perfection,' he wrote to the composer Moya Henderson. 'But wish I were not several people in one and only one life between them. Part of me wants to live in peace and silence, but various other bits need the undercurrents and intrigue of the city, and above all to do battle. So I shall never be content.'[23]

White flew home and returned to the manuscript refreshed by those days on the island. 'Any kind of artist who has been to that island will remain affected by it for ever,' he told the poet Judith Wright. He counted this a very good reason for preserving it. From this point, the writing of *A Fringe of Leaves* and the campaign for Fraser Island ran side by side. He already knew a good deal about the struggle behind the scenes, for one of the pleas for help that arrived in the mail after the Nobel was from John Sinclair, the Maryborough public servant leading the Fraser Island Defence Organisation, FIDO. White had offered then to act as a go-between with Whitlam's ministers, and gave Sinclair a little advice. 'I'm inclined to suggest you put the whole argument concisely in one document rather than send a bundle of leaflets which might make a busy man's heart sink.'[24]

White shared the general confidence that Whitlam's government would save Fraser Island. On the contrary. A few months after White's visit, Gough Whitlam and his wife were taken on a tour of the island by local enthusiasts for mining and logging. They crossed from Maryborough in great style on a 56-foot cruiser lent to them, Margaret Whitlam reported in her weekly magazine column, by 'a happy Country Party man . . . and we are indeed grateful'. She prepared an impromptu picnic of corned silverside for them all, and observed that Fraser Island seemed mostly 'barren wasteland'.[25] A few weeks later, without consulting his Cabinet, Whitlam and a couple of ministers gave Dillingham-Murphyores permission to mine and export rutile from the island, and to do so without any investigation – as required by new laws – into the impact of mining on the environment. No public announcement was made. Dillingham-Murphyores prepared to start on a two-thousand-acre patch of dunes at the southern end of the island.

When news of this broke, White wrote to Whitlam: 'I was appalled and depressed . . . As well as ruining one of the most beautiful and scientifically unique islands in the world, the move is going to cause no end of trouble to the Labor position by further embittering already disillusioned conservationists in Queensland and elsewhere. Can't something be done, please, to avert the destruction of an island which should be preserved as a national park?' The letter went straight to Whitlam's desk. A bureaucratic reply was drafted. 'Dear Patrick,' the Prime Minister wrote, 'I want to reassure you as best I can.' White was not reassured. He reported to Nin Dutton, 'I'm afraid he's very stubborn. I don't want to end our alliance, but it won't be what it was if he sells out on Fraser Island. I too, can see my way to being stubborn.'[26]

Whitlam hammered the Dillingham-Murphyore deal through the Labor caucus. White wrote again, but his letters were now unanswered. He attacked Whitlam in the press. The government from which he had expected so much, was disappointing him terribly. He wrote to Peggy Garland, 'Now they seem intent on digging out every dollar there is in the ground, destroying natural beauty which is the only thing we've got in any way distinguished.'[27]

White joined Jack Mundey in a group called Friends of the Green Bans, to try to persuade unionists not to work on any Dillingham sites in Australia. 'If we ever succeed in preventing any of this,' he told Peggy Garland, 'it's through the unions, not the Government.'[28] But Mundey's power had been broken, and the bans generally failed. An air strip and roads had been built for the new mine, plant assembled and sand bulldozed by the time Whitlam was forced, by the pressure inside and outside his government, to hold an enquiry into the impact of mining on Fraser Island.

Sinclair travelled Australia with a slide show to raise money for FIDO. Setting up his projector in Sydney one night he saw Patrick White, whom he had never met, come into the empty hall. They exchanged only a couple of sentences, but it seemed to Sinclair no more was needed to acknowledge mutuality and understanding. A few days later he had a letter from White: 'From time to time I have tried to work on those at the top, so far unsuccessfully. I shall continue to do so whenever I see the opportunity.' He enclosed a cheque for $1,000.[29]

FIDO used the money to solve in one way a problem White himself was facing as he worked on *A Fringe of Leaves*. Little was known about Aboriginal life on Fraser Island, for the tribes were now scattered and their culture extinguished. The Queensland government was reluctant to send archaeologists over to the island, apparently fearing that discoveries might hamper mining. Sinclair found an independent archaeologist to collect evidence for FIDO, and White's $1,000 paid his expenses. White, meanwhile, had to recreate the life of the tribes for his novel, and he turned to his old friend David Moore, who was now an anthropologist at the Australian Museum in Sydney. Moore confirmed what Sinclair already knew: there was almost nothing in libraries and museums. So the ceremonies and speech of the Aborigines in *A Fringe of Leaves* were a feat of White's imagination, while the cash he gave FIDO helped to reveal one of the most important Aboriginal sites yet uncovered in Australia.[30]

When Sinclair came to make FIDO's case to the enquiry, he presented White's letters, reviews of his novels, passages from *The Eye of the Storm*, even a photocopy of the $1,000 cheque, and the work of the archaeologist on Fraser Island. Seventy-four witnesses gave evidence. The Whitlam government had fallen before the enquiry reported its findings: that there must be no sand mining on Fraser Island. Every federal government since has accepted that conclusion, but the miners have not given up their leases.

Much of White's time in 1974 was taken up with arguments over the Patrick White Prize. White had diverted $20,000 of royalty income into the fund to bring it up to $100,000. He was determined that his would be the richest literary award in Australia. His lawyers, with the help of the staff of the Prime Minister, were working to make sure the income from the fund was exempt from tax. White recruited as fellow judges the historian Geoffrey Blainey and Desmond Digby's friend the librarian James Allison. 'We decide after three years whether we should be re-elected,' White told Marshall Best. 'I shall probably withdraw before very long otherwise the bitching will start.'[31] In mid-November it was announced that the first winner of the prize was Christina Stead.

White thought her 'the most brilliant and deserving of any eligible Australian writer'.[32] But by this time she was old, lonely and at a loose end. White had asked her to lunch alone at Martin Road on her first brief return to Australia in 1969. The two got on very well. 'To talk to her is more like talking to a man than a woman,' White reported afterwards to Dutton. 'Although there is nothing overtly masculine about her, and I shouldn't think anything Lesbian. Her marriage seems to have been one of the best kind.' They discussed the characters in their fiction. Stead said hers were all people she had known. 'She wasn't prepared to believe that mine, the important ones anyway, are latent bits of myself.' White gave her some books – Berryman's poems and Cyril Connolly's reflections *The Unquiet Grave* – and advised her to think carefully before burning her boats and returning permanently to Australia.[33]

Five years later she returned to live with her brother in the Sydney suburbs. She was greeted everywhere as a genius rediscovered, but she was restless and drinking. Her books were being reissued and she was toying with old manuscripts but she never really wrote again. White had asked her if he might hold a party to celebrate her return home. He thought her answer shy, so invited her again to lunch instead. She brought him wild flowers. The food was vegetarian, and she realised White had cooked this meal because her husband had been Jewish and she might be used to eating kosher. 'A delicate courtesy.'[34]

Elizabeth Harrower was their common friend, and Stead talked to her of these visits to Martin Road as 'perfect days in my recent life . . . It is, I suppose, not only his personality and delightful home and exquisite cooking but his feeling for perfection and harmony; he is able to convey it. (And he is a great scene-setter and director, but don't say that to him: he might think it meant artificial acting – no, it is himself he conveys. What genius for living!) Happy man. And he makes me happy to have seen such a thing.'[35] Stead was entirely blind on one point. Despite everything she was told, she refused to believe White was homosexual. She loved men, and loved this man. Patrick was straight, she said, and she knew this because she knew him better than anybody.

White asked Elizabeth Harrower to see if Stead would accept his prize. Stead was very touched. White, in turn, was moved by her acceptance. This was an emotional transaction for both of them. Stead was paid $6,000 and she had great pleasure spending it quickly. She liked odd clothes, good wine and good restaurants. She spoke as she always did of finishing books and getting down to new stories, but she was not writing. She drank steadily. White's New Year resolution for 1975 was to give up the booze again.

He complained that the Nobel Prize was ruining his life, and spoke as if public acclaim was turning him into a stuffed owl or a public statue like Voss in the Sydney Domain 'hung with garlands of rarest newspaper prose'.[36] Fear of this fate began to act as a release: he felt he must show he was still alive, still able to surprise and even shock, still a writer who deserved the Nobel. The sensuality of White's prose was always powerful but usually thwarted. From the time of the prize his work became saturated with a late, relaxed sensuality.

This change can be measured in the odyssey of the shipwrecked Ellen and her convict Chance. In the abandoned version of the novel White never allowed her to surrender entirely to Chance. She tortured him, 'getting unconfessed erotic satisfaction out of her mastery particularly when she worms out of him that he is a murderer. He, finally, is so horrified on consummating the relationship that he dashes back into the bush.' Now in the new version of *A Fringe of Leaves* the convict becomes Mrs Roxburgh's 'saviour-lover' and the consummation of their passion is described in prose that had never been more uninhibited. Instead of horror and frustration, there is pleasure frankly expressed. On the island one afternoon they are gathering lily roots,

> bumping, laughing, falling and rising, swallowing mouthfuls of the muddy water.
> In the gaps between the mangled lily-flesh he made the water fly in her face by cutting at it with the flat of his hand. She could not imitate his boy's trick, but followed suit after a fashion by thumping the surface and throwing clumsy handfuls at him.
> He caught her by the slippery wrists, and they kissed, and clung . . .[37]

The pond was always a sensual image for White, and now it seems the convict and the shipwrecked lady were to consummate the passion of the frustrated jackeroo in the muddy lagoon at Walgett.

He was ill in January. Many asthma sufferers in middle age believe their affliction has burnt itself out. White hoped his asthma had left him for ever, but in the early weeks of 1975 he was sick again: first with asthma and then with bronchial complications. 'As always . . . work got hold of me and I have gone ahead well (I think.) Yesterday when I was feeling particularly awful I unravelled one of the most knotted passages in the first version. Of course on these occasions I think to myself, supposing I die? the publisher may get hold of it, and in spite of the clause in my will, give it to some hack who will turn it into something quite different from what I intended. So one has to push on.' But the trouble persisted and he was compelled once again to consult Maurice Joseph, the physician who introduced him to cortisone in the 1950s. Joseph now gave him a little cortisone spray to carry in his pocket. A few weeks later White told Dutton, 'It is good to feel alive again, and to walk at my normal pace instead of crawling like a half-dead blow-fly.'[38] White was now never without his Ventolin puffer.

Some time towards the end of that summer, Jim and Freda McClelland had White to dinner at Darling Point to meet their old friend Sir John Kerr, who was now Governor-General. White knew Kerr when he was a judge, for they were together briefly on the board of the Community Theatre in the 1960s. Kerr was then a fat and rather feminine figure, 'his hair white and fluffy like a wig in one of those amateur productions of *The Rivals*'. Kerr was not much changed, but he had a brand new wife, and on that hot night in early 1975 she arrived on Darling Point in fur and long gloves. After a good dinner, Kerr took White aside for a quarter of an hour to talk about the Order of Australia. Whitlam was setting up a system of local honours in order to do away with imperial awards. White had been offered the highest of these bunyip decorations, but was hesitating. Kerr confided that he would ruin everything if he turned it down. After a few days' reflection, White accepted. 'There began a kind of love affair with the Kerrs; private telephone numbers and invitations were exchanged.'[39]

The second version of *A Fringe of Leaves* was finished in May. A few days later Frances Peck arrived from England to spend the European summer at Martin Road. She was nineteen, shy, beautiful, rather scruffy and had the family's blazing blue eyes. After only a week White had to confess to Peggy Garland that he was finding it very difficult 'dealing with somebody who only speaks when spoken to, and reveals nothing of her true self unless you winkle it out. It's impossible to know whether she's enjoying herself, or bored or unhappy or what.'[40] He blamed the English boarding schools where she had lived since her mother's death, and decided Frances needed 'to be brought out of herself and into life'. With stumbling kindness, the old bachelor set out to open another world to this wary young woman. He introduced her to books, cinema – 'I have subjected her to some pretty tough films'[41] – theatre, music, painting and the exotic visitors who came to Martin Road. He persuaded her to give up the place she had waiting at the Camberwell College of Art, and learn painting in Sydney instead. Martin Road was to be her base for nine months. This time was not without friction, but there was nothing like the blazing animosity which had, for a while, soured White's relations with her sister Gillian. He only wished Frances would *groom* herself as a beautiful, wealthy young woman should. He could not tolerate this fashion for dressing in rags.

In the midwinter of 1975 Lizzie died in the mountains. White had been a few times to the nursing home in Wentworth Falls where she passed the last couple of years. They were awful visits. 'She can hardly put six words together by now, and sees people who aren't there. At one stage when I was trying to find out, unsuccessfully, which of her relations visit her, she said "I have Paddy White – he's very nice – he comes to see me." I happen to know her saint of a brother-in-law drives over from Mount Wilson every Sunday.' The mountains which had been the paradise of his childhood, were now somewhere he went to visit the old, crippled and senile, living 'in what approaches squalor and tangled wilderness'. Lizzie was ninety-six when she died in July. Her body was taken back to Mount Wilson. 'We buried her in its purple soil, amongst the tree ferns, outside the asbestos church.'[42]

He came down that night and had dinner with Elizabeth Harrower. He was rather flat, but said nothing about Lizzie's death or the funeral. Sid Kirk had asked him if there was anything he would like of Lizzie's. He named the little worm-eaten trunk Lizzie had brought out with her from Scotland. For years he had wanted it, but did not know how to ask. Kirk appeared a few weeks later at Martin Road.

'What do you want?' White asked him at the door.

'I've got the trunk.'

'You could have given me a ring.'

He put the chest under the window of his bedroom. One day he showed it to Harrower as if it were a treasure and sorted through all old photographs with her, very moved as he told stories about Lizzie, the Carnoustie lassie who had been his real mother.[43]

He was pressing ahead with the final version of *A Fringe of Leaves* at unprecedented speed. Publishers had been warned it would not be ready until early in the New Year, but that winter it was clear the book would be finished by the end of 1975. Hurrying him on was a familiar – but now intense – conviction that things were falling apart. His eyes were bad, he was shedding teeth, the dogs had cancers, the political situation was awful, and his doctor was threatening him with a diet to cut down cholesterol. 'But I don't propose to give up food or sex for the pleasure of continuing to live in this stinking world,' he told Waters. 'I gave up smoking years ago, and haven't had a drink for nearly a year; that is enough.' Early signs of glaucoma had been detected, and this verdict was confirmed by his ophthalmic surgeon in June, but it was still too soon to be thinking of an operation. 'My eyes are in ruins,' he complained to Maschler in August. 'I've no idea what the book is like. There are days when it excites me, then the same pages can look so awful I could throw the whole thing away. Writing it has been a discipline, and I shall be glad to go on to something which will leave me free to splash about more.'[44]

He finished work alone at Martin Road in September. Elly Polymeropoulos had arrived and taken her brother to Western Australia to see the spring wild flowers. Frances went to the country to stay with a cousin. At first White thought he would collapse under the weight of typing, feeding the dogs, watering the garden and shopping, but he fell into the rhythm of the chores and had the typing finished by the time Elly and Manoly returned. The book was dedicated to Desmond Digby.

One copy of the typescript was posted to London on 24 September. O'Hea thought it was his best. Sid Nolan rang to say he would like to do the jacket. For a time White was left sweating on responses from Maschler and Lascaris: 'Manoly is reading it, but always takes six months to get through one of my books, which he does in almost total silence, commenting only at the end, which you can understand is rather unnerving.'[45] When Maschler's wire arrived enthusiastically accepting the book, White corrected a second copy and sent it off to New York.

Marshall Best found himself struggling once more with one of those 'ghastly flimsy' typescripts. He had had enough. 'I can't understand why, after all these years, you are still so cruel to your first readers! I'd gladly raise a Better Typing Fund for Nobel Prizemen for the extra paper and postage, be it three times as long. I'm really not joking now. You can't imagine what a hardship it is for all of us.' White claimed it was all an accident. 'I am always in a state of tension when starting the final version. My hand must have slipped and the spacing gadget shot up to single-spacing. I did not notice this until I had typed about twenty-five pages. As it did not seem to me to look so bad, and because it would cost much less to send, I continued typing that way.' Against this in the margin Best scrawled, 'Oh come off it!'[46]

White left his desk for the dentist's chair. 'I am shrivelling up into a He-Ancient.' The last eight teeth came out one by one for he had decided to have all false teeth top and bottom: the full rabbit trap. 'I'm sick of these dramatic breakages of single teeth and having to face the world for days on end looking like Aubrey of *Brief Lives*. One can always keep a spare set if one is completely toothless, a far better arrangement.'[47]

On the afternoon of 11 November he was cooking a soft meal to feed David Campbell, winner of the second Patrick White Prize, when he heard on the wireless that the Governor-General had sacked Gough Whitlam and installed the opposition conservatives in office. White was shattered. 'The meal', he told Manning Clark, 'went a bit astray.'[48] The opposition had again been delaying Supply in the Senate, but Whitlam seemed on the verge of victory in Parliament when Kerr made this novel intervention in Australian politics. Many were so glad to see the end of the Labor government that they welcomed the resurrection from a constitutional grave of these powers of the crown. The rest of the country saw the Prime Minister's sacking on 11 November 1975 in more conventional terms: it was an outrage and unnecessary. Malcolm Fraser had only to wait a few months before the country went to the polls and he would have won easily. Now Australia was in turmoil, Fraser was in office, and elections were to be held in December.

The 'cataclysm' as White called these events filled him with disgust: at the greed and impatience of the conservatives, at those who applauded this bizarre royal exercise, at all those Australians who continued to fawn on the Queen, and at himself for having broken his own rules by accepting an honour from Kerr. This disgust fuelled White's politics through the years ahead. After 11 November he became more absolute, a sterner political puritan and a more convinced republican. All about him he saw the evil power of money in politics. The offices of Governor and Governor-General had to go, and he urged a total boycott. Even before scanning the Deaths, he turned each morning to the vice-regal column in the *Sydney Morning Herald* to see who had broken ranks to eat with Kerr and his successors at Yarralumla.

Though almost toothless, White agreed to appear on television to speak for Labor. 'How unsuited I am to these public appearances, even with my teeth, but I shall have to do it.' The Eastern Suburbs where White had mixed happily for ten years, once looked on his enthusiasm for Labor as a sympathetic eccentricity. Now the verdict of society was that Patrick White was making a fine fool of himself. The new Prime Minister was a man of his background and class: a grazier from the western districts of Victoria. Where did his loyalties lie? Not with the tedious past to which he feared his country would return if 'that grazier and his entourage' governed in Canberra.[49] White was abused at the shops; his friends were insulted at cocktail parties.

White spoke from the stage of the Capitol Theatre on Friday 28 November as one of many artists calling for the re-election of Labor. Huge crowds were turning out for Whitlam, but the polls showed a slide to the other side. Up to the last minute White had hopes that Whitlam might just scrape home, but the country's despair over Labor's performance in office triumphed over any constitutional objections to the transfer of power. By a landslide the elections confirmed Fraser in office. 'We shall now return to everything I have always hated about Australia under the rule of sunny Philistia.' For years the rich had been complaining about the imminent bankruptcy of themselves and the country, but Lascaris suddenly observed, 'Rolls and Jaguars infest Double Bay shopping centre like snails after rain.'[50]

His false teeth – 'neither too beautiful nor too ugly' – were fitted a few days before Christmas. Even the softest food was painful to chew. 'I can barely bring myself to raise the portcullis and let some liquid down my throat,' he told James Stern. 'There's no question of eating even after a week.' He warned Stern, 'We are *planning* to leave for London after Easter . . . I have no great desire to go anywhere, and at the same time none to continue lingering in this deadly reactionary country.'[51]

TWENTY-SEVEN

Dynamite All the Way

THAT GLOOMY SUMMER, Jim Sharman appeared at Martin Road to talk about *The Season at Sarsaparilla*. He was eager, puckish, guarded and precociously successful. It seemed to the young director that he was sitting with a national monument. Opposite him, White was grappling with his own sense of disbelief and admiration. The idea of Sharman directing *Sarsaparilla* had crossed his mind years before, but the hope of ever seeing this happen had faded as Sharman became the most famous young director of his generation. 'During the talk there was a thread of I don't know what (a spider's?) hanging from one of the pink-and-white cheeks, visible when air lifted and light caught it. I have never told him about this thread, or how I wanted to lean forward and sweep it away. In one way or another I might have ruined everything . . . on my side it would be dishonest if I denied an occasional twinge of sexual jealousy in my relationship with Jim, but our collaboration settled into what I would call a perfect example of fruitful sublimation.'[1]

Though he had tried to give the impression that he was finished with the theatre, White's theatrical ambitions were only ever on ice. As his fame grew, managements were curious once again to see what Patrick White had written for the stage. Scripts were circulated. Early enthusiasm was usually followed by polite excuses and then silence. The plays brought in a trickle of royalties from American universities, English television and minor German cities. White forbade productions in South Africa.

A revival of *Sarsaparilla* in Sydney had been talked about for years. White told the Old Tote in 1967, 'I might consider it if Sharman could produce.' But the Tote backed off. Sharman was only twenty-two. The following year he directed a caustic revue at the little Jane Street Theatre. On the opening night of *Terror Australis* the audience was asked to wear decorations and when the crowd arrived in evening dress and medals it was herded into the auditorium through a sheep race while the cast stood on stage baa-ing their way through the national anthem. White loved the show and when he saw it torn to pieces in the *Sydney Morning Herald* he wrote to the paper urging all who despaired of Sydney theatre to pay *Terror Australis* a visit.[2] The two men met in King Street the day the letter was published. It was the kind of coincidence both valued.

Sharman had led a solitary and conventional life as a child in Sydney – until the holidays came and he joined his father's famous boxing troupe in the bush. Young Jim beat the drum to gather the crowd. At the age of five he watched blacks fighting whites, and crowds of blacks and whites in the tent barracking for their own. The troupe was theatre and the Sharmans were good at it. Going around the country shows with them was Sorlies, the bush vaudeville, and the Great Levante gave the boy his first lessons in magic. Then, at the end of the holidays, Sharman returned to his mother's respectable flat in Randwick and an ordinary school where the boys knew none of this other life.

At seventeen as a precocious schoolboy Sharman went to see *The Ham Funeral* at the Palace, and a couple of years later at *Sarsaparilla* he heard for the first time on the stage the language of the streets in which he lived. The English plays and American films that inundated Australia were all telling him life happened somewhere else. Not here but over there. White said it happened at home, and gave life in these Sydney streets the force of some primitive myth. It was a decisive discovery.

The morning White's letter appeared in the *Herald*, Sharman was looking through records in Edels. White was pointed out to him leaving the shop, and he ran down King Street in pursuit. 'Hey, Mr White,' he called and clapped him on the back. White turned, startled by this, but then amused to see this paint-splattered, long-haired character on the footpath. The young man thanked him for the letter. 'We stood together in the street, made awkward by our confrontation, our different worlds, the gap between our ages, in spite of what we had in common in that abrasive, shit-slinging revue. We drew apart.'[3]

Harry Miller had a spotter's eye for young talent and he shared White's hopes for Sharman. When Miller bought the Australian rights to the rock musical *Hair* he hired Sharman to direct and design it in Sydney and it was an immense success. (White stayed away, for he had thought the show an amateurish bore when he saw it in New York: 'the good bits would have squeezed into half an hour'.) Sharman staged *Hair* in Boston, Tokyo and then Melbourne, where he worked with the young Sydney designer Brian Thomson. Sharman and Thomson became a team and went on to stage productions of *Jesus Christ Super-star* around the world. Their London production ran for nine years in the West End. During the run they concocted, with Richard O'Brien,

The Rocky Horror Show which was another huge success, and their *Rocky Horror* film became the focus of an international cult. White enjoyed *Rocky Horror* when he saw it on stage in Sydney in the winter of 1974; 'most entertaining and professional'.[4]

New playwrights appearing in Australia in the early 1970s were not much to White's taste: too much conversation and not enough magic. He made sure he saw all the new Australian films and plays: he called it doing his duty by 'Strine. 'I continue with my policy of trying to find out about Australian film and theatre,' he told Ronald Waters, 'but most of it is a waste of time.' Once the Opera House opened he discovered a late passion for opera. 'The minute you get inside that Opera Theatre, there is all the glamour and excitement I expect when I go to the theatre, which I get in London, whereas usually in Sydney one is battered into a state of moral and physical despair in some Nissen hut or church hall.' His taste was catholic: Mozart, Verdi, Weill and Janácek. He was happy to wallow once in a while in Puccini. Sydney was a better place for having the Opera House, White declared – except for the hazards of infection. The building was full of viruses, 'as people who succeed in getting tickets rise from their deathbeds to use them'.[5]

While White was in this state of estrangement from local theatre, Jim Sharman came home. He had put his stamp on the three most influential musicals of the decade, and was now anxious to find 'whatever it was that was meant to come next'.[6] On an aimless evening in Sydney he was driven down Martin Road and saw White's house perched on its hill. It looked like something from a Hammer horror movie, the sort of place where no one had knocked for a long time. Sharman thought of the plays and wondered where else in the world such a writer would live and not have them revived. Later that year, when the Old Tote offered him a production, Sharman chose *Sarsaparilla*.

White wanted them to meet *at once* when he heard this news, amazed that this 'wonderkid of Australian theatre, idol of the young, should want to disturb the dust'. Sharman put him off for a few days to read some of the novels, for he feared an interrogation. There was none and they spoke only briefly about the play when he called on 8 November 1975. Finding common ground when they discussed casting, they moved on to other things. As they spoke, Sharman was reminded of his grandfather, the bush patriarch who started the boxing troupe in the Depression. He liked this in White. He, in turn, was rather awed by this young man sitting opposite, 'pink and white above a royal-blue windcheater'. He told Sharman it was good he had come home: an artist must not be alienated from the landscape in which he was brought up.[7]

A new phase of White's life began the day Sharman came to Martin

Road. White forgot none of the past troubles, indeed he raked over them as he approached this fresh collaboration. 'We got together very happily this morning and found we have the same ideas about actors,' he told Geoffrey Dutton. 'How very different from Tilly Tasker who would never contemplate anybody I suggested for a part.' But after years of hearing bullshit from producers and managements, he discovered that Sharman got things done. It seemed almost miraculous: such good fortune did not come but was *sent*. At their second meeting, White remarked that his story *The Night the Prowler* might make a good film. Sharman asked him for a screenplay. A few weeks later White wrote to Dutton, 'This is pouring out of me.'[8]

The screenplay was only a diversion. White was preparing to begin the work 'simmering' in his mind ever since the trip to Melbourne in the aftermath of the Nobel when he saw the painting of Herbert Dyce-Murphy in drag. 'I should like to use it as a novella,' he told Barry Jones at the time. 'I can see it so vividly too, as another impressionist painting.' At Jones' suggestion White consulted the Murray-Smiths, for they had discovered the old man out on Mornington Peninsula and had made a stab at disentangling fact from fiction in his life. As White was working on *A Fringe of Leaves* and fretting to be free of its constraints, he was quizzing the Murray-Smiths about Dyce-Murphy: 'I really know enough to write what I plan, but one can always glean a little more.'[9]

Dyce-Murphy was the child of a Victorian grazing family raised in Suffolk where his uncle was Lord-Lieutenant. He claimed the elderly Empress Eugénie had befriended him as a boy. This may or may not have been true, but he was certainly dog-handler on Sir Douglas Mawson's 1911–14 Antarctic expedition. Much of the time in England he lived as a woman under the name Edith. Herbert/Edith was photographed as a woman at Henley and lived with a retired ship's master in Kew. In old age Dyce-Murphy was entirely unashamed of this youthful transvestite life and boasted that the War Office had employed him for five years to travel round France in drag spying on the French railway system. He returned to Melbourne and married. His widow was still alive but White did not want to meet her. 'I think my original facts will be well enough disguised to avoid causing embarrassment or distress.' At first White referred to the project as 'the Murphy novel', but then it began to move in fresh directions and he wondered if anyone would connect the central figure of the book with Dyce-Murphy, 'except that I feel that I must use that piece of dialogue between Murphy and his mother. ("No, but I am your daughter Edith." "I'm so glad. I always wanted a daughter.")'[10]

The Twyborn Affair, White's late masterpiece, is the novel of a man cursed with unreason and a rebellious body who lives in exile wherever he settles: he is, he realises, 'the stranger of all time'. White always insisted that his novels were autobiographical to some extent. 'But the present one is more explicit than the others. There are still plenty of disguises of course, otherwise it would be the kind of humdrum documentary expected by Australians.'[11] The book was written as his dreams were coming true on the stage, and White was to dedicate it to the man responsible: Sharman.

On the evening of 16 February 1976 Max Kaufline was called to a motel in Cooma to meet a tall man of his own age who wanted to be driven around the Monaro. Kaufline had lived all his life in the High Country and knew it like the back of his hand. He was hired for three days, and returned next morning with sandwiches and coffee packed by his wife. All Kaufline knew about his passenger was that he had once jackerooed out at Bolaro and was curious to see the district again. The man said little, but sat and watched the country roll past. He took no notes and no photographs.

They stopped at the dam that drowned old Adaminaby, and drove to the new township, a neat little place where Frank Yen's son ran the picture show. Kaufline headed up to Kiandra where blackberries and snow had levelled all but the last of the goldminers' huts, and then they drove back down to Bolaro. As the taxi rattled over the bridge, the passenger pointed to a cottage on the river bank. 'That's where I wrote my first book. Thank God it was never published.' Hawthorns pressed against its walls. Rabbits shot out of the bushes as they approached. The two men peered in the windows. Kaufline expected his passenger to follow the rule of the bush and make himself known at the big house. He refused: he wanted to meet no one. The only person he asked after was Sally Venables. She had been dead for years.

When Kaufline returned to the motel next morning he knew who his passenger was – his son-in-law had recognised the name – but still White said nothing about the novel he was researching. What seemed most on his mind was a short story that was going to be made into a film. They drove over the bare, undulating hills to Nimmitabel and Bibbenluke. At Bombala White stopped the car in the drive of a homestead. Again he refused to go to the door. He looked around for a bit and said, 'That'll do.'

Kaufline's orders on the third morning were to head north to Michelago. After pausing in the drive of the Ryries' homestead under the mountains, they drove up the highway and turned off to Lanyon. When they were both young men, this old place with its noble avenue of bunya pines was the hub of a vast property. Now it lay on the edge of Canberra, open to the public as a historic homestead and hung with paintings given by Sid Nolan. White showed Kaufline the paintings and seemed very taken with them. They ate their sandwiches and drove down the back road along the Murrumbidgee. At Tharwa, White remarked that he had once camped there with a mob of sheep. They clattered over the Bolaro bridge again and crossed that great bowl of yellow grass on the way back to Cooma. The fare for the 464 miles covered in three days was $122. There was no tip.

That night White joined the Kauflines for a barbecue after quizzing Kaufline 'pretty hard' to make sure no one but family would be there. It was very relaxed. The son-in-law recited favourite lines from one of the novels, but White had no memory of writing them. He was emphatic. For many years afterwards he sent the young man copies of the novels as they appeared in new paperback editions. From Sydney White reported to Dutton that the trip 'turned out most rewarding'.[12]

His return to the Monaro was part of a larger plan to revisit the literary terrain of all his early novels: the Monaro of *Happy Valley*, the London of *The Living and the Dead* and the southern France of *The Aunt's Story*. Now, with the candour and ease of an old and distinguished writer, he might draw closer to truths explored as a young man. Though the central figure of the new novel would wear inspired disguises, there would be no hiding the bond between writer and subject: both Australians, homosexuals, at home and homeless at either end of the earth.

Bearing their splinter of Santa Teresa's staircase, White and Lascaris set out for Europe in April. White was full of worries. Would Manoly's feet stand the pace? Would the money last? At least with false teeth he was now 'less greedy and cost less to feed'. The Nolans met them at Heathrow. She was looking frightful, 'thinner than ever and in agony from her back'. Yet the best days of the next two months were spent with the Nolans: at galleries and the theatre, eating superb meals in Putney, and driving in the country. One of their marvellous trips was to Sissinghurst, which White thought inspired. 'I'm sure her ghost haunts at night.' He wrote to Dutton, 'We should really make the effort to go more to the country while we are here, but London is in my bones and I can't tear myself away from it. London is something you and David Campbell will never understand!'[13]

Because he had not shown his face in Europe since the Nobel, White was worried he would be harassed by journalists. So publishers, agents and hosts were asked to keep his presence a secret. They did, while making a great fuss of him in private. 'Lots of theatre, serious and frivolous,' White wrote home. 'We're getting fat though: too many reunion meals with friends.' Twice in those months in London White came face to face with Samuel Beckett, once as Beckett came out of a bar in Sloane Square at 11am. Neither man made a move to speak. 'We flickered at each other from a distance. I don't expect he knew who I was; he only suspected a possible predator.'[14]

Juliet O'Hea had retired. 'Agent first,' *The Times* called her, 'and friend very closely second, to half the writing establishment.' She had gone to live in a cottage in Kent. Despite his objections to Kent – 'it's dank' – White allowed himself to be driven down for the day by O'Hea's sister who expected and feared a heavy literary discussion *en route*. White raised instead the question of Hoovering rooms: how often did it have to be done? His own position was, once a week but thoroughly.[15]

Beyond the far end of Ebury Street in Chelsea, where Cheyne Walk runs down to the Thames, was one of White's favourite neighbourhoods in London, even though he suspected the damp air of those streets was bad for his lungs. Here he planned to house Eadith Trist's brothel in an imagined Beckwith Street, lying somewhere between unfashionable squares and the Embankment. The street

was not unconscious of the river as a source of life. On gloomy days, brick which might have been reduced to a sullen ruby, seemed to respond to the glimmer off the water. On brighter occasions the street acquired dash from the clatter and importance of traffic as it surged at right angles, parallel to the silent river.

Very early one morning he left his hotel and traced the path Mrs Trist would take at that hour, when business at the brothel was over for the night. From the region of Beckwith Street he crossed the river to Battersea and climbed over the railings into the park. He couldn't remember railings, and asked Peggy Garland to find if they had been there in the 1930s. They had, so Eadith Trist must carry keys 'which patronage had provided her' to stroll across the grass at dawn. 'Hair damp, a naked face somewhat haggard in a light turning from oyster to mauve.' He sat with Sid Nolan on the Embankment improvising dialogue for the novel. The painter took the part of the mother and White was his son–daughter on these evenings by the river.[16]

He had to face Stockholm. Towards the end of June White and Lascaris flew to Sweden where Artur Lundkvist and Björkstén were waiting. White could have made his Nobel oration even at this late date, but he refused and his instructions to Björkstén were that the press was not to hear of his visit until he had left the country. Stockholm was delightful. 'Everybody most agreeable and hospitable. Scandinavians seem almost incapable of the rudeness and bad temper which prevails in other countries in the Nineteen Seventies. Architecturally it is a dream, especially in those long summer nights of pale green light.' Björkstén took them to his cottage in the forest at Östervåle for the celebration of midsummer. The cottage stood beside a meadow of purple crane's-bill, buttercups and blue campanula. The light at night was very beautiful when it came closest to dark and the pines stood in pale silhouette. Mists rolled down from the north. There was singing and dancing around a maypole in the field on midsummer's night. White was faintly disappointed, 'None of the drunkenness one expected, and no Miss Julie letting down her hair.'[17]

Marseilles seemed infernal after the chaste cities of Scandinavia. White and Lascaris flew down from Oslo on 7 July and Jim Sharman was there to meet them with news that he had found a producer to film *The Night the Prowler*. White was delighted and took them to 'the best fish restaurant in the world' to celebrate. A few days later the two travellers set out from Marseilles. As a connoisseur of discomfort, White could not have chosen a better time to explore the south of France. In the hell of July they caught a bus along the coast to Hyères. 'It trundled through Bandol, grazing the double-parked cars. One could see what the place *used* to be. The same goes for Hyères: one gets a few glimpses of what it used to be. There are still the palms and the *lauriers roses* and the shell of the Parc Hôtel which is being turned into an Hôtel de Ville.' This was once a watering hole for the English and a few rich Australians. Literary consumptives favoured Hyères, and Edith Wharton (with very healthy lungs) had a château above the town, and a boulevard named in her honour. When White was a boy, he had wanted to come here for Christmas holidays rather than the dreary snows, but Ruth considered *le Midi* unsuitable for children. Now he was planning to assign Joan and E. Boyd (Curly) Golson to the best hotel in town while Joanie pursued her passion for the mysterious Eudoxia Vatatzes. The old Parc Hôtel became, in *Twyborn*, the Golsons' pub in St Mayeul: the Grand Hôtel Splendide des Ligures.[18]

But on the eve of 14 July there was no room in town for White and Lascaris. They found themselves stuck ten miles along the coast from Hyères, 'on a Florida-style highway, devoured by mosquitoes, plagued by diarrhoea in my case and surrounded by a most unsympathetic type of French bourgeoisie'. He was revolted by the French passion for *la plage* and the women exposing their 'watermelons or dried figs' as they swam topless in the sea. Yet this unsympathetic landscape was what he needed for *Twyborn*. The Vatatzes' cottage, 'shutters a washed-out blue, walls a dusty crackled pink' stood on a rutted road past the salt pans and runtish pines that lay between the hotel and the town of Giens. St Mayeul he was to confabulate from Hyères, Bandol and Giens, which stands unspoiled on a ridge above the sea.[19]

As his guide to this country, White had the letters and diaries of Katherine Mansfield. She was still one of his favourite monsters, 'very good on the feel and look of that part of the French coast, and her rather dreadful outpourings helped me when I was gathering material for the French section of *The Twyborn Affair*'. Before making this journey, he had read her stories again, and now found them overpolished and affected, but the letters and diaries, though sometimes painfully fey and self-conscious, 'do jump at one . . . At their best they're as perfect in their imagery as early morning.'[20] Katherine Mansfield spent probably the happiest months of her life with Middleton Murry in a little pink house with strange blue-grey shutters near Bandol. After tuberculosis was diagnosed, she made terrible wartime railway journeys back to convalesce in Bandol and, after the war, to Menton. White thought she was terribly good at bad railway journeys. These were absorbed into *Twyborn*.

Peter Beatson came over from Aix and met them in Hyères on a day of small calamities. Beatson's sight had been failing for many years, and he was now almost entirely blind. White was going to take them all to lunch, but the restaurant was closed. Surly taxi drivers refused to take them to see Edith Wharton's château. 'We finally sprawled on the grass in a park and talked surrounded by the strong, animal stench of monkeys or goats (we never found the source of the smell) which made Patrick grumpy because his sense of smell was so weak he hadn't noticed it. Manoly, who speaks French well, refused to interpret when dealing with taxi drivers, restaurateurs, etc., so Patrick, whose French is very, very English had to negotiate in a loud voice with the recalcitrant natives.'[21]

Once White and Lascaris were on the train to Nice the landscape seemed to put things right: 'No sign of a dreadful freeway or the endless string of cars, but real life going on as though nothing had happened.' Nice was familiar territory, and he was pleasantly surprised to find it had not turned into another hell after all these years. 'Bouncing and vulgar, but with style,' he reported to Dutton. 'There are also some excellent restaurants and intriguing streets. We found the Palais Lascaris which is now a museum. In the Seventeenth Century Manoly's ancestress the Princess Eudoxia of Nicaea married a Vintimille, and that's how Nice got its name. The custodian of the museum became quite tremulous when I told him who Manoly was.'[22] The custodian perhaps quailed at the prospect of challenging this history: Nice had had its name for over a thousand years before the arrival of the Lascarises.

White was planning to bind together in *The Twyborn Affair* the Greek and Australian strands of his life: Smyrna and Sydney, the Vatatzes on the Prokymaia and the Twyborns of Rushcutters Bay. The spice trader Angelos Vatatzes is 'a Byzantinologist by vocation and an authority on Orthodox theology, which he admits he doesn't yet understand'.[23] His chaotic reflections on the past are a history of the Lascaris emperors of Byzantium-Nicaea at the height of their power under John III Vatatzes.

The original Eudoxia was the Emperor's sister, living several unhappy lives, always in exile as the wife of foreign princes. Eudoxia is the name by which Vatatzes knows his mistress, and when they flee St Mayeul together by train, the old man sits in the carriage wearing an imperial eagle at his throat. Their last refuge is a narrow room in a narrow house in Menton.

The travellers reached Menton in the last week of July. 'It's the place we've liked best along this largely destroyed coast,' White wrote to Penny Coleing. On their first morning White called at Mansfield's villa Isola Bella, which lies outside the town towards the Italian border. In the garden is a room where writers come each year from New Zealand to work. The biographer Michael King was at the villa in 1976. White left a postcard under his door: 'I came in search of K.M. this morning . . . if you feel like it, perhaps we could have dinner one night.'[24]

They met. King found two complete pilgrims, going everywhere Mansfield had been, knowing every flower she described. 'I asked if he planned to write about her or about someone like her, but he did not answer directly.' They went walking along the beach and through the town, White scattering the Mentonais as he strode about. King found him easy, often raucously entertaining, but flaring at times into bursts of scathing derision. 'He was attentive and gentle with me, gentle too with Manoly (but bullying).' They ate that night in a restaurant where the *patronne* sang Piaf songs until White requested 'Knees up Mother Brown'. A lot of wine had been drunk. Madame expressed ignorance of the song and White invited her to hand the guitar to King, who sang that and a couple of Australasian *chansons éthniques* to a mixed response from the crowd. 'Patrick beamed like a proud grandfather. It was the only time I saw him looking mellow.'

King put a plan to White: if he exposed himself to a civic reception at the Hôtel de Ville, the French might be encouraged to restore their support for the Katherine Mansfield trust, which had been cut off when New Zealand began to object to the French exploding nuclear bombs in the Pacific. White screwed up his face in disgust, but agreed. A few days later the deputy mayor of Menton, standing beneath a frieze of mythological birds and animals painted by Jean Cocteau, mistook Lascaris for White and greeted him effusively. Order was not restored for some minutes. White was looking thunderous as they all sat down and the deputy, a former rector of the University of Algeria, began a speech of extraordinary, rather formal Gallic flattery.

'White followed every word and began to drum his fingers impatiently on the table top. After about twenty minutes the recteur ran out of words, bowed and waited for Madame Tardy, who was supposed to act as interpreter. She turned to Patrick who said that he had understood the speech. "Would you like to reply, monsieur?" And Patrick said clearly, in his beautifully modulated voice, "Actually this sort of thing gives me the shits." Manoly and I recoiled. Madame Tardy went puce, but she recovered sufficiently to say to the recteur, in French, that Monsieur White thanked him for his felicitations.' *Nice Matin* took photographs while champagne and pastries were served. White signed the *Livre d'Or*, and was presented with several volumes of the *Cahiers du Collège Poétique de Menton* plus a number of travel brochures for the Côte d'Azur, all of which he threw into a council rubbish bin at the foot of the town hall stairs. 'He was frosty when we parted.' The French did not restore the grant.[25]

The travellers hurried through Italy, for Eleanor Arrighi had died. 'I don't feel I want Rome with Nellie no longer there,' White wrote to Luciana Arrighi. The two men were back in their roof-top flat in Athens in time for Lascaris's birthday on 5 August. After the celebrations they travelled round Euboea in a taxi. 'Wonderful forests and pretty villages almost always within sight of the sea, and a number of Fourteenth Century churches tucked away. At one of the churches a convent where the abbess would have made the perfect Laura Trevelyan.' White was coughing blood on Euboea, cast down by this and anxious to hide it from Lascaris. Eating one night by the sea in the township of Nea Artaki the story of 'Fête Galante' 'erupted' around him. The taverna and a neglected chapel off the Kymi road became the settings of this tale of misplaced devotion.[26]

After Euboea they spent a few strenuous days in Lascaris country in the southern Peloponnese getting about by boat, bus and taxi. Their explorations took them back to the dazzling grandeur of Mistra. 'We found the remains of the Lascaris house and, in the church the ancestor built, his mural, or what the Turks left of it, also the place where his bones are said to lie.' In Athens White began the first draft of 'Fête Galante', grumbling that everything was so unpunctual in Greece, 'one has to put in time somehow, or else go mad'.[27]

More to the point, *A Fringe of Leaves* was about to be published and he was throwing himself into the story to calm his nerves. The book appeared to 'an astonishing reception' and sold well. The whole process was remarkably painless, apart from one or two 'very low' reviews in America and the vulgar jacket of the Viking edition which featured a *soignée* white woman and a couple of African huts. White wondered darkly if this showed the influence of Viking's new editor, Mrs Onassis, and warned Alan Williams, 'JACKIE . . . could well be your downfall.'[28]

Rehearsals for *Sarsaparilla* began a few days after the travellers returned to Sydney in October, but Sharman made White wait a fortnight before letting him into a rehearsal. He marked time unpacking, cooking and writing letters. 'Lots of awfulness in Australia,' he told his niece Alexandra Dawson, 'but at least the air is pure after the stuff we have been breathing.'[29]

He found all his faith in Sharman justified once he saw the play. They loved the same kind of theatre, a place of myth and magic with a dash of vaudeville. But Sharman's eye was cooler than White's: the failings that drove White to despair, Sharman accepted with resignation, even a grim kind of joy. He relieved White's plays of their weight of rage. The star of *Sarsaparilla* was Kate Fitzpatrick. She was very beautiful, quixotic, witty, passionate and shrewd. White had admired her from a distance, but after seeing her as Nola Boyle she became one of his passions, an actress in the line that stretched back beyond Ambrosine Phillpotts to the stars he chased as a stagestruck schoolboy. Kate and Jim were the core of the little band that was beginning to gather round him.

John Tasker was in the crowd on opening night, for he was reviewing *Sarsaparilla* for a theatre magazine. He wrote: 'Welcome back to the theatre Patrick White.' There were critics – I was one of them – who wished Roy Child the boy novelist wouldn't go on and on about life and love. And White thought the man from the *National Times* wrote 'a stinker, accusing me of pinching from Tennessee Williams what I got from my mother before T.W. began to think. "At Rosedale when I was a girl . . ."'[30] But the overwhelming response of critics and the crowds to the revival was pleasure.

In triumph White suffered amnesia. He spoke of *Sarsaparilla* being 'accepted at last' because of Jim Sharman and very good casting. 'We are doing so well we could move to another theatre if there was one but there isn't . . . the main thing is that it has been proved that the play can entertain a large number of people.'[31] But *Sarsaparilla* had done just that in Adelaide and Melbourne in the 1960s. Now Sydney was accepting the play and White was enjoying his first commercial success in the theatre in his home town. Those afternoon newspapers that had once ridiculed the plays were now silenced. White was fiercely proud of the full houses.

He had heard the enthusiastic foyer talk of Sydney society on opening night, and suspected they were watching *Sarsaparilla* through a veil of nostalgia. He said to Sharman, 'I think I might write one for them next time.' Within a few days he was at work on *Big Toys*. The germ of the play had been in his mind for some time, but now he had found an enthusiastic public, actors he wanted to write for and a director he could trust, 'It came pouring out – a rather black comedy.' At the centre of the play stands a figure rather like Jack Mundey the hero of the Green Bans, and the plot grows out of attempts to seduce such a man into joining the corrupt society around him. White finished a first draft during the *Sarsaparilla* run, and the final version was finished by Christmas Eve. Sharman declared it his best and the actors from the

Sarsaparilla cast for whom it was written were enthusiastic. 'We have everything but the right theatre,' White told Charles Osborne. 'I feel this must offer itself as everything else has happened miraculously so far.'[32]

One terrible event cut through the euphoria of these weeks. In late November Sid Nolan rang in the middle of the night to say that Cynthia had committed suicide. Stunned by the news, and intimidated by the long-distance call, White grasped little of what he was hearing. 'What do you know? How did she do it?' he asked Charles Osborne a few days later. 'Cynthia told us things from time to time, but one could never be sure if some of it might be fantasy; she was so distraught half the time, and suffering physically. It makes my relationship with Sidney very difficult. There has always been a lot in him that I felt I didn't know about. In spite of appearances, I don't find him a *candid* character. So, please, if you can throw any light on this awful business, let us know.'[33]

She had booked into a tourist hotel behind Piccadilly Circus, and from there sent a telegram to Putney: 'Off to the Orkneys in small stages. Love Cynthia.' Some hours later she took an overdose of barbiturates and her body was discovered next morning. Two police appeared at the house to give Nolan the news. He packed a few belongings and left. That night he opened another bottle of her barbiturates, swallowed a handful but recovered. At some time in those days he rang Martin Road.

White wrote in the *Australian*, 'Her death has been a shattering break in continuity for those who loved and appreciated this remarkable but in many ways complicated woman. Because, let's face it, Cynthia was difficult. She would have been less exhilarating, less special, if she had not questioned our values, put us to the test. Although capable of happiness in its most limpid forms, deeper down she was a tormented creature . . . Most memorable of all recollections are those of the resplendent English summer of 1976, the last summer of Cynthia's life. It was almost too perfect: happy meetings, simple meals . . . I shall remember her in the shimmer of her Putney garden beside the river, amongst the magnolias, the hummocks of pinks and tussocks of cornflowers, the Persian roses with their spiny canes, the perfumed cabbage-roses forgotten except by those who remember what is out of season and who are obsessed by roses. Sitting in a dappling of light and elm-leaves, talking and laughing, the two French bulldogs in attendance, is how I shall remember Cynthia, her personal colours breaking through the play of light and leaves . . . I know that my own life and work have been enriched since my path was crossed by this king-fisher of the spirit who suddenly left us while still ashimmer.'[34]

He said nothing to Nolan of his darker worries, nor did he

betray any shift in his affection as he came to realise that Cynthia was the link that had sustained his friendship with the painter. His letters were friendly, and when Nolan saw him in Sydney White seemed affectionate and concerned, but within eighteen months of her death White was complaining to Dutton that Sid was 'on with all the wrong people' and six months further down the track, when Cape was looking for a designer for the jacket of *The Twyborn Affair*, White told Maschler, 'Nolan would not be at all right, anyway, we are no longer in touch.'[35]

The characters of *The Twyborn Affair* were working so hard in White's head after Christmas that he found himself out of bed one morning wandering the house at 4am. He cleared a patch on his desk, and began writing in the New Year of 1977. The foolscap pages filled swiftly though his routine was often interrupted in the next three months by the last, sad efforts to film *Voss*. 'I'm relieved to find my suddenly chaotic life rather goes with the climate of the novel,' he told Juliet O'Hea. 'Otherwise it would be sunk.'[36]

Ken Russell never appeared in Australia. After hanging on for a time he confessed to John McGrath that it was a long way to Australia, and he hated planes.[37] With Russell out of the picture, White's choice fell on the great American director Joseph Losey who, it turned out, had admired *Voss* when it was first published and even made rough notes at the time on how it might be filmed. Harry Miller persuaded him to come out to Australia for a brief visit in 1974. Losey had said then that he would be ready to film the following summer. Harold Pinter declined to write the script, and Losey turned to David Mercer.

White's view of Harry Miller had soured over the years. He watched with amused scorn as Miller charmed his way into the heart of the grazing class. They were neighbours: Miller had bought an immense house in Martin Road and was seen hacking round Centennial Park. White said, 'Harry bullshits too much trying to make people think he's a millionaire.'[38] Harry had yet to raise the cash for *Voss*. There was no money to film in 1975. On their last trip to Europe, White flew from London to Paris to spend several days with Losey and Mercer. At this point the director was about to begin filming Pinter's adaptation of Proust, but a message came to White in Athens to say that these plans had fallen through and Losey was ready to film *Voss* as soon as Harry Miller raised $2.6 million.

The director and David Mercer arrived with a German production crew to look around in January 1977, a few weeks after White began to write *Twyborn*. White's patience with Harry was now almost exhausted, especially as Sharman seemed to raise $400,000 for *Prowler* without much fuss. There was a dinner at 'the Miller villa' in late January for White, Losey, Lascaris and Mercer, plus various Australians now attached to the *Voss* project. 'Terrible,' White called the night in a letter to Ronald Waters, 'in the ox-blood dining room with suits of armour from *Conduct Unbecoming* and family portraits from the auction rooms. Everybody got a bit drunk, I shouted a little.' This did not do his own performance justice: White *raged* at Miller about the money. Losey described the outburst as the most remarkable thing he had ever seen. By the time they left to walk home, White and Lascaris were both very drunk. Lascaris fell in the street and White staggered on. 'It is now only up to the frightful Miller to raise his part of the money,' he told Waters. 'One always heard about his rich friends. But where are they now?'[39]

White only partly grasped the difficulties of filming *Voss*. Losey had one of the great names in contemporary cinema, but everything he made after *The Go-Between* lost money. By 1977 he was almost unbankable. He was also very frail, so frail that he had asked Mercer to keep the desert scenes to a minimum. After a couple of days out in Central Australia looking at locations, Losey collapsed and was brought back to a Sydney hospital, where it was said he was suffering from viral pneumonia. Whether he had the stamina to make *Voss* was doubtful, and whether his scriptwriter would survive the film was also uncertain. Sydney put him back on the bottle. 'David Mercer lapsed into a kind of alcoholic melancholy while here,' White told Waters. 'He started ringing ex-wives on the other side of the world, who proceeded to heap shit on him. He came here to a couple of meals. We get on very well together.'[40] Mercer was drinking so heavily that after one bout in Sydney the crew had to heave him into a bath to rehydrate his collapsed body.

Everything came to hinge on Miller persuading the Australian Film Commission to invest $500,000. So much public money had never been put into a film in Australia before. Things were made very difficult by Losey insisting on having his own team, and the local film unions were hostile to the notion of so much public money going to fund an American director, German co-producer, British scriptwriter, and the German actor Maximilian Schell who was to play the explorer. The second of Miller's problems was thornier still: the commissioners did not trust him with the cash. This Miller says is rubbish, and that the obstacle was the jealousy of local film directors. Both sides agree on the grim conclusion: the Film Commission refused the money for *Voss* in late March.

White was deeply disappointed but spoke as if this were fate, or perhaps Leichhardt's revenge, and that *Voss* was not meant to be filmed. Losey went home and made *Don Giovanni*, but a few years later he was still saying he hoped to make *Voss* 'using David

Mercer's brilliant scenario'. Losey died in 1984. The collapse of *Voss* was the end of White's connection with Miller. To Waters he reported, 'Harry Bull, every time he sees me in the park, spurs his horse into a trot till he is out of danger.'[41] Miller hung on to the rights for a couple of years, but after his ticket business went bust (and he went to jail) Miller sold the *Voss* rights and they came ultimately into the hands of Sid Nolan. White still had his veto.

While the film team was in Australia, White had buried his anxieties in work, and the Riviera section of *Twyborn* was finished in three months. Most of this opening section of the book takes place just before the First World War. 'After that there is a return to Australia, and a jump in time to the Twenties,' he explained to Beatson. 'This coming week I am going down to the Monaro to have another look at it, as the second part of the novel takes place down there. I shall be flying to Canberra unfortunately. It will be the first visit to that distasteful non-city for what must be nearly thirty years. I shan't be there long, though. I shall be staying with David Campbell the poet outside Queanbeyan, and he will drive me through the country I want to see, particularly the station where I worked in my youth.'[42]

With Campbell at his side, White made himself known at Bolaro. The house had changed since he was a jackeroo. In the prosperous 1930s the Osbornes smartened it up with Venetian windows and concrete columns, built another storey and decorated rooms in the Tudor style. White used these mock-Tudor interiors for the Lushingtons' house at Bogong, but the shape of the homestead in *Twyborn* is as White knew Bolaro under its red, rambling corrugated-iron roof:

> As often happens in the approach to an Australian country house, it was difficult to decide where to breach the Lushington homestead. There were verandas, porches, lights, snatches of piano music, whingeing dogs, skittering cats, archways armed with rose-thorns, a drift of kitchen smells, but never any real indication of how to enter. Australian country architecture is in some sense a material extension of the contradictory beings who have evolved its elaborate informality, as well as a warning to those who do not belong inside the labyrinth.[43]

By a clump of sycamores in the garden, White found a graveyard built since his time. A plain iron gate in a drystone wall opened on to a little plot where Steenie Osborne and his wife Leura ('A Gracious Woman Retaineth Honour,' *Proverbs* 11:16) were buried beside their grandchild Stephen Shawn Osborne, 'Died 28 June 1940, aged three months.' White gave Bogong such a graveyard, and buried, behind its elaborately designed iron gate – 'a rich folly if ever there was one' – the offspring of Marcia Lushington by her husband and lovers. The first of the Lushington children, born on White's birthday in 1912, survives only a few months until Lascaris's birthday in August.[44]

The weather was freezing and White caught a cold that dogged him most of the winter, but he was pleased with the second trip, and on his return to Sydney he wrote to Alan Williams, 'I got what I wanted – a charge for that section of my novel which is set in the Monaro . . . It was always forbidding – now it is full of ghosts and vengeance. The cottage where I lived was deserted, unlocked and beginning to collapse. The double-seated dunny, where fowls used to roost and fall down the holes, has already done so.'[45]

White had little but hostility for the Monaro as he lay in bed in Ebury Street writing *Happy Valley*. Now he could also admit the austere beauty of the landscape and its subtleties of detail,

> a combing of cloud, a hare starting up from its nest in the tussock, a flotilla of geese rounding a bend in the river.

Bolaro became Bogong – bogongs are moths that swarm in the High Country in early summer – and he modelled the men and women of Bogong closely on those he had known as a jackeroo. His affection and respect for Steenie Osborne is clear in the grazier Greg Lushington, pear-shaped and fatherly, who warns Eddie Twyborn, as Dick had warned his son, that a jackeroo's life was 'not all violets'. Mrs Tyrell is an unflinching portrait of the old hag Sally Venables, who baked shoulders of mutton and laid out the dead. Into Prowse he put the randiness of the jackeroo Norris King, who went dancing every Saturday night in Cooma; the misery of the overseer George Irvine, whose wife and child had left him; and the golden-red beauty of Frank Loder, after whom he had lusted at Barwon Vale.[46]

He wanted more detail, and wrote to Betty Withycombe asking to see the letters he had written from Bolaro in 1930. In a frank gesture of trust by which, perhaps, she hoped to regain her cousin's affection, Betty Withycombe sent him all four hundred or so letters she had had from him in the thirty years of their friendship. She had planned to leave them to the Bodleian Library, and now she assumed White would store them together with her letters to him. She did not know these had been burnt in the pit at Dogwoods. When the boxes of his letters arrived, White stacked them on a chair in the dining room, afraid they would be too painful to open. At some point he mustered the courage to read the Bolaro letters, and wrote to Betty Withycombe to say they were neither as detailed nor as interesting as he had hoped. Betty's boxes stayed in that corner of the dining room for some years. White then destroyed them all.[47]

That winter Lascaris was recovering from a very painful attack of shingles, then his back gave way and he found himself once again in the old corset he had worn after first wrecking his back at Castle Hill. Acupuncture brought him relief. White, meanwhile, had chills that kept him in bed for a fortnight complaining but working, so that the Monaro section of the novel was drafted by the time *Big Toys* opened at the Parade Theatre in October.

The critics were not kind. *Big Toys* has the distinction of pioneering a genre – the corruption play – but Ritchie Bosanquet QC, his wife Mag and the trade union man Terry Legge seemed naïve figures to those who knew something of the real players in that corrupt city. White had questioned Jim McClelland very closely about the habits of the Sydney Bar as he was writing the play, but McClelland found the result false, and wondered ruefully if he were to blame. White took heart from seeing the little Parade Theatre full for most of the run, and the show toured to Melbourne and Canberra. He told Peggy Garland, 'I'm glad I've had my say about hypocritical, plutocratic, contemporary Sydney society. I've also been able to say what I think about uranium and atomic weapons. Now of course I'm the most awful Commo to many people.'[48]

Not that he cared. He had a new family now of actors, writers, designers, photographers, 'young enough to be my children and whom I consider as such . . . I think these children are what keeps me going and the wonderful part is they understand me much better than most of my contemporaries.'[49] He adored cool Jim, *his* director, and there were none of the exhausting tantrums his passion for Tasker had inspired. There were Luciana Arrighi, Kate Fitzpatrick, the young writer Jim Waites, Willy (William) Young (Yang) who took the truest photographs of White in these years, and the designer Brian Thomson who conceived perhaps the most memorable moment in *Big Toys* when the opulent backdrop of Sydney at dusk opens on to a void and a hot Westerly is heard blowing across the city.

After an early preview of the show, the actors and crew handed him a pillowslip marked 'Paddy' from which, very puzzled, he drew a water pistol, a mouth organ and a copy of *Robinson Crusoe*. Each little toy had made him more suspicious. Then he pulled out the mechanical mouse, and laughed and wept with joy. These were the gifts this spoilt boy had asked for in 1917. He had shown his letter 'to Santa' to Brian Thomson and the designer had memorised the list. Yang took snaps of White with the mouse in his hand. 'After that preview we all had supper together *en famille*, and last week before Brian T. flew back to London I gave a dinner for him and the pals in a private room at Le Café, the in-place, with the cast coming on after the performance. Senile delights, no doubt, but none the less delightful. I hope to continue. Next year they are going to revive a *Cheery Soul*, Jim directing.'[50]

White drafted the London section of *The Twyborn Affair* in the months between *Big Toys* and the filming of *The Night the Prowler*. This was the first time he had returned in his writing to London since the opaque pages of *The Living and the Dead* nearly forty years before. His sometimes wavering love of that city had been revived in full during his last visit. 'London is still my favourite place on earth,' he told Alan Williams. White could not join those radical republicans who, in the aftermath of Whitlam's sacking, called for a complete breach with Britain. 'I am not afraid to confess that I am sentimental to some extent,' he told a crowd at a Brisbane political rally this year. 'I value my British ties, especially to London, the great cultural centre of the world, an immense stimulus to creative art, as most Australian artists who have lived there will tell you.'[51] Old affections made him a rather muddled politician, but they were the well from which the artist drew.

This section of *Twyborn* charts the rise of the former jackeroo Mrs Eadith Trist from a West End flower shop to her brothel in Beckwith Street in the early years of the war. The spirit of Sister Teresa hovers over the brothel where Eadith Trist rules her 'vernal nuns' like a mother superior, expecting them to obey her almost 'conventual rule'. The influence on White of George Moore's double-decker about the worldly nun was unexhausted. Even in the early 1980s, he was advising Dutton to publish: 'I still think a publisher would be rewarded if he re-issued *Evelyn Innes* and *Sister Teresa* considering how fashionable opera has become in Australia, and the fascination of the Catholic Church.' White had never been inside a brothel like Trist's, but he knew the sexual pulse of wartime London, and had talked to the whores on the beat at Victoria Station and along Piccadilly as he looked for sex in the blackout.[52]

Down by the river, with the evening light turning from 'dove to violet', White placed the apotheosis of all the park-bench scenes in his novels. Why does he have strangers and lovers meeting on park benches? 'Because it happens.' Mrs Trist finds herself sitting side by side with her ancient mother Eadie outside a London church. What follows is unprecedented in White's writing: the entire acceptance by a mother of her child. Eadie scribbles a message on the flyleaf of her prayerbook: 'Are you my son Eddie?' Mrs Trist cannot trust herself to speak, so seizes the pencil and writes: 'No, but I am your daughter Edith.'

The two women continued sitting together in the gathering shadow.
    Presently Eadie said, 'I am so glad. I've always wanted a daughter.'[53]

Those who imagined White would settle down after the sacking and put politics behind him, were disappointed. He quit the Order of Australia. 'All such honours are bribes, and all honours are political,' he told Dutton. 'Everything is political unless you plump for indifference. I was indifferent until Whitlam appeared on the scene and injected life into Australia. But the last election showed that that was illusion. We shall never be anything of a nation because we are too bloody greedy and too bloody stupid. Thinking as I do, I shall get on with my dreadful fate of being an Australian, but at least without the irrelevant baubles.'[54]

He spoke to a crowd of 15,000 at a rally for constitutional change on the first anniversary of Whitlam's sacking, and when the Queen toured the country again a few months later, in March 1977, he spoke at meetings in Brisbane and Sydney, urging Australians to keep their heads in the presence of this 'myth made flesh, wearing a democratic smile'. Kate Fitzpatrick ate on the royal yacht as he had fourteen years before, and this caused a brief and painful hiatus in their friendship.[55]

White was culling out those of his friends who welcomed the Fraser government. 'Fortunately, most of our real friends think the same way as we do politically.' This sorting along political lines meant the disappearance of the Eastern Suburbs friends who had tinkled and gossiped happily at Martin Road for years. In some respects this upheaval in the White crowd followed an old pattern: in the Sharman years, as in Tasker's time, old friends were forced to make way for a new set of theatricals. But this time the process was not marked by the great quarrels of the 1960s. Margery Williams had fought White all the way on Labor and now he let their long correspondence peter out. Barry Humphries was dropped because he was now 'on with all the wrong people'. Mollie McKie, with whom he had been in easy contact since RAF Intelligence days in Alexandria, complained in 1973 of Whitlam's dictator government. White's friendship for her fizzled into nothing over the next two years. One night in a Bondi restaurant he complained to two old academic friends about their devotion to Eastern Suburbs ladies: 'I hate them,' he said. 'I want to bring them down.' The four men had shared a cab to Bondi but two cabs left the restaurant. For them it was 'like a death'. More patient friends like James Fairfax stepped aside, hoping White would 'settle down over this Whitlam thing'.[56]

He had begun to claim the prerogative of knowing who would be at the tables to which he was invited. 'Can you come to dinner on Thursday week?' Sue Du Val asked him one night. They were face to face over Hugh Paget's table during a British Council bash.

'Who's coming?'

'What does that matter?'

'Oh, you old cunt,' he snapped. They did not speak again.[57]

The Martin Road dinner party, a ritual honoured and often feared in Sydney, was now almost a thing of the past. 'We've more or less given up having people to dinner,' White told Tom Maschler. 'Unless it's four of us in the kitchen. That I can still enjoy . . . times have changed and there are no longer the people we feel we *ought* to ask.'[58]

White had finished the first draft of *The Twyborn Affair* in late October, when the Prime Minister Malcolm Fraser called fresh elections. At first the prospect filled White with dread, but then he began to feel that Whitlam had a chance of regaining office. 'Does it strike you how *common* the Liberal politicians sound on the radio?' he asked Manning Clark. 'Or perhaps it's the absence of credibility which seems to make them sound like that.' But White's hopes were entirely misplaced, and Fraser won a second handsome victory. White said, 'The fascist sheep got what they wanted; let them now reap the results.'[59]

Whitlam left politics. White flew down to a 'testimonial shivoo' in Canberra to make a last public declaration of faith in this 'great man' who had so often disappointed him. John Kerr was also leaving politics. He had cut a sad figure at Yarralumla in the two years after the sacking, and was off to be Ambassador to UNESCO. White's valediction for the Governor-General was private and bitter: 'One can only hope that guzzling pig will blow up on all the good things he will eat and drink in Paris . . . But think of what *we* shall have to shell out in the meantime.'[60]

The undertow of this rage and exasperation was almost miraculously absent from *The Twyborn Affair*. White was as angry as ever about public life in the 'Land of High Farce – and sheep shit', but he was able to vent his anger now on the podium, and return, composed, to his work. 'So much that is depressing in recent weeks,' he remarked to Dutton. 'I don't know what I'd do if I hadn't my novel to hand, like a piece of knitting.'[61]

They shot *The Night the Prowler* in seven weeks. White did not haunt the set, though he appeared a few times at the house in Vaucluse which Luciana Arrighi had turned into the Bannisters' place on Centennial Park. He stood at the barricades in the street, occasionally smiling at one of his own lines, and the locals brought him copies of his books to autograph. He told Sharman he could not imagine anyone working in the chaos of a film set.

The story of *The Prowler* grew from an odd incident in Martin Road when an intruder was found in bed with a most respectable young woman. Was this rape as claimed, White wondered, or an interrupted assignation? Out of this mystery came another of his tales of the young breaking out of their cocoons. Felicity Bannister sheds her fiancé and begins to take revenge on the local bourgeoisie. She finds wisdom of a kind among derelicts and the riff-raff of the park. Sharman had cast Kerry Walker to play Felicity. She was too old, twenty-nine, but seemed absolutely right. White met her for the first time at Le Café, and within minutes she had dropped a wine glass into his lap and found herself mopping his crotch. He liked her at once. 'Automatically! Edith Evans once said, "I was never pretty but larky, and larky's what counts in the theatre." Kerry is very larky. She is someone I always felt I could write for.'[62] Of all the Sharman theatricals 'Kero' grew closest to him in the years ahead. She was his protégée, a superb deadpan clown offstage and on, the funniest gossip in his life; a daughter to worry over, help out, quarrel with and take pride in as her career grew. She broke many of his rules, but she was adored.

Towards the end of *Prowler*, Felicity finds an old man dying in a ruined house. He was as White feared and dreamed he would himself be one day, stripped entirely bare. In dressing-room chat, White raised the idea of playing the role himself.

(*Some rags, bundles of sacking, a filthy old mattress, beside it a tea-chest on which stand a dusty bottle and set of teeth. Signs of aged flesh on the mattress – that of an old man.*)
FELICITY (*fascinated by figure on mattress*). What are you doing here?
OLD MAN (*moving his head like a tortoise against the mattress*). Living . . . or't anyrate, this is where I what they call live . . . I left off clothes some time back. Less trouble without. If you want to scratch yerself, for instance. Or pee. Or if somebody comes to the door, they go away . . . I can honestly say I never believed in or expected anything of anyone. I never loved, not even meself – which is more than can be said of most people. I'm nothing. And nothing is a noble faith.[63]

The idea of White doing the part was not taken seriously, and it was performed by an old man who had a heart attack during the filming. He checked himself out of hospital to finish the scene.

As a shield against the nervous hopes raised by the film, White began to write another screenplay called 'Monkey Puzzle'. Lately, there had been several efforts, all of them rebuffed, to have him tape archival interviews to be locked away until his death. In 'Monkey Puzzle' a writer called Will Garlick allows Mrs Henrietta Birdsell to tape his confessions. Birdsell's dim-witted regard for the Great Writer is finally routed, and Garlick is left in peace. White had a first draft of 'Monkey Puzzle' on paper in a couple of weeks. 'I'm so glad I've dropped onto this medium for my old age,' he told Manning Clark. 'So much easier on the lungs than grinding away for a couple of years at a novel.' A final draft was ready for Sharman in December. At first he assured White he liked it, but later he changed his mind: 'He says the final message is "So What?" which is, as I see it, the message today.'[64]

The rough cut of *The Night the Prowler* ran for two hours, and Sharman settled down after Christmas to cut another thirty minutes. 'We're so sick of lumbering films in which the brilliant director can't bear to sacrifice 1 cm. of his genius,' White told Ronald Waters. 'He wants this one to be dynamite all the way.' White saw another cut on 25 January, and it promised a 'terrifically good' result. He warned Peter Beatson that *Prowler* was not what people expected of an Australian film: 'The French won't look at it because there isn't a kangaroo or an Aborigine in sight, but it pleases me aesthetically, and it has the kind of shocks to which Australians at least should be subjected.'[65] Though still unfinished, *Prowler* was chosen to open the Sydney Film Festival in June 1978.

The New Year brought a blow: the Old Tote, sliding towards bankruptcy, postponed the revival of *A Cheery Soul*. Sharman resigned and White withdrew the play. 'I shall go where Sharman goes.' They decided to organise a theatre company of their own. 'I should be younger for the fights which have to be fought,' he told Peggy Garland. Yet for a man in his sixty-seventh year he was extraordinarily alive, and the thought of those battles ahead cheered him considerably. While Sharman was still cutting the film, White began the second draft of *The Twyborn Affair*. He was unusually optimistic: 'I think the novel . . . will be good, though no doubt it will horrify a lot of people, and I shall be ostracised for the rest of my life.'[66]

Homosexuals had appeared in many of his books but the closer they came to command the action the more heavily he disguised them. In *Twyborn* a homosexual was to stand centre stage in clear sight for the first time. White was taking the novel into new yet intimately familiar territory.

He was, at the same time, drawing closer than he ever had to a source of his genius. 'My homosexuality', he once told Jim McClelland, 'gives me all the insights that make me a great writer.'[67] White was one of those homosexuals who see themselves as part woman and part man: not so much a woman as to be effeminate, but enough to understand and share feminine virtues. He admired in others signs of his own ambivalence: men of unexpected gentleness, and women with masculine strength. 'True friendship,' remarked Eadith Trist, 'if there is anything wholly true – certainly in friendship – comes, I'd say, from the woman in a man and the man in a woman.'[68] Since he was a young man White had seen this ambivalence as a source of artistic strength, for he believed it gave him such insight into the feminine that he could *become* both man and woman as he wrote. 'I recognised the freedom being conferred on me to range through every variation of the human mind, to play so many roles in so many contradictory envelopes of flesh.'[69]

White always argued that he was driven by intuition and not by intellect – he made this point constantly over the years to counter a brand of literary analysis that was brought to bear on his work – and for him intuition was a powerful feminine virtue. The intuitive Patrick White was the feminine Patrick White: sexuality was not only a source of insight but one of the forces that drove him to write.

Yet he had remained reluctant for so long to write candidly about homosexuals. Friends, publishers and agents had not encouraged him in the past to challenge that native reluctance. Juliet O'Hea insisted 'such' books were not published until after the release of *Lady Chatterley*.[70] That was not true then and irrelevant now, for Lawrence's novel had been on sale in England and Australia for over a decade. The revolution had happened. Yet White held back.

In his writing as in his life, White worried that the label 'homosexual' would seem to isolate men and their affections in some territory outside the ordinary experience of the human race. The devotion of Harry Robarts to the explorer Voss needs no particular name, for it is love expressed in the most admirable way White knew, through service and sacrifice. After *Voss* White began to identify a few homosexuals more clearly in his novels. Alf Dubbo looks back with gratitude to his initiation by the Rev. Timothy Calderon. The elegant Maurice Caldicott in *The Vivisector* is gently mocked for his furtive affections. Cecil Cutbush, the masturbating grocer at the Gash, is excoriated for the sin of seeing his sexuality as a badge of brotherhood. Cutbush was not only a sad old fool, but one of those men who imagine homosexuals everywhere. He makes the mistake of thinking Hurtle Duffield is queer:

> 'Mr Duffield –' he selected the name, and held it up – 'I have never had an opportunity to tell you how much it has meant to us – to US – our comparatively small, but no less *avid* minority – to have you living in our midst.' His nostrils enjoyed it the more for smelling slightly off. 'Our confraternity may be under-privileged, and despised by some, but no one can deny that we appreciate the Higher Things. To walk past your home is, for us, a deeply moving experience. Flint Street has become a place of pilgrimage.'

> 'I suppose I'm what people would call a coward.' The grocer didn't attempt to hide the drops which were beginning to ooze. 'I've often thought Judas must have been of a homo-sex-ual

persuasion.' Poor bugger didn't seem to know the thing had caught on.[71]

Early in the 1970s Ingmar Björkstén had asked White why he had not written a novel about a homosexual. 'If I had wanted to . . . I should have written it,' he replied. 'But that is a theme which easily becomes sentimental and/or hysterical. It is, anyway, rather worn.' These literary misgivings were of long standing and it seemed no writer had earned White's admiration for tackling the subject head on. He had taken a great dislike to Genet, while admitting there were 'some glittering jewels in *Notre Dame des Fleurs* lurking amongst the shit'. James Baldwin exasperated him: 'If he had been a white queen shrieking instead of a black, the world would have shouted back, "Enough!" long ago.' Nor, for rather different reasons, could White share the American taste for Walt Whitman. 'Even his mixed-up brand of homosexuality is irritating; one longs to hear of him having an honest-to-God root with one of his bus-drivers instead of sitting there fumbling with the tickets.'[72]

On his first trip back to the Monaro in 1975, White took a copy of David Malouf's new novel *Johnno*, which he discovered was 'one of the best books I've read by an Australian'. He met Malouf soon afterwards and complimented him on finding the 'only way' to write a book about the love of two men for one another. Malouf took this to mean that he had the emotions right in *Johnno* but saved everyone from the difficulties: the special pleading of homosexuality and the messy business of writing about sex between men. Malouf saw in White a genuine æsthetic reluctance to tackle the theme.[73]

White still refused to commit himself to the campaign for homosexual law reform, despite a new spirit of public candour in Australia. This baffled those who admired his pugnacious stand against Kerr, Fraser and uranium mining. But White still found it ludicrous to think of his sexuality as a cause: 'I've marched in the streets, but only to get myself a man.' He might have remained untouched by the times and the changes that had come to his city, but for being part of his new theatrical family. Sexuality was a matter-of-fact affair in that crowd, and they were not bothered by White's innermost fear that to be seen as homosexual might leave them locked in some stifling coterie. White spoke often at this time of his fear of being ostracised – many of his letters had this flourish – but he knew he would not be ostracised by the Sharman crowd nor, perhaps, by their generation. Between Sharman and White there was a running dialogue about what they should be doing, should be thinking, should be reading. Sharman said one day, 'I am surprised you haven't dealt more openly with homosexuality in your writing.' White replied that this was one of the clichés of fiction like the Catholic childhood. But Sharman remembers him saying this with a half-smile.[74] Looking back to this exchange, Sharman realised that *Twyborn* was already under way.

The Nobel Prize continued to work its magic. He complained, as ever, that it was ruining his life but he vowed not to let acclaim turn him into a grand old man of literature. 'I hope I am launching out in a fresh direction,' he told Alan Williams as he worked on *Twyborn*. 'But of course there are many who would like to see me locked up in a museum.' Old fears mattered less now. Once he had confessed to Dutton the suspicion that deep within himself was some Elinor Glyn waiting to 'dash off a novelette to shatter the world'.[75] He had always guarded against it.

But the peculiar genius of the man was to turn an idea on its head. Purity, not love and happiness, is the goal of Eudoxia Vatatzes, the jackeroo Eddie Twyborn and the brothel keeper Eadith Trist. Sex is for them an act of kindness, a sacrifice of devotion. Towards the end of her career Mrs Trist is invited to a house party 'in the Ottoline style' in Wiltshire – the hostess has the name Untermeyer in memory of his recently dead Manhattan patron – where the fashionable madam is cornered by a forthright, very shabby member of the aristocracy,

> 'Purity . . .' she snuffled. 'That daisy at any rate is pure.' She pointed with the toe of an abraded brogue at a clump of pink-to-white daisy which had shot up since the lawn-mower razed Ursula's lawn to perfection. 'I'd like to think you were,' she turned abruptly to the bawd. 'In spite of what I hear, my instincts as a cat-lover tell me you may be. Too pure for your own good.'
>
> Eadith was aghast. 'I've never aspired to virtue. As for purity – truth – I've still to make up my mind what they amount to. But hope I may. Eventually.'
>
> 'Good for you.'[76]

The quest for purity left White free to explore without self-pity or special pleading the difficulties of his life as a homosexual: the long guilt of childhood, the innocent blunders of his family, the difficulties of self-acceptance, his determination to 'come to terms with his largely irrational nature',[77] the ambivalence that cut him off from the ordinary world of men, his sense of being a walking deception always more convincing to others than himself, and the extraordinary release of his thwarted sensuality found in landscape. Eddie Twyborn, after spending the night in Marcia Lushington's bed, left for the jackeroos' hut at the first sign of light, stumbling down the hill through the increasing green of the false dawn, the light from an outhouse window, and the scented breath of ruminating cows. In his own experience, in whichever sexual role he had been playing, self-searching had never led more than briefly to self-acceptance. He suspected that salvation most likely lay in the natural phenomena surrounding those unable to rise to the spiritual heights of a religious faith: in his present situation the shabby hills, their contours practically breathing as the light embraced them, stars fulfilled by their logical drowsing, the river never so supple as at daybreak, as dappled as the trout it camou-flaged, the whole ambience finally united by the harsh but healing epiphany of cockcrow.[78]

Two months after setting to work on the new draft White wrote to Greene, 'I'm back, peacefully, with *The Twyborn Affair*. Not that it won't be an abrasive novel, which will probably earn me complete ostracism in Australia. But it doesn't drag me as far into schizophrenia as involvement in film and theatre does.' He warned Greene that once this draft was done he would have to type and tinker some months more before the novel was ready. 'So please don't expect it too soon. Probably another year. I can't be driven.'[79]

Sydney holds its Film Festival in one of the great cinemas of the world, a Depression blockbuster in Viennese baroque. As the 1978 festival approached, Sharman was in the papers saying *The Night the Prowler* was, of everything he had ever done, 'the one thing that is most completely satisfying to me'. White had decided to be at the opening. 'I shall have to be there, but only in the shadows.'[80]

He had hoped for dynamite, but in the gaudy foyers of the State theatre after the screening the mood of the crowd was subdued and polite. White was hurt to hear that one or two old friends had slipped out of the theatre rather than face him afterwards. Critics had tough things to say. *Prowler* was called disjointed, inconsistent, condescend-ing and unforgiving. Perhaps two films were at war with one another here: a superb comedy at the Bannisters', and a stumbling search for life's meaning over in the park? In the face of such hostility, White was as resilient as ever: '*The Night the Prowler* got some good reviews on the fringe, but was slain by the Establishment critics. The *SMH* called it a "savage piece of bourgeois-bashing". Of course if the bourgeoisie had been foreign they would have swallowed it without a murmur. It's going to be released before Christmas, probably earlier overseas.'[81]

A few weeks after the festival came the magnificent débâcle of the Paris. Sharman and Rex Cramphorn found a narrow city picture theatre called the Paris to be the home of their new company. White gave $10,000 and declared the Paris Company was the 'only hope for having a living theatre in this provincial city'. The season opened in July with high hopes and great goodwill, but the play was a dud. White told the Moores they had 'got off to a shaky start with Dorothy Hewett's *Pandora's Cross*. The play is certainly rather a muddle, but full of entertainment the way Jim has produced it and the actors have responded. People are going for that reason, but it won't run as long as we hoped. After that Louis Nowra's *Visions*. Then the revival of *A Cheery Soul*.'[82]

But by the time the first show closed the company knew there would be no money to stage *A Cheery Soul*. White still continued to lobby for the theatre. The Australia Council gave $30,000 to Cramphorn's production of *Visions*, but this subsidy was exhausted after a fortnight. 'Nobody is going to the Paris Theatre and it will close at the end of the week,' White wrote to Dutton. 'Dorothy's play was open to criticism, but Louis Nowra's *Visions* is about the most imaginative and wittiest play by an Australian – also very relevant to our national mess though set in Paraguay.'[83] The Paris was an expensive failure, yet the expectations of the city had been raised.

By the time the company dispersed in the last days of August, White had taken solace in *The Twyborn Affair* and was 'bashing away' at the final version. 'I shall probably finish about February unless some dreadful diversion, illness – or even death, holds me up! I always imagine I'm going to drop dead before I finish something I'm working on.'[84] He gave up drinking spirits. A third trip to the Monaro with David Campbell had been planned, but Campbell was dying of lung cancer. White was most distressed, not only by his friend's suffering, but also because he was of a generation which counted death by cancer as somehow a violation of the proper order of dying. He could hardly come to write the word and called it, instead, 'the plague'. Nelly Arrighi, the dogs, now David Campbell. Death by the plague was the death White feared most.

As he typed the final version of the Riviera section, he was haunted by a train dream. 'I met a man carrying a paper bag who said he had a bomb he wanted thrown. I said I would, and threw it from the train when passing the target, though what the target was, the man hadn't actually explained. The following day in the same dream I met the same man who asked whether I would throw a second bomb. Again I said I would, and threw it, the target still unspecified. Nobody in the carriage appeared to notice on either occasion.'[85] Three times that winter he was brought down by flu. The third attack, in September, was vicious and left him feeling very feeble, but he kept on working.

His energy came and went. He told Peggy Garland, 'I have periods of abject despair.'[86]

His friends were checking details: the railings in Battersea, the season for marigolds in England, the newspapers read in the south of France by the English in 1914, the causes of the First and Second World Wars, the colour of Manning Clark's eyes, the dialect of Provence – provided by Patric Juillet, proprietor of Le Café – dates for presentations at court, and the proper form of address for a duke's daughter. He quizzed Maie Casey: 'Her Titles: in the beginning Lady Ursula Forrestier, then Lady Ursula Untermeyer? would she ever be referred to as Lady Untermeyer pure and simple? I'm sure you can give me this info.'[87] She did.

The typescript of *Twyborn* was finished in less than half the six months White thought he would need. When Greene arrived in Australia in November on his annual inspection of Jonathan Cape's outlying subsidiaries, White told him he was about to finish, but it might be some time before he could have it. Greene reminded him gently how much postage might be saved if he could carry the typescript to London. White saw the good sense in this and redoubled his efforts. By the middle of the month, White's hero had walked out into that first night of the Blitz. 'I can remember', he told Manning Clark as he was writing, 'coming out of the Café Royal and seeing the East End on fire.'[88] Twyborn falls in Piccadilly under the rain of bombs that White survived.

Green was given one copy of the typescript to read on the plane back to England. White took a second copy round to Sharman's flat in Bondi. He said, 'I am thinking of dedicating this to you, but I was worried what it would do to your reputation.' Then he laughed, 'But I realised you don't have a reputation.'[89] Sharman read *Twyborn* straight through that night. When he rang Martin Road in the morning, White was a little put out: this was too quick.

Greene battled with the single-spaced sheets of onion-skin paper on the flight home, and telegraphed enthusiastic acceptance from London. Quite deliberately, White delayed sending the New York copy so that London again had a head start. He was not going to put *Twyborn*'s fate into the hands of the New York critics. When Alan Williams eventually read the typescript he wired from New York, 'MOVED AND DAZZLED BY MOST MEMORABLE PROTEAN PROTAGONIST SINCE OVID. HEARTFELT CONGRATS.'[90]

Miss Docker finally had her chance in these wonderful last months of 1978. The Sydney Theatre Company offered Sharman its first production, and as White finished *Twyborn*, *A Cheery Soul* went into rehearsal. Sharman kept White away, for he had decided to abandon the author's finicky directions and do the play on an almost bare set by Brian

Thomson. 'This production won't be the least bit naturalistic,' White told David Moore. 'Nor will it make any concessions to the audience. I'm all for that!'[91] To calm his fears as he waited, White returned to the screenplay of 'Monkey Puzzle', adding a few scenes and reworking the piece in the hope of persuading Barry Humphries to take the role of Will Garlick.

White came to the first preview in January. The fire curtain was down, and on it was painted the cast list like a huge vaudeville poster. When it rose, the actors were dotted about a brilliantly lit stage, bare except for a piano. There was a soft chord. All the inhabitants of Sarsaparilla except Miss Docker turned to face the audience. They stood stock still for the second chord, and on a third Robyn Nevin's Miss Docker turned, her face locked in a silent scream. Sharman heard White gasp. A sign came down: 'A Kitchen at the Custances' and the play began. Afterwards White said to Sharman: 'I haven't been so excited in a theatre since the opening moment of *Oklahoma*.'[92]

A Cheery Soul broke all box-office records at the Drama Theatre of the Opera House. White feigned astonishment at the queues. 'We averaged 85% full during the run. A lot of people hated it of course, and some of the reviews were stinkers, but the proof was in the takings.' Robyn Nevin was electrifying: 'she gives what would be considered a great performance in any part of the world where there is a tradition of theatre'. About half-way through the season he began writing a screenplay for her. 'It's called tentatively "Last Words" because I've always been fascinated by those.'[93] This was another homage to Lizzie Clark, who appears in the guise of Eureka Steel, born on an Australian farm and brought to town as a maid to Mrs Norman (Flo) Masters. Eureka is the real mother to the Masters children and holds the family together when Norman Masters is ruined and sent to jail.

Ruin was an idea that haunted White for years – Jinny Chalmers-Robinson survived the ruin of her husband E.K. (Bags) in *Riders in the Chariot* – but the theme had fresh currency in 1979, for Harry Miller had crashed. A few months after being host to the Prince of Wales at a big bash at the Miller Villa, his computer ticket agency collapsed and he was charged and later convicted of aiding and abetting the fraudulent misappropriation of $700,000. White took grim delight in Harry's fall.

DENZIL (*coldly, toying with a news sheet*). What's 'misappropriation of funds'?
FLO MASTERS (*frowning, huddling slightly*). One forgets you're so precocious, Denzil.
DENZIL. Does it mean he *stole* the money?
FLO MASTERS. I expect it does.[94]

Eureka leaves the family, as Lizzie did, to move to the country and have a still-born child. But in 'Last Words' the old nurse returns for a time to look after the surviving Masters. In a sense, she is all that remains of the family. She dies in the street. Her last words:

> EUREKA (*head moving back and forth against pillowed coat*). Lots of people don't recognise happiness when they see it . . . or if they do . . . they can't face the . . . responsibilities.

White finished the screenplay in May. Sharman was enthusiastic and expected to be able to raise the money, but then *The Night the Prowler* opened. The film was first released in New York where it was shown at midnight in the hope of riding the cult success of *The Rocky Horror Movie*. That gambit failed. Six months later came its general release in Australia, where it was promoted as a horror movie. *Prowler* died first in Melbourne – 'city of sodden rectitude' – and then limped through a few weeks in Sydney. White blamed the petrol strike, torrential rain, and the film festivals keeping away the crowds. '*The Night the Prowler* has been driven into the ground temporarily, but I refuse to lie down. If I had obeyed *Those Who Know* I'd have written no more novels after *The Aunt's Story*, no more plays after *The Ham Funeral*. So it is now with films.'[95] But the fate of the film doomed the commercial hopes of the new screenplays and White's late career as a screenwriter.

Elly Polymeropoulos arrived in Australia for a third visit about the time *Twyborn* was finished, and White was conscious again of how little he had seen of his own country. 'I have been nowhere,' he once remarked to Dutton, 'except comfortably in my own imagination.' Lascaris and his sister spent some weeks in the far north of Queensland, exploring the reef and its hinterland. 'Much of it sounded seductive, and I feel I'd like to go one day. They found the climate like that of Egypt,' he told the Duttons' daughter Teresa. 'And the cockroaches, too, were like the big juicy Egyptian ones.'[96] With the proofs of *Twyborn* corrected, and waiting impatiently for the book to appear, White was seized with the idea of exploring the rim of Australia and then writing a last novel.

'I don't want to follow every bay and cape,' he explained to David Moore, 'but I'd like to get an idea of the shape of the whole from the air, then go over a bit of it by land later on.' Broome, the old pearling town on the coast of Western Australia, seemed the place he most needed to visit. He had no idea how this plan might be carried out until Maie Casey, now very old and living on her estate outside Melbourne, offered to lend him her plane and her pilot. The expedition might still be expensive, for White would pay for fuel and accommodation, but he confessed to Ronald Waters that he had 'raked in a bit of money lately'.[97]

The grit round which the new novel was forming in White's imagination was his irritation at Desmond Digby's refusal to paint. Digby was happy designing sets and costumes for the Australian Opera, where he had become absorbed into the court of Joan Sutherland and Richard Bonynge. White thought this a waste of his old friend's talent. Almost as much a waste were his beautiful illustrations for children's books – except that Digby brought him fascinating gossip about the people who wrote books for children. They seemed a very odd lot. The half-formed plot of White's new novel involved a man married to a children's writer who is fed up with the phoney world of children's writing. Husband and wife decide they will fly around Australia and see the reality of their country, then descend on Mount Wilson to disrupt a crowd of children's writers holding a seminar. White saw the book in terms of big circles and small circles: the country and the writers.[98]

He had always refused invitations to address literary seminars. Geoffrey Dutton's passion for them was one of those aspects of his friend's life he tolerated without ever understanding. As White was mulling over these ideas for the new novel, he was offered life membership of the Association for the Study of Australian Literature. He refused. 'Australia seems to be suffering from a sickness called seminar,' he told ASAL. 'Surely what the writer needs is orthography, grammar, and syntax, which he learns at school; after that he must read and write, read and write, and forgetting all about being a writer, live to perfect his art . . . True writers emerge of their own impetus; to encourage those who haven't got much to contribute, you are prolonging false hopes and helping destroy the forests of the world. This must appear a churlish reply to your kind letter with its offer of an honour and literary conviviality! But it's what I believe, and much as I enjoy conviviality, I suspect that more literature plops from the solitary bottle, than out of the convivial flagon.'[99]

The circumnavigation novel faced an immediate hurdle. A strike at the Caltex oil refinery in Sydney had cut off the supply of aviation fuel. This was the same strike White blamed for keeping crowds away from The Night the Prowler. Through June and July he kept hoping fuel might become available for his 'frivolous private gallivanting'.[100] But, as he waited, his enthusiasm for the new project began to fade. The fate of The Prowler rather depressed him. He began to worry his lungs might not be up to such a journey; that it would cost too much; that Maie Casey was too ill; that her pilot was unenthusiastic. By the time fuel was flowing again in August White had, without warning, turned his mind in another direction. 'I have started doodling with not so much an autobiography as a self-portrait,' he told the Duttons. 'As so many others are anxious to put in the warts, at least I can try to show where I think the real ones are.'[101]

The appearance of *The Twyborn Affair* in November 1979 brought none of the difficulties White had foretold. He was not ostracised. The book was not burnt in the streets. The worst he could claim were 'pretty glazed looks here and there from neighbours and strangers'.[102] As the year drew to its end, a tide of praise was flowing towards him – the puzzlement of the Americans still lay some months ahead, for Viking did not publish until March 1980. *Twyborn* appeared on the short list of the Booker Prize, but White removed it in order, he said, to give younger writers a chance – and he was worried the women among the judges might not favour him. Critics in London and Australia named it their book of the year. At home it was a bestseller, beaten only at the cash register by the latest Frederick Forsyth. White remarked to Ronald Waters with deep satisfaction, 'Strange goings-on indeed.'[103]

TWENTY-EIGHT

Patrick White Writes His Own Life

IN EARLY OCTOBER, as he was sketching the self-portrait, White flew to Belltrees for the weekend. Michael White was waiting with a car at Scone's little airport and the two cousins took the road that cuts along the river to Gundy. They had not seen one another since their brief conversation in Martin Place fifteen years before, and it was another fifteen years before that since Patrick had driven into Belltrees along the shallow river that Voss and Hurtle Duffield and Elizabeth Hunter followed in their journeys to Rhine Towers and Mumbelong and Kudjeri. Past Gundy they climbed to the lip of the valley and drove down to the house. Belltrees had come to be regarded as one of the great 'historic' homesteads but the house was hardly older than the man arriving that afternoon. Judy White was waiting for them on the veranda, and they went in for tea.

Michael White had been running Belltrees since his father's death in 1964. He was a very different man from the autocratic Alf: thoughtful, considerate and without side. The White blaze of blue in his eyes was muted, but he had the face of his grandfather the collector Henry. Michael White's business was cattle. He was a judge of bulls and bred at Belltrees a line of marbled beef for Tokyo restaurants. Prosperous as the place remained, it was neither as big nor as rich as it had been in his father's time. He had only a handful of men working there now. Yet life was still lived at Belltrees on a considerable scale: polo was the preoccupation of the place, touring royalty stayed the night. The Whites had declared their acres a wildlife sanctuary, and had bought the brooding black mountain over the river to save the forest on its western flank and the colony of lyre-birds that lived at the foot of the range.

Alf's widow had lived alone in the homestead for years. Michael and Judy White built a house for themselves on the site of Arthur and Milly's cottage Kioto, and it was not until the late 1970s that they and their seven children began to prepare to move down to the big house.

This involved a huge sorting of possessions and in the course of this Judy White decided she should write a book about Belltrees. She explained in the preface to *The White Family of Belltrees* that she undertook the task because she realised, 'The White men themselves inherently shy and enveloped by modern day pressures may leave forever locked away so much valuable, documented material.'[1] In the volumes of Henry's letterbooks, she found copies of the old man's fond letters to and about young Paddy White at Lulworth. Michael was surprised by these, for his grandfather's affection for the boy had been hidden by his father's hostility to the man. Michael was prompted by this discovery to bring his cousin back to Belltrees, to re-establish a forgotten bond, and let him know he was welcome.

The timing was good. The invitation from Belltrees arrived at Martin Road about six weeks after White began working on the self-portrait he was calling *Flaws in the Glass*. He wanted to 'pick the archive' at Belltrees.[2] His friend Elizabeth Riddell had already sharpened his curiosity, for she had been up there working on a series for the *Bulletin* on the big landed families of Australia. Belltrees seemed much as he had described it to her, and she convinced him he would enjoy the visit. White accepted. Manoly was invited, but would stay behind to look after the dogs. White was very matter of fact about these preparations. He told Nin Dutton bluntly, 'I'm going to Belltrees 6/8th.'[3]

Drinking tea in the den, he relaxed and began telling tales Michael and Judy had never heard about the Whites before: how uncle Arthur and his wife Milly were so mean they starved themselves on baked custard in their suite at the Australia, and how, when the dying man was being carried out on a stretcher, he told Milly she must take the tram to visit him in hospital. Michael was shocked by this for he had been brought up to regard Arthur as his patron saint. His father had gone to the Australia, shortly before the old miser's death, to persuade him not to leave his half share in Belltrees to the King's School and the Church of England. This came to Michael and his sisters instead. The school and the church still had a great deal of his fortune, and Milly gave £500 for a memorial window in St Andrew's cathedral depicting missionary efforts in the Pacific. The deal was that if Arthur's window cost less than £500 Milly would get the change.

Patrick told them nothing of the self-portrait he was preparing to write. He asked to see the photograph albums and they showed him the picture of Dick and his brothers with their drab wives taken when he was not yet one. The six White men are in striped trousers and black coats, their blue eyes burning holes in the plate: Frank of Saumarez with a great beard, Arthur and Ernest gazing away into the paddocks, and Henry slumped in his chair with the look of a familiar bookkeeper who knows their secrets. The son wondered what his father had done for sex before his marriage at forty-two: men or women? Who? The library, with H.L.'s fifty volumes of letterbooks and photo albums had been moved into Dick's old bedroom, and the cardboard tag on the key still carried the initials V.M.W.

The curse of the Whites had passed to several of Judy and Michael's children. Patrick had believed his asthma was the worse for him having a dose of White and Withycombe blood through each parent. But Judy corrected him on this detail: there was no Withycombe in Dick, only Ruth was White and Withycombe. Patrick was nonplussed: he thought brother and sister White had married brother and sister Withycombe in Somerset. Family trees were produced, and he announced he felt better at once. Unlike his last visit to Belltrees in 1948, this one did not provoke an asthmatic blow-out.

He was given his aunt Maude's old rooms which he had last seen when he was a little boy climbing the stairs to collect a little pocket money to take back to school in 1925. Now it was the guest suite, 'where how many crowned heads had slept'.[4] Judy and Michael, who were still living up at the new house, drove off to get ready for dinner. Patrick was left alone. As he prowled through the house, he found himself staring at his mother's four-poster bed, part of the consignment of furniture she sent back when she left for London. He confided to Nin Dutton that his mother's bed was the great discovery of his return to Belltrees.

Michael recorded in the station diary: 'Patrick White flew up to stay for weekend. Light frost on flats.' Next morning Patrick went out with Michael, 'rounding up a couple of old bulls to send to Texas for hamburger. No beautiful marbled beef.' A fat woman in a short dress rushed across the road as they drove through the village. 'Tell me about that woman,' said Patrick eagerly as she disappeared into the little school. 'Who is that woman? Why is she like that?' Nothing seemed to spark his interest so immediately that weekend.[5]

The wind had brought down branches on the track up Mount Woolooma. Twice as they climbed Michael had to get out of the four-wheel drive and saw through fallen timber. On a ledge at 4,500 feet, the Whites had built a glass eyrie. Here they cooked lunch on a gas ring. 'It was wonderful. A storm broke and eagles were being tossed among the clouds.' Below them lay the rich valleys of the Hunter, the Isis and the Page, running to the foot of the Mount Royal Range. The Whites had once owned all the superb landscape beneath them: it was, as Patrick used to remark, 'their corner of the world'. But it was not for him. Whenever he found himself in the bush he felt the old tug-o'-war in him between the landscape and the life: 'I feel, this would be wonderful; then I realise I couldn't stand more than a fortnight. For me, the pavement and the crowd.

You've got to have something to fight against; otherwise you'll die of bush ballads.'[6]

The weather grew worse as they drove down the mountain in the late afternoon and left Patrick at the homestead. At about 6pm a violent storm struck the district. Michael recorded 'strong winds with little rain and cold change' in the diary. The power suddenly failed in the valley and Judy drove down to find candles for her guest. She found Patrick quite unfazed in that immense house, entirely alone in the dark.

White's urgent purpose in writing *Flaws in the Glass* was to make a public and dignified declaration of his homosexuality. The confession was half-made in *Twyborn*, and what was generally known might at any minute be said. He wanted to say it first himself. 'Telling the truth about oneself is a very difficult thing to do,' he told Björkstén. 'However, I felt I had to attempt it as many people are wrong about me; even many of those who have known me fairly intimately for years, often show they have no idea what I am like.' But when the book was out he spoke more bluntly about the purpose of these confessions: 'To stop some other bastard getting in first.'[7]

The public's knowledge of Patrick White's life was scrappy but accurate. He had written his own biographical notes on the early dust jackets and he kept a sharp eye on these details once publishers took over the chore. For years he gave interviews as each novel appeared or play was produced, and any errors were corrected smartly by him with letters to the editor. After the Adelaide plays, when he broke with the press for nearly a decade, newspapers endlessly rehashed what was in their files. There was enough exotic material to keep journalists from going out digging for more. White was glad.

Over the years he had written a few brief memoirs. *Prodigal Son* was quoted so often by everyone – press, critics, academics – that the text seemed in danger of wearing out on the page like a photograph left too long in the sun. He wrote other accounts of his life, but in disguise. *Meanjin* had an essay from him when *Voss* was published, but it was cast curiously in the third person: 'Patrick White began by going to school in Sydney, but after developing asthma . . .' This was cut, rejigged and published by *Meanjin* without naming White as the author.[8] Seventeen years later he gave an 'interview' to two academics he trusted: Gerry Wilkes and his colleague at Sydney University, Thelma Herring, who was one of the pioneers of Patrick White studies at Australian universities. Wilkes took only a few notes as they talked at Martin Road, and afterwards sent a list of the questions and these jottings to White, who drafted the answers on his typewriter. The 'interview' appeared in *Southerly* in the winter of 1973. White wrote to Dutton: 'Have you come across the new *Southerly* in which I make my début, and give probably my one performance as a strip artist?'9 This was in effect a first rough sketch for *Flaws in the Glass*.

Of all the obligations normally undertaken by winners of the Nobel Prize for Literature, the only one White fulfilled was to give the Swedish Academy a biographical essay, which was a reworked and expanded version of the 'interview' of the year before. It appeared in Stockholm in 1974, but White did not want it republished: 'I think a lot of Australians would be offended by what I say,' he told Marshall Best. 'It is something that will keep.' For the Swedes, he managed at last to use the word 'I'. How odd it was, he had remarked years before to Maie Casey, that he could not write in the first person. 'I become inhibited. So I could never think of writing an autobiography. I can't feel I should be the least bit interesting as the single identity I am sup-posed to be, only as the many characters of which I am composed.'10

White began to change his mind in the course of writing *The Twyborn Affair*, and when he broke off for a few weeks to do the screenplay 'Monkey Puzzle' it was to write about a writer caught up in the business of biography and autobiography. Will Garlick has published two volumes of memoirs – 'self-indulgent shit' according to one of his fans – before he begins to tape-record his confessions with Henrietta Birdsell. Garlick is a writer. Though White had written about painters, actors and musicians at work, he had steered clear of the great cliché: writing about a writer writing. But in 'Monkey Puzzle' he made a first attempt in fiction to say something of what it is like to write.

> (*Previous eroded creek-bed becoming a tumultuous mountain stream matched by a grandiose symphonic outburst, Mahlerian massed choirs, at first full blast, then muting, and gradually fading.*)
> WILL'S VOICE. . . . when the flow is infinite . . . everything I've ever experienced . . . much that I haven't . . . and all that I hope to WILL into existence . . .
> (*Image of Will at his desk writing madly as the mountain torrent continues flowing over and around him.*)
> WILL'S VOICE. Because art – like life – if you'll allow me to say so – is an act of almost pure (*softly*) – will . . . and courage . . . the courage not to side-step one's blemishes and vices – all ALL must be shown in what amounts to a gigantic *orgasm* of honesty . . . the excremen-tal . . . as well as the purity of innocence . . . and sensuality . . . not forgetting love . . . (*cry of pain*) . . . the wounds . . . oh, the bruises and the wounds . . .11

He had been shy until now of analysing *how* he wrote: better to let it happen than risk the torrent drying up by becoming too self-conscious. So psychoanalysis had always been impossible for White, and he was disconcerted by the appearance over the last few years of books and articles probing the sources of his gift. He helped their writers with letters and interviews, but was very reluctant to open the presentation copies when they arrived at Martin Road. 'Afraid I haven't read your book,' he told Peter Beatson after *The Eye in the Mandala* appeared in 1976. 'You know my rule about not reading books about myself.' But after *Twyborn* White was less nervous of this intro-spection; perhaps he thought the big peaks in his career had been scaled and he might now risk reflecting on where all the work had come from – and there was still the need to make those public declarations. He was not embarking on an autobiography but a memoir of what made him the writer he was: *Flaws in the Glass*, he told the critic Dorothy Green, 'sets out to be a self-portrait as truthfully and simply as I can make it'.[12]

He had no diaries to work from, had never kept letters, nor did he make copies of the letters he wrote. He had only his memory, but he remembered everything. 'One could go on remembering incidents and adding thoughts for ever,' he told Alan Williams. 'I hope I can restrain myself because there are other things I have to write.' Childhood and youth were easy, but he found it more difficult as he approached the present: 'what to select and how to avoid giving offence'. A short sketch of the book was ready by January 1980, and it appeared in Geoffrey Dutton's literary supplement to the centenary edition of the *Bulletin*. White sent a copy of this 'rather dreadful magazine' to Peggy Garland: 'It's coming along and taking the shape I had envisaged. I shall have it down on paper soon very roughly. Then I shall have to work at it, perhaps for ever as I remember more.'[13]

White was not one of the tribe of novelists compelled to invent lives for themselves, nor did his view of the life he lived change much over the years. From the early jacket flaps, through the essays for *Meanjin* and Stockholm, and on into *Flaws in the Glass* ran the same themes woven into a common skein of affliction, exile, foreign-ness, hostility and misunderstanding. But early on White began covering his literary tracks. So he did still. *Flaws in the Glass* is a unique literary memoir in its refusal to celebrate the first achievements of his career. The little *Thirteen Poems* might be forgotten today but for a single copy that turned up in a bundle of books bought by Sydney University from the collector Colin Berckelman in 1969. White does not mention these poems in his self-portrait. Nor does he record his publishing debut with the poem 'The Ploughman' nor the little volume in which it later appeared. He continued to scorn all the poems as 'forgettable juvenilia' and wished the two books to oblivion. He had recently told the National Library of Australia that 'The Ploughman' was 'best forgotten. Perhaps I shall contrive to steal and destroy the book you have next time I am in Canberra.'[14]

Ruth was part of the problem here, for how could he write about his early literary efforts without admitting something of his mother's role? That she encouraged him, published his first books and produced the early plays at Bryants' is not acknowledged in *Flaws*. White credits her with little beyond giving him his love of theatre and fine food, though he does acknowledge what was more and more apparent as each year passed, that he and his mother were extraordinarily alike. As patron, benefactor, cook, gardener, gossip and authority on questions of marriage, children, education, manners and good form, Patrick and Ruth were almost at one. His mouth had set in his mother's aggrieved line; his arresting eyes and his temper were hers. They were the Withycombe in Patrick White; so were his charm, his courtliness, his deep, sudden laughter. As he neared his seventieth birthday, he looked, as one remarked who knew them both at that age, 'Like Ruth without the pearls.'

In a world of predators, Ruth was the great predator. White managed to show pity for her in *Flaws in the Glass*, he even had wry amusement, but gave no ground in the lifelong struggle with this woman to whom he was so closely bound. He cited many of Ruth's minor betrayals, but Cheltenham was the one that mattered still. 'When the gates of my expensive prison closed I lost confidence in my mother, and [I] never forgave.' When he had written about his life before, he passed over Cheltenham in a few words, but now he set out his first account of life as a Lewisite. The school had still an odd way of intruding into his existence. *If* was filmed at Cheltenham, and he thought Lindsay Anderson's fable of armed revolution at an English public school was one of the best films of his life, and he revelled in the wholesale massacre of staff with which it ends. 'Seeing the Old Coll buildings again gave it an additional touch of horror.' His memory had been refreshed on his last trip to Europe when they stopped in Oslo to see Ragnar Christophersen, and White was puzzled to find how Christophersen would 'talk endlessly about the school he hated'. Cheltenham had to be faced: no account of what made White as he was would make sense without it.[15]

Cambridge is once again passed over in a few words, but not out of hostility. His memories of the place had grown warmer as the years passed: 'I enjoyed every minute of my life at King's,' he told the Swedish Academy. Cambridge had never surfaced in his writing, except in the shadowy university career of Elyot Standish in *The Living and the Dead* and White would not write about the Cambridge years now. Why? 'They didn't interest me.' This creative indifference appears to stem from a sense of failure that cast a pall of regret over his memories.

He admitted in *Southerly*, 'I didn't make the most of Cambridge.' A sense of failure is confirmed by his companion R, who remembers White's dreams of intellectual fulfilment, and the narrow domestic life he lived instead, sheltering with R and his provincial friends. In *Flaws* White does not pass over periods of failure, observed R, 'but on the whole his descriptions of experiences of unhappiness which most inspired his pen were of those when misery was created by the insensitivity or the downright cruelty of others, often associated with crass philistinism. I do not think he cared to write, or was drawn by recollection to write, of those episodes when self-pity or self-delusion led to frustration, disappointment and disenchantment: that is, internally created, not externally imposed.'[16]

Reluctance to admit failure must be measured against the astonishing candour of his confessions of fault. Those who saw the man revealed in his fiction knew how clearly he recognised his own deep flaws. Now the time had come for confession without the disguises of fiction, and he went about it with a will – all the more so to satisfy himself that he was not blowing his own trumpet. He delivered this bleak assessment of himself, in part, to keep the world's affection at bay: 'Perhaps when *Flaws in the Glass* comes out and they see I am not the noble, stuffed figure they would like me to be, I can get on with what I still have to write and see my friends in peace.' These were not penitent confessions. He blamed fate and his family for much that was bad in him: temper from the Withycombes and an unforgiving nature from the Whites. He wrote, 'Blood is the river which cannot be crossed.'[17] Regret was muted; no promises were made for the future. As he laid bare his flaws White was saying: this is what I am, don't expect me to change, for whatever I am as a writer these flaws have made me.

Homosexuality he approached with candour and discretion in equal measure, asserting the vernacular dignity of that old Australian term of abuse, poofter. In writing to Greene he called his self-portrait *The Poof's Progress*. By this time White was cautiously concerned about the rights of homosexuals. When Angus Wilson was knighted in mid-1980, White remarked to Dutton, 'The knighthood may help advance the homosexual cause.' Demonstrations did not: 'Screaming about the streets and waving your handbag in people's faces. That gets me down.' Homosexuals in New South Wales were still being prosecuted for sodomy. The Catholic and cautious Labor Government of the state was slow to make promised reforms and White found this 'pussyfooting' appalling. 'I am compiling a list of the Superpoofs in History who have contributed to the arts, and shall spring it on this philistine colony at the end of the year.'[18] In the end, he thought it would be a waste of time. *Flaws in the Glass* would be his argument for acceptance, perhaps respect, for what is after all a commonplace of human nature.

He wrote, 'I never went through the agonies of choosing between this or that sexual way of life. I was chosen as it were, and soon accepted the fact of my homosexuality.' He only hinted at the distress, self-disgust, loneliness and self-pity he experienced living the life he knew to be inescapable. He seemed only able to speak of this in fiction – overtly in *Twyborn* for the first time, but all his fiction explores the territory of pain that lies between sensuality and its expression, between lust and love. 'I settled into the situation. I did not question the darkness in my dichotomy, though already I had begun the inevitably painful search for the twin who might bring a softer light to bear on my bleakly illuminated darkness.'[19] Lascaris was the twin.

White did not pretend that their life had been a homosexual idyll, but he gave most moving thanks to Lascaris for his survival as a writer and a human being. 'What I had always aspired to was, simply, truthfulness and trust as far as the human body and fantasies allow, and the security of permanence. So much for aspiration. My jealous, not to say violent nature, might have assured repeated wreckage, if chance or Charles de Menasce had not arranged the meeting with M. in July 1941.' At the centre of the book White placed an account of their journeys through Greece. This chunk of travelogue – not as funny about himself or as brilliantly detailed as the letters from Greece – seems eccentric at first, perhaps mere padding. Yet in this record of an ancient people in modern guise, of high hopes often dashed, Byzantine mysteries and sublime landscapes, of terrible frustration and those 'brief moments of perfection Greece offers the obsessed' – White found a way of celebrating his twin but interlocked passions for Greece and 'the small Greek of immense moral strength who became the central mandala in my life's hitherto messy design'. He told Björkstén after the book appeared, 'Some are bored by our travels through Greece, but one of the more perceptive critics described them as being like a marriage which is how I see them myself.'[20]

As he worked at *Flaws in the Glass* White was having his portrait painted by Brett Whiteley. He thought this a wonderful omen: two portraits at once. Whiteley's turned out to be the finest of the half-dozen White allowed to be painted. He caught what is almost impossible for photographs and paintings to show: the ironic play that gives life to White's basilisk face. Whiteley had asked for a list of the writer's loves and hates which, to White's fury, he pasted on to the canvas:

LOVES
Silence
The company of friends
Unexpected honesty

Reading
Going to the pictures
Dreams
Uncluttered landscapes
City streets
Faces
Good food
Cooking small meals
Whiskey
Sex
Pugs
The thought of an Australian republic
My ashes floating off at last

HATES
The PR machine
Pretentious socialites
Money grabbers
Writing
First nights & film premières
Insomnia
The 'Show' (RAS)
Sport
Noise
Motels
Liars
TV
Jet flights
Unnecessary cars
Unending worthy radio talks
The overgrown school prefects from whom we
    never escape

In October, after he had finished the second version of *Flaws* and was cleaning up his desk, Australia was plunged into another general election at which Malcolm Fraser won a third victory. White was so disgusted he began to rage that his fellow countrymen needed 'invasion, bloodshed, foreign occupation and a taste of starvation to bring them to their senses'. Explaining his politics was another of his purposes in writing *Flaws in the Glass*: 'I have to show how life in this piffling British colony has made me a republican and driven me always farther to the Left, till I am what the conservatives describe as a "traitor to my class".'[21] It was to rebut this charge, that White gave the most detailed account he had ever given of the rise of the Whites and his place in the family. Rich he admitted they were, but his purpose was to argue they were not part of the ruling class.

White had been distressed when Geoffrey Dutton accepted a commission from Mobil Oil to write the text for a book of photographs of Australia. He complained even to Dutton's children that their father had sold out to the multi-nationals. Distress turned to anger when he read *Patterns of Australia* and found himself credited with aristocratic breadth of understanding. 'That bit about the "aristocrat" was particularly blood-curdling,' he replied to Dutton. 'You can't have met many of my family . . . We were the new rich at the turn of the century. Hardly aristocracy. If I am anything of a writer it is through my homosexuality, which has given me additional insights, and through *a very strong vein of vulgarity*. All of this I hope to bring out in *Flaws in the Glass*.'[22]

Nor did White see it as a betrayal of his White past to be a republican. He claimed the unprincipled greed of conservative royalists was not part of his family's experience. 'My father and his brothers were honourable men who would not be divorced from their principles. My dowdy aunts had a moral core which could not be faulted. Even my more pretentious, more elegant mother would never have shed her principles.' He saw the shedding of principles all around him in Australia. More strongly than ever he was urging a boycott of all men, women and institutions responsible for the coup of 1975. That there was a new man as Governor-General made no difference: those who ate at Yarralumla or had truck with the Fraser government could only do so, to White's mind, by shedding their principles. 'I'd be a Rum Puff indeed if I accepted,' he told Manning Clark when an invitation came to a National Book Council dinner at which the new Governor-General would be guest of honour. 'And you'd be a Stuffed Turkey to submit.'[23]

What White had to say about the Queen and her Glücksburg consort Prince Philip did not worry his publishers, but Cape took fright at the little essay on 'amiable, rorty old, farting' Sir John Kerr. 'Politicians', observed the editorial department, 'are notoriously sensitive about drink.' White refused to make changes: 'This is one of the most important sections in the book and vital to my "self-portrait". The Kerrs' behaviour had a great influence on me. It moved me farther to the Left and made me a convinced Republican . . . All Australia knows that Kerr is a drunk. He was photographed lying on the ground at the Tamworth Agricultural Show, and on national television staggering forward to present the Melbourne Cup. The drinking habits of politicians are referred to regularly in the Australian press.' The Kerr section appeared uncut. 'If we are sued I shall go to prison rather than pay, because it may advance the Republican cause,' he declared. 'Life today is so rotten

I expect nothing more from it on a personal level. I am only afraid the homosexual aspect of the book may queer the Republican issue. But it is a risk which must be taken.'24

After working on the final version of *Flaws in the Glass* for about seven weeks, White collapsed in early December. For ten days he felt like death. Reading in his doctors' faces his own worst fears, he decided he must have cancer or tuberculosis. Joseph was called and discovered a virus mixed up with the old fungoid infection in his lungs – a virus which he told Maschler rather proudly 'South Pole penguins also develop' – and Joseph put him back on prednisone. 'Again I feel full of life.' In illness, anxiety and a euphoric haze of prednisone, the book was finished on New Year's Day, 1981. 'I hope you are not going to say that *Flaws in the Glass* will destroy my literary reputation,' he told Maschler. 'Any literary reputation that can't stand up to the truth isn't worth having.'25

White gave the typescript to Lascaris and he was shattered by what he read. The prospect of this first public acknowledgment of his relationship with White was hard to bear, though he thought it was written beautifully. More painful were White's vivid portraits of the Lascaris family. They were not untrue, but they would cause offence in Athens. White writes of the Lascaris family with pride – the pride of an in-law – but he also saw them with the eyes of a novelist. His portrait of Manoly's father is devastating and Lascaris imagined the family would think he had put White up to it. But he asked for no changes and none were made. *Flaws in the Glass* was dedicated

to Manoly
again

'Manoly's arthritis has been very bad through all these ups and downs,' White reported to Peggy Garland a few days later. 'Instead of balancing activity with rest, he drives himself all day, never stops working in the garden, and I often feel he will drive himself into the ground. My book may have something to do with it. But I felt I had to tell, among things which have made me as I am, the story of a wonderful if difficult forty-year relationship.'26

All year, in fits and starts, he worked on a new novel, but he was tired and there were many interruptions. In March he gave a television interview on 'The State of the Colony' and a deluge of letters had to be dealt with afterwards. 'Only one letter of abuse, but dirty mutterings from the Establishment are reported to me.'27 In April he put the book aside, for Jim Sharman had been appointed artistic director of the next Adelaide Festival and asked him for a play. He finished a first draft of *Signal Driver* by the end of April 1981.

'The play is about a couple who spend their lives just failing to signal the driver and escape from each other and their responsibilities,' he explained. 'Their lives also reflect the decay of Australian society from 1920 to the present day. Only four characters, the other two being a pair of music-hall clowns or timeless avatars, invisible to the humans, who act as chorus.' In New York before the Second World War he had known an actress called Dolly Purdell, who married a worthy Scot and became a script reader at RKO. When they had rows she would go down to Grand Central with her suitcase, and he would follow to coax her home.[28] That was the framework for *Signal Driver*: three acts, three arguments and three reconciliations set in a tram (later bus) stop on the edge of an Australian town.

Sharman chose Neil Armfield to direct the new play for the festival, and an early version of the script was with him in May. White had admired Armfield's early work at the Nimrod in Sydney and had written to the *Sydney Morning Herald* defending one of his productions after a cold review by Harry Kippax. The *Herald* refused to run the letter; the theatre published it as an advertisement in the same paper; and this little *cause célèbre* marked a further deterioration in the relationship between White and his first evangelist Kippax.[29]

Armfield was only twenty-six and White wondered if he would catch the allusions in a play that covered the long span of his own life. 'Of course I can go over it with him line by line, but that will not be the same.'[30] White read *Signal Driver* through to him, as he had once read *Cheery Soul* to John Sumner. He took the young man down to the old wooden bus stop on Anzac Parade. This was the shelter he had in mind as he wrote *Signal Driver*: he and Lascaris came down here to catch the bus to town or up to Taylor Square for fish and dogs' meat. It was *their* bus stop. He confessed he had often run down here to make his escape, but the young director took this to be the truth self-dramatised: White might cool off at the bus stop after a row, but he would never take the bus to freedom.

Armfield was a 1950s kid who grew up in a new suburb of Sydney where his father worked in a biscuit factory. There was no theatre in his background, but a drama teacher found him at high school, and at university he acted (enthusiastically) and directed (with distinction) until a never-finished thesis on Ben Jonson propelled him out into the theatre. The Armfields had decided early on what mattered in life: a son had died, and illnesses were endured with tough good humour, simplicity and emotional generosity. The survivors loved one another and knew that life was precious. Neil Armfield's work had a clarity that set it apart and a passion that was rare on the Australian stage.

He was willing to raise the emotional heat very high. That, and the courage to tackle difficult texts without flinching, made him an ideal interpreter of White's writing. White dedicated *Signal Driver* to Armfield.

The 1982 Adelaide Festival was to have Patrick White as its totem. *Signal Driver* was opening the festival and the Sydney Symphony Orchestra with Marilyn Richardson was to play a fragment of the uncompleted opera *Voss*. The opera had been a sub-plot of White's life for ten years, since a young nun came to him with the idea in 1972. 'Fancy if a simple nun could come up with the real thing. It is a remote possibility, but I think I shall let her try.'[31] Moya Henderson then left Queensland, the order, and then Australia to study for five years in Germany. Throughout this long preparation she composed not a note of *Voss*. When she returned home she found the Australian Opera would not commission her to write the full-scale *avant-garde* work both she and White wanted. She pulled out.

White was sick of *Voss*. The novel's fame seemed to cast a shadow over all his books and plays. He found it grating to be known always as 'the author of *Voss*' and not the novels he thought his best: *The Aunt's Story*, *The Solid Mandala* and *The Twyborn Affair*. 'It got into the hands of gushers, and I hate gush.' White was made no fonder of the book by the fact that Nolan now owned the film rights, and the painter and Harry Miller still hoped to produce 'a dazzling film to aggravate White'.[32] Tired as he was of the novel, White did not stand in the way when the Australian Opera came to him with a new plan for an opera based on *Voss*. Sharman was to direct and be involved with the project from the start; Richard Meale would write the music. White admired Meale's work, indeed he tried to convince him to collaborate on a satirical opera, *Births, Deaths & Lotteries*. But Meale wanted to tackle *Voss*. David Malouf had written the libretto.

Malouf had become one of White's friends. He was the Australian offspring of a family mostly Lebanese but partly London-Jewish, raised in the simple prosperity of Brisbane in the 1940s. White imagined him as a figure of some mystery: so open yet deeply reserved, so Australian yet thoroughly European, an academic who could write beautifully, a poet who had written some of the best Australian novels White had read. White tried unsuccessfully to persuade Viking to publish Malouf's *An Imaginary Life* in America. 'It will not be the big money-spinner, but it is literature and perhaps Viking can still afford that. Some of his recent poetry I find miraculous.' Later White decided Malouf should be considered for the Nobel, and sent a bundle of all his books to Artur Lundkvist. 'Perhaps the Nobel people will not find me acceptable,' he wrote, 'but I am convinced that Malouf is of great literary worth.'[33]

The new *Voss* team began work in July 1979. White hoped they would succeed, 'but I have a feeling that *Voss* is everybody's albatross, including my own'. He was disturbed to hear that Meale was writing tunes. More than ever, White was interested in difficult contemporary music, and had lost interest in traditional opera which he complained was ground out for subscribers and their wives. 'I don't want to see *Bohème* for ever.' He imagined a *Voss* opera as harsh as the landscape that humbled his explorer. At first he objected to anything from the opera being sung at the 1982 festival – 'I still think it a mistake to go on about one's work in advance' – but Sharman persuaded him to relent, to raise Meale's morale.[34]

Once the preparations for Adelaide were in hand, White took the new novel out of his drawer, reread it and found he liked what he had written. For a few months in the winter of 1981, working from four to six hours every morning at the dining-room table, for his desk was a mess of papers and envelopes, White carried on with the novel, taking the first draft to about the half-way point. He hoped he would have the strength to finish it. 'You don't know about old age until you're into it yourself,' he told Maschler. 'The dreadful slowing up process, and always more to do, the letters to answer, the people to stave off. Every other day I'm expected to wave a wand and save somebody or something.' But already the first rumblings were being heard from London as *Flaws in the Glass* fell into the hands of reviewers and the press. In the hullabaloo to come the novel died and White wondered if he would ever face 'the immense physical labour' of another.[35]

White's orders to Cape were: 'No films, no interviews. If the book can't speak for itself that's just too bad.'[36] *Flaws in the Glass* spoke with a roar.

Charles Osborne, arts bureaucrat, biographer and Australian Londoner, received a review copy from the *Financial Times* and was so startled by White's account of Cynthia Nolan's suicide that he rang the painter and read the passage to him. Nolan had no inkling that White's feelings towards him had shifted so fundamentally. He had seemed sympathetic when they met, quite unchanged since Cynthia's death. Now he heard Osborne read: 'What I cannot forgive is him flinging himself on another woman's breast when the ashes were scarcely cold, the chase after recognition by one who did not need it, the cameras, the public birthdays, the political hanky-panky . . . all of which, and the Athenaeum Club, would contribute to the death of any painter.'[37]

Nolan tried to stop the book. He consulted two London lawyers, Lord Goodman and the playwright-barrister John Mortimer, who, he says, advised him the book was defamatory, but urged him not to take action because the case would be expensive and very painful. Nolan claims also to have been told by one of the editors at Cape that White was prevented by the publishers from saying even worse things about him.[38] Whatever may have been said to mollify the painter, this does not appear to have been the case. Greene and White insist that no cuts were made to *Flaws in the Glass* before its publication. Nolan took his own revenge. He sent a diptych out to Australia called *Nightmare*, which had an ashen-faced White in a pale blue cap (inmate? prisoner? magician?) standing by a dog's arse. A line on the animal's haunch might be a tail curled back or a map of its bowel. A crucifix is painted on the dog's belly and its head bears a crude likeness to Manoly Lascaris. Nolan also sent out some drawings based on the *Divine Comedy* in which White is thrust into the sodomites' circle of hell. When these went on exhibition, Nolan told the press, 'I'm a good hater . . . I'll bury him . . . He doesn't understand much about life does he? He's just lived with a man for forty years.' White began to claim he had never much liked or been impressed by Sid Nolan. 'It was far more Cynthia. He's done far more harm to himself than he has to me. I didn't like what he said about Manoly and Manoly was very upset. But anyway, he will bite the dust. He already has as far as his talent goes.'[39]

White allowed Cape to sell a few chunks of the book to the *Observer*, for which the paper paid £10,000. When R read that Patrick White's memoirs were to be serialised before publication, he gathered his children about him and warned them what might be said. But R and Cambridge remain offstage. About old lovers, *Flaws in the Glass* is very discreet: Spud Johnson who died in Santa Fe in 1968 is not mentioned – indeed Lascaris had never heard of him. The Duke of Baena and San Lucar, living in his villa in Biarritz, is called merely Pepe; and Joe Rankin, about to retire from his Atlanta medical practice, is plain Joe. Editions of *The Living and the Dead* had not carried the dedication to Joe Rankin for years.

Flaws in the Glass reached the shops in October, and White's most acerbic comments were quoted in newspapers throughout the English-speaking world. The book was front-page news in England and Australia: reviews were good, and it became the bestseller of White's career. White put it down to smutty curiosity: 'People wanted to have a perv.'[40]

In Oxford Betty Withycombe had the book read to her for she was going blind. So upset was she by White's portrait of her sister Joyce – 'one of the world's masochists' – that she determined thereafter to adopt a 'deliberately unforgiving' stance to her cousin.[41] In London Sid Nolan, John Kerr and Joan Sutherland posed for a photograph in the crush bar at Covent Garden: three of White's victims out on the town. In Athens Elly Polymeropoulos wept. In Wellington the elderly Professor of History at Victoria University discovered his Lulworth tutorials had convinced young Patrick White to turn his back on history. Fred Wood sent him a gentle protest 'pointing out among other things the splendid

use he made of historical material in his own work'.[42] From Ireland
to Zimbabwe, ex-Lewisites wondered who it was among the prefects
White so loathed that fifty years after leaving school he could still
ask, 'whether that narrow, almost fleshless, borzoi skull is still above
ground, or whether it lies whitening, snapped shut on the last of its
vicious intentions'.[43] Answer: Crewe Read.

Relics of Ruth's society thought her portrait dreadfully unfair.
They remembered a gritty woman of charm who loved dogs and hats
and theatre. True, she had laughed at her son's writing, but that sort
of thing *happens* in families. Their more lasting memory was of Ruth's
early ambitions for her little genius, and the pride of the woman in his
fame. How could Patrick – Paddy, still, to some of them – say Ruth
was bitterly disappointed in him? Why could he not acknowledge the
deep attachment to his mother that lasted till her death? *Flaws in the
Glass* was just a record of spats and disagreements. She wasn't like
that! Indeed, she wasn't like that to them: Ruth was their friend but
Patrick's mother.

The book was known in some circles as *Claws in the Arse*. When
Desmond Digby – the D of the telephone gossip in *Flaws* – read the
book in typescript he begged White to cut the barbed remarks about
Joan Sutherland hating his novels and loving pulp. Now he saw the
published book and found the barbs still there. John Tasker was
wounded to find the early productions of the plays passed over with
hardly a word. It was as if they had not happened. A former equerry
to the Queen wrote to the *Sydney Morning Herald* complaining about
the account of lunch on the royal yacht: 'If Mr White's inaccurate
and ungentlemanly comments . . . represent the voice of Australian
nationalism, pray give me colonialism.' White declined with regret the
choreographer Graeme Murphy's request for the rights to *Flaws in the
Glass*: 'I only wish I could see Desmond Digby translated into ballet.'
One of White's doctors suggested an X-ray of his chest should have
been included: 'a good idea I should have thought of'. Christina Stead
discovered in *Flaws*, contrary to her stubborn belief, that Patrick White
was not a lady's man. 'Well,' said Dorothy Green, 'Patrick has been
telling us a little bit about himself.' Stead tossed her head and replied,
'Writers should never write autobiographies.'[44]

White's friendship with Stead had deteriorated as he lost patience
with her unending despair. She drank; she moved about restlessly from
friend to friend, exhausting her welcome and moving on; she talked
about writing but could not drag herself to her desk. White and Stead
met for the last time at lunch at her brother's house in Sydney. White
said a number of severe things to her that day, and Stead seemed shaken.
At one point they were talking about writers who allow their work to
be edited. Stead proudly claimed to manage it all herself: 'I've always

humped my own bluey.' White said, 'Like hell you have.'[45] As her guests left she gave them a brown paper bag of empty bottles to take with them so that her brother would not discover them in his bin.

After the fuss over *Flaws in the Glass* White did not return to the novel as he had hoped he would. 'I doubt I shall ever get back to a normal writing life,' he told Maschler. 'On top of it all, Manoly's increasing arthritis is a great worry. I should have six minds to deal with everything that arises. Of course, I could *employ* people, but neither of us could bear having a retinue around, and I'd no longer be able to support my various causes if I had to pay an army of retainers. We may come to that, however. The moral is: one should go off with a heart attack at the age of sixty-five.'[46] He did not believe this for a moment. Arthritis had reduced Lascaris' world. He was advised not to drink coffee, and they both gave it up. Acupuncture gave him some relief, but he was hobbling about with a stick, could not sit through a play or a film, and for some time was unable to wear his left shoe. Early in the New Year, 1982, the pain abated a little. He wrote to Kerry Walker, 'The Lord in all his mercy has given me a better day today after tortures during the last two. Paddy was most upset.'[47]

Rehearsals for *Signal Driver* began in February 1982. Sharman had some worries about the first act, so White rewrote it before flying over to Adelaide. He stayed, not with the Duttons, but in a house Kerry Walker shared with a friend from the theatre company. She was cast as one of the music-hall beings. None of his directors had allowed him to see so much of the rehearsal process as Armfield did now: 'Working with the actors on *Signal Driver* I learnt a lot more about theatre, and was able to explain a lot to them,' White told David Malouf. 'In the past my presence wasn't exactly encouraged.' He spent the mornings at rehearsals, sitting quietly, occasionally filling a lull with a wry comment. Sometimes he slipped over to the Adelaide railway station to buy a pie and sit eating it on a bench. In the afternoons he returned to the house for a siesta before going back to the theatre at night. 'The play is developing well, but I have no idea how it would strike an audience,' he told Elizabeth Harrower. 'It tears me to bits, so much of our life in it, and I cry all through Act III, which becomes embarrassing.'[48]

The Huebsch doctrine, to which White always subscribed, applied only to books, for there is time for them to find their own audience. Plays need promotion: they have a life of only a few weeks. Sharman persuaded White to give publicity interviews as each of the late plays opened. At first journalists expected to find a prickly, taciturn subject, but they discovered a courtly, loquacious, rather cranky, and astonishingly candid man who was happy to gossip with them for an hour or two in the sun at Martin Road, or in the foyer of an inter-state hotel. The interviews developed a pattern. White would talk about the work at hand, the state of Australia, the horrors of *nouveau riche* Sydney, old age, his chest and Lascaris' feet – 'we totter about supporting each other' – the state of theatre, his religion, his decision to write no more novels – 'it's too much, sitting there day-after-day with your bronchial tubes filling up' – and his dreams of other lives: as an actor, or a great cook or a dancer. Most insistently, he spoke of beginning again as a writer-director in the film industry: 'You can get at them best through film or the dreadful telly.'[49]

Signal Driver opened the Adelaide Festival, and White came down to take a bow with Armfield and the cast. He said nothing of the past in his brief speech from the stage. White was not interested in gloating at this final victory over the troglodytes of Adelaide. His presence was everywhere in Adelaide in 1982: in the play, in William Yang's official photographs, in the film of the festival, and in the concert fragment of *Voss*. The warmth of *Signal Driver*'s reception that night seemed to consign the old humiliations to history. Sharman was staying on in the city for two years to run the state theatre company, and White commended him to Adelaide. The audience streamed out of the theatre to watch the tail-end of a brilliant display of fireworks over the Torrens.

Critics gave the play a guarded welcome; they were more excited by the seventeen minutes of *Voss* than by *Signal Driver*. 'It is more beautiful, more grateful for the voices and more genuinely operatic than most people would have dared to hope,' wrote Roger Covell. This was not White's response. He acknowledged the scene was very beautiful, but wrote afterwards to Meale to remind him that *Voss* was 'austere and gritty, even in that gentler scene – as I remember it. Then the singers were wrong, the man downright bad, the woman too mellifluously perfect. They were like two giant waxworks standing there on the platform. I couldn't imagine them ever developing human passions. No doubt these bad impressions will be corrected when the whole work is heard as opera and not a static concert piece. You are a composer I admire, so I hope you will bring it off. My disappointment is that you haven't composed a contemporary opera instead of a romantic work based on the hateful *Voss*.' Meale replied defending the scene, and White repeated his assurances of admiration and confidence. '*Voss* is yours to do what you will with it. I hope you have a tremendous success – a success I shall enjoy, even when the members of the establishment, the company directors and their vacant women are madly clapping something they don't understand.'[50]

White had enjoyed working again with his theatrical family now transplanted by Sharman to Adelaide. To give them something new, and as a reply to the tepid critical reception for *Signal Driver*, White began a new play once he returned to Sydney. At some point during the festival he had remarked to Sharman about the new fashion for emptying lunatic asylums, and seemed exhilarated by the 'fabulously disastrous' idea that the mad should be sent out to live in the community. From this grew *Netherwood*, a play about 'the sanity in insanity and the insanity in sanity; and about the incompatibility of the orthodox Australia and the unorthodox Australia – the old-style country people and the city drop-out'. He set the play in a house in the landscape of Moss Vale and Sutton Forest, where a few mental patients are being cared for by a couple who have left the city in search of a more useful life. In their convalescent home of the spirit, White explores old themes: love in service, the woman in man, the nature of sanity, and, most urgently, the habit of violence in man. He was writing *Netherwood* after coming to believe the threat of nuclear war cast a shadow over all his achievement. 'I can't see that anything matters beside this great issue.'[51]

He had stood with poets and trade union officials on the platform of the Assembly Hall in Melbourne late in 1981 to launch People for Nuclear Disarmament. On Palm Sunday 1982 he led a march through Sydney and addressed a crowd of 30,000 for half an hour in the rain, calling for a ban on the mining of uranium and the destruction of both nuclear and conventional weapons. 'So our work will not be done until we have eradicated the *habit* of war.' The violence that breaks in on the little asylum of Netherwood, comes of ignorance and malice and habit. 'Comical bastards, us humans,' reflects the sergeant of police as he gazes at the carnage. 'Seems like we sorter *choose* ter shoot it out . . .' Corpses litter the stage as if this were a Jacobean tragedy or, indeed, the bloody climax of the first little play he wrote at Tudor House, 'The Mexican Bandits'.[52]

When Patrick White marched in a shapeless jumper and warm woollen cap, he was flanked by the leaders of the Australian Left. But on the platform he did not echo their rhetoric of weapons, treaties and solidarity. He had no plan. He preached instead the searching of hearts, the victory of the spirit and the faith in common humanity that would save the earth. 'This wonderful earth! Every morning as I stumble round the park across from the house where I live, dragged by my large, insistent dog, through frost, fog, bird calls, a sun rising through watered cloud, or later in the year, from behind solid dollops of ice-cream cumulus, to the clash of brass, the tinkle of humidity, I am strengthened by the natural phenomena I see around me. My eye is rejoiced by the texture of brick in a slum wall. Reasons for hope can even be found in those brief breathing spaces of a great city, those pocket handkerchiefs of grass littered with fragments of broken glass and the vomit from victims of the society in which we live.'[53]

As White became convinced that the prevention of nuclear war was 'the most important moral issue in history', his old political certainties were turned on their heads. His passionate support for Israel changed to sympathy for the dispossessed Palestinians. He no longer regarded the Russians as totally evil, totally cunning. 'Nobody is that. I can recognise a certain amount of evil in myself, for instance, but would lay claim to a little good. So with all of us: there is material to work on.'[54]

A common thread ran through all the political causes he had taken up since he spoke from the truck in Centennial Park in 1972. This was his fear of the power of money. The greed of developers threatened to destroy his city in the early 1970s; greedy and impatient conservatives deposed Whitlam in 1975; greed made Australians kotow to Americans and Japanese and British; greed linked governments, miners and manufacturers in the 'monstrous web' of the uranium industry which threatened the earth and its peoples. White's politics, in their condemnation of money, were the politics of an angry monk. Money: 'One of the curses of life from century to century, breeding war, despair in the poor, dishonesty in the ambitious, while the hungry are encouraged to believe they will eat if they go along with what is planned for them.' Money: 'The poison which infects and destroys all advanced societies. The money which dazzles those who manufacture armaments, deluded scientists, and politicians. Humility should be the antidote . . .'[55]

He dreamed of the bare cell in which he might live his last years, and gave an echo of this dream to Theo Vokes in *Signal Driver*,

> an empty room, bare floor-boards, a work-bench, my tools around me, and any old sort of bed to throw myself down on when desire leaves me. A monk's palliasse, some might see it as. And outside the window a view of the ocean . . .[56]

In his mirror White saw his eyes going off 'like the eyes of a stale fish'.[57] Though he had kept glaucoma at bay for six years with drops and exercises, his eyes now seemed to suffer blackouts as he worked, and in May 1982 he was told his right eye must be operated on. He put his work aside to rewrite his will, pay his tax and find a housekeeper. He feared what the surgeons might discover once they had him on the operating table.

White's seventieth birthday was celebrated that month very quietly. It was as he wished. Public fuss over birthdays was one of the counts in his indictment of Nolan in *Flaws in the Glass*, but Geoffrey Dutton had not picked up this signal and published a birthday tribute in the *Bulletin*. 'I was amazed by your effusion,' White wrote in a rage next day. 'Manoly and I both squirmed all the way through it, not only for the inaccuracies, but for its silliness and vulgarity . . . you, I should have thought, would never have sunk to the level of Andrea and Nola Dekyvere.'[58] There might have been a time when White could bear Dutton writing an article so chatty and insinuating, with a strong dash of self-promotion. But not now. The piece was fake, for it suggested a happy and continuing intimacy when, in fact, their friendship was almost exhausted.

Dutton had ignored White's advice to bury himself at Anlaby like a Russian on his estates, husband his fortune and write. Instead, Dutton continued to pursue his public literary career which took him flying about the world, and for which he was given an Order of Australia in 1976. Dutton accepted the gong just as White was returning his own. 'It is very distressing,' White wrote from Athens on hearing this news. After the failure of a last attempt to make Anlaby pay, this time by scientific pig breeding, the Duttons decided to sell and build a new house for themselves outside Adelaide. White's sympathies were engaged by their predicament. 'Getting out must be the worst of nightmares,' he wrote in February 1978. But he was so worried by this time about the Duttons and money, that he added a few offensive words of advice: 'I hope you're not going to blow all the money from Anlaby building the new house at Piers Hill; it could easily happen today.'[59]

He went down to Piers Hill after his visit to Belltrees in 1979, and was surprised to find 'the most beautiful house in the most idyllic landscape'. A few days later he learnt that Dutton had accepted money from Mobil Oil and a grant from the Australia Council. White made a few rumbling noises then, but did not erupt until he read the Mobil book a year later. As well as blasting Dutton about the 'aristocratic' comments, he accused him of putting himself in the hands of oil companies and the government in order to go on 'living it up in the old Dutton funster fashion. Australia disgusts me more and more, but what really shatters me is when those I have loved and respected shed their principles along with the others.'[60]

Dutton accused White of moral megalomania. 'It's time you recovered your sense of proportion, your sense of humour and most of all your sense of humility, which once long ago you declared to be the most essential thing of all . . . what right have you to pontificate about other people's lives? You should reread King Lear, for more than one reason − "who should 'scape whipping?" Despite your extraordinary insights, your genius in fact, you have not had enough contact with the ordinary world since you left Castle Hill. Twenty Martin Road is more of an ivory tower than Piers Hill. Your homosexuality, since you mention it, has indeed given you great insight, but it has also denied you the give and take, the interaction of love with human frailty, that comes not only from one's own life with wife and children but from those of the children's friends. Your private income has enabled you to write and you have had the strength of mind to devote yourself to writing, a grim hair-shirt that sometimes makes you oblivious of what other writers have to do to keep going.' Dutton ended, 'Unfortunately, perhaps, love cannot be destroyed, and I still feel that for you.'[61]

White gave no ground. Essentially, he was accusing Dutton of burdening and complicating his life when he should be simplifying it in order to get on with his writing. 'I had to say it otherwise our relationship would have trundled along in the unnatural way it has been going for some time.' White reminded Dutton of Liselotte's remark in *The Aunt's Story*: 'We must destroy everything, everything, even ourselves. Then at last when there is nothing perhaps we shall live.' He grappled point by point with Dutton's argument: 'You seem to imply there's no give and take in a homosexual marriage. My God if you knew!' He came to the question of money. 'As for my private income, we did have enough to live on during the years at Castle Hill, by carefully counting every penny. Since there was an income of any size, I've been giving it away. By now I give most of it – not a noble gesture when one no longer has much desire for anything beyond a roof, a bed, a table, and a few pots and pans. Yrs, Patrick.'[62]

Their intimacy ended with this exchange in late 1980, but the ghost of a friendship survived for another eighteen months. A few brief, cool letters passed between Martin Road and Piers Hill. After *Flaws* appeared, Dutton defended Nolan, and White conceded his inability to forgive – 'inherited from my Uncle James' – was one of his worst flaws. 'Every time I come to that bit about forgiveness of trespasses in the Lord's Prayer I know I can't pretend to be a Christian.' White did not write again until the birthday article appeared in the *Bulletin*, and then only to break off the friendship finally. 'I'm sorry, but I've had enough of Duttonry, and ask you not to ring me when you fly from capital to capital for what I can't see as any good reason. And please let there be no correspondence. As you know, I don't keep letters, but this one will be an exception – to show the curious why our relationship ended.'[63]

'What a vain prick you are,' Dutton replied. 'My sole aim in writing that article was to try to show that you were once a humane, generous and even good man as well as a complex artist. I realise now that unconsciously I was writing an elegy.' He complained of letters unanswered, and presents unacknowledged. 'I intend never to write or speak to you again, and as for telephoning, I wouldn't waste the ten cents on you.'[64]

Nin Dutton had been hunting for a housekeeper who could look after the two men at Martin Road once White returned from his glaucoma operation. She rang at some point in all this to give him the name of a woman she had found. White replied, 'I wouldn't want a housekeeper you'd found.'

'Why?' she asked.

'Because you're vile, vile, vile.'[65]

Ten days before the operation a flutter was discovered in White's heart, and he was put into hospital, given drugs and then electric shocks to throw his heart back into its rhythm. 'All most astonishing – that this could be happening to oneself!' The operation was then postponed a second time by a bout of bronchial flu. It took place finally in early July and was a success. He reported to Waters, 'the other specialists, heart and chest, continue hovering. Went to the heart professor last week, and he wanted to fling me into hospital to have more electric shocks for my wrong heart rhythm. I refused. I'd planned to make a vegetable strüdel with *grüne sosse* at the weekend, and nothing was going to put me off. I continue to take pills by the handful and put in eye drops every couple of hours. No time for anything else, I feel nauseated and don't seem able to get back my strength. At least I don't wet the chairs yet and they haven't chalked up cancer against me.' The housekeeper was soon dispensed with. 'She was a very worthy woman but M and I would gloom at each other across the kitchen table as she chirped away.'[66]

He returned to work on *Netherwood*, 'dribbling it out painfully over the weeks, sometimes no more than three or four lines a day'. Feeling time was short, he dispensed with the second long-hand draft and typed away as hard as he could, finishing the play in early October. Sharman was stunned. 'If I can stun somebody like that in my seventies, there must be some life left in me.'[67] They had planned to revive *The Ham Funeral* in Adelaide in 1983, but Sharman decided the new play should take the place of the old.

In the catalogue of White's infirmities, a new complaint appeared in the first days of the New Year, 1983. He seemed to have strained his back. His friends took little notice of this, for bad backs were Lascaris' department, but by the middle of January both men were having acupuncture. 'I look like a skeleton probably hiding a cancer. Manoly might be ten or fifteen years younger, but is hobbling painfully and may have to undergo a foot operation. The operation on my other eye is to come. I only have to fit it in with rehearsals and the opening of my new play at Sharman's theatre in Adelaide. Rehearsals start end of April.'[68]

Australia had been to the polls five times in the past decade. In February 1983 a sixth general election was called at which the Labor Party under Bob Hawke regained office after seven years in Opposition. White was thrilled. 'We are rid of that lying bastard Fraser,' he told Peggy Garland. 'Hawke is flash, but right for Australia.'[69]

White was invited to the inaugural celebrations at the Opera House, and at the reception afterwards was led up to the new Prime Minister. 'I brought up the subject of uranium. He appeared uneasy in spite of his political triumph, his coiffure and his sartorial splendour.' Hawke fobbed him off then, and White grew sceptical, disappointed, then bitterly angry as the months went by and he discovered Hawke would take no moral stand on nuclear war, nor work towards a republic, nor sever those ties to the United States and Britain which prevented Australia becoming the 'great independent democracy in the South' which White had once hoped to see established in his lifetime.[70]

White spent the weeks after the election drafting, then rehearsing – in front of his bathroom mirror – a speech to scientists gathering in Canberra in May to discuss nuclear war. He had never been more frightened by the prospect of delivering a speech, yet of all of them none has had such an impact as *Australians in a Nuclear War*, which was broadcast many times, sold on cassette and published in several collections.[71]

White told his congregation of scientists that they must strip themselves of the superfluous baggage that clutters their lives in order to find strength by discovering who they really were. White cited on behalf of this ethic of non-attachment to material things Gandhi, Aldous Huxley, Spinoza, the Gospels and the American poet-monk Thomas Merton. Only man stripped bare could hope to find great truths. 'I *have* known them, and shall again, but only intermittently, the result of a daily wrestling match, and then only by glimmers, as through a veil. None of the great truths can be more than half-grasped. I doubt I should have arrived anywhere near my inklings of them if it weren't for what I sense as links with a supernatural power.' He urged the scientists to continue searching for identity, moral strength, underlying spiritual truth and 'the good faith in us which may help save the world'.[72]

He returned home for a few days and then flew over to Adelaide for the opening of *Netherwood* which Sharman was directing. Kerry Walker was Mog the child-murderer, one of the afflicted inmates of this amateur asylum. White thought the show was a great success, but the verdict of critics was harsh. Time had done nothing to still the agitation bad notices provoked in White, and he saw malice everywhere in the press. Though his friend James Fairfax was now chairman of the Fairfax empire, White was convinced Fairfax's papers were out to sabotage his work. Their critic Harry Kippax he now dismissed as a 'deadhead'. Adulteries, professional disappointments, remembered snubs and cheap patriotism were held responsible for the hostile notices. 'There are reasons for everything!'[73]

Having decided he was too old and infirm to fly abroad again,

White was puzzled that other old people did not see reason and abide by his decision. When Peggy Garland said she was travelling to Egypt, White reproached her sharply: 'You would be crazy to sail up the Nile at your age, or set out on a long trip anywhere at any season. You can't imagine what the crowded planes or the airports are like.' But then Andreas Papandreou invited White to Athens to celebrate the ninth anniversary of the fall of the Colonels and he accepted. He was flown over in November: the risks to his lungs which he would not face for the Nobel he took happily for these celebrations. 'The expedition to Greece', he explained to Dorothy Green, 'could well be my last Great Experience.' Lascaris decided against the journey: 'he said it would be too complicated and too painful'.[74]

Despite the Nobel Prize, and all that he had written about Greece in the last forty years, Patrick White was little known as a writer in that country. Papandreou had cause to remember him, for when the leader-in-exile passed through Sydney in 1974 White came to his hotel room and gave him a cheque for the Greek cause. 'It was just a teaspoonful but he seemed very grateful for that.'[75] He took to Athens a tender speech about Greece. It was not delivered but Dimitri Photiades, well into his eighties and hurrying to finish the last volume of his memoirs, gave it to an Athens newspaper. White had finished with an appeal for help in the fight for peace: 'You Greeks gave the world civilisation. Since the fall of Byzantium it has been preserved by the Panayia and the Saints – as you know in your hearts, even those of you who *profess* not to "believe". Surely we must not allow the barbarians of today to destroy by holocaust this civilisation you have created.'[76]

On his last night in Athens, after Papandreou's opulent reception, White watched from the window of his room in the Grande Bretagne a huge demonstration against the Turks, 'a march of a million Athenians through the city, all ages, sexes, banners high, lots of red flags, voices chanting . . . it was a bit of an anticlimax to look out the window next morning and see the black figures of normal human beings trotting to work through the drizzle under their umbrellas. Later that day the wet season began in earnest: steep streets became torrents, and on level ground the potholes turned into a series of dangerous lakes. I spent the afternoon in bed, to be ready for departure at 2 a.m. I expect all this, and floundering to Elly's through rivers, lakes and dark, for a last supper (no chance of a taxi) brought the bronchial troubles on.'[77]

He arrived home with flu. 'After the nightmare city Athens, the traffic noise, cars driving straight at pedestrians, polluted skies, strained, desperate faces, the peace and beauty of our garden is hardly credible. Instead of screeching metal, the sound of cicadas and crickets, birdcalls, nesting doves and bulbuls, a brilliance of sky and flowers, and one of my favourite sights, bark shredding from angophoras and the lemon scented gum.'[78]

After this brief appearance on the international stage, meeting world leaders and heroes of the Greek resistance, White felt he could make more ambitious appeals for peace. He drafted open letters to the leaders of the Western world: to Ronald Reagan, Margaret Thatcher and François Mitterrand. The letters are cranky: a mixture of reminiscences and reproach and abrupt rudeness. To Reagan: 'Come on, cowboy!' And to Thatcher: 'I urge you to search your heart, Mrs Thatcher, if one exists behind the pearls . . .' The letters to Western leaders were sent for publication to the *New York Times*, *The Times*, and *Le Monde*. None appeared.

The Russians invited him to fly over for a fortnight in June 1984 to address the Writers' Union. He accepted on two conditions: that he could speak to the Foreign Minister Andrei Gromyko and that his air fares to Moscow were paid. It was impossible, he said, to meet the cost himself: 'I have too many commitments.' Elizabeth Harrower was invited to make the same journey and she pressed the Russians on White's behalf. The Embassy was silent on Gromyko and adamant about the fares. But the whole idea, Lascaris pointed out, was impossible: 'Patrick doesn't have a heavy overcoat.'[79]

A new party was being formed to work for nuclear disarmament. At first White was sceptical: wasn't it better to keep on at the Hawke government 'with every threat and any kind of blackmail we can think of'? But as the Nuclear Disarmament Party evolved in the winter of 1984 White poured money in and spoke on its behalf. The NDP wanted all foreign military bases in Australia closed; all nuclear weapons banned from the country's soil, sea and air; and an end to uranium mining. 'I am feeling exhausted after weeks of supporting the anti-nuclear movement,' he wrote to Ronald Waters in August. 'Recently I spoke at Melbourne University and a week after in Sydney Town Hall for Hiroshima Day. Packed houses and good coverage in each case. Never thought I could manage this sort of thing. It must be the frustrated actor in me added to the despair of life today.'[80]

His back was worse. He found some relief in acupuncture and chiropractic but by October the pain was so terrible that he almost called off a trip to New Zealand to present the country's first Media Peace Prize. Bob Harvey, who had organised the visit, was at Auckland airport to meet him when he arrived with Lascaris on 1 November. He found White frail, irritable and gruff. 'He was obviously a very sick man.' Next morning Harvey came to the hotel for a cup of tea. 'He was honest that he felt he was dying . . . and in a way he apologised for being so foul-tempered.' White presented the prizes the following

night, congratulating New Zealand for the brave and independent stand
it had taken against nuclear arms. He recalled Solomon Rakooka the
black yardman at Lulworth who came every day to collect him from
kindergarten, 'my small white hand in his large black spongy one as
he helped me board the tram'. This childhood alliance, he said, was
an image of a personal duty he now felt towards the people of the
Pacific.[81]

He spent a bad night, and a doctor was called to the hotel about
1am to give him some shots. He had agreed to be interviewed by
television next day, and emerged from the studio quivering with
indignation. For the first time in his life he had been quizzed publicly
about his homosexuality. To Michael King, who met the two men to
take them for a drive, White complained of intrusion and impertinence.
'Take us into the city,' he said. 'I seem to remember a long street down
the middle.' King found him very tired and ill. He had not seen White
since their time in Menton. 'In our three hours together the only time
he reveals anything like the animation of our first encounter eight
years before is discussing the peace question; and when we stop in
the Auckland domain at the garden for the blind . . . then for twenty
minutes, sore back in remission, he and Lascaris discover plants like old
friends, exclaim with pleasure, stroke them, smell them, crush fragrant
leaves. White's habitual mask, which he describes as that of an "enraged
sea lion", dissolves as he revels in nature and a shared delight. Back in
the car he is old and tired again.'[82]

When he reached home, he was given an X-ray which showed
several vertebrae in his lower spine had crumbled. Glaucoma, and now
osteoporosis, the thinning of his bones, were the price he had to pay for
the lifesaving cortisone he had been taking for twenty-five years for his
chest. 'Now at least I know it wasn't imagination and isn't cancer, but
the outlook is bleak,' he told Elizabeth Harrower. 'Rest and calcium
seem all they have to offer.' He was put into St Vincent's Hospital,
where he stayed for five weeks, reading a little, writing letters and
watching television. He was intrigued by *Neighbours*. Patients and staff
brought him copies of his books to autograph. Another round of elections was called as he lay there. Visitors and nurses were given leaflets
for the NDP. He sold badges. Opinion polls showed strong support
for the new party, but in the end only one senator was elected. 'The
NDP didn't do as well as we hoped in the election,' White told Peggy
Garland. 'But at least we gave the bastard Hawke a fight – we must
keep on.'[83]

A fortnight before Christmas he was allowed home. Instead of
his old loping stride he managed only to shuffle about 'like a maimed
cockroach'.[84] Those he once towered over now faced him eye to eye,
for he had shrunk four or five inches. He leant heavily on his stick,

which became a vaudeville prop, pointed and waved and pounded on the floor in a geriatric soft-shoe shuffle. He refused to move into one of the empty guest bedrooms, so every morning he struggled down the narrow staircase, and set himself up in the sitting room under a strong reading light. On a little table beside the armchair he had two boxes of Man Size Kleenex, a packet of peppermints, his Ventolin inhaler, a bottle of eye drops, the *Observer*, and the morning mail: 'most of them stuffers: they can get stuffed'.[85] A biro hung round his neck, and he had a long, grey device with a hook for picking up bits and pieces that fell at his feet.

'*I am trapped in this house*,' he protested to Luciana Arrighi. 'I can't get around and do and see the things which stimulate me. No films, plays, restaurants because my back couldn't last out.' His greatest luxury was a new cordless telephone. 'I can make myself heard on the cordless as far north as the Queensland border and as far South as Melbourne,' he told Peggy Garland. 'I am about to try it out on Perth where one of my plays will be revived in the Festival.'[86] He was taking calcium and vitamin D, drinking milk and doing a few exercises to help knit his spine. An Anglican nun from a community in the Hunter Valley brought him a chunky wooden cross which he also hung round his neck. The cross tangled with the biro, like the icons on the chest of an Orthodox Metropolitan.

'My life has taken a new turn,' he told Ronald Waters. 'The pain for a long time was agonising, now it is much less and I can hobble about but have to lie down a lot. At least we know it isn't cancer. The worry is that I shall have to lead, probably, a very limited life. If only I can sit long enough at desk or table to finish a few bits and pieces . . . who knows? There is so much to tidy up. M has been wonderful.'[87]

TWENTY-NINE

The Town of Jerusalem

WHITE THOUGHT HE knew all about old age. When he was young he had written confidently about old age; his early lovers were much older men; he played older than his years. 'I was never young.' In his fifties he spoke of being old, and in his sixties he claimed to be surprised to find himself still writing, reading, campaigning, cooking, feuding. 'This is what old age does to one, when I had imagined sitting about in a state of bland tranquillity listening to gramophone records.' A decade later, when he was indisputably old and the gramophone had broken down never to be repaired, he knew he had only ever known old age in theory. 'I wrote *The Eye of the Storm* from the outside.'[1]

He had not found peace, nor had a lifetime's work brought contentment, for he was still in hand-to-hand combat with doubt and pride. The wisdom of old age had not descended on him, except that, 'In a sense my disbelief is wisdom.' He still laid down the law with ferocity on small matters – the breeding of children, the vices of the *nouveaux riches*, dogs and dog care, those Sydney shysters who should be in jail, the delusions of literary academics, the vulgarity of Bob Hawke – but the big questions were still open, as unanswerable in his seventies as they had been in his youth. About himself he felt there was still 'a bit more' to understand. He was less jealous, perhaps, and more tolerant but wondered if this only meant he was 'giving in'. He knew his memory was not the infallible instrument it had been. Names escaped him now, and he feared this might be a first sign that senility was on the way.[2]

The great surprise was to find his crumpled body did not *feel* old. The cliché of the youthful geriatric, which he had resisted in his own writing, turned out to be true, and it made it seem all the more idiotic to be 'creeping about when you don't feel all that old inside'. Desire had not let him go. Christina Stead's problem, said David Malouf, was to be randy to the end. 'A terrible problem', said White, 'if you haven't got someone.' He blessed the fate that gave him his 'permanent faithful' and saved him from this worst of nightmares. Transience, he told Björkstén in the course of a general reprimand, 'can lead to a pathetic old age'. White's marriage had endured. 'Don't know what would have happened if I hadn't found him,' he told Waters. 'We still have screaming rows, but not so many.' Peggy Garland reported that her sister Betty mellowed once she turned eighty. 'She no longer snaps and snarls at me.' Lascaris remarked drily on hearing this news, 'Ah, well, we shall have to wait till eighty . . .'[3]

White went on complaining that age was a dreadful mess; that his life would be a shambles to the end, 'led between stove and desk, burnt food, and chaotic foolscap';[4] that the demands made on him were never ending; that his country was vile and the world was vile and the human race pretty appalling – but he was alive. Life itself was thrilling and he would put every ounce of his determination into the task of being alive.

In early January 1985 he was back at his desk every day, working for as long as his back would allow on a novel begun before the expedition to New Zealand. This was *Memoirs of Many in One*: 'It's about premature senility. No. No. It's a *very* funny subject. It will offend a lot of people. Does them good. I enjoy it. It is religious in a sense; they won't like my approach to religion, the ones who are orthodox religious. And it's bawdy; the ones who like the bawdiness will be offended by the religion.' He was having a lot of fun writing. His mastery of the first person was now so complete, that he made himself a figure in the book, and the self-portrait was funny and true: Patrick the old sod, the performer, the prim disapprover, the occasional bore, 'the born Mother Superior'.[5]

The conceit was that he, Patrick White, had been asked to edit the memoirs of the late Alex Xenophon Demirjian Gray of Alexandria and Sydney who, he admitted to Ronald Waters, 'is myself in my various roles and sexes. It gives me great scope.'[6] Alex Gray's forebears and offspring are also fragments of White, and these familiar figures of his imagination are gathered together in the pages of *Memoirs* as friends once gathered in Sydney after the war, holding one last party before the ship sails.

Alex Gray is going mad. The shifts of time and place, dreams and waking, are as dazzling in *Memoirs* as they were in the Jardin Exotique of *The Aunt's Story* written thirty-five years before in the flat on the Safia Zaghloul. But this writing is funnier, sharper and earthier. Theodora Goodman was drifting towards the kind of peaceful death White knew now was not to be his, but Alex Gray is demented and alive: alive to see, taste, dream, try her will, to wrestle with saints and demons – and alive to write. 'Words are what matter,' she shouts at her practical daughter Hilda,

'Even when they don't communicate. That's why I must continue writing. Somebody may understand in time. All that I experienced . . . in any of my lives, past or future – as Benedict, Magda, Dolly Formosa. Somebody . . . could understand tomorrow . . .'

Alex Gray is still trying to make sense of herself: 'to discover – by writing out – acting out my life – the reason for my presence on earth'.[7]

White took seriously the challenge of writing from inside a senile mind. His old friend Dr Ferry Grundseit told him all he knew about Alzheimer's disease, and passed him on to a neurologist, Dr Robert Ouvrier, who came one evening to Martin Road. Ouvrier had wondered if White's talk of research might be an elaborate cover for his worries, but he found White obviously in charge of his faculties, alert, curious and with a lively memory. Ouvrier discussed the disease, including a case in his own family, and left some printed case histories of Alzheimer's at Martin Road. White gave Alex Gray a vivacity which those whose minds are falling apart do not possess, but Ouvrier found the woman's delusions, illusions, wandering, forgetfulness, paranoia, her coarseness and lack of inhibition were authentic.[8]

White rescued some of the theatrical passages from 'The Binoculars and Helen Nell' abandoned fifteen years before and reworked them for *Memoirs*. Alex Gray is an actress of sorts and her career – all illusion, perhaps – ends one night in the Sand Pit Theatre. This débâcle is based on a night White spent with Armfield at the Performance Space in Sydney watching a show about national mythologies that involved a bride in a burnt wedding dress and actors emerging from drifts of sand. All this is reflected in *Memoirs*. Alex Gray, breathing through a snorkel under the sand, is supposed to emerge saying, 'I am the spirit of the land, past, present and future.' Instead she misses her cue and stumbles out shouting, 'I am the Resurrection and the Life' – an echo through White's work from the earliest days. One of the Cheltenham poems had a mad Messiah shouting that line. Children scattered then in fear, now the unbelievers at the Sand Pit break into unprecedented laughter,

Are they supposed to laugh? I suspect no one has ever dared at a venue for serious, innovative drama like the Sand Pit. But finally they can't contain themselves . . . [9]

Disguised as Alex Gray, White took revenge *inter alia* on Harry Miller, Harry Kippax and the vulgar Mary Fairfax, stepmother of James, who appears as Lady Miriam Surplus of Comebychance Hall.

Alex arrives at her party in an ocelot coat announcing herself as the Empress Theodora of Byzantium, and gallops a white horse through the smorgasbørd,

> ploughing the Double Bay hair-dos the bald pates, the hair-pieces and blow-waves, then down to the plastic scum where beach meets lantana, and up again, up. I might have been leading a cohort in which Valkyries galloped neck and neck with Sisters of the Sacred Blood . . .

Alex travels the Outback performing Shakespeare and her one-woman show *Dolly Formosa and the Happy Few*. Somewhere in the bush 'K.V.H. of the *S.M.H.*' arrives by light aircraft to catch the show. No quarter is shown the critic: he has the look of an anæmic bat, glows a little in the dark, and is said to have made his last gesture to modernity 'many years ago when he invented Brecht'. On reading these words, Kippax reflected that the only playwright he ever invented 'was an Australian, Patrick White'.[10]

White was impatient to finish the book. 'I should really spend years on it,' he told Kerry Walker. 'But my own senility might overtake me.'[11] He had worked on *Memoirs* for about three months before his back collapsed and after returning to it in the New Year of 1985 he finished a second draft in only four months. Both energy and patience were lacking for the typing of a third draft, and on 1 May he took the manuscript in his shopping bag to his agent's office. Since O'Hea's retirement, almost all his affairs had been handled by Barbara Mobbs in the Sydney branch of Curtis Brown. She was a true successor to O'Hea: an efficient, firm woman whose application to White's interests was informed by a streak of practical good humour. White called her the flying nun, and it was to Barbara Mobbs under that name that he dedicated *Memoirs*. He revised and reworked her typescript and the book went off to London in late June.

He was going to the park again, but taking only a short walk and resting on a bench by the lake while Lascaris went further over the sandhills with Nellie their possessive Jack Russell, and Eureka the mongrel stray. White mastered buses, clambering on to the 396 to go in to the bank. As he refused to have credit cards and trusted only head office, the banking took some time and effort. 'My God, the bank!' Since computers, things had gone from bad to worse at the bank. 'Soft . . . What do you call it? Software. What does it mean? They used to have *software* on the third floor of David Jones.'[12]

They followed as far as possible their old, practical routine. White was cooking again and Lascaris did the shopping. They had a cleaner every Thursday, and Lascaris was up at dawn to unlock the house for the 'Spanish treasure'. She was paid, in the best traditions of the bush, in cash and meat – usually chops. On warm days they sat under the vine drinking tea. Occasionally they saw a play or a film, and ate at a restaurant about once a week, 'but only if I know the chairs are going to be all right'.[13] Lascaris no longer drove at night, so friends collected them or they took taxis. Lascaris would stand ready in the garden – for it was as imperative as ever that taxis not be kept waiting – and signal White with a torch when the car arrived. White would appear at the top of the steep path, walking carefully with a stick while carrying a canvas hold-all that had his pills, eye drops and a rubber back cushion. All the way down to the gate, Lascaris would shine the light at his feet, and then stow the torch in the letterbox for the return journey.

Neil Armfield's productions of *Signal Driver* had drawn good crowds in Adelaide, Melbourne and Brisbane. The play went into rehearsal at the Belvoir Street Theatre in Sydney as White was toying with the last changes to *Memoirs*. The Belvoir was a new co-operative company, the third Sydney theatre White had taken a hand in establishing. He had been to the meetings as his back was failing the previous year, and liked to complain that he'd ruined his back in the cause of Belvoir Street. He was in fact but not in name the theatre's patron, and the $10,000 he contributed made him its biggest individual shareholder. *Signal Driver* was the new company's first production, and was backed by friends and actors. Armfield was again directing. Esso gave $10,000.

White gave a couple of interviews at the theatre. Happiness? 'I've had more than most people would hope for but I had the wrong chemistry for happiness. No. I haven't been a happy person. Oh, I've had wonderful bursts of happiness. But how can anyone who thinks or sees what goes on be happy? . . . Turn a blind eye and you could lead a wonderful life. I could eat and drink myself silly and debauch myself in every way and pretend everything was lovely . . . No, you're young and you've got things to do. In a way I've run out of things to do. With a broken back and failing eyesight you can't lead a very wild life . . . No I never regret having not had children. It would have been dreadful. Dreadful. I would have been a terrible parent. Too irritable. I wouldn't have wanted them round me when I was working. I would have said things they wouldn't have liked, and made them unhappy. You know those famous lines of Philip Larkin? "They fuck you up your Mum and Dad"? That's a wonderful line. I'd love to get a spray painter to spray all round the department stores before Mother's Day. A dreadful invention. Another bit of dishonesty.'[14]

Kerry Walker was Ivy Vokes in this production, and on opening night White sent her flowers and a card: 'Age beautifully.' The crowds that had always come to *Signal Driver* before did not turn out in Sydney.

Belvoir had not yet established its audience, but White blamed the small
houses squarely on H.G.K. whom he saw as the leader of a cabal of
critics: 'They got together and panned it.' Kippax was not enthusiastic
about the play on his second viewing, but his public verdict was a good
deal kinder than his private opinion, for he had come to think all White's
later plays were trash.[15]

Towards the end of the Belvoir season Walker read White the brief
account in Alan Jenkins' *The Thirties* of the fall of the vicar of Stiffkey,
thrown out of the church for lewd relations and ending his days performing with lions in a sideshow. One ate him. 'Oh, I know all about
that,' White cried impatiently. 'I was at Cambridge with his son.' But
that night he decided to write a play that was an Australian version of
the Stiffkey story. *The Budgiwank Experiment* – as its title was before
cautious friends persuaded him to call it *Shepherd on the Rocks* – was
to be another act of retaliation against the Sydney critics and a vehicle
for the stars of *Signal Driver*. White told Kerry Walker, 'I am writing
this for all of us and everything we stand for.'[16]

William Yang was to take a photograph for the jacket of *Memoirs
of Many in One*, but he had a call from Martin Road giving fresh
plans. 'She is me,' said White, 'so I thought I'd have a photo of me
as her for the frontispiece and a photo of me as Patrick on the back
flap.'[17]

The weekend before the pictures were to be taken, White suffered
a kind of breakdown and was taken to St Vincent's. He told Greene: 'I
went out to dinner on the 7th and was struck down in the night with
curiously persistent lapses of memory, Manoly with the vomits. We
got a doctor in the morning who said I only had a hangover – a pity
because we had eaten such an excellent lamb biriani. I had drunk too
much local vodka with mine, but Manoly only a little white wine to
his food. Next night M. fetched a neighbour-doctor who is also one
of the heads of this hospital. He had me admitted through the Casualty
(which I now call the Russian Dungeons) was moved up to a ward in
the thoracic that morning and finally accepted as an inmate attended
by our neighbour.'[18]

He felt weak, but his mind cleared leaving him annoyed that the
photo-session had to be postponed. As he lay there he had a new idea.
'Shall make my way to a public phone as soon as the physio leaves
me alone,' he told Greene.[19] Later that morning he had a chance to
call Yang. He explained that in *Memoirs* Alex Gray dies in hospital, and
the ward would make a good backdrop for her death scene. White was
a virtuoso of the death scene. Hardly a book or play was without a
death, and he had in his repertoire crucifixion, traffic accidents, canni-
bal feasts and cliff plunges; there are murders, committed or considered;

deaths by fire, brain fever, heart attack and 'by torture in the country of the mind'; deaths at sea, in the desert, on winter mornings, under rubble, under bombs, on a commode in jewels, in the street attended by anonymous saints 'who lift us from the gutters, wiping the vomit from our lips, who comfort us as our limbs lie paralysed on the pavement, feed us within their limited means, and close our eyes . . .'[20]

All were guesswork, perhaps inspired guesswork, for death is one subject White could only ever write from the outside.

We go nowhere when we die, for death is not a journey. In a universe without heaven or hell, our spirits may perhaps survive where we have lived and suffered. What else death offered was still unclear to White. The moment would be what mattered: at the moment of death he would (or would not) discover the Presence of which he only ever had inklings in life, the 'mysterious universal Presence ignored, cursed, derided, or intermittently worshipped by the human race'. Death for Alex Gray, tended by the nuns of St Damien's, is the moment when 'the last of human frailty makes contact with the supernatural'.[21]

He had told Dutton some years before, 'I only want to gather up the last shreds of my life into an acceptable fabric.' There was to be no hoopla: 'down the ramp at the crematorium with no ribald jangle of gongs and hollow applause'. Then his ashes were to be brought back and scattered on one of the lakes in Centennial Park. 'The park is the place which means most to me. I hope I shall haunt it, and protect it.'

Under Yang's instructions, the nurses moved White's bed next to the sink and under a plain crucifix. White played dead, but Yang was disappointed with the photographs. The corpse of Alex Gray looked like a fairly healthy Patrick White. So when White was back at Martin Road a few days later, they had another session, this time in Lascaris's bare bedroom. Icons were arranged at the head of the bed, and the corpse wore a nightdress with a bit of lace showing above the sheet. Kerry Walker painted his face and gave him a blood capsule to chew. A stream of stage blood ran down his jaw.

Lascaris disapproved. Sharman thought the photographs a terrible idea. So did Desmond Digby. Barbara Mobbs was amused at first but then very cool: 'He'd be leaving himself wide open.' White agreed the death-bed shots were unsuitable, but thought the frontispiece of Alex in a kerchief was tactful and witty. 'She looks Greek, she could have been a nun, she could be an actress, and she could be a bitch.' No one but Yang was keen in the end, so White gave up the idea. 'Various people feel having the nun as frontispiece could backfire,' White told Greene. 'So I am retreating, regretfully. I have nothing to lose at the end of my life, and only look forward to leaving a diabolical world and a piddling country.'[22]

Memoirs ends with Hilda and Patrick taking a trip round the world to lay a few ghosts in those places that had meant most to Alex. In Assisi they visit the Basilica of San Francesco and are then directed by an urbane Franciscan to the church of Santa Chiara – down a steep hill. Jonathan Cape changed this to up a steep hill. White protested: 'We were directed by the cynical Franciscan and I seem to remember walking down hill. While approaching the end of *Memoirs* I consulted David Malouf, who lives part of the year in Tuscany. A friend of his produced photocopies from a guide book, and we have our own Blue Guide. What to do???? Are you or your informant *sure*?'

'I was in Assisi myself last summer,' replied Liz Cowen from Cape. 'I am absolutely sure that the church of Santa Chiara is *up* the hill at the other end of the town to the basilica of San Francesco.'

'Barbara, who is a practising R.C., says she remembers it being *down*hill. So I think we'll have to leave it that way. Hilda is a disturbed rationalist and Patrick not all that different from Alex in one of her more senile roles. So what?' Cape insisted. White gave way.[23]

Both Cape and Viking wanted to credit White as the author on the cover of *Memoirs*. They tried hard to persuade him. He said he did not care if being called editor cut sales. Would he allow inverted commas on the jacket? No. As White was checking Viking's blurb he found himself described as the 'Nobelist Patrick White'. He scrawled in the margin, 'No! NO! NO! One of the most horrible words I've ever heard.' This was corrected with apologies. Cape was to publish on April Fool's Day 1986, Viking not till the fall.

Spring in the park was miraculously beautiful that year, 'all this gum blossom and birdcall'. White was able to take long walks and look forward to marching in the Peace March on Palm Sunday. He was the stronger for having given up drink again after the night of the local vodka. 'I'm also stroking a play,' he told the Sterns on New Year's Day, 1986. 'A few lines a day in between cooking our meals and trying to deal with correspondence. I could employ at least four slaves, but shouldn't have anything left to give away.' Six weeks later he told Greene, 'I have almost got my new play down on paper. So much happening or threatened. I am stuck in the last scene. It will come with a rush eventually.'[24]

White was hard at work to calm his nerves as he faced another opening. The pattern was an old one; what was looming was the 'wretched' opera *Voss*. So hostile had he become to the project since a little of Act One was sung at the 1982 Adelaide Festival that he spoke of refusing to go near it. His whole response to *Voss* was coloured by the fact that Nolan now owned the film rights. 'Too many dishonest fingers have dabbled in *Voss* and I've come to hate it,' he told Ronald Waters. White was also disparaging the composer Richard Meale in public, accusing him of turning down his satiric libretto in order to be 'an establishment darling'.[25] But Sharman, with great tact, drew White back towards the project in the early weeks of 1986. There were, in any case, too many of the old crowd involved for White to turn his back entirely: besides Sharman and Malouf, there was Brian Thomson designing the sets and Luciana Arrighi the costumes.

One night in mid-February White and Lascaris saw a run-through under industrial lights at the Australia Opera's paint shop in Surry Hills. There were two pianos and a few bits of costumes. White was dreading this, but Sharman thought he arrived that night open to what lay ahead. He wept. 'We spent a thrilling evening,' he wrote next day to Greene. 'The complete thing will open at Adelaide Festival on March 1st . . . I shall not be there as I can't appear at a Festival which invites the Queen of England. However, I shall see the complete version when it comes to Sydney later in the year.'[26] He relished the prospect. Every conceivable monster would be there, including the stars of the Sydney new rich and most of the politicians he had fallen out with. On the morning of the day he spent some time practising what he called his 'looking-without-seeing' look.

White was now a landmark. No face at the Opera House was more famous, but he had a way of walking through a crowd without causing a stir, deploying a pre-emptive surliness that kept people at bay. The Opera's invitations said black tie; White wore corduroy trousers, a heavy jumper and a blue cotton jacket. His pen hung round his neck. He sat very still during the performance, occasionally chewing his gums. He leant forward to hush a matron. When the audience was roaring at the end, he fished in his pocket and brought out his eye drops. He did not take a bow. White, Lascaris and their party left for home. The opening had confirmed the triumph *Voss* enjoyed in Adelaide. 'It was a stupendous occasion,' he told Elizabeth Falkenberg. 'It took me three days to recover both physically and emotionally; I relived so much.'[27]

Memoirs appeared. Critics were puzzled, amused, scathing, angry, wry and delighted. A Melbourne Jungian broke new ground by birching White in the *Age* for being gay.[28]

Some time that winter, White had a letter from the editors of the Melbourne magazine *Scripsi* asking him to write for a special edition of the magazine to be published by Penguin in 1987. *Scripsi* liked his work, and he liked the magazine's international yet Australian outlook, while complaining at the same time it was 'so intellectual I can't understand half of what goes on in it'. He wrote *Three Uneasy Pieces*. They are an old man's reflections on the failure of age to bring wisdom, certainty or rest,

Prayer and vegies ought to help towards atonement. But don't.
There is the chopping to be done. Memories rise to the surface . . .

Some of these reached his fiction for the first time: memories of life in
Cheltenham and Cambridge, of the opulent existence at the hotel in
Villars-sur-Bex, of the imagined ash heap of Hiroshima as he described
it to anti-nuclear rallies, and the miserable home in the Blue Mountains
where Lizzie Clark died. The second *Uneasy Piece* has an appearance by
Mrs Ethel Kelly as the Contessa del Castelmarino, alias Gladys (Baby)
Horsfall of Gundy, New South Wales. The third is an old writer's nightmare of the 'stuffed turkey' he has become and the saint he always
aspired to be. These little pieces, 'prose poems' White called them,
are haunted by age and decay, yet are astonishingly alive:

> I lay down my sticks on the dishwasher which no longer works.
> I am dancing again, almost without knowing it, in collusion with
> the radio. I am dancing, but cautiously, with both feet on the
> ground . . .

White sent the *Uneasy Pieces* down to Melbourne by the end of
September.[29] Of all the writers *Scripsi* approached, White was the
only one to meet his deadline. White was a professional to the end.

He was back on the platform. A clumsy monorail was being
built along Sydney's narrow streets and White campaigned against
it and marched with 10,000 demonstrators along its route through
the city. The monorail was built. In November White spoke to a
peace conference at the Australian Defence Forces Academy in Canberra. He met there and enjoyed a *rapprochement* with the writer Thea
Astley. 'Catching a politician's ear is a trick I've never mastered,' he
confessed to the conference. 'They see me, I suspect, as a ratbag to use
and discard.' He ended with a prayer for peace and justice. He said, 'I
believe in prayer.'[30]

The year ended badly. For about six weeks he worked at a new
novel. The characters had been rehearsing noisily in his imagination,
but he left off when he realised that to write the book 'would take a
lifetime when there is so little of that left to me'.[31] In November 1986,
one of the partners of Curtis Brown had appeared from London and she
came to tea at Martin Road. There had been tensions in the Sydney office
for some years and London had decided to resolve them by dismissing
Barbara Mobbs. White was appalled and broke with Curtis Brown after
fifty years. One of the senior partners offered to fly out to try to persuade
him to stay, but White warned him not to waste his time. There was talk
of litigation. White declared he would spend his last penny fighting for
the right to take all his business to Mobbs. Curtis Brown shied away

from the prospect of fighting the old man through the courts.

White collapsed. A long run of bronchial asthma ended in pleurisy. 'This did my bone ailment no good as I had to stop my exercises and the things I eat to build up my bones,' he told Waters. 'Finally I developed endless diarrhoea as the result of all the antibiotics I had been taking.' He felt in the early weeks of the New Year that he was on top of most of these troubles, 'Not the osteoporosis, which will be with me for ever.'[32] He hoped now he had the strength to get over to Adelaide in April for rehearsals of *Shepherd on the Rocks*.

The new play, on which he had been working intermittently for nearly two years, followed very closely Jenkins' brief account of the fall of the vicar of Stiffkey in *The Thirties*. White took names, characters, even lines of dialogue from Jenkins, but translated the story into an epic religious revue to suit his own purposes. Danny Shepherd has a parish called Budgiwank, 'really a kind of Castle Hill-by-the-sea. Before he became a priest he was a performer and he's really always been a performer and the Budgiwank Experiment is a crazy idea he has of converting prostitutes and junkies at the Cross and bringing them down to the parish where they can mix with virtuous parishioners. He wants to see what effect it has, if they'll learn something about life and the spirit through rubbing on each other – but he falls foul of the archbishop and the dean.'[33] When Shepherd is defrocked, he returns to the stage, preaching and tap-dancing his way towards Jerusalem.

White never quite made it to the holy places of Jerusalem for it was always his fate to be stopped at the border dividing the city. By the time Danny Shepherd reaches Jerusalem, the town has been hijacked by greed. Jerusalem is a market town: 'Lovely. Big new supermarket. Speciality shops. And Now it's Showtime.'[34] In White's calendar, the most detested event of the year was still the Royal Easter Show, that fortnight when he felt trapped in his own house by horse floats and tourists. He sends Danny Shepherd to end his days as an act at the Jerusalem Easter Show.

When he flew to Adelaide in early April, he booked himself into the Gateway Hotel. He felt too old to stay with friends. The first week of rehearsals was exhausting, but he was pleased with the cast and Armfield's approach. John Gaden was the fallen Shepherd and Kerry Walker the prostitute Queenie. It worried him that Brian Thomson's design followed so much the circus theme: 'I had to remind them that it is a play about the varieties of religious experience.'[35] He flew home and returned a fortnight later. For the first time, Lascaris was with him for one of his Adelaide opening nights. John Gaden brought White on to the stage to take a bow. 'You have been in our hands all night,' said the playwright to the first-night audience, 'now we are in yours.'

'*Shepherd on the Rocks* brought in the public,' he reported to

Moya Henderson. 'As far as I'm concerned, it was a great success: design, music, acting, direction – all that I could have wished. Perth, Brisbane, and the Sydney Festival want it for next year, but I won't have anything of mine performed during the nauseating Bi. I'd like to see it done eventually in Sydney, the city to which it belongs.' White had decided that nothing of his would be performed or published in Australia in the bicentennial year of white settlement. He was boycotting the Bi. 'I hope I am dead before 1988 when we are supposed to celebrate our emptiness in a great shower of bullshit.'[36]

Coughing, he said, had given him a hernia, and he faced this minor operation with morbid dread. What might the surgeons find once they open him up? 'Mrs Flack,' suggested David Malouf, 'Mrs Jolley, Stan Parker . . .' There was no cancer, but he caught pneumonia and was in hospital for a fortnight. He had a telephone and television. 'I realise what gaps there have been in my life. All the things I've missed. Ads telling you to stuff your kids with sugar.' He worried the flowers visitors were bringing made too much work for the nurses. 'Not FLOWERS?!'[37]

At home again, he worked on four short 'very black' theatre pieces he was writing for Kerry Walker.[38] He called them *Four Love Songs*. An old woman sits talking on a park bench; a man enters and sits beside her. He departs; she keeps talking; he returns and kills her. A cat lies on a waterbed – White had heard of an arthritic cat that could only be comfortable on its own little waterbed – while the voice of its mistress is heard talking about her lovers. There were defamation worries with 'The Whore's Cat' for the lovers were politicians. In the third *Love Song*, 'My Big American', two girls fuck American soldiers on leave in Sydney. The fourth was to be 'A Nun's Monologue', a satire on the life of Mary McKillop, but after Barbara Mobbs had done a great deal of research at convents, White found he admired this Australian candidate for sainthood too much to write the satire. He was taken to the McKillop shrine in north Sydney: 'It was wonderful.' White believed in saints: on this point the 'lapsed Anglican egotist agnostic pantheist occultist existentialist' was at one with the Orthodox Lascaris.[39]

Cambridge and Sydney Universities had both offered White honorary doctorates in the previous twelve months. He turned them down. Soundings were made by King's College about an honorary fellowship, but these appeared to cease with the appearance of *Flaws in the Glass*. Now, in late 1987, Melbourne University offered him a doctorate of letters. White thanked the university but again declined. 'Years ago the Australian National University offered me this degree which I refused, partly out of shyness, partly from sensing I should be surrendering some of my independence. Having refused the ANU, I felt I must refuse any other offers both at home and overseas. Though no longer shy, my instinct was right on the other count: independence, particularly in Australia, is a person's most important weapon.'[40]

As White saw the millions being 'squandered' on preparations for 1988, his disapproval of the Bicentennial set hard.[41] What was planned seemed expensive, vulgar and embarrassing, a clone of the American Bicentennial with cricket and royalty thrown in. The year-long party was to begin on Australia Day, 26 January, with a replica of the First Fleet sailing into Sydney Harbour.

Beneath White's monkish distaste for the celebrations lay a deep hostility to any exercise of official patriotism. He had lived a very long time, and remembered Germans being pelted with vegetables in the First World War. 'Dachshunds were stoned.'[42] Since he was a boy at Tudor House, joining the other boys to mock old Skuse, he had known the temptation to betray himself by joining the mob. Everyone runs that risk of betraying their better selves in a crowd, cheering the victors or ridiculing the defenceless, the afflicted, the foreigners – those whom White saw as his own kind. For forty years he had been trying to show his country it was not as it believed itself to be. He was not now going to accept the official version being put about for these celebrations. Where were the poofters, the republicans, the pessimists?

'It all starts with the question of identity. In recent years we have been served up a lot of clap trap about the need for a *national* identity. We have been urged to sing imbecile jingles, flex our muscles like the sportsmen from telly commercials, and display hearty optimism totally unconvincing because so superficial and unnatural. Those who preach this doctrine are usually the kind of chauvinist who is preparing his country, not to avert war, but to engage in it. Anyhow, this is not the way to cultivate an Australian identity. For one thing, we are still in the melting pot, a rich but not yet blended stew of disparate nationalities. And most of us who were transplanted here generations ago, either willingly or unwillingly, the white overlords and their slave whites, are still too uncertain *in ourselves*. Australia will never acquire a national identity until enough *individual* Australians acquire identities of their own. It is a question of spiritual values and must come from within before it can convince and influence others.'[43]

On makeshift poles in the garden he hoisted two flags a fortnight before Australia Day: the black and red Aboriginal flag with a sun at its centre, and the blue and white Eureka cross which many republicans hope to make the national flag. The night before a television crew was to interview him in the garden, the flags were stolen. Replacements were quickly found in the morning: an old Eureka from the Builders' Labourers Federation, and a magnificent Aboriginal flag from the black and white protesters occupying a headland on the Harbour for the Australia Day celebrations. Beneath the flags White spoke for those who wanted justice, integrity and peace before celebrations. 'Circuses don't solve serious problems. When the tents are taken down, we'll be left with the dark, the emptiness – and probably a two-dollar loaf.'[44] Brief grabs from the interview were shown around the world.

On Australia Day he watched the arrival of the fleet on television and found something positive and stimulating in the moment, 'when for a few hours Australians seemed to forget their squabbles and to become more or less reconciled to one another'. But the moment passed. He called 1988 the year of the great Australian lie.[45] His publishing and performance boycott held. *Scripsi* had so dithered over their special issue that there was a danger the *Three Uneasy Pieces* would appear in 1988. In late November 1987 White suddenly withdrew the pieces, and Bruce Pascoe, a Melbourne publisher, issued them in a little paperback before Christmas. White dedicated them to an old friend, Thea Waddell. Cape republished them in Britain, but White did not give them to Viking, for his old American publishers continued to feed his royalties through Curtis Brown.

He was ill again in late summer and in March spent a few days in hospital. When he returned home, he spent days in bed, only coming downstairs for meals. He complained of being a geriatric bundle: 'I shall be going through the motions for the rest of my life.' The weather was terrible at that worst time of year in Sydney, sweltering heat and days of grey rain. He read Salvatore Satta's posthumous novel *The Day of Judgement* – 'a remarkable book'; the letters of Gertrude Bell; Edmund Wilson's criticism – 'I never tire of him'; Michael Ondaatje; the latest Nadine Gordimer – 'Very good, but visions of the future are always dangerous'; plus new Australian novels – 'You've got to find out about things.' The best of these Australians was Kate Grenville's *Joan Makes History* – 'it delighted me all along'.[46] His accountant came to tell him he was giving too much money away. Nellie was run over and both White and Lascaris were distraught: 'She was part of our lives, more than any dog we've ever had.'[47] Their great friend Penny Coleing found them a new Jack Russell, christened Milly.

When the cool weather arrived after Easter, more or less on time according to the old calendar, White rallied. He was gathering his strength for a speech at La Trobe University in July. 'I've got some rather explosive stuff I've come by.' From a fellow member of a group called Writers Against Nuclear Arms he had heard that new telephone exchanges being built in the capital cities were to be used for electronic surveillance, 'invading the nation's privacy on an unimaginable scale'. He had a look at the new exchange in Pitt Street: 'I went down there as an innocent old man wanting to write about stress in telephone exchanges. There was quite a lot of laughter in the background when I said that and I was told I'd have to get permission. There was a chair there. I said, I can wait. They said I'd better go down to Telecom head office and see the PR there. I knew that would be no good so I left.'[48] Unfamiliar with the routine bars and cameras that guarded the entrance, White concluded that some sinister purpose was at work here. This was the explosive revelation he had for La Trobe in July.

So great was the crowd trying to force its way in to hear him that the aisles and stage filled with people. The doors were locked, unlocked and locked again. White seemed by about half a century the oldest figure in the theatre. 'Very kind of you,' he said as the applause died away. 'I hope we're still friends at the end.' His theme was the need to face up to lies – the lies of parents to children, the lies of politicians, advertisers and the Bi. He ended with a prayer for the old, sick, the poor and the Aborigines. 'I believe most people hunger after spirituality, even if that hunger remains in many cases unconscious. If those who dragoon us ignore that longing of the human psyche, they are running a great risk. The sense of real purpose – the life force – could be expelled from a society whose leaders are obsessed by money, muscle and machinery. That society could – quite simply – die.'[49] He stood at the lectern for half an hour signing his books – mostly copies of Flaws in the Glass.

Ile Krieger wanted to see him while he was in Melbourne. Fritz had died after a long bout of Alzheimer's, and White had written tenderly to her in the months before his death. It was their first contact for many years, but he did not want to see her now. John Tasker had read Three Uneasy Pieces as he was waiting to die of liver cancer. He wondered if White was signalling a general amnesty with the reconciliation scene at the book's end,

> He is holding my hands in his. I who was once the reason for the world's existence am no longer this sterile end-all. As the world darkens, the evil in me is dying. I understand. Along with the prisoners, sufferers, survivors. It is no longer I it is we . . .

But Tasker's death in June 1988 provoked bitter memories in White. He said the eulogy Kippax delivered at the funeral was 'a long oration full of lies'.[50]

Soon after White returned from Melbourne, Clem Withycombe's widow Mag died at the age of 101. White took a hire car for the long drive to the Northern Suburbs Crematorium, the trip that always brought to mind lines from A Cheery Soul,

> So they rode to the funeral in the hired cars. Their grief was ever

so gently, ever so expensively sprung . . . Those whom habit, or a
sense of duty, would not leave in peace, drove . . . and drove . . .
in the funeral procession.

Only a handful of people had gathered at the Spanish incinerator, for
his aunt had outlived her friends. The one profoundly unconventional
act of Mag Withycombe's life was to live so long. White remarked, 'I
suppose I'm next.'[51]

He had bronchitis in August and after a couple of days became
confused again. Now it was worse than the night of the local vodka.
Words were failing him, and he was not able to grasp what Lascaris
was saying. 'Patrick just lies there like an inanimate thing.' Lascaris
hoped this was no more than a reaction to new antibiotics, but he
spoke to the doctor who called an ambulance.

The two men were waiting, for the umpteenth time in their lives,
with White's hospital bag packed. He had shed weight over the last few
days and shrunk. His hand gripping the blanket was a knot of bones
and veins. His teeth were out. Once or twice he smiled and said, 'Oh
dear.' His voice was soft and clear. Though it was hot in the attic,
he wore a singlet under his blue Viyella pyjamas and there was a
fan trained on him. Kerry Walker was reading to him, but he was
not paying much attention. Birds outside the window were making a
cheerful racket. The garden smelled of jasmine. It was a perfect spring
afternoon.

He pulled back the covers. At first it seemed he wanted to cool
off, but he sat bolt upright and swung his legs off the bed. Lascaris
supported him and asked, 'Do you want your stick?' He made no
sign or reply, but quite forcefully and neatly lay down again. He did
this several times. Walker tried to get him to drink some barley water
from a spoon, but Lascaris stopped her. He did not want it. She read
to him. He seemed to be trying to apologise. 'Oh dear,' he said. 'Oh
dear.'

The ambulance arrived. Wendy, a short New Zealander with a
silver oxygen case under her arm, came into the attic, and asked,
'What's the story?' Lascaris began at the beginning. She interrupted
him. 'Have you got a letter?' There was no doctor's letter. She was
sceptical. Her off-sider arrived. Troy was a big bloke who held White's
wrist very gently in his hand to take his pulse. There was no rush to
any of this. Wendy unleashed the blood pressure straps, and they put
an oxygen mask over White's nose and mouth.

'Is there a back entrance?'

Lascaris started to explain about the back way to the hospital.

Wendy said, 'We know the way to Vincent's.'

She and Troy lifted White from the bed in a boatswain's chair. He was breathing very heavily, and his arms kept dropping. Wendy said, 'No. Patrick, mate, hold me round the shoulders.' They gave him a spell at the head of the stairs, and then began to manœuvre him down, pausing to rest every few steps. It took five minutes, perhaps more, for them to reach the hall. The back door was unbolted and in the light that streamed into the house, White looked like a sack of bones. His face was blank, but his eyes were full of fear. They carried him through the garden and down to the ambulance waiting in the lane.

Barbara Mobbs was standing by the open ambulance. As they lifted him on to the stretcher, White shook himself from their grip. As Walker caught his arms, Mobbs took his ankles and between them all he was hoisted untidily into the ambulance. His bag and the oxygen were stowed beside him. The door came down and the ambulance drove off. Lascaris followed them to St Vincent's in one of the cars.

Walker was performing that night, and Mobbs drove her to the theatre. In Oxford Street they found themselves behind the ambulance. White was sitting high up with his face under a light. Wendy was giving him oxygen. Mobbs was supposed to be going to the theatre with him that night to see *Fiddler on the Roof* – Desmond Digby had done the costumes – and she thought she should still go. She was certain he would pull through again and didn't want to be accused of wasting the ticket.

White stayed that night in a corner of the casualty ward at St Vincent's. His condition was a mystery. 'They can't tell if he's had a stroke or not,' Lascaris reported. 'They won't be able to tell till they've cleared his chest, and his chest infection is terribly bad.' He had been warned to prepare himself. 'I don't believe it. I think he will pull through this time.'

Tests made over the next few days revealed pneumonia, glaucoma, pulmonary fibrosis – ruined lungs – a collapsed spine, chronic wheezes and rheumy eyes. There was no sign of a stroke. The severe confusion of those hours was the result of hypoxaemia: pneumonia and battered lungs between them had brought the oxygen in the blood reaching his brain to an abnormally low level.[52] For thirty-six hours it was uncertain if he would survive, then his lungs and brain slowly cleared. He was back from the brink again, very weak but lucid. An oxygen mask was kept strapped to his face, and he was fed through a green tube in his nose. Pads on his chest connected him to a monitor in the corridor: his heart was on television.

He stayed in hospital for three weeks. The room filled with baskets of spring flowers stripped from the gardens of those women Lascaris called with wry affection, 'Patrick's lady disciples'. He was emaciated. Elizabeth Riddell took him oysters. Greek neighbours brought a dish of spinach rice prepared for the Feast of Holy Cross. When he had regained a little strength, he was released to go home with a plastic bag stuffed full of pill bottles, tubes and droppers.

'Well Patrick, look after yourself,' said the sister. She had a dry manner and lavender-grey skin. 'It has been a pleasure.'

'I'm sure it hasn't.'

'Always pessimistic! His attitude – ' She paused and then began, as if determined to have this out once and for all, 'Why are you – ' But perhaps she sensed this was an enquiry without end, for she broke off, smiled and drifted out.

White arrived back at Martin Road weak but resolute. That night he had a relapse, and his doctor tried to re-admit him to St Vincent's. White refused to go, but agreed under duress to have a nurse in the house. Jill Bailey appeared next day and an arrangement which White insisted was for the time being continued till his death. She enforced the pharmaceutical regimen under which he had to live, and made him eat again, big meals plus snacks and a glass of stout before lunch. There were reverses – a blood clot in his leg put him back into bed for a fortnight – but he grew a little stronger every week. His memory had frayed in the crisis, and as it was restored he became more cheerful. That her patient was tractable and enjoyed having a nurse about the house was a relief to Bailey: she had read *The Eye of the Storm*.

He found it lonely at first, for while he was in hospital his friends could drop by and gossip as they had never been free to do before at Martin Road. The rules relaxed a little. The silent number seemed to be public knowledge now but White did not mind enough to have it changed, and only exploded when he was rung during the siesta. The cordless had been abandoned, and when he was downstairs he dragged himself the length of the house once again to answer the telephone in the kitchen. For a time it was the best exercise he had. Lascaris never touched the telephone if he could help it: this was White's prerogative. The flow of letters from Martin Road dried up.

He began sorting his papers with Barbara Mobbs's help. Most flat surfaces in the house – the dining-room table, the passing-out couch, his desk – were covered in layers of letters, empty envelopes, magazines, pamphlets and books. These were cleared away. In the course of the operation Paddy's letter to Father Christmas came to light, and he was delighted to see it again for he had thought it lost for ever. He collected all his speeches and gave them to Paul Brennan, who was to publish them in 1989 at his Primavera Press in Sydney. 'My God,' he said, 'how did I spout all that over the years?'[53]

In early summer he began taking short walks along Martin Road with his nurse. Neighbours came to their gates to congratulate him as he shuffled vigorously along. Over the next few weeks their expeditions together became more ambitious: to Bondi Junction to buy fish and oysters, or up to the Cross to order books at Norma Chapman's spotless, crowded little shop. He was very fond of Norma Chapman, and there is something of her in the formidable Miss Clitheroe of the English Tea-room and Library in St Mayeul: 'She was so thin, so high-toned, so assured . . .'[54] In the weeks before Christmas, patient and nurse were out buying cards at the gallery, pastries, perfect white peaches, and jewellery for his friends.

Gallimard was publishing *The Living and the Dead*, and in the New Year he had to reread chunks of the book to help the translator work out what he had meant nearly fifty years before. Reacquainting himself with his least favourite novel was not a happy experience. His verdict was unchanged: it probably should not have been written, and certainly not written when it was.

The proofs of the book of speeches arrived at Martin Road in March. After the La Trobe speech, Barry Jones the Minister for Science had convinced him that rumours about the telephone exchanges were unfounded. White was at first sceptical, but Jones was the only member of the government he still trusted, so he deleted the allegations from the published speech and denounced instead this 'fantasy of an irresponsible fanatic'.[55] Jones gave him an enormous Eureka flag to fly in the garden on Australia Day.

By the end of summer White and Lascaris were again going occasionally to the theatre and out to dinner. White was visiting the sick again, which at this point in his life seemed more chutzpah than charity. He still had days of misery, but he was gathering strength and putting on weight all the time. 'I have my ups and downs,' he said, but his mind was sharp, and he was showing an astonishing determination to live. There were then some bad days in October when he was coughing so much he burst a blood vessel in his lung. This meant a lot of time in doctors' waiting rooms spent reading magazines. '*Mode*, that's a loathsome magazine. They had a piece on who's up and who's down. Barry Humphries is on his way down.' He paused. 'Nosh* is on his way up.' Pause. 'I'm steady.'[56]

His nurse began sorting through the cupboards. Out went all the old jumpers eaten by moths. He sent some books, including volumes of George Moore, to be sold: 'There's no point in them all sitting here gathering dust.'[57] He gave away a stash of paintings he had never liked and stored in a cupboard. He found the cap worn by one of the chorus girls in the old Sydney production of *The Ham Funeral* and thought it should go to a theatre museum. The

*The food critic and Wagnerian, Leo Schofield.

most exciting discovery was a target map of Gondar in Eritrea, drawn for the squadron at Kassala by Abyssinian patriots. Barry Jones was given this to hand to the Australian War Memorial in Canberra.

He was in good shape, but no longer had the strength to speak or march for his causes. He continued to campaign in his own way. He sent politicians in Australia and abroad copies of Mary Benson's book on South Africa, *A Far Cry*. Bob Hawke wrote to say the need to end apartheid was one point on which they were close. White thought this reply gracious. Through the post came a Bicentennial medal honouring him as a Great Australian, which he threw into the bin. In June the speeches were published as *Patrick White Speaks* and he bought 109 copies to send to friends, politicians, actors, critics and relatives all over the world. Many arrived inscribed with the pithy message, 'Last Words.'

That winter he had a letter from Geoffrey Dutton, whose life had undergone great changes. He and Nin were divorced; he had left South Australia to live with his new wife in Mudgee over the Blue Mountains from Sydney; he was concentrating once again on his writing. To White he wrote, 'I've been reading the collection of your prose pieces, and thought that I would write to you, but not intending that you should answer. The book brought back a lot of memories. I am thinking in particular of the letter you wrote me which resulted in the end of communication between us. I was enraged at the time. Now I think you were quite right. My life was all wrong, and you had been trying to tell me so for some time.' Dutton had just finished his biography of the poet Ken Slessor: 'His was a sad life like that of most writers in this country.' White did not reply.[58]

AIDS killed the first of his friends. This left White numb: here was another horror in a world already so full of horrors. The choir of King's College was touring Australia, and in a photograph promoting the concerts he saw the window of his old room looking over the Backs. He wept. In October a hearse tore off the front bumper-bar of their new car.

All 1989 White was waiting for things to happen: for this book, for the speeches, for the memoirs James Fairfax was writing – White was suggesting chapter headings: 'Can Miriam's Boy Pull it Off?' – but most anxiously of all for Neil Armfield's production of *The Ham Funeral* at the Wharf Theatre in November.

The chance for fresh vindication was still welcomed and this production by the Sydney Theatre Company offered him particular satisfaction for the company had turned down both *Signal Driver* and *Netherwood*. For years White had condemned both the company and the glossy, often camp style of its director Richard Wherrett. 'I have walked out of so many of their plays.'[59] Now Wherrett and the company had invited Armfield to revive *The Ham Funeral*. The play had not been done in Sydney for twenty-eight years. A new generation would see it for the first time, and everyone would have a chance to see what the play was *really* like now that it was out of the hands of the still-reviled Tilly Tasker.

White was apprehensive. In May he read the play for the first time in years, and was pleased. He had a forceful say in the casting, and between them White and Armfield gathered many of the old crew who had served the plays so well in the past: Kerry Walker was the landlady Alma Lusty; Max Cullen, for whom he had written the role of Terry Legge in *Big Toys*, was her landlord; Robyn Nevin, last of the Cheery Souls, came on as one of the old vaudeville girls rootling through the garbage bins like the Mad Woman of Lulworth who so scared and intrigued Paddy White. Tyler Coppin was White's choice to play the young poet.

The day rehearsals began in October, White and Wherrett came face to face. White turned away after a few words. It was a gesture of calculated rudeness. As Wherrett made a speech of welcome, he rattled in his bag looking for eye drops. Armfield asked White to take Nevin's part in the first read through. 'Robyn can't be here today.' At the break White was pleased by the actors' compliments: pitch was a problem but the rhythm was good. He said, 'I've always wanted to be an actor.'[60] White sat there for a week as Armfield took the cast through the text with painstaking care. White untangled some of the mysteries, and made small changes to a few lines. 'I know it pays off in the end,' he said. 'But there are times I never wanted to hear another word of that play again.'[61] For the next fortnight he stayed away, and tried to keep it all out of his mind by looking at the *Four Love Songs* again. He had some new ideas.

'I hate first nights, with all those avoidable people. I loathe them,' he told the press. He would only be there to support the company.[62] A television camera trailed him from the moment he arrived. Lascaris was with him, and Barbara Mobbs. As they reached the foyer, a gusher sprang forward to introduce himself and White turned to stone. He spoke quietly to a few friends, ignored the camera and climbed the stairs to the theatre. Armfield's production was miraculous. The difficulties of the text seemed to vanish as White's young poet fought his way out of the 'great, damp, crumbling house', struggling free to pursue his fate as artists must again and again at whatever cost.

White was happy. He did not acknowledge the applause, nor did he speak, but he answered half-a-dozen questions for the ABC television crew. 'I can't hope for a better production than this,' he said. 'It is the great night of my life.'

'The young poet is looking for answers. You wrote this when you were thirty-five. Do you think you have found any answers?'

'No, I don't.'

'What do you think is the purpose of life?'

'Waiting to die, really. That may sound pessimistic, but it's also realistic. It has some good moments.'

'What . . . ?'

'Tonight for one thing. And my relationship with a wonderful partner of forty-seven years, which is more than most people can chalk up.'

'How important is love to life?'

'It's all important – but not lust.'

'What type of love is important?'

'Affection, I think. Yes, affection.'

'Do you have any expectations left?'

'No. To die comfortably, to die in my own bed.' He broke off and gave a deep, breathy laugh. 'Not in the bath!'[63]

There was applause as he came down the stairs into the foyer. The cast trickled in to join the audience. White had been planning his gift to the cast for months: a cake with Dobell's dead landlord in icing sugar. The two Alma Lustys would cut it together. Joan Bruce and Kerry Walker each took a hand on the knife. Armfield spoke. White autographed programmes, talked, sipped a glass of white wine, and said again, 'This is the most exciting night of my life.' Lascaris was beaming and his face was wet with tears.

Barbara Mobbs gathered up a sheaf of lilies in cellophane. Lascaris had the carry-all bag with the night's supply of pills, drops, inhalers and cushions. White fished his beret out of his pocket. It was time to go. The camera followed them a little way down the long corridor, and then turned back to the party. The television lights were doused. White made fair time towards the street, leaning on his stick, grim, pleased and exhausted.

'Are you for magic?' Danny Shepherd asks the crowd as he is about to throw himself into the lions' cage for the last time at the Jerusalem Show,

Are you for magic? I am. Inadmissible when we are taught to believe in science or nothing. Nothing is better. Science may explode in our faces. So I am for magic. For dream. For love . . . At the gates of death – which is not hell, as Church voices have so often promised, I hope to shed my doubts, fears, obstinacy, lust. I do not expect an easy transition. I believe that renewal can only be reached through blood and ash. While many of us will continue pursuing false dreams – that's where the votes are to be caught (all you need is a shrimping net and a fair measure of hypocrisy). I pray for grace – for the deceived shrimps – the monsters of power – and the least deserving creature – myself.[64]

A few days after he finished reading the typescript of this book, White had a mild bout of pleurisy which triggered a bronchial collapse. He said, 'My lungs have packed up.' A physiotherapist called at the house every afternoon and there was a new doctor who fascinated him: 'He treats cardinals.' On most days he sat in a silk paisley dressing gown in the chair by his bed. Friends rang to ask how he was. 'Not wonderful.' By his pillow was a stack of books, including a *New Testament*. 'I'm not reading much,' he said. 'Mainly cookbooks.' His temper was vile much of the time. His appetite was finicky. The delicate meals he ordered were not what he wanted when they arrived. All his energy went into the hard work of getting air into his lungs.

In late August there was an attempt to patch up his quarrel with Sidney Nolan. Barry Jones offered himself as a go-between and brought a message to Martin Road that the painter was in Australia and would welcome a reconciliation. White rejected the idea with scorn and a muted tirade against the man: Sir Neddy Nolan of Herefordshire, O.M.

He grew so frail and tired by the middle of September that he was barely able to leave his bed. A night nurse was engaged and then dismissed as an outrageous expense a few days later when the patient rallied enough to regain control of the household. Three times he refused to go to hospital. He refused to have a commode in the attic, for Ruth had died on the commode. Two nurses – Jill Bailey and a colleague – looked after him during the day and on the worst nights a nurse appeared and Patrick did not protest. All the time now his hands were cold and Lascaris sat for hours warming them in his own. Patrick said to his visitors, 'Manoly has kind hands.'

As he grew weaker he shed his anger, but he remained entirely himself: curious, tart, demanding, very funny and alert. He gossiped, talked about his family and the people he missed. 'I miss *Zoe*!' On one calm morning he pointed out his favourite picture in the room: Max Watters' grey painting of a country church. 'It's from the country round Belltrees.'

The business on which he was engaged was exhausting and some-times humiliating. He was pleased at least to be spared two fates that had horrified him for years: cancer and senility. 'I want to have my wits to the end.' His breath churned through his lungs and in the last week he could only manage to raise a finger or two in greeting and farewell.

The night nurse on 29 September was a strong young man wearing a T-shirt of the Virgin and Child. At about nine Lascaris went to sleep in his room across the landing. He was exhausted. At five the next morning he heard a disturbance and went in to help. White stopped breathing a few minutes later. He died at dawn, the best time of day.

White asked that there be no speeches, no ceremonies, no epitaphs and no public announcement for a week. The secret was impossible to keep. Papers around the world had the news next day on page one. His notices in death, as in life, were mixed.

The body was cremated a couple of days later. No one was present. He had laid all this out in the will. Early the following morning, the feast of St Francis of Assisi, Lascaris and Barbara Mobbs took the ashes over to the park. White had chosen a scruffy stretch of water near the bench on which he used to rest in a clump of melaleucas. Could it not be one of the beautiful lakes, Lascaris had asked? It had to be this: heavy with lilies, with a scurf of plastic and broken glass along the bank.

The sun was not yet up and a mist was on the water. Barbara Mobbs kicked aside a few empty cans and prayed. As Manoly poured out the ashes a pair of ducks swam over to investigate, hoping for bread. Lascaris said, 'I think that's it.' He crossed himself three times and turned to Mobbs. 'We have done the heroic deed and now we can have breakfast.' They made their way back up to the house with Milly the terrier leaping ahead of them through the grass.

A Note on the Book

My PURPOSE IN writing Patrick White's life was to find what made him a writer and where his writing came from. So the book is not only an account of White's own experience but the insights, misconceptions – and there were many – characters encountered and stories heard on which he drew to write his novels, plays and poetry.

Patrick White had gone to great lengths to get me access to both his friends and enemies as I wrote his life. Doors were opened which would otherwise have stayed bolted against any biographer.

In May 1986 he gave me authority to collect his letters. White had been asking – though less and less forcibly as the years passed – that all these be destroyed. Many were, but a great deal of this wonderful correspondence survives. The 2,500 letters I collected in Australia, New Zealand, the United States, France and Britain are the backbone of this book.

I spent six years researching and writing. Towards the end I asked White why he had allowed *anyone* to write his life after saying so often and so vehemently that biographers should wait until he was dead. He replied that he was sick of the books academics had written about him and hoped a biographer might show him as a 'real' person. 'And I thought it might be just as well to be around when that person is writing about this person.'

He had no veto on the text, but we agreed early on that he could check the book for errors once it was with the publishers. When I began collecting his letters there was the additional complication that as copyright owner White might forbid me to use some, perhaps all, of them.

I brought the book to him on 17 July 1990. He read it over the next few days, then asked me to sit with him at home while we read it through together a second time. We spent nine days together. He corrected many spelling mistakes – in English, German, Greek and

French – and identified about twenty-five errors of detail. These I have corrected. He confessed he found the book so painful that he often found himself reading through tears. He did not ask me to cut or change a line.

D.E.M.

Acknowledgments

I OWE THE greatest debt to Manoly Lascaris. He never welcomed his life being laid bare in this way, yet he helped me with great generosity. His forbearance makes it possible for this story to be told and I honour him for that.

For the last six years Peggy Garland has been my shrewd and forthright guide to her cousin's life. The day we met in her cottage in Oxfordshire she put into my hands the first, thrilling bundle of his letters that I had seen. Peggy Garland showed me what this book might be. Her sister Betty Withycombe found much of this process painful – not least my discovery that White had destroyed their thirty-year correspondence – but she gave me unfailing and candid assistance.

Michael and Judy White let me have the run of the remarkable library at Belltrees and guided me through the sprawling history of the Whites. Their generosity and good humour have meant a great deal.

All my friends have had a difficult time in the last few years. I owe them thanks and apologies in about equal measure. Nick Enright had the worst of it, for he was my sounding board. He read drafts of every chapter and helped me face their shortcomings. Most of all I want to thank him for helping me through the miserable times when I thought my work would never be over. He urged me to stay calm, keep it plain and trust the story would find its readers.

My work was assisted for two years by fellowships from the Literature Board of the Australia Council, the Australian Government's arts funding and advisory body.

To do justice to the contributions of all those who helped me write Patrick White's life would add dozens more pages to an already long book. The Notes show the individual debts I owe. Here may I merely thank the following women and men for their recollections, letters, diaries, advice, financial records and photographs.

In Australia: Pauline Allen, Don Anderson, Rosemary Annable of

St James's King Street, Neil Armfield, Jean Arundel, Thea Astley, the Australian Archives, the Australian Broadcasting Corporation, the Australian Defence Force Academy Library and the Library of the Australian War Memorial, Murray Bail, Richard Barrett, Adrian Basser, the Berrima District Historical Society, Helen Bettington, Nerida Bettington, Bill Blackett-Smith, Ron Blair, Franca Bopf, John Bowen, Brigadier G.P.H. Boycott, Veronica Brady, Paul Brennan, Katharine Brisbane and the staff of Currency Press, Joan Bruce, Janine Burke, Margaret Cameron, Sylvia Cameron, Rita Camilleri, Judy Campbell, Martha Campbell, Elizabeth Carter, Stuart Challender, Mabel Chapman, John Clark, Manning Clark, Trixie and Ron Clugston, Anne Cobden, Penny Coleing, Mrs Frank Crago, old boys and staff of Cranbrook, Peter Craven, Peter Crayford, G.C. Cullis-Hill, Tim Curnow, Bob Darke, James Davenport, Lawrence Daws, the Department of Defence, Rae de Teliga, Wendy Dickson, Desmond Digby and James Allison, E.L. Dixon and the staff of Tudor House, Geoff Dutton, Nin Dutton, Sue Du Val, Alvie Egan, David English and his colleagues in the Association for the Study of Australian Literature, Anthony Estorffe, James Fairfax, John Fairfax Group Ltd, Suzanne Fairfax (née Stogdale), Noni Farwell, Gretel Feher, Moira Ferguson, Margaret Fink, Dr Andrew Fisher, Fisher Library and the archives of Sydney University, Kate Fitzpatrick, Carol George, Gary and Helen Ghent of Withycombe, Harry Gillet, Lucrecia Gonzalez, Fay Gosse, the Embassy of Greece, Dorothy Green, Ferry and Hannah Grunseit, Richard Victor Hall, Alice Halmagyi, Georgina Haralambous, Norman (Pat) Hardy, Elizabeth Harrower, Jill Hellyer, Moya Henderson, Hazel Hollander, John Holroyd, Alec Hope, Major-General Ron Hopkins, Geoffrey Ingleton, John Iremonger, Heather Johnson, Barry Jones, Maurice Joseph, Clayton Joyce, Max Kaufline, Tony Kaurin of Bolero, Nancy Keesing, Jim Kell, Brian Kiernan, Norris King, Harry Kippax, Tom Kirk, Paul Knobel, Ile Krieger, La Trobe Library, John Lavender, Alan Lawson, Reg Livermore, Angus and Stephen Lloyd, Nance Loney, John Lonie, Mary Lord, Robin Lucas, His Excellency José Luis Pardos, Morris Lurie, Tara McCarthy, Jim McClelland, Frank McDonald, Liz McDonald, Jane Macgowan, Manfred Mackenzie, Stephanie McLarty, Ian Mcpherson, Beatrice McPhillamy, Humphrey McQueen, the Maitland and District Historical Society, David Malouf, Eva Mandel, Peter Manning, Lyster Martin, Philip Martin, Kay Maxwell, Anne Mayor, Richard Meale, the Meanjin Archive at the Baillieu Library of Melbourne University, Rosemary Meares, Harry Medlin, Barbara Mobbs, David and Gwen Moore, Craig Munro, Stephen and Nita Murray-Smith, the National Australia Bank, Lauri Neal, Marlene Norst, Alan Oldfield, Silvya Ordoñez, Robert Ouvrier, Sir Jock Pagan, Kevin Palmer, Nita Pannell, Cathy Peake,

Frances Peck, Barry Pierce and the staff of the Art Gallery of New South Wales, Stan Pierce, Nicholas Pounder and Simon Taaffe, Maria Prerauer, the Prime Minister's Department, John Douglas Pringle, Peter Quartermain, Helen Railton, Barrett Reid, Elizabeth Riddell, Frances Riordan, Julie Rose of Rosetrans, Glyn Rutherford, the Ruttys of Mittabah, St Luke's Hospital, St Philip's Church Hill, Ian Sanderson of Walgett, Peter Sculthorpe, Clem Semmler, Geoffrey Serle, Bob Sessions, Tom Shapcott, Jim Sharman, Dinah Shearing and Rod Milgate, John Sinclair, Bruce Skurray, Adair Slatyer, Jane Smart, Ralph Smith, Vivian Smith, Sasha Soldatow, Gavin Souter, Keith Stephens, Dal Stivens, John Sumner, John Tasker, Kylie Tennant, Ken Thomas, John Thompson and the staff of the National Library of Australia, Brian Thomson, Robert Tickle of the Muswellbrook Historical Society, G. Topp, Richard Turnley of Boscobel, Peter Valder, John Vallentine, Kath Vallentine, Mary Vallentine, Renate Wagner, Jim Waites, Kerry Walker, Richard Walsh, Joan Watkins, Frank Watters, Rodney Wetherell, Jim and Margaret White, Patricia White, Pat Wilcox of Barwon Vale, Gerry Wilkes, Marian Wilkinson, Peter Withycombe, Robert Withycombe, Gary Wotherspoon, William Yang, P.J. Yeend at the King's School, Geoff Yen, John Young, Patsy Zeppel, Mrs R. Zilahi.

In Britain: Luciana Arrighi, Associated Book Publishers, Ray Bloomfield, the British Library, the British Red Cross Archives, the British Theatre Association, the Britten-Pears Library, James Byam Shaw, John Byrne of Bertram Rota, the Library of Cambridge University, Anne Chisholm, Liz Cowen, Robert Cross, Curtis Brown Group Ltd, 162–8 Regent Street, London, Joyce Cummings, Elizabeth David, Gwenda David, Dilys Daws, Alexandra Dawson, Richard de Mestre, Raymond Duveen, Chuck Elliott, Shelton Fernando, Colin Franklin, Nick Garland, Tom Garland, Sally Gell, Sir John Gielgud, Victoria Glendinning, Grahame C. Greene, his successors and the staff of Jonathan Cape, Jane Grigson, the Imperial War Museum, Lord Harewood, Harrap Ltd, Frank Hauser, Otto Herschan, Patrick Hewlings, Christopher Hogwood, Barry Humphries, the Central Library of the Isle of Wight, Agnes Lachlan, Charles Levi, Harry Lewin, Anne Lloyd, Edmanson Lodge, Alison Mansbridge, John McGrath, Seamus McManus of the Dorchester, Keith Michell, the Ministry of Defence, Anthea Morton-Saner, Nigel Nicolson, Juliet O'Hea, Charles Osborne, Tim Pearce and the staff of Cheltenham College, Ellen Pollock, Gillian Pope, the Public Records Office, the Raymond Mander and Joe Mitchenson Theatre Collection, Amanda Reiss, Routledge & Keegan Paul, the Royal Academy of Dramatic Art, Rosy Runciman of Glyndebourne, Sir Steven Runciman, George Rylands, Peter Schryver, Mrs K.B. Sewell, Alan Seymour, W.H. Smith Limited, James Stern, Maurice Temple Smith, the Theatre Museum, Robert Tod, the libraries of the University of Reading and University College London, Ronald Waters, Robert Wellington, Westminster City Library, Lt-Col A.E. Wilkinson, Margery Williams, Ted Wiltshire, H.D.B. Wood, John Wyse.

In the United States: Chilton Anderson, the *Atlanta Constitution*, John Beston, Zoe Caldwell and Robert Whitehead, the Rare Book and Manuscript Library of the Butler Library at Columbia University, the Library of Congress, Sumner Locke Elliott, Eleanore Fox, Donald Gallup, the Harry Ransom Humanities Research Center in the University of Texas at Austin, the Harvard Theatre Collection, the Harwood Foundation of the University of New Mexico, Genevieve Janssen, Perry Knowlton of Curtis Brown, George Minkoff, the New York Public Library, James K. Rankin, the *Taos News*, Colonel Peter Teesdale-Smith, Amanda Vaill and the staff of the Viking Press, Jenny Vogel and Steven Koltai, Alan Williams.

In New Zealand: Peter Beatson, Bob Harvey, the Department of Health, Janet Frame, Michael King, Gordon McLauchlan, Keith Thomson, Mark Williams, Fred and Joan Wood.

In South Africa: the Ministry of Defence, John Hewitson, Tommy Irvine, Mr Justice H.C. (Nick) Nicholas.

In Sweden: Per Anger, Ingmar Björkstén, David Harry, Bertil Käll of Forum Publishers, Artur Lundkvist, Ingegärd Martinell, Anders Ryberg of the Swedish Academy's Nobel Library, the staff of the Swedish Institute.

In France: Madame la vicomtesse d'Artois, Xavier Garcia-Larrache, the staff of the Hostellerie de Ciboure, the detectives of Itxassou Léa and Camille Irigoyen, François Laurent of Editions Gallimard, the staff of *Sud-Ouest*.

In Spain: Ragnar Christophersen.

In Germany: Elizabeth Falkenberg, Dr Jürgen and Ruth Oertel.

In Greece: Effie Lambadaridou, Robert Liddell.

In Italy: His Holiness the Pope, Father Pierre Riches, Patricia Contessa Volterra.

In Ireland: the Office of Censorship of Publications, the Most Rev. Archbishop George Simms.

Abbreviations

Arrighi	Luciana Arrighi
Aunt's	*The Aunt's Story*
Beatson	Peter Beatson
Best	Marshall Best
BL	Belltrees' letterbook
Burnt	*The Burnt Ones*
Casey	Maie Casey
Clark	Manning Clark
Coleing	Penny Coleing
Columbia	Rare Book and Manuscript Library of the Butler Library at Columbia University
Congress	Library of Congress
Cushman	John Cushman
Digby	Desmond Digby
Dutton	Geoffrey Dutton
EGL	Manoly Lascaris
Eye	*The Eye of the Storm*
Falkenberg	Elizabeth Falkenberg
Flaws	*Flaws in the Glass*
Fringe	*A Fringe of Leaves*
Garland	Peggy Garland
Green	Dorothy Green
Greene	Graham C. Greene
Happy	*Happy Valley*
Harrower	Elizabeth Harrower
Henderson	Moya Henderson
HRHRC	Harry Ransom Humanities Research Center, University of Texas at Austin
Huebsch	Ben Huebsch
Johnson	Walter Willard (Spud) Johnson

King	Michael King
Living	*The Living and the Dead*
McKie	Mollie McKie
Malouf	David Malouf
Mamblas	José Ruiz de Arana y Bauer, Viscount Mamblas, later Duke of Baena and San Lucar
Mandala	*The Solid Mandala*
Maschler	Tom Maschler
Medlin	Harry Medlin
Memoirs	*Memoirs of Many in One*
Moores	Gwen and David Moore
Murray-Smith	Stephen Murray-Smith
NL	National Library of Australia
NSW	New South Wales
NT	*National Times*
Osborne	Charles Osborne
Plays	*Four Plays*
Ploughman	*The Ploughman and Other Poems*
PW	Patrick White
Riders	*Riders in the Chariot*
Sculthorpe	Peter Sculthorpe
Semmler	Dr Clem Semmler
Sharman	Jim Sharman
Signal	*Signal Driver*
SMH	*Sydney Morning Herald*
Southerly	*Southerly*, vol. 33, no. 2 (1973)
Speaks	*Patrick White Speaks*
Stern	James Stern
Tasker	John Tasker
Tree	*The Tree of Man*
Twyborn	*The Twyborn Affair*
Uneasy	*Three Uneasy Pieces*
Viking	Viking Press
Waters	Ronald Waters (Waterall)
Williams	Margery Williams

Letters are distinguished from other sources by being dated in the notes thus: 11.ix.1985. All other quotations – from books, diaries, interviews and so on – are dated thus: 11 Sept 1985.

Editions of White's Work

UNFORTUNATELY WHITE'S EARLY novels have different page numbers in the London and New York editions. When referring in the notes to these novels I give both numbers: the UK/Australian number first and the US page number in square brackets afterwards: e.g. *Aunt's* p.33 [42]. Thankfully, his publishers shared the same plates from *The Eye of the Storm* onwards, so the page numbers then tally. These I give only once: e.g. *Fringe*, p.67. The editions of White's work referred to in the notes are:

	UK and Australia	North America
Happy Valley	George G. Harrap, 1939	Viking, 1940
The Living and the Dead	Eyre & Spottiswoode, 1962	Viking, 1941
The Aunt's Story	Eyre & Spottiswoode, 1958	Viking, 1948
The Tree of Man	Eyre & Spottiswoode, 1956	Viking, 1955
Voss	Eyre & Spottiswoode, 1957	Viking, 1957
Riders in the Chariot	Eyre & Spottiswoode, 1961	Viking, 1961
The Burnt Ones	Eyre & Spottiswoode, 1964	Viking, 1964
Four Plays	Eyre & Spottiswoode, 1965	Viking, 1966
The Solid Mandala	Eyre & Spottiswoode, 1966	Viking, 1966
The Vivisector	Jonathan Cape, 1970	Viking, 1970
The Eye of the Storm	Jonathan Cape, 1973	Viking, 1973
The Cockatoos	Jonathan Cape, 1974	Viking, 1975
A Fringe of Leaves	Jonathan Cape, 1976	Viking, 1976
The Night the Prowler	Penguin Books/Cape, 1978	
The Twyborn Affair	Jonathan Cape, 1979	Viking, 1979
Flaws in the Glass	Jonathan Cape, 1981	Viking, 1981
Memoirs of Many in One	Jonathan Cape, 1986	Viking, 1986

Three Uneasy Pieces	Australia: Pascoe Publishing, Melbourne, 1987
	UK: Jonathan Cape, 1988
Patrick White Speaks	Australia: Primavera Press, Sydney, 1989
	UK: Jonathan Cape, 1990

Published only in Australia

Thirteen Poems	Private, *c.*1930
The Ploughman and Other Poems	Beacon Press, 1935
Big Toys	Currency Press, Sydney, 1978
Netherwood	Currency Press, 1983
Signal Driver	Currency Press, 1983

The Letters

THE ESTATE OF Patrick White retains the copyright in his letters and I thank the estate and his literary executor Barbara Mobbs for allowing me to quote from them in the book. For the most part White's letters remain in private hands and I thank the recipients and their heirs for giving me access and permission to use them. Many batches of White's letters have passed into public collections. My use of them in these pages is with the kind permission of the following institutions where they are now held:

Marcel Aurousseau	National Library of Australia
Ruth Bedford	Mitchell Library, State Library of NSW
Marshall Best	The Viking Press
Naomi Burton	Rare Book and Manuscript Library of the Butler Library at Columbia University
David Campbell	National Library of Australia
Alec Chisholm	Mitchell Library, State Library of NSW
Clem Christesen	Meanjin Archive of the Baillieu Library, University of Melbourne
Douglas Cooper	Getty Museum, California
Curtis Brown, New York	Rare Book and Manuscript Library of the Butler Library at Columbia University
John Cushman	Rare Book and Manuscript Library of the Butler Library at Columbia University
Geoffrey and Nin Dutton	National Library of Australia
Graham C. Greene	Jonathan Cape papers, Reading University
Alice Halmagyi	National Library of Australia
Ben Huebsch	Library at Congress, Viking Press and Rare Book and Manuscript Library of the Butler Library at Columbia University

Spud Johnson	Harry Ransom Humanities Research Center Library at the University of Texas at Austin
Nancy Keesing	Mitchell Library, State Library of NSW
Mollie McKie	National Library of Australia
Pepe Mamblas	National Library of Australia
Tom Maschler	Jonathan Cape papers, Reading University
Stephen Murray-Smith	La Trobe Collection, State Library of Victoria
Charles Osborne	Harry Ransom Humanities Research Center Library at the University of Texas at Austin, and the Library of Cambridge University
Ralph Smith	The Library, the Australian Defence Force Academy, Canberra
P.R. (Inky) Stephensen	Mitchell Library, State Library of NSW
John Tasker	National Institute of Dramatic Art, Sydney
Alan Williams	Viking Press

Notes

1 Ruth

1   *Bulletin* (24 March 1910), p.20.
2   *Flaws*, p.10; *Eye*, pp.423, 123.
3   PW to Moores, 12.i.1958.
4   Asthma: PW to me, 8 Oct 1986.
5   Owen Wright, *Wongwibinda*, University of New England History Series (Armidale, 1985), p.66.
6   *Maitland Daily Mercury* (3 Jan 1913), p.4.
7   *Flaws*, p.8.
8   *Aunt's*, p.70 [60].
9   Ibid., p.20 [13].
10   *Illustrated Sydney News* (7 June 1890), p.25.
11   Alan Clark, *Archer* (Shoalhaven Historical Society, Nowra, 1979), p.13.
12   *Aunt's*, pp.19–20 [12–13].
13   Alan Newton of Denman to me, 21 April 1987.
14   *Maitland Daily Mercury* (24 Nov 1899), p.3; John B. Beston, *Descent*, vol. 7 (Society of Australian Genealogists, Sydney, 1974), pp.18, 19.
15   *Maitland Daily Mercury* (24 Nov 1899), p.3. William Lipscomb, brother of Winifred Withycombe, was trustee for the family of T.W. Tucker, former senior proprietor of the *Maitland Daily Mercury*. Another affectionate but brief obituary was carried in the *Muswellbrook Chronicle* (25 Nov 1899), p.2.
16   *Vivisector*, p.124 [106].
17   PW to me, 6 May 1986.
18   PW to me, 1 April 1987.
19   *Tree*, pp.31–3.
20   *Scone Advocate* (10 Aug 1909), p.4.
21   Ibid. (15 June 1909), p.2.
22   Ibid. (16 July 1909); Belltrees Station diary, 15 July 1909; PW to me, 6 May 1986.
23   *Maitland Daily Mercury* (29 July 1909), p.3; Belltrees Station Diary, 28 July 1909.
24   *Scone Advocate* (24 Aug 1909), p.2.
25   H.L. White to his solicitor Charles Ebsworth, 12.xii.1909, BL vol. 20.
26   PW to Dutton, 28.xi.1965.
27   *Australian Financial Review* (11 July 1972), p.2.
28   PW to Maschler, 20.ix.1973.
29   *The Young Ardizzone: an autobiographical fragment* (Studio Vista, London, 1970), pp.51–2.
30   *Flaws*, p.10.

31   PW to Williams, 21.vi.1970; PW to me, 26 Jan 1987. I have not been able to find the hotel or the fire.
32   *Voss*, p.137 [123–4].

2 The Happy Valley

1   *Aunt's*, p.19 [12].
2   Edwin J. Brady, *Australia Unlimited* (George Robertson & Co., Melbourne, 1918), p.942.
3   *Australian Dictionary of Biography*, vol. 6 (Melbourne University Press, 1976), p.387.
4   Stephen Roberts, *The Squatting Age in Australia, 1835–1847* (Melbourne University Press, 1964), p.193.
5   A.P. Elkin, *The Diocese of Newcastle* (Australasian Medical Publishing Co. Ltd, 1955), pp. 111–12, quoting the 1843 Committee on Monetary Confusion.
6   Roberts, *Squatting Age*, p.204.
7   Brady, *Australia Unlimited*, p.942.
8   *Maitland Daily Mercury* (6 May 1875), p.2.
9   Margaret (Mrs Jim) White to me, 20 April 1987.
10   *Australian Dictionary of Biography*, vol. 6, p.388. The house is now called Camelot. That it was one of several sources for Xanadu, PW to me, 10 Feb 1987.
11   Dr W.H. Lang, Ken Austin and Stewart McKay (eds), *Racehorses in Australia* (Art in Australia Ltd, Sydney, 1922), pp.24–6.
12   J.P. Abbott to Parkes, 2.iii.1872. Parkes papers, Mitchell Library – quoted in Stevan Eldred-Grigg's ANU thesis *The Pastoral Families of the Hunter Valley, 1880–1914*, p.242.
13   *Maitland Daily Mercury* (26 Dec 1874), p.1.
14   Ibid.
15   Ibid.
16   Ibid. (6 May 1875), p.2.
17   *Eye*, p.10; *Mandala*, p.164 [155]; *Voss*, p.21 [15].
18   *King's School Magazine* (May 1938).
19   Brady, *Australia Unlimited*, p.944, and Judy White, *The White Family of Belltrees* (Seven Press, Sydney, 1981), p.35. I am indebted to her book for this entire chapter.
20   The identification of the Scone/Belltrees team with Paterson's Geebung team was made in Ernest's obituary in the *Scone Advocate* (13 Jan 1914). Many others claim the privilege. The poet married a relative of the Whites.
21   White, *White Family*, p.57.
22   BL, vol. 44, 15.i.1921 and vol. 26, 29.iv.1912.
23   H.L. White to John Patterson, BL, vol. 28, 5.v.1913.
24   H.L. White to Angus & Robertson, BL, vol. 28, 25.v.1913.
25   BL, vol. 43., Feb 1920.
26   BL, vol. 14, 20.xi.1905.
27   White, *White Family*, p.95.
28   H.L. White to J.H. Bettington, BL, vol. 42, 21.ix.1919.
29   23 March 1909.
30   BL, vol. 48, 8.iv.1923.
31   *Muswellbrook Chronicle* (6 Oct 1909), p.2.
32   *Scone Advocate* (12 Nov 1909), p.3.
33   H.L. White to *Sydney Mail* (26 April 1913), BL, vol. 28.
34   *Eye*, p.25 ('Here there is no life'); *Vivisector*, p.34 [27].
35   H.L. White's entries in station diaries for 1, 6, 14, 17, 20 & 23 May 1913; also BL, vol. 28, 26.iv.1913 onwards.

3 The Bunya Bunya Tree

1   *Vivisector*, p.108 [93], linked to this visit by PW to me, 4 Aug 1986.
2   12 Jan 1914.
3   BL, vol. 30, 11.i.1914.
4   Michael White to me, 31 July 1986.
5   H.L. White to the egg collector Lawson Whitlock, BL, vol. 30, 22.vi.1913.
6   PW to Dutton, 30.iii.1965.
7   *Flaws*, p.4.
8   *Vivisector*, pp.84–5 [72]; compare with the almost identical account of Lul-worth nursery, *Flaws*, pp.14–15.
9   Tom Kirk to me, 4 Oct 1986; *Flaws*, p.14.
10 PW to me re Robert Clark putting up his age, 10 Sept 1987; Oliver Halliday doing the same thing in *Happy*, pp.16–17 [17–18] and Duffield ditto in *Vivisector*, p.173 [150].
11 BL, vol. 35, 1.iv.1917.
12 *Speaks*, p.139.
13 *Flaws*, p.133.
14 *Vivisector*, pp.86–7 [73–4]; PW identifies Lulworth as the source of the Courtneys' house in *Southerly*, p.132; compare PW's description of the Sunningdale garden with the Lulworth garden, *Flaws*, p.16.
15 Mr Voss, *Voss*, p.60 [50]; neglected spikes, *Vivisector*, p.79 [67]; Theo's joke, *Aunt's*, p.11 [5]; Paddy's protector and home of God, *Flaws*, p.70; Aborigines gathering seeds, *Voss*, p.224 [205]. The tree survived, hemmed in by a wing of St Luke's Hospital, until 1986.
16 *Twyborn*, p.122; PW linked the circumstances of his and Twyborn's first asthma attacks to me, 8 Oct 1986.
17 Sharman interview, *NT* (30 June 1979), p.26; *Flaws*, p.5.
18 *John O'London's Weekly* (Nov 1940), p.132.
19 PW to Williams, 21.vi.1970.
20 *Speaks*, p.171.
21 *Flaws*, p.23; *Tree*, p.233; *Vivisector*, pp.8–9 [4–5].
22 *Flaws*, p.21.
23 *Speaks*, p.171.
24 PW to Keith Michell, 9.x.1957.
25 *Twyborn*, p.168, connection approved by PW to me, 28 July 1990.
26 *Voss*, p.22 [15].
27 The sighing door, *Eye*, p.20; the table, *The Ham Funeral* in *Plays*, p.27.
28 'Nora Barnacle . . .', PW to Huebsch, 11.x.1960, Congress; 'sloppy Australian . . .', *Mandala*, p.99 [91]; PW discusses his mother's strictures about Australian slang in letters to Casey, 1.xii.1968 and to Best, 27.ii.1961, Viking Press.
29 *Voss*, p.382 [353]; PW identifies Lulworth as the basis for the Bonners' house in *Southerly*, p.132 and *Flaws*, p.153.
30 See *Vivisector*, pp.94, 241 [80, 210]. White says the scene differed from the ritual at Lulworth only in that Ruth never pushed his head into the cupboard to smell the dresses.
31 PW to me, 1 May 1985; Kelly in *Smith's Weekly* (24 March 1923), p.20. Kelly edited the women's pages of this paper for a couple of years.
32 *SMH* (17 Oct 1918), p.7.
33 *Australasian* (26 Oct 1918), p.821.
34 Ibid.
35 *Eye*, p.91; PW to me about Bertie's playing, 1 May 1985.
36 'suggesting the . . .', *SMH* (21 June 1918), p.8; about accuracy, her daughter, Mrs Beatrice McPhillamy to me, 27 Aug 1986;

the impression of the Pompadour, PW to Dutton, 30.iii.1965.

37   *Daily Guardian* (26 July 1923), p.7.
38   Ethel Kelly, *Twelve Milestones, Being the Peregrinations of Ethel Knight Kelly* (Brentano's Ltd, London, 1929), p.178.
39   *Flaws*, p.244.
40   PW to me, 1 May 1985; *Flaws*, pp.20, 244; PW to Johnson, 22.iv.1940.
41   PW to me, 13 Sept 1989; *Chu Chin Chow* opened in Sydney on 26 March 1921.
42   'She infected me . . .', *Speaks*, p.74; 'lithe and muscular . . .', *Flaws*, p.70.
43   *Speaks*, p.76.
44   Patrick White collection, Mitchell Library, Sydney.
45   'Everything happened . . .', *Australian Book Review* (1962), Children's Book and Educational Supplement, p.4; 'One seems . . .', PW to Huebsch, 25.ii.1957, Viking.
46   'as earthly . . .', *Twyborn*, p.97; the portrait of the wet-nurse draws on a number of Lizzie's characteristics, and her burial is in the same purple soil in which Lizzie was buried at Mount Wilson in 1975, *Flaws*, p.30; 'If I was shy . . .', *Flaws*, p.5; re a Catholic nurse instead, PW to Dutton, 1.x.1969.
47   PW to me, 13 Sept 1989; *Flaws*, p.41.
48   PW to me, 8 Oct 1986; *Mandala*, p.252 [243].
49   *Vivisector*, p.148 [128].
50   'all the crinkled . . .', *Bulletin* (12 June 1919), p.42; 'It was . . .', *Daily Telegraph* (6 June 1919), p.5.
51   *Flaws*, p.42.
52   H.L. White to Dick White, BL, vol. 34, 5.xii.1915; BL, vol. 39, 7.xii.1918; station diary 12 Aug 1921.
53   Scabbing, H.L. to Whitlock, BL, vol. 35; PW to tooth fairy, Patrick White collection, Mitchell Library, Sydney.
54   *Speaks*, p.74.
55   'I have a small . . .', H.L. White to J. Hagen, BL, vol. 42, 6.ix.1919; H.L.'s reply to PW, BL, vol. 43, 24.xi.1919.
56   *Tree*, p.257; linked by PW to me – see Chapter 14.
57   BL, vol. 47, 13.viii.1923; BL, vol. 48, 14.v.1923 and 17.vii.1923.
58   BL, vol. 51, 12.xi.1924.
59   *Flaws*, p.25; *Aunt's*, p.19 [12].
60   PW to Casey, 9.ii.1967.
61   PW to Dutton, 18.i.1962.
62   PW to Dutton, 25.i.1970.

4   The Best Years

1   *Fringe*, p.90; identified as the source, PW to me.
2   *Bulletin* (31 Aug 1922), p.42.
3   *Australian Book Review* (1962), Children's Book and Educational Supplement, p.4; *Mandala*, p.196 [186]; *Southerly*, p.136, *Happy*, p.189 [185]; *Flaws*, p.24.
4   *Aunt's*, p.9 [3]; PW linked old Mesdames Morrice and Goodman, to me, 8 March 1990.
5   Morrices as a source in PW's writing: Gertrude was the 'starting point' for Theodora Goodman, *Flaws*, p.25; Browley was 'biscuit' at *Flaws*, p.25, as was the Goodmans' Meroë, *Aunt's*, p.19 [12]; nearby Moss Vale became Sorrel Vale, *Southerly*, p.132. Old Mrs Morrice's life and skills: notes of Frederick John Morrice on his father and mother: file 11/6/3/686 in the Society of Australian Genealogists library, Sydney. The Dubocs: Dr Marlene Norst discovered their papers in the State Library of NSW. I quote her translation of Julius Duboc's letter from her account of his life in *Commonwealth*, vol. 6,

no 2 (Spring 1984), pp.11–19, at p.14.

6   *The River and Other Verses* (Australasian Authors' Agency, Melbourne, 1912).

7   *Fruh- und Abendroth* (C.U. Koch's Verlagsbuchhandlung, Dresden and Leipzig, 1899).

8   Sister Mary Assumpta O'Hanlon, *Dominican Pioneers in NSW* (Sydney, 1949), p.140.

9   *Flaws*, p.25.

10   Richard de Mestre to me, 27.x.1986.

11   PW to me, 29 June 1989; Nance and Hurtle, *Vivisector*, p.187 [162–3]; Waldo refused another of those waterside assignations when a woman of vague age said, 'Come down by the water, brother . . . under oner those Moreton Bay ffiggs, and we'll root together so good you'll shoot out the other side of Christmas,' *Mandala*, pp.184–5 [175]. Sometimes the park bench is in the Sydney Botanic Gardens, e.g. the courtship of Rodney Halliday and Hilda, *Happy*, p.103 [102]; and the park bench scene in *Vivisector*, p.264 [231] is set at 'the Gash'; the poet Wetherby 'smiled for the clerks in parks who expose themselves regularly, in words, on benches', *Aunt's*, p.236 [219]. The consummation of all the park-bench meetings is, of course, in London, where Twyborn's mother recognises her daughter/son, *Twyborn*, p.420.

12   *Flaws*, p.24.

13   On the Manly ferry Hurtle Duffield confesses to the printer, *Vivisector*, p.416 [365]; Dowson confesses to Fazackerley in 'A Woman's Hand', *Cockatoos*, pp.75–6; Sir Basil Hunter, 'womb-happy', decides at the last minute against taking the ferry, *Eye*, p.271.

14   Other side of the world, *Eye*, p.271; Walter Quong seduced Ethel at Manly, *Happy*, pp.91–2 [91], and Stan Parker began such a beach seduction on Manly in *Tree*, but it nearly ended in strangulation, p.341; Stan brought his wife Amy on their first and last holiday 'beneath those pine trees', p.414.

15   'mooning, dreaming . . . observing, always observing', *Flaws*, pp.244, 245; Joyce and Dublin, PW to Huebsch, 11.x.1960, Congress.

16   'trudging these streets . . .', *Speaks*, p.35.

17   *Flaws*, p.28.

18   PW to Beatson, 29.xi.1970.

19   *Flaws*, pp.32–3.

20   PW to Dutton, 18.i.1962 and 8.vi.1963.

21   Quoted by Peter Valder in *The Blue Mountains, Grand Adventure for All*, ed. Peter Stanbury and Lydia Bushell (The Macleay Museum, University of Sydney, 1985), p.74.

22   *Sunday Times* (29 Jan 1922), Comic and Children's Section, p.7; White linked *Uneasy*, p.29, to 'Red Admiral' on 15 June 1988. I owe a great debt to Carol George, who spent many weeks working from White's vague clues in order to track these pieces down.

23   Ibid. (22 Oct 1922). When I read this to PW he was silent for a time then remarked, 'Well, I can say that none of the adults there could have written it for me.'

24   Golson and Vatatzes, *Twyborn*, p.110; Mrs Standish in *Living*, pp.106–7 [114]; also Sister de Santis's stiff white skirt brushed the iron stair railing of Mrs Hunter's house, *Eye*, p.16; a nun's hem raises the scent of basil on the island of Perialos, *Vivisector*, p.401 [351].

25   Both 'Susan' and 'Long Ago: A Reminiscence' were written at Cheltenham when PW was sixteen. In *Thirteen Poems*, privately published by Ruth about 1929. The only copy available to the public appears to be at Fisher Library, University of Sydney.

26   'this picture . . .', *Flaws*, p.31; 'the sweet . . .', *Voss*, p.15 [9]. Wynne at his bench was an image White remembered for life. In the Melbourne magazine

Tension (April 1984), p.23, he speculates that it gave him his interest in furniture and was the source of the tables that crop up all the time in his work. Two further examples of good men at their benches: Joe Barnett in *Living*, pp.185, 192 [205–6, 214], and Stan Parker in *Tree*, p.406.

27   'Her dress', *Twyborn*, pp.170–1; cf. *Flaws*, p.31; 'Lopokova', *Flaws*, p.31.
28   'Mount Wilson tick', Tom Kirk, *SMH*, Good Weekend (23 Feb 1985), p.23; explorations and tall tales, PW to Beatson, 29.xi.1970; 'bush silence', *Flaws*, p.32.
29   Tom Kirk to me, 4 Oct 1986.
30   *Vivisector*, p.105 [89–90].
31   Triumph, *Flaws*, p.50, which becomes an opportunity refused in *Vivisector*, p.78 [66]; on putting the Aborigines out of his mind, *Speaks*, p.184.
32   *Flaws*, p.107.
33   Advertisement, *SMH* (1925), undated clipping in the Tudor House archives at Moss Vale.
34   *Aunt's*, pp.23, 28 [16, 20]; linked by PW to this view, *Southerly*, p.132.
35   W.J. Meyer and E.C. Dixon, *Tudor House, the First Fifty Years, 1898–1948* (Waite & Bull Printers, Sydney, 1948), p.8.
36   The timing, PW to me, 19 Feb 1985; the plot, PW to Sharman, *NT* (30 June 1979), p.26.
37   C.G. Cullis-Hill to me, 3 Feb 1986.
38   PW to me, 29 April 1987, linking Dubbo/Calderon at *Riders*, p.365 [348–9], to himself and Skuse. He insisted he remembered the encounter with gratitude; 'anti-climax', *Flaws*, p.18.
39   *Flaws*, p.5.
40   *Vivisector*, p.628 [554].
41   Moss Vale *Scrutineer* (31 May 1922), p.2.
42   C.G. Cullis-Hill.
43   'How Clem . . .', 'A Woman's Hand', *Cockatoos*, p.20; 'round and good . . .', PW to me, 15 June 1988; the Parker boy in *Tree*, pp.51, 265, and Theodora in *Aunt's*, p.24 [16–17].
44   'Serious pungency', *Aunt's*, p.32 [25], identified by PW to me as his own response; ferrets 'turning and rattling' appear at a crucial moment in *Tree*, p.422.
45   Bill Blackett-Smith to me, 27 May 1986.
46   PW to me, 14.viii.1985.
47   *Flaws*, p.27.
48   PW to Nita Pannell, 31.viii.1961.
49   *Aunt's*, pp.38–9 [31] and *Voss*, p.55 [46]; PW identified the Tudor House incident as the origin of these to me, 14 July 1988.
50   *Flaws*, p.26 and *Australian Book Review (1962)*, Children's Book and Educational Supplement, p.4.
51   PW to Sharman, *NT* (30 June 1979), p.26.
52   This pale blue White gave to the God of Stan Parker's mother at *Tree*, p.5: PW to Kylie Tennant, *SMH* (22 Sept 1956), p.10.
53   *Aunt's*, p.56 [48].
54   *Aunt's*, p.56 [47–8], identified by PW to me as drawn from these Bong Bong Sundays.
55   PW to McKie, 27.vi.1956.
56   H.L. White to Dick White, BL, vol. 48, 19.v.1923.
57   The promise, *Scrutineer* (28 Feb 1923), p.2; the avoidance, ibid. (19 Dec 1923), p.2.
58   Ibid. (3 Oct 1923), p.2.
59   Dick as a chauvinist, PW to Green, 1.v.1984; 'pure Australian',

H.L. White to W.G. Carpenter, BL, vol. 46, 14.vii.1922.

60 Ruth's glove, PW to me, 5 Feb 1986; 'a little pin . . .', PW's Australia Day message, 1984, *Speaks*, p.139.
61 *Speaks*, p.40.
62 *Flaws*, pp.16–17.
63 Sept 1924.
64 Ibid.
65 Ibid.
66 Ellerston was bought by the father of the painter Donald Friend, and is now the polo headquarters of Kerry Packer.
67 H.L. to Dick White, BL, vol. 48, 24.vii.1924.
68 'If yer luck . . .', 'Last Words', unpublished screenplay by PW, scenes 2 and 3.
69 *Flaws*, p.19.
70 Meyer and Dixon, *Tudor House*, p.11.
71 *Flaws*, p.30.
72 Beasts, PW to me, 4 Aug 1986; 'have always believed . . .', PW to Nita Pannell, 31.viii.1961.
73 'one of the Furlows . . .', PW to Johnson, 20.viii.1939; 'leave the child . . .', *Happy*, p.82 [82].
74 'Sue's way . . .', Kirk to me, 4 Oct 1986; 'That boy's . . .', PW to Sharman, *NT* (30 June 1979), p.26.

5 Exile

1   H.L. White to Dick White, BL, vol. 51, 19.vi.1925; Harry Courtney goes off on a similar expedition in *Vivisector*, p.138 [118].
2   PW to the Duttons, 2.ii.1975.
3   *Flaws*, p.12.
4   PW to Janet Hawley: 'I'm a terrible typist . . . started on two fingers at the age of 13', *Age* Extra (8 Feb 1986), p.9.
5   'melancholy . . .', PW to McKie, 18.viii.1951.
6   Brigadier G.P.H. Boycott, a contemporary of PW's, to me, 23 May 1986.
7   E. Humphris and D. Sladen, *The Life of Adam Lindsay Gordon* (Eric Partridge, London, 1912), p.38.
8   Southwood House Book, p.175, Cheltenham College archives.
9   The Most Rev. George Simms to me, 29.x.1986.
10 Ragnar Christophersen to me, 17 Nov 1986.
11 Ibid.
12 Simms to me, 29.x.1986.
13 PW to Clark, reported to me, 23 Nov 1988.
14 Christophersen.
15 *Australia and New Zealand Weekly* (8 July 1926), p.15.
16 PW to Mamblas, 5.ii.1946.
17 *Southerly*, p.133.
18 *Uneasy*, p.38 [UK 38–9].
19 *Australian Book Review* (1962), Children's Book and Educational Supplement, p.4.
20 'The Maelstrom': *NT* (30 June 1979), p.26 and White to me, 19 Feb 1985; 'The Bird of Prey', *Southerly*, p.136, *Flaws*, pp.26, 41, PW to me, 19 Feb 1985.
21 'amused . . .', *Flaws*, p.4; 'Ruth was . . .', Pauline Allen (McDonald) to me, 3 Oct 1986. 'I fluctuated . . .', *Flaws*, p.1.
22 'I never . . .', *Flaws*, pp.34–5.
23 Plain and vain, *Flaws*, p.41; 'handsome . . .', *Flaws*, p.3; 'I settled . . .', *Flaws*, p.35.
24 Betty Withycombe to me: at her first meeting with PW in 1928 his

misanthropy was already fixed as it was to remain for the rest of the time they remained in contact (i.e. to 1959); she thought a fair summary of this misanthropy was Laura Trevelyan's list of humanity's appalling qualities: greedy, shoddy etc, *Voss*, p.411 [380–1].

25 *Flaws*, p.34.
26 Ibid.
27 *Uneasy*, p.20; PW to me, 8 Oct 1986, of this holiday in Villars, 'It's all in "Dancing with Both Feet on the Ground".'
28 *Uneasy*, p.22 [UK 23].
29 Ibid., p.18 [UK 18–19].
30 Ibid., p.18 [UK 18].
31 *Living*, p.174 [192].
32 H.L. White to Dick White, BL, vol. 51, 12.vii.1925.
33 *Flaws*, p.14.
34 Christophersen.
35 Link with Miss Hare's fan in *Riders*, PW to me, 29 Nov 1988.
36 PW to Williams, 2.i.1971.
37 PW to Dutton, 7.x.1969.
38 Hailing's notes on the dust jacket of *Voss* in his scrapbook now in the Cheltenham College archives.
39 Peter Schryver to me, 30 Oct 1986.
40 Ronald Waters to me, 30 Sept 1985. When Waters came to know her later on, she was unable even to remember receiving it.
41 Christophersen.
42 Ibid.
43 *Thirteen Poems*, privately published *c.*1929, pp.3–4. Copy in Fisher Library, University of Sydney.
44 Ibid., p.5; lilacs are associated in his work with Mount Wilson, with adolescent sentimentality and his first attempts at writing. Lilacs are a crucial image in *The Ham Funeral*: 'the long, bosomy sprays of lilac would press against your soaking shirt . . . the dreamy scents drench you with words and longing.' *Plays*, p.31. See Chapter 18.
45 PW to Clark, 19.iii.1978.
46 *The Times* (14 Aug 1928), p.7.
47 PW to King Carl Gustav and the Swedish Academy, 24.xi.1973.
48 In *Twyborn* the grazier Don Lushington of Bogong takes the same train and sends a poem about a glacier home to his wife, p.243.
49 PW to Harrower, 3.vi.1971.
50 Major Harry Lewin to me, 6.x.1986.
51 Tod to me, Dec 1987.
52 PW to Sharman, *NT* (30 June 1979), p.27.
53 *Flaws*, p.66.
54 *Daily Mail* (8 Aug 1924), quoted in *Said and Done* (Weidenfeld & Nicolson, London, 1955), where the archaeologist O.G.S. Crawford pays a tribute to Withycombe, pp.162–5, 218–20, 236.
55 *Flaws*, p.64.
56 Garland to me, 9 Dec 1986.
57 *Flaws*, p.66, also PW to me.
58 'most spectacular', *Flaws*, p.67; 'bluestocking', *NT* (30 June 1979), p.27.
59 PW to me, 6 May 1986.
60 Betty Withycombe to me, 14 Oct 1985.
61 Betty Withycombe to me, 14 and 25 Oct 1985, 16 Nov 1987.
62 Garland to me, 9 Dec 1986.
63 *Thirteen Poems*, p.15.
64 Ibid., p.16.

65   S.J. Kunitz and H. Haycraft (eds), *Twentieth Century Authors* (H.W. Wilson, 1942/1956), p.1509.
66   PW to Best, 20.ii.1961, Viking.
67   'to such . . .', *Flaws*, pp.13, 64; 'discovered . . .', PW to McKie, 6.xi.1961.
68   Christophersen to me, 17 Nov 1986, 20 Jan 1987.
69   *Flaws*, pp.38, 36.
70   'St Jacques, Dieppe', *Thirteen Poems*, p.21.
71   *Flaws*, p.37.
72   *Living*, pp.59–62 [59–62], 148–51 [164–7].
73   *The Lewisite* (Winter 1930), p.14.
74   PW to me, 8 Oct 1986.
75   *Thirteen Poems*, p.18.
76   *Twyborn*, p.133; PW to me, 8 March 1990, 'This was *my* habit.'
77   *Flaws*, pp.14, 27, 47.
78   PW to me, 1 May 1986.

6   The World of Sheep

1   PW to me, 8 March 1990.
2   *Twyborn*, p.149.
3   PW to me, 8 March 1990.
4   *Aunt's*, p.11 [5].
5   PW to me, 1 May 1985. He was uncertain whether *Thirteen Poems* was printed before or after his return, but the date of publication was either 1929 or 1930.
6   White to Johnson, 20.viii.1939.
7   *Flaws*, p.47.
8   PW to me, 3 Aug 1990.
9   Undated clipping from *The Women's Weekly*, early 1930s.
10   *Aunt's*, p.79 [70]. PW to me that he heard this at one of these unhappy dances in 1930.
11   'The Letters', *Burnt*, p.233 [225–6]; that this passage was based on Ruth grilling him, PW to me, 26 Jan 1987.
12   *Flaws*, p.48.
13   Peter Valder to me, 15 May 1986.
14   'English' inhibitions, *Flaws*, p.47; 'the disease . . .', *Eye*, p.212; 'a stranger . . .', *Flaws*, pp.46, 47.
15   A favourite phrase, e.g. *Twyborn*, p.174.
16   Michael White to me, Aug 1986.
17   PW to me, 19 Feb 1985.
18   *Twyborn*, p.179: this is the scene at Bolaro as it was in 1930. Later the house was altered, and the garden grew up to hide it from the road.
19   PW re Irving to me, 5 Feb 1986; emerges in *Twyborn*, p.187.
20   *Twyborn*, p.279.
21   'she revealed . . .', *Twyborn*, p.180; Venables as the original for Peggy Tyrell, PW to me; 'fucked for fat', Sally Venables probably the source for this expression in *Vivisector*, p.193 [167], PW to me, 8 March 1990.
22   *Twyborn*, p.201.
23   Norris King to me, 27 Feb 1986.
24   This crops up several times, e.g. *Happy*, p.25 [27].
25   'lost and found', *Flaws*, p.194; good rider, PW to me, 30 July 1990; 'he could . . .', *Twyborn*, p.272.
26   The tramp's account, *Aunt's*, p.43 [35–6].
27   *Twyborn*, p.194.

28   PW to me, 1 May 1985.
29   PW to Dutton, 25.vii.1961.
30   *Southerly*, p.136, *Flaws*, p.46, PW to me, 19 Feb and 1 May 1985.
31   PW to Dutton, 21.ii.1976.
32   *Happy*, pp.28–9 [29].
33   *Twyborn*, pp.247–8.
34   PW to the Moores, 9.iv.1957.
35   PW to me, 22 Oct 1988; 'too exquisite . . .', PW to Richard King, 26.ii.1984.
36   *SMH* (13 Feb 1930), p.13; (14 Feb), p.12.
37   PW to me, 10 Feb 1987.
38   A full list of Ruth's and Dick's friends is in *SMH* (18 May 1935), p.9.
39   *Eye*; identification of Ebsworth to me as the model of Wyburd, and of
      his daughters as sources for Laura and Belle in *Voss*, PW to me, 30 Sept
      1988.
40   PW's biographical note sent to Clem Christesen, 15 June 1956, Meanjin
      Library, Melbourne University.
41   *Truth* (2 Dec 1934), p.29. PW insisted she only used the monocle to read menus.
42   *Memoirs*, p.38.
43   PW to me, 1 May 1985.
44   Waters to me, 30 Sept 1985. Alas all destroyed.
45   *Vivisector*, p.62 [51–2].
46   *Tree*, p.444.
47   PW to Johnson, 17.viii.1939.
48   Ray Hartley in *Being Different* (Hale & Iremonger, Sydney, 1986) gives
      an account of homosexual Sydney in the 1930s. Garry Wotherspoon, the
      book's editor, also provided information to me, Nov 1986.
49   The diary remains with the Sanderson and Wilcox families at Barwon Vale.
50   Ian Sanderson to me, 1 Dec 1986.
51   *Flaws*, p.51.
52   Ibid.
53   PW to me, 23 Dec 1986.
54   *Speaks*, p.40.
55   Sanderson.
56   'two sisters . . .', PW to me, 23 Dec 1986; 'beginning to . . .', *Southerly*,
      p.136.
57   *Vivisector*, p.112 [96]; PW to me, 8 March 1990, 'This was my experience.'
58   PW to me, 8 Oct 1986
59   PW to me, 27 Nov 1986.
60   Parrott, *Aunt's*, pp.72–3 [63], 82–5 [72–5]; the salesman, *Tree*, p.308; Prowse,
      Twyborn, pp.235, 284. Loder married and was killed in Borneo during the
      Second World War.
61   *Flaws*, p.51–2.
62   PW to Tasker, 26.iv.1963.
63   The Ridley girls surpassed their mother's ambitions. The younger married
      a cousin of PW's, 'lives in great style, accepted everywhere': PW to Tasker,
      26 April 1963.
64   *Aunt's*, p.72 [63].
65   Sanderson.
66   *Twyborn*, p.158. That this was based on his own experience with Dick, PW
      to me, 8 March 1990. And moonlight? 'Allow me some creative latitude!'
67   'would not have regretted . . .', *Twyborn*, p.206; 'A cock, a dog . . .',
      Eye, pp.194–5; that his night in Scone was also the source for Mrs Hunter's
      sleepless night, PW to me, 29 April 1987, 8 March 1990.
68   *Vivisector*, pp.191 [166], 208–9 [180–1]; that all his arrivals at Belltrees
      seemed to be early in the morning, PW to me, 29 April 1987.

69   PW to me, 8 Oct 1986.
70   Tim Whitney to me, 26 Dec 1989.
71   'He'll probably . . .', *Flaws*, p.170; diplomat and writer, PW to me, 14
     Aug 1985.
72   Wood to me in Wellington, June 1985.
73   PW to me, 2 Oct 1989.
74   *Southerly*, p.133.
75   PW to Garland, 5.iii.1952.
76   Guy Innes, interview with PW, 1939, unidentified clipping in Ruth White's
     scrapbook; PW to me, 19 Feb 1985, and biographical note to Clem Christesen,
     Meanjin Library.
77   *Flaws*, p.29.
78   PW wrote of having to run away, but without giving reasons, PW to
     Dutton, 10.iii.1974; discontent with isolation, S.J. Kunitz and H. Haycraft
     (eds), *Twentieth Century Authors* (H.W. Wilson, 1942/1956), p.1509; 'peculiar
     tastes', *Meanjin* (June 1956), p.223; 'There was nothing . . .', to me, 8 Oct
     1986.
79   PW to Williams, 4.ix.1963.

7   King's Men

1   Waters to me, 4 Oct 1985, 29 Nov 1987.
2   PW to Garland, 25.vi.1952.
3   *Flaws*, p.68.
4   To me, 16 Nov 1987.
5   'with a wry . . .', PW to me, 1 May 1985; the landscape for *Twyborn*
     and Kitty Goose in *Living*, PW to me, 8 May 1989.
6   *Flaws*, p.38; *Southerly*, p.133.
7   Waters to me, 4 Oct 1985.
8   *Living*, p.163.
9   George Rylands to me, 27 Nov 1987.
10   'who are deaf', *Riders*, p.262 [250]; lungs, PW to Beatson, 5.xii.1971;
     Bread and Butter Women, PW did not remember when he wrote it. That R
     does not recall PW working on the play while they were together suggests
     it was written before May or June 1933. This is supported by an unidentified
     newspaper clipping in my possession which says that PW was 'a youth of
     twenty when he wrote this piece' in his spare time at Cambridge.
11   'I stayed . . .', PW to me, 14 Aug 1985; 'happy here' from 'Lines Written
     on Leaving the Scilly Islands', *Ploughman*.
12   'If I Could Tell You', *Ploughman*.
13   'Futility', *Ploughman*.
14   A.E. Housman, *The Name and Nature of Poetry* (Cambridge University
     Press, 1933), p.49.
15   'Lovely, Lovely You May Be', *Ploughman*. R says the date 'October 1933' is
     impossible, principally because he was shown what may have been an earlier
     version of the poem in May or June that year. The date may refer to a final,
     polished version.
16   R to me, 2.i.1989.
17   'human contact', S.J. Kunitz and H. Haycraft (eds), *Twentieth Century
     Authors* (H.W. Wilson, 1942/1956), p.1509; 'The sun smote . . .', *Plough-
     man*.
18   'Rain in Summer', 'If You Would See' and 'I Walked in the Garden',
     Ploughman.
19   Mrs Oertel, quoted in the *Hannoversche Allgemeine Zeitung* (15/16 Nov
     1975), p.15.

20   *Living*, p.115 [125]; Herr Richter is based on Herr Oertel, PW to me,
      10 Sept 1987.
21   *Riders*, p.162 [152]; cf. PW's recollection of the words of the crazed army
      officer in the block of flats in Hanover, to me, 10 Sept 1987.
22   'Taking root', White writing in *Twentieth Century Authors*, p.1509; PW
      identifies Hanover as the Heimat of Voss and Himmelfarb in *Flaws*, p.39;
      he identified Elyot Standish of *Living* as studying in Hanover to me, 10 Sept
      1987; the quotation from *Living* is from p.116 [126].
23   'Sadness that . . .', from 'After Rain', *Ploughman*; 'comic . . .', *Flaws*, p.39.
24   *The Times* (15 June 1977), p.1.
25   Katherine Mansfield, *Letters and Journals*, ed. C.K. Stead (Penguin, 1977),
      p.76.
26   'a rather . . .', PW to Stern, 2.ix.1976; Franz Grillparzer, Austrian
      dramatic poet, 1791–1872; the gloomy verses were 'Bitter were the tears
      she wept' and 'Lament in Winter'; 'I saw . . .', from 'The Ploughman' –
      all verse from *Ploughman*.
27   Re Squire: Patrick Howarth, *Squire, Most Generous of Men* (Hutchinson,
      London, 1963): 'traditional, yet . . .', p.125; 'whisky', p.217. 'I kept . . .',
      PW to me, 10 Sept 1987.
28   PW to me, 19 Feb 1985.
29   R to me, 23.v.1988.
30   'They involved . . .', PW to me, 1 May 1985; 'Was it . . .', *Uneasy*,
      pp.15–16 [UK 16].
31   To me, 16 Nov 1987.
32   'Trio', *Ploughman*.
33   R to me, 23.v.1988
34   'Interlude', *Ploughman*.
35   PW to Mary Lord, then President of the Association for the Study of
      Australian Literature, 17.vi.1979; PW, address to the librarians of Australia,
      Sydney, 19 Sept 1980, PW's autobiographical note, *Twentieth Century Authors*,
      p.1509.
36   Proust, PW to Dutton, 10.ii.1962; other books, *Southerly*, p.133, Reha
      Himmelfarb's taste for Fontane, *Riders*, p.153 [144], cf. *Flaws*, p.40.
37   PW to Dutton, 1.v.1967; Flaubert, PW to Sharman, *NT* (30 June 1979),
      p.27; *La Chartreuse*, PW to Dutton, 21.vi.1970; Fournier, *Southerly*, p.139;
      Gide, PW to Falkenberg, 1.vii.1985.
38   To me, April 1989.
39   Stephensen to W.T. Baker & Co, Sydney, 6.vii.1934. Mitchell Library,
      Stephensen papers, box Y2144. An example of Ruth's attempts to recruit
      for the company is PRS to Alexander Gordon, 2 June 1934, box Y2123.
      Details of shareholders are in box Y2117.
40   PW to Stephensen, 21.x.1934, Mitchell, box Y2144.
41   PW to me, 10 Sept 1987.
42   'Oram's Grave', *Ploughman*.
43   'would it be . . .', PW to Stephensen, 21.x.1934, Mitchell, box Y2144;
      'Great Australian novel . . .', Craig Munro, *Wild Man of Letters, The Story
      of P.R. Stephensen* (Melbourne University Press, 1984), p.138.
44   Red Page, *Bulletin* (10 July 1935), p.4; *SMH* (23 Feb 1935), p.10.
45   Ruth White to Stephensen, 8.iii.1935, Mitchell, box Y2144.
46   *Opinion*, vol. 1, no.1 (15 May 1935), p.5. The writer was identified only
      as A.D.C. It may have been Stephensen himself.
47   'It deals . . .', *Sydney Sunday Sun and Guardian*, Colour Section (16 Dec
      1934), p.2; 'bludging males . . .', PW to me, 19 Feb 1985, plus a number
      of unidentified press clippings in my possession.
48   *The Playbox* (March 1935), p.13.

49 *Sydney Mail* (30 Jan 1935), p.17 (another review was in *SMH* (24 Jan 1935), p.8.); *Smith's Weekly* (16 Feb 1935), p.23.
50 *Smith's Weekly* (16 Feb 1935), p.23; ibid. (29 Jan 1935), p.22.
51 Unidentified newspaper clipping in my possession.
52 PW to Peter Beatson, 5.xii.1971.
53 PW to Stern, 20.x.1974.
54 George Moore, *Sister Teresa* (F. Fisher Unwin, London, 1901), p.42.
55 Ibid., p.233.
56 *Flaws*, p.57.
57 R to me, 14.iii.1989.
58 *SMH* (18 May 1935), p.9.
59 Mrs H.D. Fairfax (née Stogdale) to me, 29 July 1986, letter Sept 1986.
60 PW could not recall the name of this play, and said no copies of it survive; 'poor Dick', *Flaws*, p.58; the name and Dick's deal, PW to me, 6 May 1986.
61 PW to me, 19 Feb 1985.
62 'We laughed . . .', *Flaws*, p.39; 'to honour . . .', diary of the late Mrs Oertel, in the collection of her son Dr Jürgen Oertel, Hanover.
63 *Aunt's*, p.145 [133].
64 PW to Sharman, *NT* (30 June 1979), p.27.

8 The Mouse and Roy

1 *Living*, p.321 [366].
2 'artists of domesticity . . .', *Flaws*, p.56; 'a rackety . . .', PW to Casey, 9.vii.1978.
3 PW to me, 8 Oct 1986.
4 'obdurate . . .', 'The Twitching Colonel', *London Mercury* (April 1937), p.602; PW identified the setting of *The Ham Funeral* to Williams, 4.ix.1963; 'still a respectable . . .', *Living*, p.38 [34]; PW identified the geography of Part III of *Twyborn*, to me, 30 Sept 1988.
5 Betty Withycombe to me, 25 Oct 1985; Waters to me, 4 Oct 1985.
6 *Flaws*, pp.56, 59, 60, 63; 'at the edge . . .', Waters to me, 30 Sept 1985.
7 'too frightened . . .', PW to me, 19 Feb 1985; 'nothing else . . .', PW to Johnson, 11.viii.1939.
8 *Flaws*, p.80; resilient, PW to Williams, 21.vi.1970.
9 Graham Greene (ed.), *The Old School, Essays by Divers Hands* (Jonathan Cape, 1934), p.14; *Letters from Iceland* (Faber & Faber, 1937), p.253.
10 White has given two accounts of this brush-off. In *Flaws*, p.55, he says the production was *Dance of Death*, but in *Southerly*, p.134, he says it was *The Dog Beneath the Skin*. As the former opened in Feb 1934 while White was still at Cambridge, the latter must be the production concerned. It opened on 30 Jan 1936.
11 PW to Garland, 5.iii.1952.
12 PW to me, 8 March 1990.
13 'all those . . .', PW to Beatson, 5.xii.1971; 'this morning . . .', PW to Betty Withycombe, 29.vi.1936, collection of Peggy Garland.
14 Visits to the brothel, PW to me, 29 June 1989; fascination with the make-up, PW to Gerry Wilkes, 8.viii.1973.
15 'romantic reconstruction . . .', *Flaws*, pp.39–40; 'At night . . .', PW to me, 10 Sept 1987.
16 Repulsive, PW to Huebsch, 11.x.1960, Congress; 'God', PW to Best, 25.ii.1960.
17 'an intellectual . . .', *Flaws*, p.60; 'I always . . .', PW to Stern, 18.iii.1968.
18 Heather Johnson, *Roy de Maistre: The Australian Years, 1894–1930* (Craftsman's Press, Roseville, 1988), p.5. Johnson, a great-niece of the painter,

gave me very generous help with this account of de Maistre's life.

19   Discharge details, Major-General W.O. Rodgers, Director General Army Health Services to me, 19.ii.1987; techniques for treating shell-shock, J.O. Fairfax, *NSW Red Cross Annual Report* (1919–20), p.10.

20   Sir John Rothenstein, *Modern English Painters, Lewis to Moore* (Eyre & Spottiswoode, 1956), p.249.

21   Daniel Thomas, *SMH* (14 Sept 1976), p.7; the picture hangs in the Art Gallery of NSW; 'In Sydney . . .', *SMH* (9 Aug 1919), p.8.

22   'preordained . . .', Rothenstein, *Modern English Painters*, p.253; 'Roy was . . .', PW to me, 19 Feb 1985.

23   Grace Bros leaflet advertising the disc, in the files of the Art Gallery of NSW.

24   *The Home*, Sydney (1 Nov 1929), p.54.

25   'De Mestre is . . .', de Maistre to Daniel Thomas, 21.x.1960, Art Gallery of NSW; 'aristocratic . . .', Rothenstein, *Modern English Painters*, p.255.

26   Bacon/de Maistre exhibition, 'The 1930 Look in British Decoration', *The Studio*, vol. 100 (Aug 1930), pp.140–1; 'with the reverence . . .', John Richardson, *New York Review of Books* (25 April 1985), p.24; 'He has a good . . .', PW to Johnson, 4.viii.1939.

27   Bethia Ogden to Heather Johnson, 29.vii.1986.

28   PW to Williams, 28.vi.1961.

29   'He himself . . .', PW to Stern, 18.iii.1968; liking for older men, PW to me, 26 Jan 1987; 'not because . . .', *Australian* (1 Aug 1970), p.15; 'with one . . .', *Flaws*, p.60.

30   'He persuaded . . .', *Flaws*, p.60; 'seduced by . . .', PW to Stern, 18.iii.1968.

31   'The Good . . .', de Maistre, *Art in Australia*, no. 14 (1928), unnumbered pages; 'the fragmentation . . .', PW to Casey, 26.xi.1967.

32   PW to Dutton, 19.ix.1960.

33   *Flaws*, p.52.

34   'I don't think . . .', PW to Jill Hellyer, 12.iii.1972; 'When I was . . .', PW to Dutton, 15.ii.1961; 'drunk with . . .', PW to Keith Michell, 10.vii.1957.

35   PW to Hellyer, 26.iii.1972.

36   PW to Casey, 23.ix.1969.

37   'dark cave', PW to Maschler, 23.viii.1973; loss of creative self, PW to Jill Hellyer, 17.vi.1981.

38   *London Mercury* (April 1937), p.609.

39   PW to Clem Christesen, 3.ii.1962.

40   *Happy*, pp.83–4 [83].

41   Ibid., p.81 [81].

42   PW to Johnson, 20.viii.1939.

43   'My downfall . . .', PW to Garland, 16.i.1972; 'Rodney Halliday . . .', PW to Johnson, 20.viii.1939: 'was very . . .', PW to Johnson, 11.viii.1939.

44   *Happy*, p.268 [260–1].

45   PW to Keith Michell, 10.vii.1957.

46   *Eye*, p.432: Mrs Hunter says of the Macrorys: 'A girl married an overseer, and her father bought a place for them. This was "Kudjeri".' Also cf. *Eye*, p.478.

47   *Happy*, p.327 [317].

48   PW to Sharman, *NT* (30 June 1979), p.30.

49   Sir John Rothenstein, *Time's Thievish Progress* (Cassell, London, 1970), pp.96–7.

50   *Flaws*, p.62.

51   Waters to me, 30 Sept 1985; Withycombe to me, 14 Oct 1985, 16 Nov 1987.

52   'Betty was . . .', PW to me, 23 Dec 1986; 'All my youth . . .', PW to Garland, 30.viii.1970.

53   To me, 30 Sept 1985.
54   Waters.
55   *Sketches from 'Nine Sharp'* (Samuel French Ltd, London, 1938), p.45. This may not be the precise text performed at the Arts Theatre Club in 1937, as Waters recalled some different lines in his impromptu performance over lunch in a London restaurant in 1985.
56   'three bitching . . .', PW to me, Feb 1985. The judges were George Mackaness, an anthologist and popular historian, and Ben Sullivan, head of talks at the Australian Broadcasting Commission. *School for Friends* was performed on 14, 21 April, 26 May, 2, 9 June 1937. No copy of the play is known to have survived.
57   'Cleverly written . . .', Trafford W. Whitelock, *Everyone's* (9 June 1937), p.42; 'Mrs Victor White . . .', Sydney *Daily Telegraph* (10 June 1937), p.14.

9   Spanish Eyes

1   R de M to Daniel Thomas, 21 Oct 1960, in the archives of the Art Gallery of NSW. The painting now hangs with the Hinton collection in the Armidale gallery in NSW.
2   In the possession of Heather Johnson.
3   PW identifies the Hostellerie as the original of Theodora's Hôtel du Midi, *Flaws*, pp.128–9; 'a tight fit', *Aunt's*, p.142 [129–30]; the clock which was still ticking in 1987, *Aunt's*, p.142 [130]; 'beaucoup de fleurs', Léa and Camille Irigoyen, nieces of the late Madame Jacquet, to me, 22 Dec 1987; the cross-currents making up 'The Jardin Exotique', PW to Dutton, 12.viii.1959.
4   Léa and Camille Irigoyen.
5   *Happy*, p.65 [65].
6   Diary of the Duke of San Lucar, X. Garcia-Larrache – Archivo de Baena – Bayonne.
7   Mamblas, *Sud-Ouest*, Bordeaux (31 Oct 1973), p.11.
8   'colonial . . .', Mamblas diary, 3 Sept. Both poems were written on 28 August; neither has been published. The poems are now in National Library of Australia with White's letters to Mamblas.
9   *Sud-Ouest*.
10   PW to me, 8 March 1990.
11   *Flaws*, p.63.
12   This was written in 1973 in the *Sud-Ouest* article celebrating White's Nobel Prize. According to the material provided to me by the Archivo de Baena, the details in *Sud-Ouest* were not drawn from contemporary diary entries or letters. I showed the article to White on 30 Sept 1988 and asked him if it was accurate. He skimmed the translation. His only comment: 'How embarrassing.'
13   To me, 22 Oct 1988; cf. *Living*, p.199 [222].
14   *Living*, p.195–6 [218].
15   Archivo de Baena.
16   A.S.G. Butler, *The Architecture of Sir Edwin Lutyens*, vol. 1 (Country Life, London, 1950), p.59.
17   PW to me, 30 Sept 1988.
18   PW to me, 3 Sept 1987.
19   *Sketch* (29 Sept 1937), p.626. The reviewer attributed *Parties*, as the sketch was then called, to Cooper himself. See PW complaining to Mamblas, 10.xi.1937. Date of the first performance was 12 Sept 1937.
20   PW to me, 19 Feb 1985; the Lord Chamberlain approved the script on 4 Oct, some days before the Manchester opening. Some small cuts

including a reference to Queen Mary were ordered. The script is with the Lord Chamberlain's papers in the British Library.

21 'Dreariness . . .', PW to me, 19 Feb 1985; 'I can . . .', PW to Waters, 28.vi.1970.
22 *Manchester Guardian* (13 Oct 1937), p.11.
23 PW to me, 19 Feb 1985.
24 PW to Johnson, 20.viii.1939.
25 PW to Mamblas, 10.xi.1937.
26 Ibid.
27 To Mamblas, 4.i.1938.
28 To Mamblas, 13.i.1938.
29 'a lot . . .', PW to Mamblas, 10.xi.1937; 'But you . . .', PW to Mamblas, 13.i.1938; 'I have . . .', PW to Mamblas, 19.xi.1937.
30 To Mamblas, 2.xii.1937.
31 *SMH* (2 Dec 1937), p.7.
32 PW to Dutton, 19.ix.1965.
33 NSW Probate number 227125.
34 PW to Mamblas, 2.xii.1937.
35 Waters to me, 30 Sept 1985.
36 27.i.1938.
37 PW to Mamblas, 27.i.1938.
38 *Home* (May 1938), p.82.
39 *SMH* (26 March 1938), p.6.
40 Clipping in Ruth White's scrapbook. Collection of Alexandra Dawson.
41 27.i.1938.
42 To Mamblas, 27.i.1938.
43 Guy Innes, 'Notable Australian Novelist', clipping in Ruth White's scrapbook in collection of Alexandra Dawson. Date line: London, 10 March 1939.
44 3.ii.1938.
45 *Southerly*, p.134.
46 The pictures from the Eccleston Street flat are now all in the Art Gallery of NSW: the furniture is dispersed.
47 PW to Mamblas, 2.iii.1938.
48 *Aunt's*. The identification of the admiral and Sokolnikov is made by White, e.g. in *Flaws*, pp.76–7.
49 *Living*, pp.64–5 [65].
50 *Flaws*, p.77.
51 PW to me, 22 Oct 1988; *Southerly*, p.136. No manuscript of 'Nightside' appears to survive.
52 PW to Mamblas, 23.ii.1938.
53 2.iii.1938.
54 PW to Mamblas, 16.ii.1938.
55 *Bookseller* (26 Jan 1939), p.84.
56 'The House Behind the Barricades', *New Verse*, no. 30 (Summer 1938), p.9.
57 Geoffrey Grigson, *The Crest on the Silver, an Autobiography* (Cresset Press, London, 1950), p.181.
58 'I fear . . .', PW to Mamblas, 17.iii.1938; 'It ain't . . .', Mamblas to PW, 24.i.1938; 'I must . . .', PW to Mamblas, 23.iii.1938.
59 War caused by human vileness, PW to Mamblas, 23.iii.1936; 'I have no head . . .', 17.iii.1938; 'dreary looking . . .', PW to Mamblas, 23.ii.1938.
60 'There were . . .', PW to Mamblas, 23.ii.1938; Eden losing his nerve, Mamblas's diary, 23 April 1938; 'just an excuse . . .', PW to Mamblas, 6.iii.1938; Gollancz meeting, PW to Mamblas, 17.iii.1938.
61 Peggy Garland to me, 27.ii.1990: 'Wystan . . . was terrified at the thought of seeing wounded people in pain and thought he would be able to help if

he could give them a shot of morphine or whatever it was.' Did he use it himself, I asked? Peggy Garland to me, 9.iii.1990: 'I am sure Wystan did not use any drugs except tobacco. He was oddly careful about health and needed no stimulants: so in the time we knew him [before his departure for USA] he hardly drank alcohol (as far as I can tell).'

62 *Flaws*, pp.67–8.
63 PW to Mamblas, 17.iii.1938.
64 'I found . . .', Mamblas' diary, 18 April 1938; 'there must . . .', PW to me, 1 Aug 1990.
65 PW to me, 14 Nov 1988; PW to Björkstén, 20.vi.1984.
66 This was probably the third play he wrote after coming down from Cambridge. PW was uncertain how many he wrote at this time, though he said *Return to Abyssinia* was the third or fourth. By my calculations one was written before Ruth and Dick arrived in 1935, another before he met de Maistre in 1936, and then *Return to Abyssinia*.
67 PW to Dutton, 19.xi.1960.
68 Beauval based on Sorel, PW to me, 19 Feb 1985; Wyse to me, 1 Oct 1985.
69 *The Story of the Boltons Theatre First Season* (Marsland Publications Ltd, London, 1947), p.28.
70 That White read *Rasselas* only after finishing *Happy Valley* has been the cause of some confusion among scholars. PW to Manfred Mackenzie, 22.vii.1962, 5.i.1963; to Ian Donaldson, 20.i.1964; and to me, 6 May 1986. See also the exchange between Donaldson and Mackenzie in *Essays in Criticism* (July 1963, April 1964, Oct 1964).
71 PW to Dutton, 13.i.1964.
72 PW to me, 19 Feb 1985. These two paintings, along with de Maistre's portraits of White himself, are in the Art Gallery of NSW.
73 *Living*, p.202 [225].
74 Ibid., p.222 [249–50]; that Walsh was the source of Collins, PW to me, 5 Feb 1986.
75 *Sud-Ouest*.
76 *Sud-Ouest*.
77 'England is very puzzling . . .', *Living*, p.204 [228]; 'living and the dead' p.286 [325]. PW identified Mamblas to me as the source of this exchange, 3 Sept 1987.
78 PW to Mamblas, 7.ii.1939.
79 *Liverpool Post* (13 Feb 1939), p.5.
80 To me, 27 Nov 1987.
81 *Bystander* (8 Feb 1939), p.206.
82 PW to Johnson, 24.vii.1939.
83 Sales figures for *Happy Valley* do not survive either in UK or Australia. We know the size of print runs and the dates on which the second printing became available. That Australian booksellers took 500 copies before publication is reported by PW to Mamblas, 7.ii.1939. John Holroyd, an authority on the book trade in Australia, recalled to me, 14 Feb 1986, that Dymock's secured distribution rights in Australia. 'It had a fair sale.'
84 Unfair to country towns: *SMH* (1 April 1939), p.20; protest to *John O'London's Weekly* (5 May 1939), p.190; the letter was signed 'Reader'.
85 'Surely a little . . .', 'Mail Magazine', *Adelaide Mail* (18 March 1939), p.9; 'consciousness of . . .', Australian *Tribune* reviewing *Riders in the Chariot* (2 May 1962).
86 Melbourne *Herald* (18 Feb 1939), p.36.
87 *Bohemia* (June 1939), p.18.
88 *Bonniers Litterära Magasin*, vol. 8, no. 5 (May 1939), pp.352–3.
89 6.iii.1939.

90   'Notable Australian Novelist', London, 10 March [1939], unidentified clipping
      in Ruth White's scrapbook. White remembered Innes's prediction in his essay
      'Prodigal Son', republished in *Speaks*, p.16.
91   To me, 14 Oct 1985.
92   PW to me, 22 Oct 1988.
93   Unidentified press clipping.

10 Crossings

1   PW to Johnson, 4.viii.1939.
2   PW to Johnson, 24.vii.1939.
3   April 1939; this is one of the very few letters White kept.
4   'I got to know . . .' and 'I remember . . .', PW, unpublished open letter to
      President Reagan, 29.v.1984; 'might be . . .', PW to Johnson, 15.ix.1939.
5   'three arseholes . . .', PW to me, 3 Oct 1987 – the other two are Miami
      and Honolulu; Holstius, *Southerly*, p.141; 'horrifyingly touristy . . .', PW
      to me, 29 April 1987; Alex Gray in *Memoirs*, pp.135–6 and Eddie Twyborn
      in *Twyborn*, p.141.
6   This is Taos through Theodora Goodman's eyes, *Aunt's*, pp.275 [255],
      276 [256]; PW identified this as Taos to me, 8 Oct 1986.
7   *Aunt's*, p.277 [256].
8   Sean Hignett, *Brett, from Bloomsbury to New Mexico* (Hodder & Stoughton,
      London, 1984), p.215.
9   *Aunt's*, p.289 [268].
10   'disintegrating . . .', *Aunt's*, p.290 [269]; the Jackson/Johnsons, *Aunt's*,
      pp.279–88 [258–67]. PW identified the Jacksons as the Johnsons of the
      novel to me, 29 April 1987.
11   PW to Johnson, 4.viii.1939.
12   *Laughing Horse*, no.20 (Summer 1938), courtesy Laurence Pollinger Ltd
      and the estate of Mrs Frieda Lawrence Ravagli.
13   'Trailing up . . .', PW to Johnson, 26.vi.1939; 'all through . . .', *Aunt's*,
      p.269 [249].
14   PW to Johnson, 26.vi.1939.
15   'I went . . .', PW to me, 29 April 1987; 'with letters . . .', PW to
      Johnson, 8.vii.1939; 'a cheap . . .', PW to me, 8 March 1990.
16   PW to Johnson, 8.vii.1939.
17   PW to Johnson, 24.vii.1939.
18   PW to Harrower, 1.vi.1972.
19   PW to Johnson, 24.vii.1939.
20   Ibid.
21   Ibid.
22   PW to Mamblas, 15.ii.1940.
23   London the chief character, PW to me, 12 May 1988; the life of Goose/Stand-
      ish, *Living*, pp.24–34 [17–30]; not aware of the parallels, PW to me, 8 March
      1990; 'not badly done', PW to Aurousseau, 23.v.1967.
24   PW to Mamblas, 15.ii.1940; the Spanish attaché appears in *Living*, p.204 [228].
25   PW to Johnson, 17.viii.1939.
26   PW to Johnson, 24.vii.1939.
27   PW to Johnson, 4.viii.1939.
28   PW to Johnson, 11.viii.1939.
29   Ibid.
30   PW to Johnson, 17.viii.1939.
31   PW to Johnson, 20.viii.1939.
32   PW to Johnson, 24.viii.1939.
33   11.viii.1939.

34   20.viii.1939.

35   17.viii.1939.

36   7.viii.1939.

37   PW to Johnson, 4.viii.1939.

38   7.viii.1939.

39   PW to Johnson, 29.viii.1939.

40   Johnson papers, Harry Ransom Humanities Research Center, University of Texas at Austin.

41   'Carried away . . .', *Flaws*, p.74, where White's chronology is awry; 'I'm so glad . . .', PW to Johnson, 6.ix.1939.

42   PW to Johnson, 6.ix.1939.

43   *Flaws*, p.77.

44   PW to Johnson, 2.x.1939.

45   Ibid.

46   'if it hasn't . . .' and 'I have been . . .', PW to Johnson, 12.xi.1939; also PW to Johnson, 27.x.1939; 'there is so much . . .', PW to Mamblas, 15.ii.1940.

47   PW to Johnson, 13.x.1939 – though the letter is dated in error 13.ix.1939.

48   'all the French . . .', PW to Johnson, 13.x.1939; 'I shall . . .', to Mamblas, 15.ii.1940; 'BAD TIME . . .', *SMH* (14 Dec 1939).

49   'Why we . . .', PW to Johnson, 22.i.1940; 'The book . . .', PW to Johnson, 24.xii.1939.

50   PW to Aurousseau, 23.v.1962; also PW to me, 12 May 1988, 24 Jan 1989.

51   Standish's homosexuality, PW to me, 12 May 1988; 'It was funny . . .', *Living*, pp.192–3 [214]; 'the drunken . . .', pp.286–7 [326]; no more than a possibility, PW to me, 12 May 1988.

52   'in case . . .', PW to Johnson, 29.x.1939; 'on the verge . . .', *Living*, p.116 [125]; 'pale eyes . . .', p.117 [127].

53   'You could feel . . .', *Living*, p.284 [323]; 'He did a lot . . .', PW to me, 13 Sept 1989.

54   'Into a . . .', PW to Johnson, 24.xii.1939; 'in fact . . .', PW to Johnson, 22.i.1940.

55   PW to Mamblas, 15.ii.1940.

56   From the script of *Swinging the Gate* in the Lord Chamberlain's papers, British Library. Charles Zwar wrote the music. The show opened on 22 May 1940 and was thought by the critics to be a pale successor to the very successful *Gate Revue*. The critics no more than mentioned White's song in passing.

57   'I'm afraid . . .', PW to Johnson, 27.x.1939; 'It reminds . . .', PW to Johnson, 12.x.1939. The portrait was begun about 20 Oct and finished about 10 Nov 1939.

58   PW to Johnson, 24.xii.1939.

59   PW to Johnson, 30.iii.1940.

60   PW to Mamblas, 15.ii.1940.

61   30.iii.1940.

62   PW to Johnson, 3.xii.1940.

63   PW to Stern, 29.x.1961.

64   'One of a breed . . .', *Flaws*, p.75; 'He took me . . .', *B.W. Huebsch, 1876–1964, A Record of a Meeting of His Friends at the Grolier Club, New York City, on December 9, 1964* (privately printed, New York, 1964), p.30.

65   PW to Maschler, 16.viii.1970.

66   PW to Johnson, 22.iv.1940.

67   Ibid.

68   *Flaws*, p.78.

69   'orgiastic . . .', PW to Reagan, 29.v.1984; electrifying, PW to me, 29
      Nov 1988; *Living*, p.222 [249].
70   PW to Huebsch, 28.v.1940. This is the only letter of White's to Huebsch
      about *Happy Valley* that I have been able to find. Copy provided to me by
      Antipodean Books, Cold Springs, New York.
71   *New York Times Book Review* (26 May 1940), p.7.
72   Betty Withycombe to me, 16 Nov 1987.
73   *Living*, p.257 [291].
74   *Living*, p.288 [328].
75   PW to Johnson, 22.iv.1940.
76   'Immense . . .', *Flaws*, p.79; 'My plans . . .', PW to Johnson, 26.vii.1940.

11   **Love and War**

 1   *Flaws*, p.81.
 2   *Twyborn*, p.402.
 3   PW to Johnson, 26.vii.1940 and 12.ix.1940.
 4   'But this takes time . . .', PW to Huebsch, 23.ix.1940, Viking; 'often
      tragic . . .', PW to Johnson, 12.ix.1940.
 5   *Flaws*, p.82.
 6   'There we lay . . .', PW to Johnson, 12.ix.1940; *Flaws*, pp.82–3; Eadith
      Trist in *Twyborn*, p.430; *Riders*, p.190 [179].
 7   Wyse to me, 1 Oct 1985.
 8   PW to Huebsch, 23.ix.1940, Viking.
 9   12.ix.1940.
10   PW has given many accounts of how he first conceived the explorer novel;
      e.g. to Huebsch, 11.ix.1956, Congress, to Aurousseau, 10.iii.1958, to Dutton,
      18.xi.1964, 7.i.1968, and in *Flaws*, pp.83, 103.
11   PW to his New York agent Naomi Burton, undated copy about 11.ix.1940,
      Viking.
12   'something lively . . .', PW to Johnson, 12.ix.1940; 'I learned . . .', *Flaws*,
      p.85.
13   PW to Huebsch, 23.ix.1940, Viking.
14   *Flaws*, p.81.
15   PW to Johnson, 12.ix.1940 and 3.xii.1940.
16   3.xii.1940.
17   *Flaws*, p.86.
18   Squadron view of White: Captain Vivian Voss, MBE, *The Story of No.1
      Squadron S.A.A.F. (Sometimes known as the Billy Boys)* (Mercantile Atlas Pty
      Ltd, Cape Town, 1952), pp.110, 39; 'I was soon . . .', *Flaws*, p.89.
19   James Ambrose Brown, *A Gathering of Eagles*, vol. II (Purnell, Cape
      Town, 1970), p.137; *Flaws*, p.88.
20   PW to Johnson, 29.viii.1939.
21   *Flaws*, p.90.
22   Minutes of the Australian Literature Society, late 1939 ('infection from the
      prevalent . . .'), Sept 1940 (The Great Singer), 17 February, 13, 17 March,
      14 Aug 1941, La Trobe.
23   Serle's son and his eventual successor at the *Australian Dictionary of Biography*
      wrote to me on 26.vi.1986; 'I doubt if *Happy Valley* would have appealed
      much to my father who was by then elderly, but he could appreciate good
      writing and originality. Wilmot was something of an experimental modern-
      ist, however. And Arthur (A.A.) Phillips, a great critic of the future, would
      very likely have approved. Maybe, it wasn't a very good year in the judges'
      eyes. The ALS was of course very amateur and stuffy but a minority of able
      people did belong, hung on trying to make something of it, and very likely

kept a close eye on appointment of judges of the Crouch Prize – the list of winners is pretty sound.'

24   *New York Times* (9 Feb 1941), p.6; *Nation* (8 March 1941), p.276.
25   Routledge to PW, 1.iii.1946, Reading University MS 1489, box 1869, MS 1487, MS 1489, box 1812; *Living and the Dead*, 'PJ card' held by Routledge; Royalty account cards, Routledge, Keegan Paul Archive, University College London.
26   'dowdy', Kate O'Brien, *Spectator* (11 July 1941), p.44; cherished, PW to Dutton, 1.viii.1960; Muir's review, *Listener* (31 July 1941), p.175.
27   The royalty cards show total colonial sales – including South Africa, India and New Zealand – of 354, Routledge, Keegan Paul archive, University College London.
28   Douglas Stewart, *Bulletin* (22 Oct 1941), p.2.
29   PW to Huebsch, 17.iv.1942, Congress.
30   PW to Dutton, 19.ix.1965.
31   'Last Words', unpublished screenplay, scene 183.
32   PW to the Sydney newspaper columnist Andrea, *Sydney Sun and Guardian* (10 Aug 1941), p.18.
33   Idyllic, PW to Garland, 25.vi.1952; 'I was obsessed . . .', Australia Day Message, *SMH* (26 Jan 1984); 'the purest well . . .', *Speaks*, p.14; 'I am thinking of coming out . . .', *Sydney Sun and Guardian* (10 Aug 1941), p.18.
34   Diary in possession of the Hon. Mr Justice H.C. Nicholas.
35   PW to Andrea, *Sydney Sun and Guardian* (10 Aug 1941), p.18.
36   *Flaws*, p.99–100.
37   *Tree*, p.164; *Aunt's*, p.210 [194]; *Flaws*, p.99.
38   *Flaws*, p.100.
39   Ibid.
40   *Uneasy*, p.15 [UK 15].
41   EGL to me.
42   *Twyborn*, p.25.
43   'Being Kind to Titina', *Burnt*, p.188 [181]; see PW's treatment of the same story in *Flaws*, pp.100–2.
44   EGL to me, 12 Dec 1985.
45   'Being Kind to Titina', *Burnt*, pp.188–9 [181–2].
46   'A Glass of Tea', *Burnt*, pp.96–7 [89–90]; PW always believed incorrectly she was taken off on a destroyer – see *Flaws*, p.102 – and that is the detail that appears in his versions of Despo's story.
47   EGL to me, 29 June 1989.
48   Edited transcript of an interview by Tim Bowden for the ABC in 1975. EGL was discussing Durrell's *Alexandria Quartet*.
49   *Australia*, ed. S. Ure Smith and G.M. Spencer, Sydney. The magazine ceased publication in Oct 1947.
50   *Across the Wire*, A special report by PW (1945), p.2, Public Record Office AIR20/5845 123974.
51   Ibid., p.1.
52   Ibid., p.3.
53   *Flaws*, pp.92–3.
54   *Across the Wire*, p.3.
55   Ibid., p.4.
56   'The Sewing Machine of Tobruk', *Australia* (1 Jan 1942), p.65.
57   *Flaws*, p.96.
58   PW to Alexandra Dawson, 16.ii.1970.
59   *Across the Wire*, pp.4–6.
60   Ibid., p.8.

61   To me, 16 Aug 1990.
62   *Flaws*, p.105.
63   PW to Casey, 8.ix.1969.
64   *Flaws*, p.106.
65   Five novels queuing, PW to Andrea, *Sydney Sun and Guardian* (10 Aug 1941), p.18; seven, PW to Johnson, 20.vii.1942.
66   17.iv.1942.
67   *Flaws*, pp.103–4; 'his love affair . . .', PW to Aurousseau, 10.iii.1958; 'grand passion' and 'in my bones', PW to Huebsch, 11.ix.1956, Congress.
68   'its pages gritty . . .', *Flaws*, p.106; 'Nobody will touch . . .', PW to Johnson, 17.xi.1944.
69   *Flaws*, p.105.
70   Ibid.
71   Ibid., p.111.
72   *Riders*, p.191 [180], *Flaws*, p.110; link identified by PW to me, 14 Aug 1985.
73   *Flaws*, p.112.
74   *Riders*, pp.159–60 [150].
75   PW to Johnson, 17.xi.1944.
76   'the sky . . .', 'After Alep', *Bugle Blast*, Third Series (Allen & Unwin, London, 1945), p.147; 'listening to . . .', *Flaws*, p.108; 'Dearest Fred . . .', *Bugle Blast*, p.154; the war novel, PW to Len Radic, *The Age*, Saturday Extra (13 March 1982), p.1; source for Voss and Laura, PW to Tara McCarthy, Canadian Broadcasting Commission, Sept 1973.
77   *Flaws*, p.112.
78   lying . . . , PW to Williams, 16 July 1967; treacherous, etc, PW to Tom Uren, mid-1985. These expressions of distaste postdated the war with Israel, but in conversation PW maintained that such were always his views of Egyptians.
79   'There is nothing . . .', PW to me, 22 Oct 1987; 'White of NSW', McKie to her brother William McKie, undated.
80   'read and write' and 'I have written very little . . .', PW to Johnson, 17.xi.1944.
81   EGL to me, 16 Aug 1990; 'In the end . . .', *Burnt*, p.92 [85]. PW identified EGL's experience as the source of this passage in *Flaws*, p.178. The prophecy of the broken glasses was made to a cousin of EGL's who once had a set of beautiful glasses, and the gipsy said to him: 'You will live . . . till the last of the twelve glasses breaks.' The cousin had gone to live in Geneva – hence the setting of the story.
82   EGL to me, 12 Dec 1985.
83   PW to Peggy Garland, 18.xii.1944.
84   'was like . . .' and all he could desire, PW to McKie, 17.iii.1945; 'I watched . . .', *Flaws*, p.113.
85   *Flaws*, pp.115–18.
86   'Greece – My Other Country', *Speaks*, p.134.
87   PW to McKie, 1.vi.1945.
88   'blue heavens . . .', PW to me, 22 Dec 1988; 'At times . . .', *Speaks*, p.134.
89   18.xii.1944.
90   24.x.1945.
91   *Flaws*: George, p.101; Despo, p.122.
92   *Flaws*, p.116.
93   EGL to me, 16 Aug 1990.
94   *Flaws*, pp.172–3.

12 **Return to Abyssinia**

1 EGL to me, 12 Dec 1987.
2 Chief obsession, PW to Huebsch, 6.x.1945, Viking; 'not only the perfection . . .', 'Prodigal Son', *Speaks*, p.14.
3 The Prime Minister's Department was advised by the Assistant Secretary of the Department of Commerce and Agriculture that export was impossible. The Secretary of the PM's Department wrote to White, 'in view of the Government's policy to restrict rigidly the exportation of merino sheep, it is regretted that your suggestion cannot be approved'. Australian Archives: PW's letter, accession A1066 item 1.C.45/61/90; reply by the secretary of the Prime Minister's Department, G305/1/3.
4 PW to Johnson, 24.x.1945.
5 PW to Huebsch, 6.x.1945, Viking.
6 PW to Johnson, 24.x.1945.
7 Ibid.
8 'The Woman Who Wasn't Allowed to Keep Cats', *Burnt*, p.276 [269].
9 Betty Withycombe to me, 14 Oct 1985, 16 Nov 1987.
10 *Flaws*, p.125.
11 PW to Huebsch, 11.i.1947, Viking.
12 PW to Mamblas, 5.ii.1946.
13 'The Prodigal Son', *Speaks*, p.14.
14 24.xi.1945, copy of the letter in the possession of Heather Johnson. Kent's mistress Madame de St Laurent had no children by the Duke; the Comte Jean Charles André de Mestre was not a husband of de St Laurent, nor is there any traced connection between him and the painter's ancestors.
15 *Flaws*, p.62.
16 Title: PW to Huebsch, 30.vi.1947, Viking; 'My creative . . .', *Flaws*, p.127.
17 Gertrude Morrice as the starting point for Theodora Goodman, *Flaws*, p.25; 'distinguished creature . . .', PW to Dutton, 13.xii.1959; 'mostly sat . . .', *Aunt's*, p.68 [58–9]; origins of Meroë, *Flaws*, p.127; its name, PW to Mackenzie, 22.vii.1962.
18 'there were . . .', PW to me, 23 Dec 1986; 'red-gold . . .', *Aunt's*, pp.70–1 [60–1]; the ingredients of Loder and Clem Withycombe in Frank Parrott, PW to me, 8 March 1990.
19 *Aunt's*, p.112 [101–2].
20 5.ii.1946.
21 PW to Sharman, *NT* (30 June 1979), p.30; in *Southerly*, p.135, he said, 'To fill my belly may have been the chief and ignoble reason why I decided to re-visit Australia to see whether I could settle there.'
22 'I said to Patrick . . .', EGL to me, 29 Aug 1988; 'the pots . . .', *Flaws*, p.128.
23 PW to me, 10 Feb 1987.
24 *Aunt's*, p.174 [160].
25 Cross-currents, PW to Dutton, 12.viii.1959; 'figment or facet' and 'I had lived in London . . .', PW to Dutton, 20.x.1980.
26 'Then we all . . .', *Flaws*, p.128.
27 Sokolnikov, *Flaws*, p.76; 'we shall walk in the lanes . . .', *Aunt's*, p.166 [153], linked to his own time on the Cape, PW to Mackenzie, 22.vii.1962; Grigg and the monkey, PW to me, 26 June 1989; 'a thin . . .', *Aunt's*, p.244 [226]; 'Perhaps you . . .', p.173 [159], linked to Auden by PW to me, 8 March 1990.
28 PW to Huebsch, 20.v.1947, Viking.
29 EGL to me, 16 Aug 1990.
30 'great goal . . .', PW to Mamblas, 5.ii.1946; 'his illusion . . .', *Flaws*, p.123; 'I asked . . .' and 'it wasn't really possible . . .', EGL to me, 12 Dec 1985.

31   *Aunt's*, pp.264-5 [246].

32   PW to Manfred Mackenzie, 8.vi.1964.

33   *SMH* (25 Oct 1946), p.4.

34   'This way . . .', *Aunt's*, p.284 [263]; the geography of Theodora's climb, PW to me, 29 April 1987.

35   'Because I see perfection . . .', PW to Manfred Mackenzie, 26.ix.1965; 'a delusion arising . . .', PW to Manfred Mackenzie, 8.vi.1964; 'I knew a man . . .', *Southerly*, p.141.

36   *Twyborn*, p.142; PW to me, 8 March 1990, 'That was my experience.'

37   *Flaws*, p.129.

38   'She was . . .', Meekes to me, 20 Sept 1989; curiosity, fear etc, *Flaws*, p.130.

39   The crystal bird, *Flaws*, p.130, *Vivisector*, p.330 [288]; half-singing, *Flaws*, p.132; 'got himself . . .', Kirk to me, 4 Oct 1986.

40   11.i.1947.

41   The complaints about the *Strathmore* appeared in the *SMH* (25 Oct 1946), p.4; a letter defending came the following day, p.2; attacking, 29 Oct, p.2; and PW appeared, 30 Oct 1946, p.2.

42   26.i.1947.

43   11.i.1947.

44   To me, 11 Nov 1987.

45   *Twyborn*, p.228.

46   'outcast . . .', PW to Ingmar Björkstén, Swedish television, Oct 1973.

47   26.i.1947.

48   *Mandala*, p.182 [173].

49   'nourished by months . . .', 'The Prodigal Son', *Speaks*, p.15; *Strange New World* (Angus & Robertson, Sydney, 1941); 'because I know German . . .', PW to Aurousseau, 10.iii.1958; knowing the character from the journals, PW to Dutton, 21.viii.1968; PW to Huebsch, 11.ix.1956, Congress.

50   PW's note-taking, to Aurousseau, 10.iii.1958; PW to Chisholm, 31.i.1947; a copy of Chisholm's late reply is with his papers in the Mitchell Library; Topp, in *Voss*, p.44 [36].

51   *Flaws*, p.112, and PW's speech, 'The Search for an Alternative to Futility', *Speaks*, pp.151-8, at p.156.

52   *Daily Mirror* (27 Feb 1947), p.21.

53   Ibid.

54   Harrower to me, 17 April 1989.

55   Wyse to me, 1 Oct 1985.

56   Ibid.

57   'the comedy . . .', *The Times* (13 March 1947), p.10; 'wildly remote . . .', *Observer* (16 March 1947), p.2; *Stage* (13 March 1947), p.5. See also *What's On* (21 March 1947) and *Daily Mail* (12 March 1947), p.3.

58   The Queen's verdict, Wyse to me, 1 Oct 1985; the Queen and Mamblas, *Sud-Ouest* (31 Oct 1973), p.11.

59   PW to Jean Scott Rogers, 3.iv.1947.

60   20.v.1947.

61   The telegram, 9.v.1947, missed PW in Sydney, was forwarded airmail to Alexandria, arriving 19.v.1947; 'Those of us . . .', Huebsch to PW, 19.v.1947; re dedication, PW to Huebsch, 20.v.1947. All at Viking Press. 'only a few . . .', PW to Mamblas, 9.v.1947.

62   O'Hea to me, 29 Sept 1985.

63   PW to McKie, 9.ii.1948.

64   Betty Withycombe to me, 14 Oct 1985, 16 Nov 1987.

65   26.i.1947.

66   PW to me, 12 May 1988.

67   PW in *B.W. Huebsch, 1876-1964* (privately printed, New York,

1965), p.31; PW to Huebsch, 16.vi.1955, Congress.
68   'too slight . . .', PW to Mamblas, 9.v.1947; the painting was done in
     Pimlico, PW to Williams, 4.ix.1963; 'Out of these . . .', programme note
     for *The Ham Funeral*, Adelaide, Nov 1961.
69   PW to Dutton, 3.x.1960.
70   PW to me, 7 Feb 1990.
71   Author's programme note, Adelaide, 1961.
72   'with its . . .', programme note; 'there is nothing . . .', *Southerly*, p.135;
     'no one ever . . .', Act II, scene 6: *Plays*, p.64.
73   PW to me, 2 Aug 1990.
74   Act II, scene 8: *Plays*, pp.69–70.
75   Act II, scenes 9 and 10: *Plays*, pp.73–4.
76   *Speaks*, p.16.
77   PW to Huebsch, 30.vi.1947, Viking.
78   Best to PW, 8.ix.1947; PW to Best, 17.ix.1947; John Holstius to Best,
     20.x.1947. All Viking.
79   PW to Best, 8.xi.1947.
80   4.xi.1947.
81   *New York Times Book Review* (11 Jan 1948), pp.5, 33.
82   PW to Huebsch, 4.iii.1948 (misdated 1947) and 9.iii.1948, Viking.
83   Liddell to me, 30 Dec 1987.
84   *Flaws*, p.128.
85   EGL to Tim Bowden, ABC radio, 1975.
86   EGL to me, 12 Dec 1985.
87   To me, 20 April 1987.
88   EGL to me, 20 Feb 1986.
89   PW to Huebsch, 4.iii.1948, Viking.
90   9.iii.1948.
91   'her floods . . .', PW to Garland, 24.x.1948; 'lidy', PW to McKie,
     27.x.1948; link between Lumsden and Jolley in *Riders* made by PW to me,
     12 Dec 1985.
92   6.viii.1948.
93   *SMH* (7 Aug 1948), p.6.
94   6.viii.1948.
95   PW told me no copy of this poem survives.
96   2.v.1949.

13 Dogwoods

1   PW to McKie, 11.vi.1948.
2   *Tree*, p.12.
3   Arthur Brown says to his mother, 'It's my vocation, isn't it, Mother?'
     Mandala, p.35 [29].
4   *Flaws*, p.138.
5   PW in *People* (12 Dec 1956), p.48.
6   *Mandala*, pp.36–7 [30–1].
7   PW to Garland, 1.v.1953.
8   EGL to me, 20 Feb 1986.
9   PW to Garland, 25.vi.1952.
10   To me, 10 June 1986.
11   PW to Garland, 18.vii.1949.
12   PW to Garland, 11.ii.1949.
13   14.viii.1949.
14   PW to Garland, 11.ii.1949.
15   2.v.1949.

16   *Tree*, pp.317–18.
17   PW to Garland, 14.viii.1949.
18   *Tree*, p.101.
19   PW to Garland, 15.xi.1953.
20   *Mandala*, p.35 [29].
21   *Flaws*, p.140.
22   The song 'To Watch the River' from *Six Urban Songs*, published in the programme for the Sydney Symphony Orchestra, 12–15 April 1986.
23   PW to me, 15 June 1988.
24   'spidery . . .', *Mandala*, p.55 [48], 'flumping', p.18 [10], 'The bus became a comfort . . .', p.12 [4].
25   *Mandala*, p.83 [76].
26   Moira Ferguson to me, 8 Feb 1989.
27   'I had never . . .', *Speaks*, p.43; 'pretending to be . . .', PW to Huebsch, 5.ii.1961, Congress.
28   'always amazed . . .', PW to Best, 27.xi.1964; PW's explanations of EGL: in *Meanjin* biographical note, 15 June 1956, Meanjin Library, Melbourne University. In early press interviews Lascaris was referred to as White's 'partner on the land', *People* (12 Dec 1956), p.49; 'wartime friend and partner . . . former Greek Army man', *SMH* (24 Aug 1957), p.2, and *New York Times Book Review* (18 Aug 1957), p.18; and 'a Greek friend whom he met during the War', *Observer* (21 March 1959), p.176.
29   *Vivisector*, Nellie Arrighi as the model for Boo Hollingrake confirmed by PW to me, 29 June 1989.
30   Luciana Arrighi Chetwynd, to me, Oct 1985 and 8.viii.1989.
31   *Darlings, I've had a Ball!*, Andrea as told to Trish Sheppard (Ure Smith, Sydney, 1975), pp.260–1.
32   PW to Huebsch, 28.viii.1955, Congress.
33   21.viii.1954.
34   25.vi.1952.
35   PW to Betty Withycombe, 14.iv.1961. Garland collection.
36   18.vii.1949.
37   21.v.1949.
38   *Woman* (22 Nov 1948), p.19.
39   'We took . . .', PW to McKie, 13.xi.1949; 'One stands . . .', PW to Garland, 22.ii.1951.
40   PW to me, 19 Feb 1985.
41   Royalty account cards, Routledge, Keegan Paul Archive, University College London Library.
42   5.iii.1958.
43   David Moore to me, 15 Sept 1988.
44   PW to McKie, 6.i.1950.
45   PW to Stern, 24.ix.1958.
46   PW to Garland, 14.viii.1949.
47   PW to Garland, 25.i.1950.
48   Ibid.
49   His despair, *Flaws*, p.143; PW to Garland, 1.v.1953.
50   To me, 29 Sept 1985.
51   PW to Williams, 16.vii.1967.
52   *Speaks*, p.15.
53   1.vii.1950.
54   29.iii.1950, Viking.
55   1.vii.1950.
56   PW to Garland, 13.xii.1950.
57   PW to McKie, 12.x.1950.

58   *Flaws*, p.144.
59   PW to Garland, 3.vi.1951.
60   Ibid.
61   Ibid.
62   Ibid.
63   PW to Garland, 15.viii.1951.
64   PW to me, 7 Dec 1989.
65   PW to Garland, 15.viii.1951.

14 Life Sentence

1   PW to Stern, 16.x.1961.
2   *Tree*, p.152; PW links this passage with the day he cursed God in *Southerly*, p.138.
3   *Southerly*, p.137; *Flaws*, p.144.
4   PW to Gordon McLauchlan, Television New Zealand, Nov 1984.
5   To Garland, 25.vi.1952.
6   1.v.1953.
7   *Tree*, p.427. Craven-Sands as a source for Purbrick, PW to me, 15 June 1988.
8   PW to Garland, 1.v.1953.
9   *Flaws*, p.73.
10   PW to Stern, 16.x.1961.
11   *Flaws*, p.145.
12   'Australians in a Nuclear War', *Speaks*, p.116.
13   PW to Garland, 30.v.1957.
14   *Southerly*, p.136.
15   To Garland, 1.v.1953.
16   3.iv.1952, Viking.
17   'perfectly literate', PW to Craig Macgregor, *In the Making* (Thomas Nelson, Melbourne, 1969), p.218; 'My aim . . .', PW's answers to queries on *Tree* from Magnus Lindberg, his Swedish translator, undated 1971.
18   'The Prodigal Son', *Speaks*, pp.16–17.
19   'instead of . . .', PW to McKie, 10.ix.1953; 'Because the . . .', 'Prodigal Son', *Speaks*, p.15.
20   Details of routine, drinking and rages: Ile Krieger to me, 22 July 1988.
21   EGL to me, 20 Feb 1986.
22   25.vi.1952.
23   To Huebsch, 3.iv.1952, Viking.
24   'in a frosty . . .', *Tree*, p.7.
25   *Tree*, p.139.
26   PW to Michael le Moignan, *SMH* (23 July 1983), p.33.
27   PW to me, 7 Dec 1989.
28   'with her . . .', PW to McKie, 21.v.1949; 'I called . . .', to Garland, 2.v.1949; *Tree*, p.293.
29   *Tree*, p.469; PW identifies this as a version of the other farmhouse in *Flaws*, p.137.
30   *Tree*, p.148.
31   28.xii.1955.
32   15.xi.1953.
33   Sydney *Observer* (21 March 1959), p.176.
34   2.xii.1953, Viking.
35   PW to Garland, 28.xii.1955.
36   *Tree*, p.495.
37   *Flaws*, p.144.
38   PW to Huebsch, 2.xii.1953, Viking.

39 'Everyone . . .', PW to me, 8 March 1990; *Tree*, pp.247, 256.
40 *Tree*, p.257; PW to me linking Bourke and England in an interview by Michael le Moignan, *SMH* (23 July 1983), p.33.
41 *Flaws*, p.23; *Tree*, p.233.
42 *Tree*, p.135.
43 *Tree*, p.66; *Flaws*, p.138.
44 *Tree*, p.196.
45 *Tree*, p.409.
46 To 'Ashley Owen', Brian Dale, in *Australian Financial Review* (11 July 1972), p.2.
47 24.xi.1954.
48 Ile Krieger to me, 22 July 1988.
49 PW to me, 15 June 1988.
50 15.i.1953.
51 PW to Garland, 25.vi.1952.
52 PW to Garland, 15.vi.1954.
53 15.xi.1953.
54 PW to Dutton, 18.iv.1961.
55 PW to Cooper, 9.v.1954; *Drawings and Watercolours by Vincent Van Gogh: a Selection of Thirty-Two Plates in Colour*, with notes by Douglas Cooper (Macmillan, New York; Holbein, Basel, 1955).
56 PW to Garland, 15.vi.1954.
57 PW to Garland, 1.v.1953.
58 PW to Huebsch, 8.xii.1952, Viking.
59 2.xii.1953.
60 'really the only . . .', PW to Garland, 1.v.1953; 'about the sort . . .', PW to Tara McCarthy, interviewing him for the Canadian Broadcasting Commission, Sept 1973. 'For the first . . .', PW to Huebsch, 2.xii.1953, Viking.
61 'a stone . . .', PW to Garland, 15.xi.1953; 'endless red . . .', to Garland, 15.vi.1954; the desk is now in the Mitchell Library in Sydney.
62 PW to Garland, 15.vi.1954.
63 PW to Naomi Burton, 21.viii.1954.
64 PW to me, 15 June 1988.
65 *Tree*, p.497.
66 *Tree*, p.499.
67 PW to Garland, 15.vi.1954.
68 François Laurent, Gallimard, to me, 22.iv.1988.
69 10.vi.1954, Viking.
70 PW to Garland, 15.vi.1954.
71 11.xi.1954, Viking.
72 27.xi.1954.
73 PW to Garland, 27.xi.1954.
74 O'Hea to me, 29 Sept 1985.
75 19.xi.1954.
76 24.xi.1954.

15 Dead Centre

1 PW to Naomi Burton, 23.xi.1954.
2 PW to me, 20 Aug 1988.
3 Colin Franklin to me, 9.ii.1988.
4 Rejections: Temple Smith to me, 17.xii.1987; 'It is all a matter . . .', PW to Huebsch, 15.ii.1955, Viking; agents re cutting, Naomi Burton to PW, 15.x.1954; 'Not a comma', O'Hea to me, 29 Sept 1985.

5 *Flaws*, pp.103–4.
6 PW to Huebsch, 15.ii.1955, Viking.
7 To me, 29 Sept 1985.
8 15.iv.1955, Viking.
9 PW to Naomi Burton, 19.viii.1955.
10 'I am . . .', PW to Huebsch, 24.xi.1954; 'Where is . . .', Huebsch to PW, 22.xii.1954. Both Viking.
11 PW to Huebsch, 16.vi.1955, Congress.
12 Stern to Patricia MacManus, 14.v.1955, and MacManus to Stern, 18.v.1955, both Viking; on Stern's standing among New York critics, Constantine Fitzgibbon quoting John Davenport in *James Stern, Some Letters for his Seventieth Birthday* (privately printed, London, Boxing Day 1974), p.6.
13 PW to Williams, 15.v.1963.
14 Mongrel family, Stern to me, 7.iii.1988; Humphrey Carpenter, *W.H. Auden* (Unwin Paperbacks, London, 1983), p.221.
15 *London Magazine* (June 1958), p.49.
16 *Post*, magazine section (14 Aug 1955), p.4; *Herald Tribune Book Review* (14 Aug 1955), p.1; *New York Times* (15 Aug 1955), p.13.
17 'Stupid . . .', PW to Naomi Burton, 19.viii.1955; 'author White's . . .', *Time*, Pacific edition (15 Aug 1955), pp.54–5; 'In spite . . .', PW to Huebsch, 28.viii.1955, Congress.
18 'I am having . . .', PW to Huebsch, 29.xii.1955, Viking; re truck drivers, PW to Huebsch, 2.ix.1957, Congress; opening windows, PW in 'Prodigal Son', *Speaks*, p.17.
19 PW to Garland, 27.xi.1954 and 12.x.1955.
20 Stern to MacManus, 4.ix.1955; Huebsch to PW, 24.i.1956, both Viking.
21 Stern to MacManus, 26.ix.1955, Viking.
22 'All corners . . .', Stern to MacManus, 4.ix.1955, Viking; 'must really . . .', PW to J.K. Ewers, 17.vi.1956, as quoted by Ewers to Christesen, 7.i.1973.
23 Pringle to me, 22 and 31 Jan 1986.
24 Stephen Murray-Smith to me, 22 July 1988.
25 PW to me, 29 April 1987.
26 PW to Barnard, 15.vi.1956, copy in Meanjin Library, Melbourne University.
27 Pringle to me, 22 Jan 1986.
28 *Age* (12 May 1956), p.17; PW to Ewers, 17.vi.1956.
29 Hope to me, 17 May 1985.
30 *SMH* (16 June 1956), p.15.
31 Peacock, PW to Christesen, 20.vi.1956; pack of dingoes, to Garland, 10.ix.1956; 'an embittered . . .', to Huebsch, 30.vi.1956, Congress; 'The only thing . . .', to Ewers, 17.vi.1956; 'not nearly . . .', PW to Craig Macgregor, *In the Making*; answers to Magnus Lindberg's queries to *Tree*, p.3.
32 'fairer review', Hope to me, 17 May 1985; *Native Companions* (Angus & Robertson, Sydney, 1974), pp.75–9.
33 PW to Nancy Keesing, 17.x.1959.
34 'until everyone . . .', PW to Huebsch, 30.vi.1956, Congress; sales figures, PW to Huebsch, 11.ix.1956, Congress.
35 Tennant to me, 21 Feb 1986.
36 *SMH* (22 Sept 1956), p.10.
37 'Lines from Egypt', *Australia* magazine (1 Sept 1941), p.43:

> Much will remain when all the agonies
> Receive in time a shape and past. This is the way of pain
> Carving and leaving the moments like a frieze,
> That half depicts a Persian massacre.

'I have always found in my own case . . .', PW to Beatson, 28.vi.1972. Note this is a reworking of an almost identical passage in PW to Garland, 1.v.1953.

38   PW on the writing of *Tree*, 'Prodigal Son', *Speaks*, pp.15–16; 'every man has a genius . . .', *Voss*, p.38 [31].

39   *Speaks*, p.16.

40   Unpublished public letter to Reagan, 29.v.1984.

41   *Voss*, p.475 [440].

42   PW to Huebsch, 11.ix.1956, Congress.

43   'bits of . . .', PW to Aurousseau, 18.vii.1970; the town, *Voss*, p.16 [10].

44   'a dry man . . .', *Tree*, p.390; PW to Michael le Moignan, *SMH* (23 July 1983), p.33; PW to me, 30 Sept 1988; 'poor old Paddy', Lyster Martin to me, 26 Oct and 4 Nov 1988.

45   PW to me, 30 Sept 1988; Lyster Martin to me, 26 Oct and 4 Nov 1988.

46   *Voss*, pp.22 [15], 59 [49–50], 92 [81].

47   PW to me, 30 Sept 1988.

48   By which PW meant having children by black women; to me, 30 Sept 1988.

49   *Daily Telegraph* (7 April 1950), p.8.

50   PW to me, 30 Sept 1988: he was most excited at this time by Nolan's bushranger paintings and would have bought one from the Macquarie Galleries, but was short of cash after paying his income tax; Brian Adams, *Sidney Nolan, Such is Life* (Hutchinson Australia, Melbourne, 1987), p.134, plus Nolan interview material in Adams' possession.

51   12.i.1956.

52   PW to Aurousseau, 10.iii.1958; *Voss*, p.402 [372].

53   'Intellectual passion . . .', PW to Murray-Smith, 26.ii.1962; 'you have . . .', PW to Johnson, 17.viii.1939; 'I am . . .', *Southerly*, p.138.

54   'Most of . . .' and 'arrived at . . .', PW to Manfred Mackenzie, 5.i.1963; 'when I . . .', PW to Moores, 8.ii.1958.

55   To the Moores, 8.ii.1958; Manfred Mackenzie, 5.i.1963.

56   'In the last . . .', PW to Huebsch, 8.ii.1957, Viking; 'Always something . . .', *Speaks*, p.16; 'only that . . .', PW to Dutton, 19.ix.1960; Berg, *Listener* (25 Oct 1973), p.545; 'I couldn't . . .', *Listener* plus *Flaws*, p.141, where PW adds 'a virulent review' to the list of influences that triggered Voss's death.

57   5.ix.1956, Congress.

58   'Why they . . .', PW to McKie, 6.v.1956; 'You have . . .', to Garland, 18.xi.1956.

59   Rosy Runciman, Glyndebourne, to me, 10.vi.1988.

60   7.iii.1957 (misdated by PW, 7.iii.1956).

61   8.ii.1957, Viking.

62   'It seemed to me . . .', PW to Huebsch, 8.ii.1957; 'against the need', Huebsch to PW, 14.iii.1957, both Viking.

63   Krieger to me, 22 July 1988.

64   PW to Fritz and Ile Krieger, 17.xii.1983. Fritz was dying when PW wrote this to him.

65   *Flaws*, pp.142–3.

66   Cats in season, PW to the Moores, 7.iii.1957; 'followed round . . .', PW to Huebsch, 31.iii.1957, Congress.

67   'We realise . . .', memo from Best to Huebsch, 12.iii.1957, Viking; 'rather laboured', PW to Huebsch, 25.iii.1957, Congress.

68   *Harper's Bazaar* (Aug 1957), p.112.

69   PW to Huebsch, 7.v.1957, Viking.

70   To me, 17 Dec 1987.

71 PW to Dutton, 13.xii.1959.
72 PW to Moores, 9.iv.1957.
73 PW to Huebsch, 19.viii.1957, Congress.
74 'an insufferable . . .', PW to Huebsch, 11.vi.1957, Viking and Congress; 'I shall . . .', PW to Huebsch, 2.ix.1957, Congress.
75 'a kind . . .', PW to Huebsch, 19.viii.1957, Congress; 'I am still . . .', PW to Garland, 13.xi.1957; 'My Jewish . . .', PW to Huebsch, 8.ii.1957, Viking.
76 30.v.1957.
77 PW to Garland, 30.v.1957.
78 PW to Huebsch, 2.ix.1957, copy in Viking.
79 *New Yorker* (5 Oct 1957), p.185.
80 PW to Best, 28.x.1957.
81 PW to Naomi Burton, 4.iii.1958.
82 Temple Smith to me, 17 Dec 1987.
83 PW to the Moores, 12.i.1958.
84 *Bulletin* (5 March 1958), p.2.
85 *Age* (1 Feb 1958), p.17.
86 *Bulletin* (5 March 1958), p.2; PW's admiration, to Casey, 31.x.1966.
87 'shaping and . . .' and 'There are times . . .', PW to Huebsch, 11.ii.1958, Viking; 'I . . . don't . . .', PW to Moores, 12.i.1958.
88 'expressive . . .' and hate getting the better of him, PW to Stern, 16.x.1961; 'As the darkness . . .', *Riders*, pp.440–1 [421].
89 *Speaks*, pp.16–17.
90 'after all . . .', *Speaks*, p.14; 'How sick . . .', PW to Moores, 8.ii.1958.
91 Cable, 8.iv.1958; PW to Huebsch, 9.iv.1958. Both Viking.
92 *SMH* (4 April 1958), p.1.

16 Letters and Cards

1 Material from Adams' manuscript, reworked at p.142, *Sidney Nolan, Such is Life* (Hutchinson Australia, Melbourne, 1987).

17 Public View

1 *Australian* (7 Dec 1976), p.7.
2 'Of course . . .', PW to Waters, 28.vii.1960; 'Leichhardt's revenge . . .', PW to Malouf, 21.ii.1981.
3 9.ii.1959.
4 'I am in no way . . .', PW to Medlin, 15.viii.1961; 'a monotonous . . .', PW to Osborne, 29.iv.1962, HRHRC.
5 'Those who . . .', PW to Prof. Philip Martin, 17.vii.1974; 'a vast . . .' and 'I could not . . .', PW to Huebsch, 5.i.1957, Congress.
6 To Dutton, 2.vi.1962.
7 Curtis Brown Group Ltd, New York, to PW, 8.iv.1960; PW to Curtis Brown, 25.iv.1960.
8 PW to Huebsch, 5.ix.1956, Congress.
9 PW to Curtis Brown, New York, 9.ii.1962.
10 10.x.1957, Congress.
11 'It was . . .', PW to Garland, 7.i.1960; 'must have . . .', PW to Huebsch, 20.i.1960, Congress.
12 To Garland, 7.i.1960.
13 W.H. Smith's house magazine, *The Newsbasket* (Dec 1959), p.18.
14 5.i.1960.
15 'A constant . . .', PW to McKie, 23.vi.1960; 'I have been . . .', Tennant to me, 21 Feb 1986.
16 'He could remember . . .', Gwen Moore to me, 15 Sept 1988; 'I think

. . .', PW to Garland, 25.x.1964.

17   To me, 13 Oct 1989.
18   Pure being, *Vivisector*, p.627 [554]; 'My flawed . . .', *Speaks*, p.42.
19   'In some ways . . .', PW to Garland, 13.xi.1957; Humphries to me, 3 Dec 1987.
20   Gwen Moore to me, 15 Sept 1988.
21   'It is the face . . .', Clark to the Patrick White seminar, Newcastle University, 1988; 'a hunger for . . .', Clark to me, 23 Nov 1988.
22   Joyce, PW to Best, 25.ii.1960; 'diseased . . .', PW to Huebsch, 11.v.1959, Congress.
23   16.x.1961.
24   *Riders*, pp.383-4 [366].
25   'Gerry Lewers has Left Us', *SMH* (18 Aug 1962), p.12; Lewers had been killed in a riding accident in Queensland.
26   Gretel Feher to me, 12 Aug 1988.
27   Astley to me, 26 Aug 1989.
28   Ibid.
29   Maria Prerauer to me, 13 Oct 1989.
30   'I know . . .' and 'Patrick can't be judged . . .', EGL to me, 20 Feb 1986; 'It is the pleasure . . .', EGL to Sharman, Sharman to me, 24 July 1985.
31   'looking for a church . . .', PW to Harrower, 16.vii.1972; considering conversion to Catholicism and Judaism, Joseph to me, 21 Aug 1986; 'I did not return . . .', PW to Stern, 16.x.1961.
32   'for someone . . .', PW to Tara McCarthy, Sept 1973; 'we suddenly . . .', PW to McKie, 21.iv.1959; 'I am . . .', PW to McKie, 6.vi.1959.
33   To Garland, 1.v.1964.
34   To Stern, 16.x.1961.
35   PW to Garland, 20.v.1960.

18   Diaspora

1   Numburra, *Riders*, p.351 [336], the painting, pp.360-1 [344-5] both identified by PW as sources.
2   11.v.1959, Congress.
3   Perfect servant, PW to me, 30 Sept 1988; 'the most positive . . .', *Riders*, p.72 [66]; debt to Hilda Richardson, PW to me, 10 Feb 1987; sunset as the chariot, *Riders*, p.551 [531].
4   'The earth . . .', *Riders*, p.172 [162]; looked at, PW to Casey, 30.xii.1966; choice of name, PW in *Southerly*, p.141; impressed by Jung, PW to Garland, 18.xii.1944.
5   'an ecstasy . . .', *Riders*, p.152 [143].
6   *Riders*, pp.221-2 [211].
7   'first a child . . .', PW to Huebsch, 5.ii.1961, Congress; 'Then I knew . . .', PW at La Trobe University, 1984, *Speaks*, p.156; 'Go Home . . .', *Riders*, p.460 [439]; 'added insight . . .', PW at La Trobe, pp.156-7; apostasy back to belief, PW to Stern, 16.x.1961.
8   PW to Huebsch, 20.i.1960, Congress.
9   To Huebsch, 11.v.1959, Congress.
10 *Riders*, p.155 [145]; identification of Holunderthal, *Flaws*, p.39.
11 Dr Jürgen Oertel to me, 12 and 13 Dec 1987.
12 *Riders*, p.161 [151].
13 PW to me, 10 Feb 1987.
14 PW to Huebsch, 11.v.1959, Congress.
15 Dr Ferry and Hannah Grunseit to me, 24 Nov 1988.

16   11.v.1959, Congress.
17   PW to Dutton, 13.ii.1972.
18   'It was strange . . .', PW to Garland, 5.x.1959; 'They still . . .', PW to Huebsch, 20.i.1960, Congress.
19   'to know . . .', PW to Best, 27.ii.1961; 'the peak', PW to McKie, 22.vii.1959; 'a wonderful . . .' and 'I think . . .', PW to Garland, 7.i.1960; Bach and Berg, PW to Garland, 5.x.1959; 'for whom . . .', PW to Best, 27.ii.1961.
20   Detail, *Southerly*, p.139; decoration, *In the Making*, p.121.
21   PW approved, 13 Aug 1990.
22   'I still . . .', PW to Garland, 9.ii.1959; 'without a . . .', PW to Huebsch, 11.v.1959, Congress.
23   PW to Garland, 3.viii.1963.
24   Betty Withycombe to me, 16 Nov 1987.
25   'Your style . . .', quoted by PW to David Moore, 31.viii.1957; 'The cold . . .', PW to Garland, 16.xii.1957.
26   The incidents in Oxford and at Kew: PW to Garland, 17.vi.1959; Garland to me, 2–6 Oct 1985; Betty Withycombe to me, 18.iv.1988.
27   Garland to me, 2–6 Oct 1985, 10.v.1990.
28   PW to Garland, 17.vi.1959; PW's letters to Betty Withycombe have not survived. See Chapter 26.
29   PW to Garland, 9.vii.1959.
30   PW to Huebsch, 20.i.1960, Congress.
31   Ibid.
32   Ibid.
33   To Huebsch, 11.v.1960, Congress.
34   PW to Clem Christesen, 10.i.1961.
35   'elation . . .', PW to Huebsch, 11.v.1960, Congress; 'the first . . .' and 'always a sober', PW to Huebsch, 3.viii.1960, Congress; 'Manoly says . . .', PW to Dutton, 1.viii.1960.
36   PW to Stern, 16.x.1961.
37   Ibid.
38   *Riders*, p.456 [436].
39   'The chives', PW to Barbara Fisher, 23.ii.1960; 'Who wants . . .', *Riders*, p.233 [222].
40   'but the idea . . .', PW to Huebsch, 5.ii.1961, Congress; Mrs Lumsden's contribution, PW to me, 12 Dec 1985.
41   *Riders*, p.85 [78].
42   PW to Stern, 16.x.1961.
43   PW to Best, 27.ii.1961.
44   'Bursting . . .', PW to Waters, 9.viii.1960; language and the final draft, PW to Waters, 28.vii.1960 and Dutton, 1.viii.1960.
45   Pasternak and Durrell: PW to Huebsch, 3.viii.1960, Congress.
46   1.viii.1960.
47   PW to Dutton, 30.v.1958.
48   'The Letters', *Burnt*, p.229 [222]; identified as based on Mrs Dutton to me by PW, 30 Oct 1986.
49   PW to Dutton, 1.v.1960.
50   *Bulletin* (1 June 1982), p.62.
51   PW to Huebsch, 31.viii.1962, Congress.
52   PW to Greene, 25.vi.1986.
53   PW to Huebsch, 20.i.1960, Congress.
54   'dragged out . . .', PW to Stern, 20.iii.1966; 'at loggerheads . . .', PW to McKie, 27.x.1958; 'the flashes', PW to Dutton, 9.i.1972, where he said that in the second draft the benefits of alcohol had passed; 'cut the knots', *Vivisector*, p.344 [301]; 'I hate . . .', PW to Dutton, 15.i.1959.

55 Weeks on a phrase: EGL to Brother G.C. Davy, 'Guests of Patrick White', *Our Studies* (Christian Brothers of Australia and New Zealand Provinces, Sydney, May 1964), p.55.
56 PW to Dutton, 2.ii.1969.
57 'very slovenly . . .', PW to Dutton, 3.x.1960; 'one suddenly . . .', PW to Harrower, 16.vii.1972.
58 PW to Best, 27.ii.1961.
59 PW to me, 8 Oct 1986.
60 To Dutton, 5.i.1961.
61 Draft of telegram with PW, correspondence in Library of Congress.
62 5.ii.1961, Congress; Huebsch, of course, accepted.
63 To Huebsch, 5.ii.1961, Congress.
64 To Huebsch, 15.iii.1961, Congress.
65 'more in a short . . .', PW to Dutton, 2.iv.1961; 'His wife . . .', PW to Krieger, 25.iii.1961. Alpers had written, *Katherine Mansfield: A Biography* (Knopf, New York, 1953); later he wrote *The Life of Katherine Mansfield* (Viking, New York, 1980).
66 7.iv.1961.
67 To Huebsch, 15.iii.1961, Congress.
68 'Now you . . .', PW to Philip Garland, 19.v.1961; 'expedition . . .', PW to Peggy Garland, 16.v.1966.
69 'kills . . .', PW to Best, 25.v.1961; 'We have . . .', PW to Best, 27.ii.1961.
70 14.iv.1961.
71 To Dutton, 25.vii.1961.
72 'The Cynthia I Knew', *Australian* (7 Dec 1976), p.7.
73 Ibid.
74 Ibid.
75 To Best, 7.iv.1961.
76 Temple Smith to me, 17 Dec 1987; PW to Dutton, 18.iv.1961.
77 PW to Garland, 22.vi.1961.
78 19.v.1961; Garland collection.
79 PW to Williams, 28.vi.1961.
80 PW to me, 13 Sept 1989.
81 To Garland, 22.vi.1961.
82 'Emmett bomb . . .', PW to Garland, 22.vi.1961; 'the columns . . .', *Eye*, pp.374–5; 'I now know . . .', PW to Garland, 22.vi.1961.
83 *The Legends of Moonie Jarl* (Jacaranda Press, Brisbane, 1964).
84 PW to Garland, 27.vi.1961.
85 Best to PW, 7.viii.1961 and 12.ix.1961.
86 21.ix.1961.
87 'Their worshippers . . .', *New Yorker* (9 Dec 1961), p.244; 'little civil . . .', *Time* (6 Oct 1961), p.66; sales figures: Viking internal memo setting out PW's sales as at about Sept 1969.
88 18 April 1962.
89 Tennant to me, 21 Feb 1986.
90 Prescott's words, *New York Times* (6 Oct 1961), p.33; 'As an aside . . .', Best to PW, 10.x.1961; 'packaged dinner', PW to Best, 16.x.1961.
91 Ile Krieger to me, 22 July 1988.
92 23.viii.1962.
93 *Flaws*, p.140; Ile Krieger to me, 22 July 1988.
94 PW to Huebsch, 2.ii.1962, Congress.
95 Ile Krieger.
96 *Flaws*, pp.140–1.
97 28.vi.1961.

19 Stage Struck

1 'pull it off . . .', PW to Keith Michell, 5.i.1957; 'one great . . .', Waters to me, 30 Sept 1985.

2 'That does . . .', PW to Michell, 5.i.1957; 'because we . . .', to Michell, 9.x.1957.

3 Report by Mathilde Burry, 24 March 1948, Salisbury Collection, Columbia University Library.

4 PW to Wendy Dickson, 27.iv.1963.

5 'and was burnt . . .', PW to the Moores, 8.ii.1958; 'a dreadful . . .', PW to Waters, 28.vii.1960.

6 PW to Naomi Burton, 29.i.1958.

7 'As acted . . .', PW to Michell, 9.x.1957; 'imagination . . .', PW to the Moores, 12.i.1958; 'in the accents . . .', PW to Naomi Burton, 29.i.1958.

8 Michell to me, 3.xi.1988; 'refurbish it . . .', PW's 'Author's Note on *The Ham Funeral*' supplied to John Tasker; in the possession of Frances Riordan, Sydney.

9 19.iii.1958, Viking.

10 Michell to me, 3.xi.1988.

11 PW to Dutton, 15.i.1959.

12 'a precursor . . .', PW to Wendy Dickson, 27.iv.1963; 'I finally . . .', PW to Dutton, 3.x.1960.

13 To me, 11 March 1986.

14 30.x.1960.

15 Charles Wicks to Beale, 5.i.1961, South Australian Archives, GRG 153/36/1.

16 Minutes of the executive committee meeting, 16 March 1961, South Australian Archives, GRG 153/27/2.

17 Dyson to Wicks, 21 March 1961, South Australian Archives, GRG 153/36/1.

18 Moore to me, 15 Sept 1988.

19 Hutchison to Wicks, 15 April 1961, South Australian Archives, GRG 153/36/1.

20 *Nation*, Sydney (22 April 1961), p.5.

21 'Of course . . .', PW to Wicks, 26.iv.1961, South Australian Archives, GRG 153/36/1; 'I am not . . .', PW to Dutton, 18.iv.1961.

22 'suburban . . .', PW to Williams, 28.vi.1961; 'The new one . . .', PW to Garland, 22.vi.1961.

23 'not that that . . .', PW to Dutton, 28.v.1961; 'purely Australian . . .', PW to Dutton, 2.v.1961 (misdated 2.iv.1961).

24 PW to Dutton, 8.vi.1961.

25 'He is . . .', PW to Dutton, 5.i.1961; 'Tasker was . . .', EGL to me.

26 'loosened some . . .', PW to Medlin, 31.viii.1961; 'I thought . . .', PW to Medlin, 13.ix.1961.

27 To Garland, 21.ix.1961.

28 30.x.1961.

29 'I have . . .', Ninette (Nin) Dutton to me, 12 March 1986; 'The vibrations . . .', 14.xi.1961.

30 Harry Kippax in his introduction to *Four Plays* (Sun Books, Melbourne, 1967), p.2.

31 *Bulletin* (1 June 1982), p.64.

32 *Plays*, p.15.

33 'It turned out . . .', PW to Medlin, 24.xii.1961; 'Mr White can write . . .', 'Brek' in *Nation*, Sydney (2 Dec 1961), p.18.

34 '*most* amiable . . .', PW to Dutton, 28.xi.1961; the poodle, PW to Garland, 20.xi.1961; 'Are you going . . .', PW to Tasker, 19.xi.1961; being cold, PW to Garland, 20.x.1961.

35   'one about bodgies . . .', PW to Beryl Pearce, 4.xii.1961; 'flourish', PW
      to Medlin, 24.xii.1961.
36   'I was well . . .', PW to Dutton, 18.vii.1962; 'I am not . . .', *Nation*,
      Sydney (28 July 1962), p.18.
37   Sydney *Sunday Telegraph* (15 July 1962), p.51.
38   PW's refusal, *Sunday Mirror* (29 July 1962), p.1; Dekyvere's disappoint-
      ment, *Sunday Telegraph* (15 July 1962), p.51; gallery confrontation, *Sunday
      Telegraph* (22 July 1962), p.49; 'Society Feud,' *Sunday Mirror* (29 July 1962), p.1.
39   Introduction to *Four Plays*, p.8.
40   'My eyes . . .', PW to Dutton, 24.vi.1962; 'I am . . .', PW to Huebsch,
      9.iv.1962, Congress.
41   'The characters . . .', PW to Huebsch, 3.xi.1961, Congress; 'burrow into
      . . .', PW to Duttons, 18.vii.1962; 'those admirable . . .', PW to Dutton,
      28.ix.1961.
42   'I have . . .', PW to Huebsch, 3.xi.1961, Congress; 'I can't stop . . .',
      PW to Tasker, 30.x.1961.
43   PW to Huebsch, 3.xi.1961, Congress.
44   PW to Medlin, 24.xii.1961.
45   To me, 9 Nov 1987.
46   29.iv.1962, Congress.
47   PW to Dutton, 13.xii.1961.
48   Sir John Gielgud to me, 25.v.1988.
49   Williams to me, 20 Nov 1987.
50   PW to Garland, 20.xi.1961.
51   Robert Craft, *Stravinsky, Chronicle of a Friendship, 1948-1971* (Knopf,
      New York, 1972), p.139.
52   Before the next, PW to Medlin, 13.i.1962; 'I think . . .', PW to Dutton,
      18.i.1962.
53   Williams to me, 20 Nov 1987.
54   PW to me, 30 Oct 1986.
55   To the Duttons, 18.i.1962.
56   'too far . . .', Curtis Brown Group Ltd, New York, to PW, 27.ii.1962;
      'I'd like . . .', PW to Osborne, 30.xi.1962, HRHRC.
57   Mortal fear and identification of the Photiades with the Alexiou, PW to
      Williams, 16.viii.1964; 'Of course . . .', PW to Curtis Brown, New York,
      17.viii.1962; 'It also . . .', PW to Aurousseau, 5.x.1962.
58   Begging for changes, Christesen to PW, 27.ii.1963; 'Surely I . . .', PW
      to Christesen, 1.iii.1963.
59   PW to Dutton, 9.iii.1962.
60   'charade . . .', PW to Huebsch, 1.viii.1961, Congress; 'Those dogs!', Act
      I, *Plays*, p.79.
61   PW to Tasker, 26.iv.1963.
62   'Suburban . . .', PW to Huebsch, 1.viii.1961, Congress.
63   Ibid.
64   Act II, *Plays*, p.175.
65   'We have terrible . . .' and 'He has managed . . .', PW to Waters, 31.viii.1962;
      'walk round . . .', PW to Dutton, 18.vii.1962.
66   PW to Waters, 31.viii.1962.
67   'not a part . . .' and 'Zoe is . . .', PW to Medlin, 15.v.1962; 'I hope
      . . .', PW to Beryl Pearce, 24.vii.1962.
68   PW to Dutton, 17.viii.1962.
69   PW to Beryl Pearce, 30.viii.1962.
70   Harry Kippax, *Nation* (22 Sept 1962), p.17.
71   'Far more . . .', PW to Wendy Dickson, 18.ix.1962; 'It's all . . .', PW
      to Christesen, 4.x.1962.

72 'Zoe drove . . .', PW to the Duttons, 26.x.1962; 'has a strain . . .', PW to Tasker, 18.x.1962.

73 'puritanical . . .', PW to McKie, 2.xii.1962; 'lunching . . .', to Dutton, 26.x.1962; 'it has . . .', to Dutton, 6.xi.1962; *Age* review (17 Oct 1962), p.5; 'No flowers . . .' and 'I am pocketing . . .', to Dutton 6.xi.1962.

74 PW to Dutton, 8.x.1962.

75 Sumner to me, 16 Dec 1988; 'he seemed . . .', PW to Tasker, 18.x.1962.

76 PW to Dutton, 6.xi.1962.

77 'flights in other . . .', Best to PW, 24.ix.1964; 'I have been so . . .', PW to Huebsch, 31.viii.1962, Congress; 'as I want . . .', Best to PW, 12.ix.1961.

78 To Stern, Christmas 1961; to Christesen, 23.v.1962; to Dutton, 9.iii.1962; 'so many . . .', PW to Stern, Christmas 1961; 'right kind . . .', PW to Dutton, 2.vi.1962; 'do regret . . .', PW to Williams, 28.vi.1963.

79 'His life . . .', PW to Dutton, 6.xi.1962; unstageable, PW to Beryl Pearce, 24.vii.1962; 'loutish . . .', PW to Dutton, 6.xi.1962; 'hell of a lot . . .', Tasker to Medlin, 17.x.1962.

80 PW to me, 12 Dec 1985.

81 'Before that . . .', PW to me, 12 Dec 1985 (the line appears in *Burnt*, p.158 [152]); the pruning, PW to me, 12 Dec 1985 (see *A Cheery Soul*, Act I, *Plays*, p.194.)

82 PW to Dutton, 24.vi.1962.

83 PW to me, 23 Feb 1989.

84 'If it comes off . . .', PW to Nita Pannell, 17.vi.1962; 'I read . . .', Pannell to me, undated letter, March 1989.

85 'inwardness . . .', PW to Medlin, 27.vi.1962; 'More like . . .', Medlin to me, 11 March 1986; 'The university . . .', PW to Garland, 11.xi.1962.

86 PW to Osborne, 30.xi.1962, HRHRC.

87 'I don't want . . .', PW to Dutton, 6.xi.1962; 'The title . . .', PW to Garland, 11.xi.1962.

88 'Very meticulous . . .', Nin Dutton to me, 12 March 1986; 'Fortunately there . . .', PW to Stern, 6.i.1963.

89 PW to the Duttons, linking the stay to 'Dead Roses', 17.iii.1963; Nin Dutton to me, 12 March 1986.

90 PW to Curtis Brown, New York, 1.i.1963.

91 'How shattering . . .' and 'The worst part . . .', PW to the Duttons, 12.ii.1963.

92 PW to Tasker, 12.ii.1963.

93 8.iii.1963.

94 'It has made me . . .', PW to Digby, 15.iii.1963; 'aura . . .', PW to Tasker, 12.ii.1963.

95 'a sense . . .', PW to Tasker, 12.ii.1963; the commission to open the Opera House, PW to Huebsch, 17.ii.1963, Congress; 'one can . . .', PW to Tasker, 26.iv.1963; 'at the opening . . .', PW to Dutton, 17.iii.1963.

21 Ruth, Death and the Afterlife

1 14.viii.1963.

2 PW to Stern, 6.i.1963.

3 'I hope . . .', *Flaws*, p.150; 'All this . . .', PW to Huebsch, 26.vii.1963, Congress; gifts of cash, PW to me, 19 Feb 1985; 'because Sydney . . .', *Flaws*, p.149.

4 PW to Huebsch, 26.vii.1963, Congress.

5 *B.W. Huebsch, 1876–1964, Grolier Club, New York, Dec 9 1964* (privately printed, New York, 1964).

6 John Rothenstein, *Time's Thievish Progress* (Cassell, London, 1970), p.94.

7   PW to Huebsch, 26.vii.1963, Congress.
8   *Mirror* (23 May 1963).
9   *Nation*, Sydney (1 June 1963), p.18.
10   The arguments, Colin Ballantyne to me, 13 March 1986; 'All very . . .',
     PW to Williams, 28.vi.1963.
11   Medlin to me, 11 March 1986.
12   'Australia would . . .', PW to Zoe Caldwell, 14.viii.1963; 'like a . . .',
     PW to Osborne, 7.ii.1964, HRHRC.
13   'Although we . . .', PW to Stern, 6.i.1963; 'the prettiest . . .', *Fringe*,
     pp.326–7; linked to the Nolans' garden by PW, to me, 13 Sept 1989.
14   'rather guarded . . .', PW to Zoe Caldwell, 14.viii.1963; 'working hard
     . . .', PW to Williams, 4.ix.1963.
15   Nolan's account: to Brian Adams, and him to me, 24 Sept 1987; PW's
     account to me, 12 May 1988; 'Poor Madge' in *Eye*, p.213, is 'so tahd.'
16   'Although I . . .', PW to Williams, 4.ix.1963; 'My mother . . .', PW
     to Duttons, 28.ix.1963.
17   To Osborne, 1.x.1963, HRHRC.
18   'slipped sideways . . .', *Eye*, p.552, identified by EGL to me as the cir-
     cumstances of Ruth's death; 'It is . . .', PW to Garland, 21.xi.1963.
19   'It was so . . .', Sumner to me, 16 Dec 1988; 'Why does . . .', Pannell
     to me; 'brilliant . . .' and 'willing to . . .', PW to Garland, 21.xi.1963.
20   'I was . . .', PW to Ian Donaldson, 20.i.1964; 'there were people . . .',
     'Almost all . . .' and 'trial by . . .', PW to Garland, 21.xi.1963; 'bruised',
     PW to Sumner, to me, 16 Dec 1988. Reviews: *Age* (21 Nov 1963), p.5; *Sunday
     Telegraph* (24 Nov), p.92; the one-line review was by Howard Palmer in the
     Melbourne *Sun*, the full text of which was, '*A Cheery Soul* is a sad play' (20
     Nov), p.18.
21   PW to Tasker, 28.xi.1963.
22   PW to Alice Halmagyi, 8.xi.1962.
23   AA and Mrs S's guile, PW to me, 29 June 1989; 'Where you . . .',
     PW to Halmagyi, 8.xi.1962; Halmagyi to me, 12 Sept 1988.
24   PW to Tasker, 28.xi.1963.
25   PW to Dutton, 5.ii.1964; confession of hatred, to Wendy Dickson, 21.ii.1964.
26   'I couldn't . . .', PW to Dutton, 13.iii.1964; 'a number . . .', PW to Huebsch,
     18.iii.1964, Columbia.
27   *Nation* (21 March 1964), p.19.
28   PW to Dutton, 29.iii.1964.
29   The dinner: Kippax to me, 7 Nov 1988 and Prerauer to me, 17 Oct
     1989; 'Harry is . . .', PW to Dutton, 29.iii.1964.
30   Kippax to me, 7 Nov 1988; Frances Riordan to me, 5 Oct 1988.
31   PW to me, 15 June 1988.
32   To Dutton, 24.v.1964.
33   'all the details' and 'Mystification . . .', PW to Best, 27.xi.1964; 'None
     of that . . .', *Burnt*, pp.96–7 [90].
34   *London Magazine* (March 1982), pp.45, 47–8.
35   To Huebsch, 16.xii.1963, Columbia.
36   'low life . . .', Viking memo to Best, 3.iii.1964; 'There is a lot . . .',
     PW to Best, 3.vii.1964; 'the whole . . .', PW to Best, 17.i.1965.
37   'the first . . .', PW to Ian Donaldson, 20.i.1964; 'Let us . . .', PW to
     Sculthorpe, 21.xii.1963.
38   'All Sunday . . .', PW to Dutton, 5.xii.1963; 'to help . . .', PW to Sculthorpe,
     21.xii.1963.
39   'Urban Songs' have only been published as programme notes for the
     first performance of Moya Henderson's song cycle, Sydney Symphony
     Orchestra, 12, 14 and 15 April 1986.

40   To Sculthorpe, 21.xii.1963.
41   PW's reassurances, to Dutton, 5.xii.1963; Sculthorpe's recall of the libretto, to me, 28 Nov 1988.
42   3.iv.1964.
43   'I am . . .', PW to Garland, 7.iv.1964; 'I think . . .', PW to O'Hea, 20.iv.1964.
44   6.x.1964.
45   'rich people . . .', PW to Zoe Caldwell, 14.viii.1963; 'He is not easy . . .', O'Hea, internal memo, Curtis Brown, 31.iii.1964.
46   The affair: information to me following PW's death; 'Everything which . . .', PW to Murray-Smith, 2.v.1964.
47   7.iv.1964.
48   'For me . . .', PW to Huebsch, 12.vi.1964, Columbia; 'sophisticated audiences . . . ', PW to Sculthorpe, 24.i.1965; 'What the hell . . .', PW to Nita Pannell, 30.i.1966. This television version was written by Jonquil Anthony who at one time was the wife of John Wyse, producer of *Return to Abyssinia* at The Boltons.
49   £600 was quoted by PW to Sculthorpe, 21.xii.1963, i.e. before *Bald Mountain*.
50   PW to Dutton, 19.iii.1964.
51   24.v.1964.
52   'stirring . . .' and 'the last of . . .', PW to Huebsch, 12.vi.1964; 'very peaceful . . .', PW to Dutton, 9.viii.1964; evolution from novella to novel, PW to Best, 13.ix.1964.
53   *B.W. Huebsch, 1876–1964*.
54   PW to Dutton, 19.iii.1964.
55   PW to Stern, 19.ii.1964.
56   'She is . . .', PW to Waters, 26.ii.1962; 'You should . . .', PW to Waters, 31.viii.1962.
57   PW to Dutton, 20.x.1963.
58   'Fanny gave . . .', PW to Sculthorpe, 21.xii.1963; 'Pugs are probably . . .', PW to Osborne, 7.ii.1964, HRHRC.
59   7.iv.1964.
60   'right down . . .', *Riders*, p.545 [526]; 'I am . . .', PW to Best, 30.iv.1964.
61   'I expect . . .', PW to Huebsch, 12.vi.1964, Columbia; 'a complete . . .', PW to Best, 13.ix.1964.
62   'was starting to look . . .', PW to Williams, 27.ix.1964; 'I have accumulated . . .', PW to Clark, 13.viii.1964; 'We discarded . . .', *Flaws*, p.147.
63   Details of the bonfire, PW to Dutton, 21.viii.1968; 'They should . . .', PW to Ingleton, Oct 1971, quoted by Ingleton to me, 19 April 1987.
64   *Tree*, p.213.
65   EGL to me, 29 Aug 1988.
66   *Mandala*, p.213 [203].
67   *Flaws*, p.147.
68   To Williams, 6.xi.1964.

22   Twins

1   PW to Dutton, 18.xi.1964.
2   PW to Dutton, 1.vi.1964.
3   PW to Dutton, 30.xi.1964 – Ezekiel was the Orthodox Archbishop of Australia.
4   'a pergola covered with . . .', PW to Garland, 25.x.1964; 'what has been . . .', PW to Stern, 14.xii.1964.
5   'A hibiscus . . .', PW to Dutton, 30.xi.1964; 'which we . . .', PW to Dutton, 21.iii.1965; 'a gale . . .', PW to Christesen, 26.i.1965; 'misused

...', PW to Dutton, 11.ix.1966.

6   PW to Williams, 6.xi.1964.

7   To Dutton, 18.xi.1964.

8   'But of course . . .', PW to Dutton, 4.x.1964; 'dreadful', PW to Williams, 6.xi.1964; 'I expect . . .', PW to Dutton, 18.xi.1964.

9   18.xi.1964.

10   'symbol chasers' and 'it must . . .', PW to the Duttons, 18.i.1965.

11   *Flaws*, p.146.

12   'childish wisdom', *Flaws*, p.146; 'You must . . .', *Mandala*, p.315 [307]; the walk to the zoo, PW to Garland, 16.v.1966.

13   PW to Dutton, 9.v.1965.

14   'I *am* . . .', PW to Dutton, 13.xi.1966; 'veiled bride', PW to Gerry Wilkes, 20.x.1969, and to me that that meant closeted homosexual, 13 Sept 1989.

15   'Waldo . . . was based . . .', PW to Björkstén, 15.ii.1983; 'on the basis . . .' and 'a rather nasty . . .', PW to me, 14 Nov 1988; 'Physically . . .', PW to Stern, 20.iii.1966; 'the face . . .', PW to Semmler, 11.vi.1967.

16   PW to O'Hea, 26.i.1965; *Mandala*, pp.150 [142], 171–2 [163].

17   Grey and stodgy, PW to Nin Dutton, 23.i.1965; 'I think . . .' and 'or perhaps . . .', PW to Duttons, 14.ii.1965; 'Arthur said . . .', *Mandala*, pp.57–8 [51]; 'I have . . .', PW to Dutton, 28.ii.1965.

18   'a Corot . . .' and 'All sorts . . .', PW to the Duttons, 18.xi.1964.

19   'little flames . . .', PW to Dutton, 18.i.1965; 'horse-and-buggy . . .', PW to Dutton, 21.iii.1965.

20   'I went down . . .', PW to Garland, 18.iv.1965; the wheel-tree, *Mandala*, pp.13 [5], 145 [137].

21   'the sterility . . .', *Flaws*, p.146; 'God reveals . . .', PW to Dutton, 24.vi.1962.

22   PW to Garland, 3.viii.1963.

23   Daws to me, 16.ix.1989.

24   PW to Björkstén, 27.v.1973.

25   'all the symbols . . .', PW to Williams, 27.ix.1964; 'He seems to me . . .', PW to Stern, 14.xii.1964.

26   PW to Walker, 24.vi.1982.

27   PW to Stern, 14.xii.1964.

28   'in a lush . . .', PW to Dutton, 9.v.1965; 'transitoriness', *Flaws*, p.146.

29   'I find . . .', PW to O'Hea, 6.iv.1965; 'Now I . . .', PW to Dutton, 21.iii.1965.

30   'The world . . .', *Aunt's*, p.123 [111]; shooting ducks, *Aunt's*, p.124 [113]; hopes for Ethel, PW to Dutton, 24.v.1964; 'Of course . . .', PW to Garland, 18.iv.1965.

31   'Yesterday . . .', PW to Dutton, 26.iii.1967; 'I think . . .', PW to Waters, Christmas 1969.

32   'I am still . . .', PW to Best, 6.vi.1965; the Scots, PW to me, 15 June 1988.

33   'You won't be too pleased . . .', Moores to me, 20 Oct 1988; 'I think it is . . .', Best to PW, 15.vii.1965; 'The title is . . .', PW to O'Hea, 21.vii.1965; Digby to me, 5 Aug 1988.

34   'about the . . .', PW to Dutton, 27.ii.1966; *Time* (11 Feb 1966), p.49 (Asian edition), p.58 (Aust.), p.87 (US); 'were only so-so . . .', Best to O'Hea, 9.vi.1966.

35   'You never want . . .', the Grunseits to me, 24 Nov 1988; 'I don't . . .', Prerauer to me, 13 Oct 1989.

36   'full of . . .', PW to Dutton, 23.ix.1965; 'Patrick did . . .', Dutton to me, 21.ix.1990; 'that miserable . . .', PW to Dutton, 12.xi.1965; 'the most appalling . . .', PW to Stern, 20.iii.1966.

37   Escaping the contracts, PW to Dutton, 4.vii.1965; 'I don't feel . . .', PW to Garland, 23.viii.1965.

38   PW to Dutton, 6.viii.1965.

39 'one of those . . .', PW to Stern, 29.xii.1966; 'I expect . . .', PW to Dutton, 17.x.1965; 'or else . . .', PW to Dutton, 12.xi.1965.

40 'a surfeit . . .', PW to Garland, 19.xii.1965; 'Also . . .', to Dutton, 18.xi.1965; 'the right . . .', to Beatson, 23.x.1972.

41 PW to Dutton, 2.i.1966.

42 PW to Dutton, 13.iii.1966.

43 Yevtushenko's speech, diary of David Moore; 'tirade of hate . . .', PW to Dutton, 3.iv.1966.

44 Inscription, PW to Stern, 20.iii.1966; 'love arias . . .', PW to Dutton, 3.iv.1966.

45 'some of . . . ', PW to Dutton, 30.xi.1964; 'along the lines . . .', PW to Best, 6.vi.1965.

46 'bloody awful' and 'when she . . .', PW to Dutton, 24.v.1964; 'Oh, said Manoly . . .', PW to Dutton, 30.xi.1964.

47 *Vivisector*, p.308 [269].

48 PW to Dutton, 1.v.1967.

49 PW to Dutton, 1.viii.1965.

50 PW to Dutton, 17.x.1965.

51 W.J. Hudson, *Casey* (Oxford University Press, Melbourne, 1986), p.312.

52 PW to Casey, 12.vii.1966.

53 'late in . . .', PW to Casey, 24.vi.1966; 'Canberra must . . .', PW to Casey, 12.vii.1966; 'we had chlorophyll . . .', PW to Ralph Smith, 1.viii.1966.

54 'She is . . .', PW to Dutton, 28.xi.1965; 'I am an . . .', PW to Dutton, 6.xii.1965.

55 PW to me, 12 May 1988.

56 *Mandala*, p.182 [173].

57 PW to Ralph Smith, 14.vi.1966.

58 'In the book . . .', PW to Casey, 17.x.1966; the Bentley, PW to Casey, 30.xii.1966.

59 PW to Stern, 27.v.1966.

60 Rising to the surface, PW to Casey, 12.vii.1966; 'very fresh . . .', PW to O'Hea, 16.viii.1966; 'Haste is . . .', PW to Dutton, 11.ix.1966.

61 17.vii.1966.

62 23.ix.1966.

63 Complaints, to Stern, 29.xii.1966; 'The flow . . .', PW to Dutton, 13.xi.1966; 'All sorts . . .', PW to Stern, 29.xii.1966; the welter, PW to Dutton, 1.i.1967; the canter, PW to Casey, 30.xii.1966; 'I think . . .', PW to Dutton, 25.i.1967.

64 PW to Dutton, 25.i.1967.

65 Eyre's phone call and 'Then there was a silence . . .', PW to O'Hea, 7.v.1967; PW telegram to Davis, 9.iv.1967.

66 O'Hea to PW, 21.ii.1967.

67 7.v.1967.

68 PW to Dutton, 23.iii.1969.

23 Working with Paint

1 PW to Garland, 23.i.1957.

2 PW to Dutton, 5.iii.1972.

3 Not searching for beauty, *Flaws*, pp.194–5; omens, PW to Dutton, 5.ii.1967; 'I have just bought . . .', PW to Dutton, 30.iii.1965.

4 Pushing Blackman in the right direction, PW to Casey, 8.viii.1966; Digby as Daumier, PW to Dutton, 1.vi.1964; 'Now, as I . . .', PW to Casey, 20.iii.1967.

5 'name game . . .', PW to Casey, 9.ii.1967; 'Certainly we . . .', PW to Garland, 19.xii.1965; visitors to Dogwoods, G.C. Davey, *Our Studies*, Sydney

(May 1964), p.54; also on the Fairweather, PW to Rodney Wetherell, ABC Sunday Night Radio 2, 9 Dec 1973.

6   'mink locusts . . .', PW to Casey, 8.viii.1966; 'Nowadays . . .', PW to Ralph Smith, 1.viii.1966.

7   'recede . . .', Davey, *Our Studies*, p.54; 'pubic hair . . .', PW to me; Dickerson, PW to Garland, 20.v.1960; Olsen, PW to Garland, 30.x.1960.

8   PW to Osborne, 31.viii.1961, HRHRC.

9   'we don't have . . .', PW to Dutton, 14.ii.1965; 'able to . . .', PW to the Moores, 8.vi.1969.

10   PW re Swanton, to me, 10 Feb 1987; steel eagle and red ferret, *Vivisector*, p.510 [449]; ritual animosity, Frank Watters to me, 17 May 1989; 'I adore . . .', *Vivisector*, p.603 [532].

11   'Viennese spiv', PW to Dutton, 30.iii.1965; Loebel link to Komon, PW to me, 29 June 1989; 'Zese faht . . .', *Vivisector*, p.479 [421].

12   PW to the Duttons, 28.xi.1965 – 'Williams' is Fred Williams.

13   PW to Casey, 14.xi.1966.

14   'Poor Sid . . .', PW to Duttons, 8.v.1966; 'Of all . . .', PW to Luciana Arrighi, 16.x.1967.

15   PW to Stern, 18.iii.1968.

16   7.v.1967.

17   24.i.1967.

18   'We have . . .', PW to Williams, 20.ii.1967; 'I am enjoying . . .', PW to Best, 21.iv.1967.

19   'genius at work', PW to Waters, 28.vi.1970; 'I think . . .', *Vivisector*, p.536 [472].

20   PW to Dutton, 30.viii.1970.

21   PW to Björkstén, 10.xi.1969.

22   Sunningdale growing out of Lulworth, *Southerly*, p.132; Ruth and Dick as sources for the Courtneys, PW to me, 7 May 1990; 'Suzanne had . . .', PW to me, 29 June 1989.

23   *Vivisector*, p.95 [81].

24   Perv, p.223 [194]; honest, p.315 [276]; cruel, p.304 [266]; 'I was trying . . .', p.538 [473].

25   'unbelievers' and 'As an old man . . .', PW to Dutton, 10.v.1970; 'everyone can . . .' and Frankenstein monster, PW interviewed by Craig McGregor in *In the Making* (Thomas Nelson, Melbourne, 1969), p.218; 'Otherwise, how . . .', *Vivisector*, p.269 [236]; 'Which can . . .', PW to Semmler, 10.v.1970; depicting squalor and beauty, *Southerly*, p.142.

26   'physically . . .', PW to Campbell, 1.xi.1970; 'I was glad . . .', PW to Casey, 12.vii.1966.

27   PW to me, 29 June 1989.

28   Miller lived at 89 Sutherland Street: Duffield's house, *Vivisector*, pp.273–4 [239–40]: PW took the exterior of the house from a big place elsewhere in Paddington, *Flaws*, p.154.

29   'very complicated . . .', PW to me, 29 June 1989; first visit, PW to Dutton, 30.iii.1962; second visit, PW to me, 10 Feb 1987; Fairfax visit, James Fairfax to me, 22 March 1988.

30   Bacon's paintings as Duffield's, PW to me, 29 June 1989; 'the most bearable . . .', PW to Dutton, 14.ii.1965; 'random arabesques', *Southerly*, p.134; not liking 1963 paintings, PW to Garland, 3.viii.1963; 'right touch . . .', PW to Colwell, Cape, 15.iii.1970.

31   *Vivisector*, p.561 [494].

32   'Not in the least,' PW to Maschler, 20.i.1970, Cape; 'all these paintings . . .', *Vivisector*, p.594 [524]; 'It was staggering . . .', PW to Luciana Arrighi,

16.x.1967.

33 'blaze . . .', *Vivisector*, p.594 [524]; 'I suppose . . .', PW to Casey, 30.vii.1967; *SMH* (13 Sept 1967), p.16.

34 'national monument,' *Vivisector*, p.589 [520]; use of Stockhausen, Beatson to me, 18.vii.1988, and the Moores to me, 20 Oct 1988; 'into that silence . . .', *Vivisector*, p.622 [549].

35 PW to Stern, 22.ii.1970; *Vivisector*, p.489 [430].

36 'Still, there . . .', PW to Dutton, 26.iii.1967; 'so perhaps . . .', PW to Williams, 16.vii.1967.

37 Art schools, 9.ii.1967; Sargent and Lautrec, 7.v.1967; telephones, 7.v.1967; toothpaste, 19.iv.1967; 'smoodge', 1.xii.1968; 'I visualised . . .', 28.v.1967.

38 Read, PW to Dutton, 14.iv.1968; Flaubert, PW to Dutton, undated, March 1968; 'one of those . . .', PW to Waters, 2.vii.1967; Casey's book, PW to Casey, 19.iv.1967.

39 Rushcutters Bay and Cooper Park, PW to me, 29 June 1989; 'unlit gas fires', *Vivisector*, p.267 [234].

40 Russell for Shuard, PW to me, 10 Nov 1988; Honeysett for Missingham, PW to me, 29 June 1989; 'I must . . .', PW to Dutton, 12.xi.1967; Caldicott, PW to me, 4 Oct 1988; 'They would . . .', Smith to me, 4 Oct 1988.

41 'Zoe at the . . .', PW to Waters, 28.vi.1970; 'would a man . . .', Halmagyi to me, 12 Sept 1988; a great novel, PW to Dutton, 13.xi.1966.

42 Luciana Arrighi to me, 8.viii.1989.

43 'scratching . . .', *Vivisector*, p.427 [375]; 'densely . . .', PW in *Bulletin* (22 Jan 1966); 'she in . . .', PW to Best, 21.iv.1967; 'pathetic . . .', PW to Garland, 19.xii.1965; 'all wait . . .', PW to Dutton, 7.x.1965.

44 *Vivisector*, p.427 [375]; Mortimer as Williams, PW to me, 29 June 1989.

45 21.vi.1970.

46 PW to me, 29 June 1989.

47 'too much . . .', PW to Casey, 26.xi.1967; 'Five Twenty' appeared in *Southerly*, vol. 28, no.1 (1968), *Coast to Coast, 1967–1968* (Angus & Robertson, 1968); and *Oxford Book of Short Stories* (Oxford University Press, 1981).

48 'It begins . . .', PW to Best, 5.xi.1967; 'The end . . .', PW to Casey, 26.xi.1967.

49 PW to Dutton, 27.viii.1967.

50 PW to Dutton, 8.v.1972: to Alan Williams, 21.x.1979, Viking; to Manning Clark, 31.x.1979.

51 PW to Dal Stivens, 11.ii.1968.

52 Baynton, PW to Casey, 9.ii.1967; 'I have always . . .', PW to Clark, 7.iv.1968; 'Interesting to see . . .', PW to Clark, Christmas 1968.

53 'one of . . .', PW to Björkstén, 26.i.1975; 'Tell me . . .', John Young to me, 29 June 1988.

54 'disgusting . . .', PW to Casey, 26.xi.1967; 'Higher Junta . . .', *SMH* (13 Dec 1967), p.2.

55 'to renew . . .', *Vivisector*, p.184 [160]; go away for a while, McGregor, *In the Making*, p.219; 'They are the wise . . .', PW to Casey, 22.x.1967; 'This incredible . . .', PW to Dutton, 3.xii.1967.

56 PW to Garland, 29.i.1968.

57 Nin Dutton to me, 12 March 1986.

58 *Vivisector*, p.248 [216].

59 'I wish . . .', PW to Best, 18.ii.1968; 'but oxywelding . . .', PW to Casey, 26.ii.1968; 'but as it . . .', PW to Dutton, undated, March 1968.

60 PW to Best, 7.iv.1968.

61 'Life has . . .', from the speech 'Greece – My Other Country', *Speaks*,

p.135; 'As he is . . .', PW to Casey, 18.vi.1968.

62 19.vi.1968.
63 'the scaly . . .', *Vivisector*, p.406 [355]; the identification of Hero, Hurtle and Perialos with PW, EGL and Patmos, *Flaws*, pp.180–1; 'intent on . . .', ibid., p.180.
64 PW to the Moores, 1.viii.1968.
65 'I must say . . .', PW to Halmagyi, 23.v.1968; an orgy, PW to the Moores, 1.viii.1968; 'of people sitting . . .' and 'I can read . . .', PW to Dutton, 12.viii.1968.
66 PW to the Moores, 8.viii.1968.
67 Ibid.
68 'looks cold . . .', PW to the Moores, 8.viii.1968; 'I thought . . .', PW to Dutton, 21.viii.1968.
69 'the part . . .' and 'perhaps that . . .', PW to Williams, 28.ix.1968; 'We only seem . . .', PW to Stern, 16.ix.1968.
70 PW to the Moores, 8.viii.1968.
71 Yaddo, PW to Osborne, 10.x.1968, Cambridge; 'he does have . . .', Cushman to O'Hea, 25.x.1968, Curtis Brown Ltd papers, Columbia.
72 PW to the Duttons, 16.x.1968.
73 'what a cunt . . .', PW to me; 'I haven't . . .', PW to Cushman, 21.x.1968.
74 'mucking . . .', PW to Waters, 31.x.1968; 'He . . . didn't . . .', PW to Casey, 13.vii.1969.
75 1.xii.1968.
76 'Fortunately . . .', PW to Dutton, 5.i.1969; Godlike, PW to Dutton, 2.ii.1969.
77 2.iii.1969.
78 Kirk to me, 4 Oct 1986.
79 Michael White to me, 28 July 1986.
80 *Vivisector*, p.106 [91].
81 'When we . . .', PW to Waters, 2.iii.1969; *Vivisector*, p.585 [516].
82 'one of . . .', PW to Stern, 7.v.1969; 'feeling cold . . .', PW to Casey, 7.v.1969; 'the most . . .', PW to Dutton, 5.i.1969; 'suddenly . . .' and 'How easy . . .', PW to Casey, 1.xii.1968.
83 PW to the Duttons, undated, early June 1969.
84 'Why did . . .', PW to Dutton, 14.vi.1969; 'is lugging . . .', PW to Casey, 13.vii.1969; 'I have been . . .', PW to Casey, 17.viii.1969.
85 *Vivisector*, p.642 [566].
86 PW to the Moores, 15.ix.1969.
87 'they expect . . .', PW to O'Hea, 10 Sept 1969; 'I notice . . .', PW to O'Hea, 5.x.1969.
88 'Until Patrick . . .', O'Hea to me, 29 Sept 1985; 'I can't think . . .', Maschler to O'Hea, 5.i.1968.
89 'very much . . .', PW to Casey, 17.viii.1969; 'I think . . .', Maschler to PW, June 1969.
90 'Poor things . . .', PW to Dutton, 7.x.1969; 'I don't . . .', PW to the Moores, 13.x.1969.
91 'It was an austere . . .', Greene to Maschler, 19.x.1969, Cape; 'what with . . .', PW to O'Hea, 20.x.1969.
92 O'Hea to Cushman, 28.x.1969, Curtis Brown Ltd papers, Columbia.
93 PW to Stern, 22.ii.1970.
94 PW to Dutton, 11.xii.1969.
95 11.xii.1969.

24 Storms

1 'My political . . .' and 'art is art . . .', PW to Garland, 10.v.1956.

2 Israel's triumphs, PW to Williams, 16.vii.1967; Cyprus, PW to *SMH* (2 June 1956), p.2; South Africa, PW to *SMH* (20 March 1968), p.11; US colony, PW to Garland, 31.x.1966.

3 To Gerry Wilkes, Nov 1966.

4 Origins of the war, PW to Best, 1.ii.1967; sincerity of witnesses and 'I . . . see . . .', PW to Dutton, 20.xi.1966.

5 'because they . . .', Best to PW, 21.ii.1967; 'I have always . . .', PW to Holt, 24.iv.1967, Prime Minister's Office, 66/2310.

6 McEwen's remark, on a memo dated 31.v.1967; final reply to PW, 29.vi.1967, both Prime Minister's Office, file 66/2310.

7 'Of course . . .', PW to Williams, 16.vii.1967; 'It is all . . .', PW to Dutton, 3.vi.1967.

8 PW to Dutton, 3.viii.1969.

9 'One can . . .', PW to O'Hea, 4.xii.1969; health, O'Hea to PW, 9.xii.1969, Curtis Brown Group Ltd.

10 *SMH* (10 Dec 1969), p.9.

11 Never a novel he knew so much, PW to Dutton, 4.i.1970; 'the novel tends . . .', PW to Maschler, 15.xi.1972.

12 'to give . . .', PW to Williams, 2.i.1971; 'While I . . .', PW to Waters, 28.vi.1970.

13 PW to Rodney Wetherell, ABC Sunday Night Radio 2, 9 Dec 1973.

14 'stuffed with . . .', *Eye*, p.131; 'Perhaps you . . .', p.127; 'Given a . . .', p.130.

15 PW to Dutton, 23.iv.1970.

16 A Wolfit ham, PW to Waters, 21.xi.1971; the biography was by Ronald Harwood, *Sir Donald Wolfit, C.B.E.: His Life and Work in the Unfashionable Theatre* (Secker & Warburg, London, 1971); 'a fascinating . . .' and 'I suspect . . .', PW to Garland, 16.i.1972; 'What should . . .', PW to Waters, 28.vi.1970.

17 'one of . . .', PW to Rodney Wetherell, ABC Sunday Night Radio 2, 9 Dec 1973; 'the same . . .', PW to Waters, 21.xi.1971; Dutton as a source, Dutton to me, 12 Dec 1988, reporting PW to him; Lady Sackville as a source, PW to me, 30 Sept 1988; 'I shall . . .', PW to the Duttons, 12.xi.1972.

18 Fairfax to me, 22 March 1988; 'with houses . . .', PW to me, 12 May 1988.

19 'a steamy . . .', *Eye*, p.544; 'that too . . .', p.83; 'strong enough . . .', p.151; 'but understands . . .', p.150; 'There is . . .', PW to me, 29 Nov 1988.

20 Ebsworth as source for Wyburd, PW to me, 30 Sept 1988; as a source for Forsdyke, PW to le Moignan, *SMH* (23 July 1983), p.33; 'splendid, slender', *Eye*, p.37; 'restricted . . .', p.30.

21 'all of . . .', *Flaws*, p.154; Martin Road for the Feinsteins, PW to Stern, 20.iii.1966; for Duffield, *Flaws*, p.154; for Mrs Gray, approved by PW, 14 Aug 1990; 'Kudjeri in . . .', PW to Maschler, 9.xii.1974; Havilah, PW to me, 29 April 1988; 'Our family . . .', PW to Maschler, 9.xii.1974.

22 'only by . . .', *Eye*, p.473; 'mineral hills' and 'You've got . . .', p.527.

23 PW to Waters, 2.viii.1970.

24 Harry M. Miller, *My Story*, as told to Denis O'Brien (Macmillan, Australia, 1983), p.239.

25 PW to Dutton, 2.ii.1969.

26 PW to Arrighi, 5.iv.1970.

27 'The Australian . . .' and 'but it . . .', PW to Waters, 2.viii.1970; 'He was . . .', McGrath to me, Oct 1985.

28 'Patrick was . . .', McGrath to me, Oct 1985; 'riding down . . .', PW to Keith Michell, 9.x.1957.

29 22.xi.1970.

30 'The garden . . .', and 'He still . . .', PW to Beatson, 29.xi.1970.

31 PW to Dutton, 27.xii.1970.

32   'He arrived . . .', PW to Dutton, 27.xii.1970; 'I . . . told . . .', PW to
      Waters, 8.i.1971.
33   'on the other . . .', PW to Dutton, 25.i.1970; 'One is inclined . . .', PW
      to Maschler, 18.ii.1970.
34   Beatson to me, 18.vii.1988.
35   1.xi.1970.
36   Transcript of evidence, *R. v. Angus & Robertson*, Sydney Quarter Sessions
      before Judge Goran, 10 Feb 1971, pp.162–6.
37   10.ii.1971.
38   'Nowhere does . . .', PW to Dutton, 25.iv.1971; Viking advance, PW
      to O'Hea, 19.viii.1971; 'It seems . . .', PW to Cushman, 22.viii.1970.
39   'M. has . . .' and 'a certain . . .', PW to Dutton, 25.iv.1971; 'They want
      . . .', PW to David Moore, 23.v.1971.
40   'We lunched . . .', PW to Dutton, 4.vii.1971; 'much improved . . .' and
      'the heaviest . . .', PW to Harrower, 3.vi.1971.
41   'At least . . .' and 'Naturally he . . .', PW to Harrower, 3.vi.1971; 'to
      alter . . .', PW to Dutton, 25.iv.1971.
42   'The only . . .' and 'like a . . .', McGrath to me, 15 Oct 1985; 'It makes
      . . .', PW to Dutton, 4.vii.1971.
43   'I suppose . . .', PW to Greene, 12.vii.1971.
44   'unless I . . .', PW to Casey, 30.vii.1967; 'Proust may not . . .', PW to
      Tara McCarthy, Canadian Broadcasting Commission, Sept 1973; 'All his
      . . .', PW to Stern, 18.vii.1971.
45   'I can . . .', PW to Duttons, 11.viii.1971; 'one of . . .', PW to Halmagyi,
      25.viii.1971.
46   12.viii.1971.
47   'a bit . . .', PW to Green, 1.v.1984; 'one of . . .', PW to Semmler, 10.iv.1969;
      'Martin Boyd . . .', PW to Kelson, sec. of CLF, 7.xi.1971, Australian
      Archives, CRS A 3753, item 71/1405, 'Martin Boyd'; pension decision,
      Australian Archives, CRS A463, item 73/1984.
48   'like a . . .', *Flaws*, p.200; very painful, PW to Coleing, 30.ix.1971.
49   'The view . . .', PW to Dutton, 24.ix.1971; 'Greece is . . .', PW to Stern,
      8.x.1971.
50   21.xi.1971.
51   PW to Beatson, 5.xii.1971.
52   PW to Dutton, 9.i.1972.
53   PW to Harrower, 19.iii.1972.
54   Ibid.
55   PW to Garland, 2.v.1972.
56   'In a way . . .', PW to Dutton, 9.iv.1972; 'a most . . .', PW to Garland,
      12.xi.1971; skeins, *Eye*, p.208, and convents, p.115.
57   'Hippies also . . .', PW to Dutton, 8.v.1972; 'To ask . . .', PW to Harrower,
      1.vi.1972.
58   *Speaks*, p.28.
59   *Speaks*, pp.31–3.
60   'the first citizen . . .', *Speaks*, p.48; Legge and Mundey, approved by
      PW, 14 Aug 1990.
61   'the usual . . .', PW to Dutton, 9.vii.1972; 'Now I . . .', PW to Beatson,
      28.vi.1972.
62   'peace and . . .', PW to Björkstén, 27.v.1973; 'I am . . .', PW to Casey,
      1.ii.1970.
63   'ocean perpetually . . .', *Eye*, p.375; 'the skeleton . . .', PW to Dutton,
      4.x.1970.
64   PW to Wetherell, ABC Sunday Night Radio 2, 9 Dec 1973.
65   *Eye*, p.20.

66 'sensuality won't . . .', PW to Charles Osborne, 4.v.1964, HRHRC; Hughes' review, *London Magazine*, 4 (2 May 1964), pp.60–3; 'It was a relief . . .', *Vivisector*, p.239.
67 'Lust and disgust . . .', *Eye*, p.405; 'Personally I . . .', PW to Björkstén, 20.vi.1984; 'Love is . . .', *Eye*, p.162.
68 *Eye*, p.202.
69 The questions to Halmagyi: Halmagyi to me, 12 Sept 1988; 'Sue and I . . .', PW to me; 'It wouldn't . . .', *Eye*, p.459; 'a fleshy . . .', p.550.
70 'Still working . . .', PW to Garland, 29.x.1972; 'blood all . . .', PW to Dutton, 22.x.1972; 'Knowing all . . .', PW to Dutton, 12.xi.1972.
71 PW to Maschler, 31.xii.1972.
72 'give a . . .', PW to O'Hea, 9.xii.1972; 'I can't help . . .', PW to O'Hea, 31.xii.1972; 'everyone at . . .', O'Hea to PW, 10.i.1973, Curtis Brown Group Ltd; 'Have just . . .', Alan Williams to PW, 14.ii.1973, Viking.
73 *Speaks*, pp.51–2.
74 McClelland to me, 19 June 1987.
75 Christmas card, 1972.

25 The Prize

1 PW to Arrighi, 6.vi.1972.
2 'There was . . .', PW to Arrighi, 6.vi.1972; 'The only kind . . .', PW to Dutton, 14.vi.1969.
3 'we are . . .', PW to Harrower, 1.vi.1972.
4 *Australian Financial Review* (11 July 1972), pp.2–3, by Brian Dale writing under the name Ashley Owen.
5 24.xi.1974.
6 PW to me, 1 May 1985.
7 *Snow Country*, PW to Williams, 21.vi.1970; 'Discovering the . . .', PW to Lindberg, 1.v.1971.
8 'dreadful mistakes', PW to Ingegärd Martinell, 4.iv.1968.
9 Ibid.
10 PW to Dutton, 5.iii.1972.
11 PW to Harrower, 19.iii.1972.
12 PW to Dutton, 12.viii.1968.
13 16.ii.1969.
14 *Hardbacks:* this can only be an approximate figure as Eyre & Spottiswoode kept no sale records and Curtis Brown trashed its royalty records before 1965. Sales figures for the British editions – up to and including *Solid Mandala* – I compiled from scattered correspondence and later Curtis Brown records. The US sales records are more complete at Viking and in the Curtis Brown papers at Columbia University.

	USA		UK and Australia	
	Sales	Earnings	Sales	Earnings
Riders in the Chariot	7,000	$US4,130	24,000	£2,500
Burnt Ones	2,300	1,200	?	£1,000
Four Plays	495	250	?	£350
Solid Mandala	5,700	2,670	12,700	£2,400
Vivisector	4,000	3,500	22,000+	£5,700+

Paperbacks: the ratio of 60:40 was supplied by White's agent and literary executor Barbara Mobbs. Penguin and other paperback publishers of his work have not kept complete records. Again this is an approximate figure.
Total Income: Allowing $20,000 as a notional figure for translations and

other odds and ends, this brings the earnings to $150,000. This was the equivalent then of about UK £60,000 and US $135,000.

15 'hardly a . . .' and 'I think . . .', PW to Dutton, 18.xi.1965; 'I . . . would . . .', PW to Coleing, 13.vi.1986; teeth and underclothes, PW to Best, 29.ii.1976; 'cautious blood . . .', PW to Nin Dutton, 13.iv.1975.

16 PW to Dutton, 18.xi.1965.

17 William Yang, *Starting Again* (William Heinemann, Australia, 1989), p.96.

18 7.v.1967.

19 The Boudin, *Vivisector*, pp.50 [41] and 62 [51]; 'so obviously . . .', PW to me, 20 May 1989; menstruation, Penny Coleing to me, 22 Aug 88, *Eye*, p.573.

20 PW to Dutton, 18.ii.1973.

21 Watters to me, 17 May 1988.

22 Anne (le Guay) Cobden to me, 17 Aug 1989.

23 Beatson to me, 18.vii.1988.

24 Gosse to me, 9 Aug 1989.

25 Garland to me, 2.vi.1990.

26 1.ii.1971.

27 Nin Dutton to me, 12 March 1986; 'ashamed . . .', PW to Beatson, 28.vi.1972.

28 Psychotherapy, Beatson to me, 18.vii.1988; 'It is a burden . . .', ABC, Sunday Night Radio 2, 9 Dec 1973.

29 Mescalin, PW to Dutton, 19.ix.1965; LSD, PW to Beatson, 29.xi.1970.

30 'I was terribly . . .', *Age* (24 Sept 1983); 'I am even . . .', PW to O'Hea, misdated, 9.ii.1966, probably 9.i.1966.

31 'that ingrown . . .', PW to Stern, 22.xi.1970; 'that thug', PW to Maschler, 29.iv.1973; 'she is . . .', PW to Maschler, 31.iii.1974; 'I believe . . .', PW to Maschler, 20.ix.1973.

32 Garland to me, 2–7 May 1987.

33 'Manoly fortunately . . .', PW to Waters, 24.i.1967; 'means endless . . .', PW to Beatson, c.10.x.1978; 'Laughter, love . . .', PW to me, 22 Oct 1987; 'M. took . . .', Moore to me, 15 Sept 1988.

34 'if Manoly . . .', PW to Williams, 21.vi.1970; 'an incorrect . . .', *Time* (25 March 1974), p.2; a copy of the full text went to Alan Williams, 17.ii.1974.

35 28.vi.1970.

36 29.iii.1973.

37 David Campbell, *Deaths and Pretty Cousins* (Australian National University Press, Canberra, 1975), pp.15–16.

38 Air France, Cape to White, 26.i.1973; nigger, PW to Viking, 1.vii.1973; French princes, PW to Viking, 18.iii.1973; the blurb, PW to Cape, 25.ii.1973.

39 'to get . . .', PW to me, 14 Aug 1985; 'words . . .', PW to Maschler, 27.v.1973; 'fully fledged', PW to Campbell, 13.v.1973; 'The latest story . . .', PW to Maschler, 29.iv.1973; 'My life . . .', PW to Campbell, 13.v.1973.

40 Waters to me, 30 Sept 1985.

41 The mauling of librettists etc, PW to Aurousseau, 18.vii.1970; 'immersed in . . .', PW to Dutton, 15.vii.1973; 'one buttock . . .', PW to O'Hea, 21.viii.1973.

42 'This is the . . .', PW to Halmagyi, 17.viii.1973; 'It is every . . .', PW to Maschler, 23.viii.1973.

43 PW to Maschler, 23.viii.1973.

44 Artur Lundkvist, *Utflykter med utländska författara* (Stockholm, Bonniers, 1969), p.189. All Swedish quotes have been translated for me by David Harry.

45 *Bonniers Litterära Magasin*, vol. 8, no. 5 (May 1939), pp.352–3.

46 *Utflykter med utländska författara*, p.189.

47 Steven P. Sondrup, *World Literature Today*, University of Oklahoma, vol. 55, no. 2 (Spring 1981), p.233. I am indebted to Sondrup's account of Lundkvist's life.

48 *Aftonbladet* (22 Oct 1969), p.18.

49 10.xi.1969.

50 Refusal to visit Sweden, PW to Magnus Lindberg, 10.viii.1971; 'very well-behaved . . .', PW to the Moores, 29.vi.1969; 'only be . . .', PW to Maschler, 1.xi.1970.

51 'Many would . . .', Lundkvist to me, 8 Dec 1987; confirmed by Lundkvist in Björkstén's letter to me, 14.viii.1989; 'I don't . . .', PW to Best, 31.iii.1970 and Dutton, 5.iv.1970.

52 *Expressen* (11 Oct 1970), p.4.

53 Christophersen to me, 17.xi.1986.

54 10.ix.1972.

55 'No doubt . . .', PW to Dutton, 22.x.1972; 'I no longer . . .', PW to Björkstén, Christmas card, 1972.

56 *Dagens Nyheter* (6 Sept 1973), p.4; these quotes from Harry's translation in the *Australian* (17 Oct 1973), p.14.

57 Ramel to PW, 18.x.1973.

58 Riddell, *Australian* (20 Oct 1973), p.3.

59 PW to Maschler, 23.x.1973.

60 Australian Broadcasting Commission, TR 107/10/73, PNS 237, PNR, 1129/10/73.

61 'extraordinary . . .', PW to O'Hea, 22.x.1973; 'I am amazed . . .', PW to Maschler, 23.x.1973.

62 PW to Jim Cope, Parliamentary Debates, House of Representatives, 29 Nov 1973, p.4081.

63 'My sister . . .', PW to Maschler, 17.xi.1973; PW to Gierow, 25.x.1973, and to the King and Academy, 24.xi.1973.

64 Interview with Gordon McLauchlan, TV-1, New Zealand, Nov 1984.

65 'What does . . .', O'Hea to PW, 18.x.1973, Curtis Brown Group Ltd; Penguin sales, O'Hea to PW, 25.x.1973; 'It will . . .', PW to Maschler, 10.xi.1974.

66 'Mysterious . . .', PW to Waters, 18.xii.1973; 'very impressive . . .', Curtis Brown Group Ltd.

67 PW to Garland, 9.xi.1973.

68 'Aber das . . .', Jürgen Oertel to me, 12 Dec 1987; *Sud-Ouest* (31 Oct 1973), p.11; *Tudorian* (1973), p.5; R to me, 26.viii.1987.

69 'paradise lost . . .', PW to Casey, 9.ii.1967; *Sir William Heans* and 'I only . . .', PW to Casey, 31.x.1966.

70 'bland rural . . .', postcard, 9.xi.1973; characters talking, PW to Alan Williams, 22.xi.1973; quotes from *Fringe*, pp.84, 85, the passage identified as arising out of his own explorations by PW to me, 1 May 1985; 'I could have . . .', PW to O'Hea, 16.xi.1973.

71 'returned to abnormal', PW to Alan Williams, 22.xi.1973; Björkstén's book was published in English under the title *Patrick White: A General Introduction* (University of Queensland Press, 1976); trailing round Sydney, *Veckojournalen* (12 Dec 1973).

72 Barrett Reid to me, 18 Dec 1988; paroxysm, Murray-Smith to me, 22 July 1988; 'It wasn't . . .', PW to Murray-Smith, 23.xii.1973.

26 The Biggest Sandbank in the World

1 Discipline, PW to Maschler, 31.viii.1975; 'returning to . . .', PW to Dutton, 12.i.1974; 'Today . . .', PW to Maschler, 2.i.1974.

2   'I feel . . .' and 'I know . . .', PW to Alan Williams, 11.i.1976; tribute
     to Ellen Withycombe, *Flaws*, p.64; ordering Rowse, PW to Maschler,
     10.iii.1974.
3   'Her mind's . . .', *Fringe*, pp.50–1; 'It was a wonderful . . .',
     PW to Coleing, 23.vi.1971; his night at the opera, PW to me, 3 Sept 1987.
4   'and turn . . .', PW to Alan Williams, 11.i.1976; 'in the hopes . . .', *Fringe*,
     p.71.
5   PW to Huebsch, 3.xi.1961, Congress.
6   Ibid.
7   'I was . . .', PW to Dutton, 20.i.1974; 'to tell . . .', PW to the Duttons,
     12.i.1974; 'I had . . .', PW to Björkstén, 27.i.1974.
8   *Speaks*, pp.47–8.
9   I had written that PW learnt of Dyce-Murphy from Murray-Smith at
     the *Overland* dinner. PW queried this when he read the ts but eventually
     concurred. That version was published in *Overland*, 121, pp.6–7. Barry
     Jones was able to correct me after PW's death. Jones to me, 2.i.1991
     and 18.i.1991; PW to Jones, 8.v.1983; cf *Twyborn*, pp.422–3; the
     painting is *The Arbour* by E. Phillips Fox, but in *E. Phillips Fox and His
     Family*, a memoir privately published by Len Fox in Melbourne in 1958,
     doubts are raised at p.70 about Dyce-Murphy's claim to be the figure in
     white. Stephen Murray-Smith suggests there that Fox's *Al Fresco* is the
     painting Murphy had in mind.
10   'with dinner . . .', PW to Dutton, 3.iii.1974; 'I shall keep . . .', PW to
     Dutton, 10.iii.1974; 'We had . . .', PW to Waters, 17.iii.1974.
11   'I am asked . . .', PW to Alexandra Dawson, 17.iii.1974; 'reducing, reducing',
     PW to Alan Williams, 10.xi.1974; '*Between ourselves* . . .', PW to Björkstén,
     6.i.1974.
12   Guinzburg to O'Hea, 5.iii.1974.
13   'If you . . .', O'Hea to Maschler, 2.i.1974, Curtis Brown Group Ltd; 'I had
     . . .', PW to O'Hea, 25.iii.1973; PW to me, 5 Feb and Tennant to me, 21
     Feb 1986; 'took drugs . . .', *Ride on Stranger* (Victor Gollancz, London,
     1943), p.157.
14   8.v.1974.
15   McClelland to me, 19 June 1987.
16   *Speaks*, pp.51–2.
17   'I could . . .', PW to Waters, 7.vii.1974.
18   *Grenfell Record* (19 June 1974), p.2; Lawson's poems and the myth, PW
     to Dutton, 30.iii.1962; 'It backs . . .', 4.iii.1974.
19   *Speaks*, pp.55–7.
20   7.vii.1974.
21   'It was . . .', PW to Waters, 7.vii.1974; 'Some of . . .', PW to the Duttons,
     14.vii.1974.
22   *Fringe*, p.234.
23   'One's feet . . .', PW to Stephen Murray-Smith, 15.vii.1974; 'along the
     . . .', PW to Coleing, 17.vii.1974; 'I enjoyed . . .', PW to Henderson,
     15.vii.1974.
24   'Any kind . . .', PW to Judith Wright, 14.ix.1975; 'I'm inclined . . .',
     PW to Sinclair, 10.ii.1974.
25   *Woman's Day* (2 Dec 1974), p.19.
26   'I was . . .', PW to Whitlam, 18.iii.1975; 'I want . . .', Whitlam to PW,
     1.iv.1975; 'I'm afraid . . .', PW to Nin Dutton, 13.iv.1975.
27   PW to Garland, 25.v.1975.
28   Ibid.
29   'From time . . .', PW to Sinclair, 15.vii.1975.
30   Sinclair to me, 12 Sept 1989, and Moore to me, 15 Sept 1988.

31   PW to Best, 9.ii.1975.
32   Ibid.
33   PW to Dutton, 22.ix.1969.
34   Stead to Harrower, Oct 1974.
35   Stead to Harrower, 3.ix.1975.
36   *Voss*, p.468 [434].
37   'getting unconfessed . . .', PW to Huebsch, 3.xi.1961, Congress; 'saviour-lover' and 'bumping, laughing . . .', *Fringe*, p.317.
38   'As always . . .', PW to Dutton, 13.i.1975; 'It is good . . .', PW to the Duttons, 2.ii.1975.
39   'his hair . . .', *Flaws*, p.227; Australian grandees are often called 'bunyip aristocrats' after those comic mythical creatures of local legend; 'There began . . .', p.230.
40   25.v.1975.
41   'to be brought . . .' and 'I have subjected . . .', PW to Alexandra Dawson, 6.vii.1975.
42   'She can . . .', PW to Dutton, 20.v.1973; 'in what . . .', PW to Nin Dutton, 13.iv.1975; 'We buried . . .', *Flaws*, p.30.
43   Wanting the trunk, PW to Beatson, 29.xi.1970; 'What do you . . .', Kirk to me, 4 Oct 1986; showing the trunk, Harrower to me, 10 April 1989.
44   'But I don't . . .', PW to Waters, 30.ix.1975; 'My eyes . . .', PW to Maschler, 31.viii.1975.
45   Nolan, PW to Maschler, 30.ix.1975; 'Manoly is . . .', PW to Moya Henderson, 1.x.1975.
46   'I can't . . .', Best to PW, 2.ii.1976; 'I am always . . .', PW to Best, 29.ii.1976.
47   'I am shrivelling . . .', PW to Dutton, 8.xi.1975; 'I'm sick . . .', PW to Dutton, 21.ix.1975.
48   'The meal . . .', PW to Clark, 15.xi.1975.
49   'How unsuited . . .', PW to Beatson, 20.xi.1975; 'that grazier . . .', PW to Maschler, 11.xii.1975.
50   'We shall . . .', PW to O'Hea, 21.xii.1975; 'Rolls and . . .', PW to Dutton, 22.xii.1975.
51   'neither too . . .', PW to O'Hea, 21.xii.1975; 'I can barely . . .', PW to Stern, 28.xii.1975.

27 Dynamite All the Way

1   *Flaws*, p.246.
2   'I might . . .', PW to Dutton, 15.x.1967; PW to *SMH* (16 March 1968), p.2.
3   *Flaws*, p.244.
4   'the good . . .', PW to Charles Osborne, 10.x.1968, Cambridge; 'most entertaining . . .', PW to John Clark, 22.v.1974.
5   Duty by 'Strine, PW to Dutton, 19.iv.1973; 'I continue . . .', PW to Waters, 1.xii.1974. 'The minute . . .', PW to Dutton, 20.i.1974; tolerance of Puccini, PW to Alan Williams, 17.ii.1974; 'as people . . .', PW to Alan Williams, 9.ii.1975.
6   Sharman to me, 29 Oct 1989.
7   'wonderkid of . . .', *Flaws*, p.245; 'pink and . . .', p.245; artists returning home, *Australian* (3 Nov 1976), p.10.
8   'We got . . .', PW to Dutton, 8.xi.1975; 'This is . . .', PW to Dutton, 4.iv.1976.
9   'simmering' and 'I really . . .', PW to Murray-Smith, 5.i.1975; 'I should . . .', PW to Barry Jones, 3.ii.1974.
10 'I think . . .', PW to Murray-Smith, 5.i.1975; 'except that . . .', PW to Murray-Smith, 30.iii.1975.

11   'the stranger . . .', *Twyborn*, p.142; 'But the . . .', PW to Clark, 19.iii.1978.
12   Kaufline to me, 3 Sept 1989; 'turned out . . .', PW to Dutton, 21.ii.1976.
13   Travelling with the relic, PW to Arrighi, 22.vii.1976; 'less greedy . . .', PW to Alan Williams, 11.i.1976; 'thinner than . . .', PW to Harrower, 7.v.1976; 'I'm sure . . .', PW to Dutton, 5.v.1976.
14   'Lots of . . .', PW to Clark, 18.v.1976; 'We flickered . . .', PW to Dutton, 5.v.1976.
15   'Agent first . . .', *The Times* (31 May 1976), p.6; 'it's dank', reported by O'Hea to me, 29 Sept 1985.
16   'was not unconscious . . .', *Twyborn*, pp.318-19; the railings, PW to Garland, 8.vii.1978; Trist's strolls, *Twyborn*, pp.309-10; details of Embankment conversations, Barry Jones to me, 7 Jan 1991.
17   'Everybody most . . .', PW to Harrower, 1.vii.1976; 'None of . . .', PW to Gwen Moore, 22.vi.1976.
18   'It trundled . . .', PW to Stern, 15.vii.1976; the Golsons' pub, PW to me, 10 Sept 1987.
19   'on a Florida . . .', PW to Dutton, 19.vii.1976; 'watermelons . . .', PW to Stern, 15.vii.1976; 'shutters . . .', *Twyborn*, p.14; sources for St Mayeul, PW to Alan Williams, 2.ix.1979.
20   'very good . . .', PW to Alan Williams, 2.ix.1979; PW on the stories, to Stern, 18.iii.1968; 'do jump . . .', PW to Garland, 8.x.1975.
21   Beatson to me, 18.vii.1988.
22   19.vii.1976.
23   *Twyborn*, p.88.
24   'It's the place . . .', PW to Coleing, 26.vii.1976; 'I came . . .', PW to King, 24.vii.1976.
25   King to me, 7.x.1989, quoting from a letter of Aug 1976.
26   'I don't . . .', 22.vii.1976; 'Wonderful forests . . .', PW to the Moores, 24.viii.76; the birth of 'Fête Galante', *Flaws*, p.198.
27   'We found . . .', PW to Harrower, 1.ix.1976; 'one has . . .', PW to Grose, 15.ix.1976, Curtis Brown Group Ltd.
28   'astonishing reception . . .', PW to Garland, 9.x.1976; 'very low' and 'JACKIE . . .', PW to Alan Williams, 20.ii.1977.
29   17.x.1976.
30   'Welcome back . . .', *Theatre Australia* (Nov/Dec 1976), p.17; me in the *Bulletin* (13 Nov 1976), p.56; 'a stinker', PW to Penny Coleing, 21.xi.1976.
31   PW to Waters, 28.xi.1976.
32   'I think . . .', reported by Sharman to me, 29 Oct 1989; 'It came . . .', PW to Waters, 28.xi.1976; 'We have . . .', PW to Osborne, 26.xii.1976, Cambridge.
33   2.xii.1976.
34   *Australian* (7 Dec 1976), p.7.
35   White apparently unchanged, Nolan to Brian Adams, mss material for *Sidney Nolan, Such is Life* (Hutchinson Australia, Melbourne, 1987); 'on with . . .', PW to Dutton, 9.iv.1978; 'Nolan would . . .', PW to Maschler, 31.xii.1978.
36   Wandering the house, PW to Alan Williams, 26.xii.1976; 'I'm relieved . . .', PW to O'Hea, 16.i.1977.
37   Reported by McGrath to me, 15 Oct 1985.
38   PW to Dutton, 9.xi.1974.
39   6.ii.1977.
40   Ibid.
41   'using David . . .', Michel Ciment, *Conversations with Losey* (Methuen, London, 1985), p.404; 'Harry Bull . . .', PW to Waters, 18.ix.1977.
42   16.iv.1977.

43　*Twyborn*, p.212.
44　'a rich folly . . .', *Twyborn*, p.184; the birthdays, p.230.
45　24.iv.1977.
46　'a combing . . .', *Twyborn*, p.207; 'not all violets', PW to me, 14 Aug 1985, *Twyborn*, p.174; Tyrell and Prowse, PW to me, 8 March 1990.
47　Too painful to open, PW to Peggy Garland, 11.ix.1977; PW's response on reading the Bolaro letters, Betty Withycombe to me, 14 Oct 1985; destruction, PW to me, 28 Nov 1985 and thereafter.
48　McClelland's input, McClelland to me, 19 June 1987; 'I'm glad . . .', PW to Garland, 11.ix.1977.
49　PW to Dutton, 20.x.1980.
50　PW to Waters, 31.vii.1977.
51　'London is still . . .', PW to Alan Williams, 11.x.1976; 'I am not . . .', *Speaks*, pp.65–6.
52　'vernal nuns', *Twyborn*, p.324 and 'conventual rule', p.322; 'I still think . . .', PW to Dutton, 9.viii.1981.
53　*Twyborn*, pp.422–3.
54　6.viii.1976.
55　Address for Citizens for Democracy delivered in Brisbane, 7 March 1977, and Sydney in an amended form, 8 March 1977, *Speaks*, pp.63–7; PW thought it a wild success, PW to Geraldine O'Brien, *SMH* (10 Dec 1983), p.31.
56　'Fortunately, most . . .', PW to Coleing, 1.i.1976; 'on with . . .', PW to Dutton, 9.iv.1978; 'I hate . . .' and 'like a death', information to me, 29 June 1988; 'settle down . . .', Fairfax to me, 22 March 1988.
57　Duval to me, 20 Sept 1989.
58　18.vii.1978.
59　'Does it . . .', PW to Clark, 27.xi.1977; 'The fascist sheep . . .', PW to Clark, 27.xii.1977.
60　'testimonial shivoo' and 'one can . . .', PW to Dutton, 12.ii.1978; 'great man', *Speaks*, pp.70–1.
61　'Land of . . .', PW to Manning Clark, 27.xii.1977; 'So much . . .', PW to Dutton, 12.ii.1978.
62　Rape or assignation, PW to me, 23 Feb 1989; 'Automatically!', PW to me, 7 Dec 1989.
63　Scenes 160–2.
64　'I'm so glad . . .', PW to Manning Clark, 27.xi.1977; 'he says . . .', PW to Dutton, 12.ii.1978.
65　'We're so . . .', PW to Waters, 11.i.1978; 'terrifically good', PW to Garland, 29.i.1978; 'The French . . .', PW to Beatson, 1.ii.1978.
66　'I shall . . .', PW to Maschler, 8.i.1978; 'I should . . .' and 'I think . . .', PW to Garland, 10.i.1978.
67　McClelland to me, 19 June 1987.
68　'True friendship . . .', *Twyborn*, p.360.
69　PW to ANU, March 1984: 'If some of the arguments are intuitive and emotional, that too, is good. For the hard bones of reason can be more powerful when fleshed out with feminine virtues', *Speaks*, p.147; 'I recognised . . .', *Flaws*, p.35.
70　O'Hea to me, 29 Sept 1985.
71　*Vivisector*, pp.582–3 [513–14].
72　'If I had . . .', PW to Björkstén, 27.v.1973; Genet, PW to Dutton, 18.xi.1964; Baldwin, PW to Dutton, 9.iii.1975; Whitman, PW to Dutton, 30.x.1961.
73　'one of . . .', PW to Dutton, 21.ii.1976; Malouf to me, 25 Feb 1988.
74　Sharman to me, 29 Oct 1989.

75 'I hope I am . . .', PW to Williams, 9.iv.1978; 'dash off . . .', PW to Dutton, 12.viii.1968.
76 'Ottoline . . .', PW to Casey, 9.vii.1978; 'Purity . . .', *Twyborn*, pp.380–1.
77 *Twyborn*, p.160.
78 Ibid., p.223.
79 12.iii.1978.
80 'the one . . .', *SMH* (2 June 1978), p.4; 'I shall . . .', PW to Dutton, 30.iv.1978.
81 Critics, *SMH* (5 June 1978), *Australian* (5 June 1978); 'some good reviews on the fringe . . .', PW to Malouf, 17.vii.1978.
82 'Only hope . . .', PW to Waters, 11.i.1978; 'got off to . . .', PW to Moores, 24.vii.1978.
83 27.viii.1978.
84 'I shall probably . . .', PW to Dutton, 27.viii.1978.
85 To Clark, 3.ix.1978.
86 3.xii.1978.
87 9.vii.1978.
88 17.x.1977.
89 Sharman to me, 29 Oct 1989.
90 13.iii.1979.
91 9.xii.1978.
92 Sharman to me, 29 Oct 1989.
93 'We averaged . . .' and 'It's called . . .', PW to David Moore, 4.iii.1979; 'she gives . . .', PW to Manning Clark, 18.i.1979; the average was, in fact, 88.4 per cent, but this record was broken soon after by Nick Enright's version of Goldoni's *The Venetian Twins* with 88.9 per cent.
94 Scene 60.
95 'city of . . .', PW to Greene, 13.vi.1979; '*The Night* . . .', PW to Dymphna Clark, 15.vii.1979.
96 'I have . . .', PW to Dutton, 18.xi.1964; 'Much of it . . .', PW to Teresa Dutton, 3.xii.1978.
97 'I don't want . . .', PW to David Moore, 4.iii.1979; 'raked in . . .', PW to Waters, 12.vi.1979.
98 PW to me, 29 Nov 1988 and 6 July 1989.
99 PW to Mary Lord, Hon. Sec. ASAL, 17.vi.1979.
100 PW to Falkenberg, 30.vii.1979.
101 12.viii.1979.
102 PW to Henderson, 25.xi.1979.
103 16.xii.1979.

28 Patrick White Writes His Own Life

1 Judy White, *The White Family of Belltrees* (Seven Press, Sydney, 1981), p.13.
2 PW to me, 18 Jan 1985.
3 20.ix.1979.
4 PW to me, 18 Jan 1985.
5 'Patrick White . . .', station diary; 'rounding up . . .', PW to me, 16 Aug 1990; 'Tell me . . .', Michael White to me.
6 'It was . . .', PW to me, 22 Dec 1988; 'I feel . . .', PW to Semmler, 24.v.1977.
7 'Telling the truth . . .', PW to Björkstén, c.Nov 1980; 'To stop . . .', *NZ Listener* (19 Jan 1985); also Peter Ward, *Australian* (18–19 April 1987), Weekend 1; and to me on several occasions.
8 The original version is in the Meanjin Library, Melbourne, with PW's letter to Clem Christesen, 15.vi.1956; the published version is in *Meanjin*

(June 1956), p.223.

9　The original notes and White's final version are in Wilkes' possession. The 'interview' was published in *Southerly*, vol. 33, no. 2 (1973), pp.132–43; 'Have you come . . .', PW to Dutton, 9.vi.1973.

10　'I think . . .', PW to Best, 9.ii.1975; the essay is now published in *Speaks*, pp.39–44; 'I become . . .', PW to Casey, 26.xi.1967.

11　'The Monkey Puzzle, a Comedy for the Screen', final typescript, pp.64, 66–8.

12　'Afraid I . . .', PW to Beatson, undated, late Dec 1976; 'sets out . . .', PW to Green, 25.i.1981.

13　'One could . . .', PW to Alan Williams, 2.iii.1980; 'what to . . .', PW to Garland, 21.xii.1979; *Bulletin* (29 Jan 1980), pp.146–54; 'rather dreadful' and 'It's coming . . .', PW to Garland, 2.iii.1980.

14　'forgettable . . .', PW to H.M. Pharabet, 19.x.1977, copy in Fisher Library, Sydney; 'best forgotten . . .', PW to Kenny, NLA, 4.vi.1978.

15　'When the gates . . .', *Flaws*, p.12; 'Seeing the . . .', PW to Waters, 1.x.1969; 'talk endlessly . . .', PW to Harrower, 1.vii.1976.

16　'I enjoyed . . .', *Speaks*, p.41; 'They didn't . . .', PW to me; 'I didn't make . . .', *Southerly*, p.133; 'but on the . . .', R to me, 23.v.1988.

17　'Perhaps when . . .', PW to Falkenberg, 1.ix.1980; 'Blood is . . .', *Flaws*, p.251.

18　*The Poof's Progress*, PW to Greene, 14.iv.1981; 'The knighthood . . .', PW to Dutton, 13.vii.1980; 'Screaming about . . .', to Gordon McLauchlan, TV-1 NZ interview, Nov 1984; 'I am compiling . . .', PW to Greene, 14.iv.1981.

19　'I never went . . .' and 'I settled . . .', *Flaws*, pp.34–5.

20　'What I had . . .', *Flaws*, p.100; 'brief moments . . .', *Flaws*, p.214; 'the small . . .', p.100; 'Some are . . .', PW to Björkstén, 19.xi.1981.

21　'invasion . . .', PW to Björkstén, c.Nov 1980; 'I have . . .', PW to Garland, 5.i.1981.

22　PW to Dutton, 17.ix.1980, *Patterns of Australia* (Macmillan, Australia, 1980), p.63.

23　'My father . . .', *Flaws*, p.153; 'I'd be a Rum . . .', PW to Clark, 16.vi.1980.

24　'amiable, rorty . . .', *Flaws*, p.229; 'Politicians . . .', Shepherd to PW, 26.iii.1981; 'This is one . . .', PW to Shepherd, 1.iv.1981; 'If we are sued . . .', PW to Falkenberg, 19.iv.1981.

25　PW to Maschler, 2.i.1981.

26　5.i.1981.

27　PW to O'Hea, 5.iv.1981.

28　'The play is . . .', PW to Falkenberg, 31.iii.1982; the Dolly Purdell (married name, Peggy Stewart) parallel, PW to me, 10 Feb 1987.

29　*SMH* (6 Sept 1980), p.19.

30　PW to Kerry Walker, 27.v.1981.

31　PW to Dutton, 12.xi.1972.

32　'It got . . .', PW to Michael Billington, *Guardian* (14 Aug 1982), p.8; 'a dazzling . . .', Miller to me, 11 July 1990.

33　'It will not . . .', PW to Alan Williams, 20.ii.1977; 'I am convinced . . .', PW to Björkstén, 13.xi.1982.

34　'but I have . . .', PW to Henderson, 5.vii.1979; 'I don't want . . .', PW to Geraldine O'Brien, *SMH* (10 Dec 1983), p.31, also PW to Le Moignan, *SMH* (23 July 1983), p.33; 'I still . . .', PW to Malouf, 21.ii.1981.

35　'The dreadful . . .', PW to Maschler, Aug 1981; 'immense physical . . .', PW to Len Radic, *Age* (13 March 1982).

36　PW to Maschler, Aug 1981.

37　*Flaws*, p.237.

38　Brian Adams, *Sidney Nolan, Such is Life* (Hutchinson Australia, Melbourne, 1987), p.238; and Nolan's June 1986 interview to Adams.

39   'I'm a good hater . . .', Nolan to Janet Hawley, *Age* (11 June 1983), Saturday Extra, p.1; 'It was far more . . .', PW to Margaret Simons, Sept 1983, published in *Tension*, vol. 3 (Virgin Press, Toorak, April 1984), p.3; *Nightmare* was shown at the Festival of Perth in 1982, and the Dante drawings at Rex Irwin's gallery in Sydney in May that year.

40   To Michael Le Moignan, *SMH* (23 July 1983), p.33.

41   'one of . . .', *Flaws*, p.67; 'deliberately unforgiving', Withycombe to me, 16 Nov 1987.

42   Wood to me, 31.x.1985.

43   *Flaws*, p.55.

44   'If Mr White's . . .', *SMH* (26 Oct 1981), p.6; 'I only wish . . .', PW to Kerry Walker, late March, early April 1982; 'a good . . .', PW to Maschler and Greene, 30.xii.1981; 'Patrick has been telling . . .', Green to me, 5 May 1989.

45   PW to me, 16 March 1987; Harrower to me, 17 April 1989.

46   25.xi.1981.

47   25.i.1982.

48   'Working with . . .', PW to Malouf, 8.xi.1982; 'The play is . . .', PW to Harrower, 28.ii.1982.

49   'we totter . . .', PW to Simons, *Age* (24 Sept 1983), Saturday Extra, p.3; 'it's too much . . .' and 'You can get . . .', PW to O'Brien, *SMH* (10 Dec 1983), p.31.

50   'It is more . . .', *SMH* (8 March 1982), p.8; 'austere and gritty . . .', PW to Meale, 9.iii.1982; '*Voss* is yours . . .', PW to Meale, 19.iv.1982.

51   'fabulously disastrous' reported by Sharman to me, 29 Oct 1989; 'the sanity in insanity . . .', PW to Geraldine O'Brien, *SMH* (10 Dec 1983), p.31; 'I can't . . .', PW to James Stern, 17.xii.1981.

52   'So our work . . .', *Speaks*, p.110; 'Comical bastards . . .', *Netherwood*, p.52; re 'Mexican Bandits', PW to Geraldine O'Brien, *SMH* (10 Dec 1983), p.31.

53   PW to La Trobe University, Aug 1984, *Speaks*, pp.151–2.

54   'the most important . . .', PW to La Trobe University, Aug 1984, *Speaks*, p.157; 'Nobody is that . . .', PW to ANU, 1983, *Speaks*, p.122.

55   'monstrous web', *Speaks*, p.106; 'One of the curses . . .', *SMH* (26 Jan 1984); 'The poison . . .', PW to President Reagan, 29.v.1984.

56   *Signal*, p.15.

57   To Björkstén, 20.v.1982.

58   1.vi.1982.

59   'It is very. . .', PW to Dutton, 6.viii.1976; 'Getting out . . .', PW to Dutton, 21.ii.1978.

60   17.ix.1980.

61   Dutton to PW, 25.ix.1980.

62   20.x.1980.

63   'inherited from . . .', PW to Dutton, 28.x.1981; 'I'm sorry . . .', PW to Dutton, 1.vi.1982.

64   4.vi.1982.

65   Nin Dutton to me, 12 March 1986.

66   'All most . . .', PW to Garland, 21.v.1982; 'the other specialists . . .', PW to Waters, 3.viii.1982.

67   'dribbling . . .', PW to Garland, 3.ix.1982; 'If I can . . .', PW to Falkenberg, 15.x.1982.

68   PW to Waters, 8.i.1983.

69   PW to Garland, 12.iii.1983.

70   'I brought up . . .', PW to La Trobe University, Aug 1984, *Speaks*, p.154; 'great independent . . .', PW to Paul Murphy *Nationwide*, ABC

TV, 12 March 1981.

71　*The Best of the Science Show* (Nelson, 1983); *Australians and Nuclear War* (Centre for Continuing Education at ANU and Croom Helm Australia Pty Ltd, 1983); and *Speaks*, p.113–26.

72　*Speaks*, p.116–17.

73　PW to Green, 30.vii.1983.

74　'You would . . .', PW to Garland, 12.iii.1983; 'The expedition . . .', PW to Green, 25.xi.1983; 'he said . . .', PW to Falkenberg, 15.xii.1983.

75　PW to me, 7 Dec 1989.

76　*Speaks*, p.136.

77　PW to Green, 25.xi.1983.

78　Ibid.

79　'I have . . .', PW to Green, 13.vi.1984; the overcoat, PW to Björkstén, 20.vi.1984.

80　'with every . . .', PW to Green, 1.v.1984; 'I am . . .', PW to Waters, 16.viii.1984.

81　'He was honest . . .', Harvey to me, 13.x.1989; 'my small white . . .', *Speaks*, p.171.

82　*NZ Listener* (19 Jan 1985), p.20.

83　'Now at least . . .', PW to Harrower, 14.xi.1984; 'The NDP didn't . . .', PW to Garland, 15.xii.1984.

84　To Falkenberg, 28.xii.1984.

85　To me on several occasions.

86　'*I am trapped* . . .', PW to Arrighi, 28.i.1985; 'I can make . . .', PW to Garland, 28.xii.1984.

87　14.xii.1984.

29　The Town of Jerusalem

1　'I was never . . .', *Uneasy*, p.15; 'This is . . .', PW to Gwen Moore, 22.vii.1973; re knowing in theory, PW to Crisp, *National Times* (17 May 1985), p.18; 'I wrote . . .', PW to Simons, *Age* (24 Sept 1983), Saturday Extra, p.3.

2　'In a sense . . .', *Uneasy*, p.11; 'a bit more' and forgetting names, PW to Glover, *SMH*, Good Weekend (18 May 1985), p.27; 'giving in', *Age* (24 Sept 1983), Saturday Extra, p.3.

3　'creeping about . . .', PW to Crisp, *NT*, p.20; 'terrible problem . . .', PW to me, 15 June 1988; 'permanent faithful' and 'can lead . . .', PW to Björkstén, *c.*Nov 1980; 'Don't know . . .' and Garland news and Lascaris response, PW to Waters, 16.viii.1984.

4　PW to Malouf, 3.xi.1982.

5　'It's about . . .', PW to Crisp, *NT*, p.20; Mother Superior, *Memoirs*, p.87.

6　To Waters, 16.viii.1984.

7　'Words are . . .', *Memoirs*, pp.86–7; 'to discover . . .', p.157.

8　Ouvrier to me, 20 June 1990.

9　Use of 'Binoculars', PW to me, 12 May 1988; 'I am the Resurrection . . .', *Memoirs*, p.151 and 'Orchard Row', *Thirteen Poems* (privately published *c.* 1929), p.18.

10　'Ploughing the . . .', *Memoirs*, p.72; KVH, pp.130, 135, 166; Kippax to me, 7 Nov 1988.

11　17.viii.1984.

12　PW to Simons, *Age*, p.3.

13　PW to Crisp, *NT*, p.18.

14　Ibid., pp.18, 20.

15　'They got together . . .', PW to Peter Ward, *Australian*, Weekend, 1 (18–19

April 1987); 'trash', Kippax to me, 7 Nov 1988.

16 'Oh, I know . . .' and 'I am writing . . .', reported by Walker to me; written as retaliation, PW to Peter Ward, *Australian* (18–19 April 1987).

17 *Starting Again, a Time in the Life of William Yang* (William Heinemann, Australia, 1989), p.92.

18 11.ix.1985.

19 Ibid.

20 'by torture . . .', *Voss*, p.440; 'who lift us . . .', 'Credo', *Speaks*, p.197.

21 'mysterious . . .', 'Credo', *Speaks*, p.197; 'the last of . . .', *Memoirs*, p.183; 'I only . . .', PW to Dutton, 15.i.1978; 'The park . . .', PW to Garland, 12.iv.1981.

22 'He'd be . . .' and 'She looks . . .', Yang, *Starting Again*, p.96; 'Various people . . .', PW to Greene, 8.x.1985.

23 'While approaching . . .', PW to Liz Cowen, Cape, 13.ix.1985; 'I was in . . .', Cowen to PW, 27.ix.1985; 'Barbara, who . . .', PW to Cowen, 1.x.1985.

24 'all this gum . . .', PW to Greene, 8.x.1985; 'I'm also . . .', PW to Stern, 1.i.1986; 'I have . . .', PW to Greene, 14.ii.1986.

25 'Too many . . .', PW to Waters, 20.xi.1985; 'an establishment . . .', PW to Richard Glover, *SMH*, Good Weekend (18 May 1985), p.27.

26 14.ii.1986.

27 13.vi.1986.

28 David Tacey, *Age* (19 July 1986), Saturday Extra, p.13. In 1988, Oxford University Press in Australia published Tacey's *Patrick White, Fiction and the Unconscious*.

29 'so intellectual . . .', PW to Falkenberg, 1.xi.1986; 'Prayer and vegies . . .', p.12; Kelly as Castelmarino, PW to me, 8 Oct 1986; 'stuffed turkey', p.45; 'prose poems', PW to Ile Krieger, 9.viii.1986; 'I lay . . .', p.15.

30 *Speaks*, p.180.

31 To Falkenberg, 11.ix.1987.

32 6.i.1987.

33 PW to Peter Ward, *Australian* (18–19 April 1987), Weekend, 1.

34 Scene XIII.

35 PW to me, 15 April 1987.

36 'Shepherd . . .', PW to Henderson, 10.vi.1987; 'I hope . . .', PW to Falkenberg, 26.xii.1985.

37 PW to Kerry Walker.

38 PW to Falkenberg, 11.ix.1987.

39 'It was . . .', PW to me, 12 July 1990; 'lapsed Anglican . . .', *Flaws*, p.102.

40 Draft reply, Christmas 1987.

41 PW to Ile Krieger, 9.viii.1986.

42 *Speaks*, p.139.

43 Ibid., p.114.

44 Ibid., p.186.

45 Ibid., p.190.

46 'I shall . . .', PW to me, 8 March 1988; Satta, *Speaks*, p.192; Wilson, PW to me, 15 Feb; Gordimer, PW to me, 28 April; new Australians, PW to me, 4 July; Grenville, PW to Greene, 21.v.1988.

47 PW to Green, 21.v.1988.

48 'I've got . . .', PW to me, 10 June 1988; 'invading the . . .', text as delivered; 'I went . . .', PW to me, 30 July 1988.

49 *Speaks*, p.195.

50   'He is . . .', *Uneasy*, pp.58–9; 'a long . . .', PW to me,
     1 July 1988.
51   *Cheery Soul*, p.225; 'I suppose . . .', PW to me, 31 July 1988.
52   St Vincent's Hospital Summary of Admission – provided by PW.
53   PW to me, 14 Dec 1988.
54   *Twyborn*, p.46; PW to me, 18 Oct 1989.
55   *Speaks*, p.193.
56   PW to me, 6 Oct 1989.
57   To me, 11 April 1989.
58   Dutton to PW, 25.vi.1989.
59   PW to Bennie, *SMH* (11 Nov 1989), p.89.
60   Walker to me, 25 Oct 1989.
61   To me, 14 Oct 1989.
62   PW to Bennie, *SMH*.
63   PW to Sally Beggbie, ABC Television.
64   Scene XIV.

Picture Credits

I thank the following photographers for allowing me to use their pictures:
Max Dupain 77; Branco Gaica 78; Robert McFarlane 61; Ern McQuillan 68; Margaret Olah 75; Ken Thomson 67; David Wilson 76; William Yang 69, 70, 71, 72, 73, 74, 79.

I thank the following for allowing me to use pictures from their collections (where the photographer's name is known I give it after the picture number):
Pauline Allen 20; Archivo de Baena, Bayonne 34; Art Gallery of New South Wales, 29: Roy de Maistre, *Patrick White*, 1940, oil on canvas, 76 x 50cm, gift of his niece Frances Peck, reproduced by kind permission of Belinda Price and Caroline Walker (Photograph by A. C. Cooper & Sons, London); Australian Consolidated Press 62; Nerida Bettington 22; Mabel Chapman 48; Cheltenham College 18; Nin Dutton 58; John Fairfax Group 56, 63 (Barry Gilmour); Dr Andrew Fisher 60; Peggy Garland 19, 49, 50, 55; Helen and Gary Ghent 9; Harry Ransom Humanities Center, The University of Texas 36; Harvard Theatre Collection 35 (Angus McBean); Ian Huebsch 38; Léa and Camille Irigoyen 33; Norris King 21; Tom Kirk 6, 8 (Notman Studios, Sydney), 14, 17 (Debenham Morgan, Cheltenham), 27; Manoly Lascaris 42, 43, 44, 45; Beatrice McPhillamy 10; Magnum 66 (Inge Morath); Dr Eva Mandel 59 (Leopold Pavlovic); Dr Jürgen Oertel 30; Helen Railton 7; Frances Riordan 64; Jane Smart of Wynstay 13; The Whites at Belltrees 1 (Sidney Jackson), 2, 3, 4; Pat White 31; The Estate of Patrick White 11, 12, 25, 26 (R), 28 & 32 (A. C. Cooper & Sons), 39 (Apkar Studio, Alexandria), 40, 41, 46, 51, 52, 53, 54, 57, 65, 68; Pat Wilcox of Barwon Vale 15; Col. A. E. Wilkinson 16; Betty Withycombe 24 (Ramsey & Muspratt, Cambridge); The Rev. Dr Robert Withycombe 5; John Wyse 47 (Herbert Paul).

Index

Throughout the index, Patrick White is noted as PW. The works of Patrick White are indexed directly under titles. Titles of published novels and plays are noted in *italic*. Titles of short stories, poems and unpublished material appear in single quotation marks.

719